Gangster Doodles

GANGSTER DOODLES

HarperCollins books may be purchased for educational, business, or sales promotional use. For information please email the Special Markets Department at SPsales@harpercollins.com.

Published in 2019 by
Harper Design

An Imprint of HarperCollinsPublishers
195 Broadway
New York, NY 10007

Tel: (212) 207-7000
Fax: (855) 746-6023

harperdesign@harpercollins.com
www.hc.com

Distributed throughout the world by
HarperCollins Publishers
195 Broadway
New York, NY 10007

ISBN 978-0-06-285655-5
Library of Congress Control Number:
2019932424

Designed by Brian O'Tuama
www.bot.graphics

Printed in China

First Printing, 2019

Gangster Doodles

by Marlon $a$$y

HARPER DESIGN
An Imprint of HarperCollinsPublishers

Foreword by David Choe

I went to "heaven" when I was thirteen. Heaven was a store inside the Beverly Center with novelty T-shirts and tchotchkes like rubber dog poo and zapping gum. Because of the store's proximity to the escalators—the perfect getaway—heaven was heavily shoplifted... by me. Because I hated myself like a proper pockmarked emo teen, I stole a happy-face shirt with a bullet hole between the eyes and blood trickling down. I wore that shirt almost every day till senior year. It was an iconic image that became synonymous with me and how I saw myself.

I went to "hell" when I was forty. I had purchased a thirteen-floor office building in Los Angeles and had transformed every floor and room into a creative figment of my imagination, an experience I called the Choe Show. I used the building and my art as a healing safe place to express and exorcise all my demons. It was a free-for-all—all you had to do for admission was be open and vulnerable and give me your soul. So many came, but many more were turned away. There were hundreds of rooms with very heavy spiritual creative work happening in all of them. I couldn't be with all the hundreds of guests at once... or could I? It was my office building, so I did what I wanted. I punched holes in every room. I dug and burrowed through different walls and floors throughout the entire building, so I could be everywhere all at once. It was the most cardio I've ever done in my life, and I never knew where I'd end up or whom I'd meet.

One night, I burrowed through a wall and tumbled into a confessional room. There was a seated figure there who hadn't heard me come in. He was expressing his fears and dreams: he wanted to be a good father and husband, he wanted to provide for his family and love them and not repeat the cycle of trauma in his life, and he was worried about his art and his career. I didn't know his name or his face, but it was Gangster Doodles. There was a sheet between us, so I have never seen this name's face nor do I know his real name, but I cried and bowed and surrendered myself to him. He was the smiling happy face with the bullet hole between the eyes.

Gangster Doodles is everything I'm not.

My art is messy and dirty

His art is clean and crisp

My art looks horrible as a tattoo

His art is made to be tattooed

My art is suffocating

His art breathes

My art is labored over, my brushstrokes layered and layered to hide all my fears and insecurities

His art is iconic, confident, and to the point; his visual vocabulary is something I've strived for my whole life

The happy face with splattered blood

So simple and stupid and complex and memorable all at once. I wish I could,
but I can't

That is why he is a fucking gangster

Of doodles

Oh, teach me Gangster Doodles

Through your lines

Through your colors

Through your composition

I can see you

I can feel you

I can learn from you

I will never forget you

Thank you.

Love,

David Choe

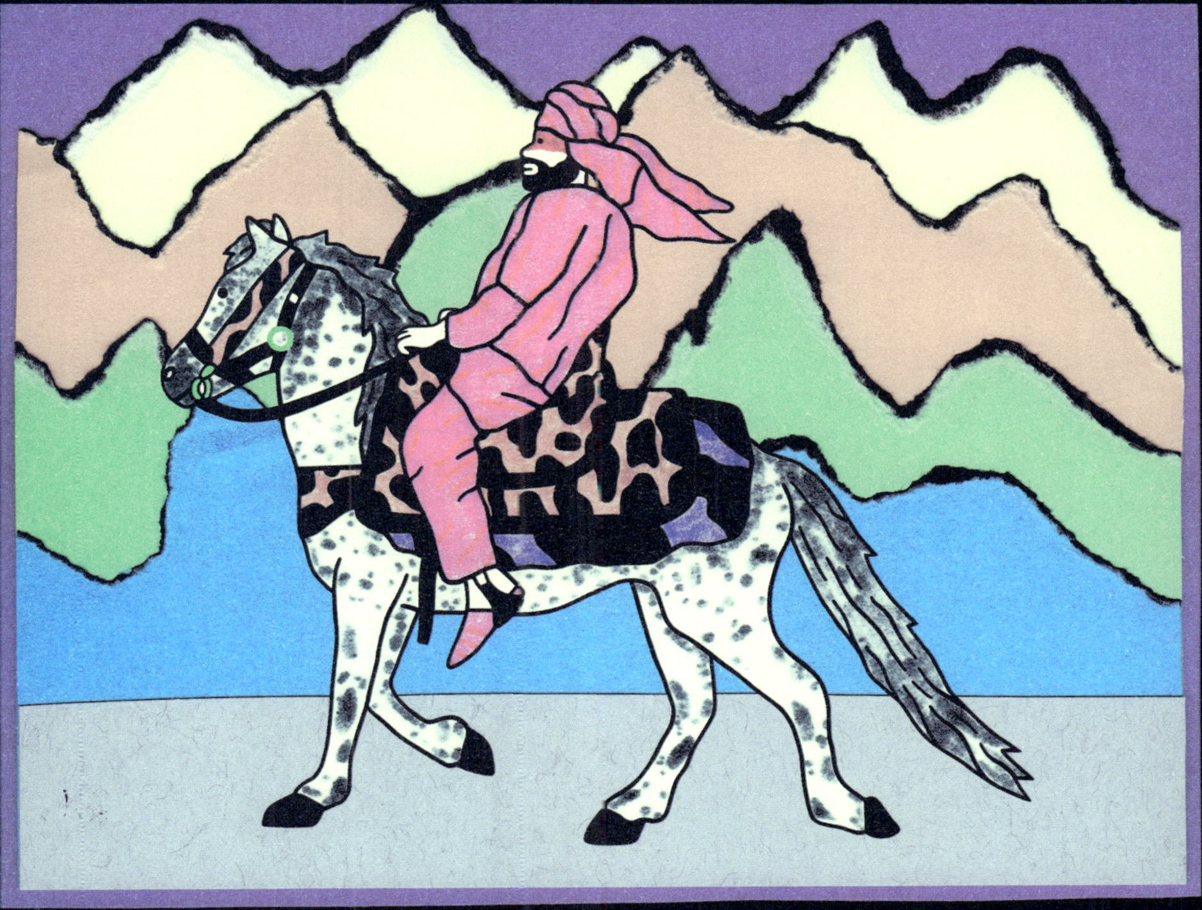

Introduction

Hello, my name is Marlon Sassy. I draw stuff on three-by-three-inch yellow Post-it notes. Let's go way, way, way back to when I first started to take drawing seriously.

I grew up in a very small town on the east coast (of Canada), population 200 at best. To do anything interesting you had to drive fifteen minutes to get into the city or jump on your twelve-speed and bike for one to two hours, depending on weather. If it was winter, you were fucked, which sucked 'cause winter usually lasted for seven months of the year. I hated the feeling of being trapped with nowhere to go.

As a kid growing up in the eighties and nineties in a small town with nothing to do, Saturday morning cartoons were my life. I remember waking up at 5:30 a.m. to watch *Astro Boy* on a really fuzzy channel 8 in my downstairs family room. For the next six to seven hours I was glued to the television, soaking up every episode of *Biker Mice from Mars, G.I. Joe, ThunderCats, Looney Tunes, Animaniacs, Spider-Man, Darkwing Duck, Teenage Mutant Ninja Turtles, Batman: The Animated Series,* and on and on. This was my happy place, my fortress of solitude. This was the golden age of everything good in the world. These shows, these memories are what shaped my young mind and helped influence the artist I am today. (Special shout-out to *Ren & Stimpy!*)

Cut to grade twelve. I took a few drawing classes but never thought about doing it on a professional level. In my mind, drawing for a living was the equivalent of being an astronaut or the mysterious sixth member of Limp Bizkit. My art teacher said I had talent and encouraged me to pursue it, but I just couldn't see it.

After graduating, I knew that I had to get the fuck outta my small town and move to a larger city to expand my horizons. At the age of nineteen, I moved to the opposite end of Canada to the west coast to attend film school. At first the culture shock was real—going from 200 to two million people was a crazy trip. While attending film school I took an elective life-drawing class that helped me rediscover my love for drawing and set me on a new creative path.

Straight outta graduating film school I got a one-month contract working at a TV production company. Month after month my contract kept getting extended. I put my head down and kept my nose to the grindstone 'cause I knew I had to pay my astronomical student loans and insane living costs.

A year into my job, I knew I needed some sort of outlet to help destress and get out all my creative shit, so I decided to figure out how to be a successful/working artist. I started my first art project using the twenty rough sketches I made in my elective art-drawing class in college. My initial goal was to draw two hours every day, which eventually turned into three hours, then four hours. At the four-year mark I was drawing every night for five to six hours. Over the course of eight years I created hundreds of paintings without any real success. During this time, I participated in two group shows and sold one painting. Creatively I hit a fucking wall, absolutely nothing I was doing was working. The creative process wasn't fun anymore.

The idea of Gangster Doodles came as an afterthought. While working at an office, I spent a lot of time on the phone making and taking calls. I also spent a lot of time ordering office supplies. My way of passing the time was to draw little doodles on Post-it notes with my stash of office pens, highlighters, and Sharpies while mindlessly taking other people's messages and calling Roto-Rooter to come to unclog the ladies' toilets. My desk was always a high-traffic area for people copping a fresh stack of Post-its or a new Sharpie.

I drew my first Gangster Doodle on a lunch break. While eating a PB&J sandwich and listening to Snoop Dogg's *Tha Doggfather* in my office cubicle, I quickly drew the album's cover on a Post-it with a Sharpie and a highlighter. Something clicked—a happy accident. I kept at it. One day, I decided I was ready to put them out there. I got into the office around 9:30 a.m. and went about my normal morning routine. After finishing all my office manager duties, I sat down at my desk and decided to pick out five different doodles to upload to Tumblr. Once the doodles were uploaded, I went back to my regularly scheduled work activities. The next morning, I was shocked and delighted to find out they had started to gain traction on the interwebs. Every day after that, I made it a point to post at least one new doodle a day. They continued to pick up momentum, and one year into drawing Gangster Doodles, I came to the proverbial fork in the road. Do I stay at my job with the guaranteed bi-weekly check and health benefits or do I take the leap of faith and put it all on motherfuckin' black?

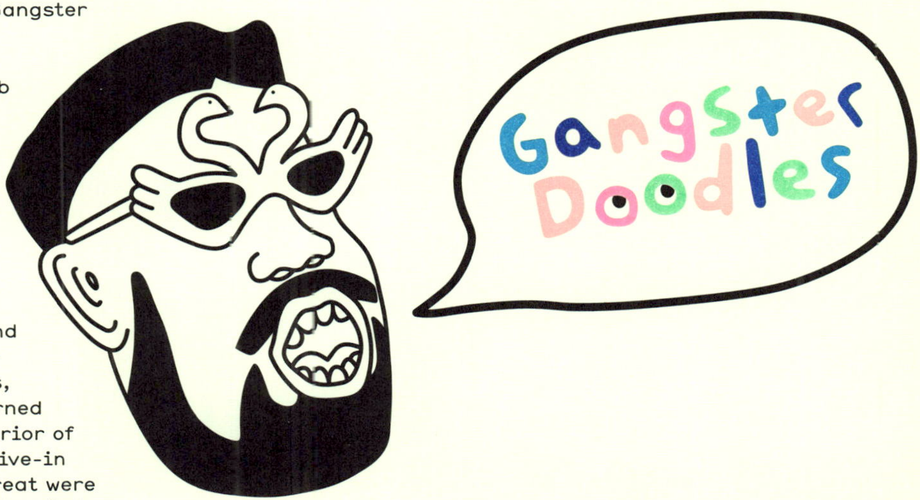

While all this was happening, I applied and was accepted to a nine-day art retreat in Wells, a small mining town turned art commune in the interior of British Columbia. The live-in art mentors for the retreat were Wayne White and his wife, Mimi Pond, multitalented artists, writers, and puppeteers who created some of the most iconic set designs and characters on the kids' TV show *Pee-Wee's Playhouse*. This was my chance to test out the idea of Gangster Doodles on a larger audience filled with hardened professional artists and people that were just like me (struggling artists trying to make it). In my bones I felt this was something I had to do in order to advance my goal of becoming an artist. Three months after the art retreat, I quit my job and started to pursue Gangster Doodles full-time.

Five years into my "art" career, I can honestly say I owe it all to Uncle Snoop. And now, in *Gangster Doodles*, I'm extremely proud to share with you some of my greatest doodle hits of the last five years in all their neon glory. 1 Luv.

Marlon Sassy

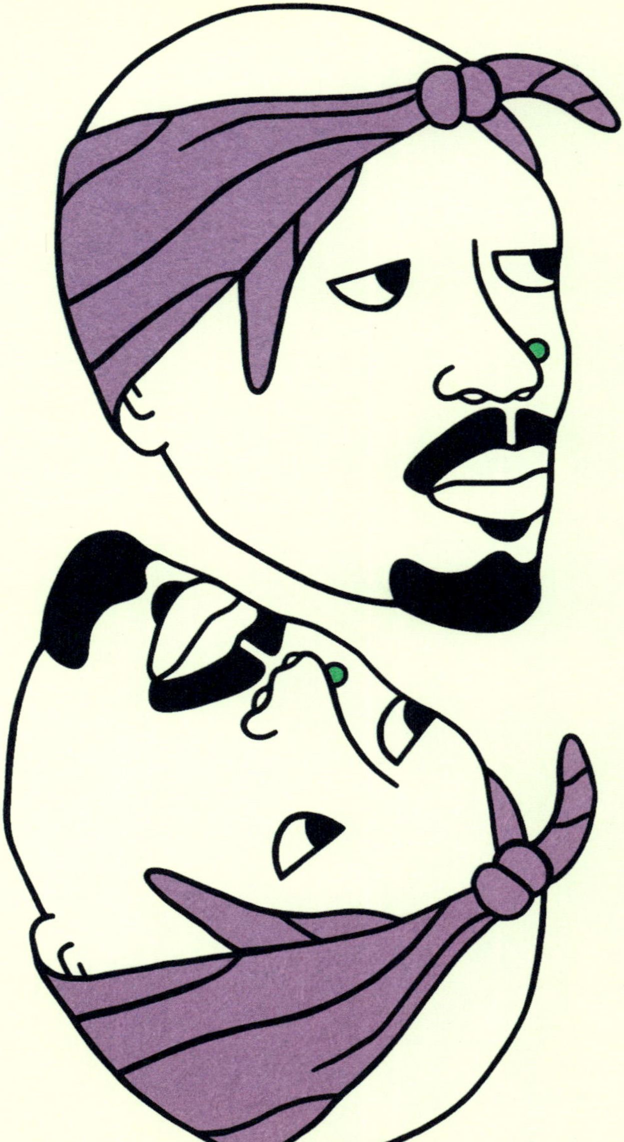

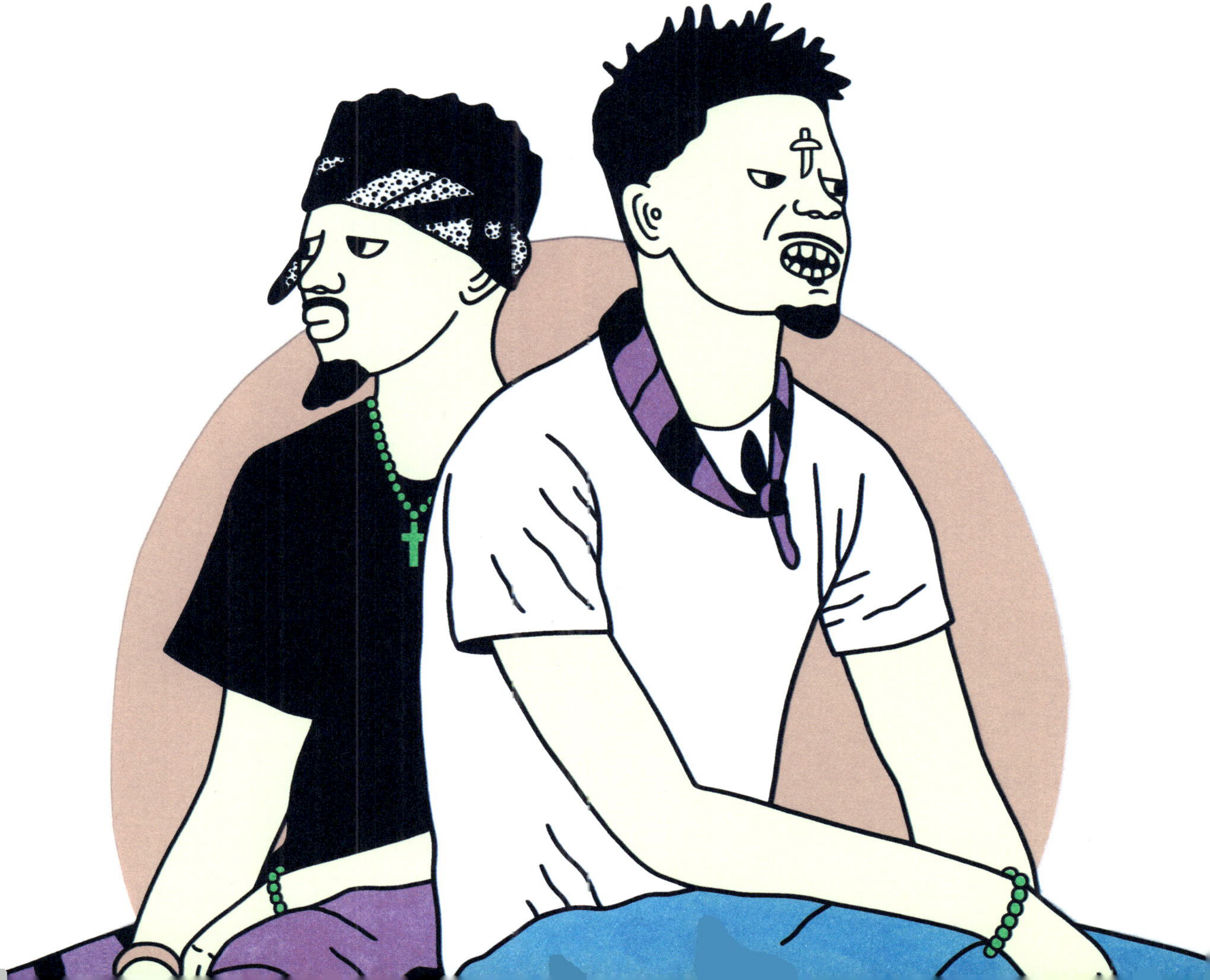

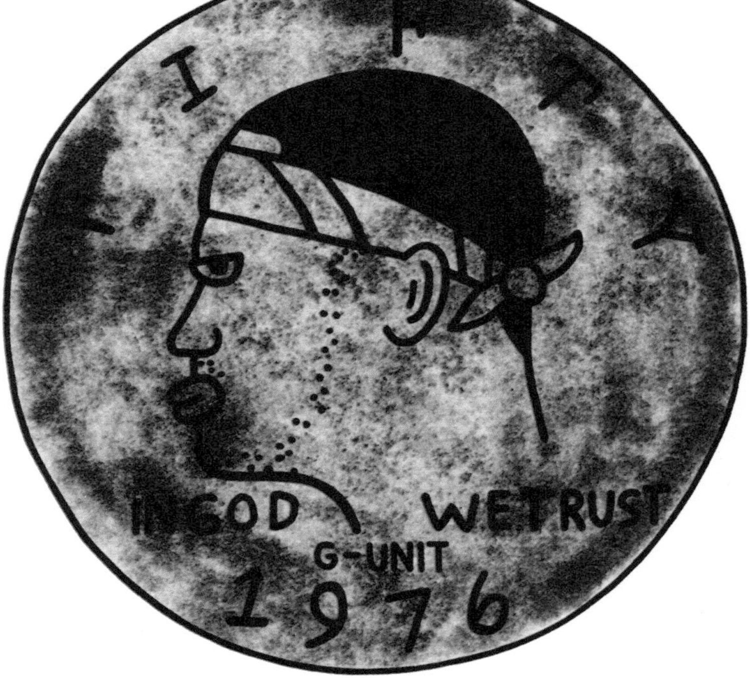
IN GOD
WE TRUST
G-UNIT
1976

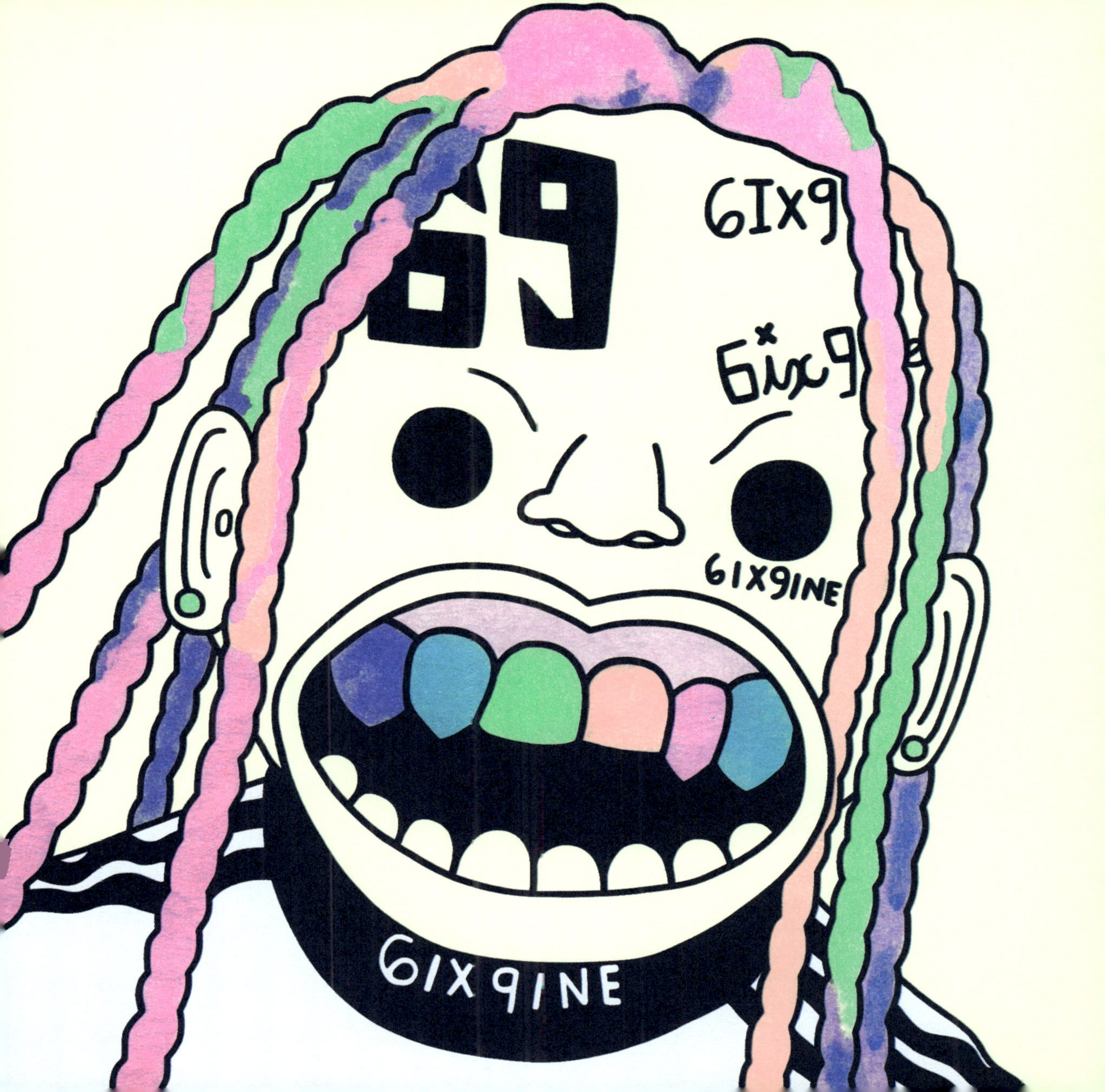
69
6IX9
6ix9
6IX9INE
6IX9INE

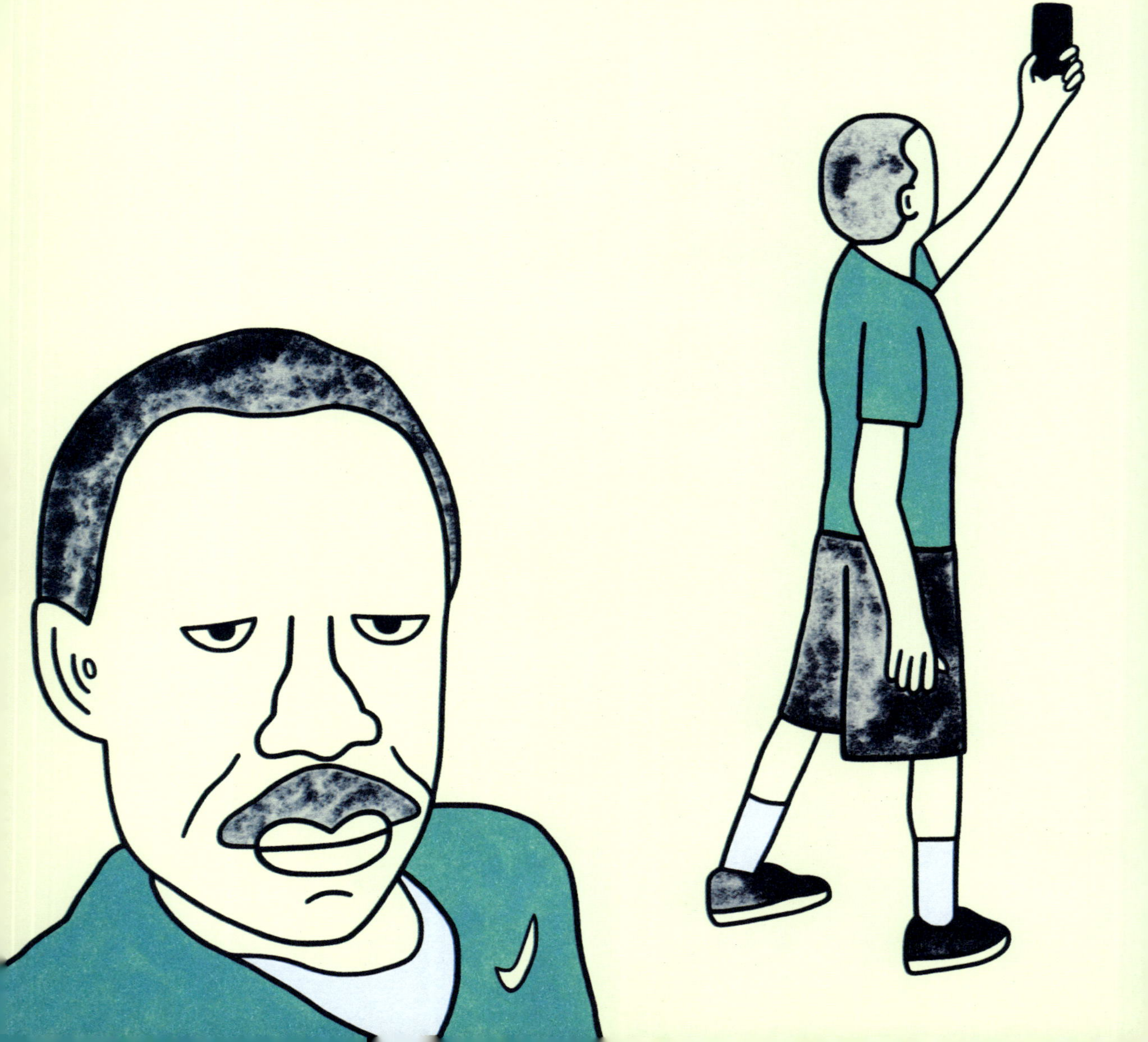

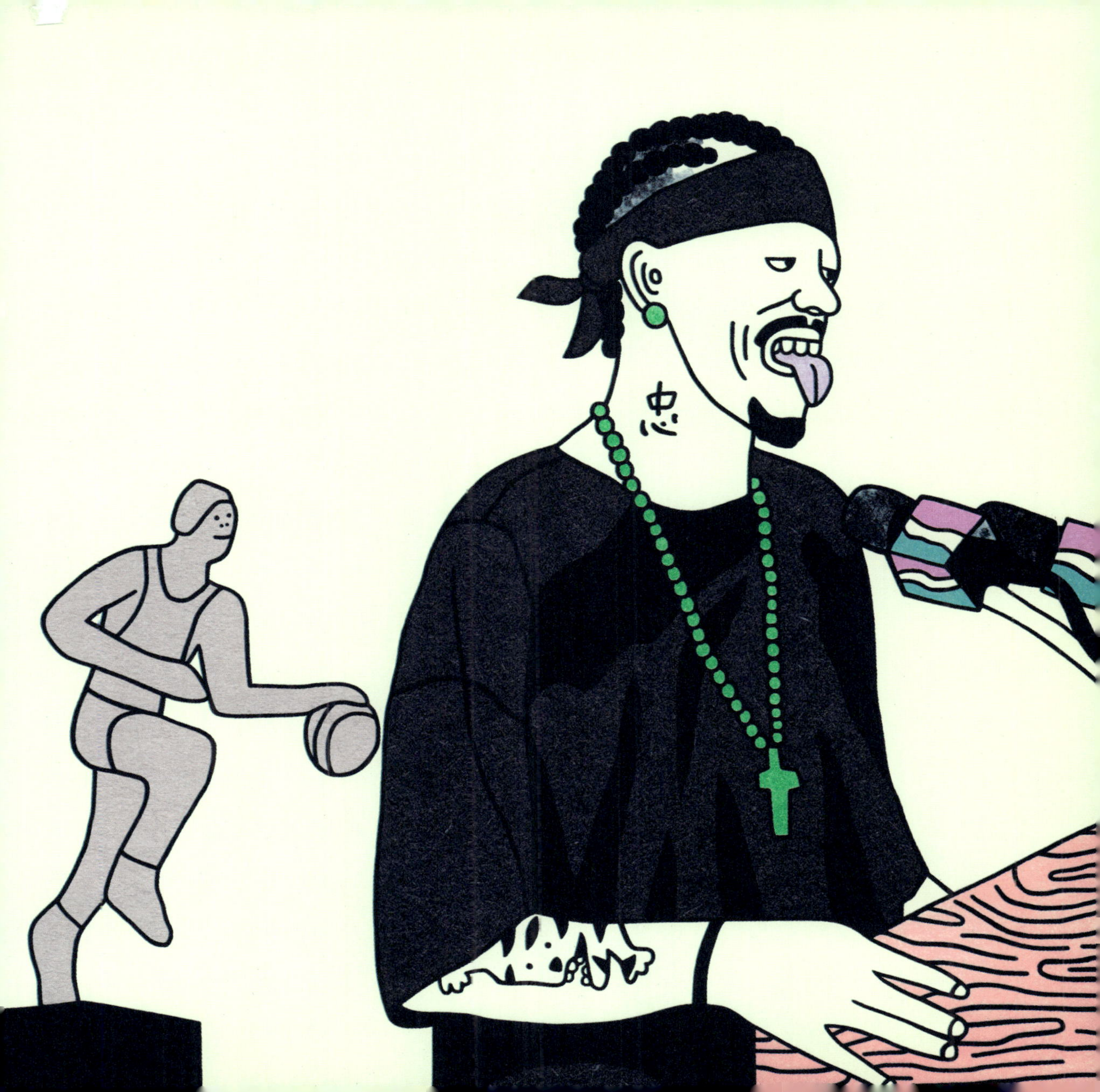
忠

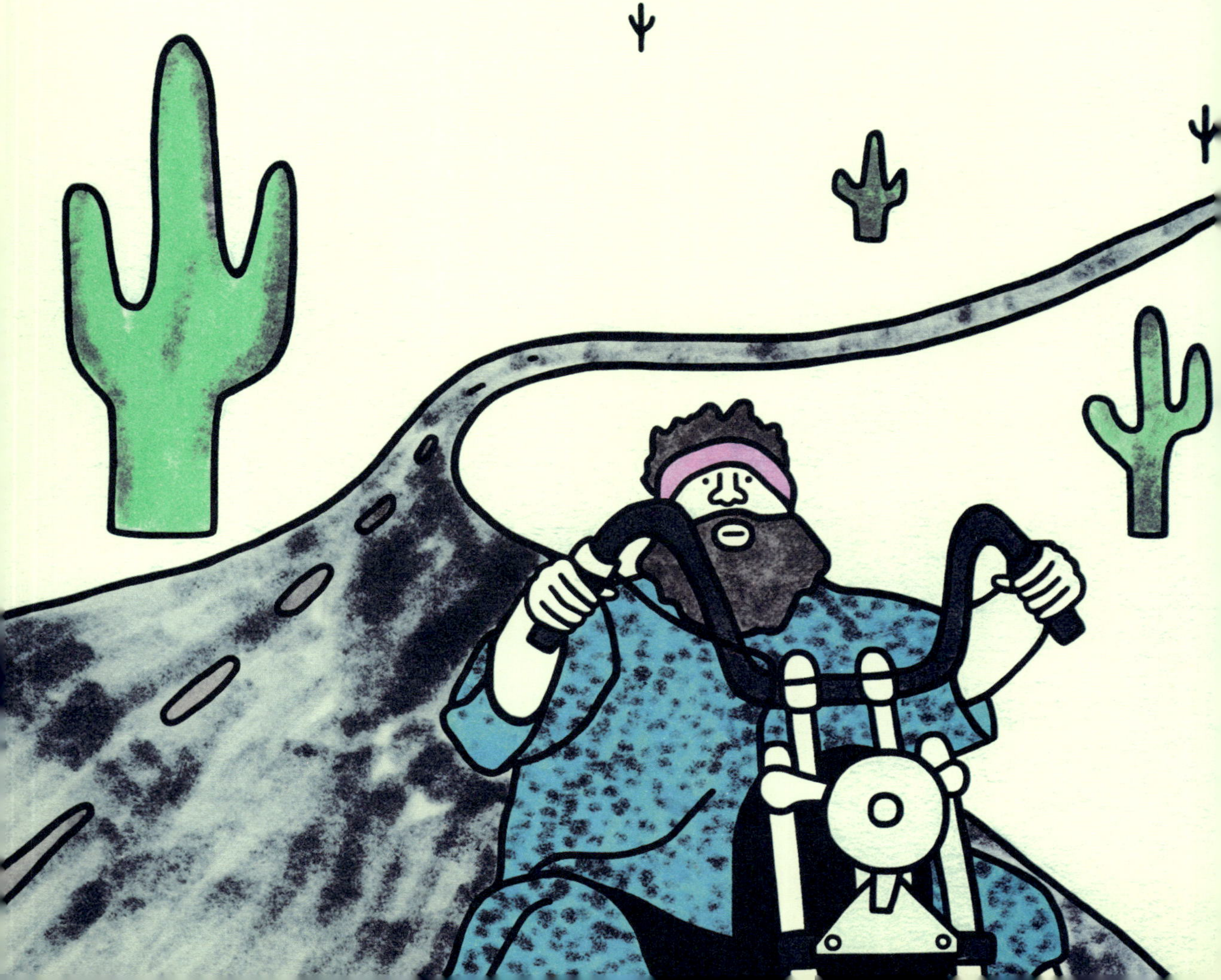

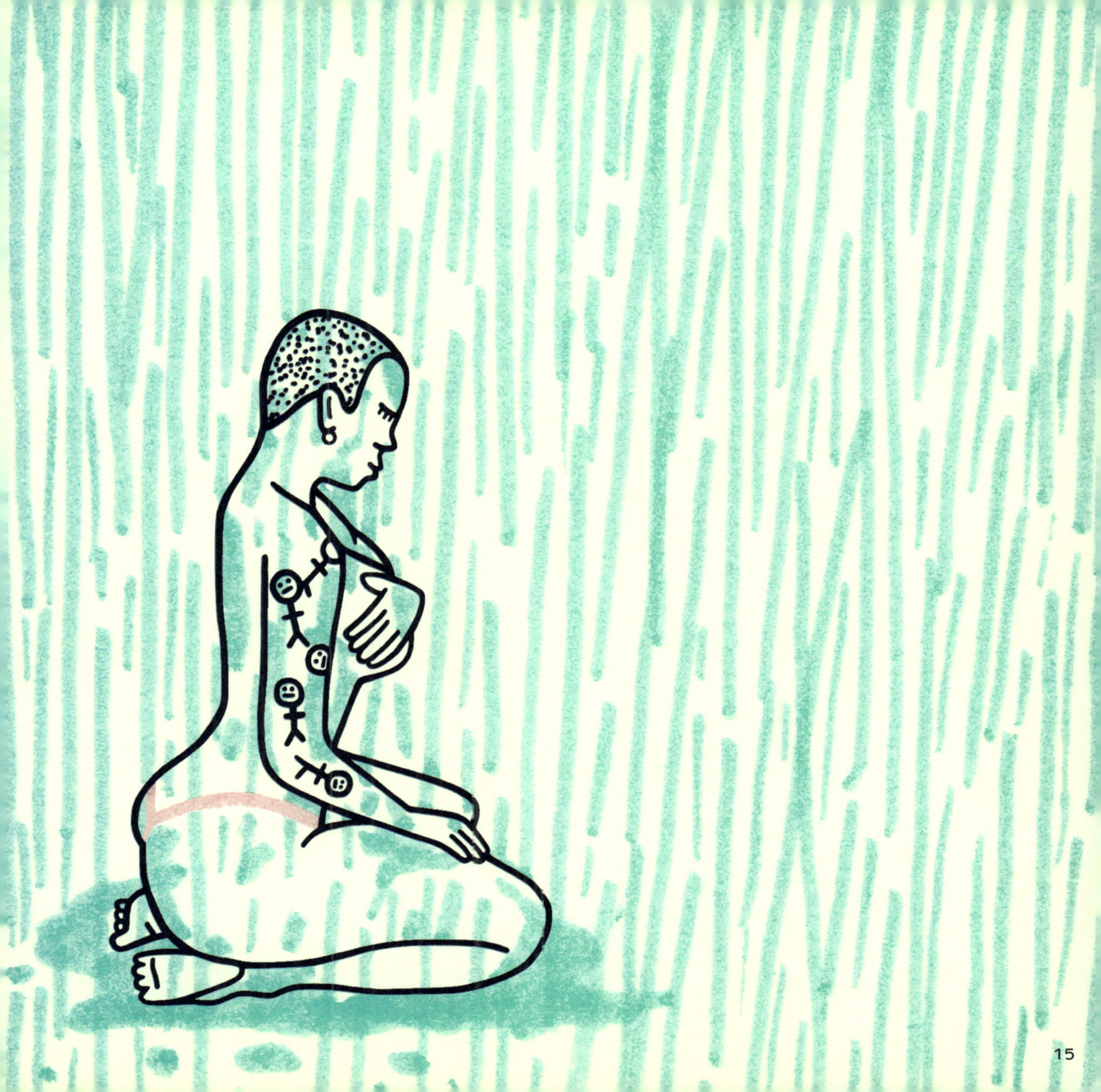

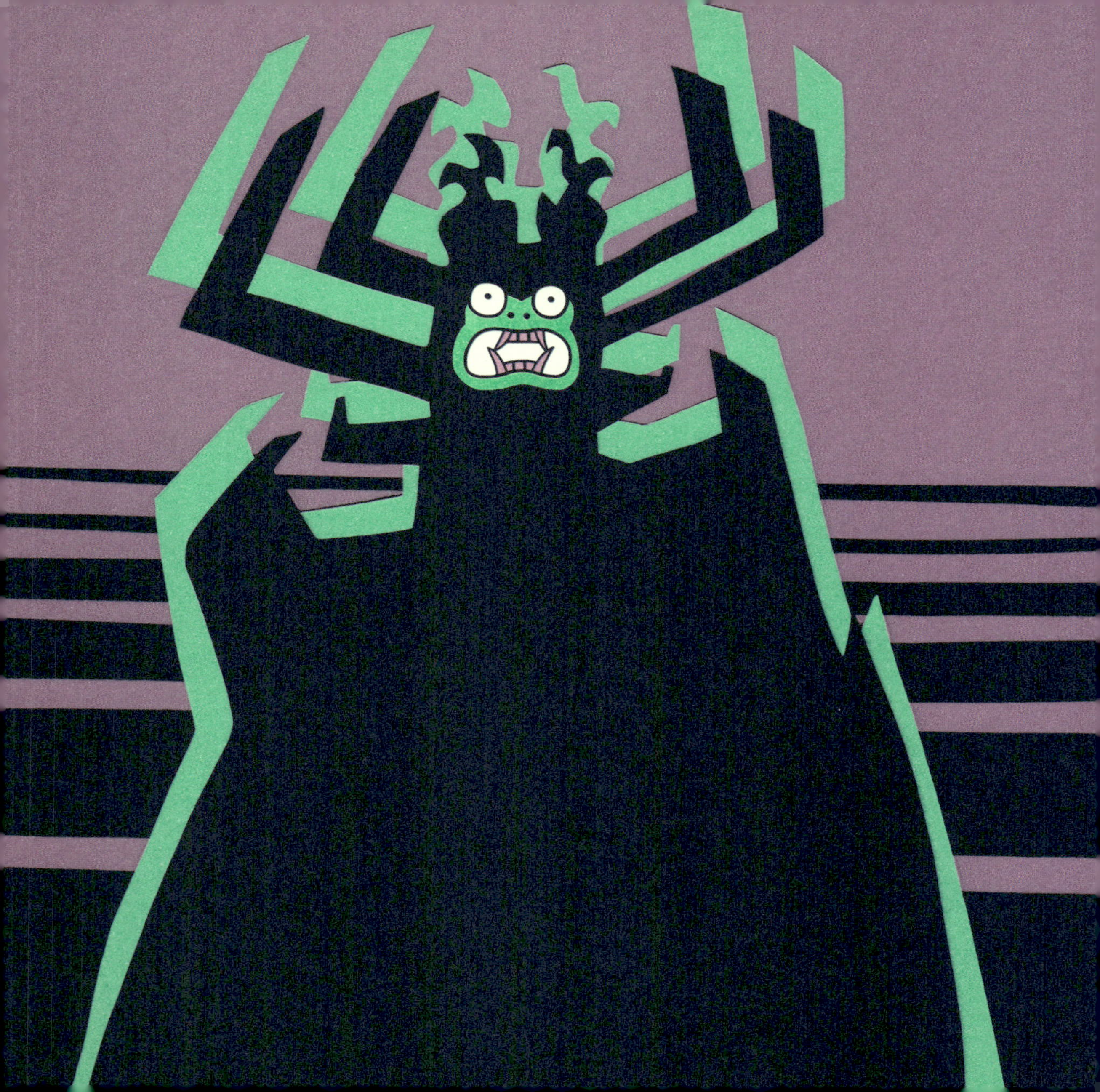

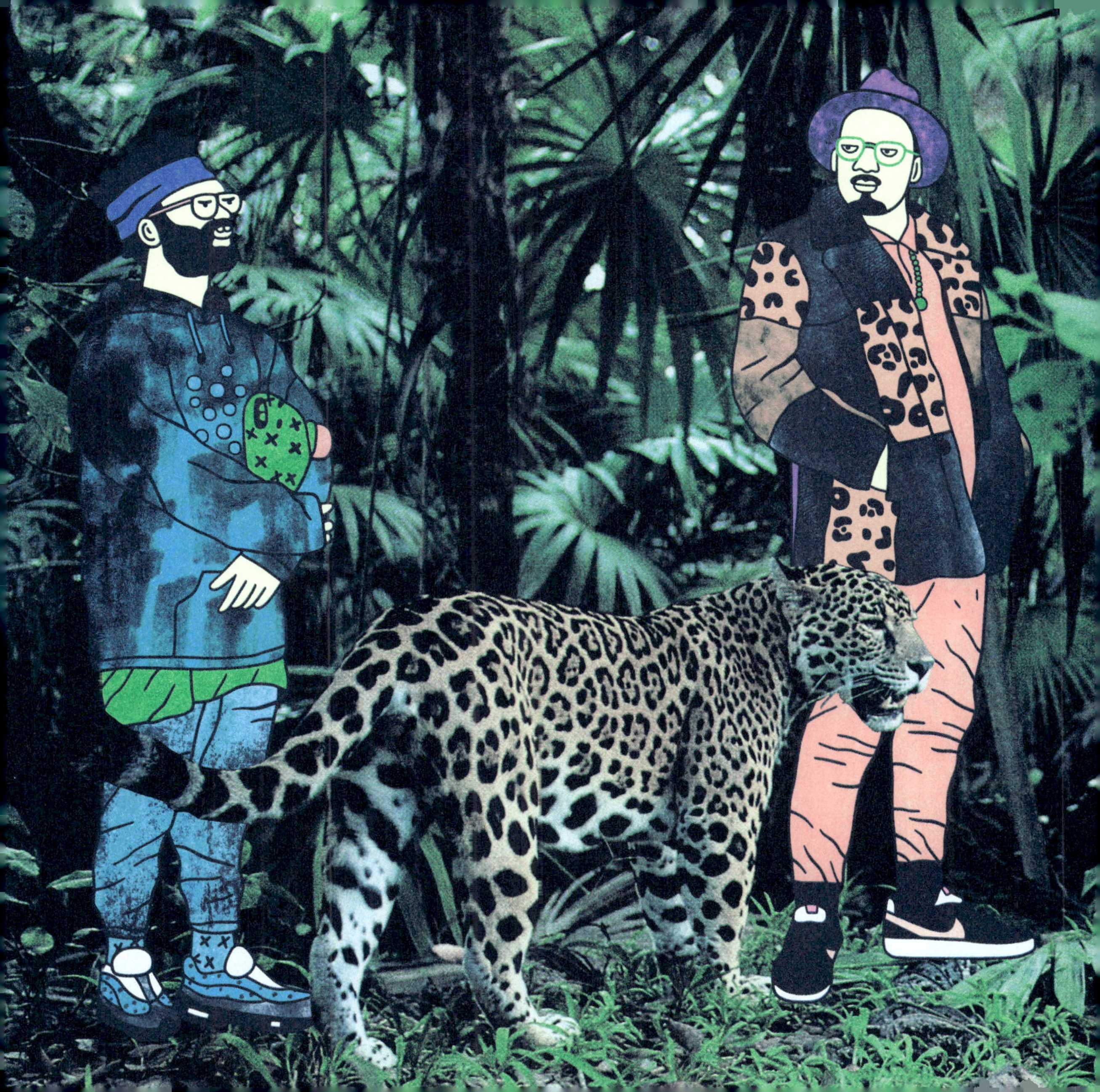

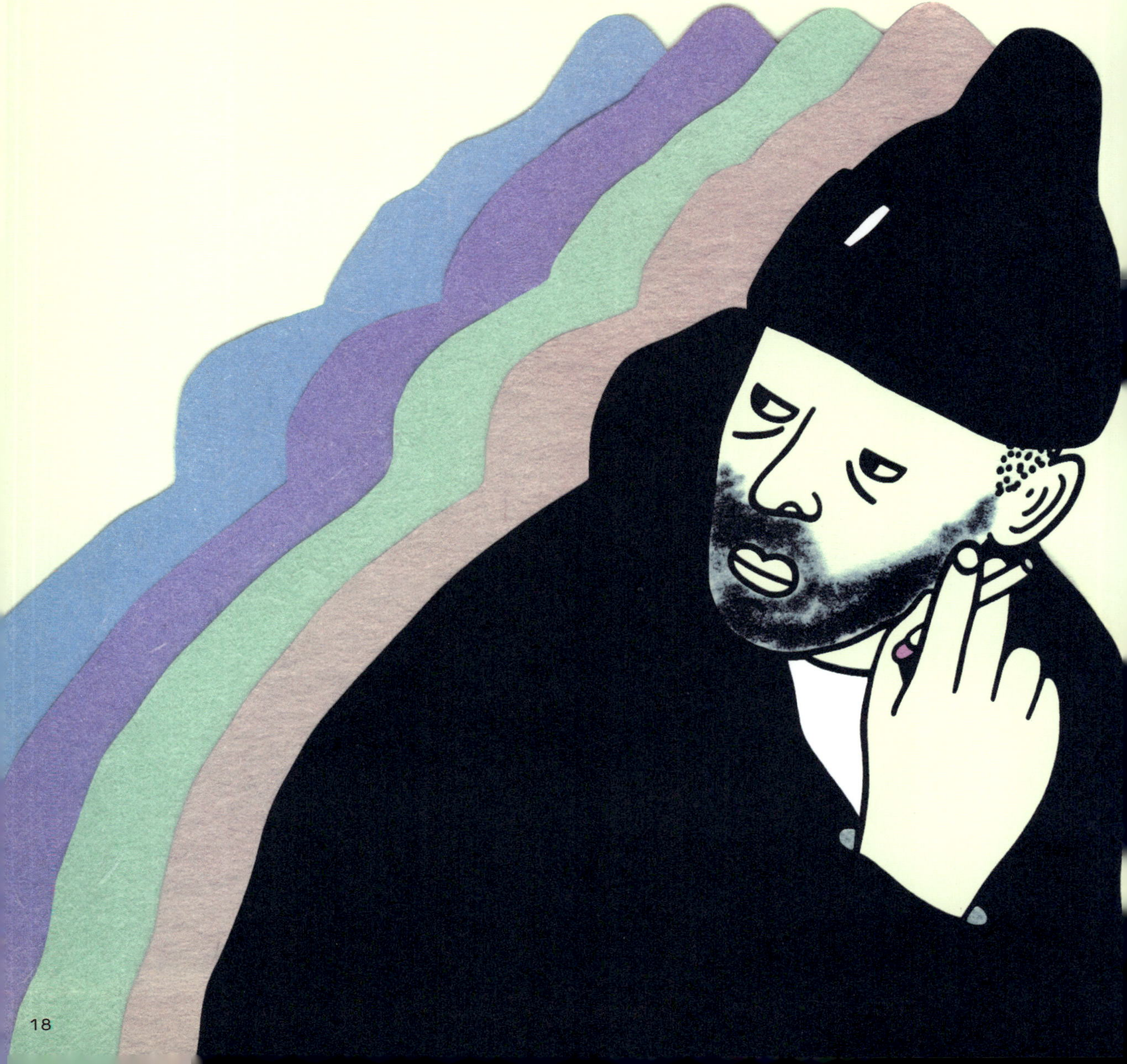

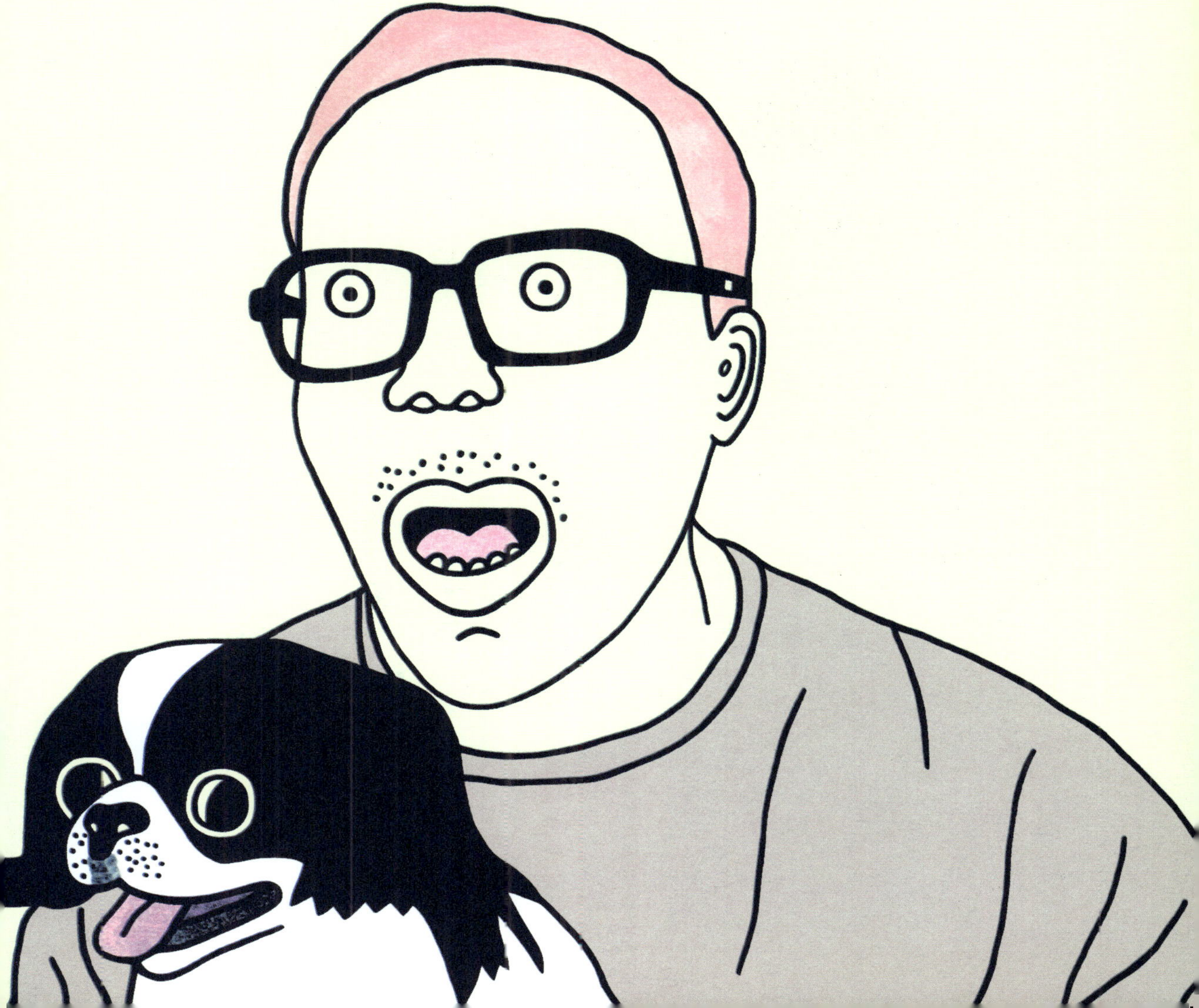

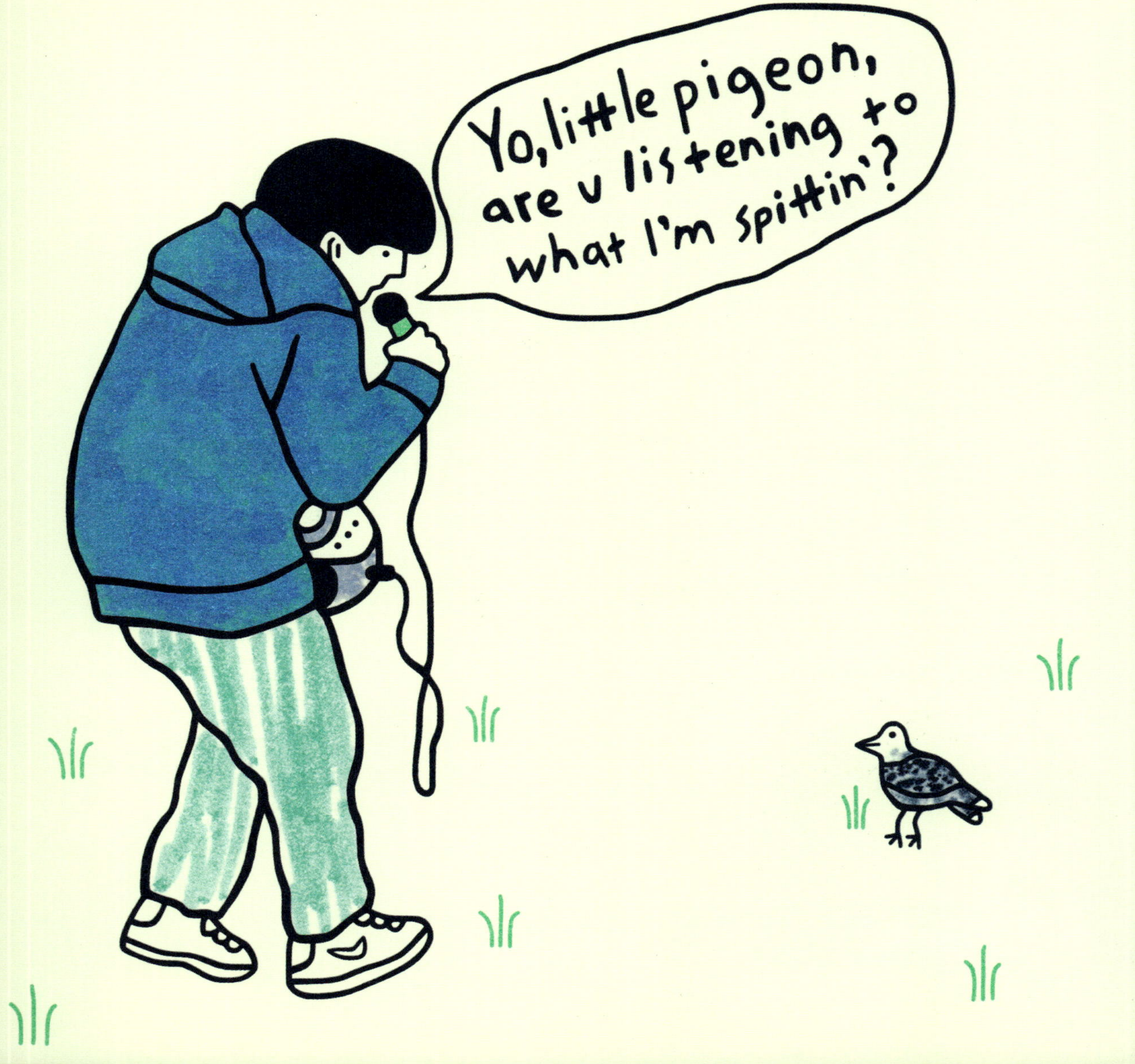
Yo, little pigeon, are u listening to what I'm spittin'?

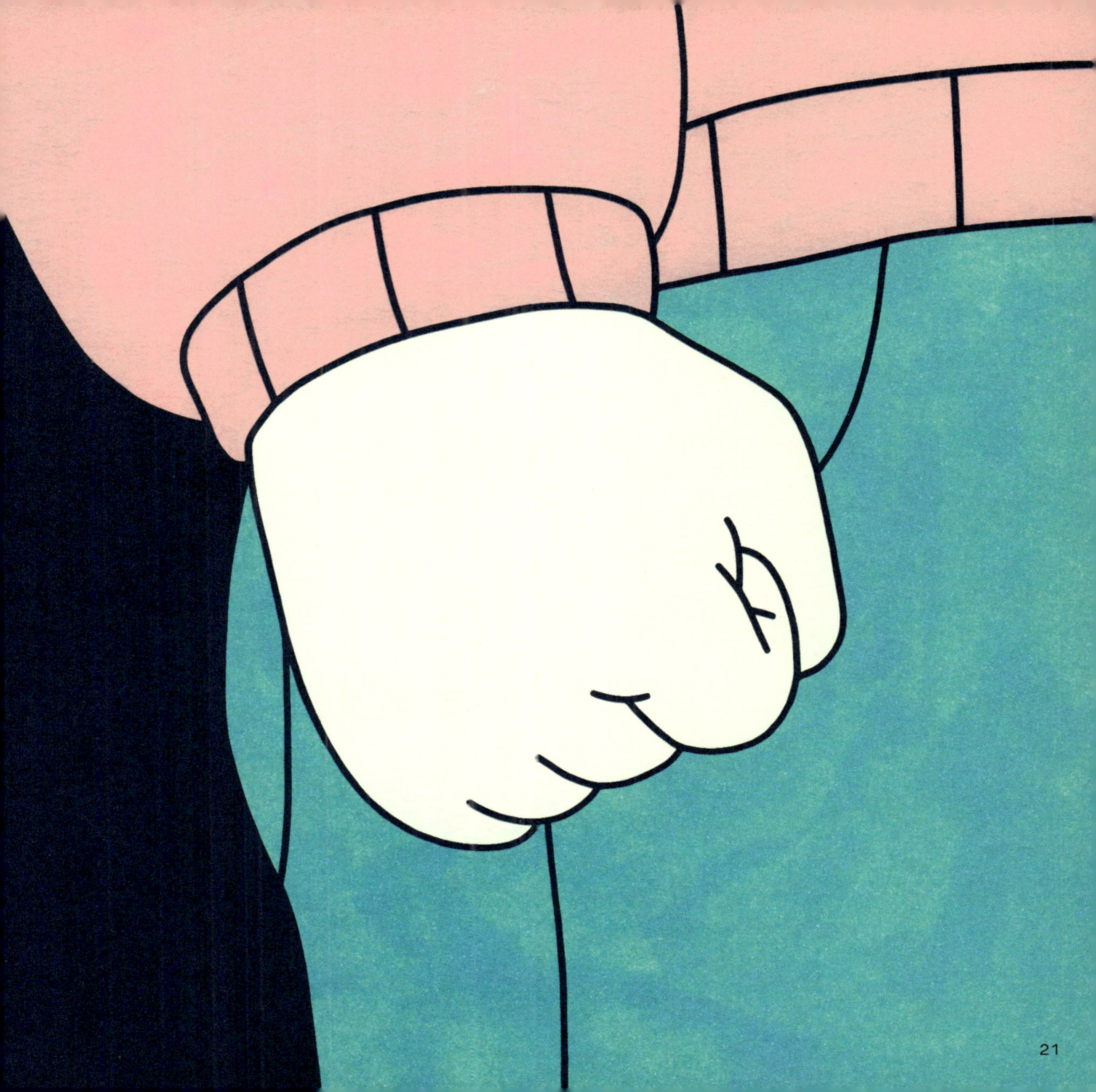

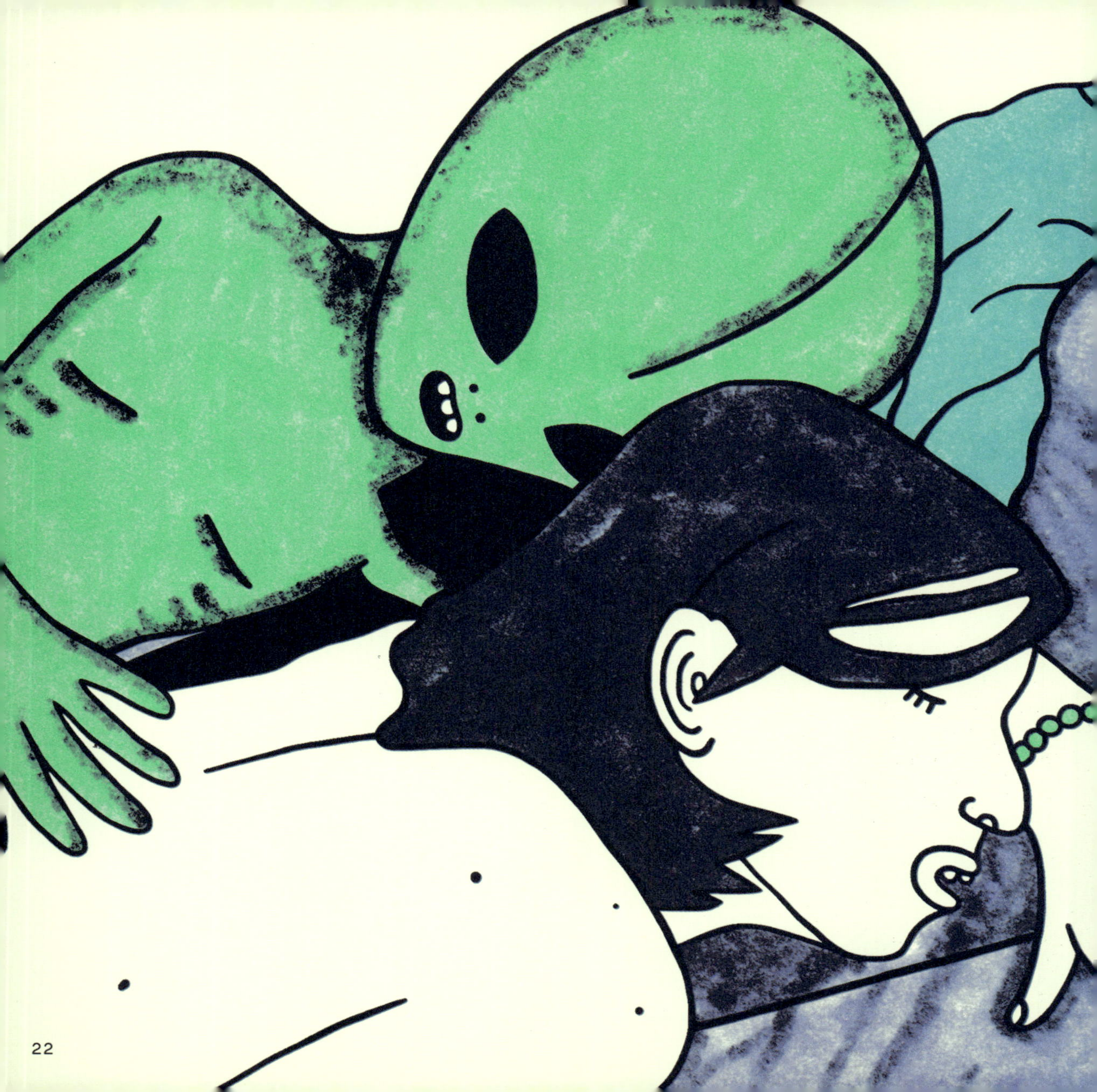

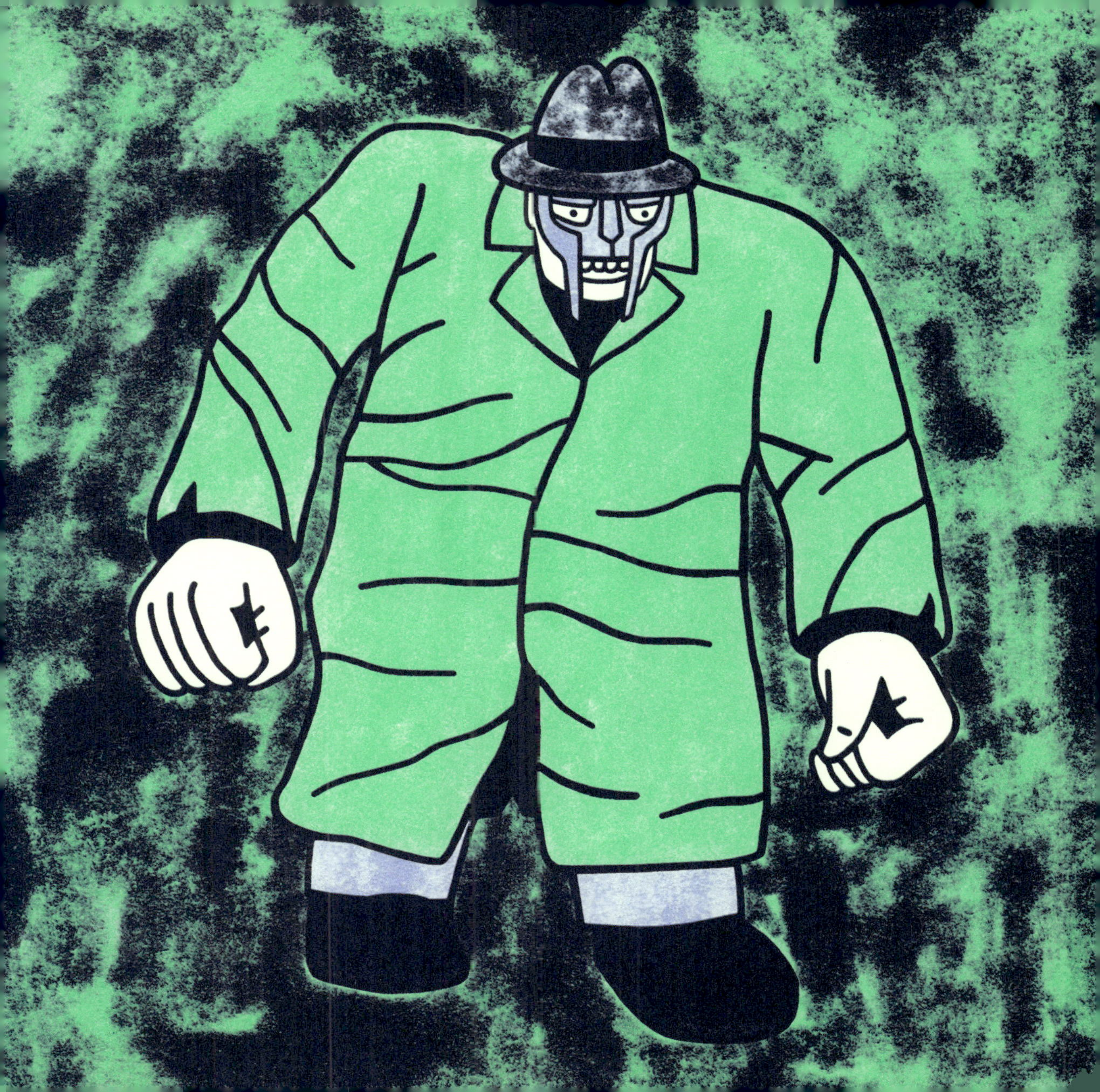

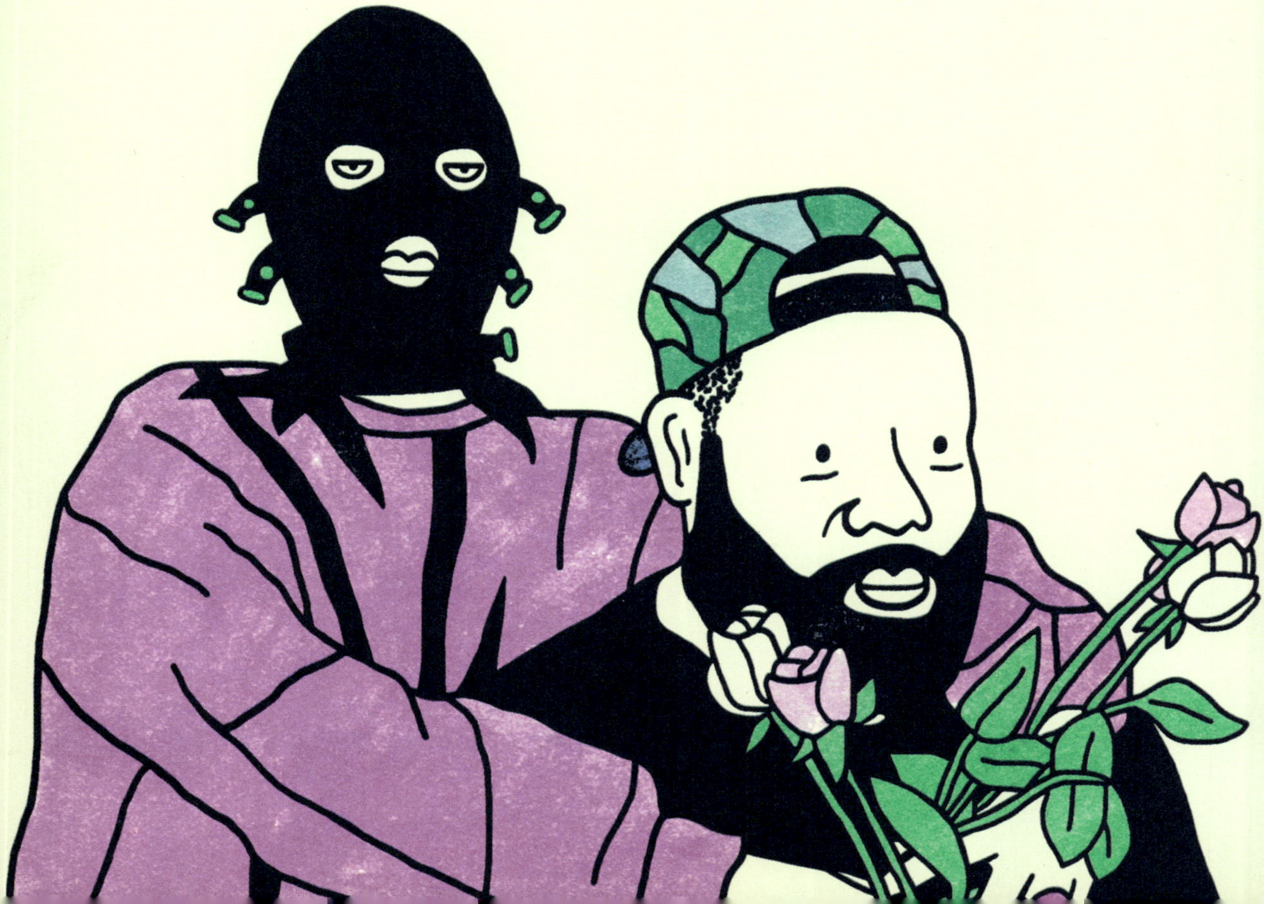

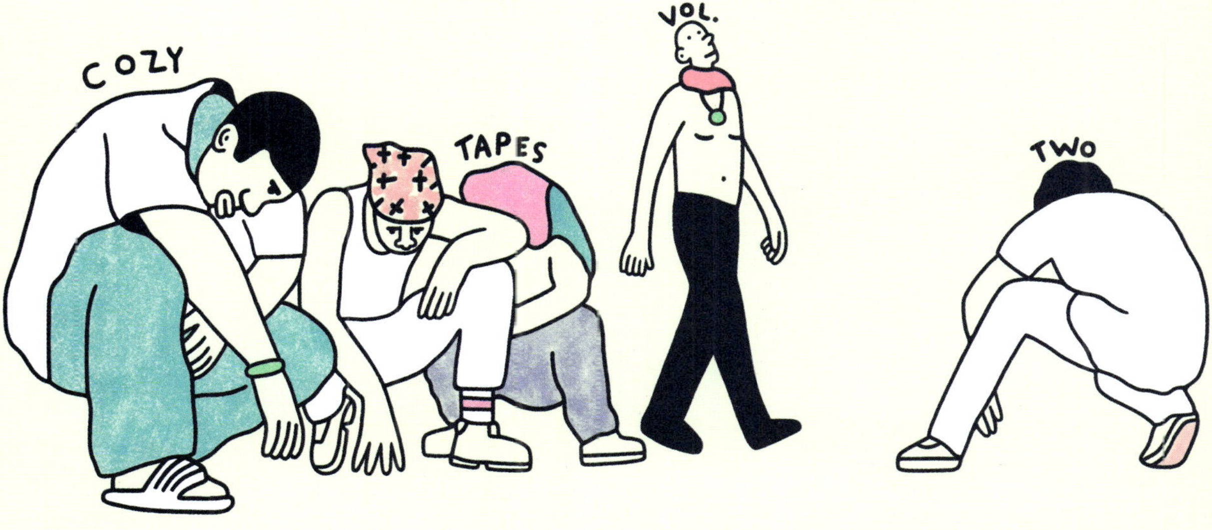
COZY
TAPES
VOL.
TWO

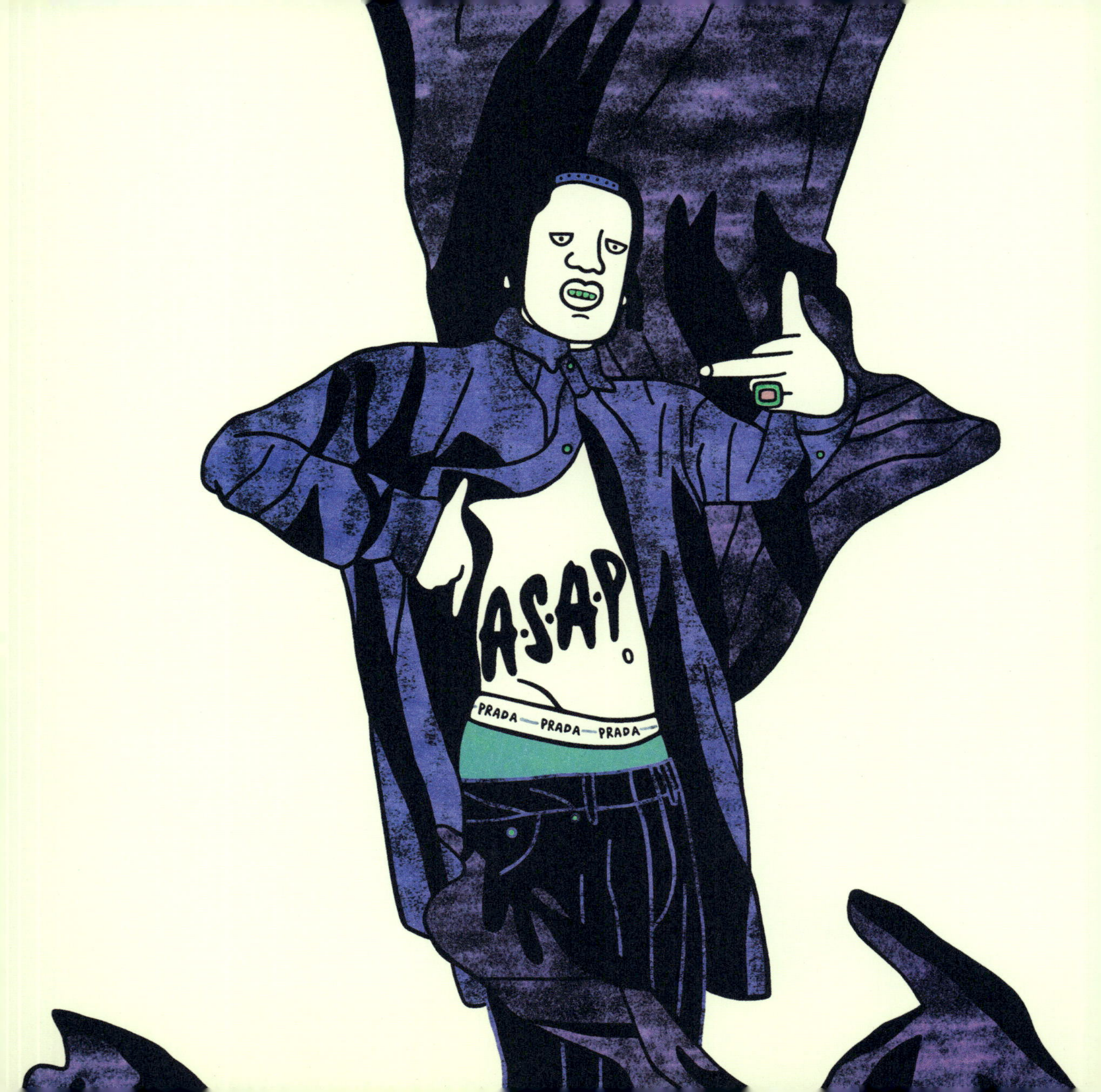
A·S·A·P
PRADA PRADA PRADA

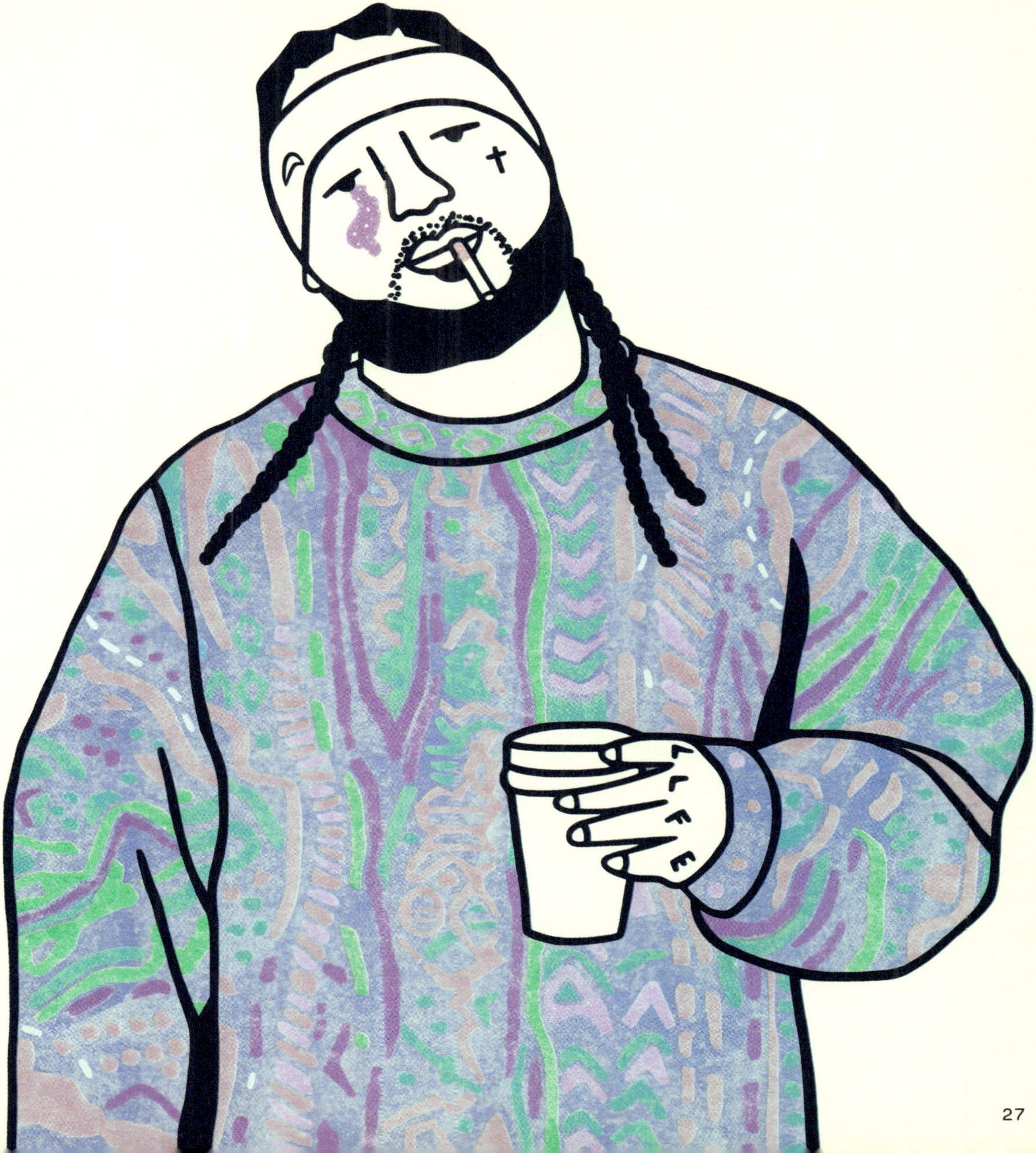
LLFE

PIZZA

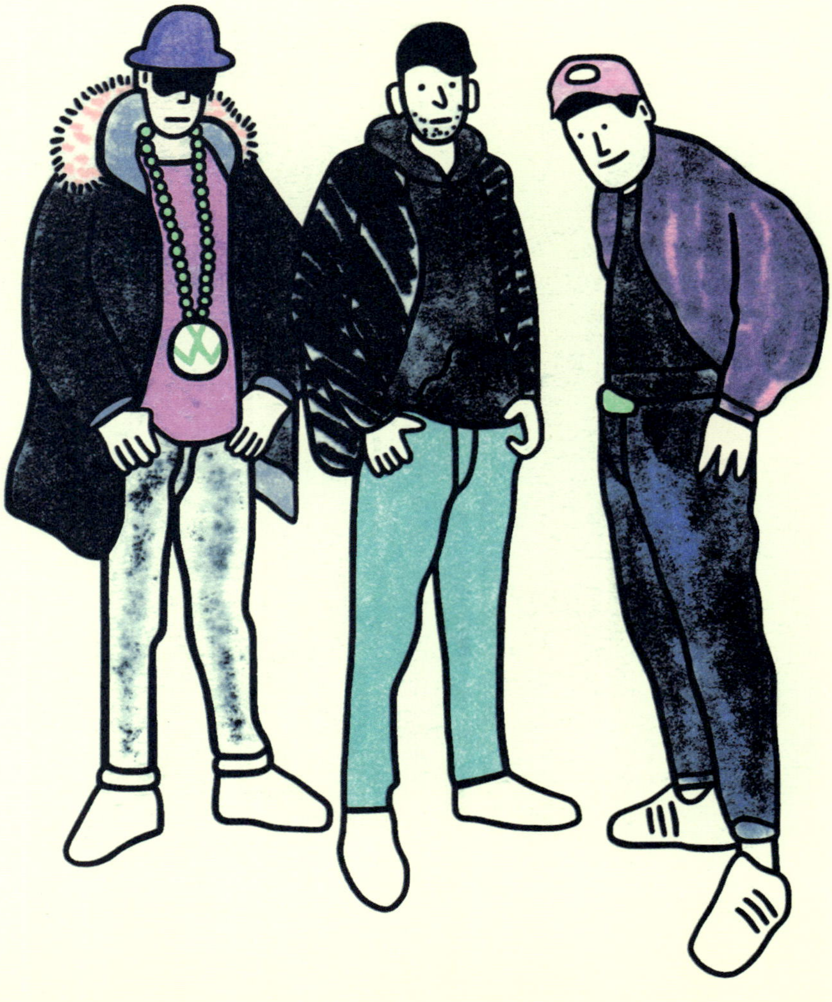

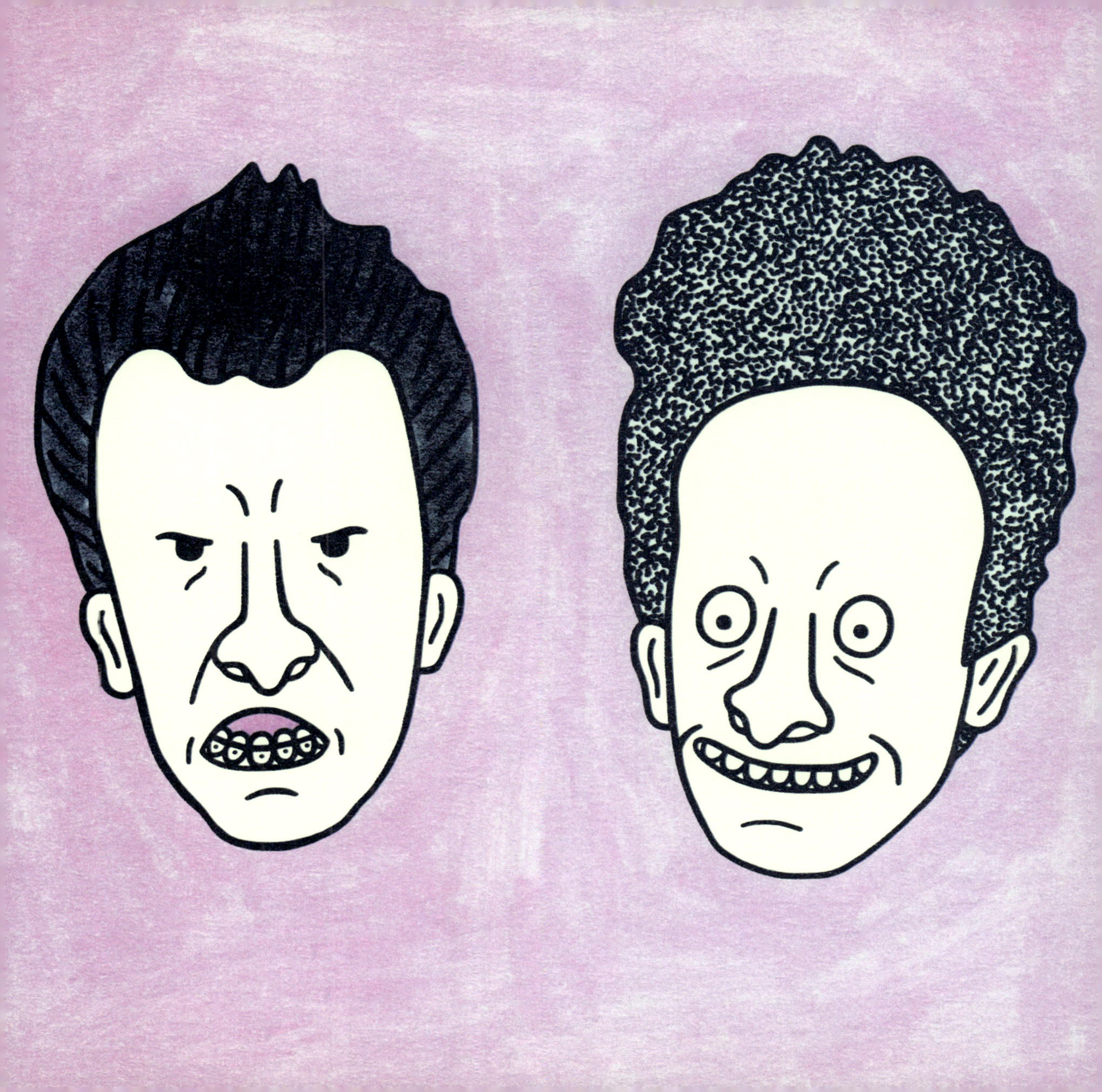

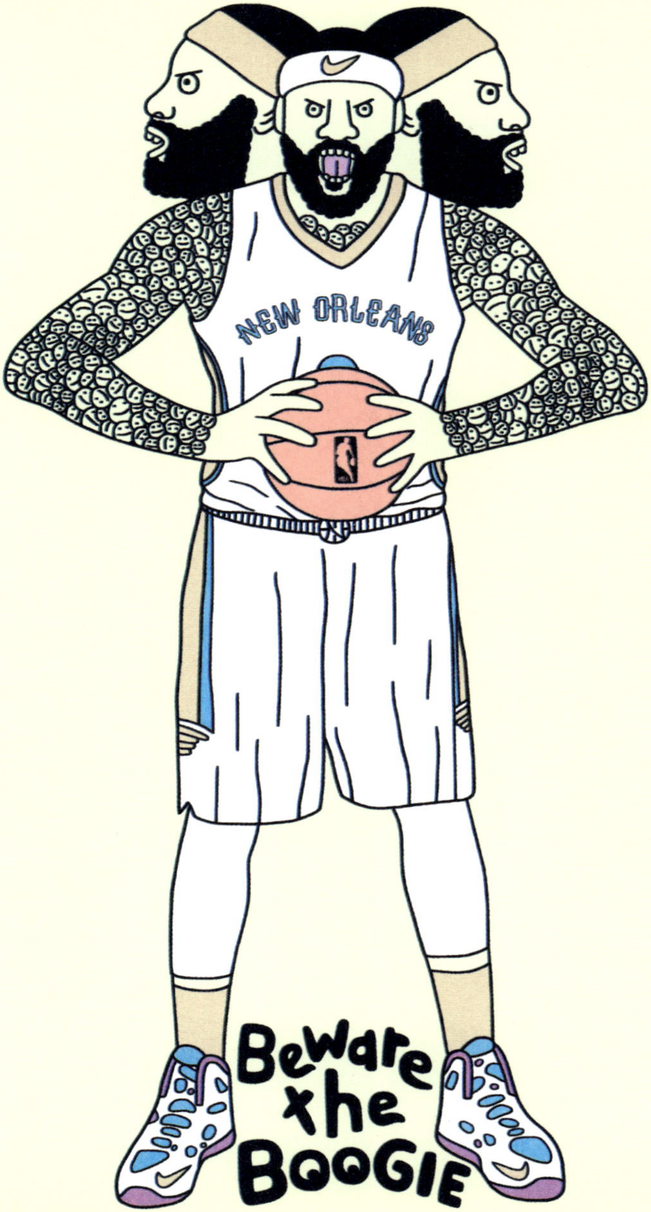
NEW ORLEANS
Beware
the
BOOGIE

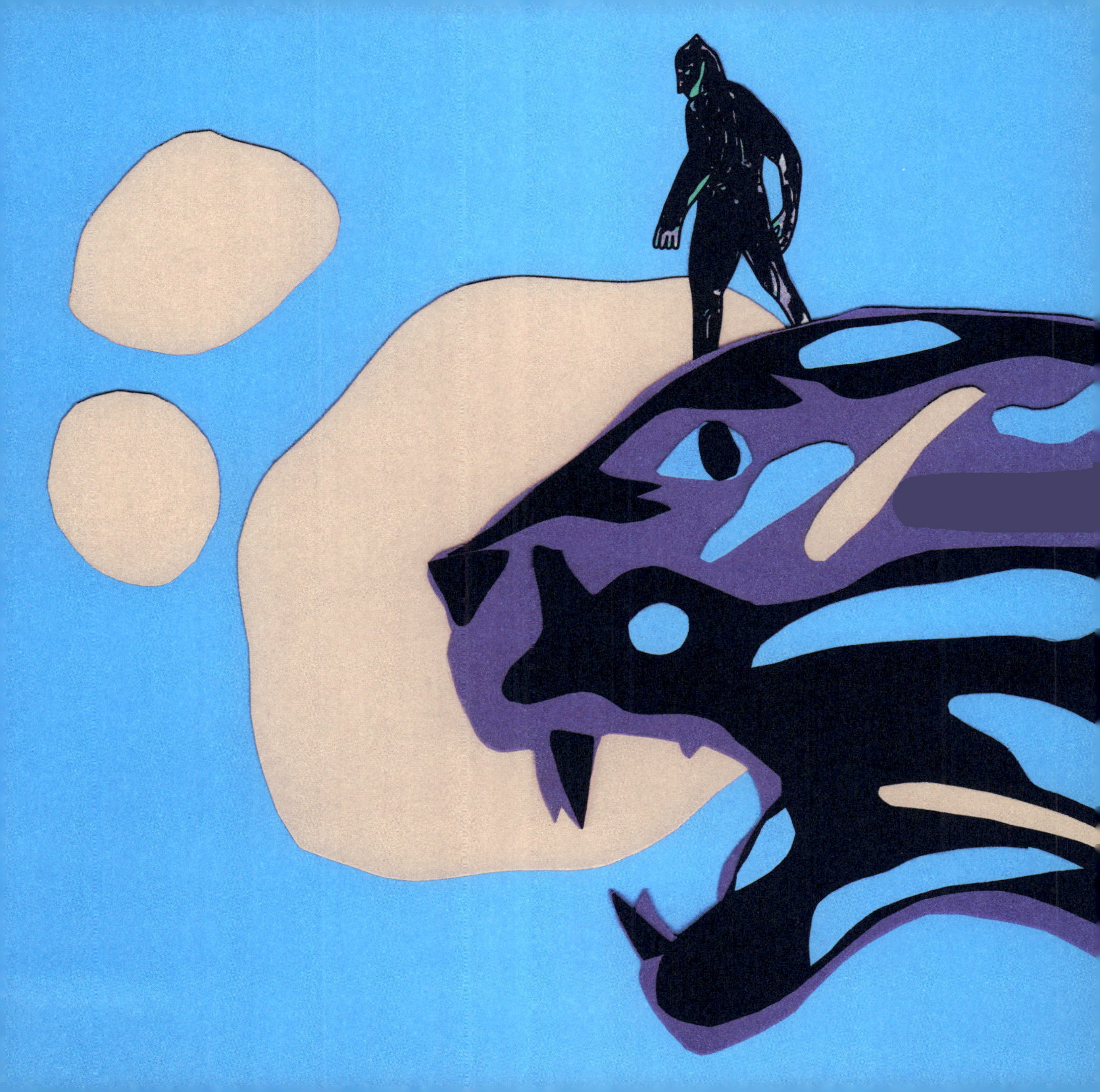

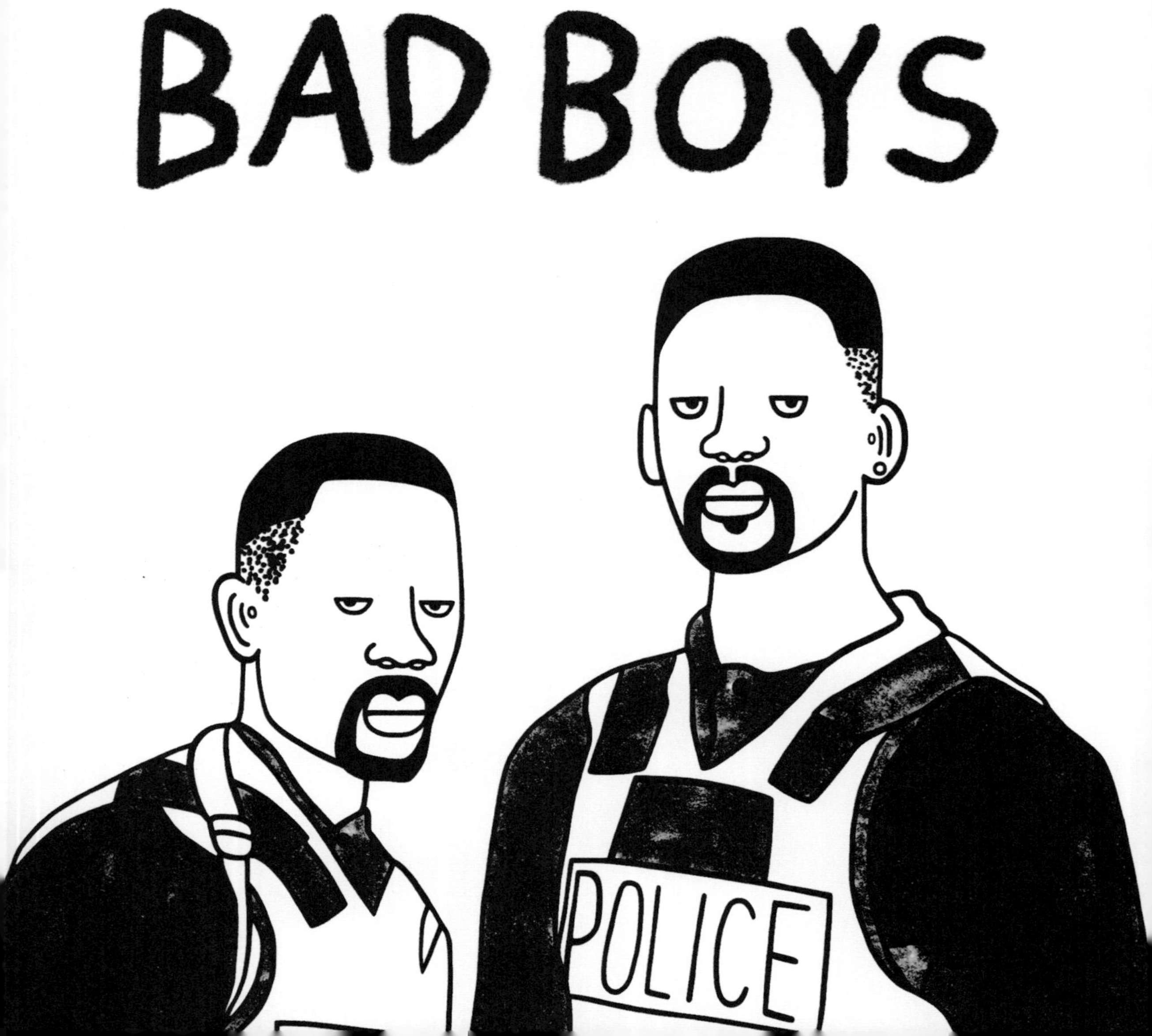
BAD BOYS
POLICE

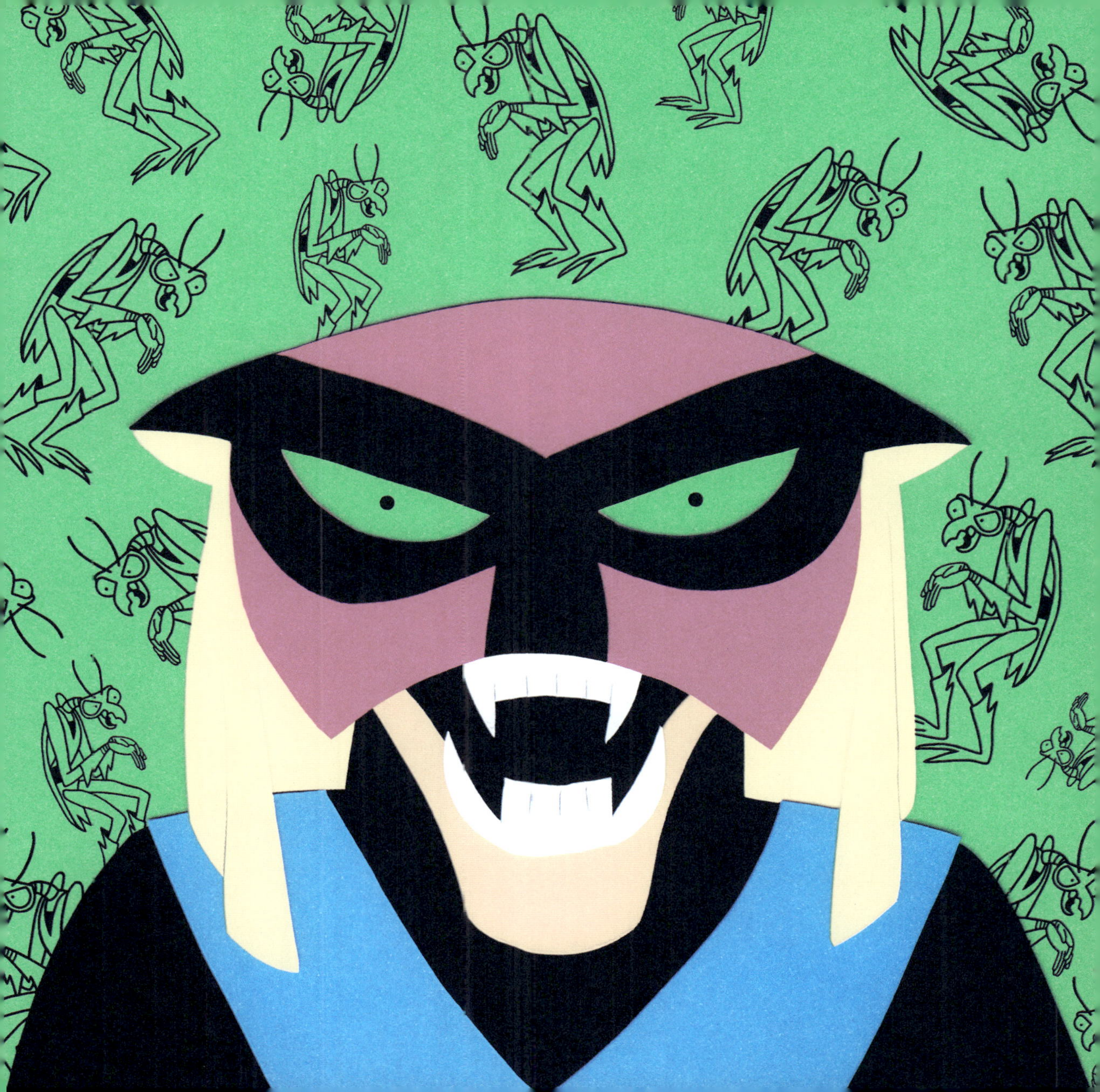

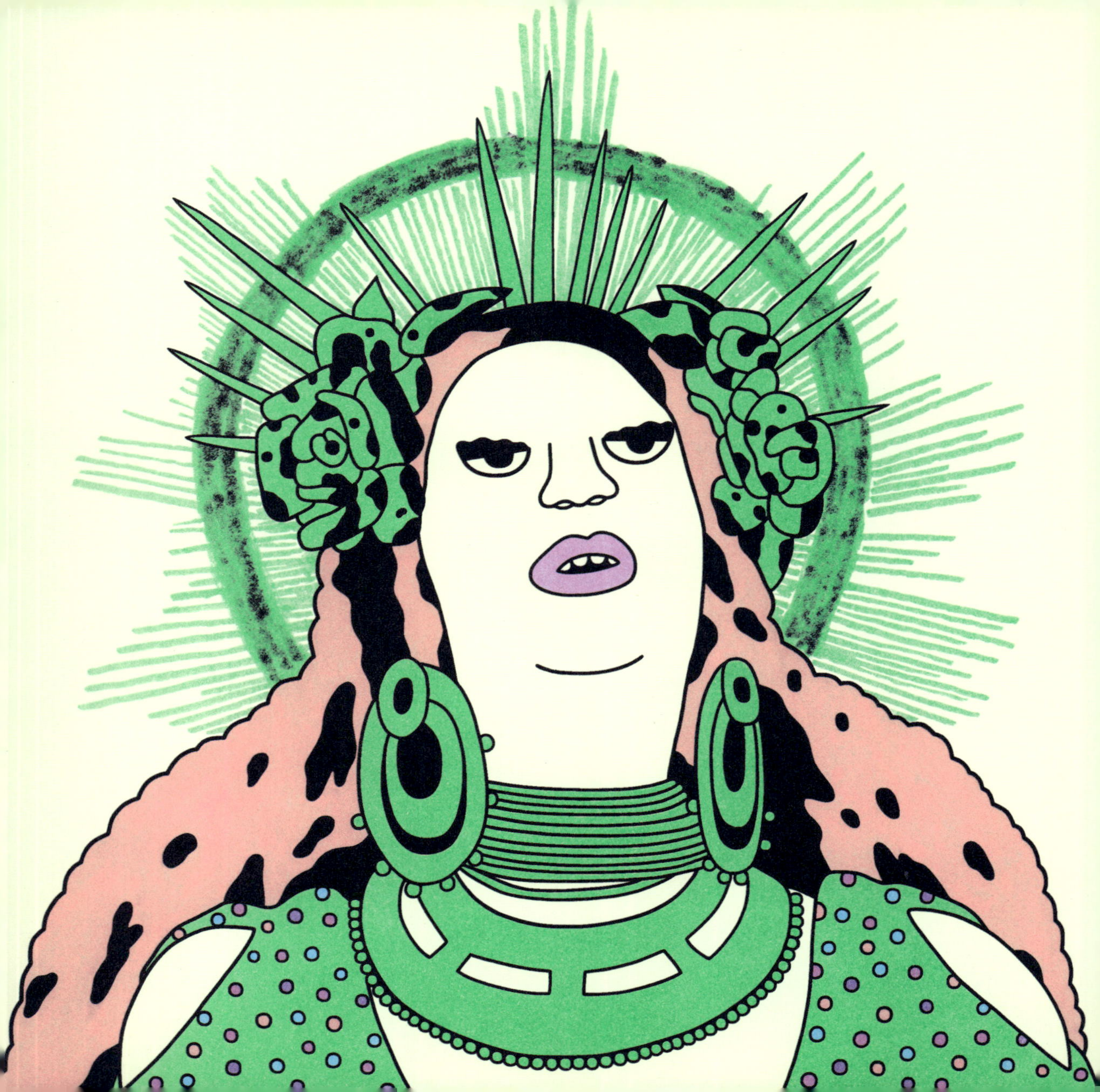

I ain't scared of you Motherfuckas

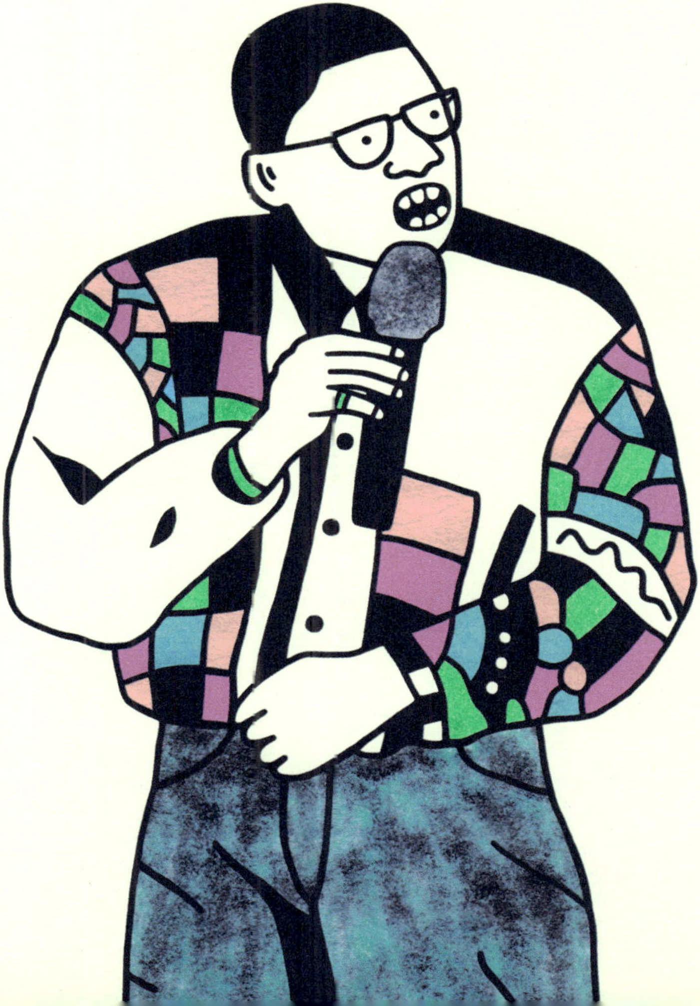

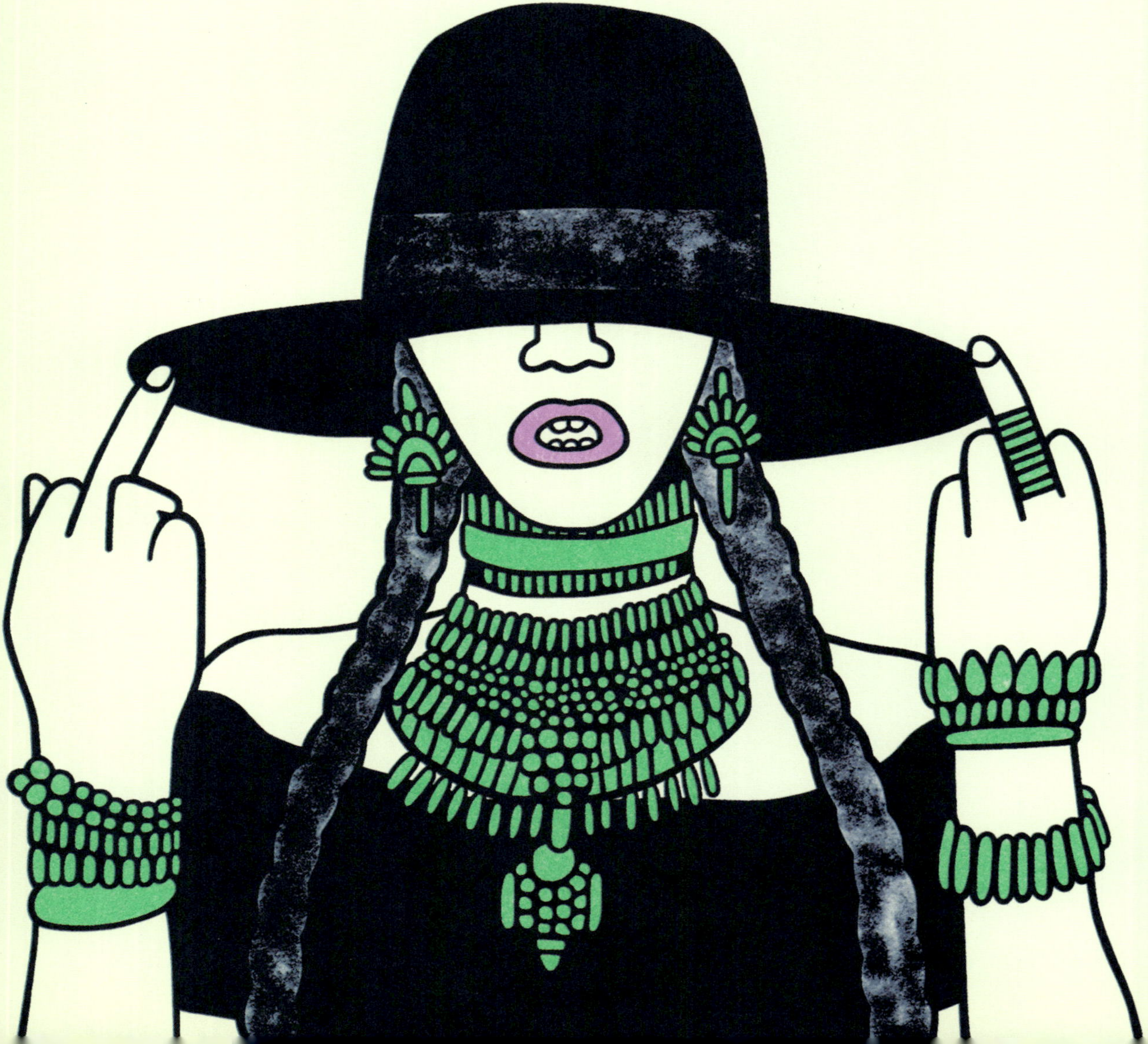

@BigSean more like big fucking douche.

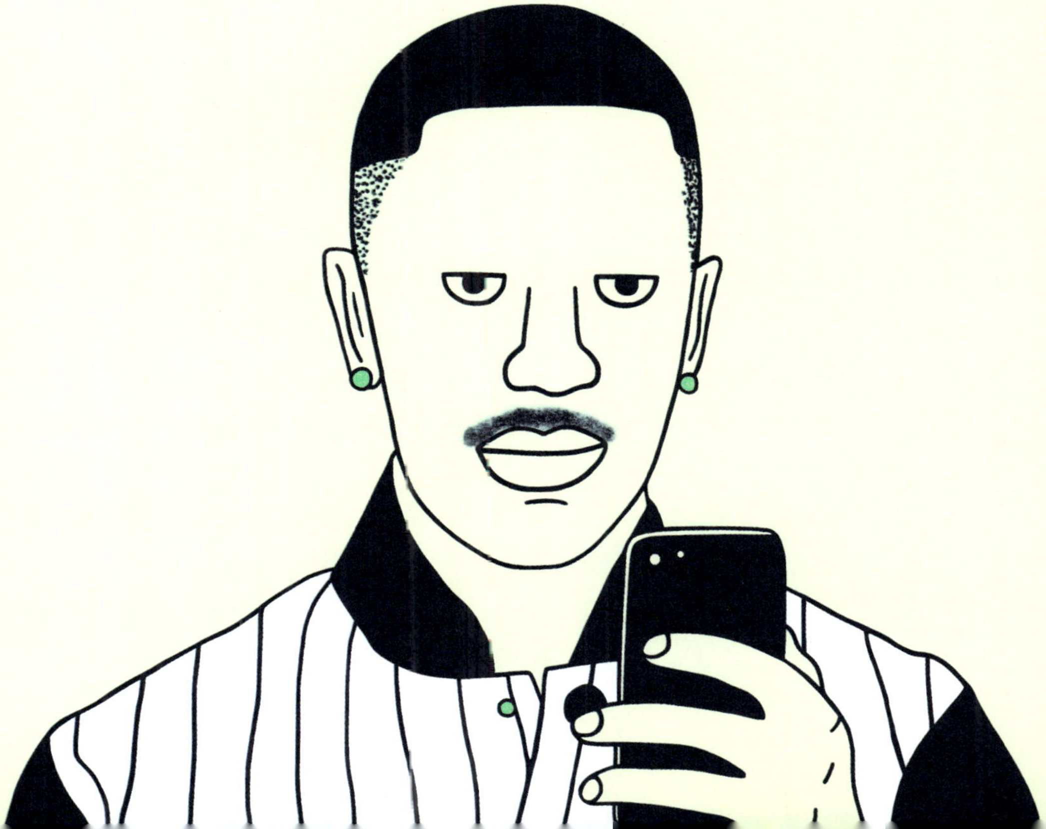

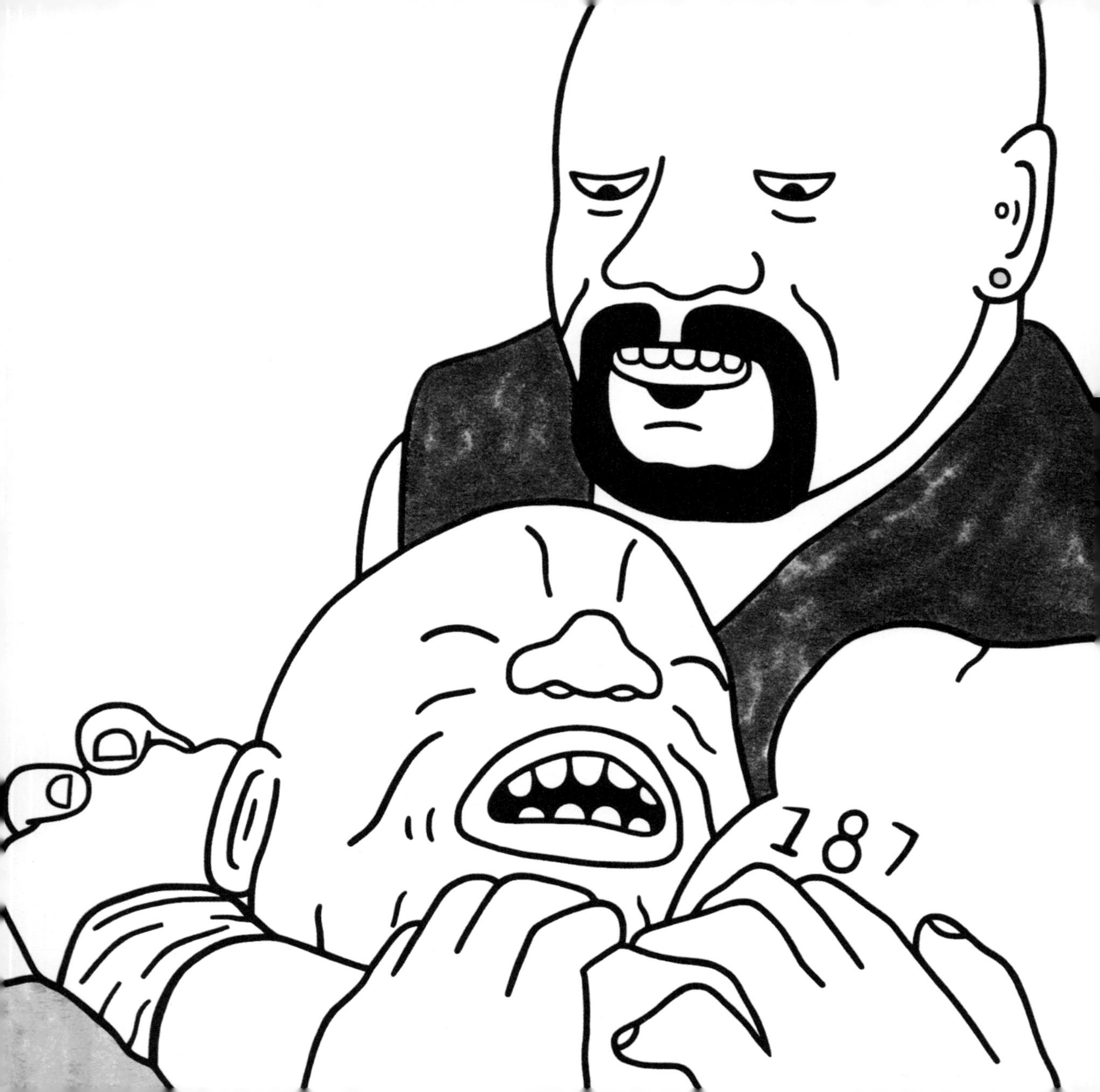
187

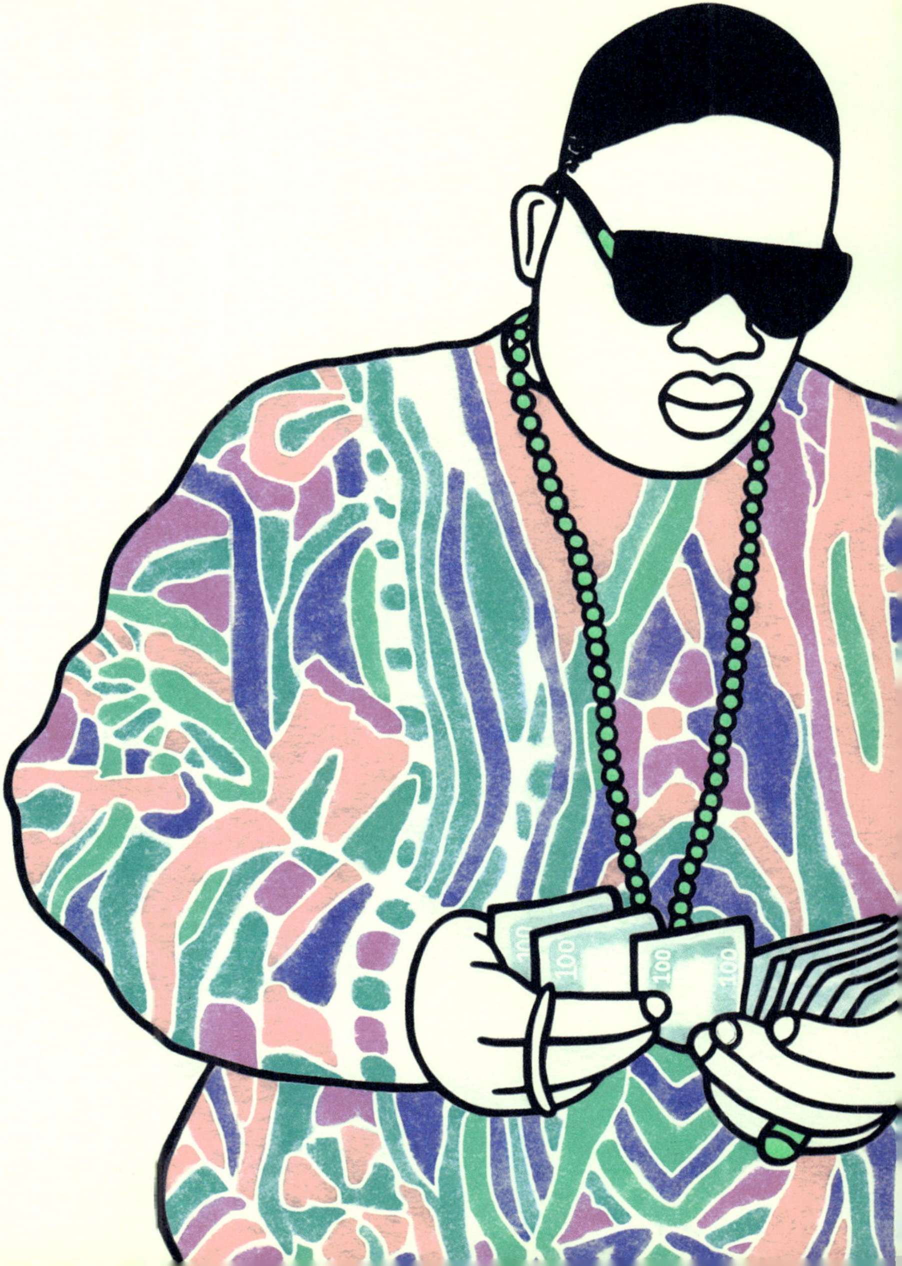
100
100
100

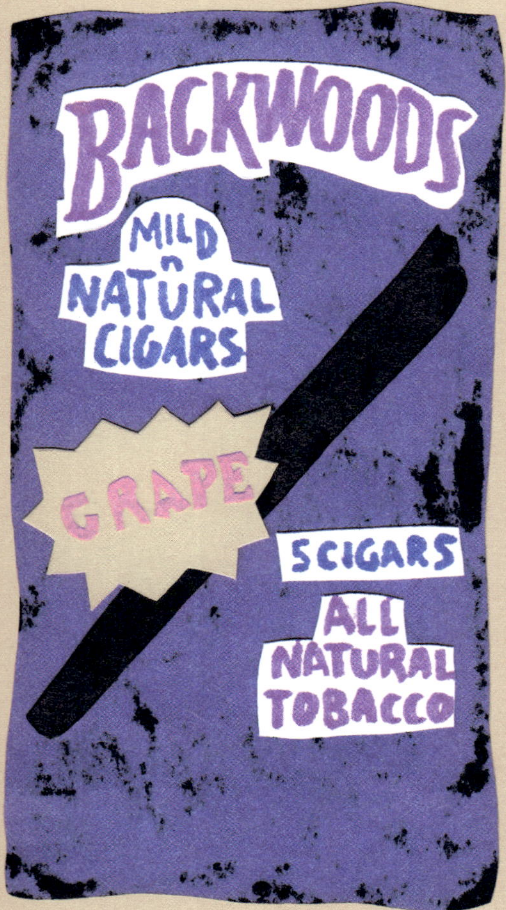
BACKWOODS
MILD n NATURAL CIGARS
GRAPE
5 CIGARS
ALL NATURAL TOBACCO

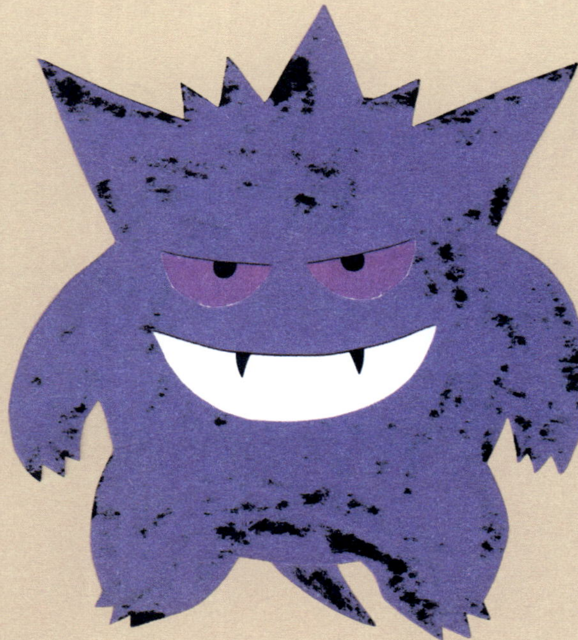

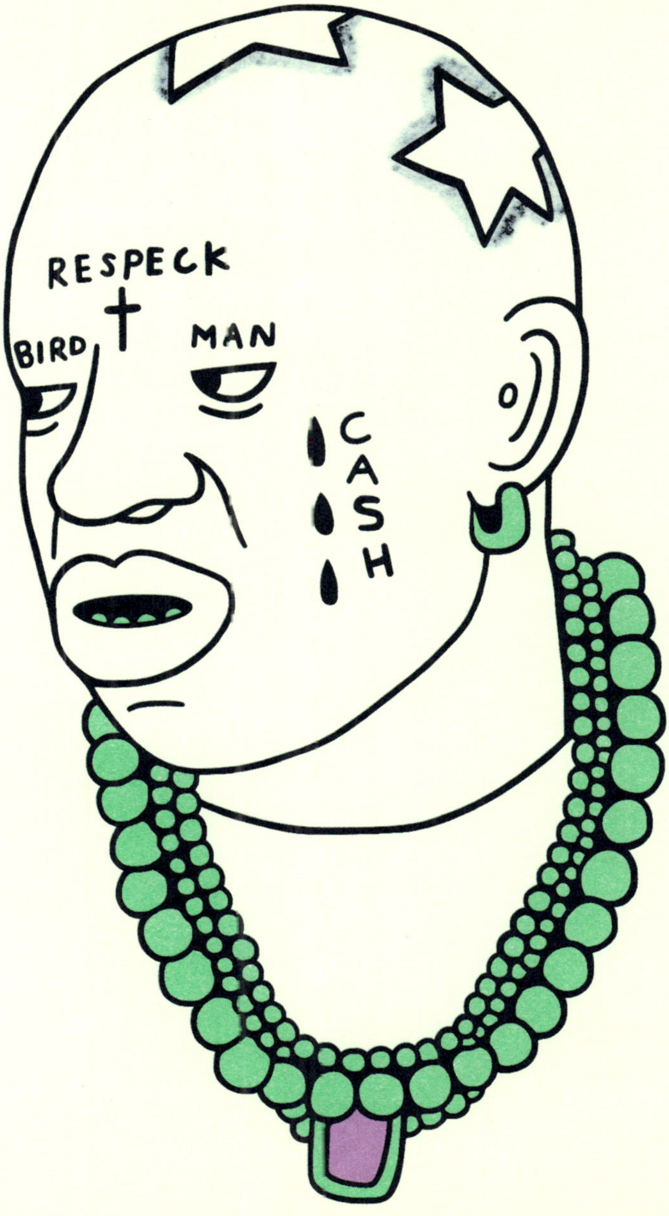
RESPECK
BIRD
MAN
CASH

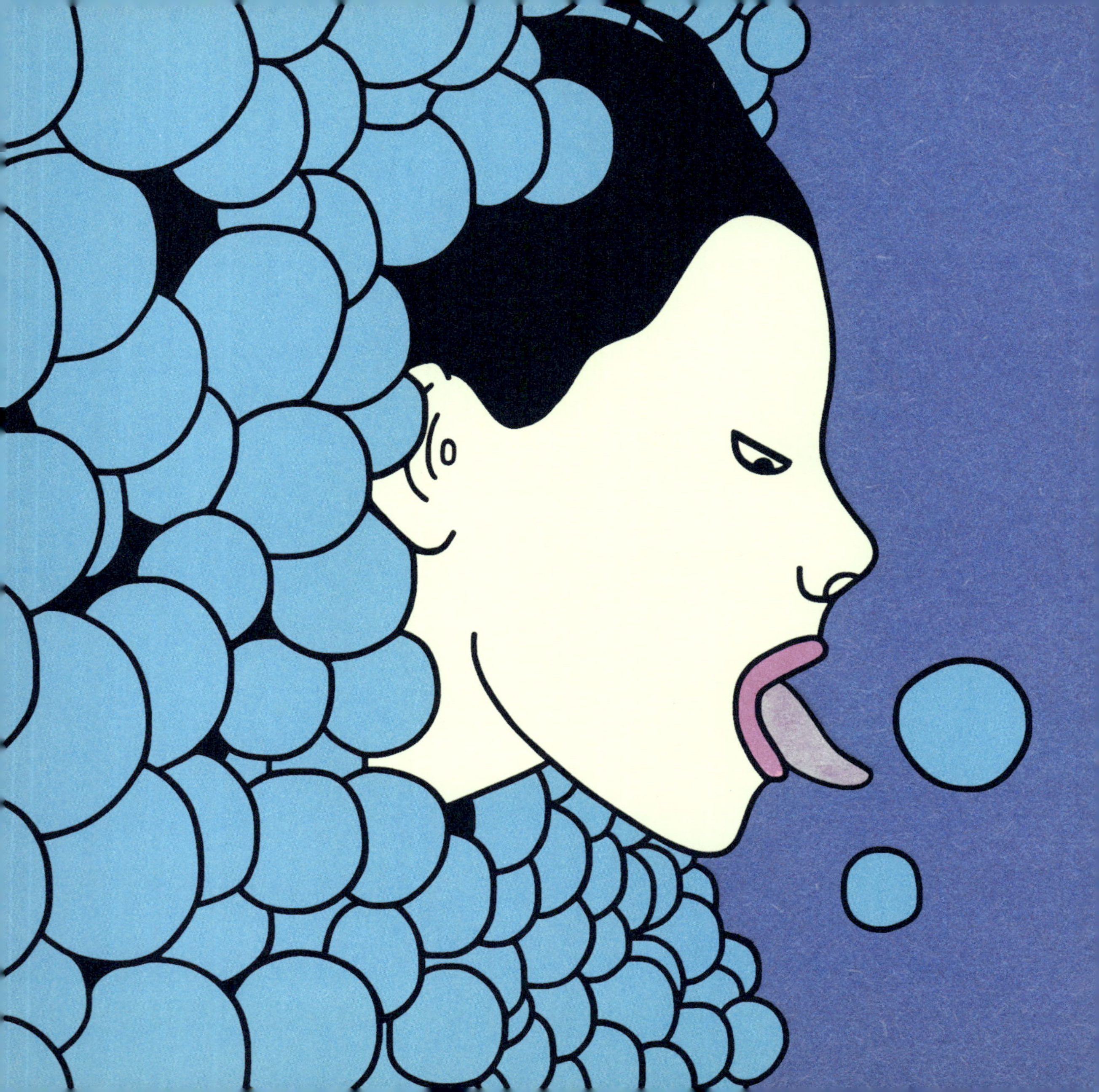

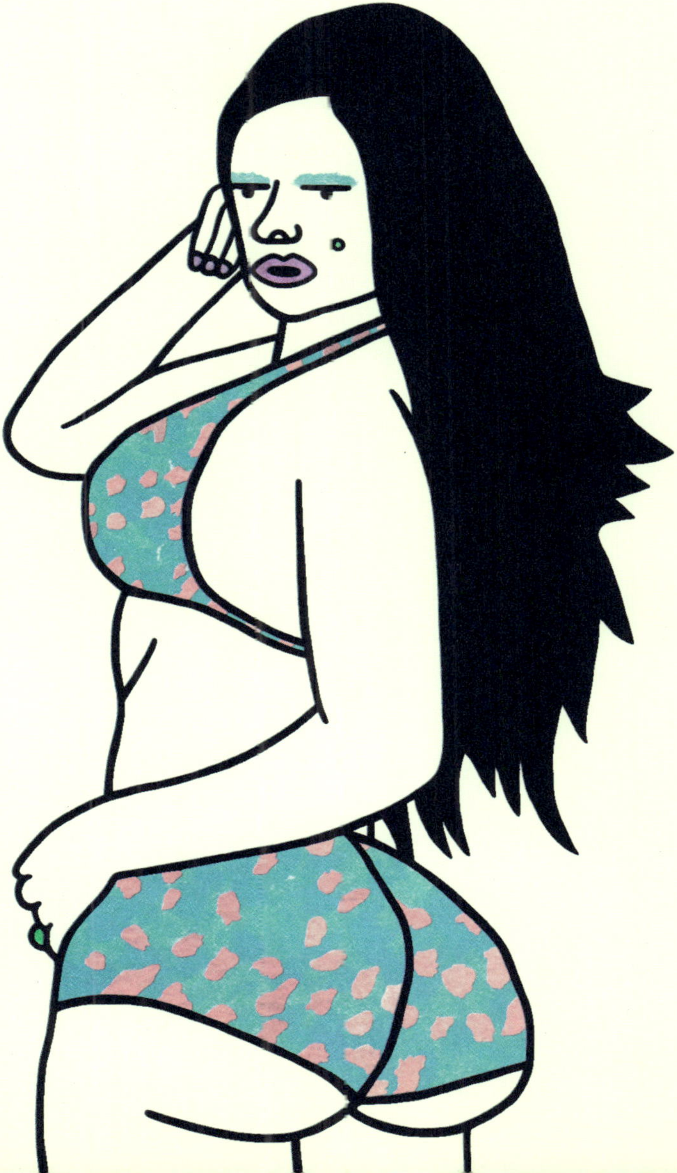

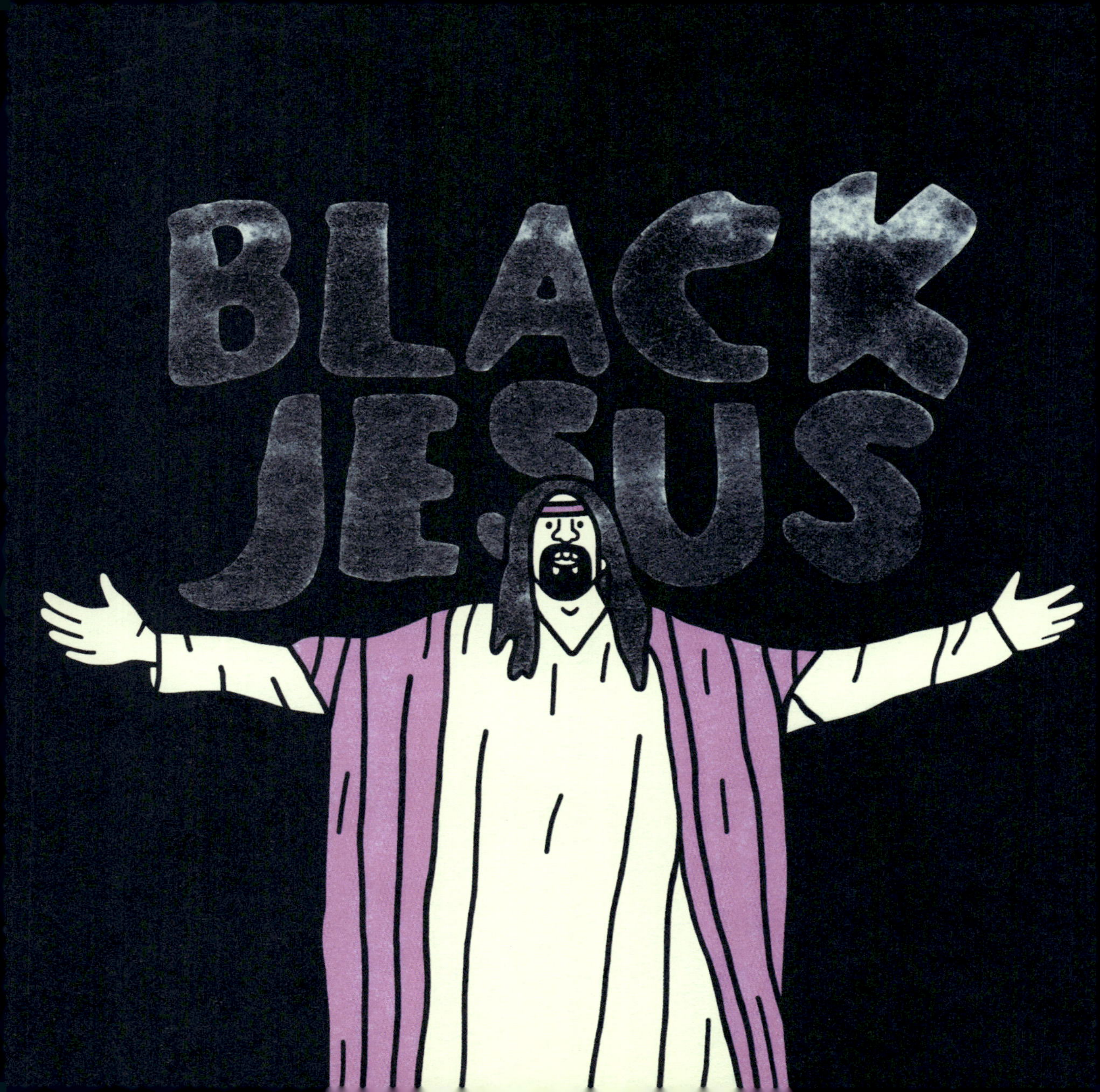
BLACK
JESUS

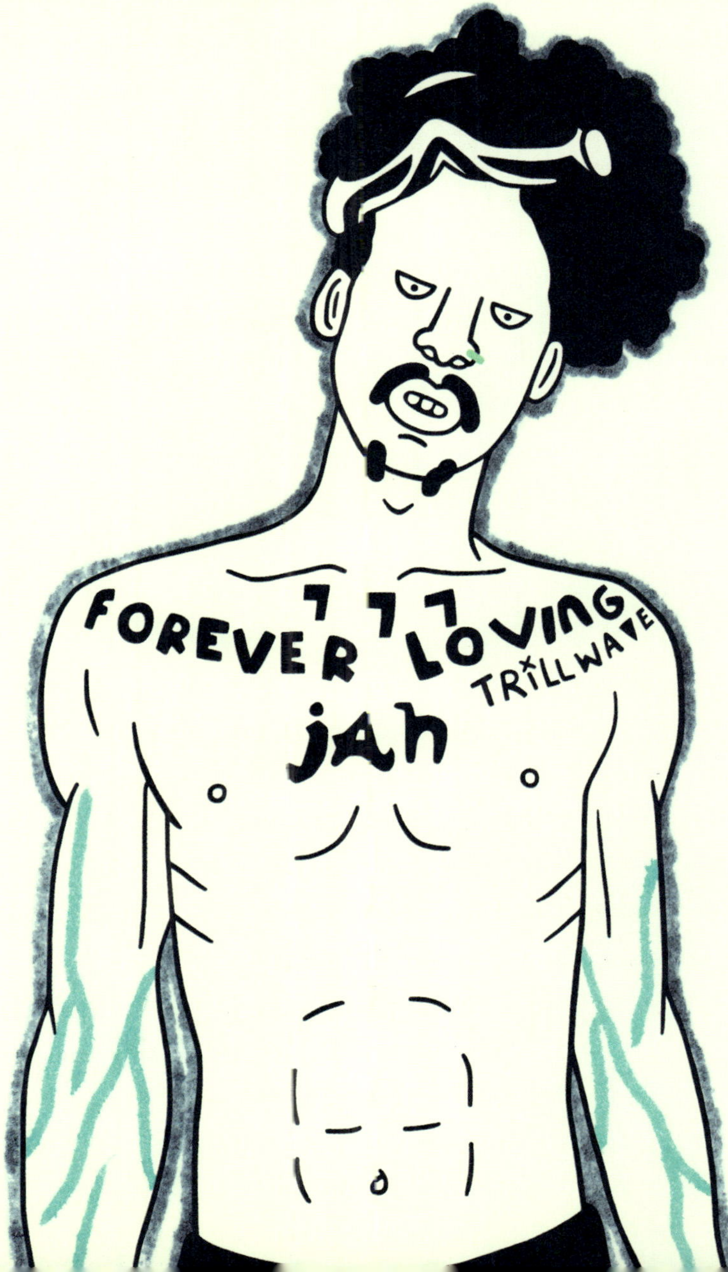
FOREVER 777 LOVING
TRILLWAVE
jah

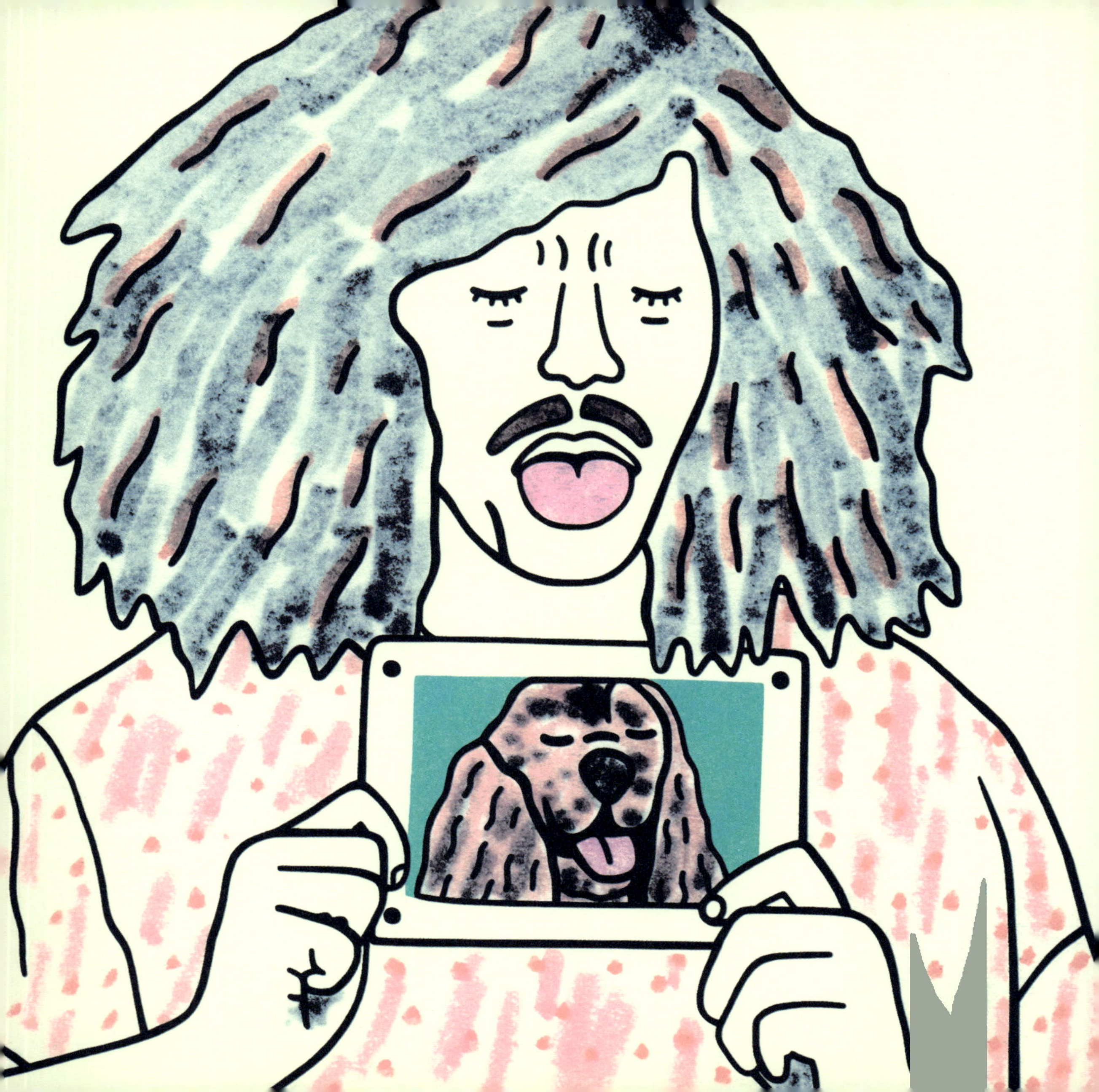

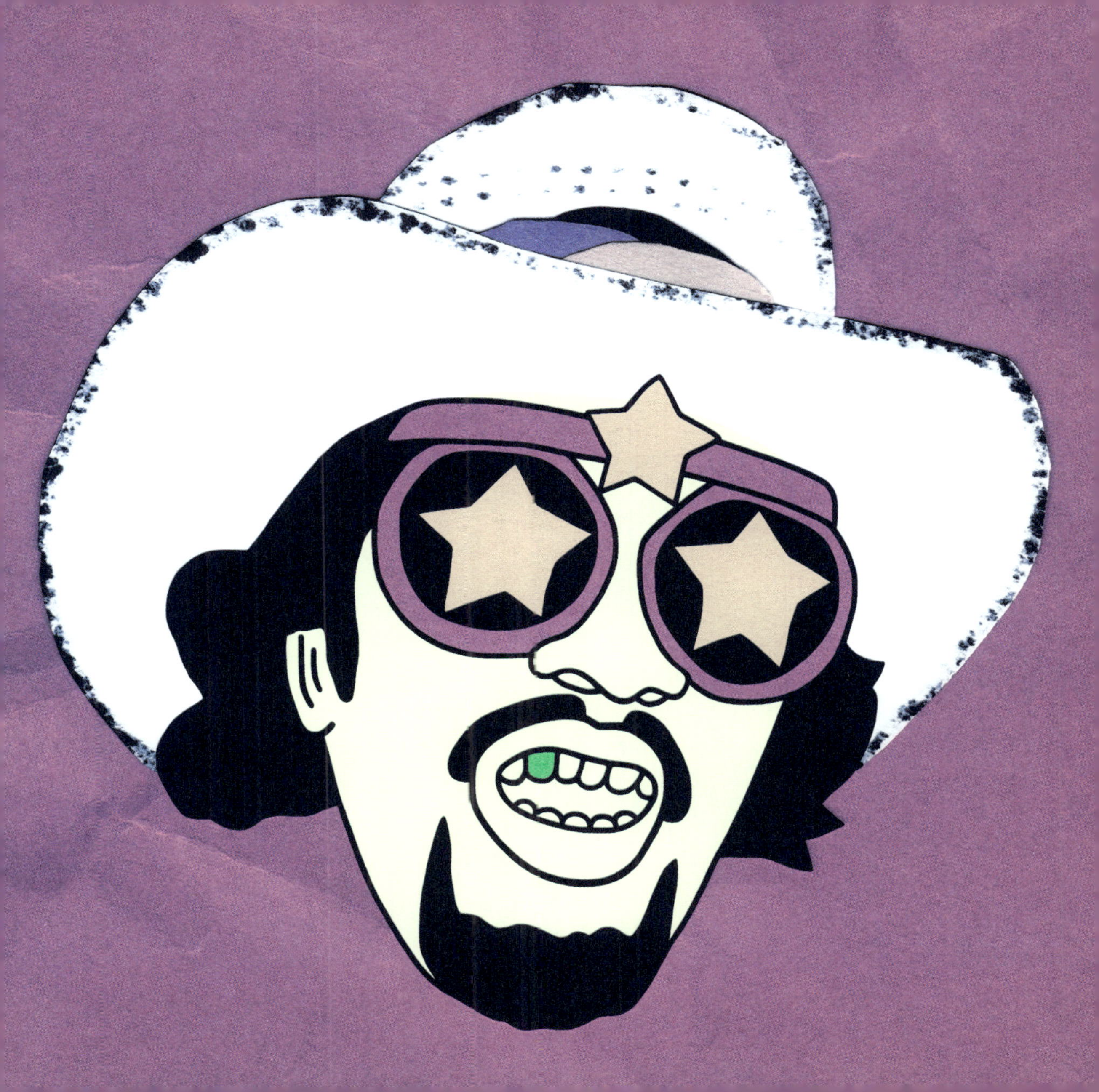

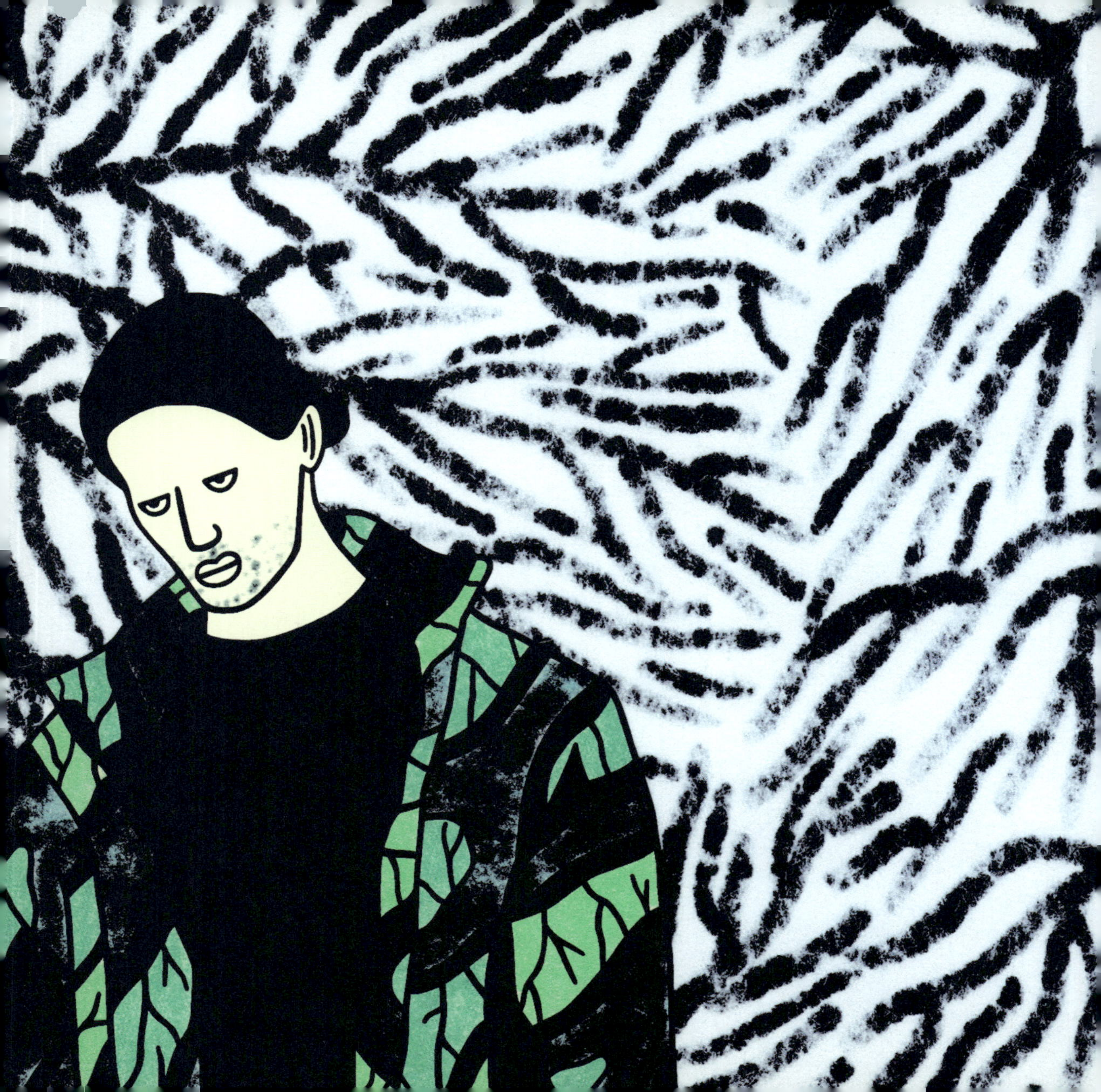

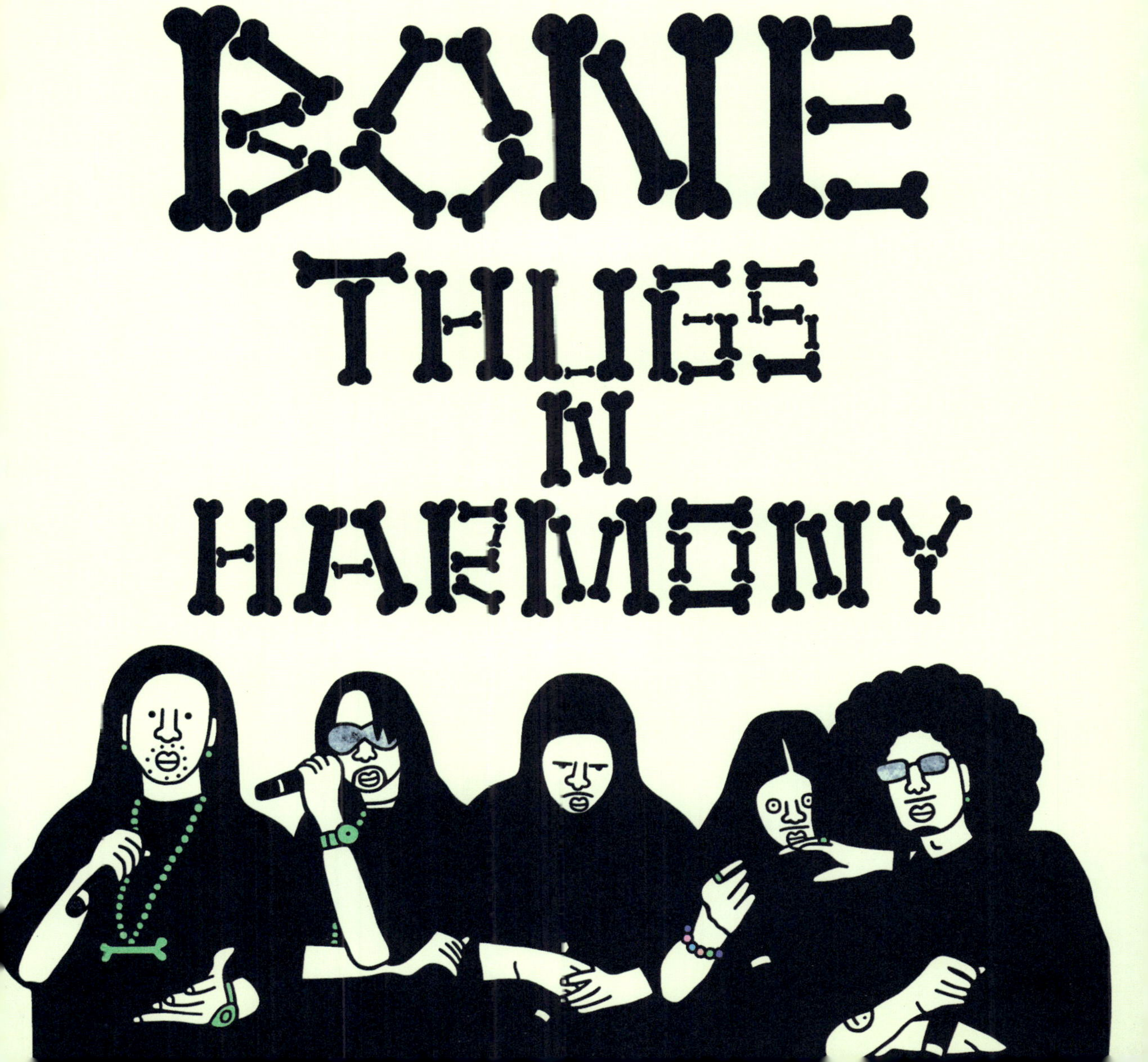
BONE
THUGS
N
HARMONY

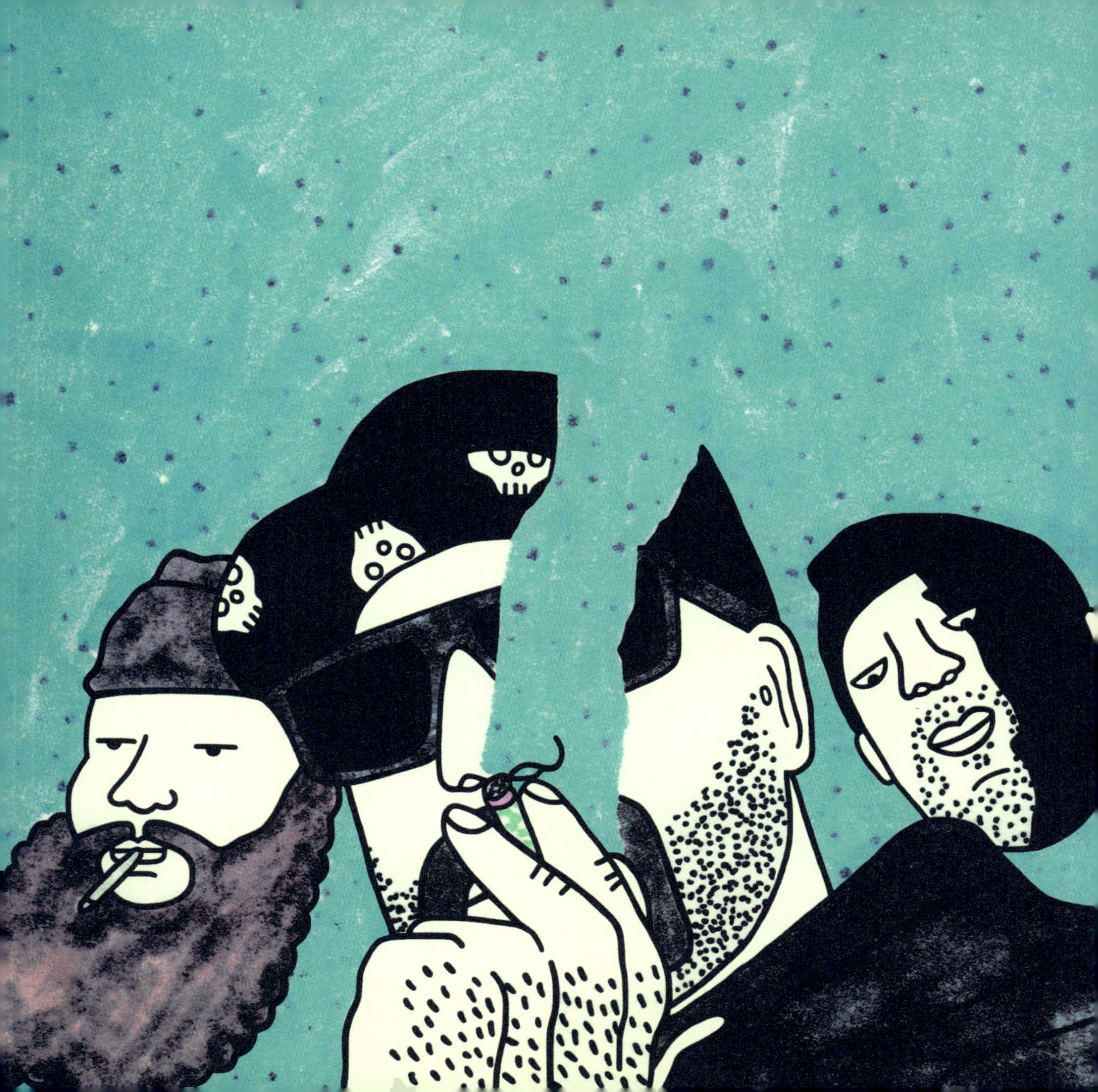

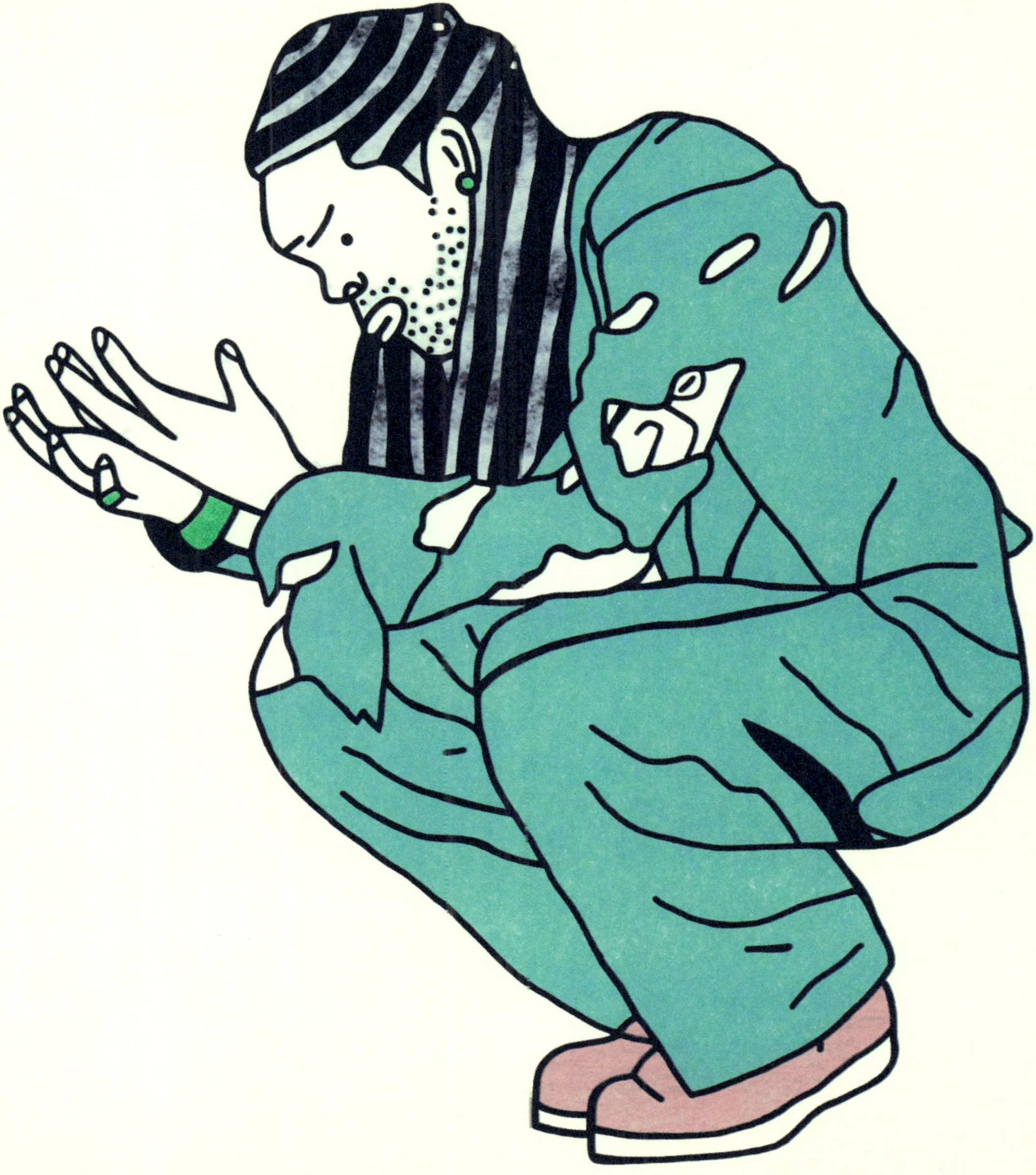

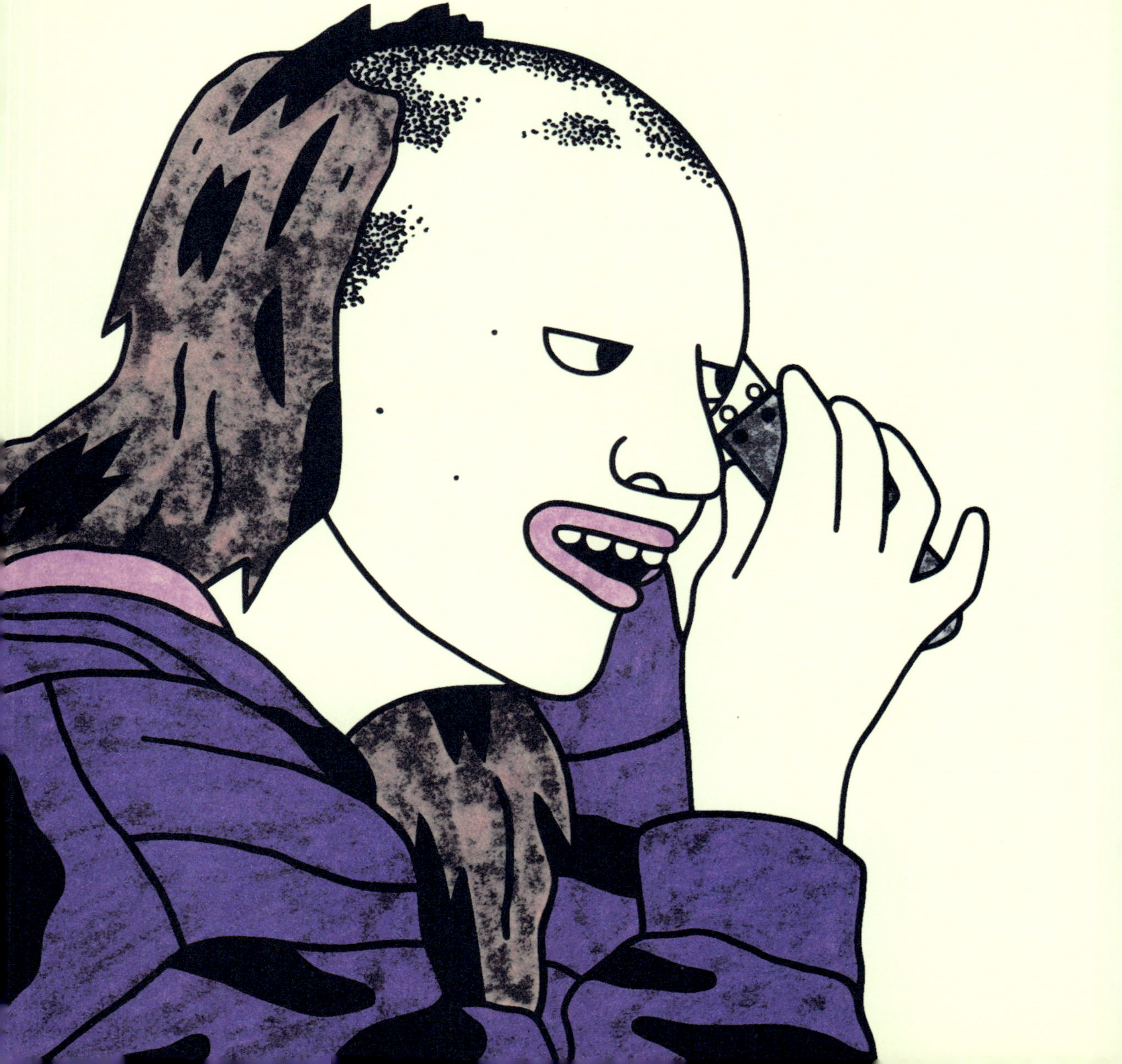

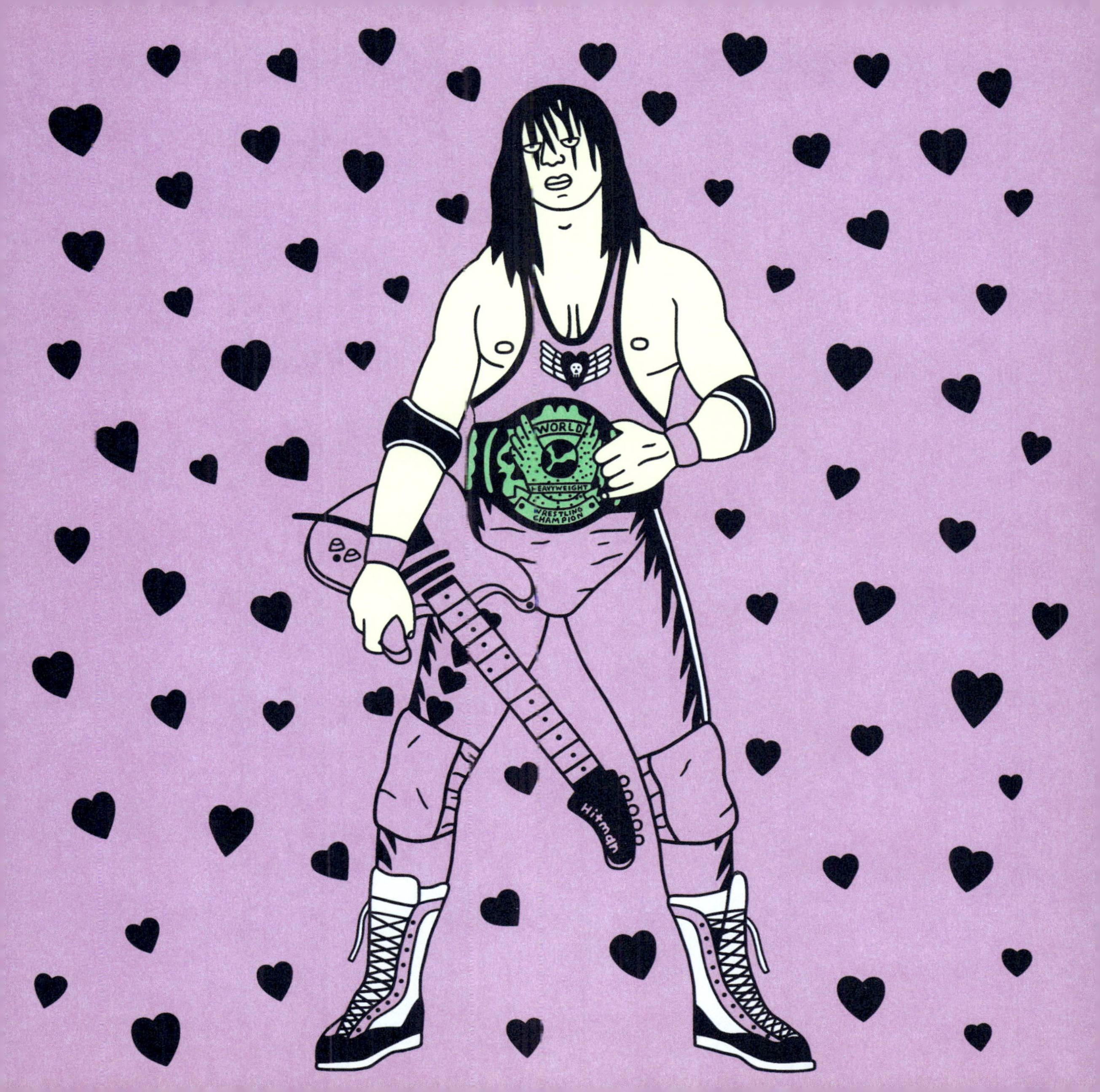
WORLD
HEAVYWEIGHT
WRESTLING
CHAMPION
Hitman

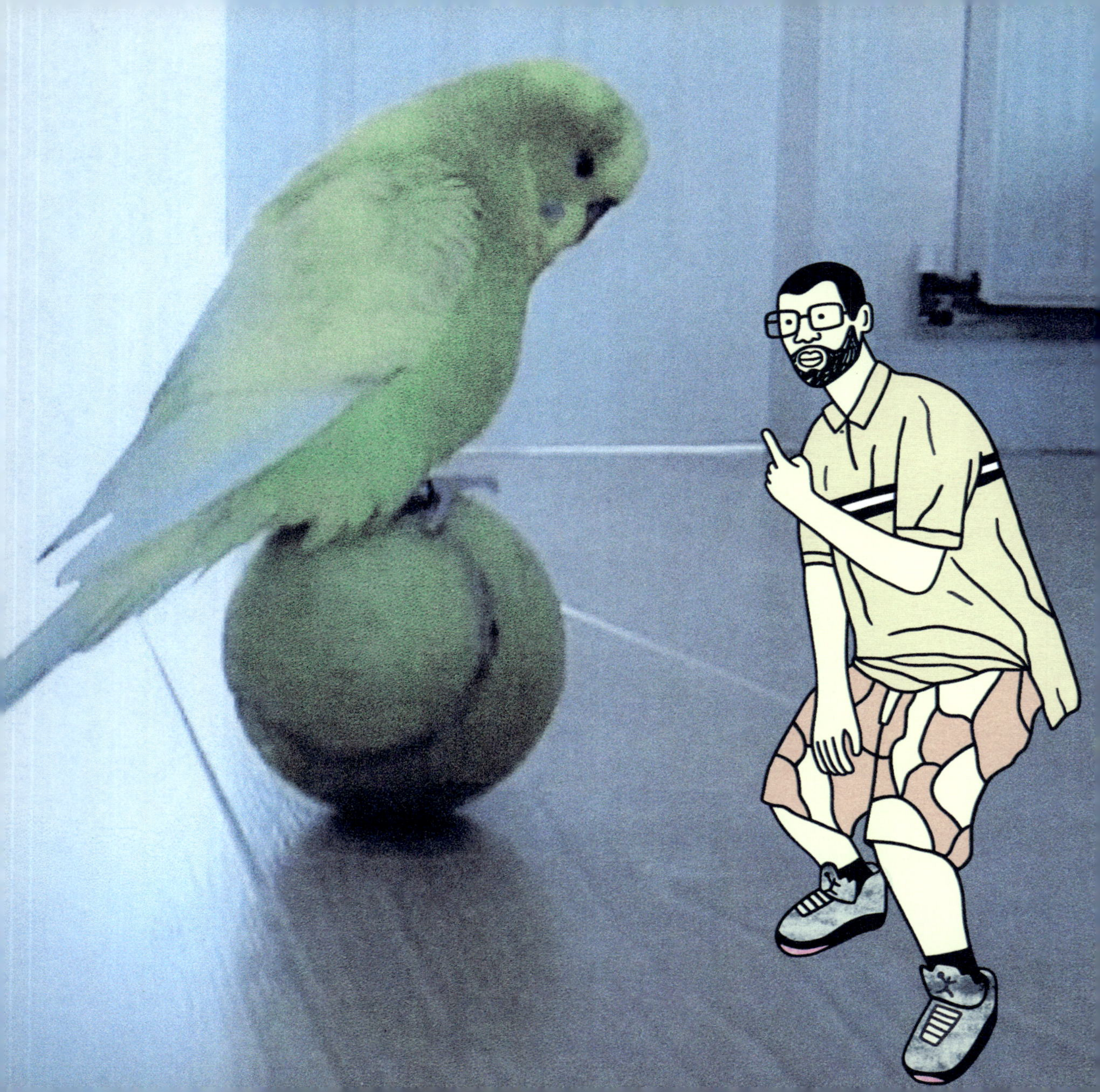

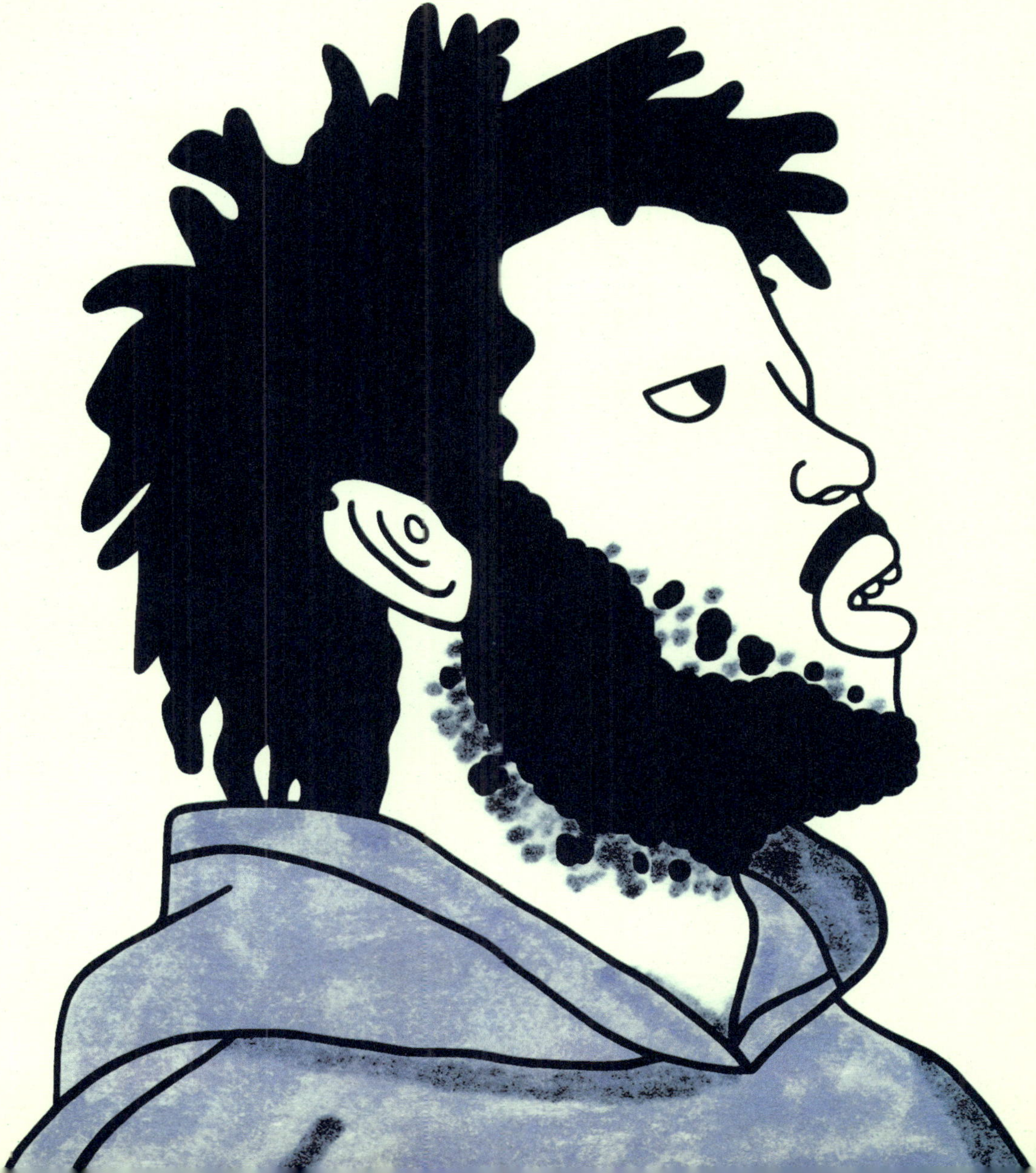

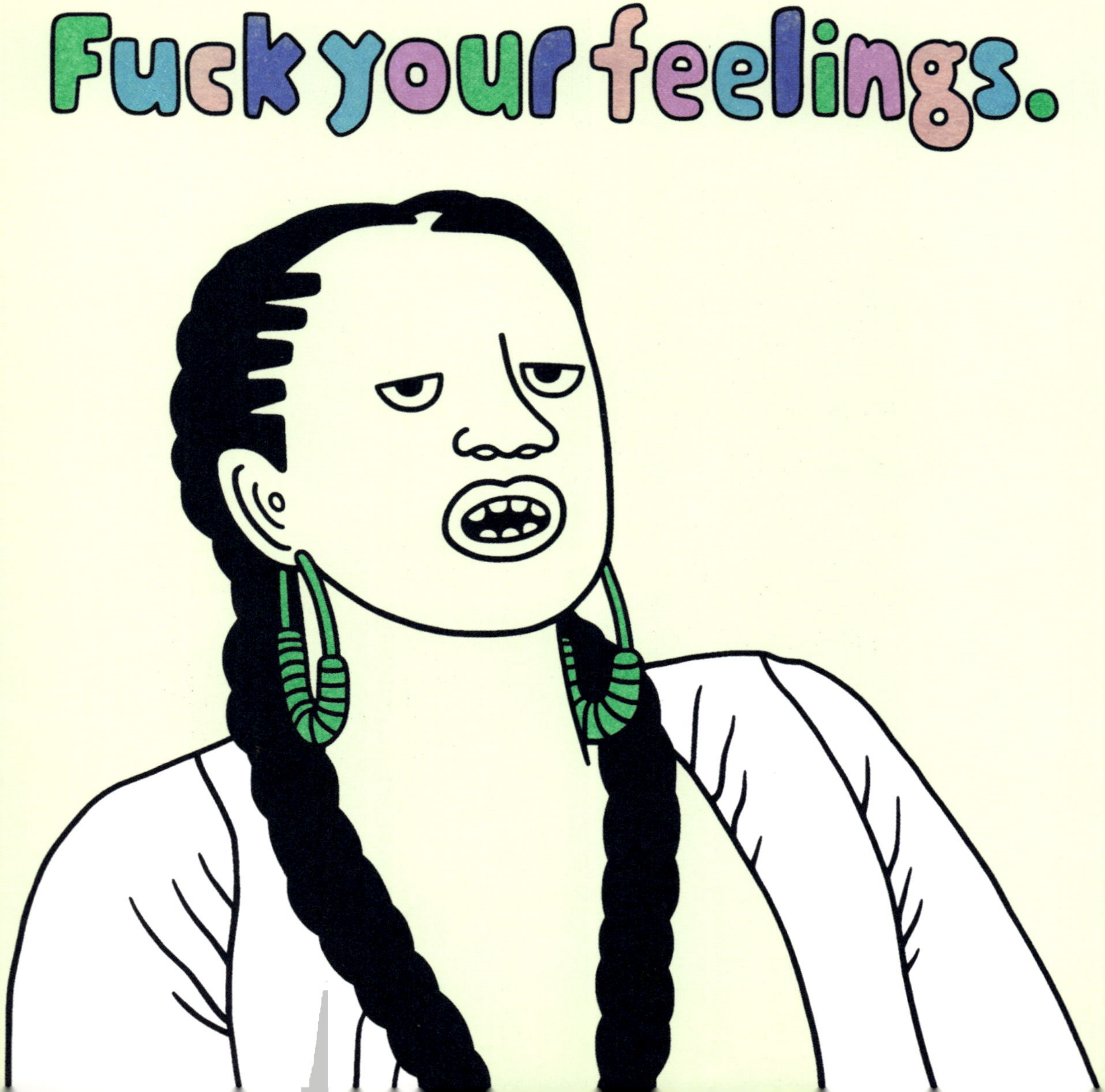
Fuck your feelings.

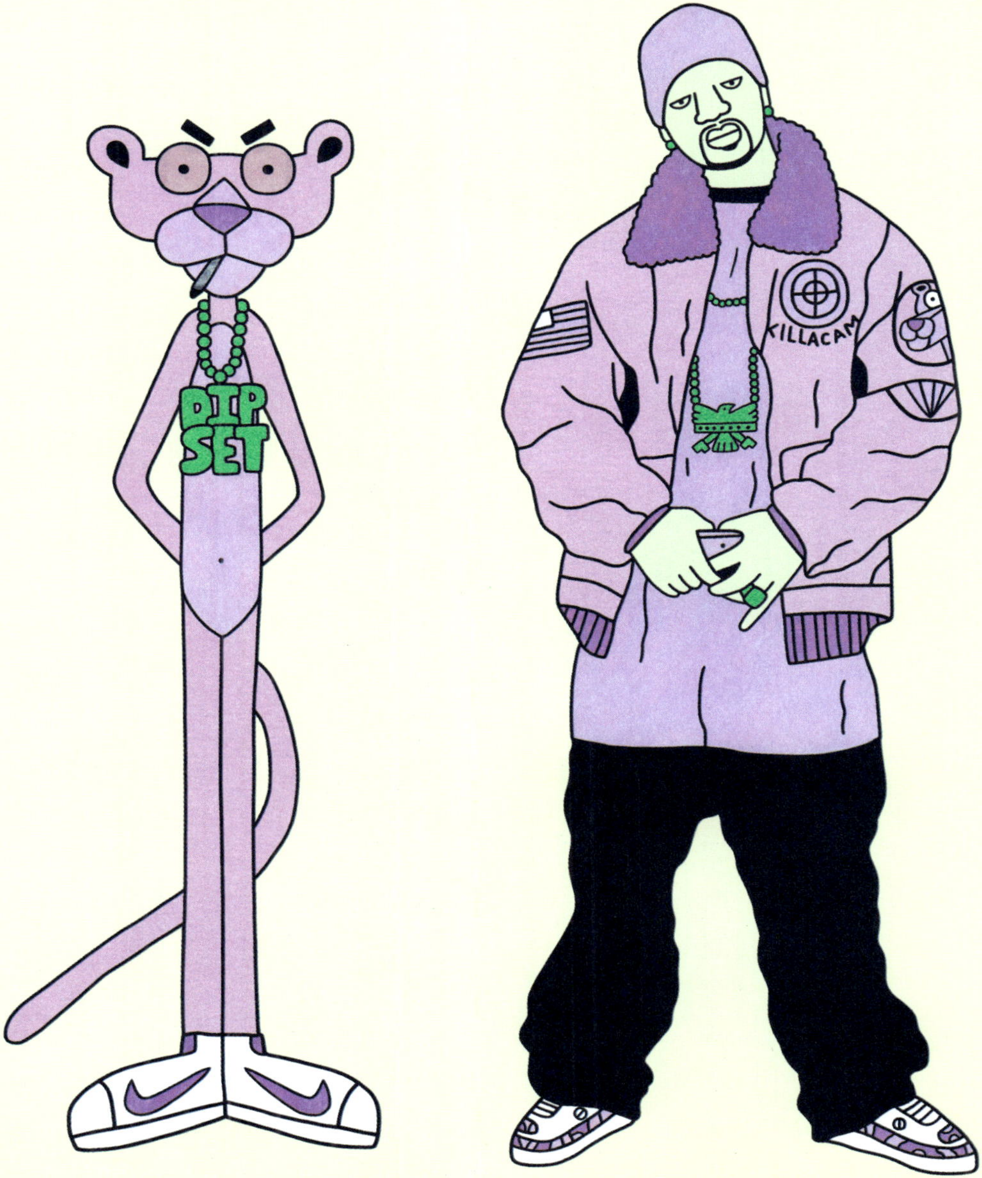
DIP SET
KILLACAM

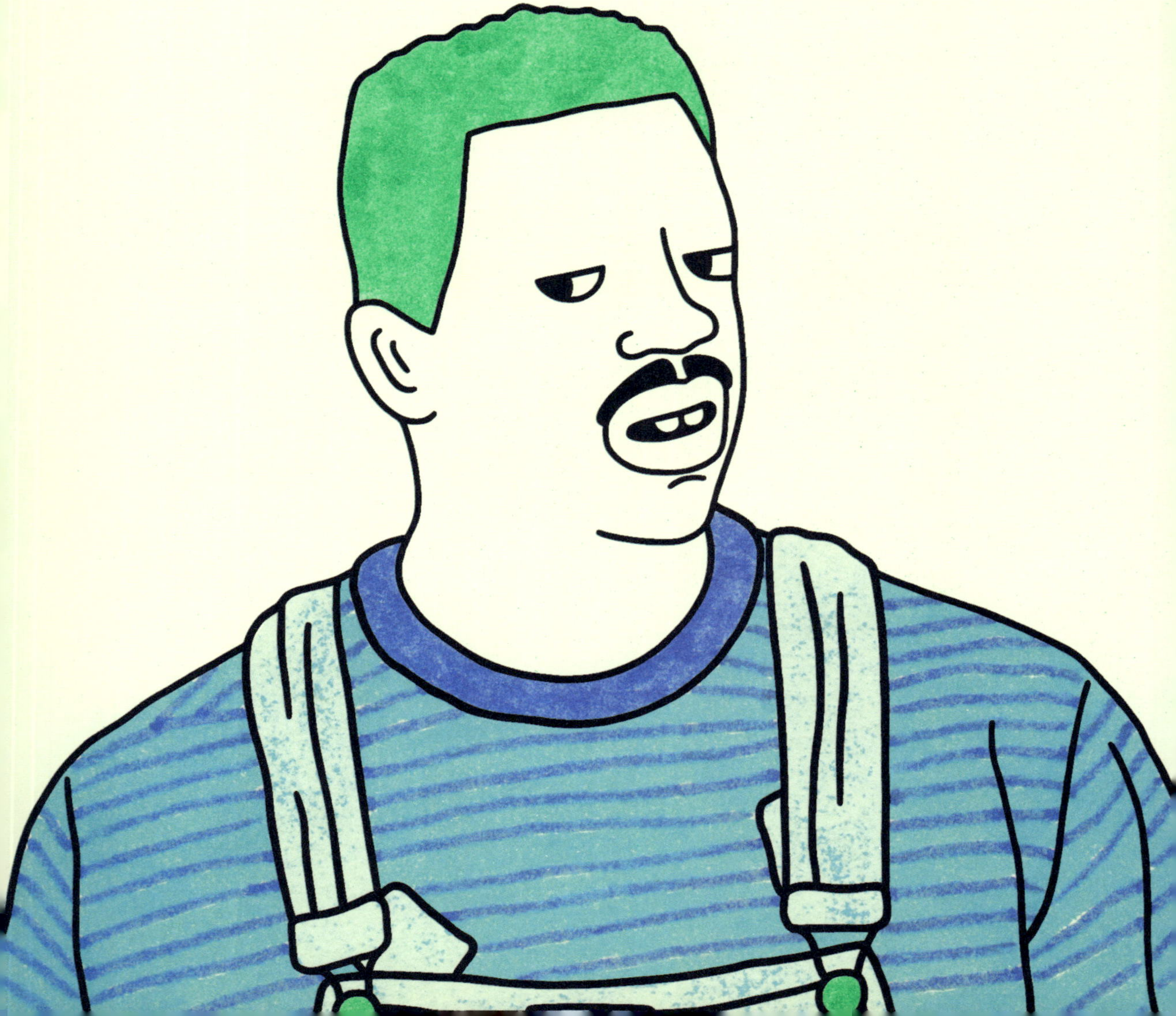

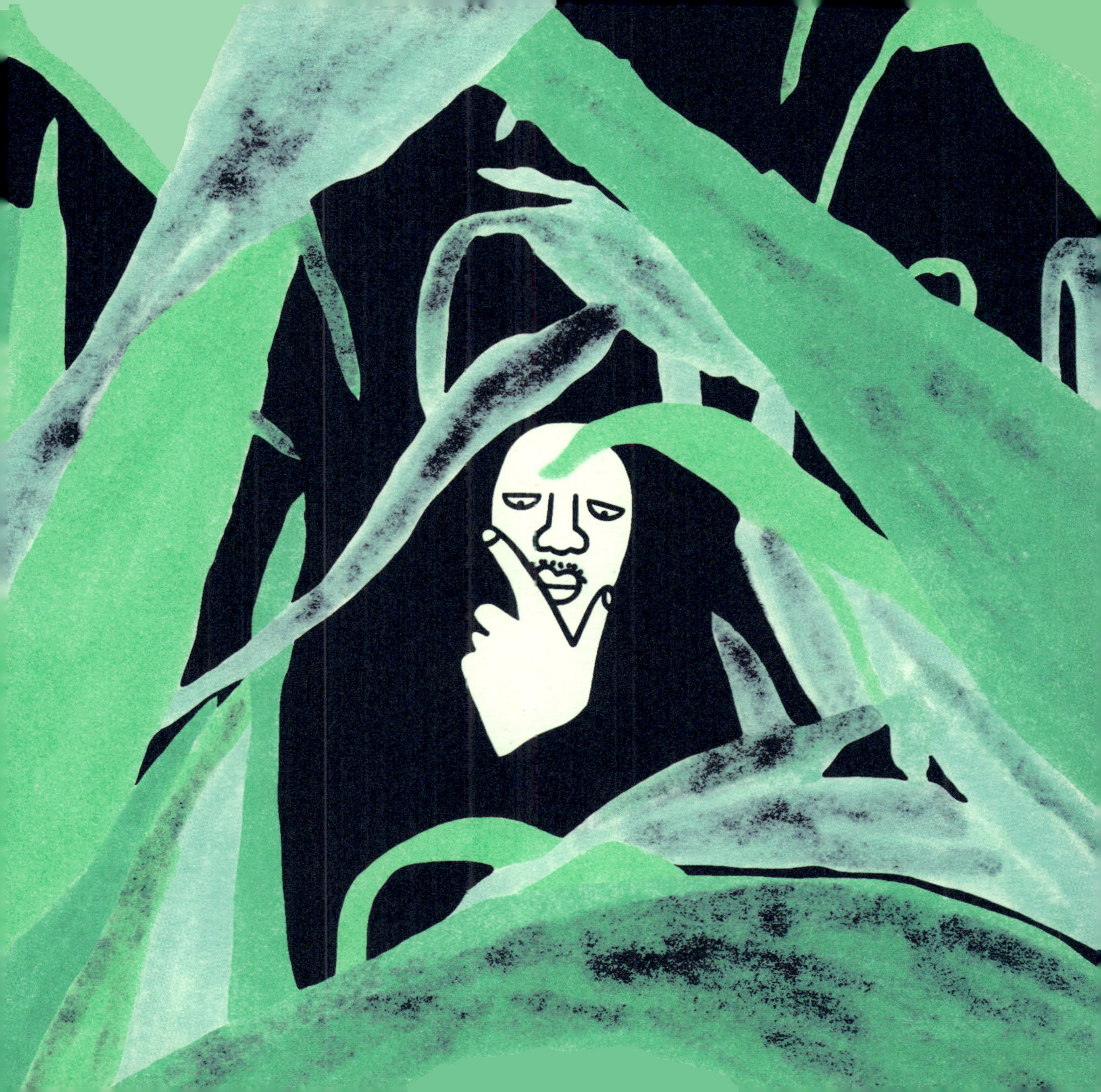

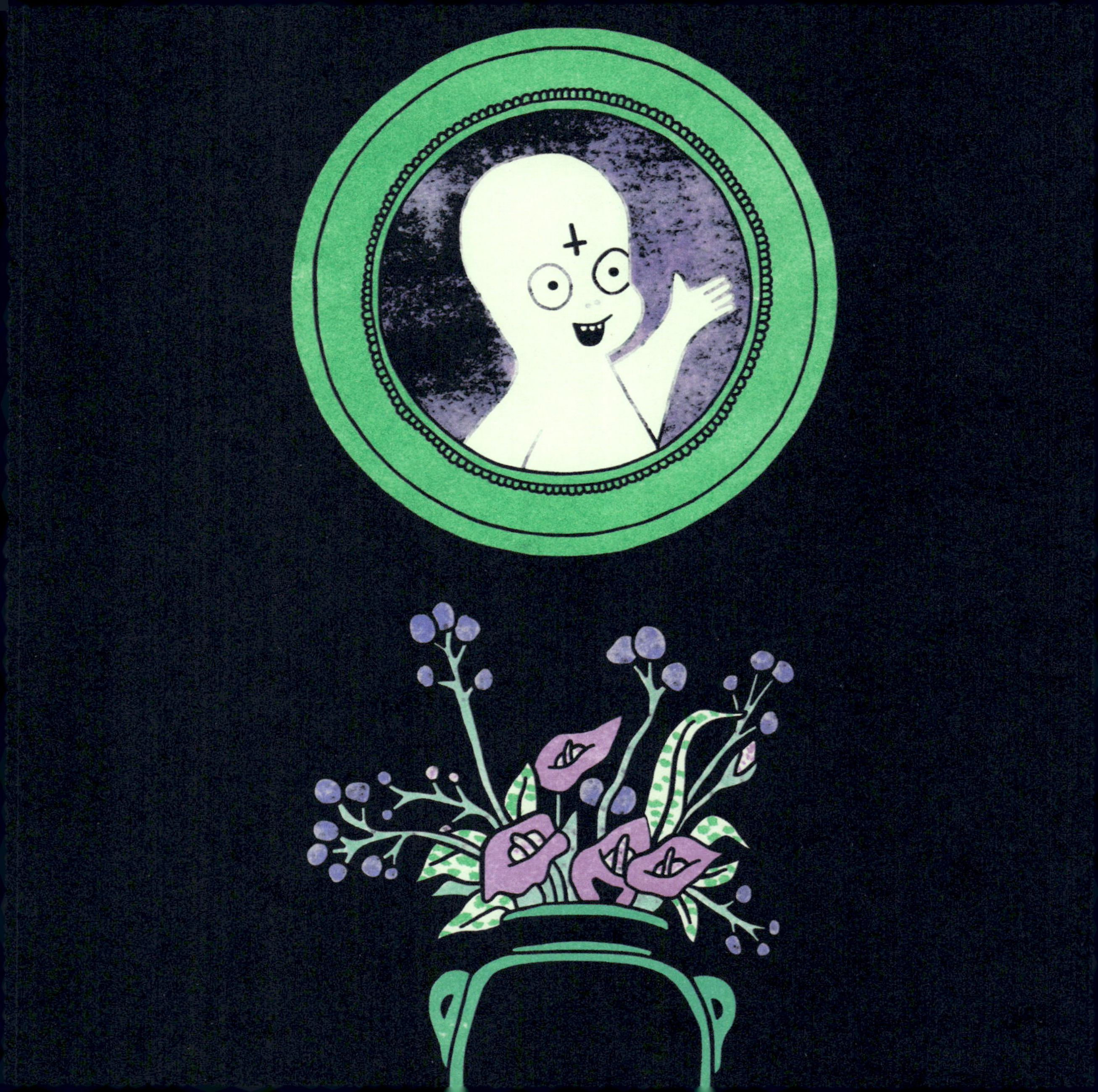

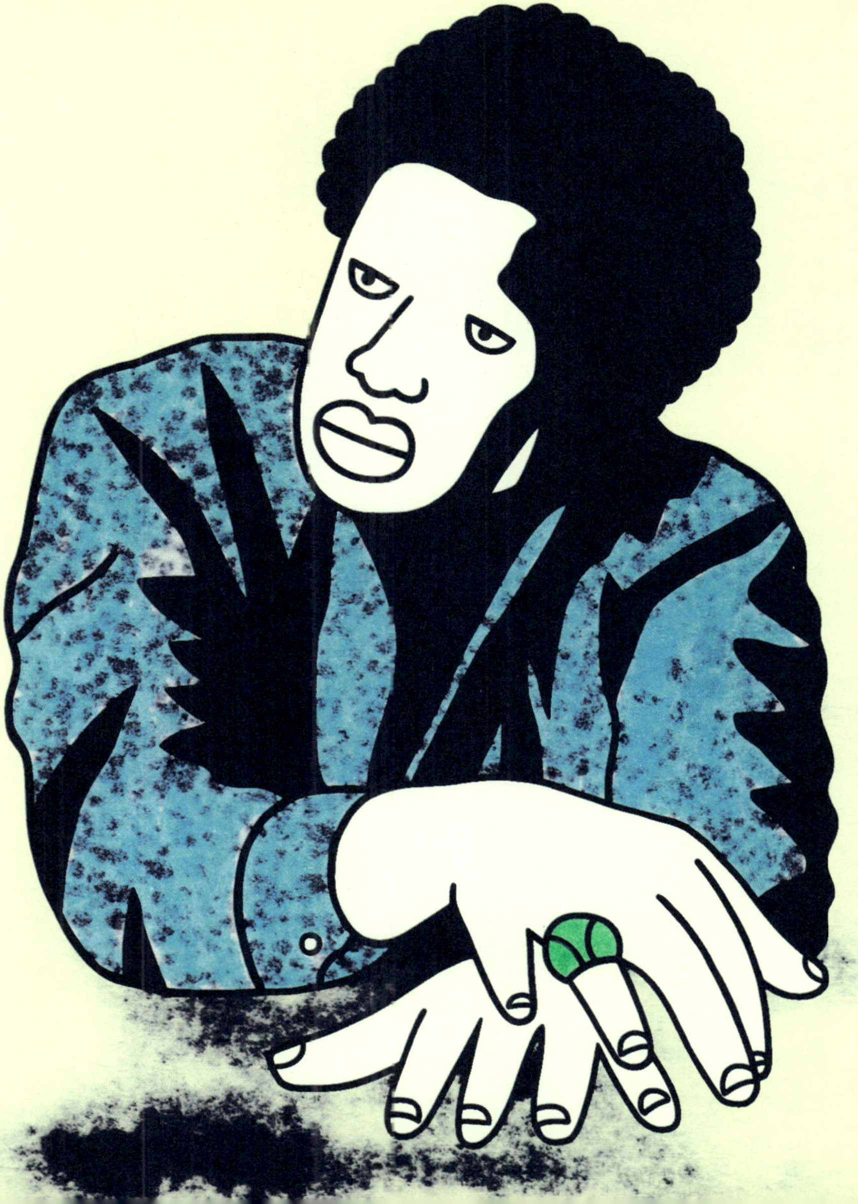

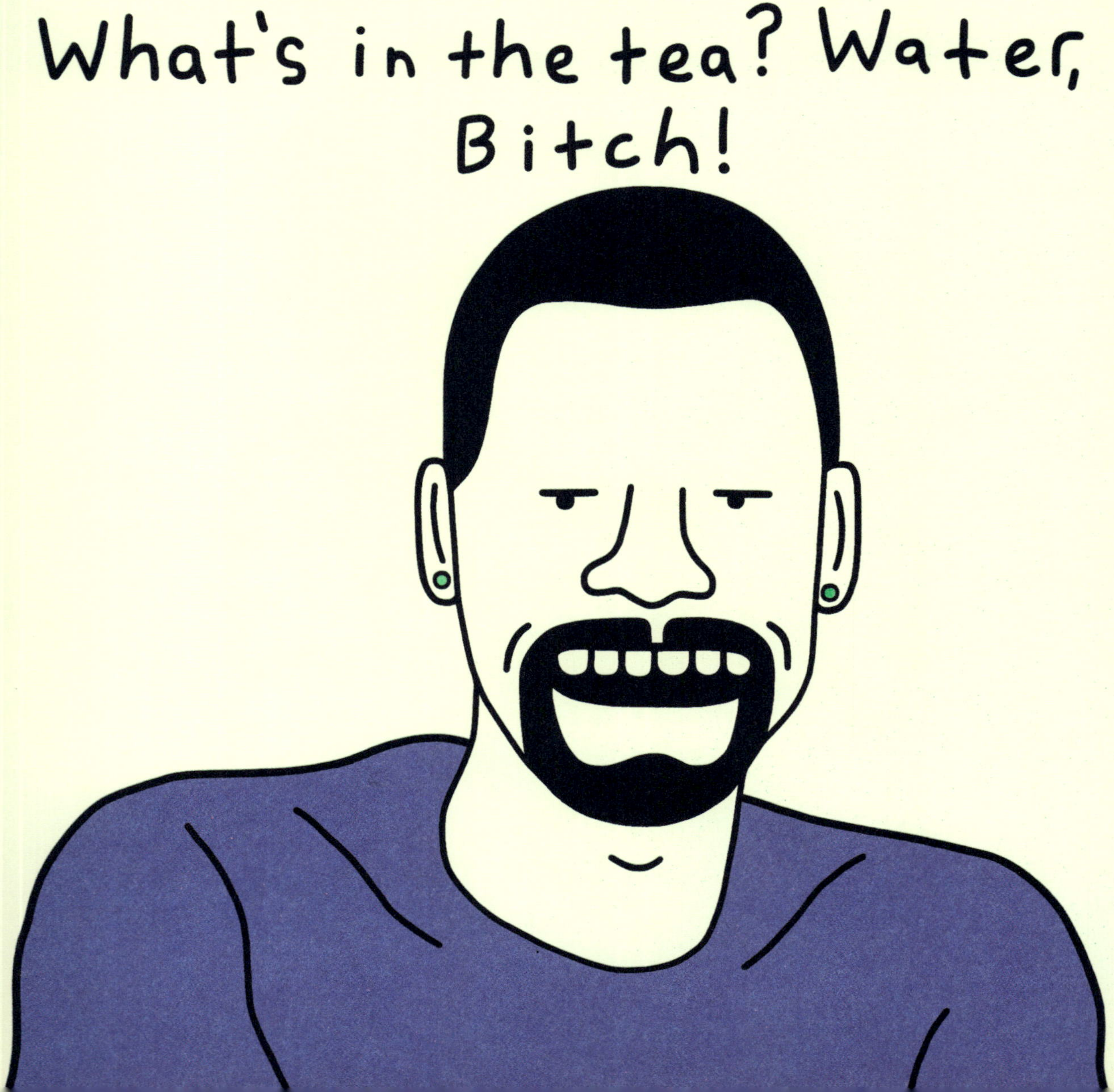
What's in the tea? Water,
Bitch!

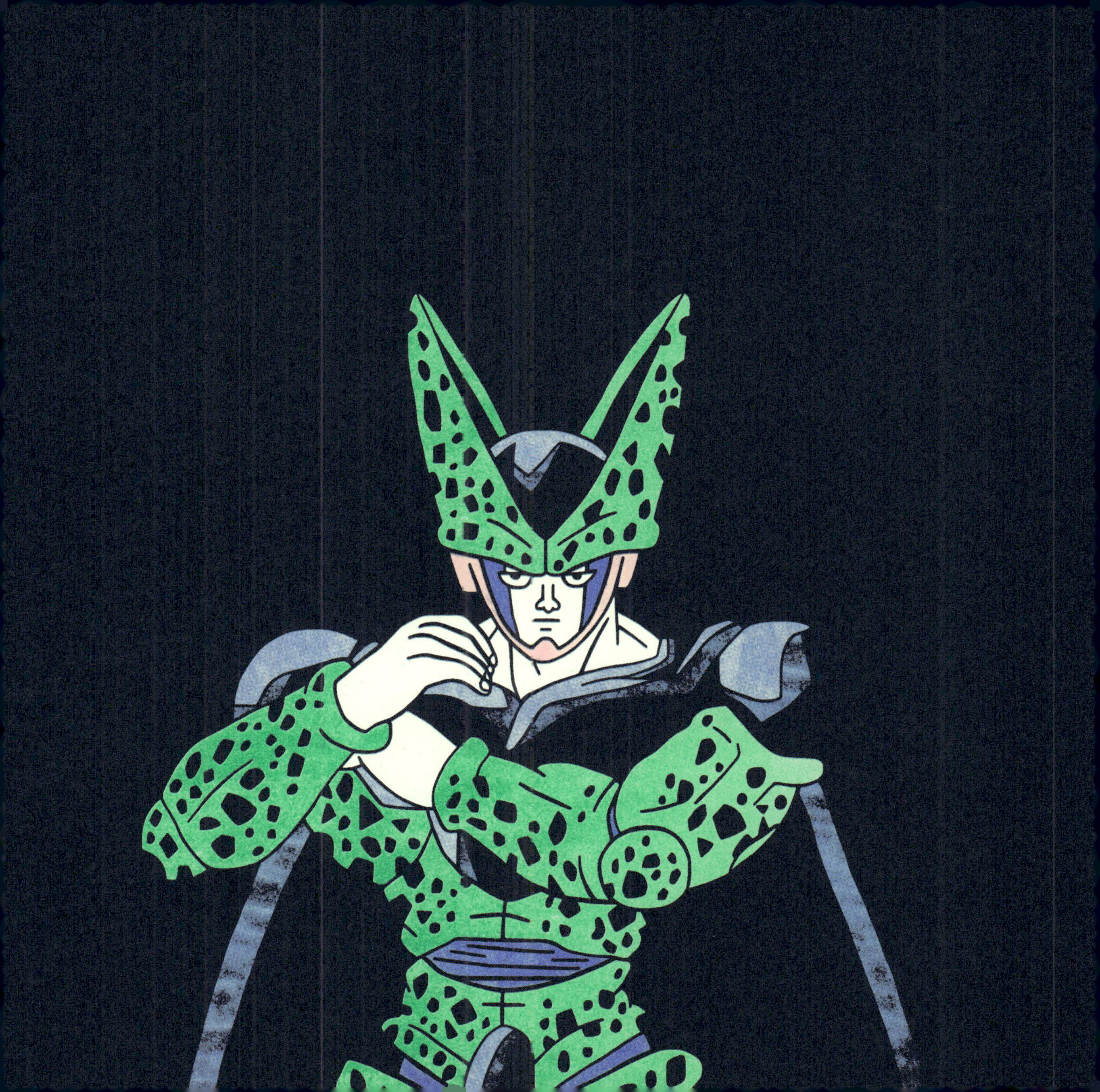

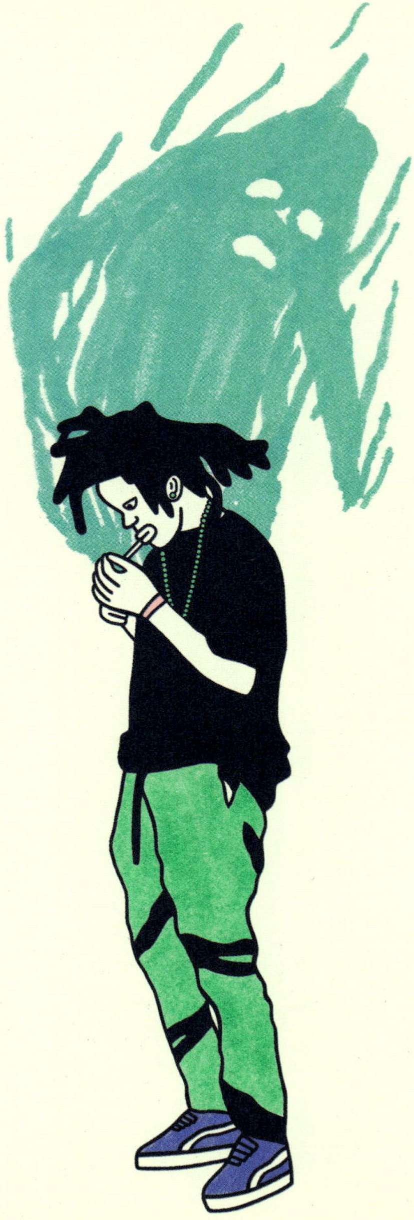

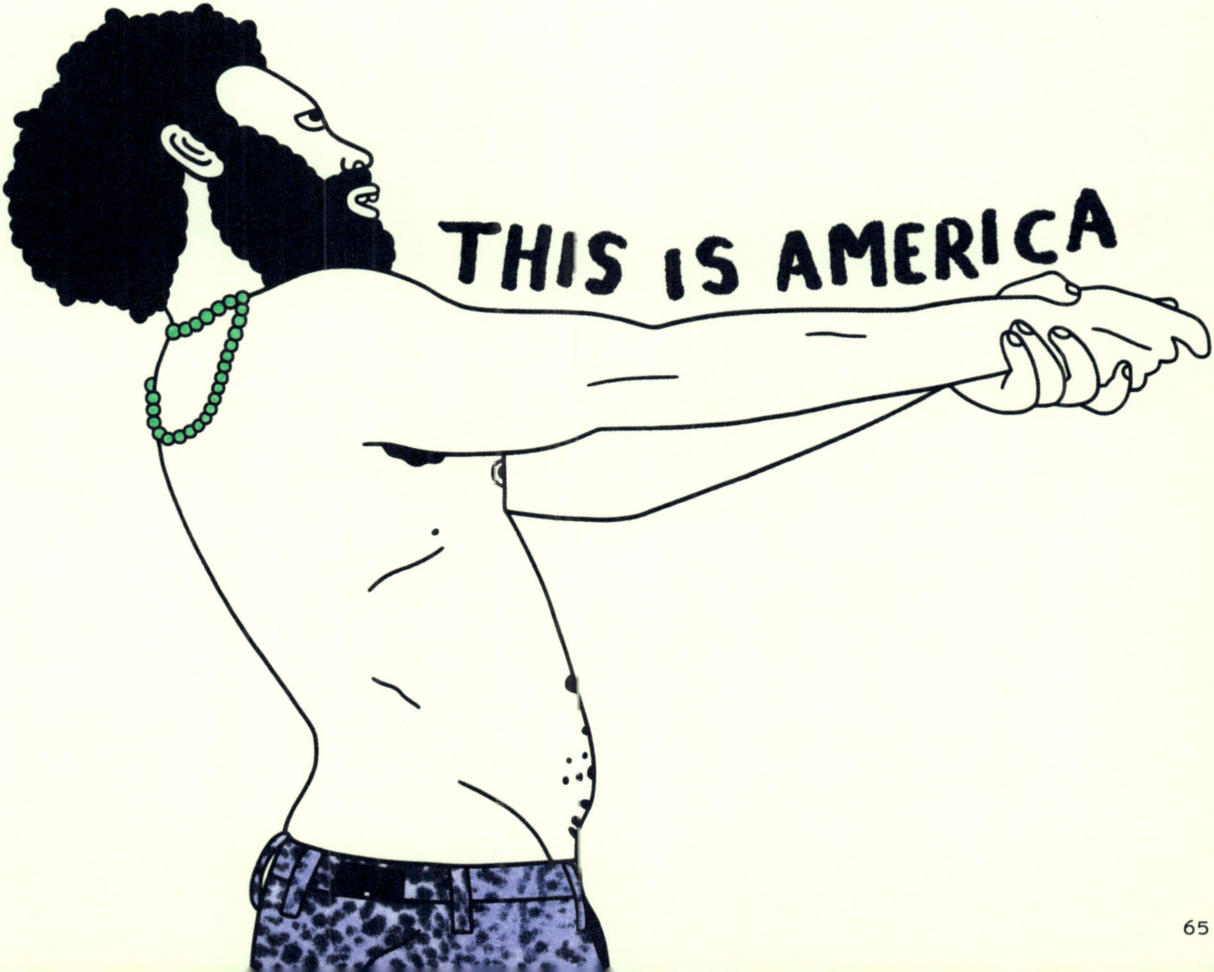
THIS IS AMERICA

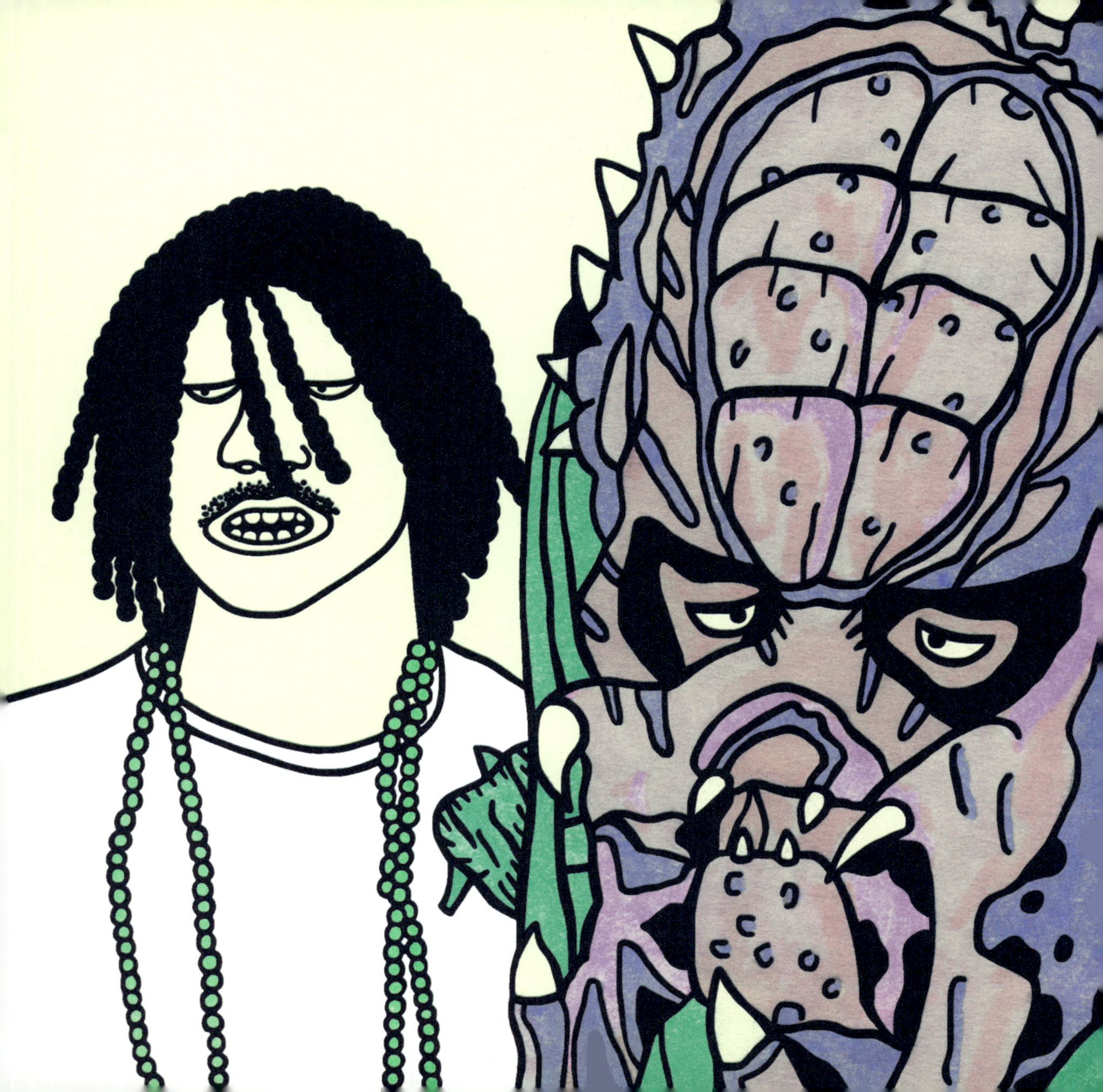

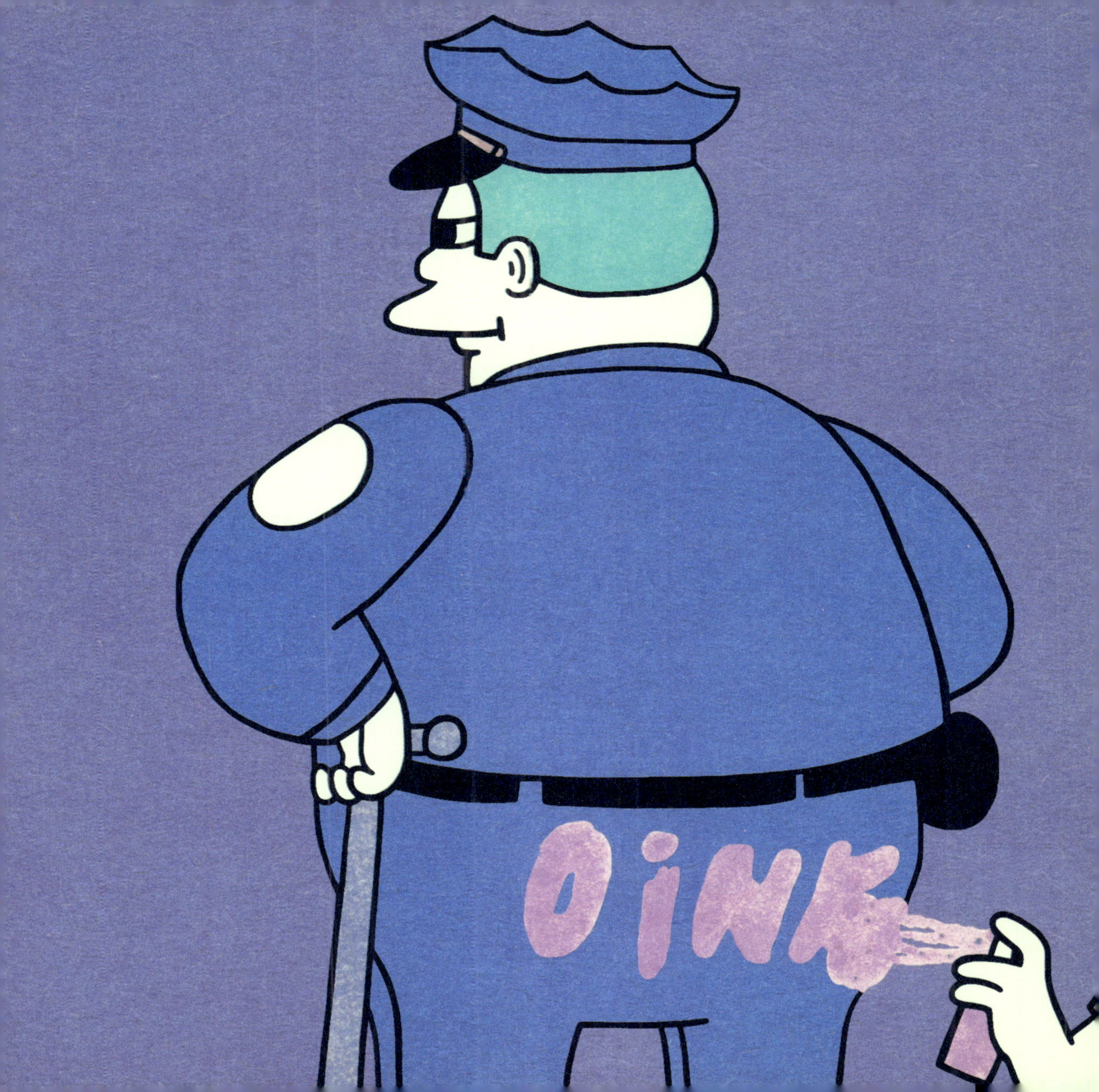
OINK

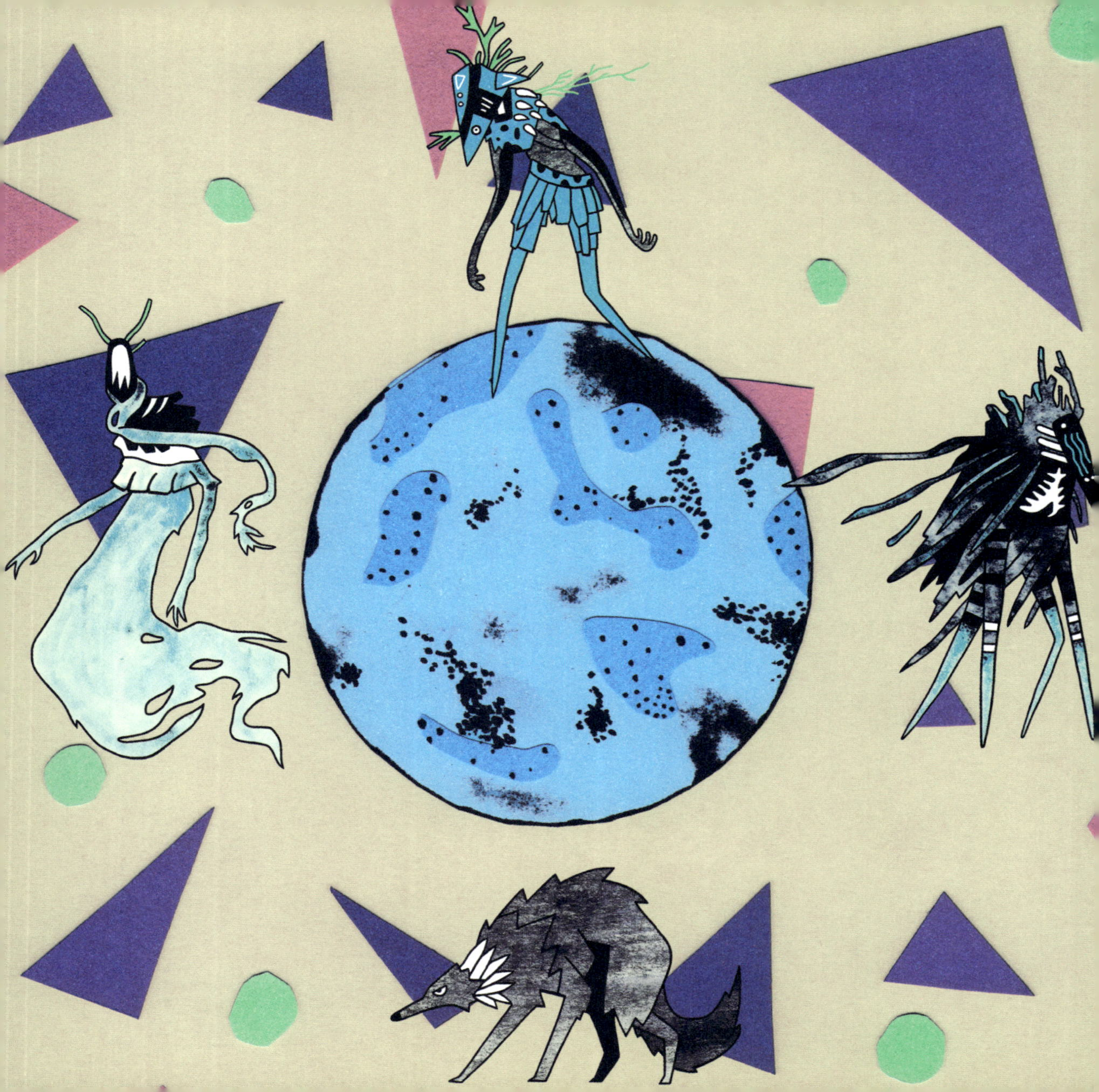

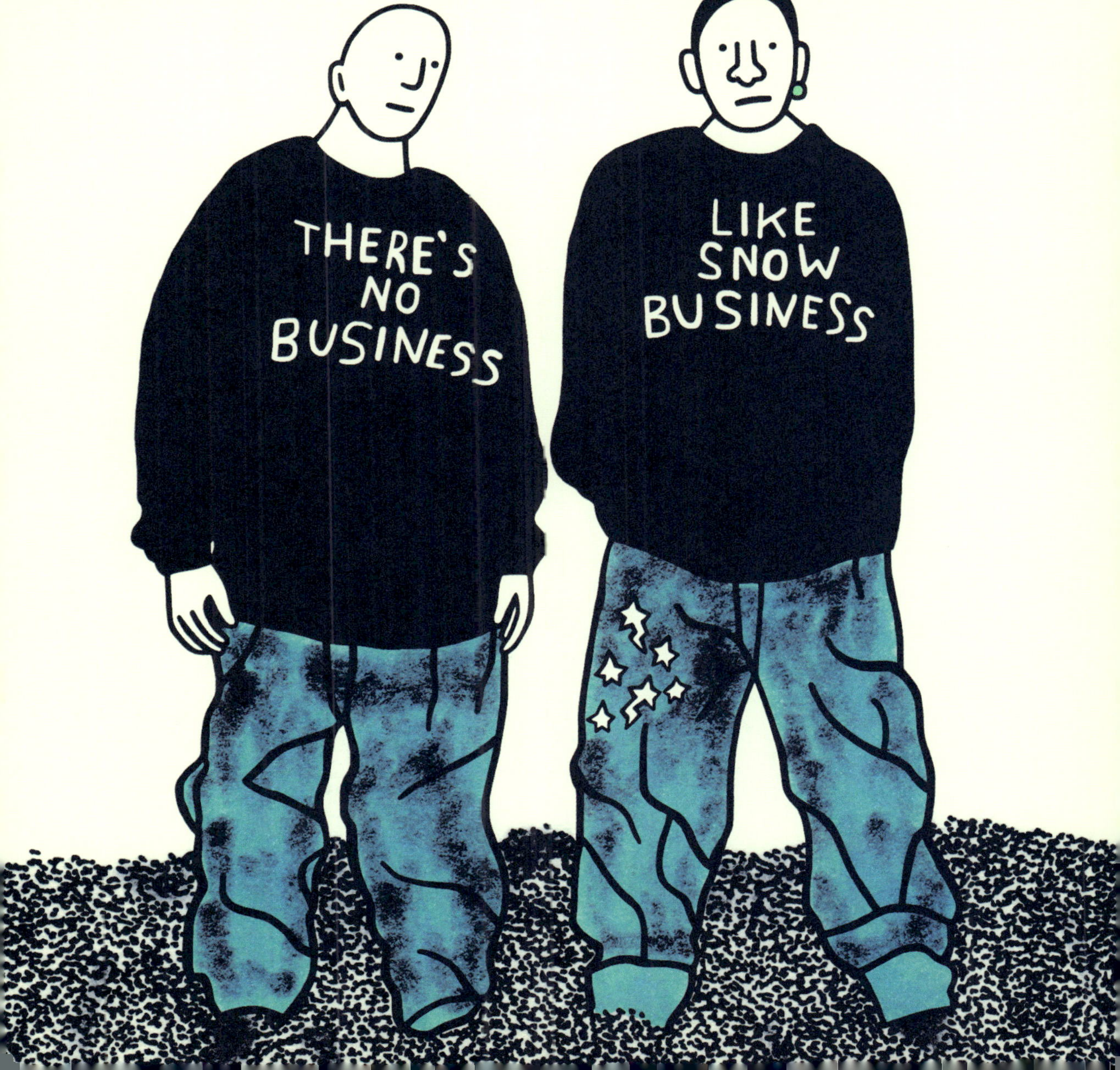
THERE'S NO BUSINESS
LIKE SNOW BUSINESS

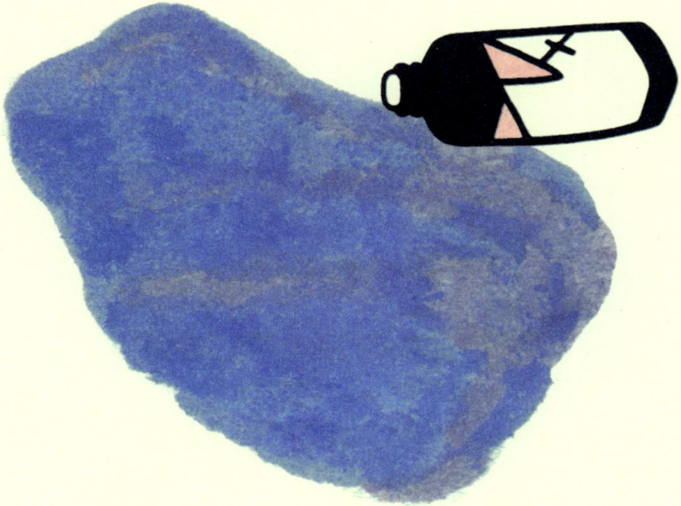

COCO IS SO MUCH MORE THAN A DOG HE IS OUR TEACHER OUR HEALER AND OUR SPIRITUAL LEADER

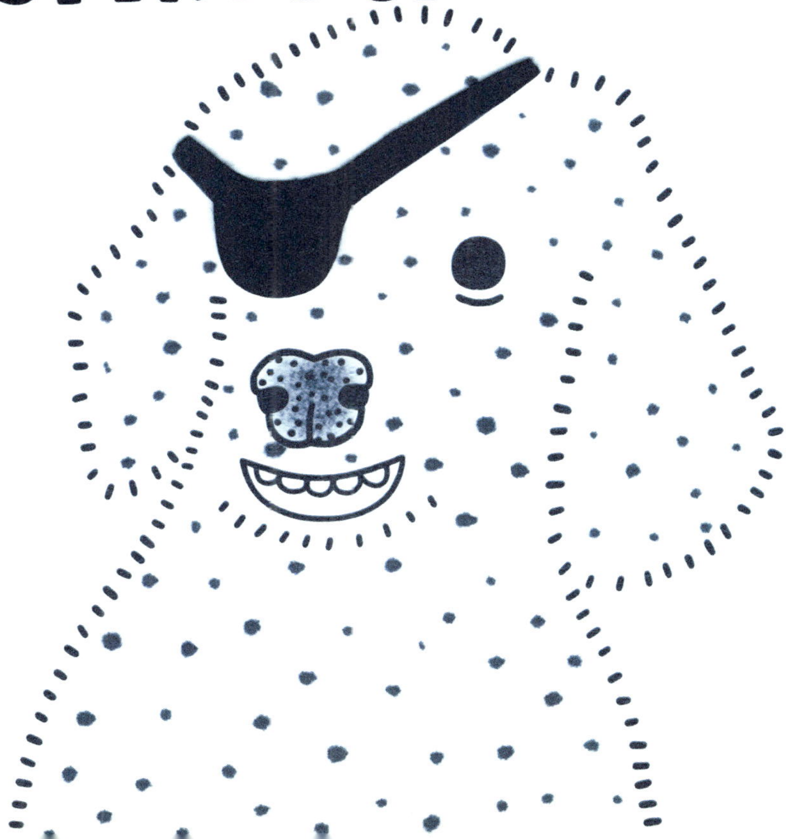

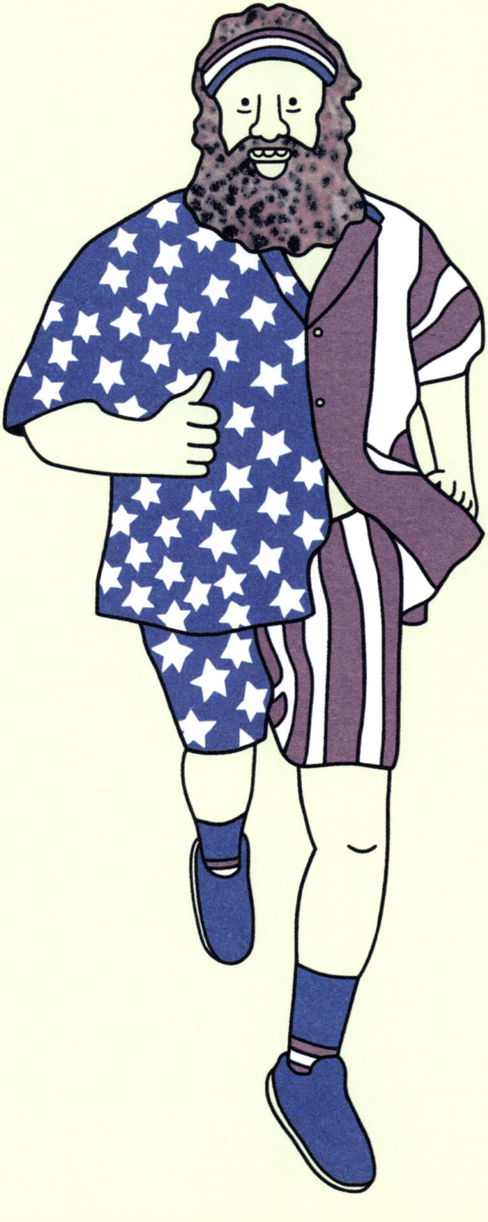

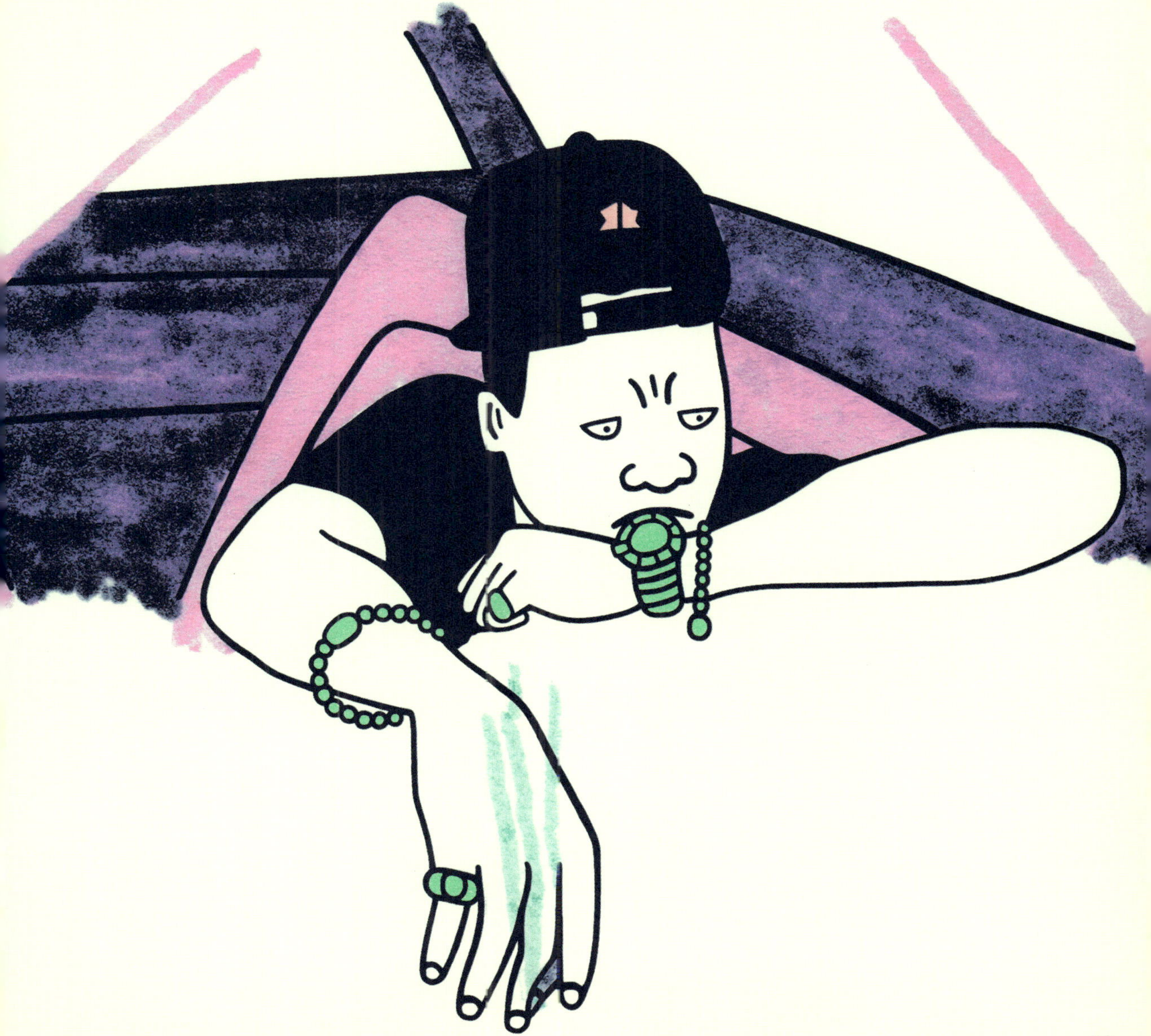

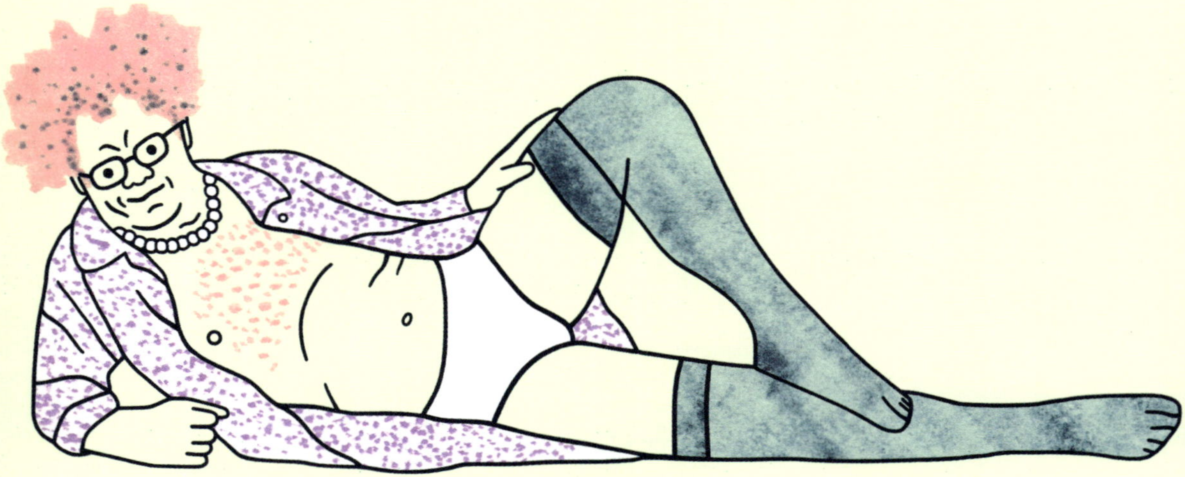

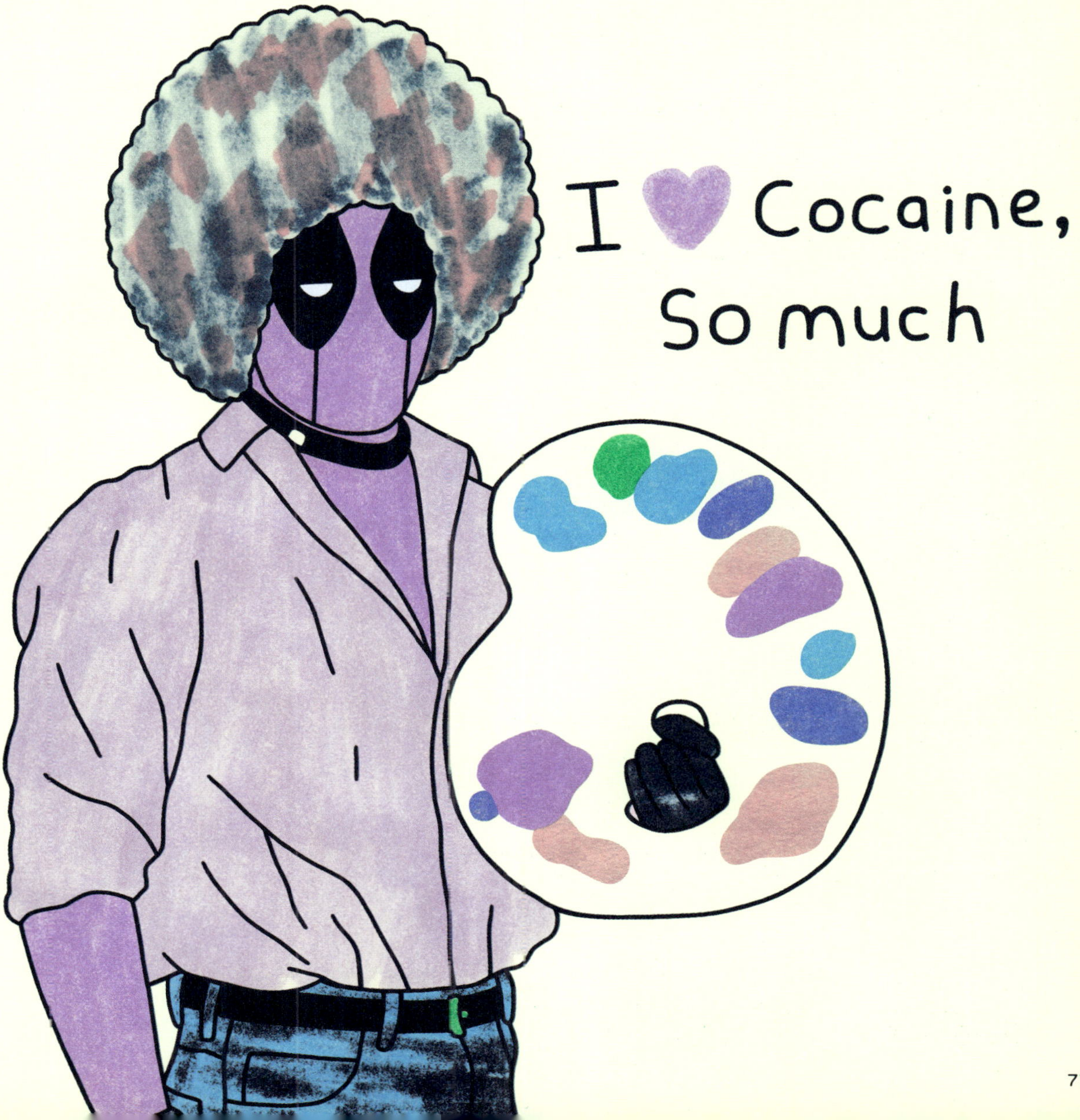
I ♥ Cocaine,
So much

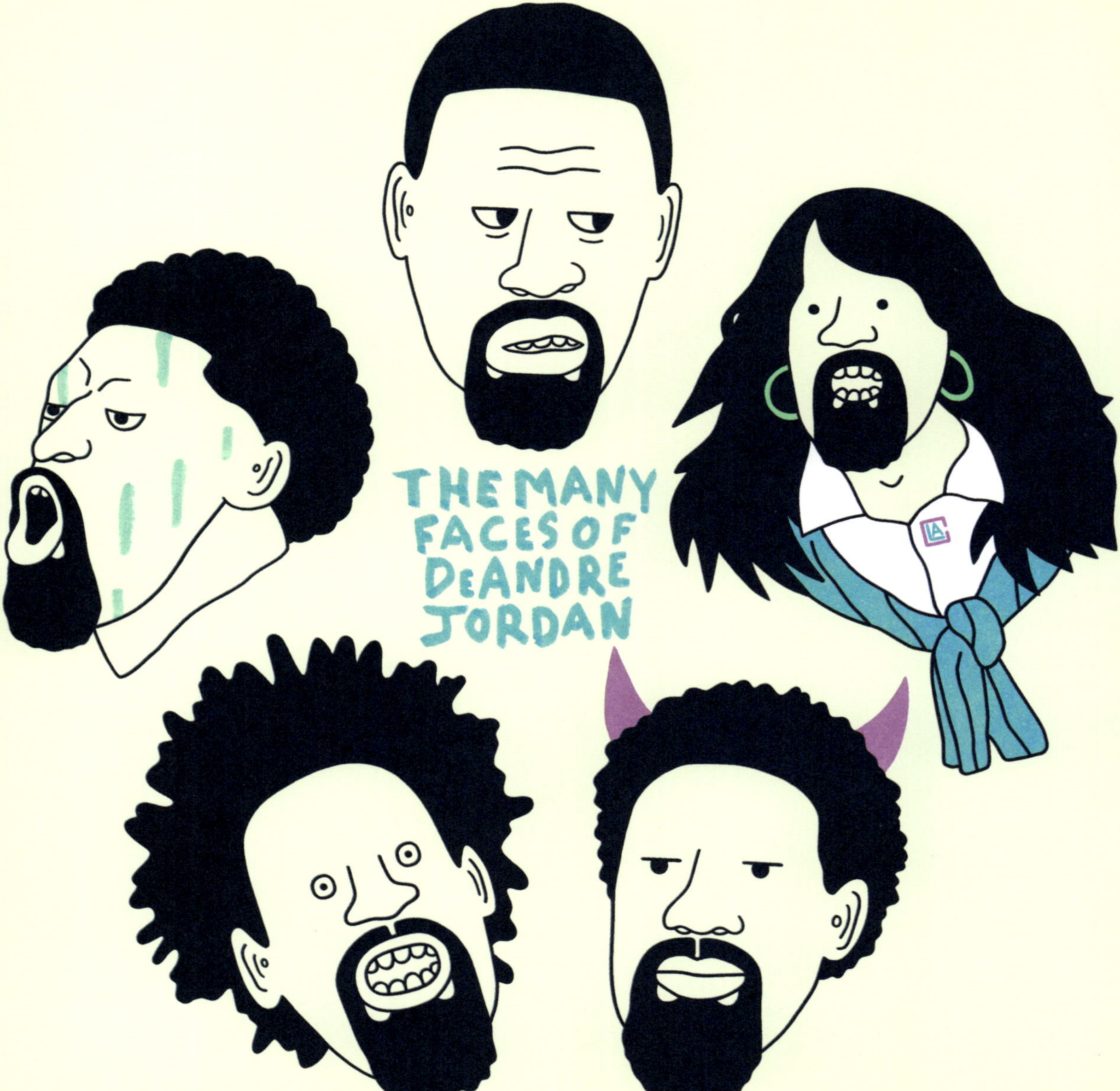
THE MANY
FACES OF
DeANDRE
JORDAN

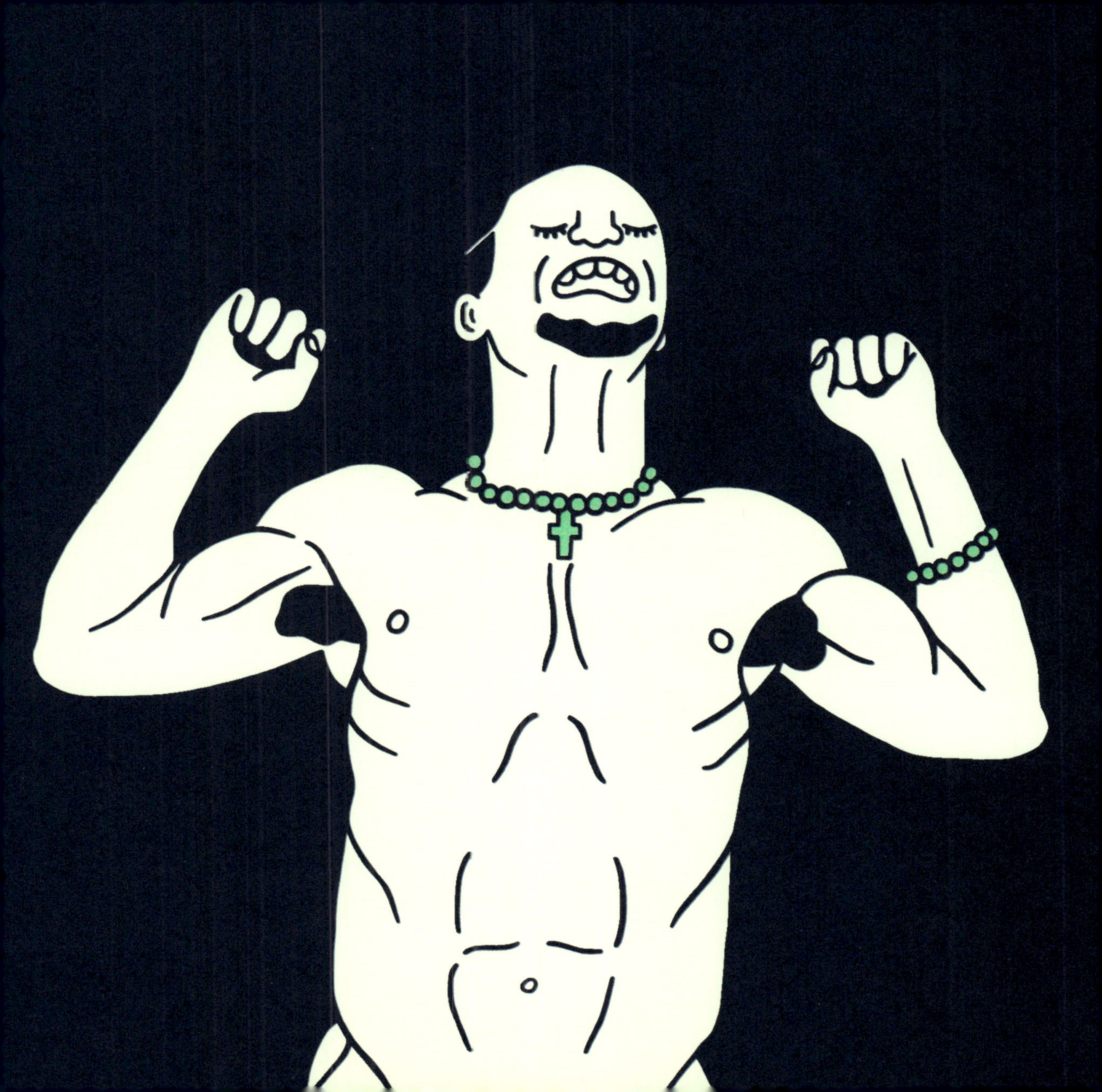

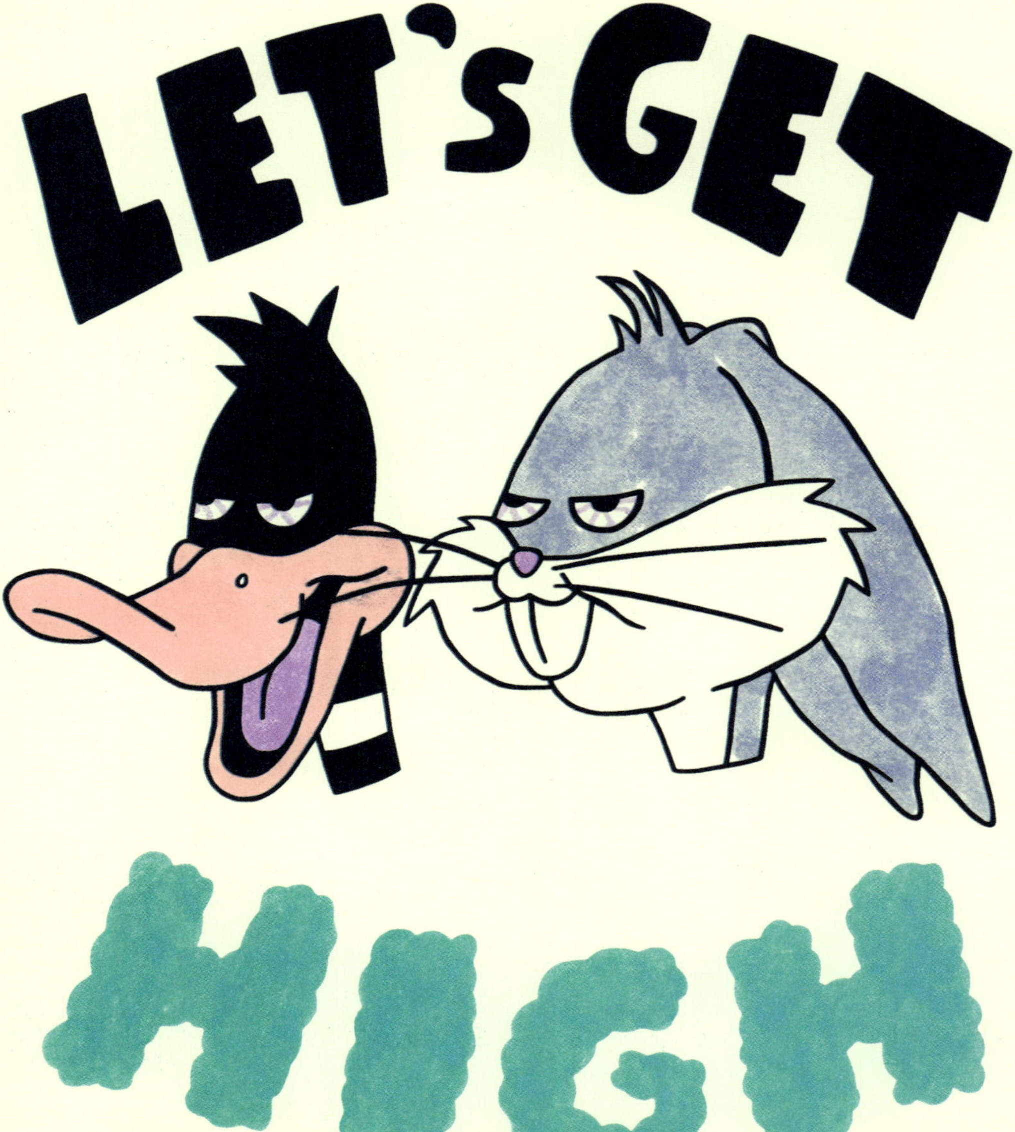
LET'S GET
HIGH

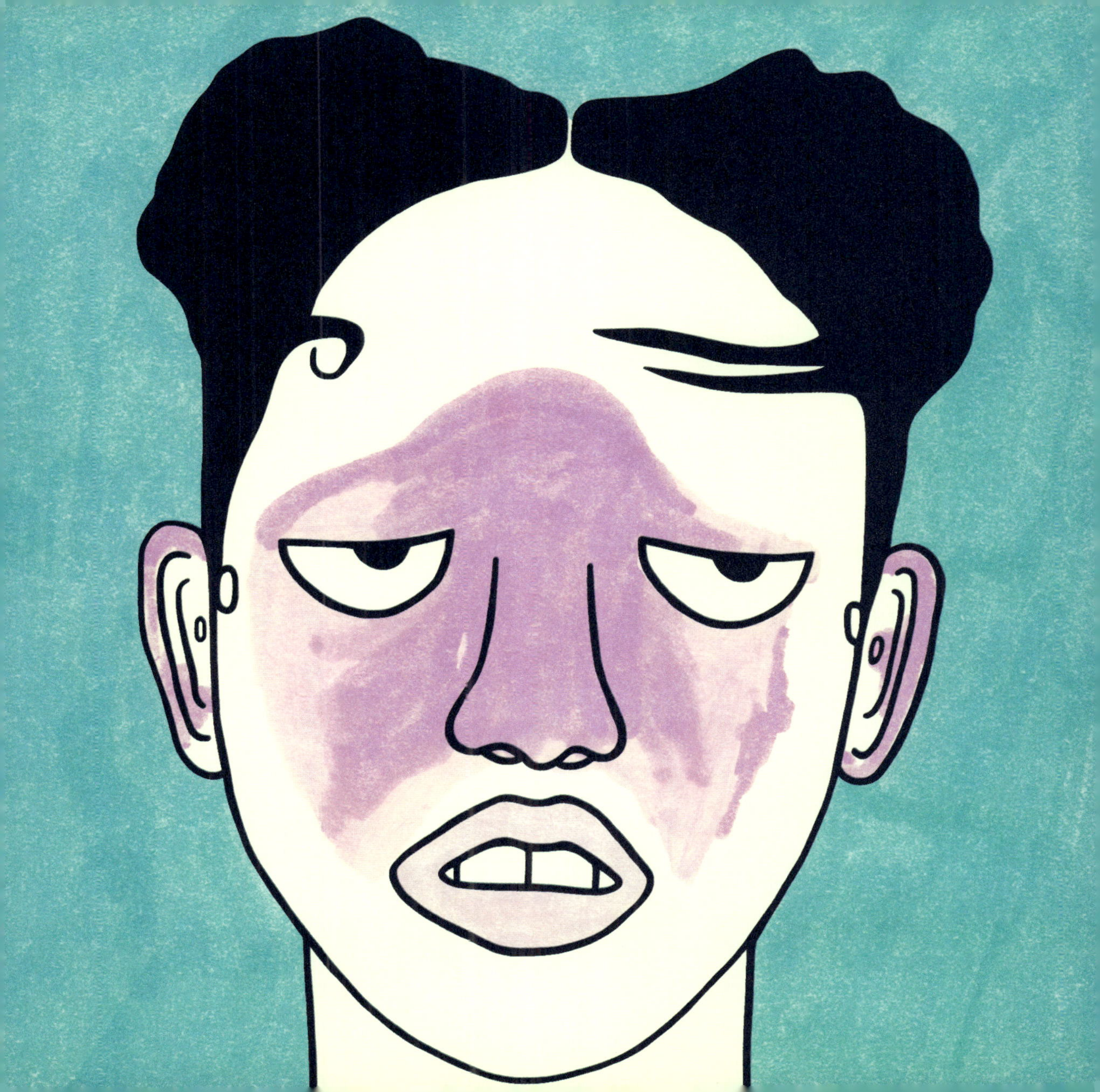

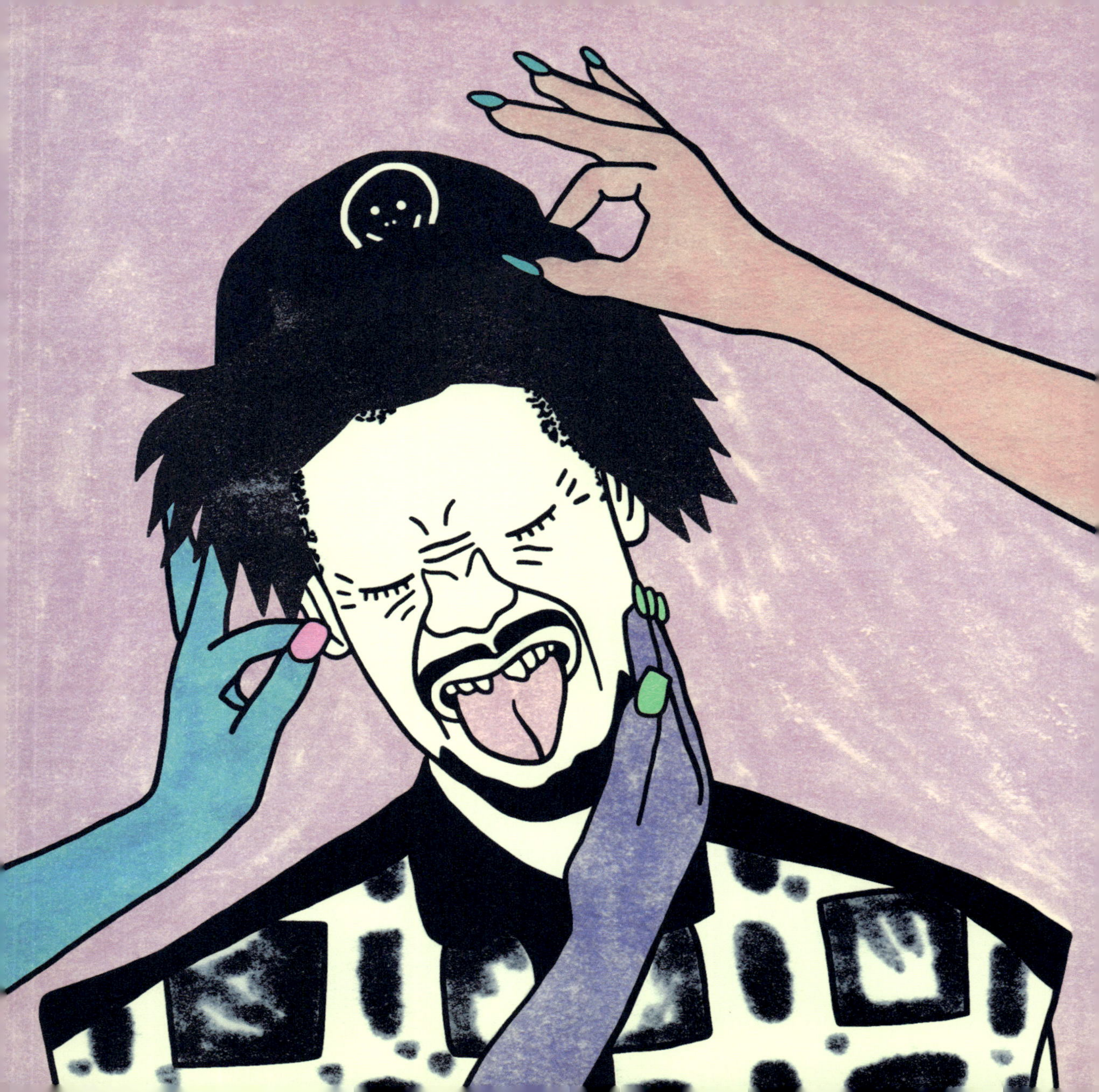

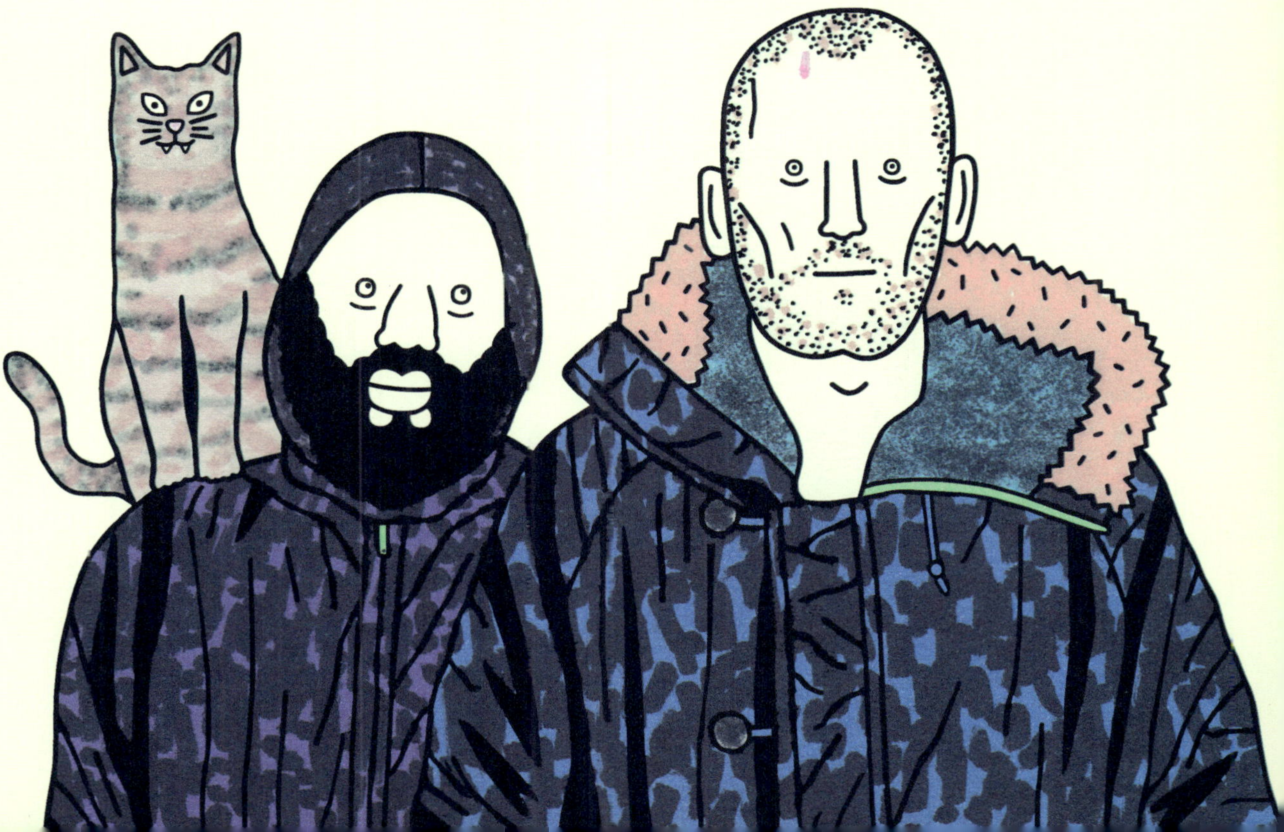

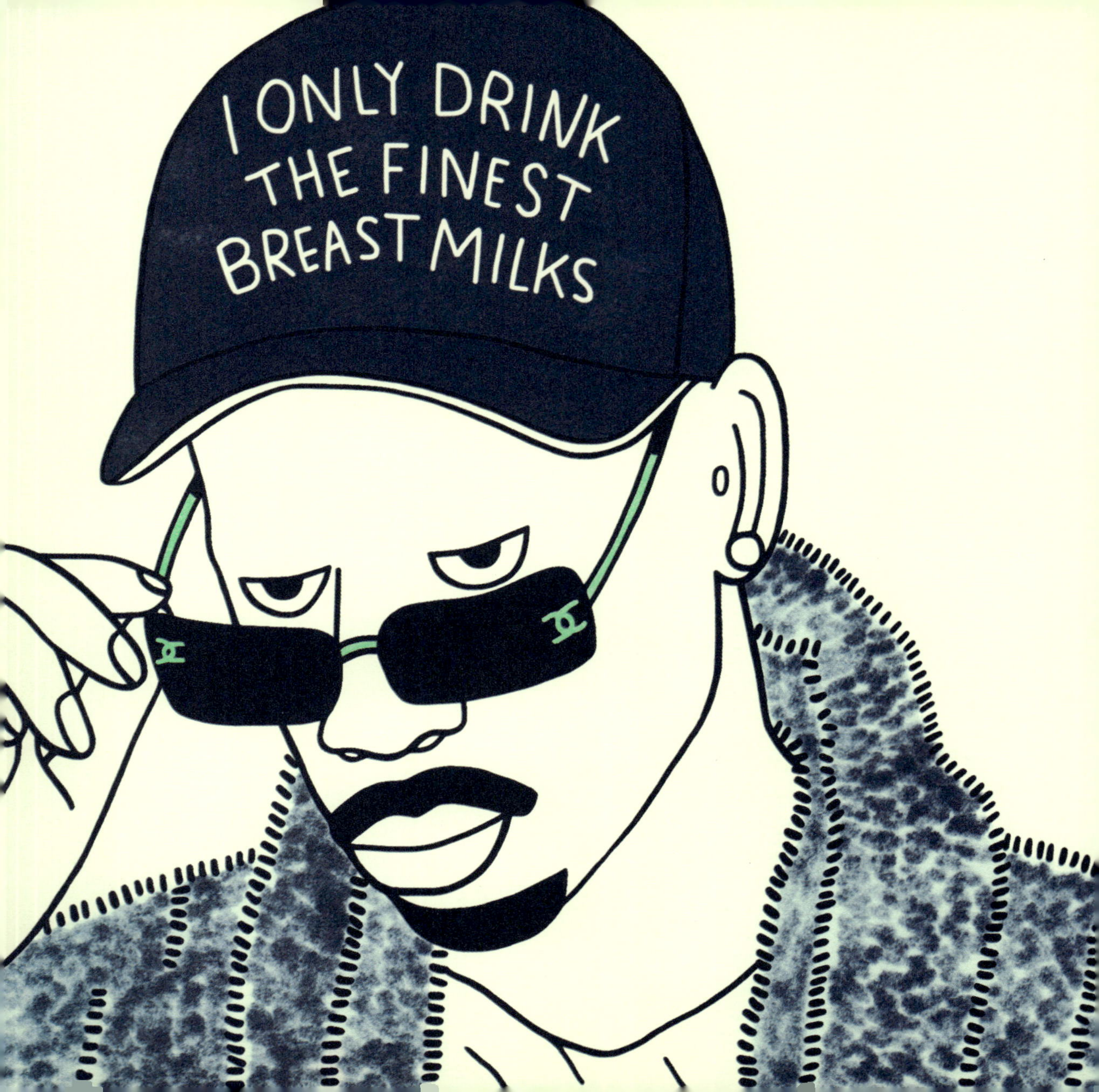
I ONLY DRINK
THE FINEST
BREAST MILKS

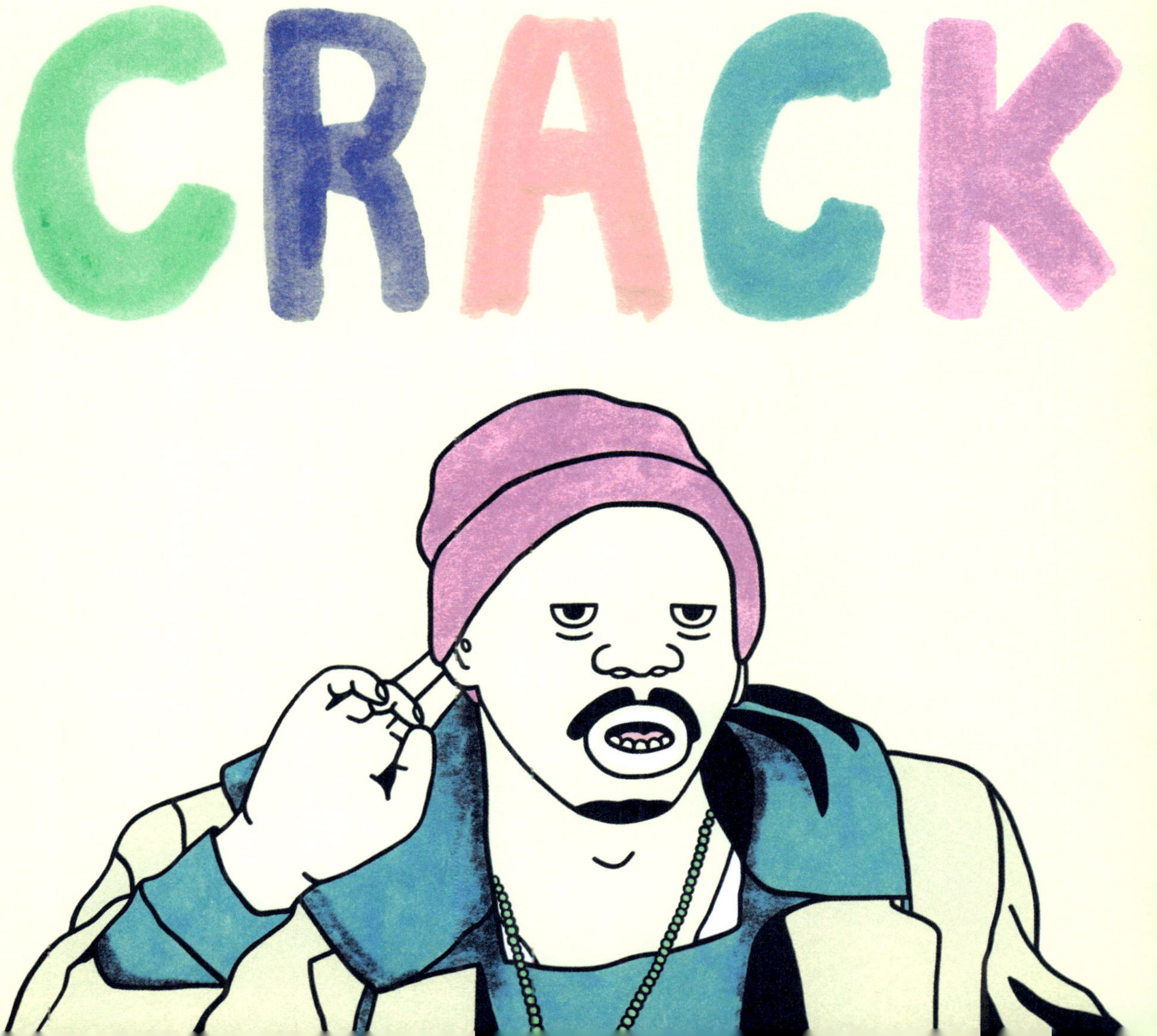
CRACK

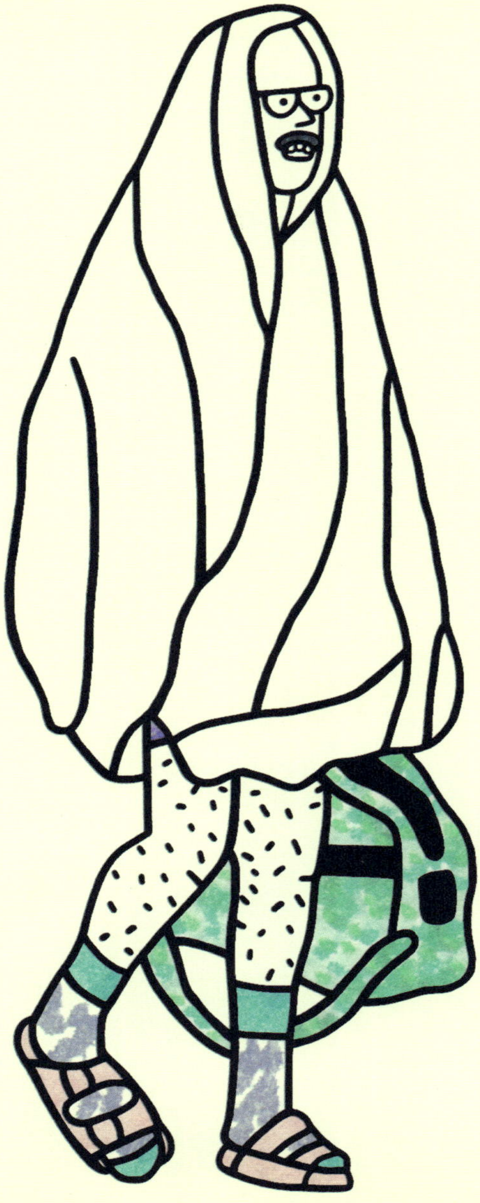

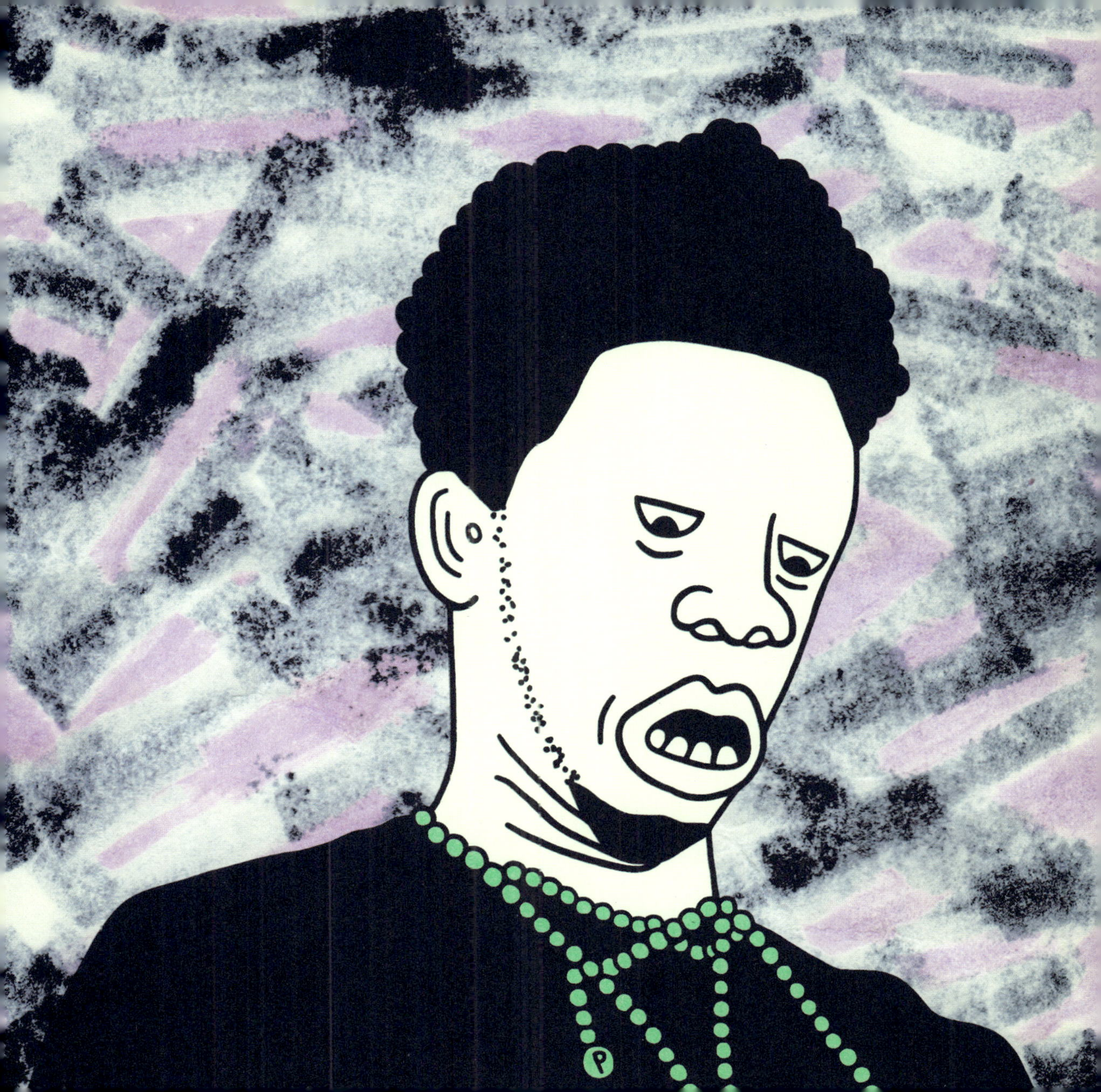

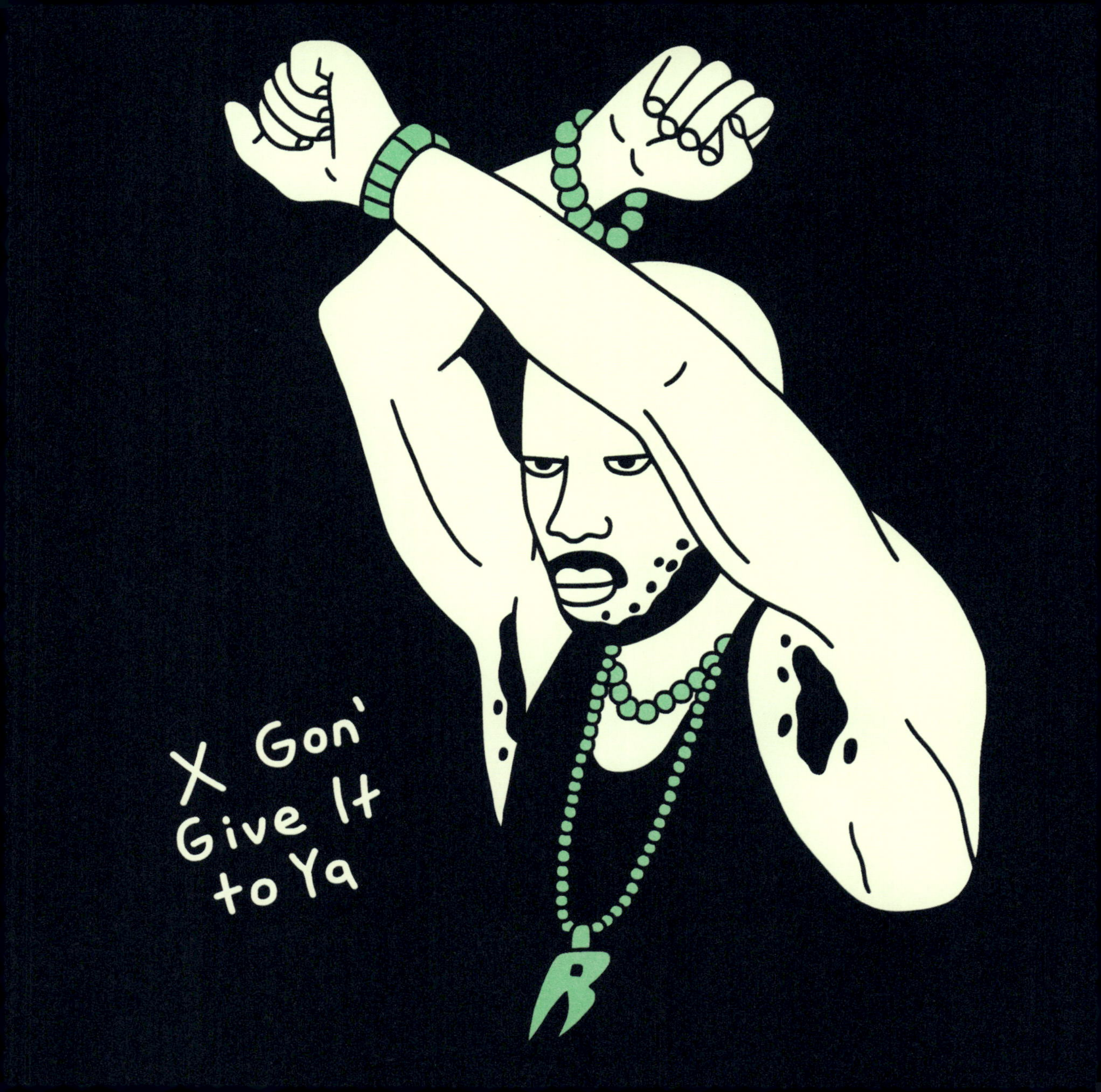
X Gon' Give It to Ya

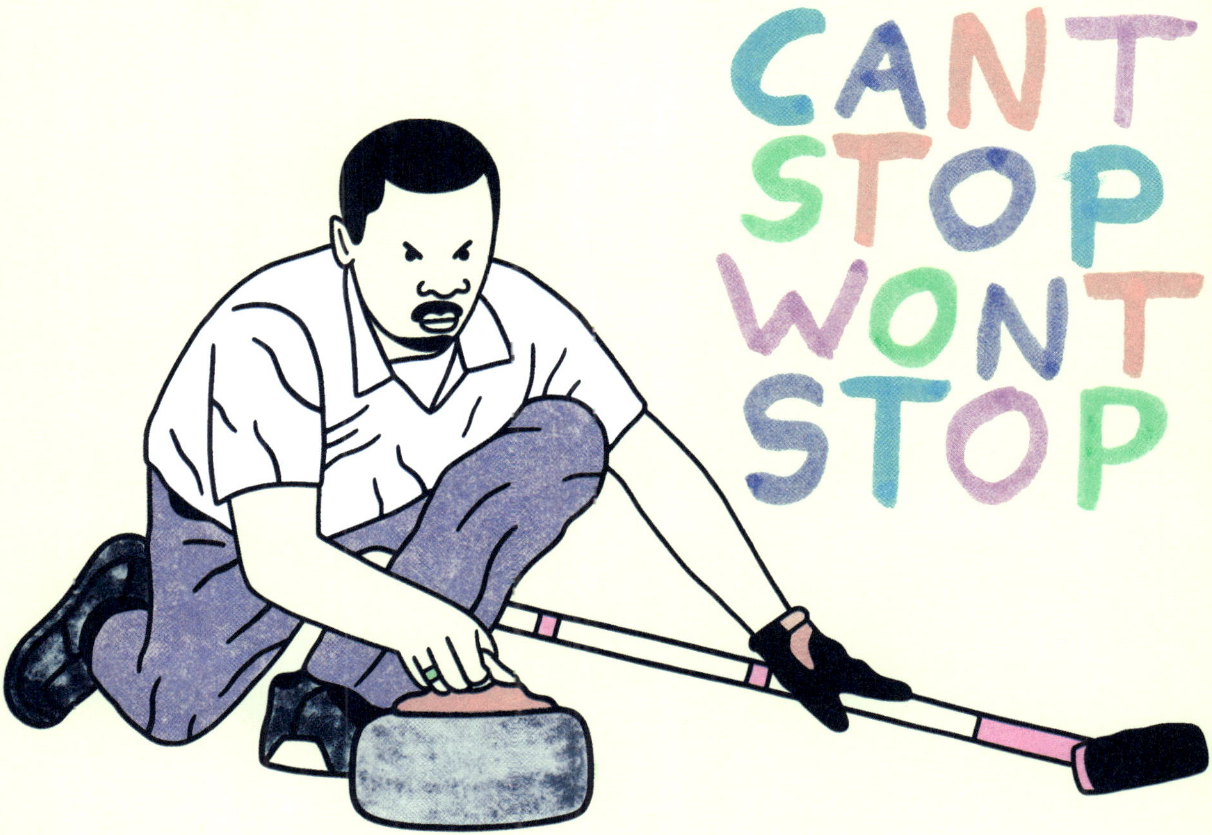
CANT
STOP
WONT
STOP

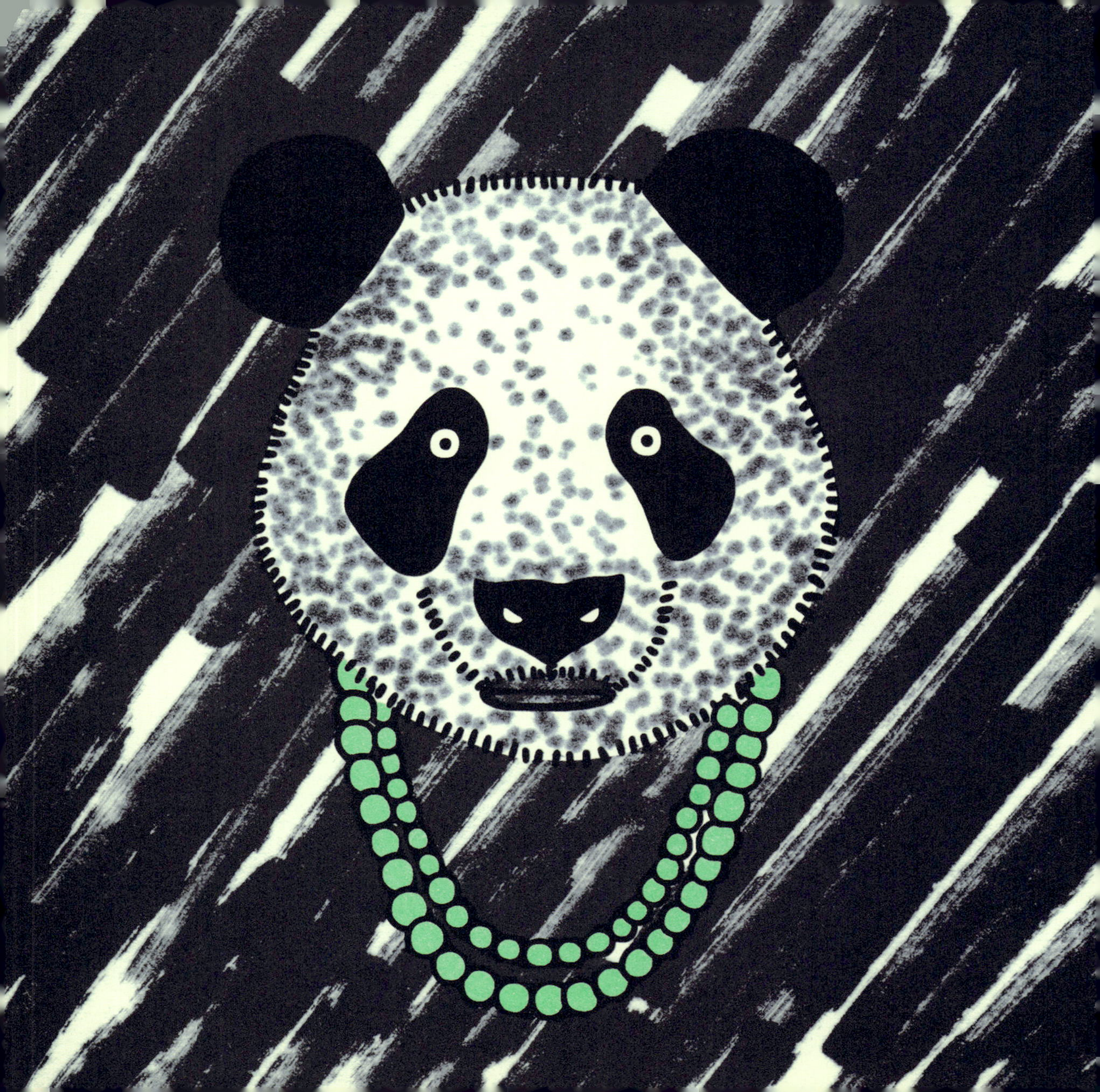

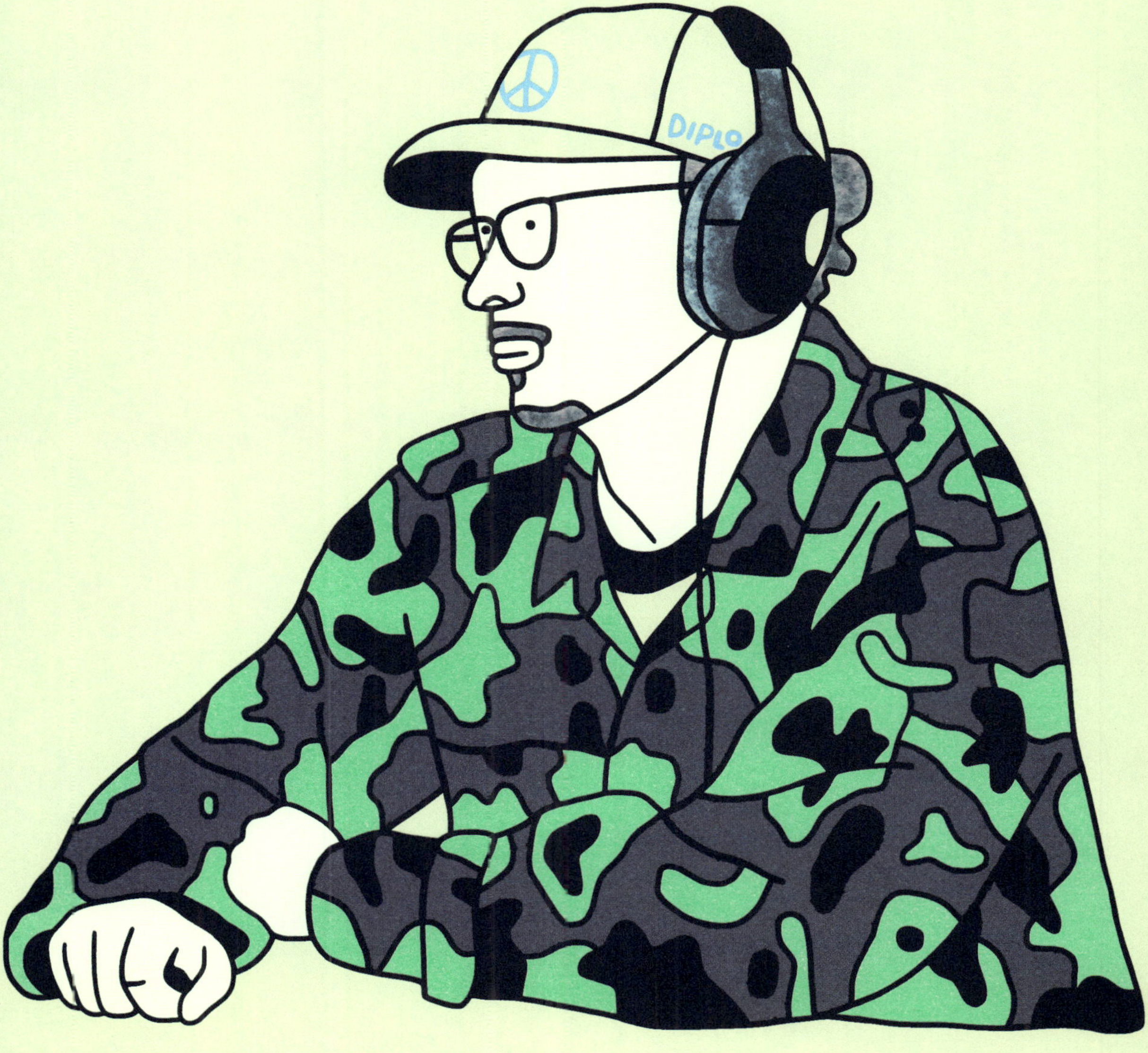
DIPLO

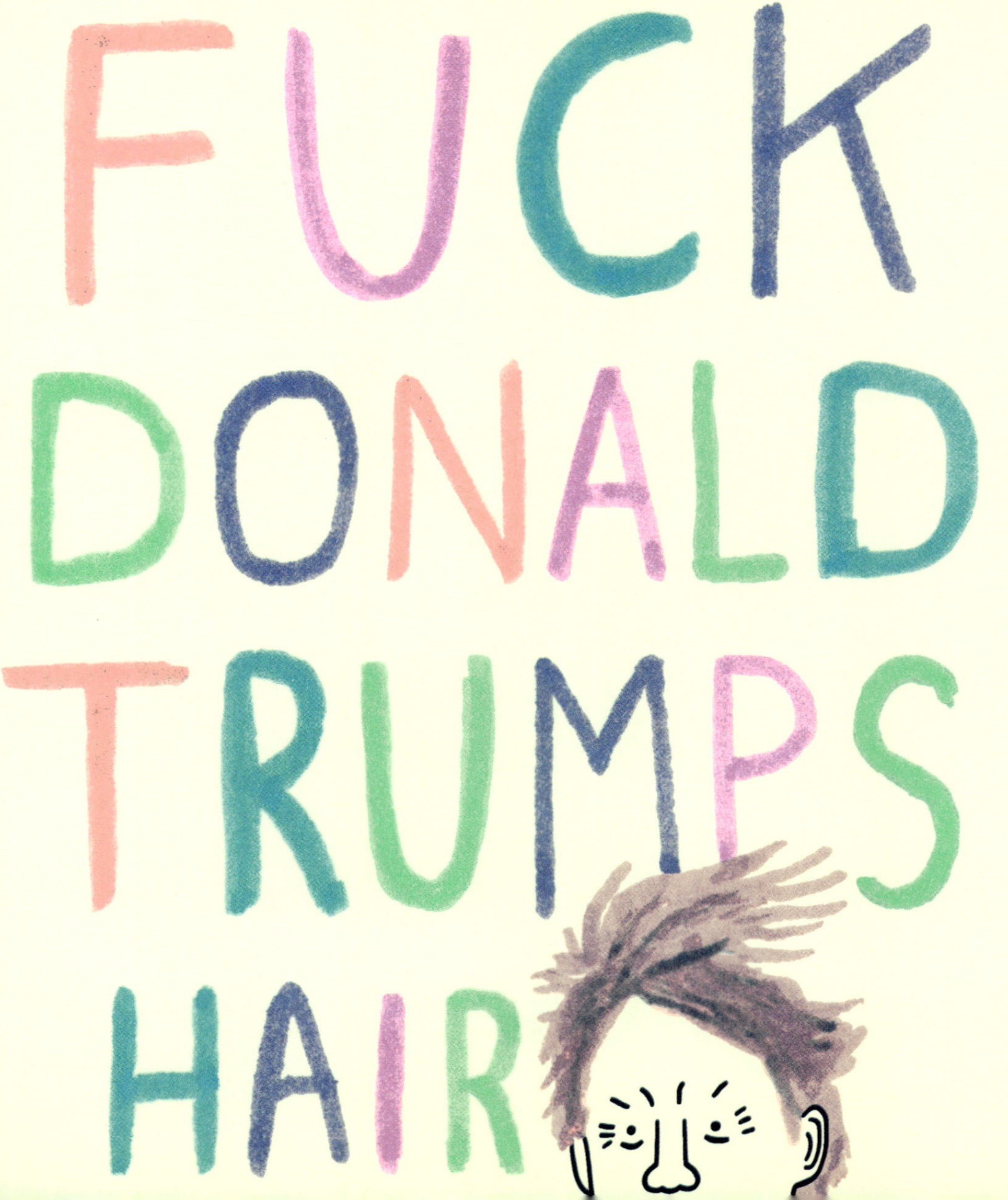
FUCK
DONALD
TRUMPS
HAIR

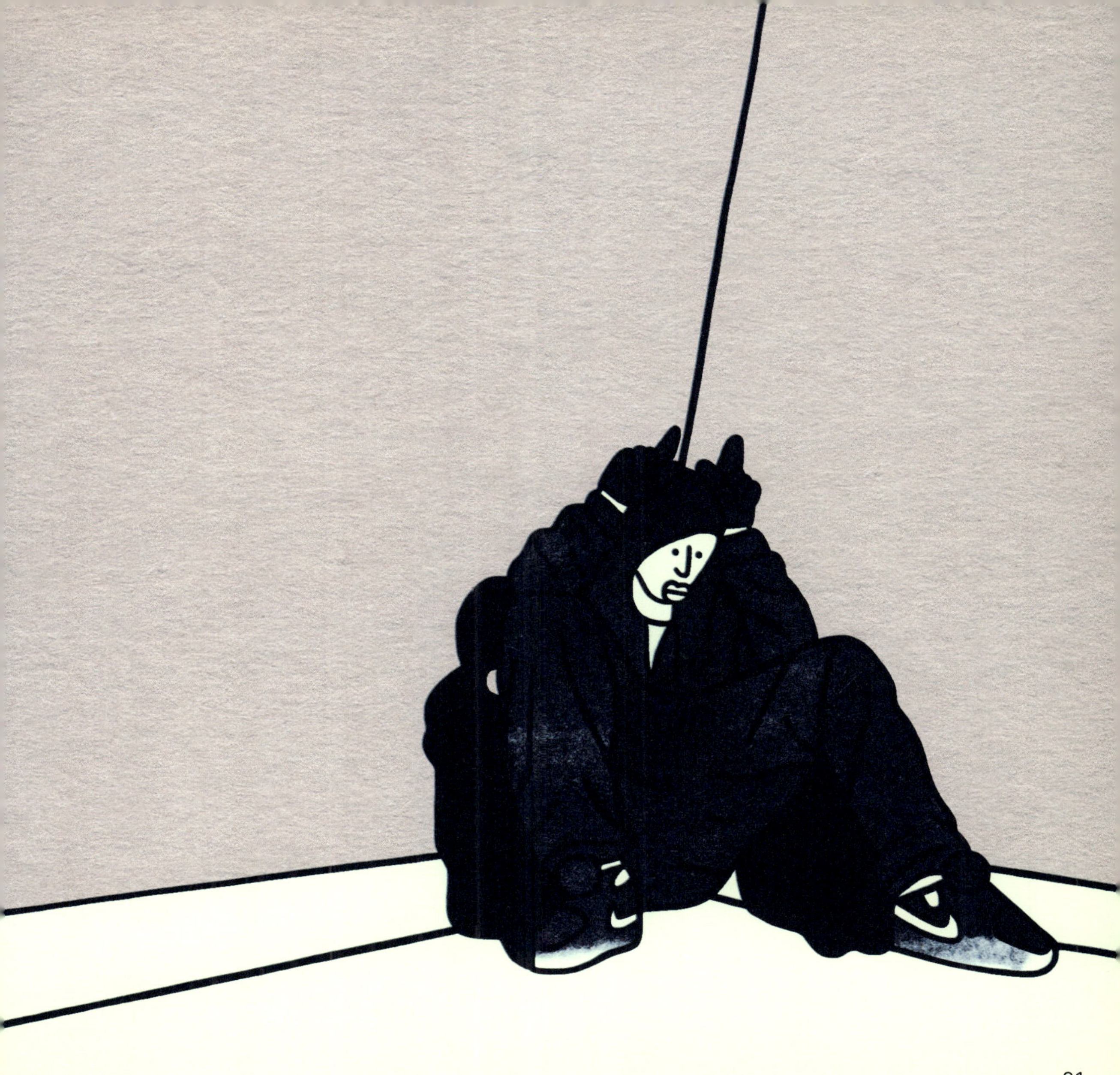

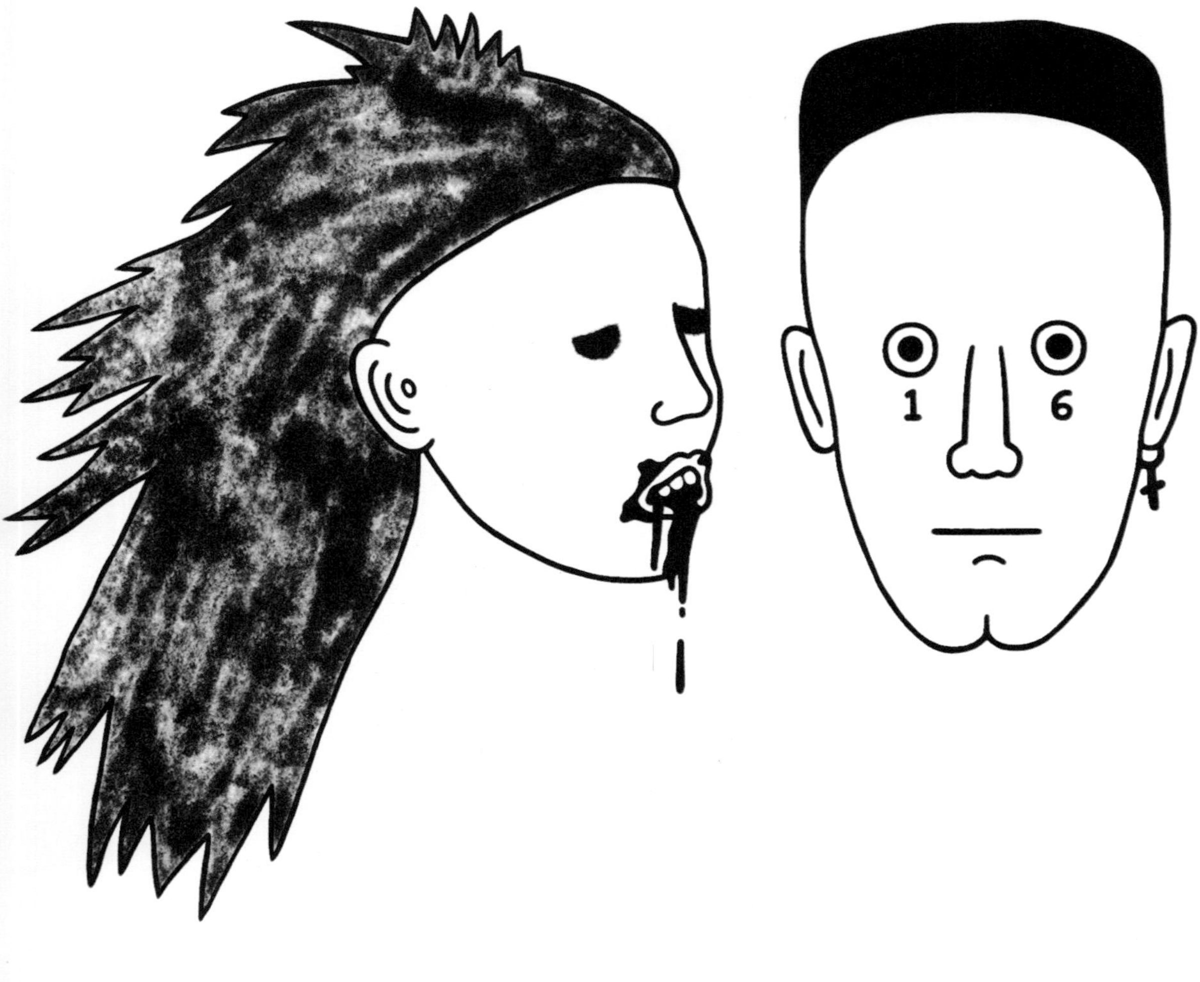
1
6

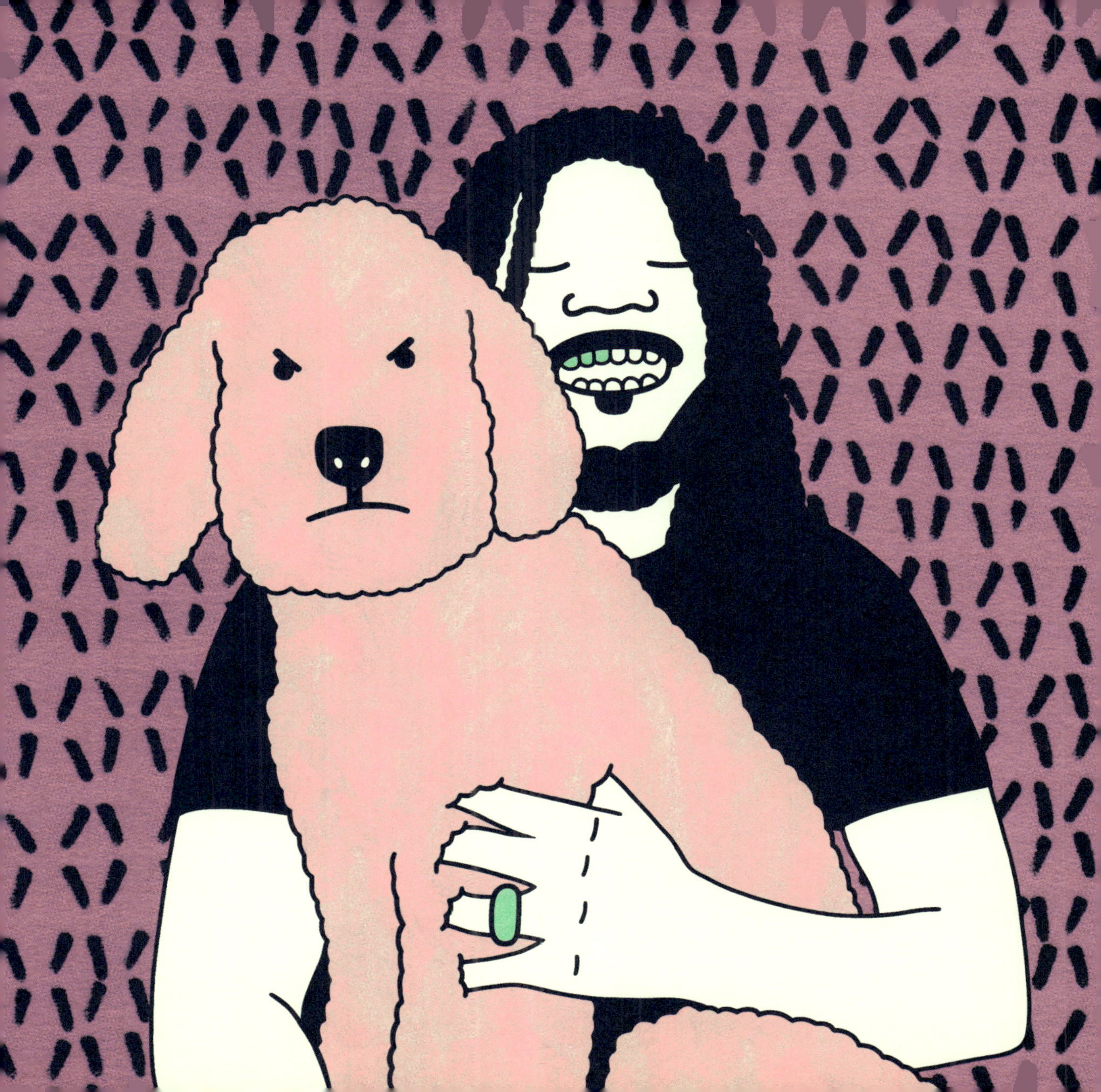

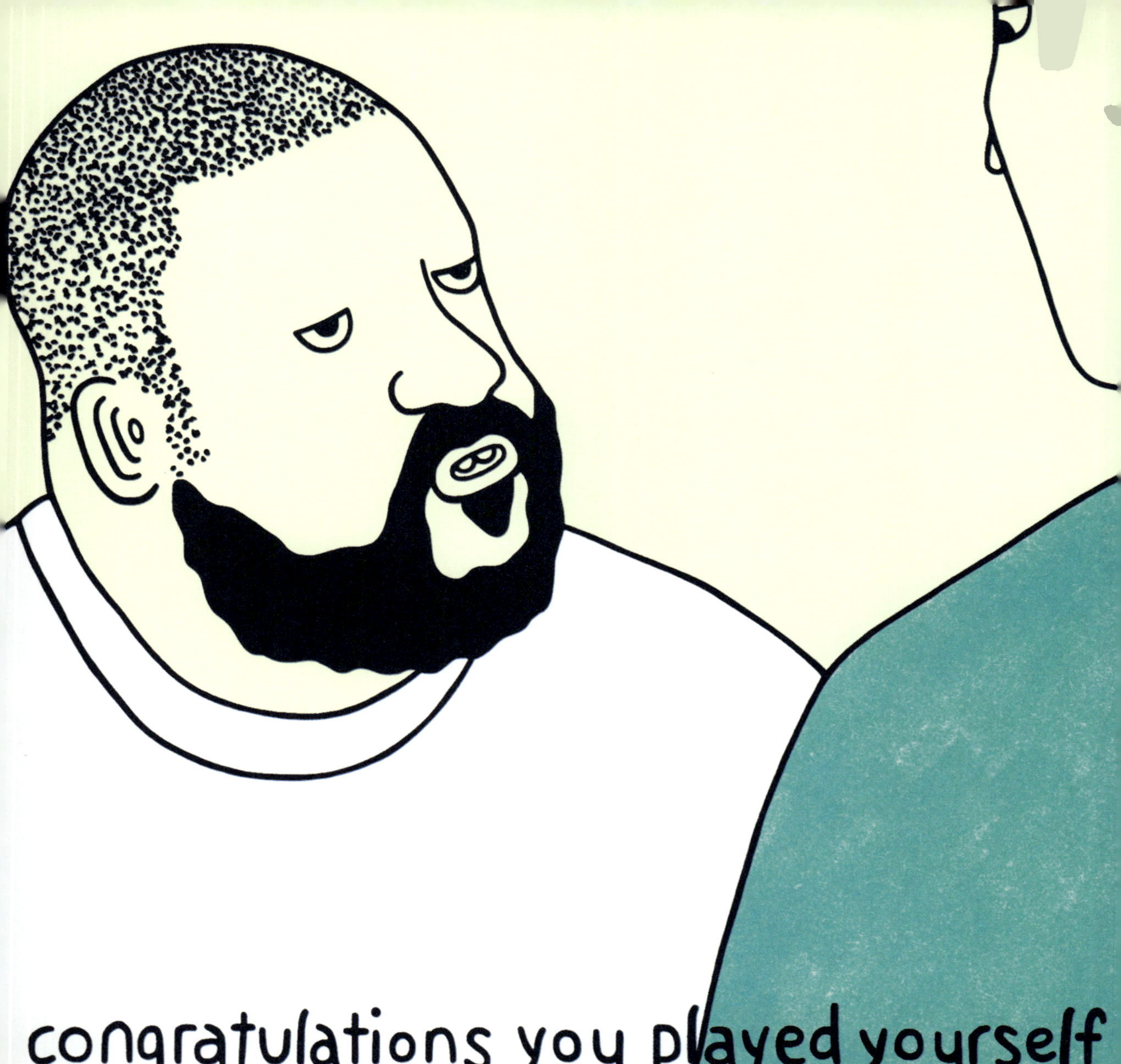

congratulations you played yourself

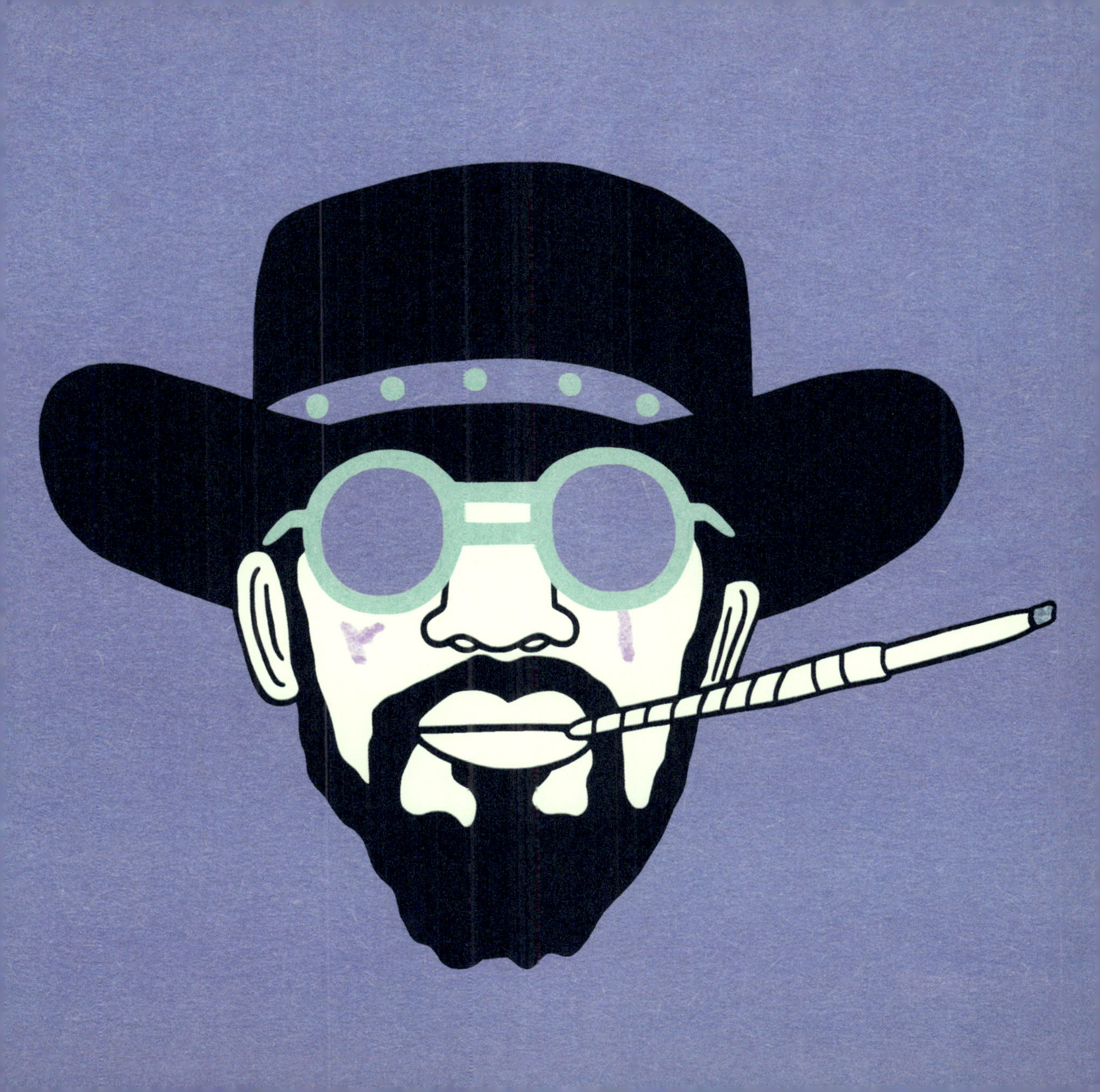

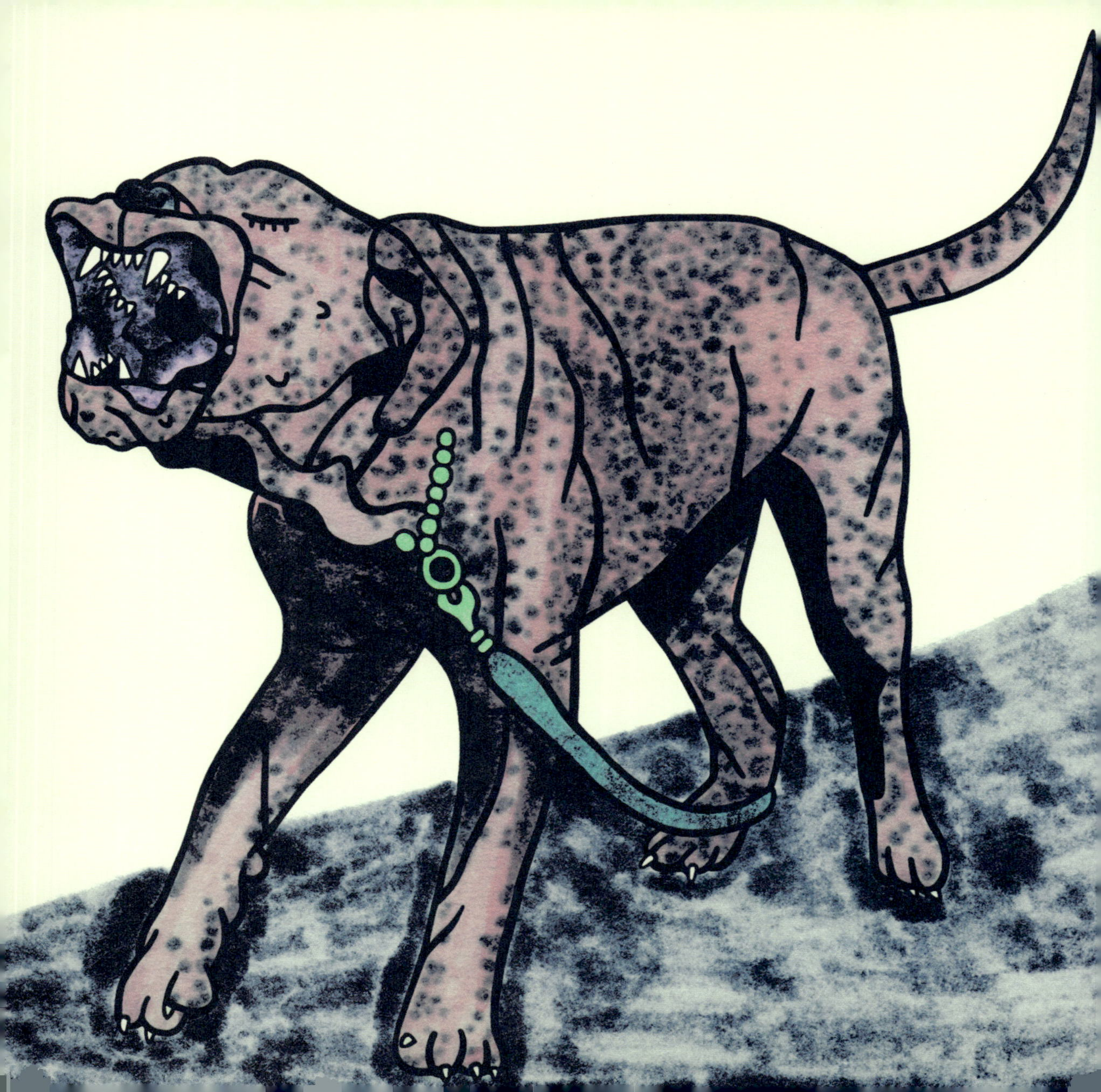

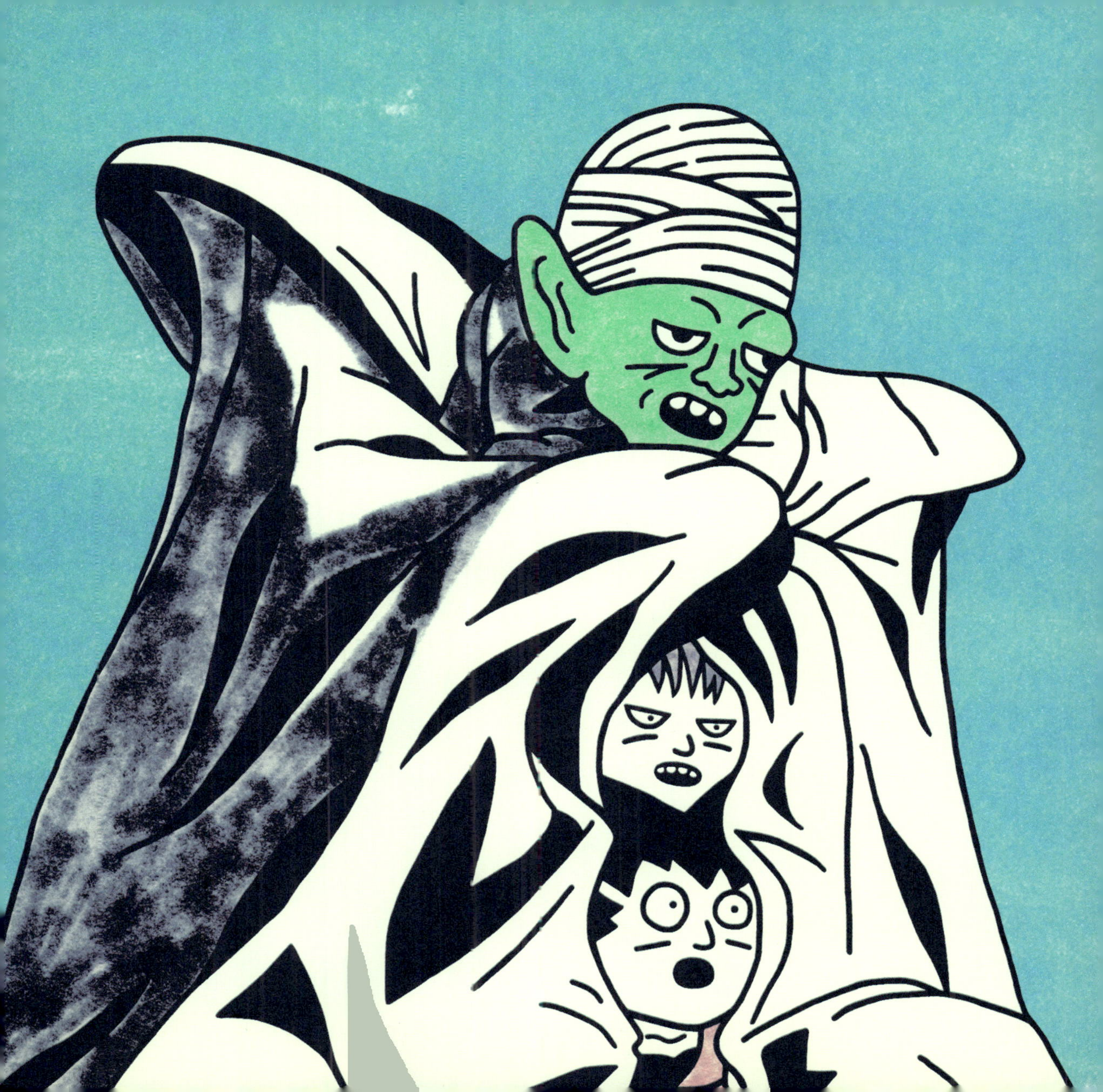

#ChargedUp

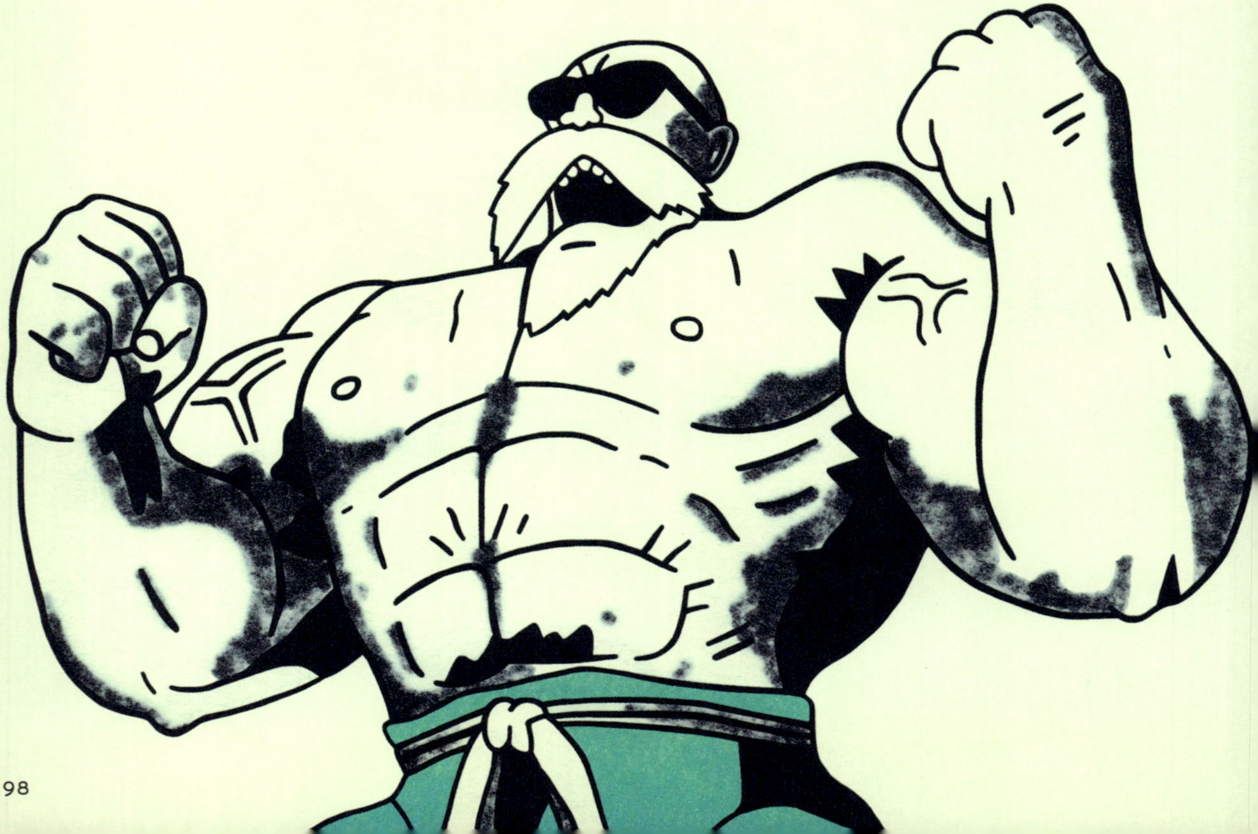

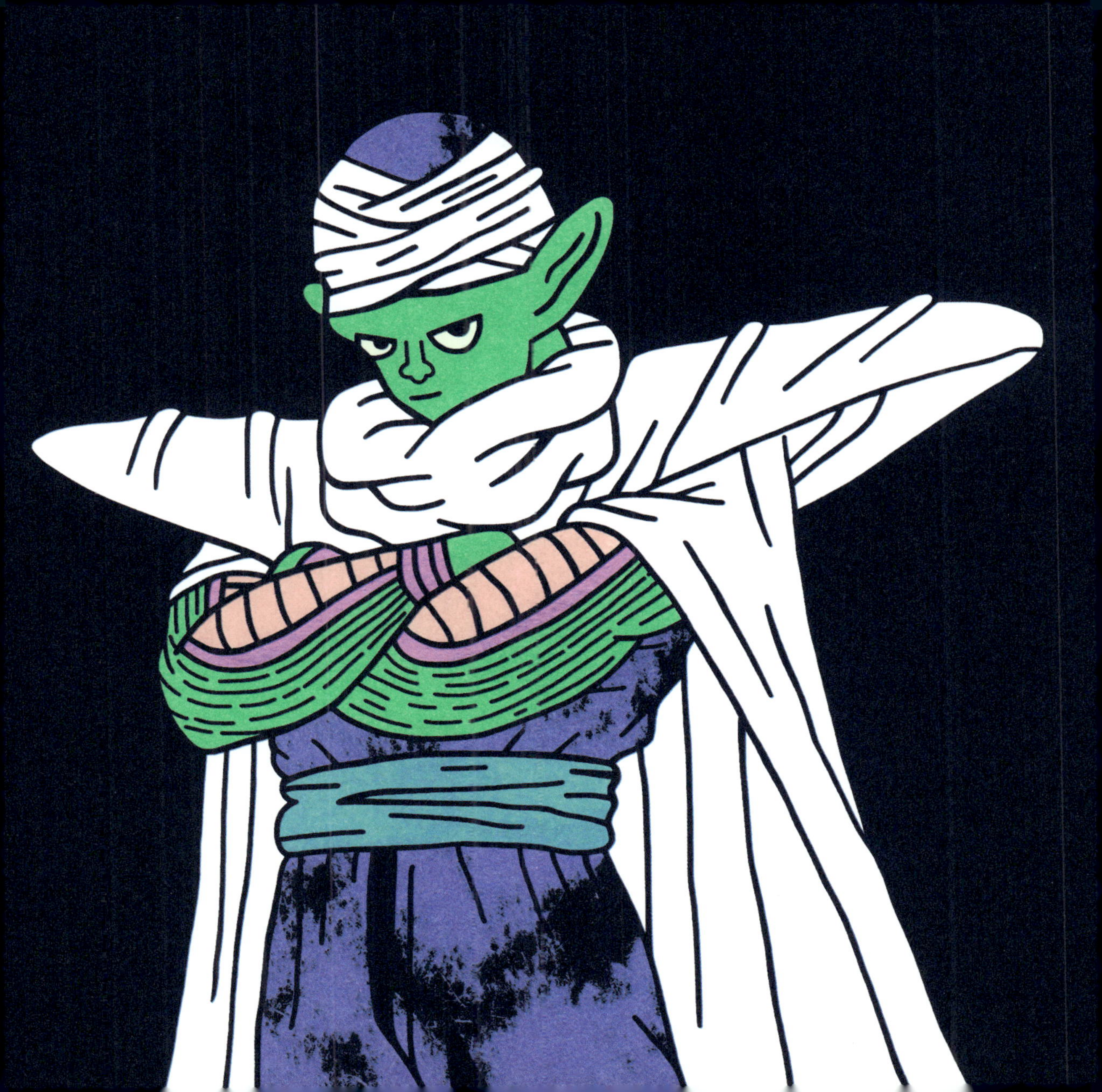

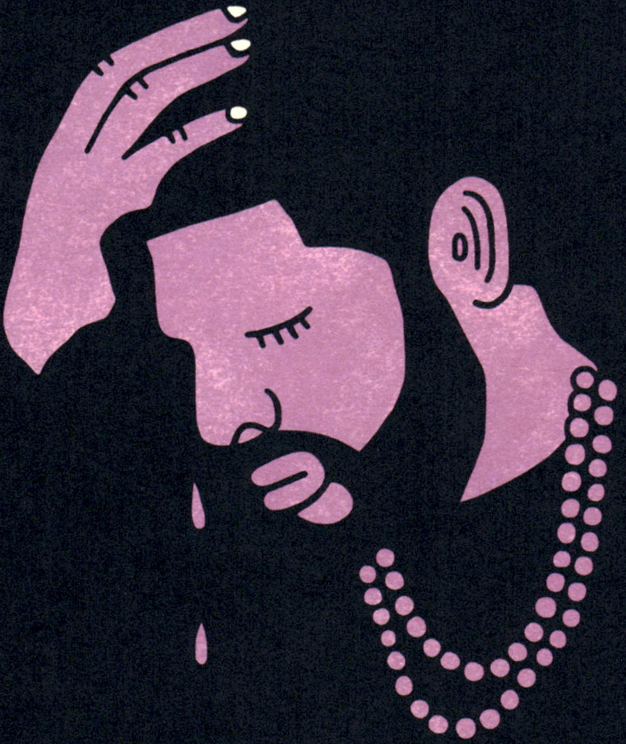

6

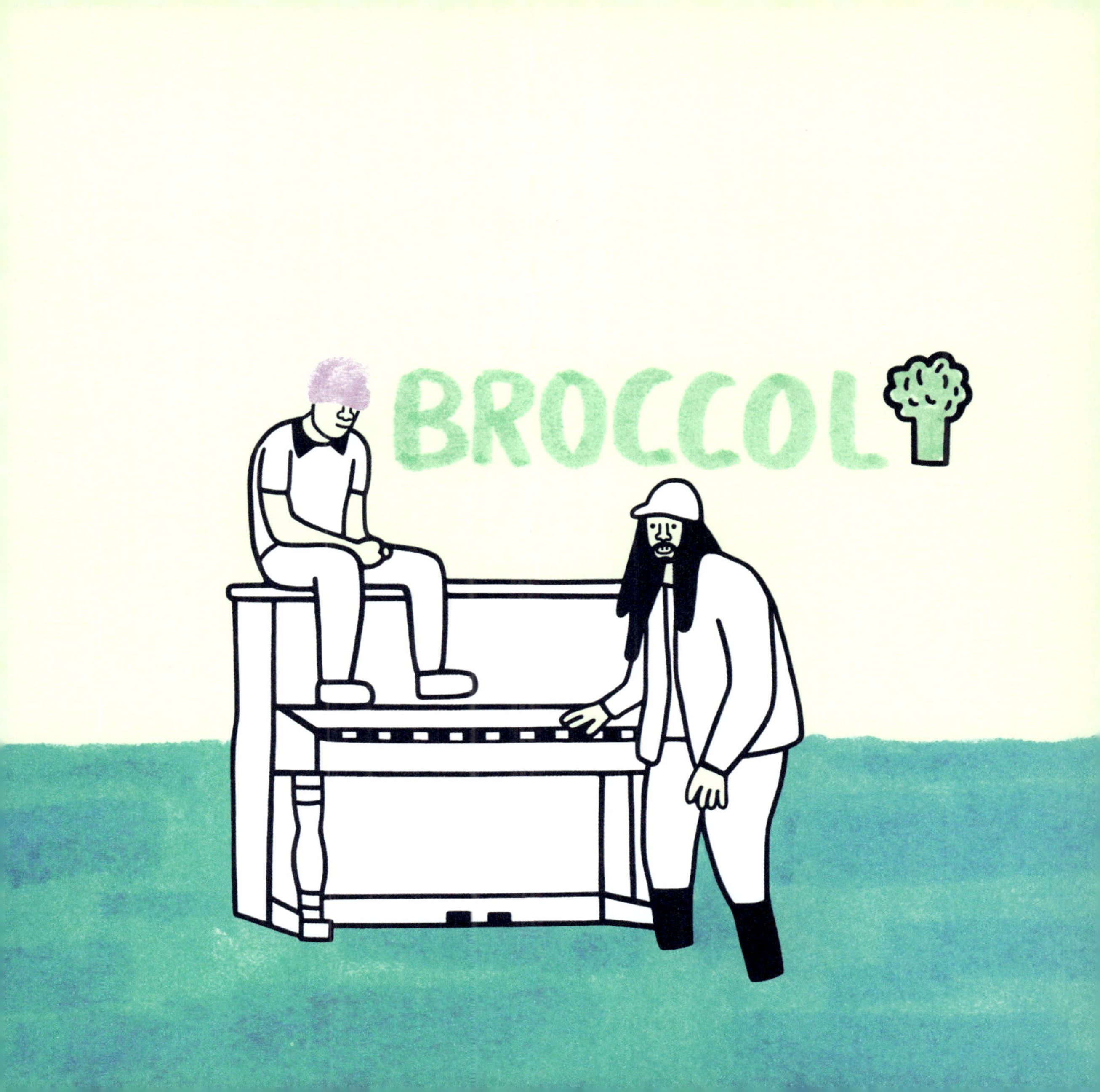
BROCCOL

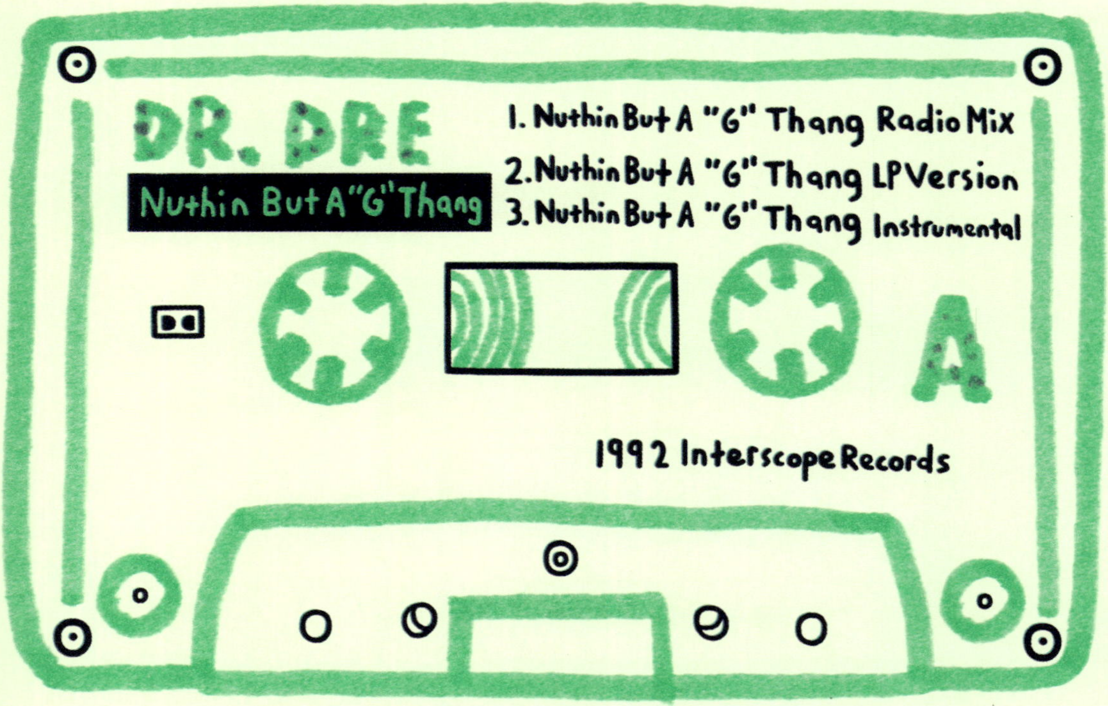
DR. DRE
Nuthin But A "G" Thang
1. Nuthin But A "G" Thang Radio Mix
2. Nuthin But A "G" Thang LP Version
3. Nuthin But A "G" Thang Instrumental
A
1992 Interscope Records

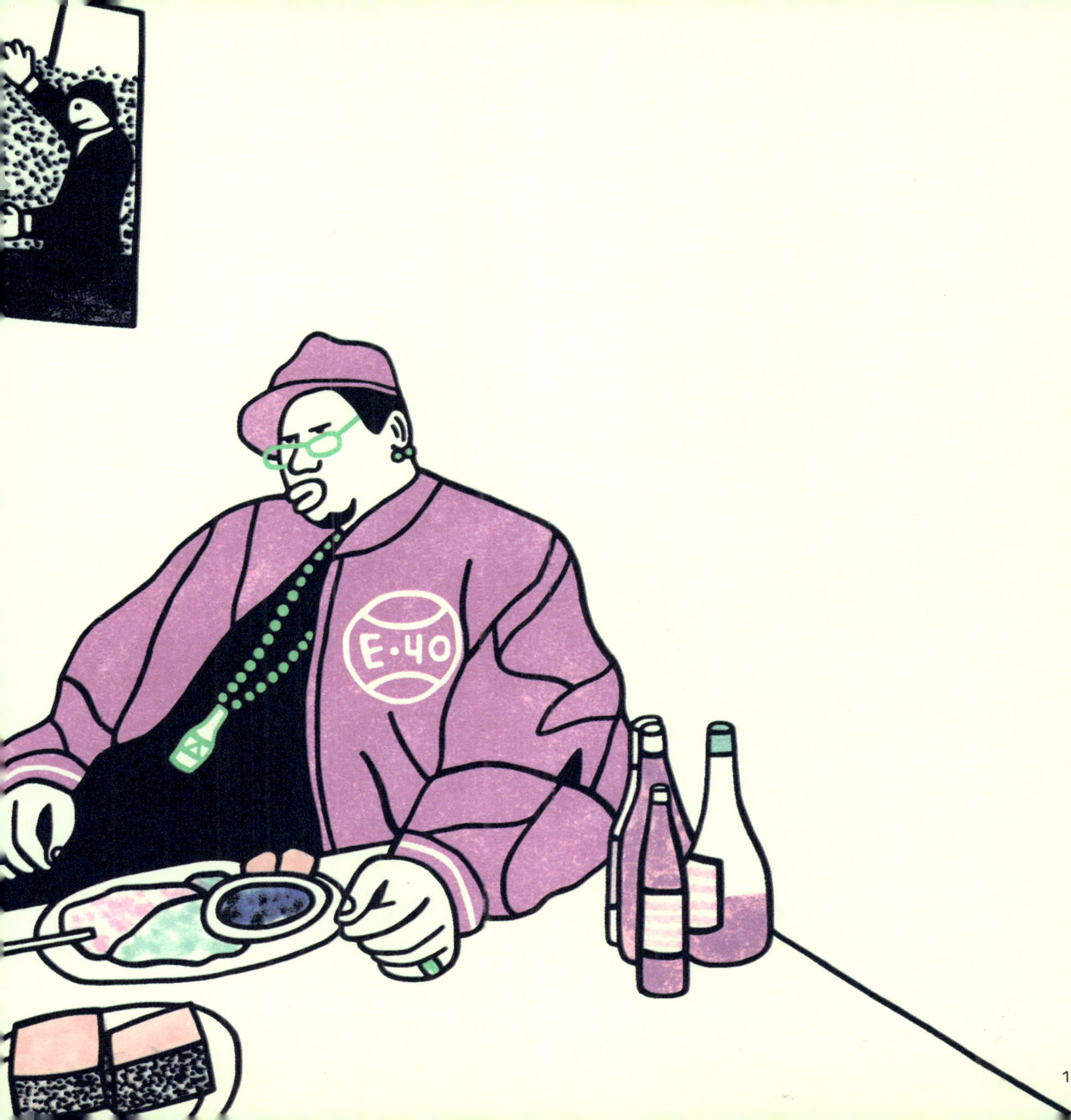
E·40

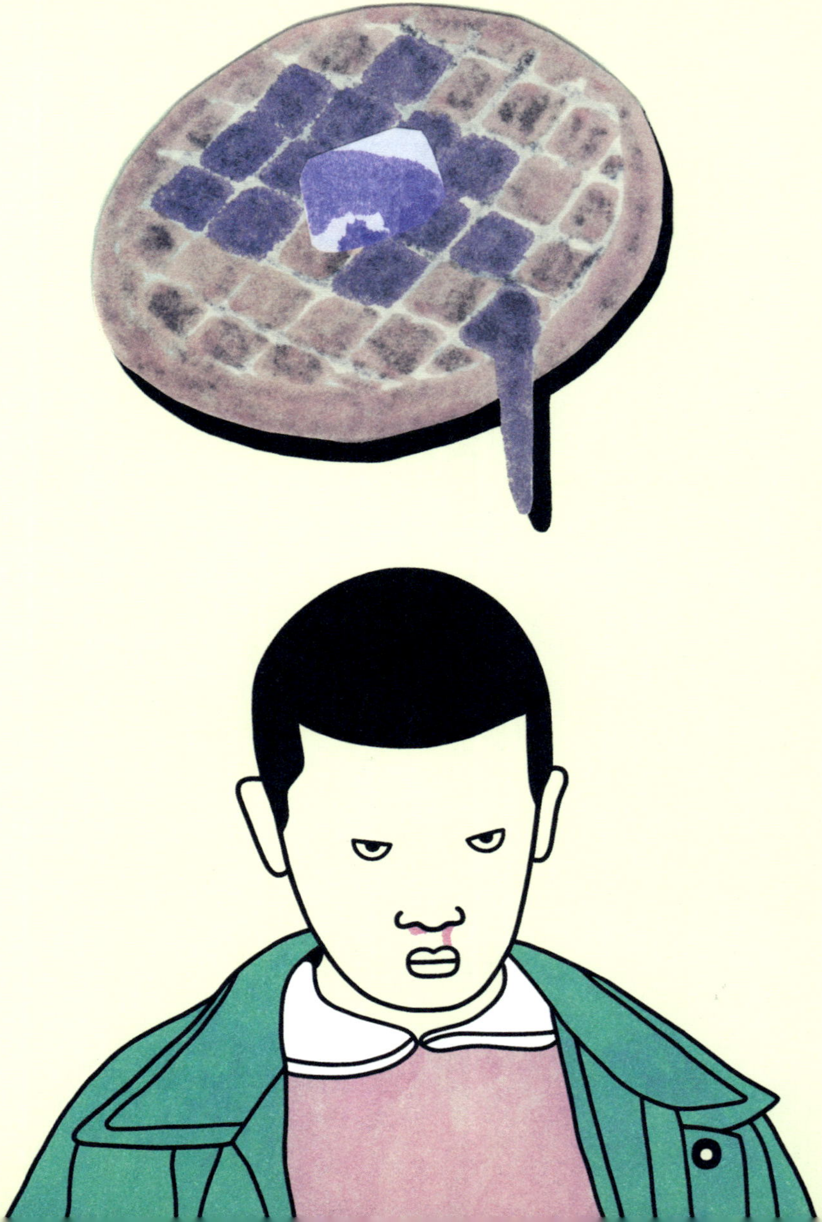

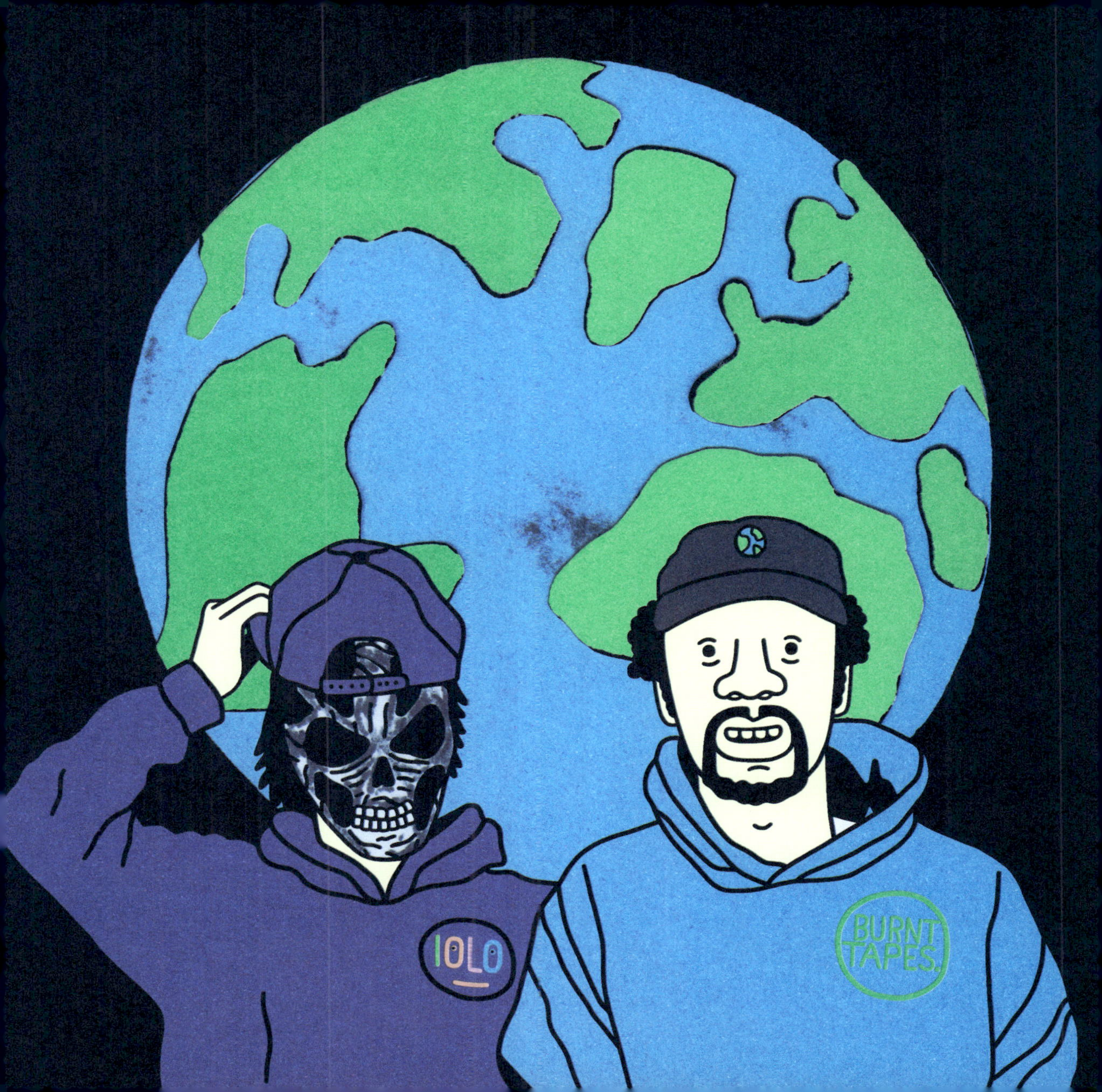
IOLO
BURNT TAPES.

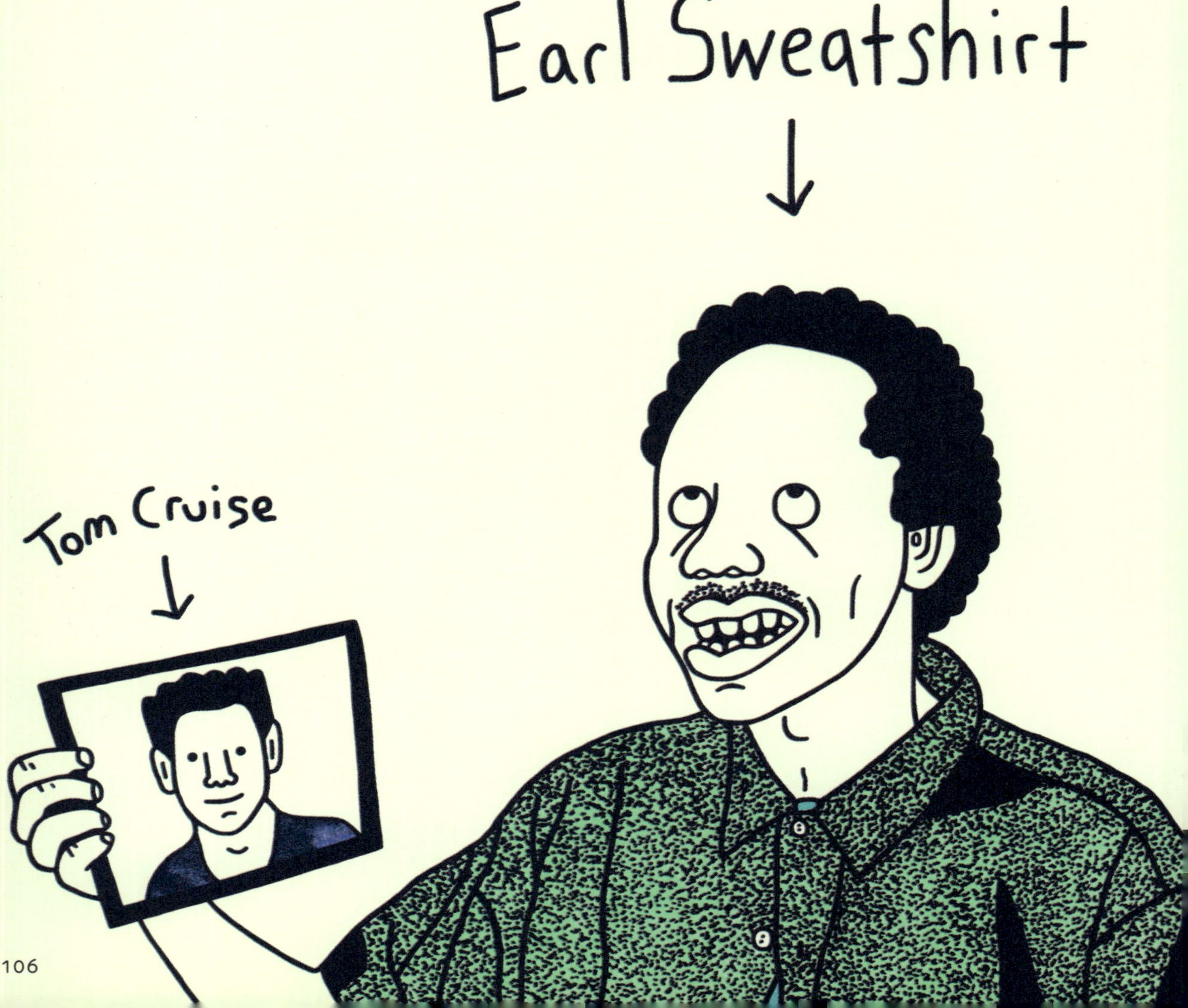
Earl Sweatshirt
Tom Cruise

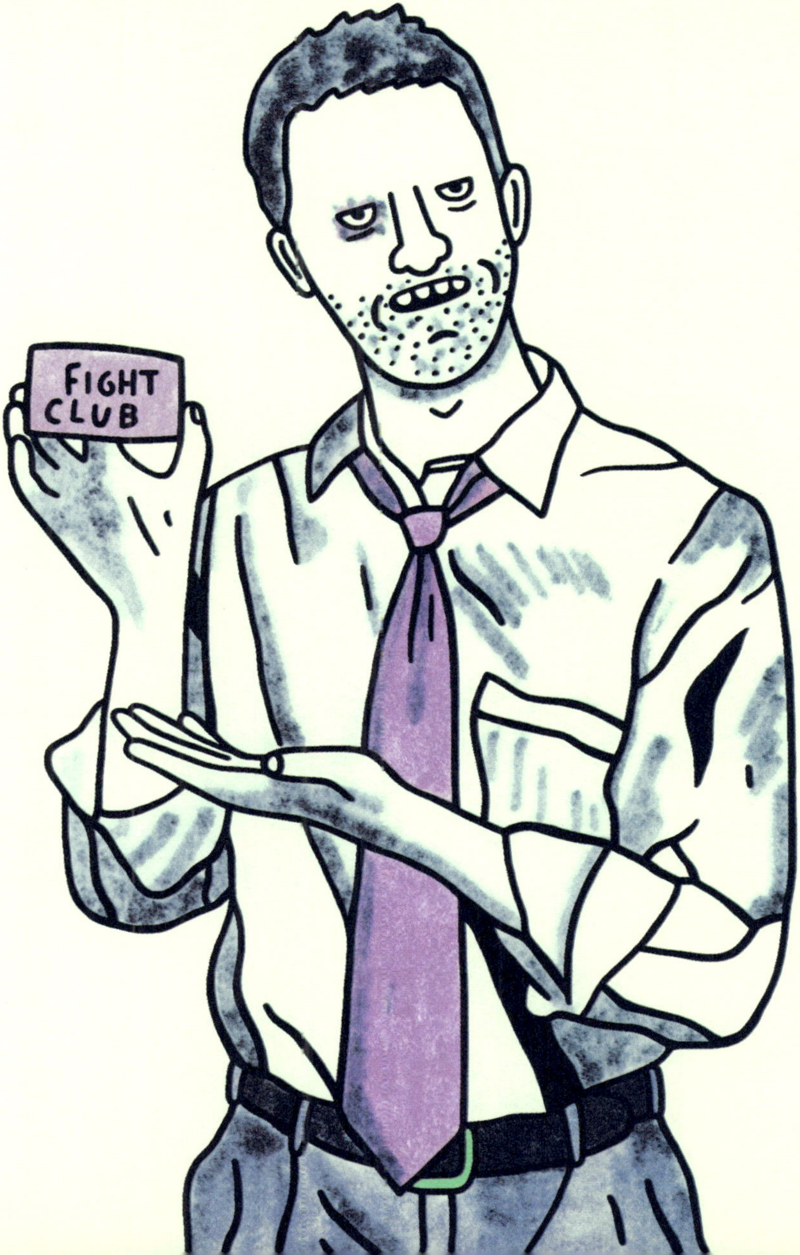
FIGHT
CLUB

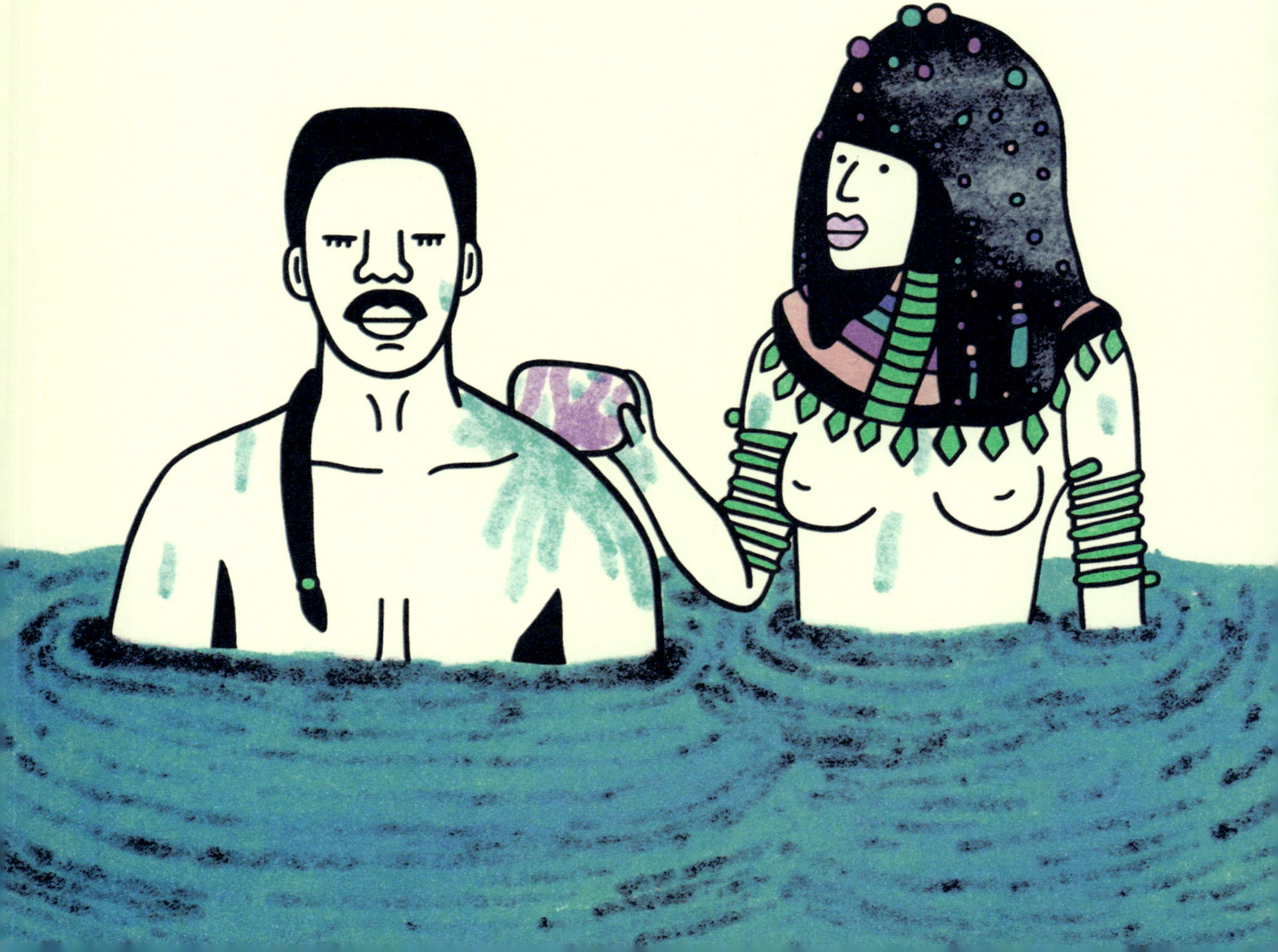

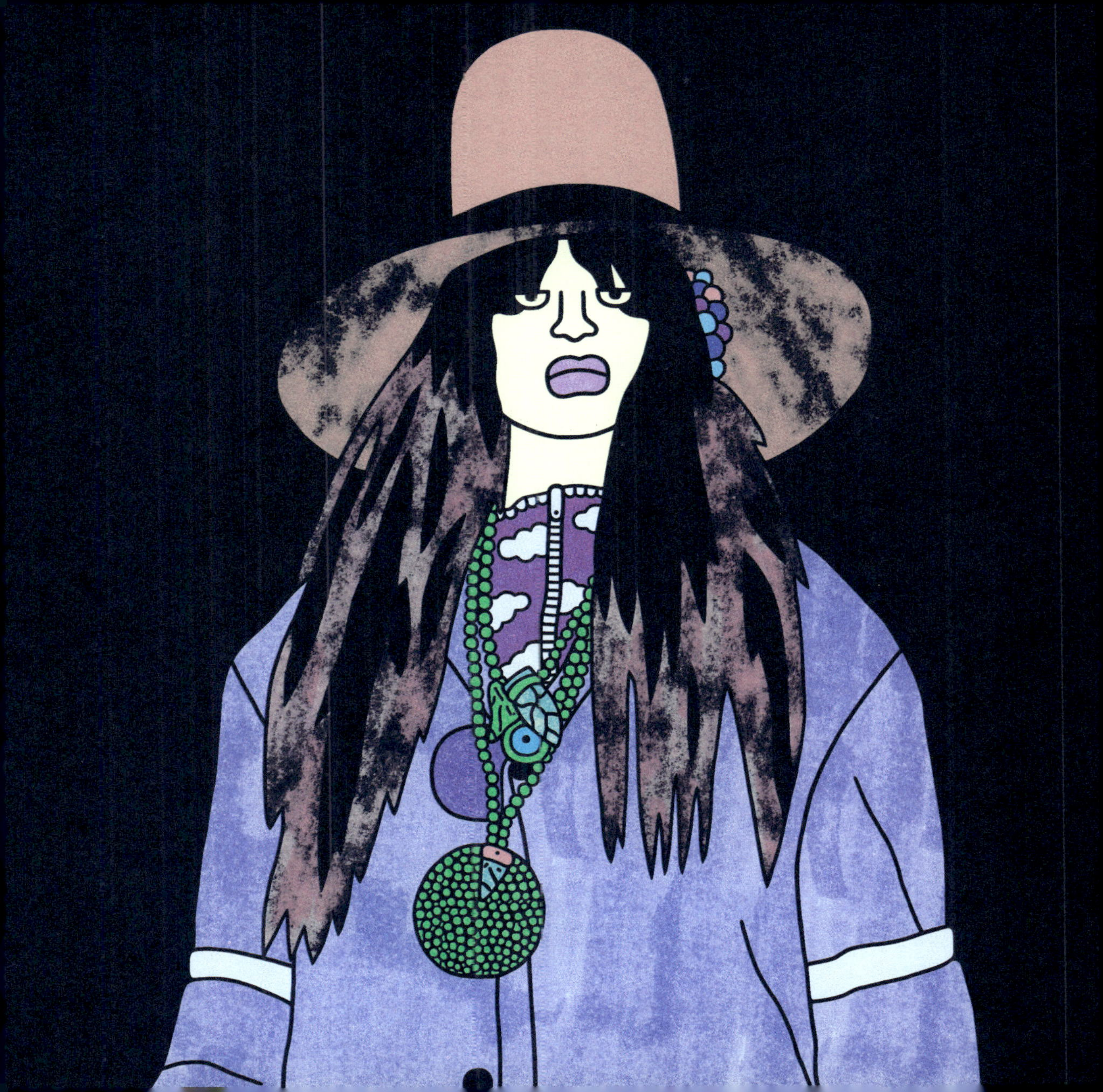

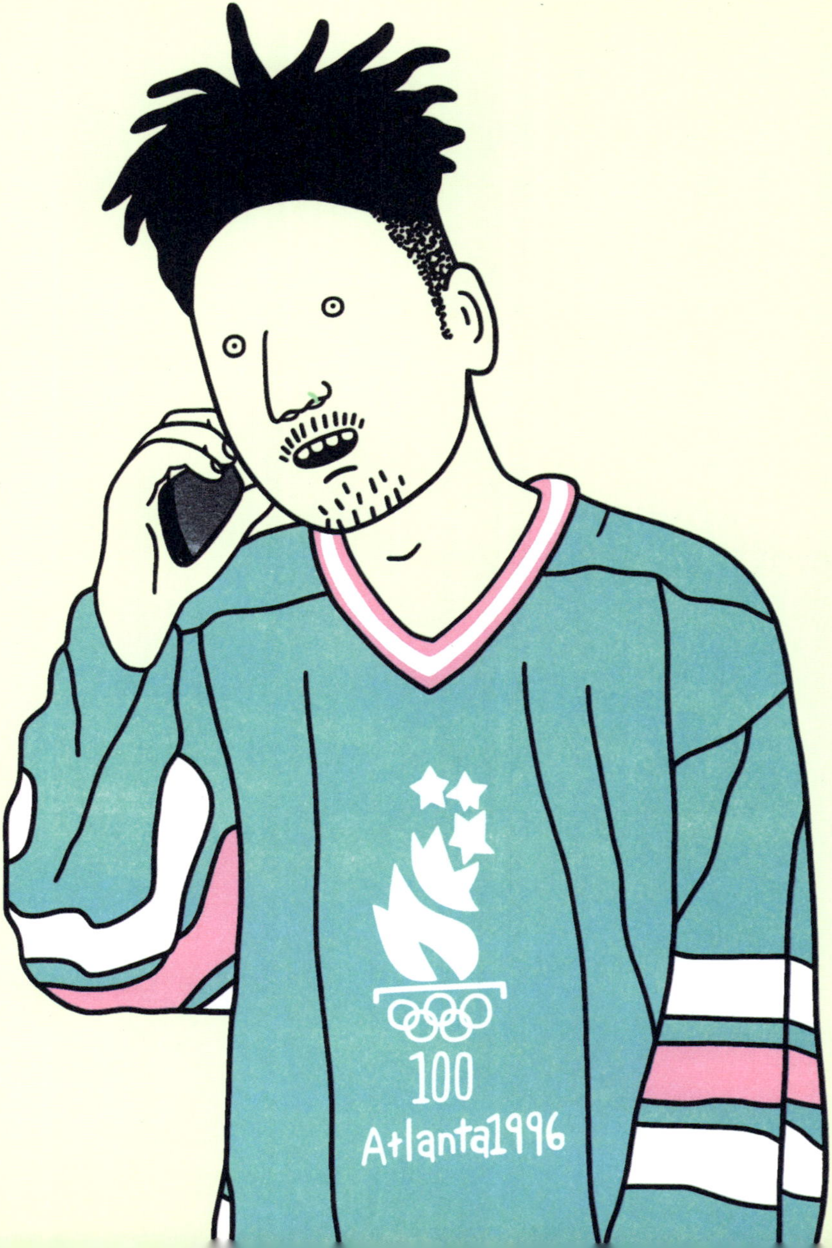
100
Atlanta1996

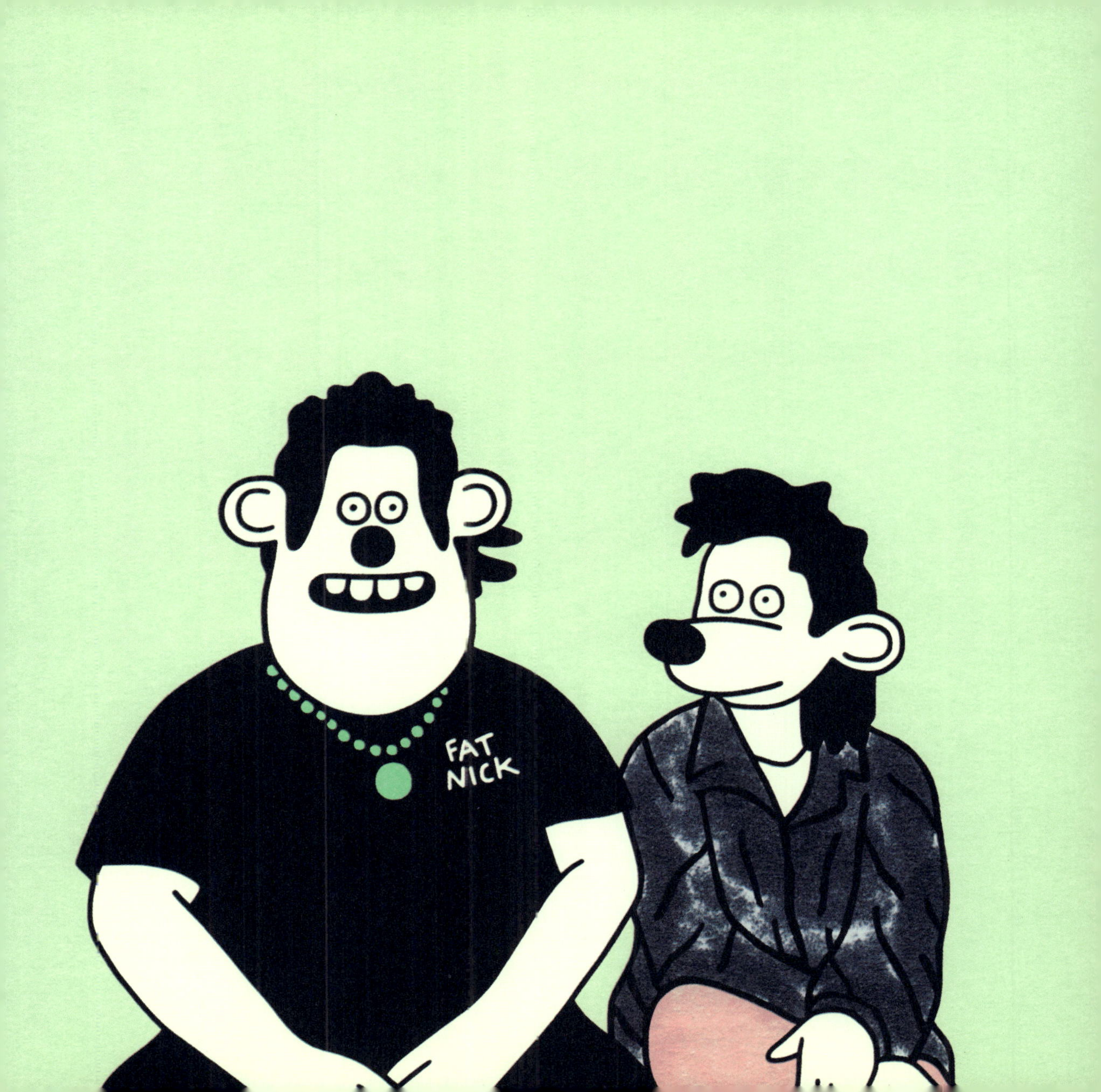
FAT
NICK

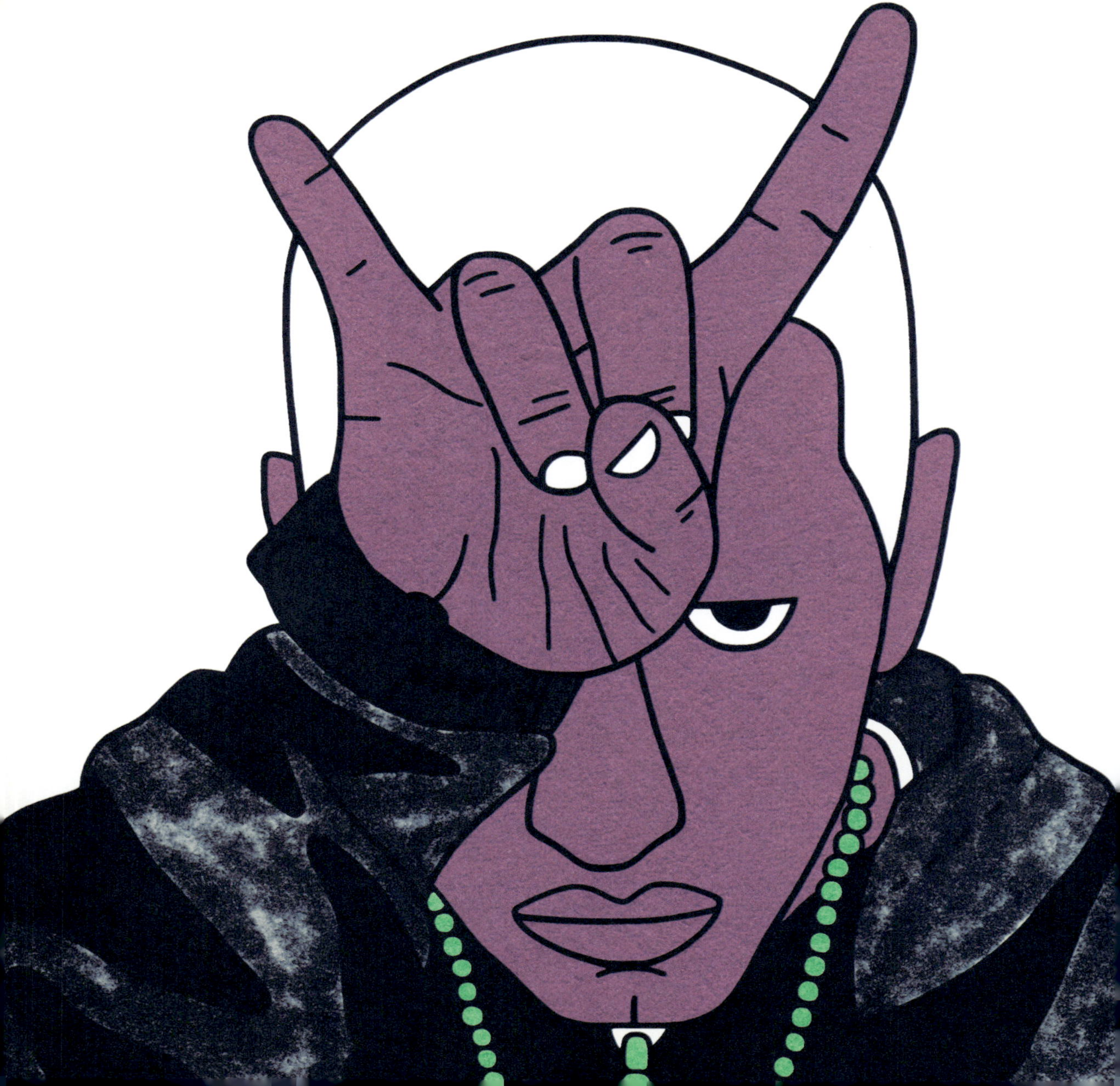

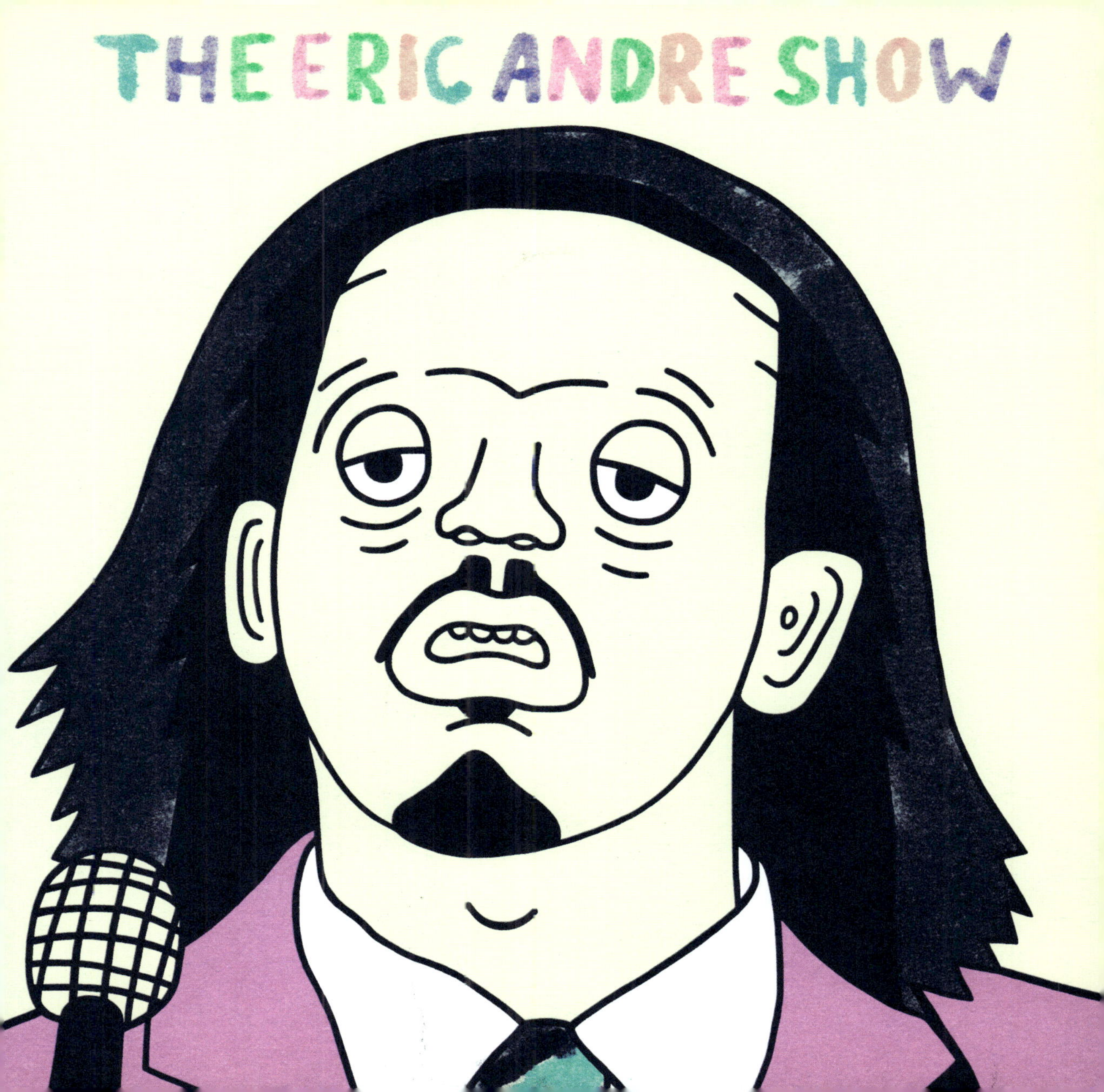
THE ERIC ANDRE SHOW

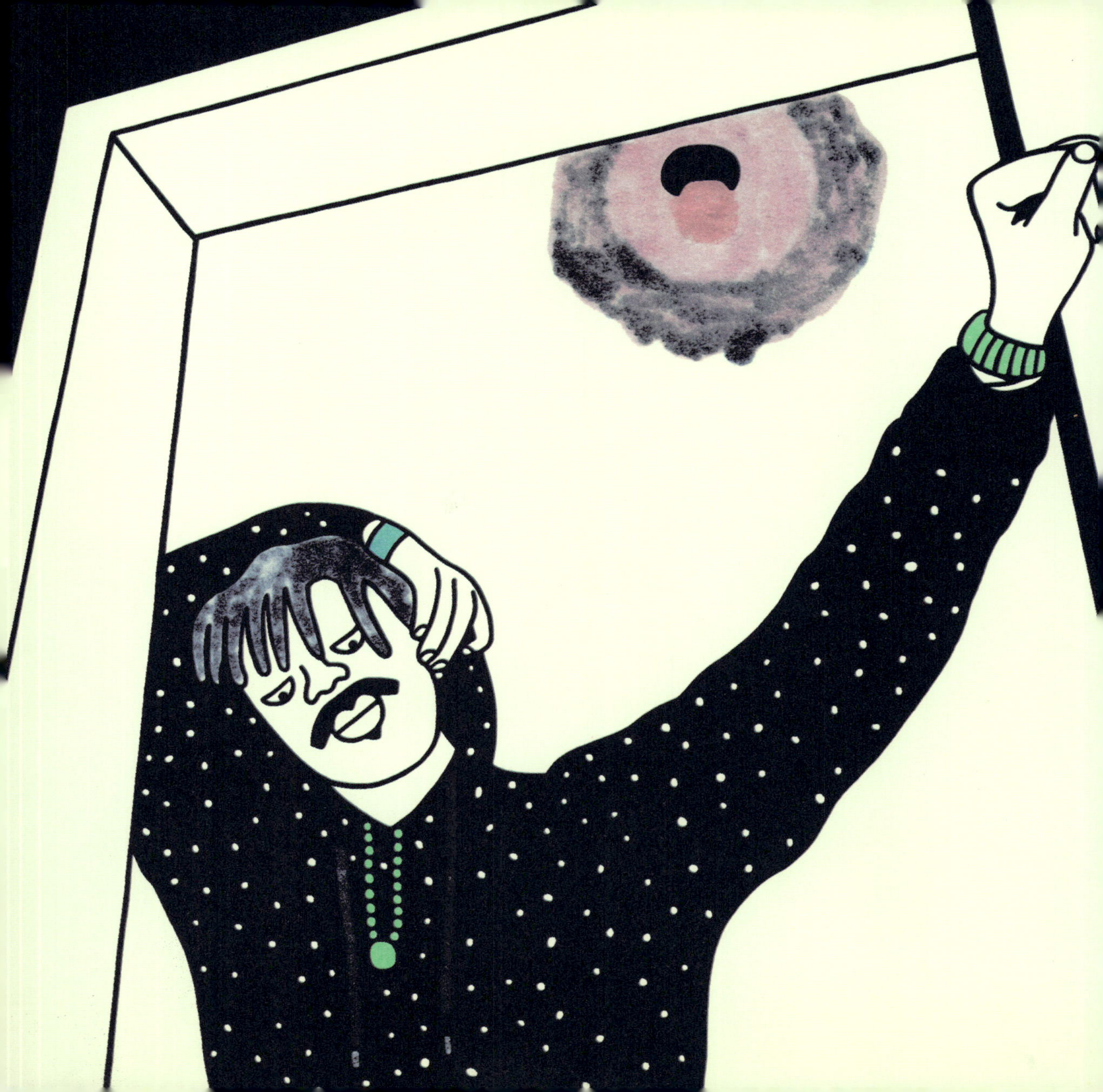

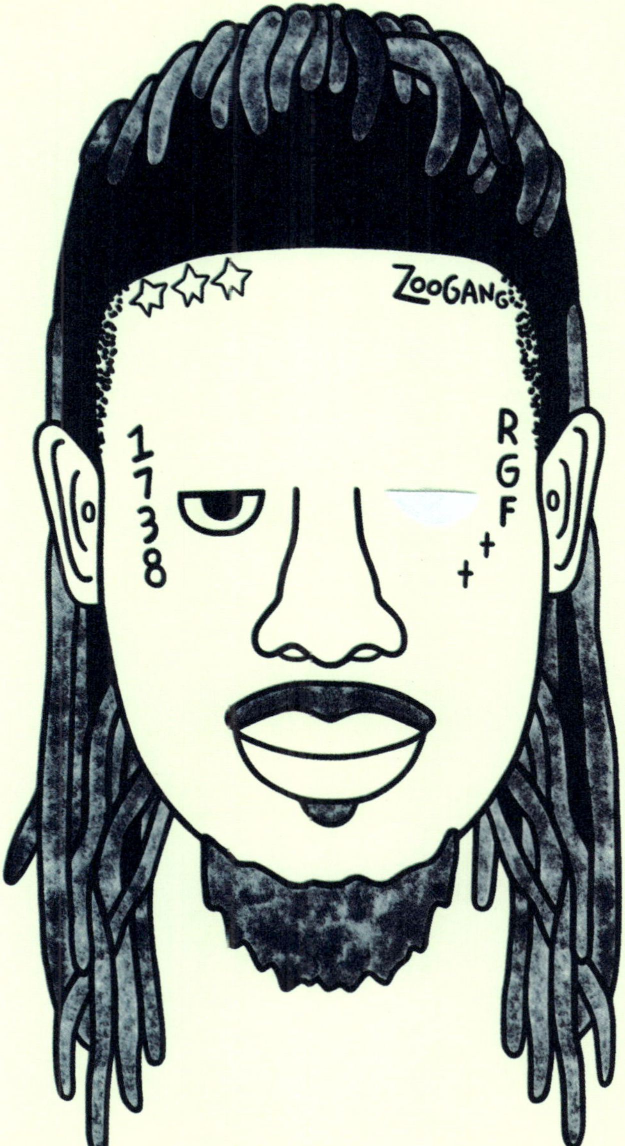
ZOOGANG
1738
RGF

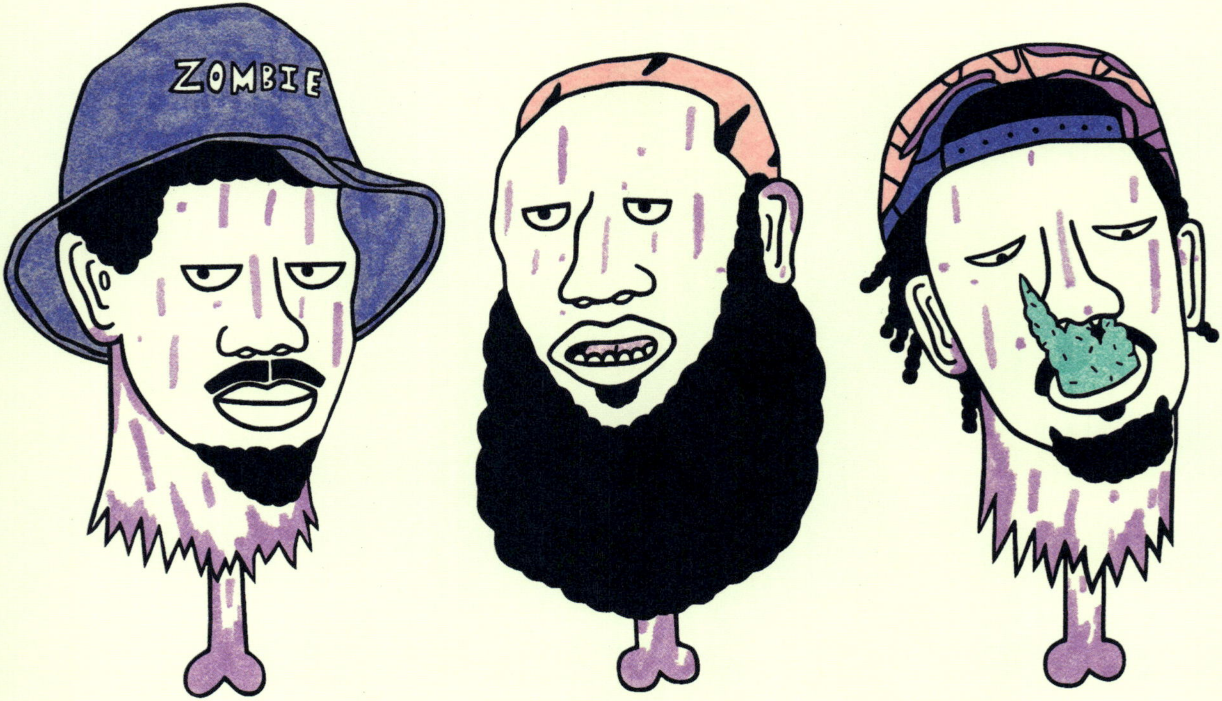
ZOMBIE

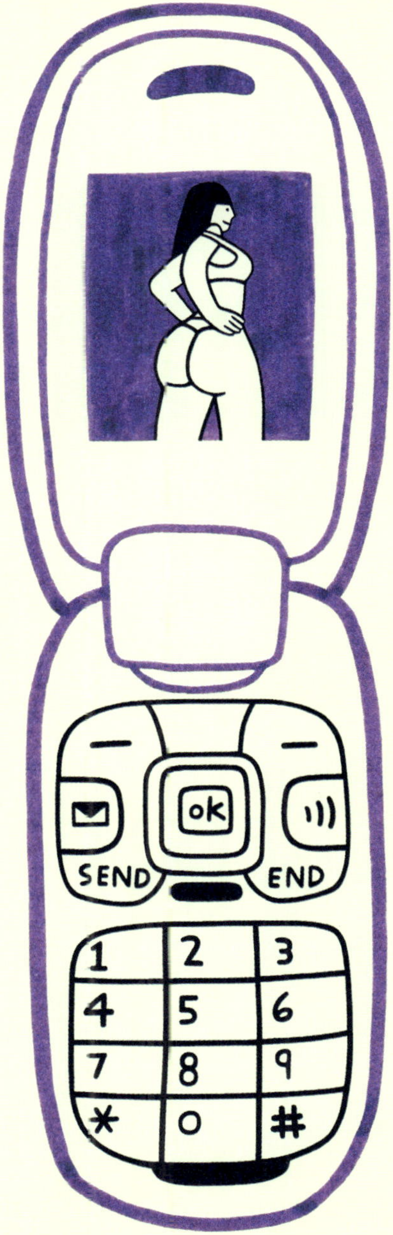
ok
SEND
END
1
2
3
4
5
6
7
8
9
*
0
#

I do not like this painting, Charlie. Its smug aura mocks me.

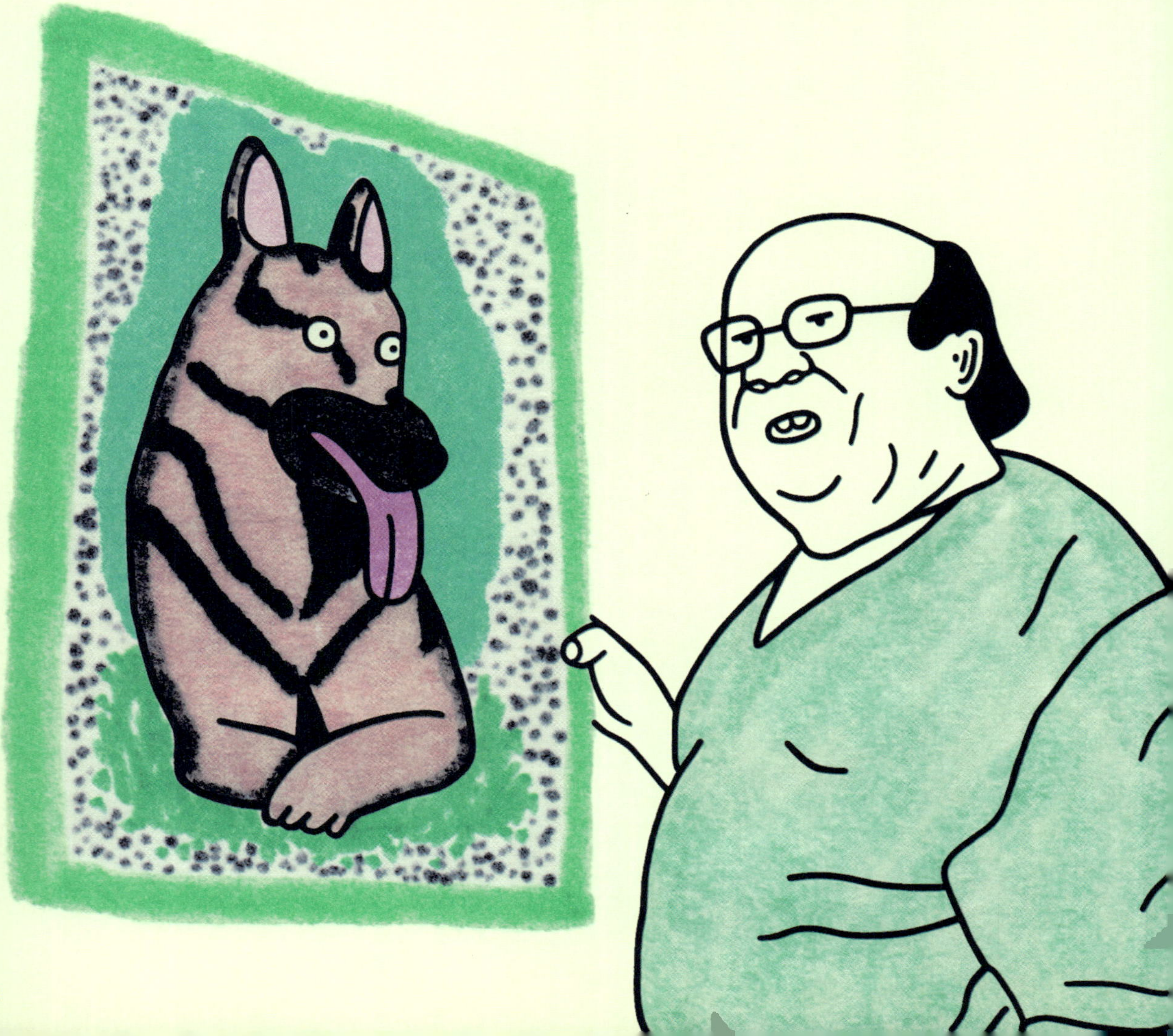

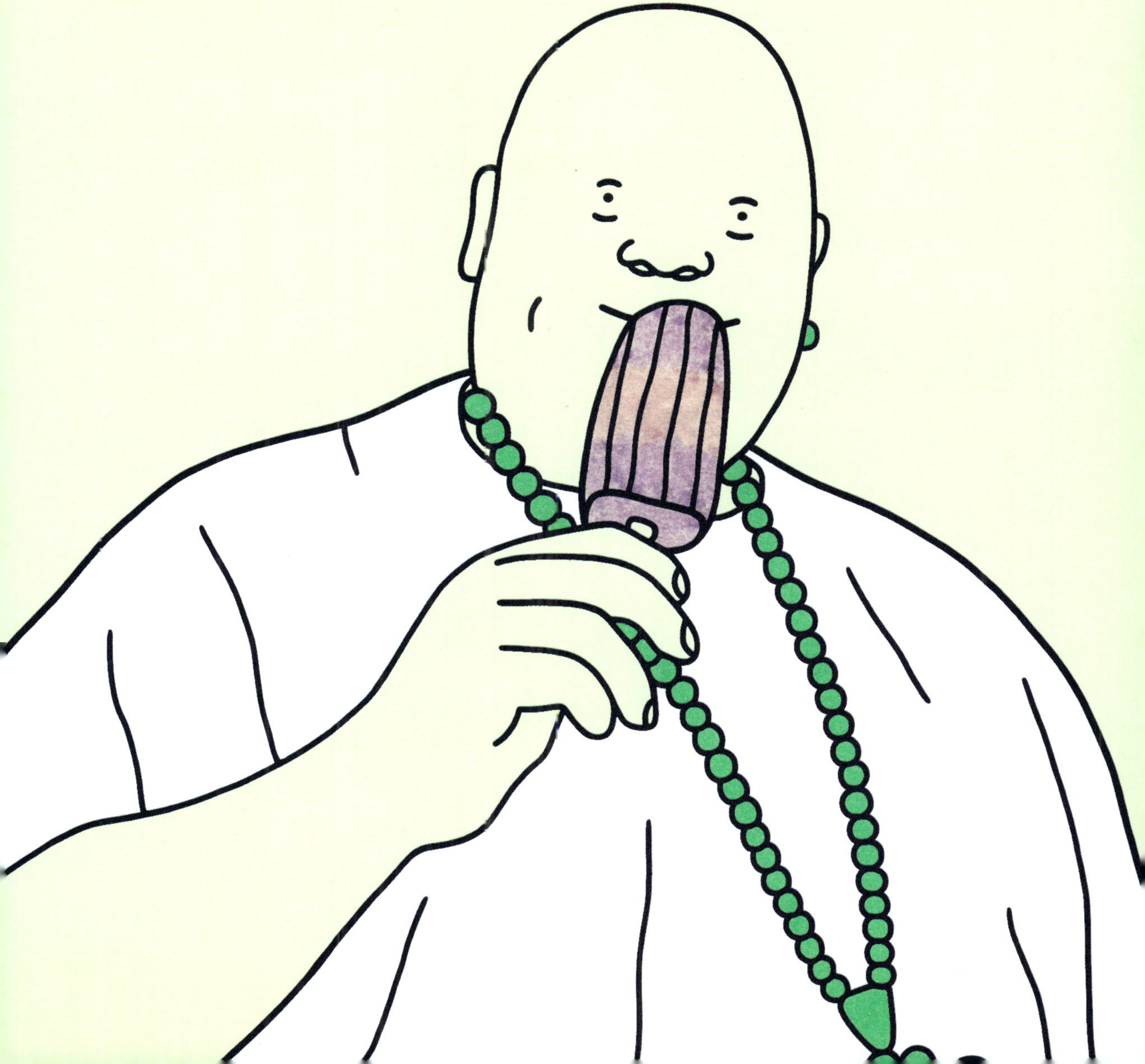

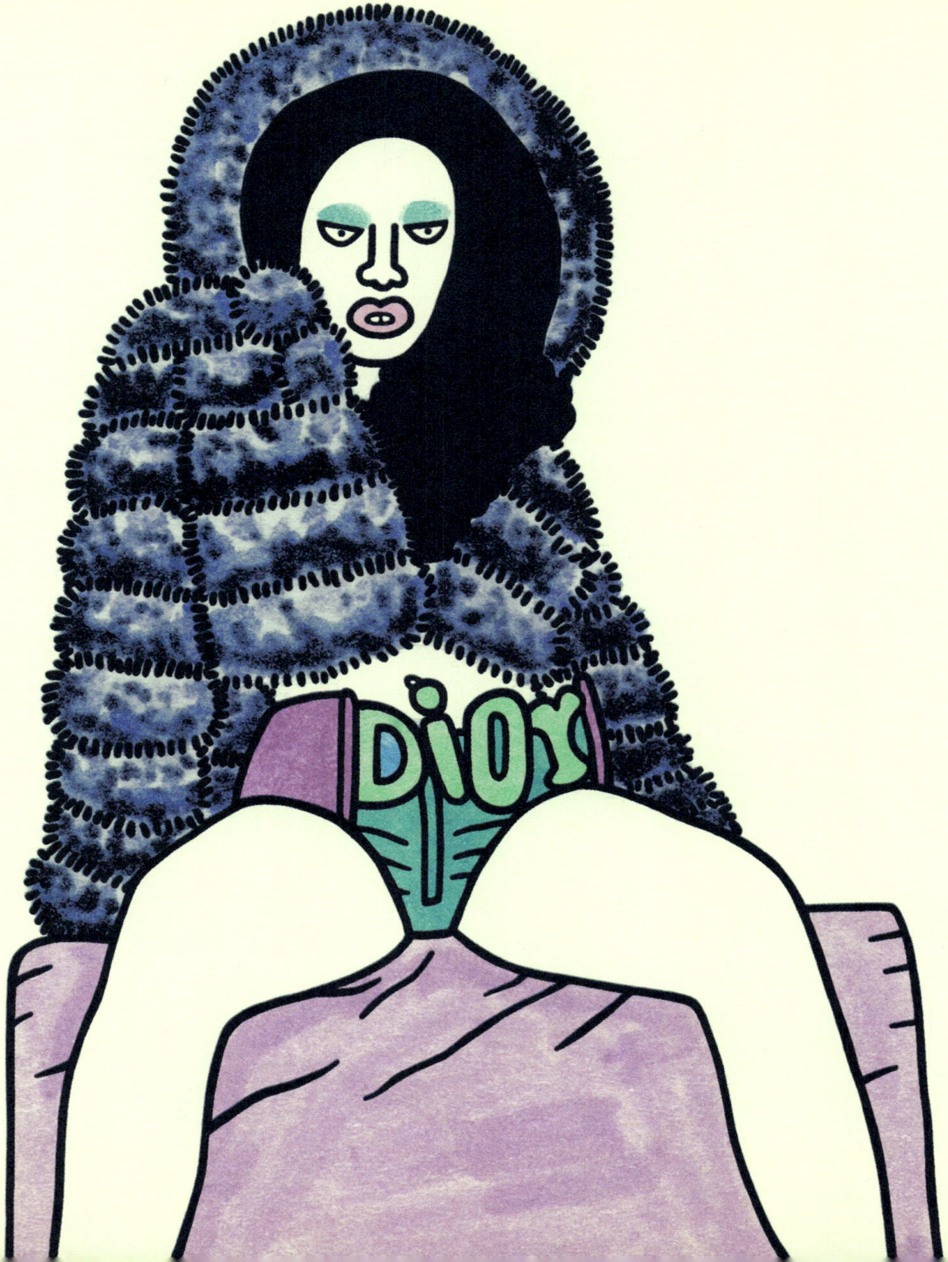
DiOr

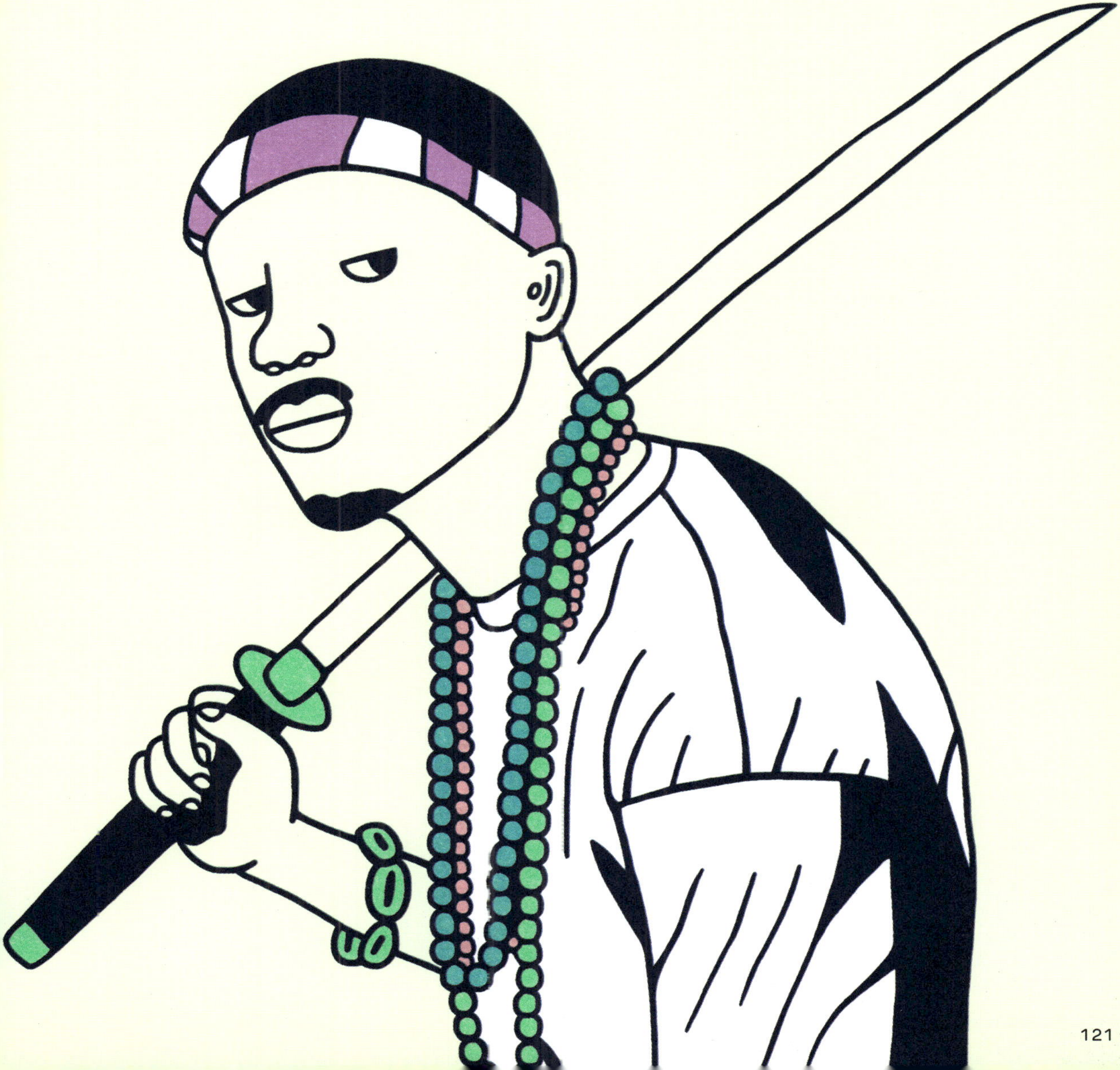

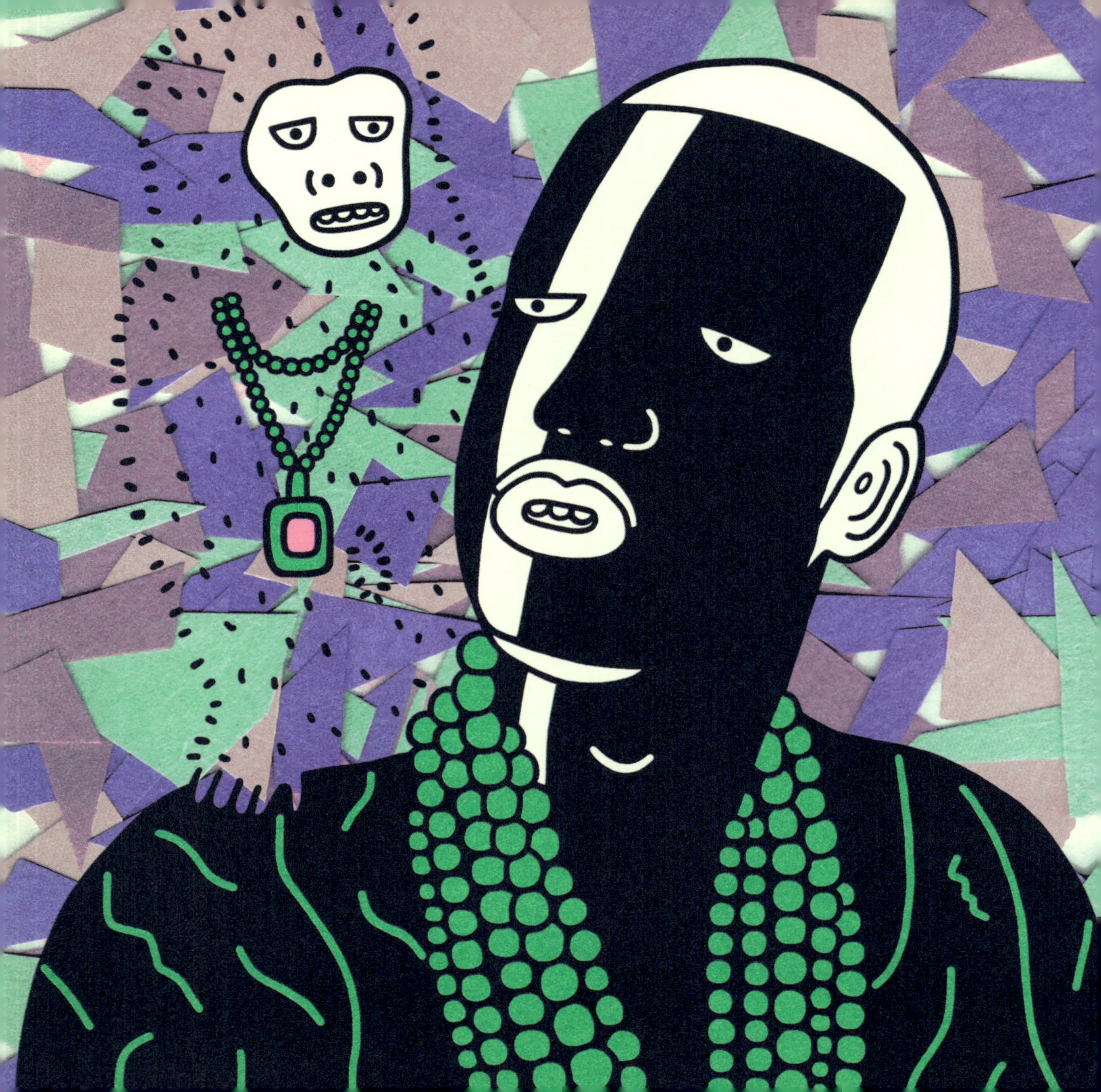

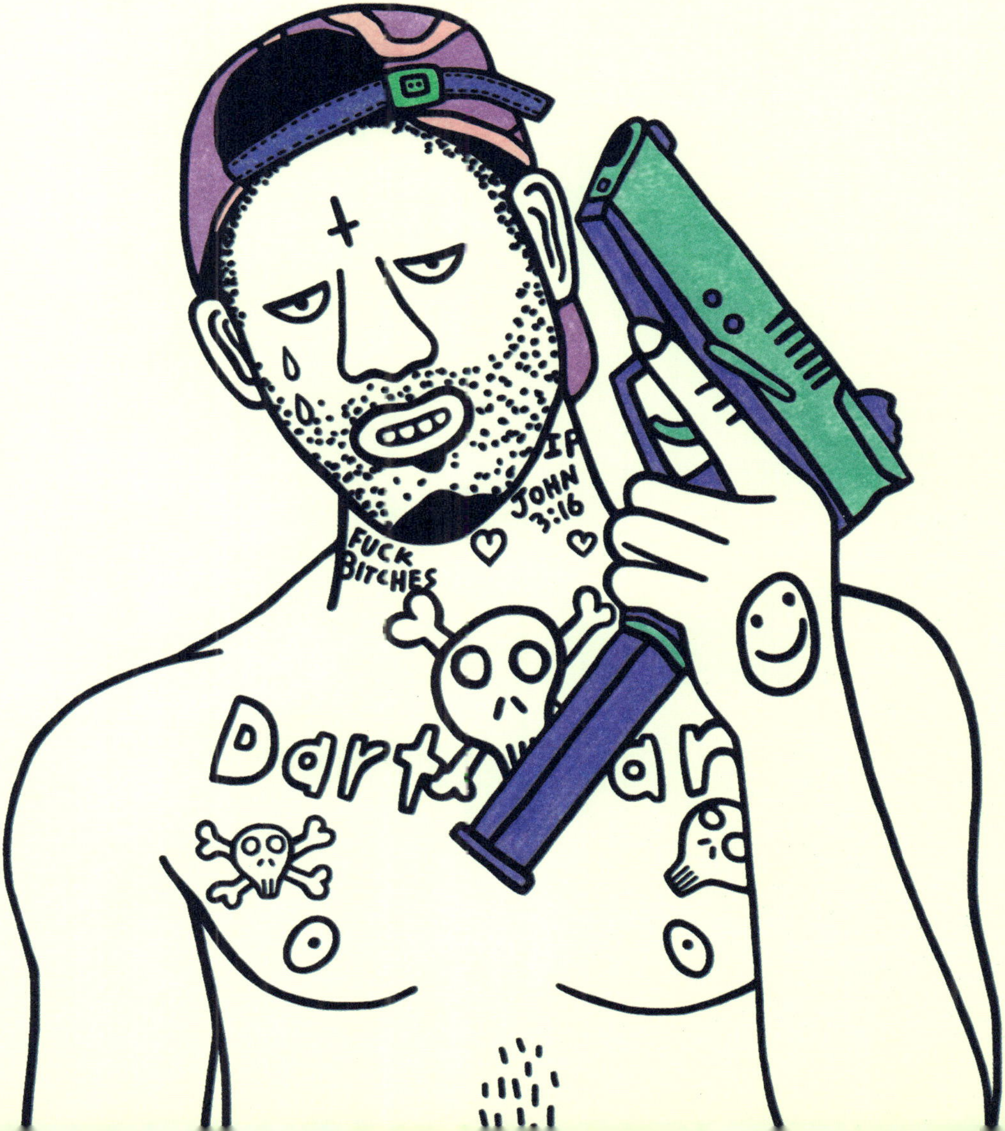
JOHN
3:16
FUCK
BITCHES

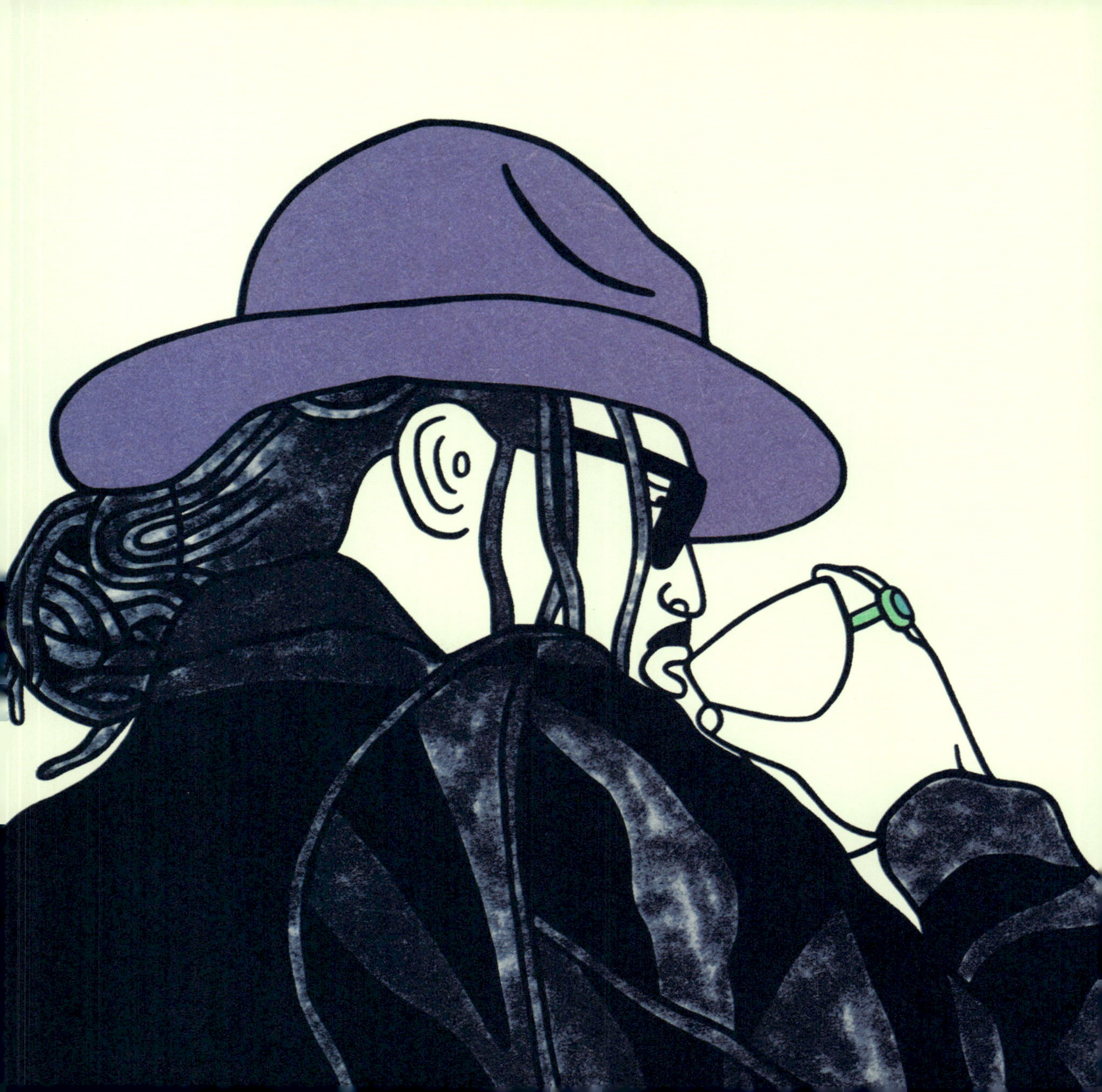

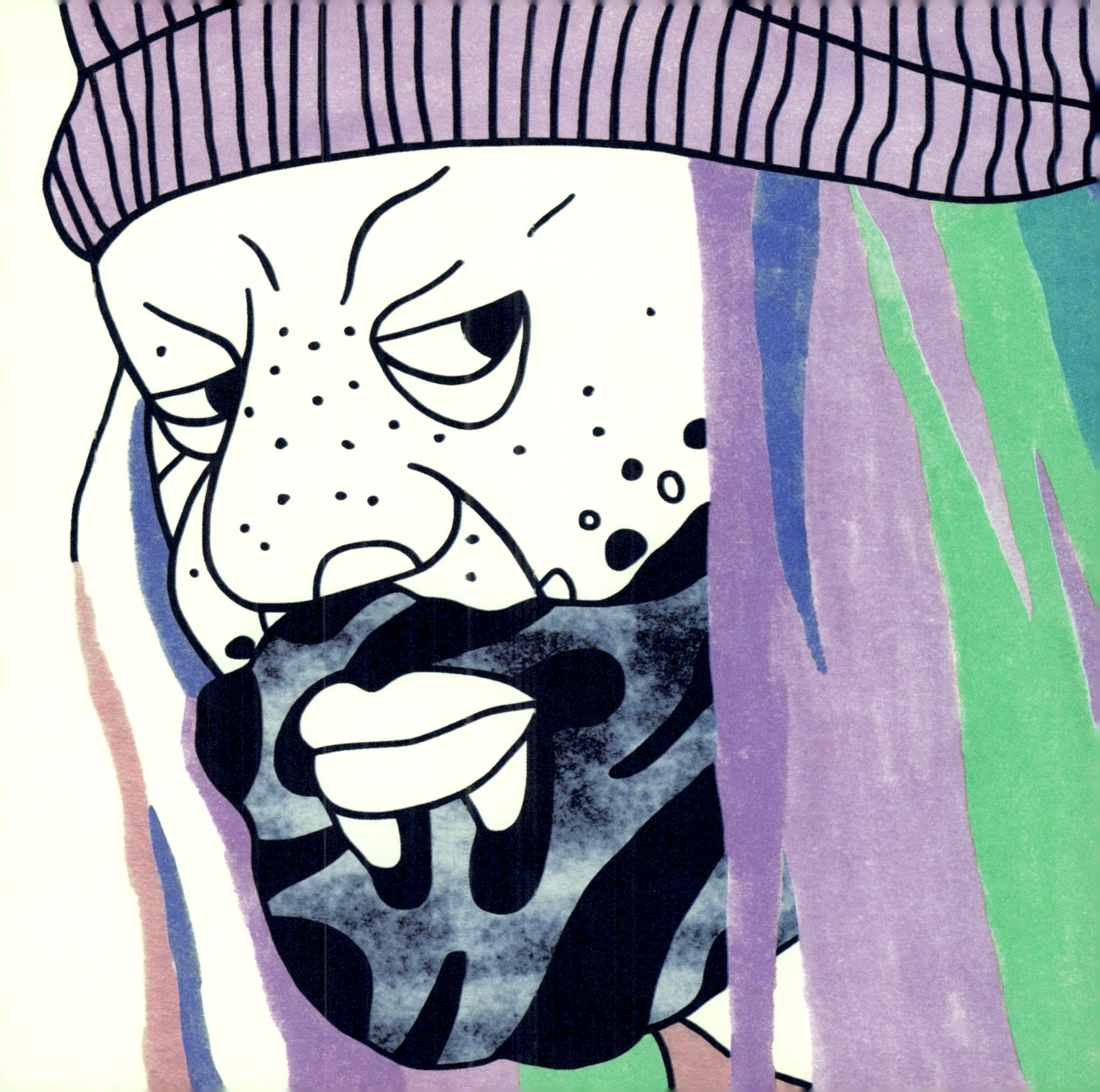

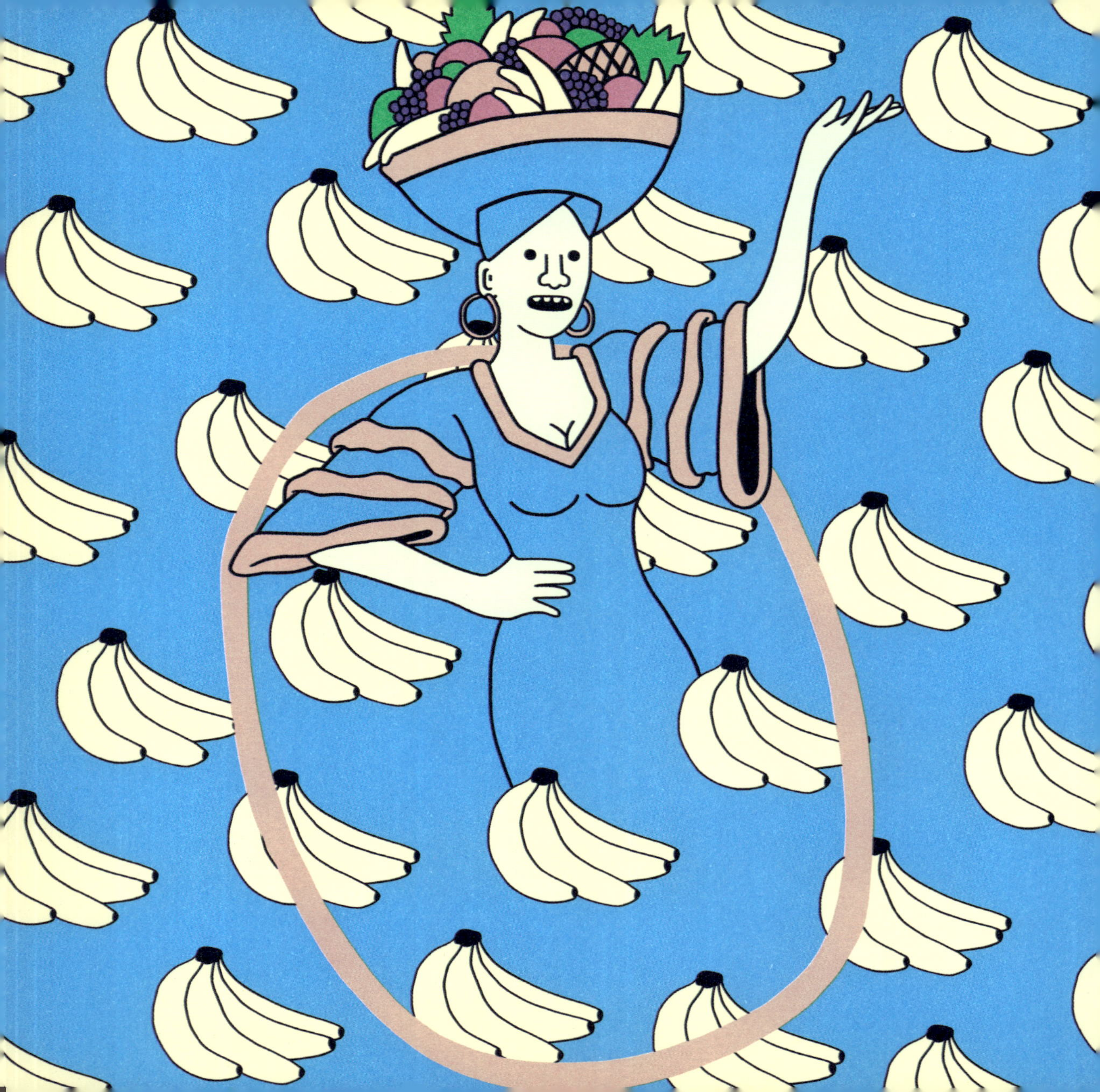

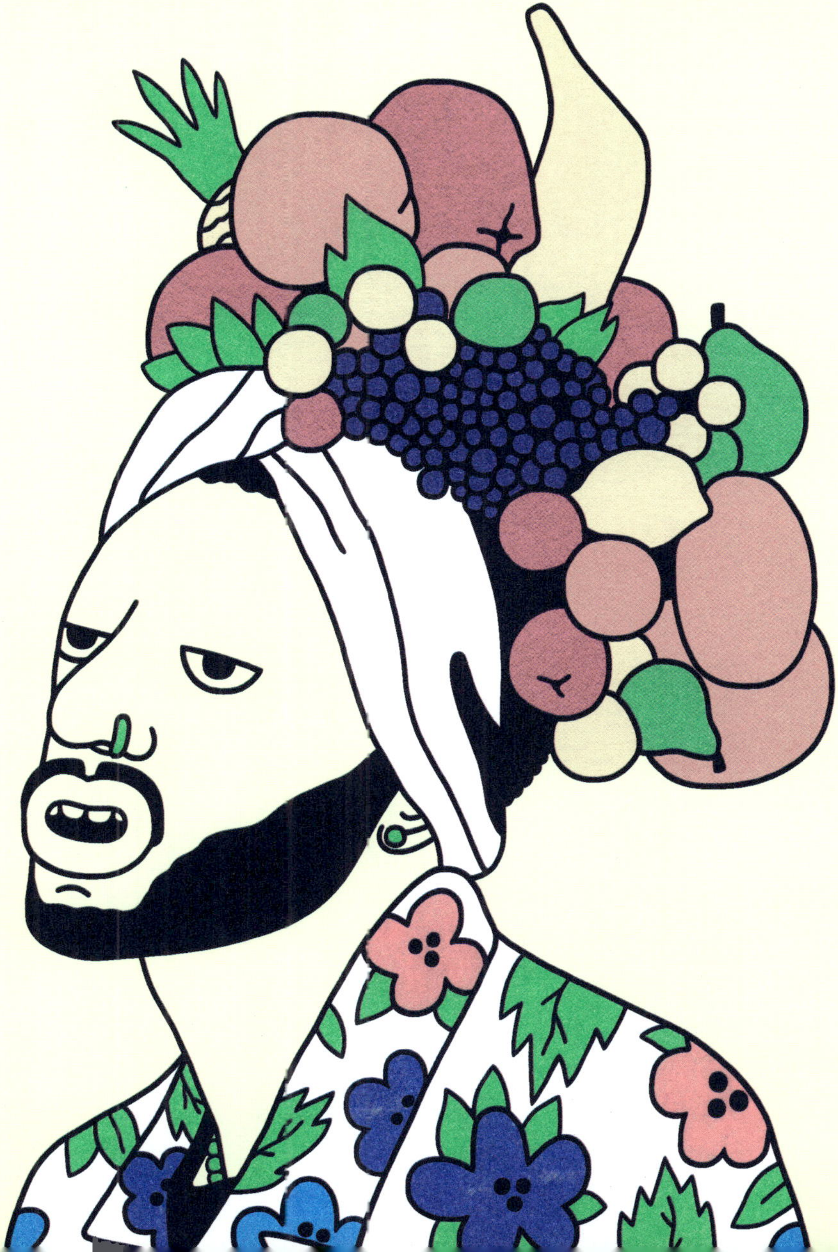

It's Gore-Tex

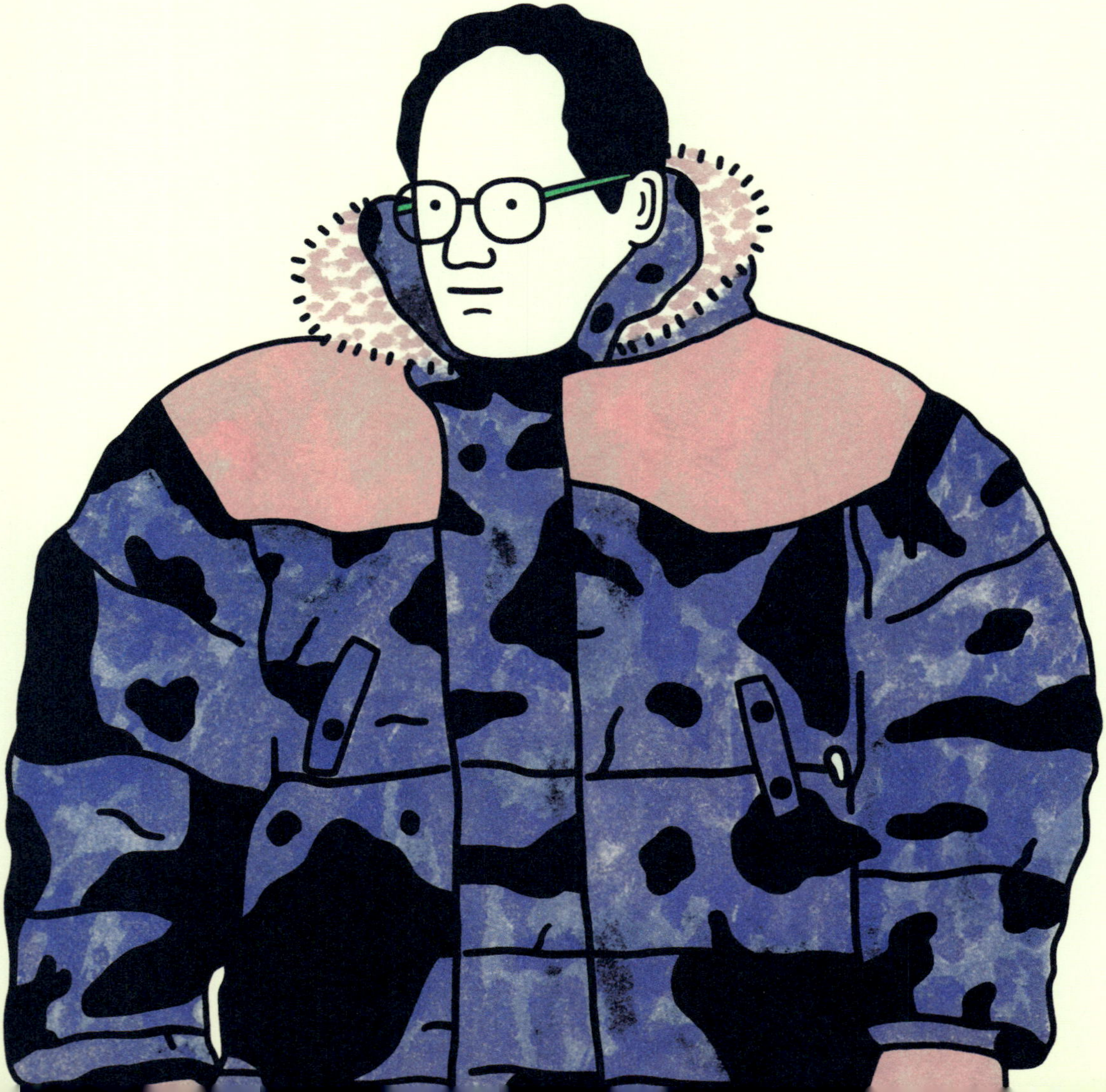

Bron' u done made a mistake
boy, u done fucked up
man...
I'm makin' this a
Ghost/Action Bronson thing...

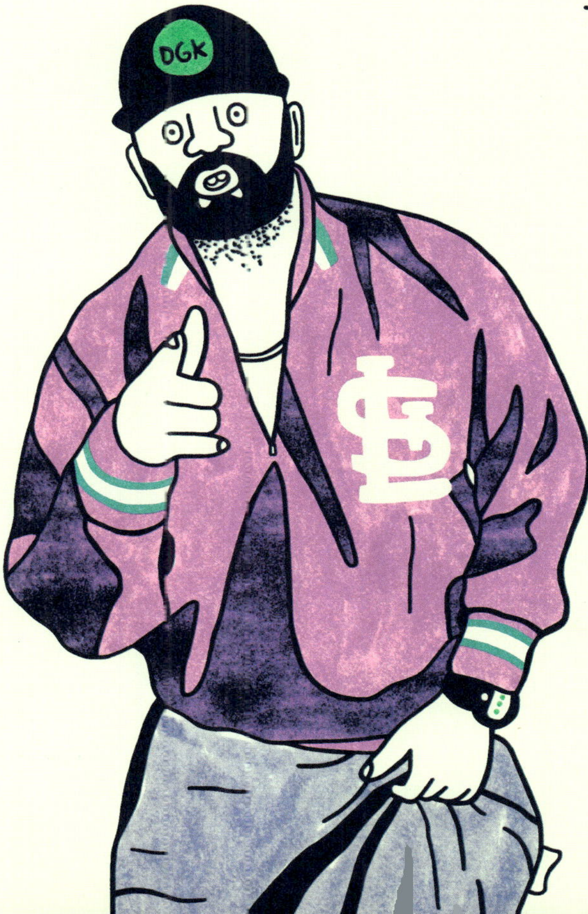

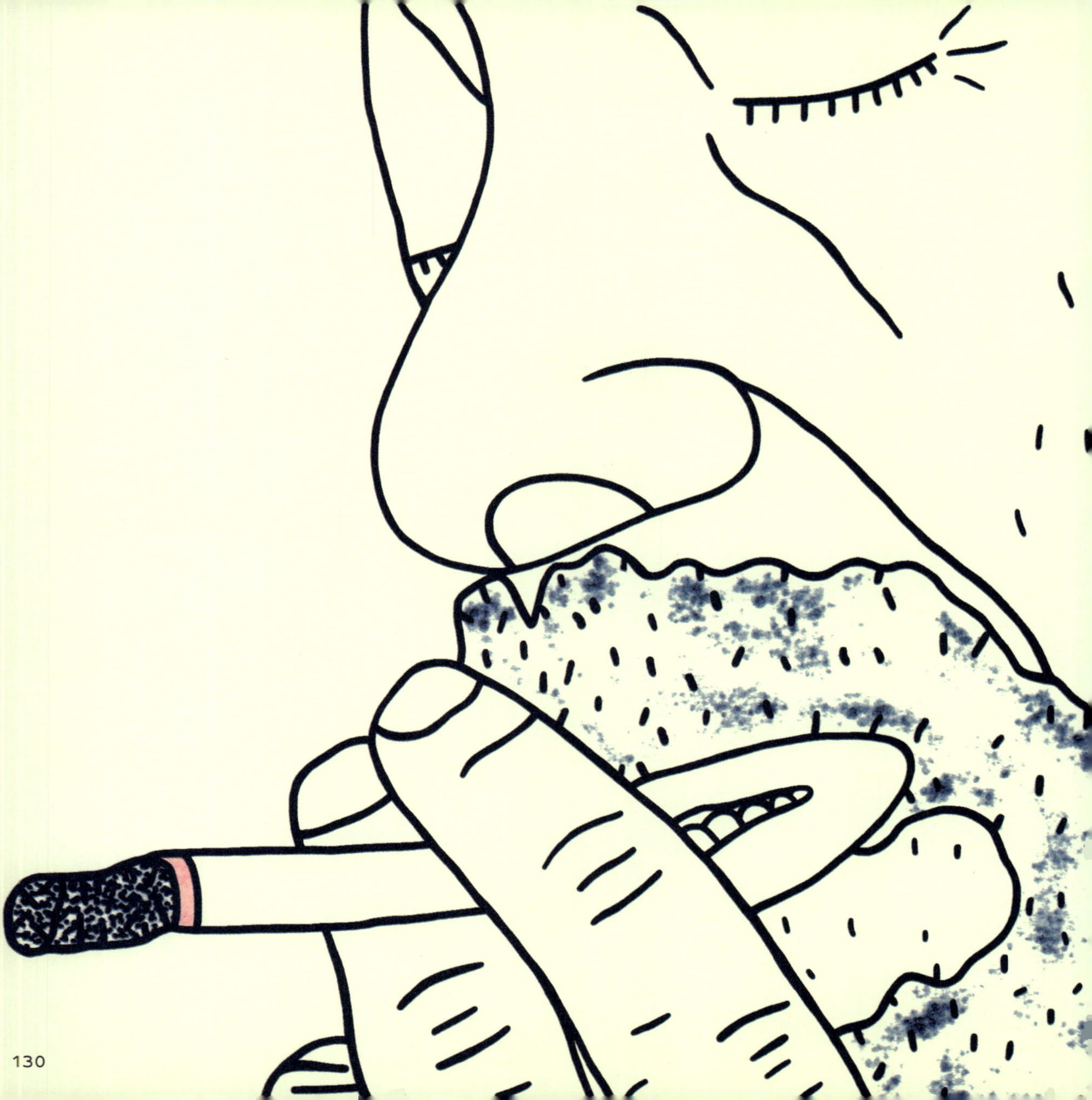

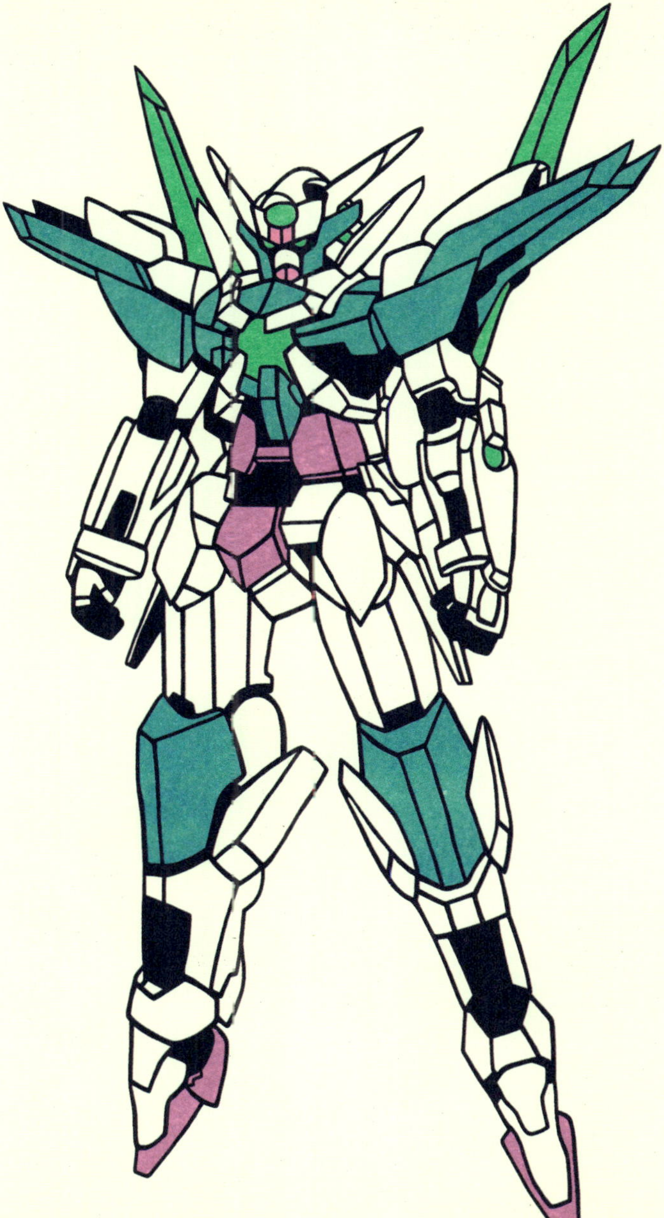

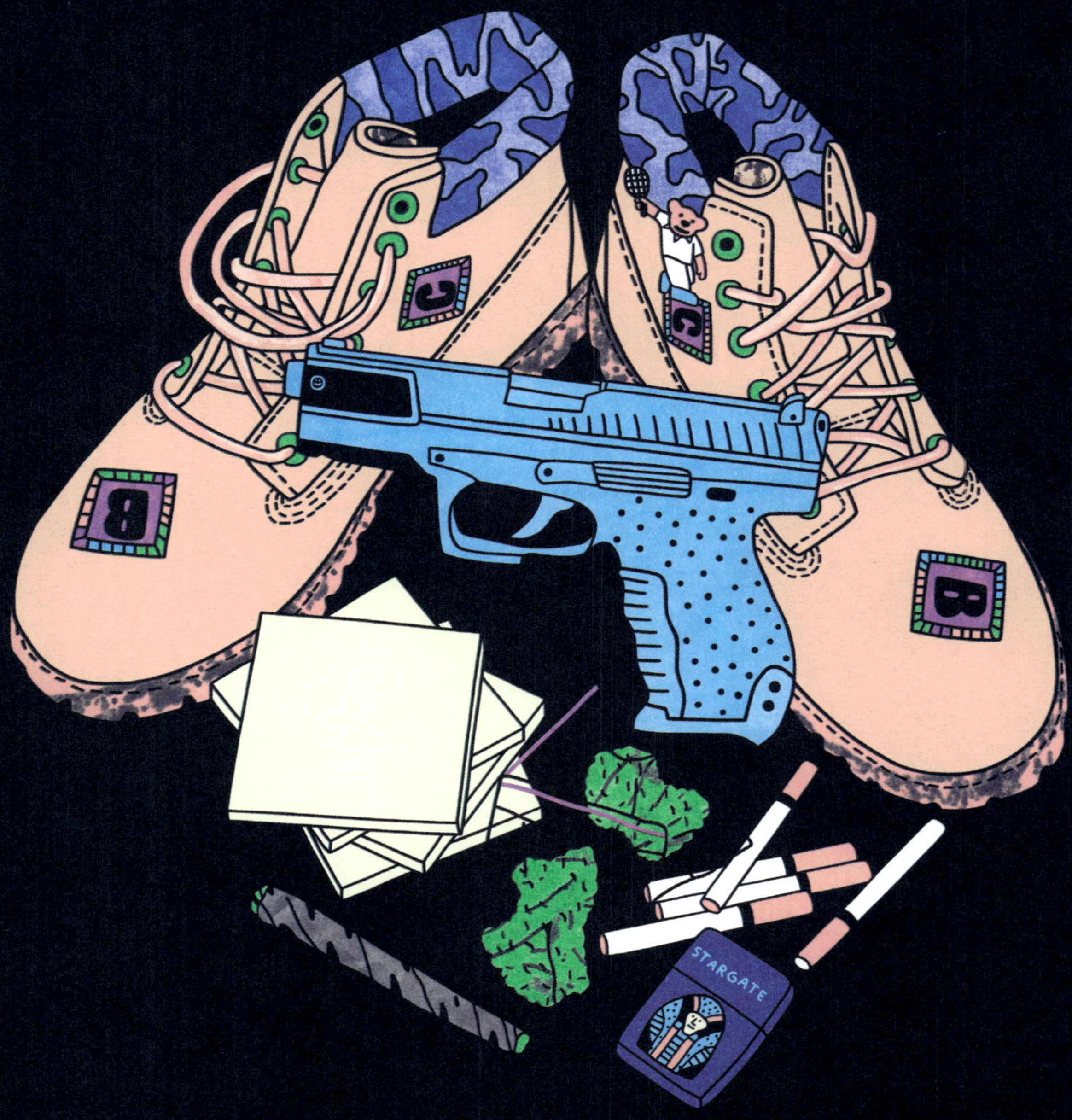
STARGATE

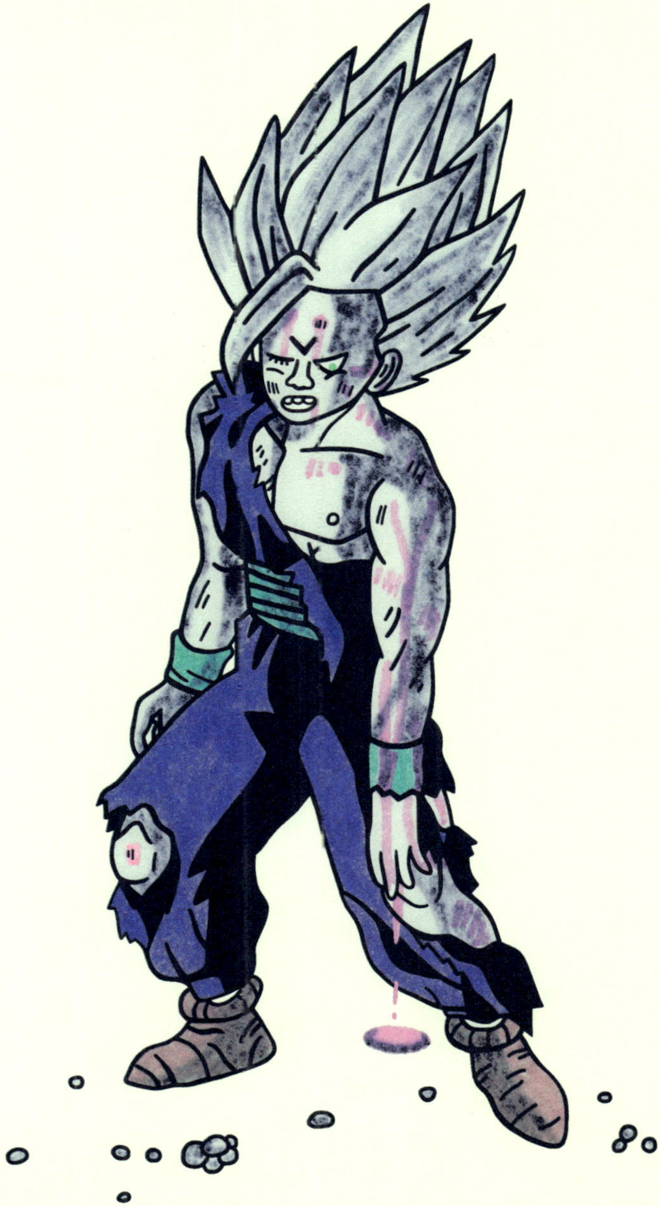

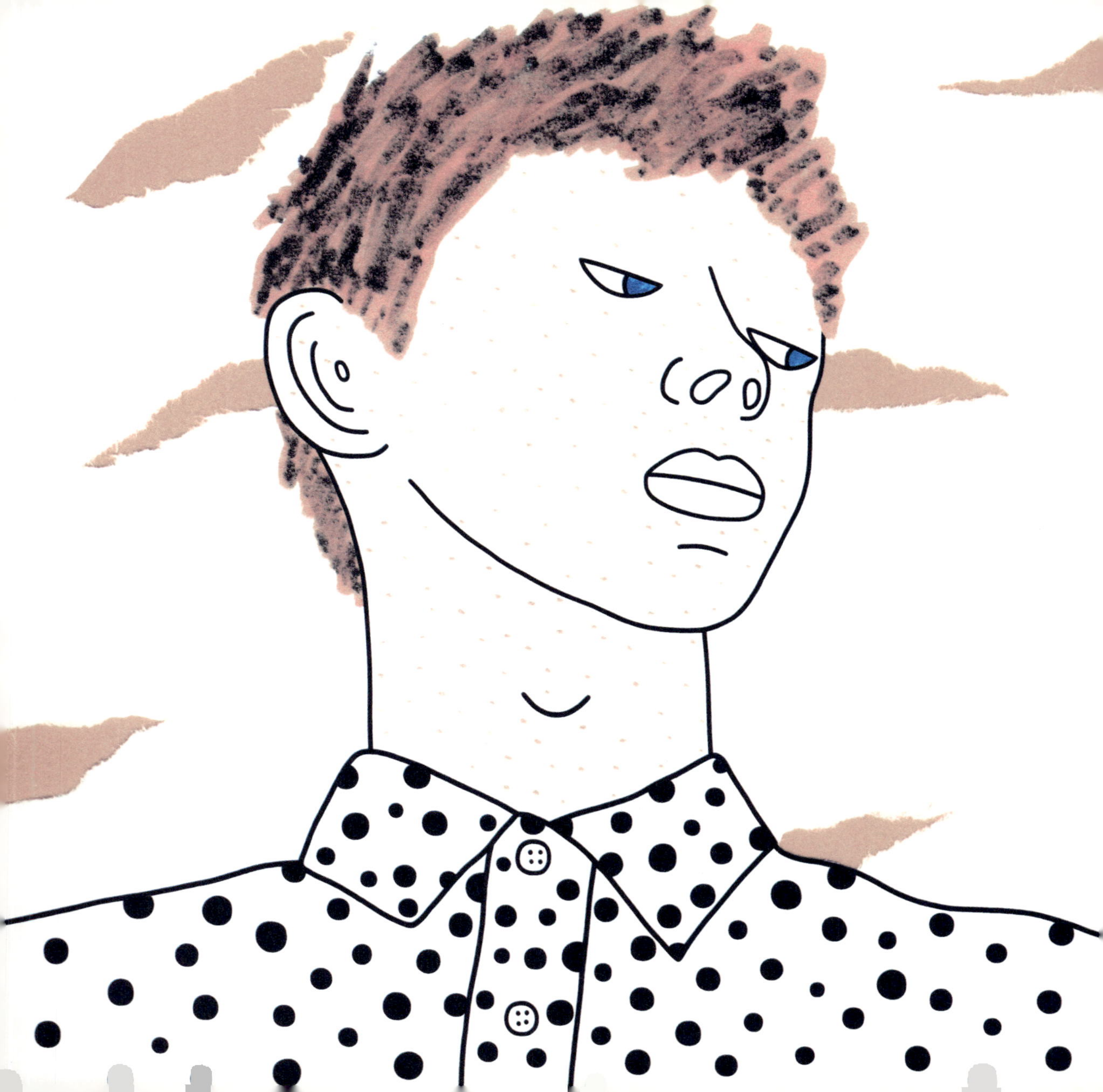

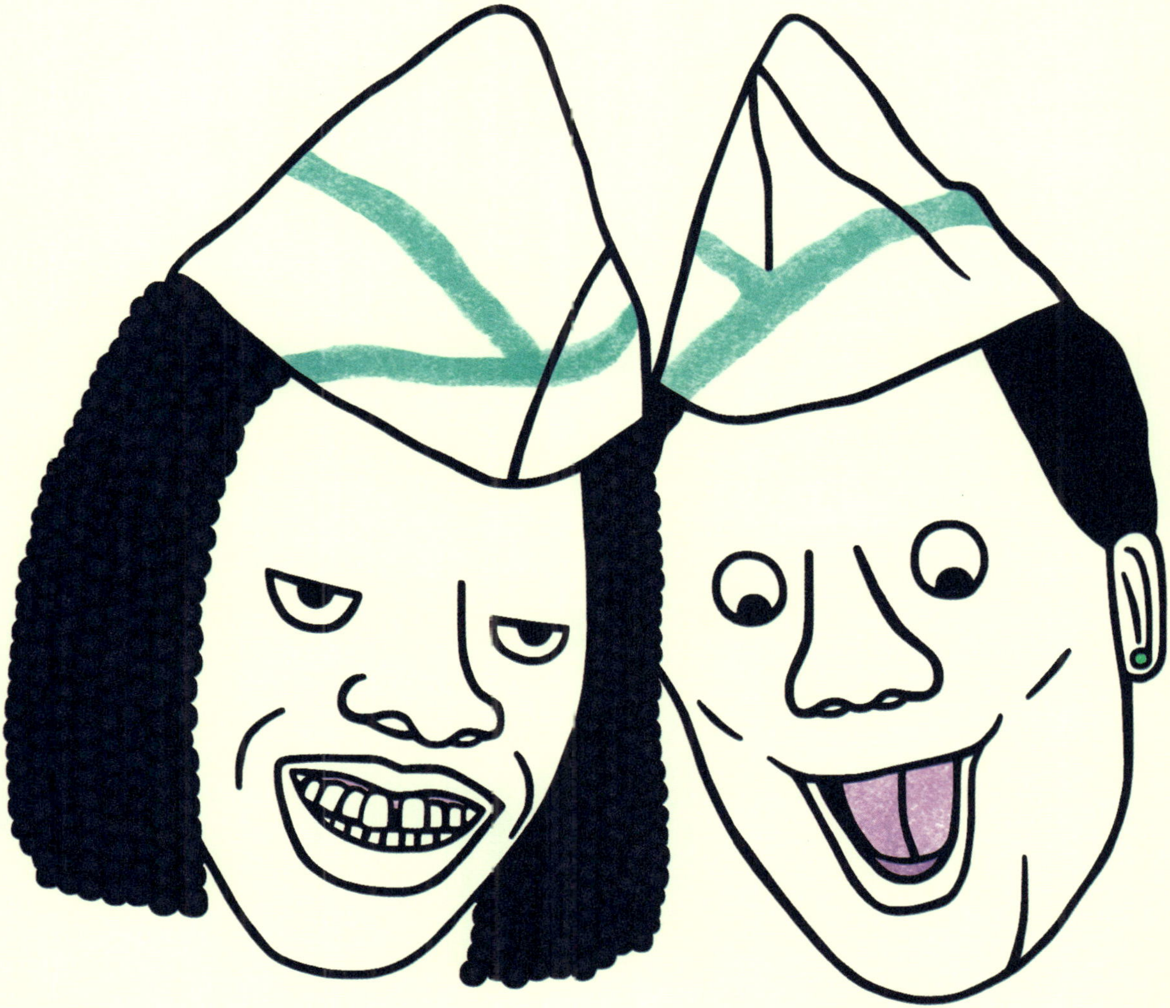

DO NOT EAT
-GRONK

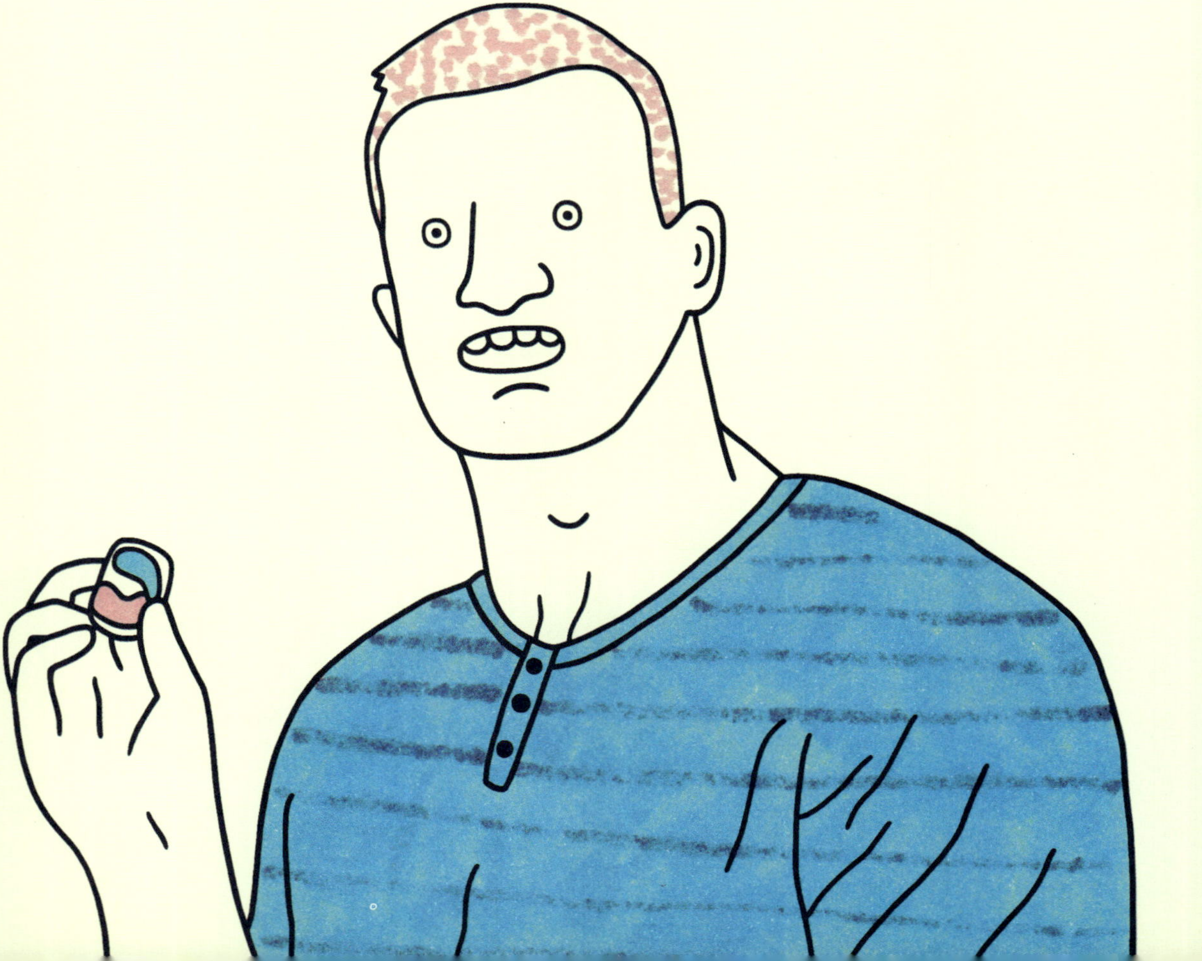

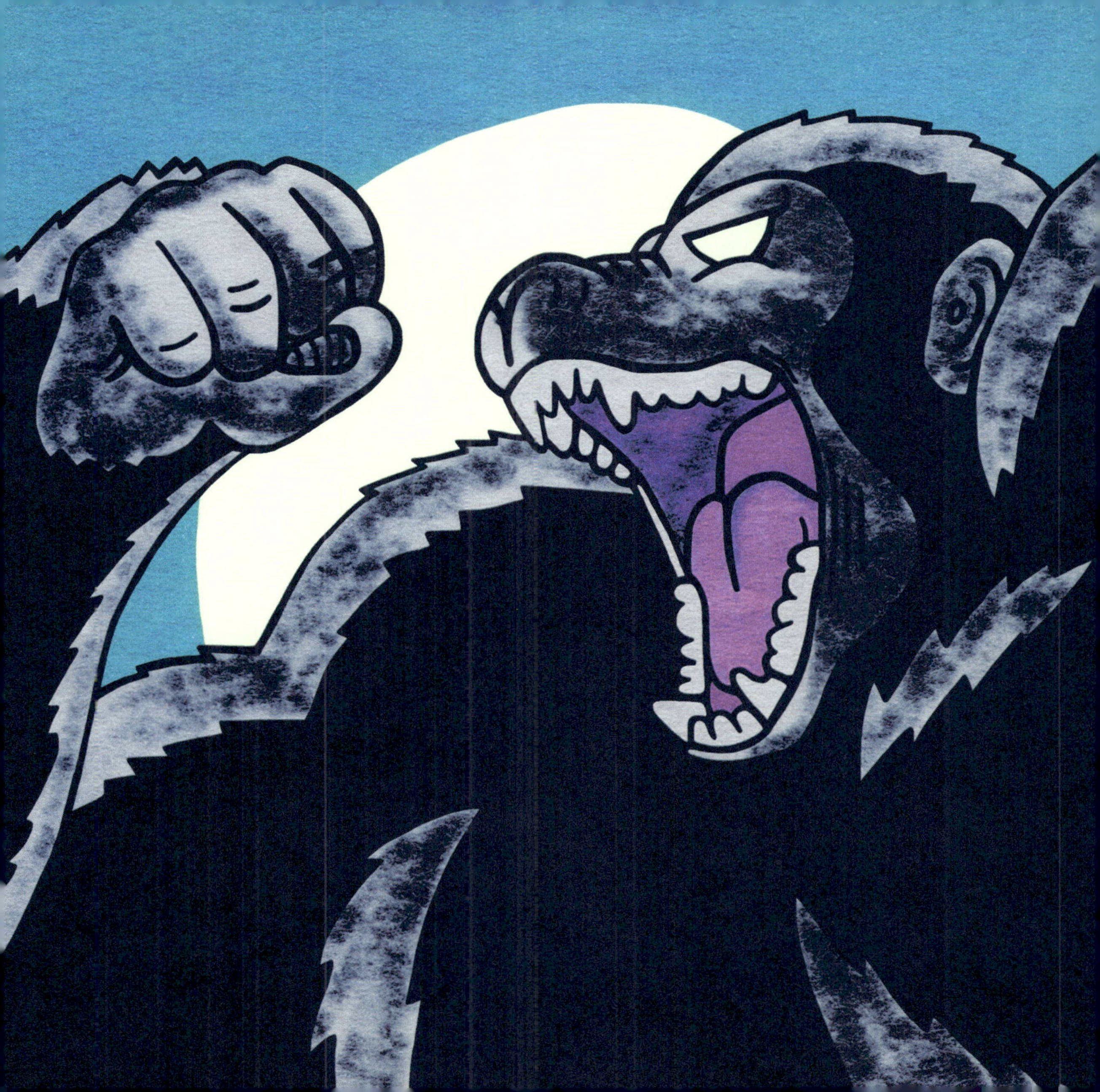

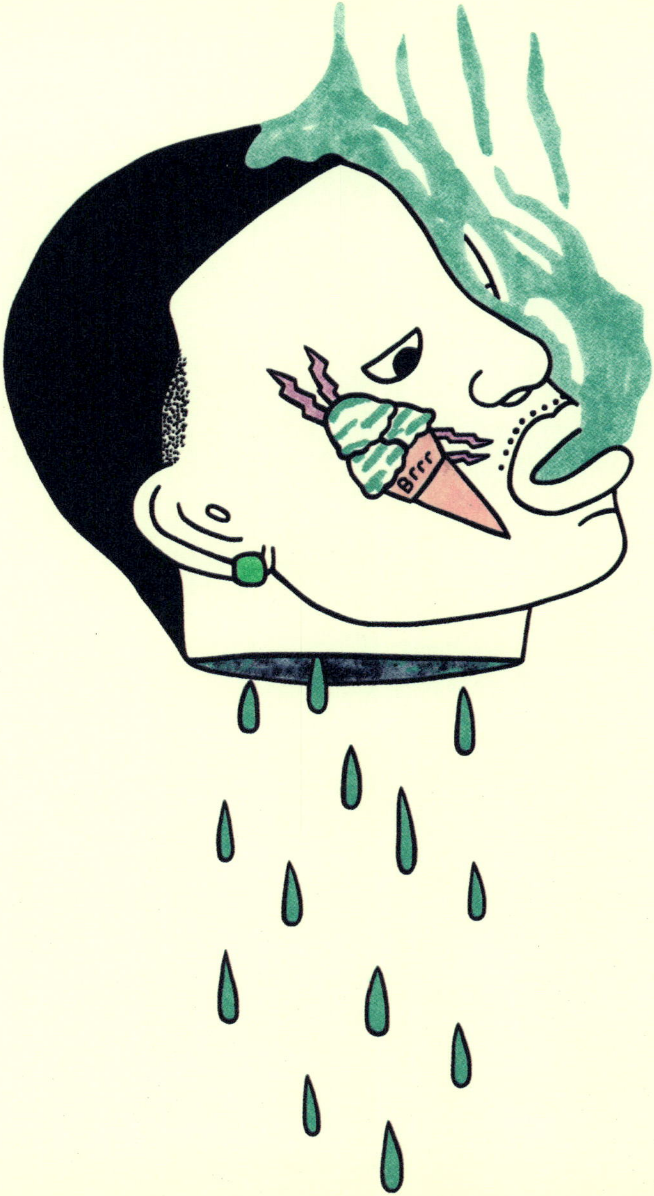
Brrr

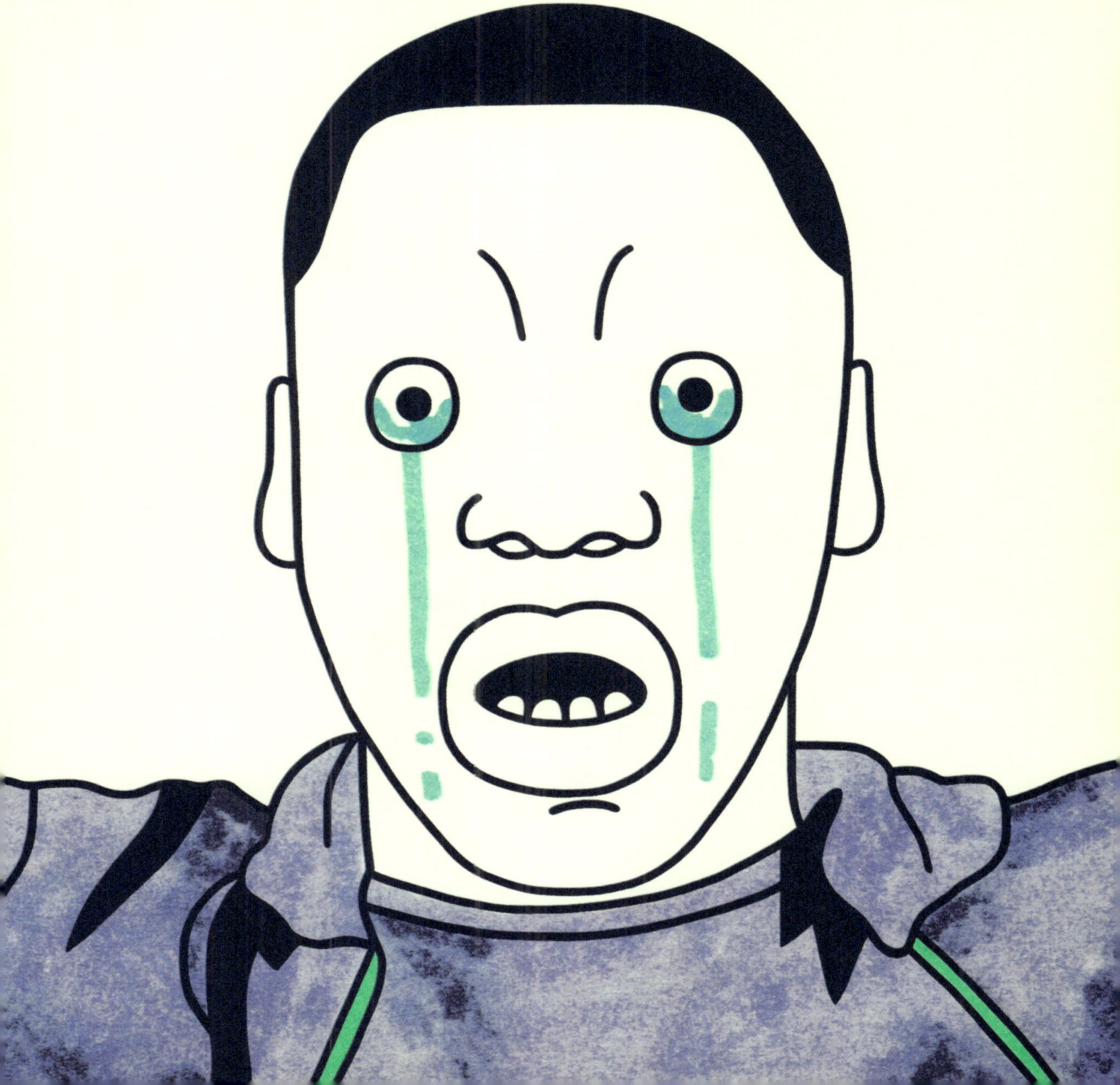

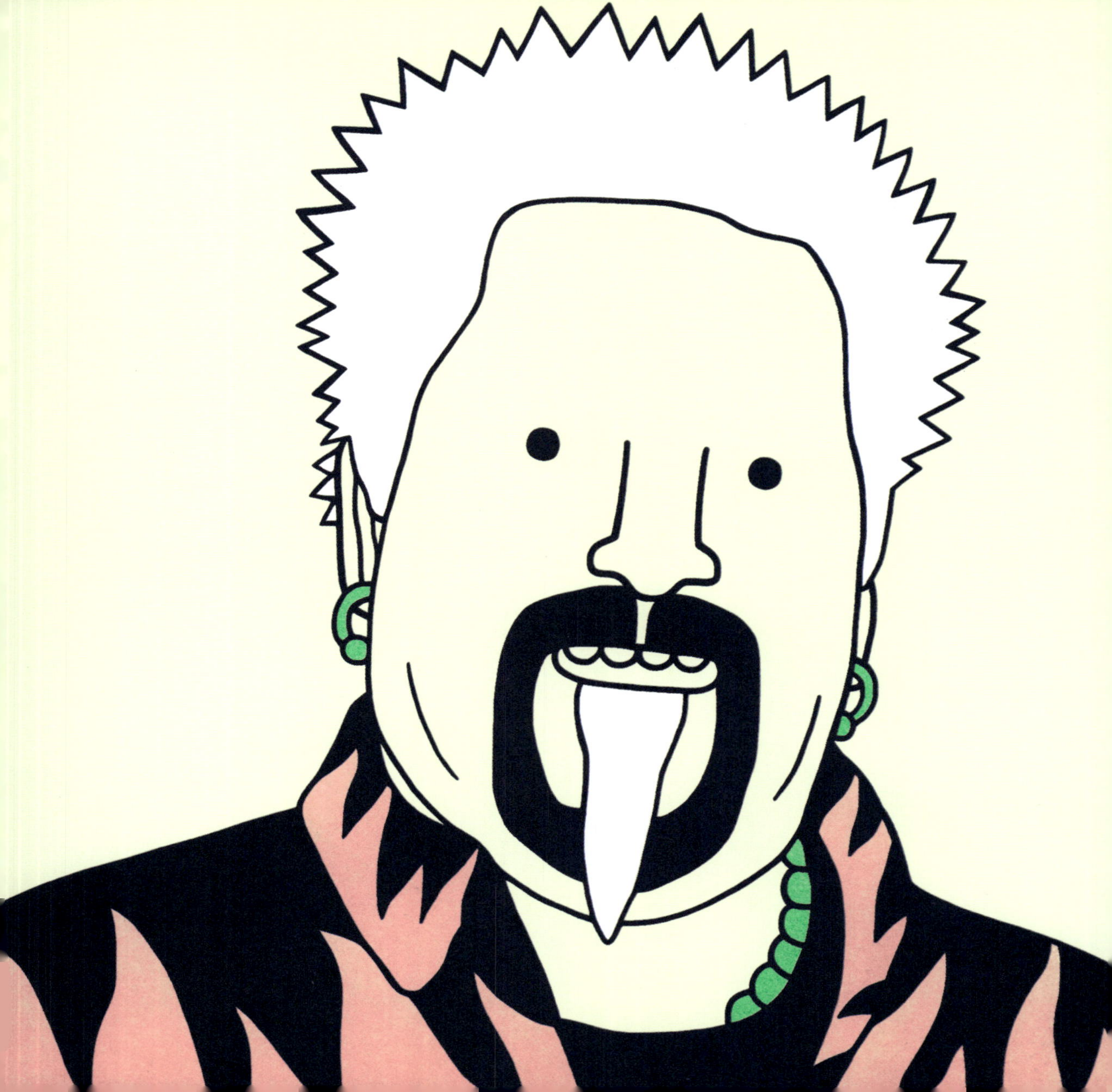

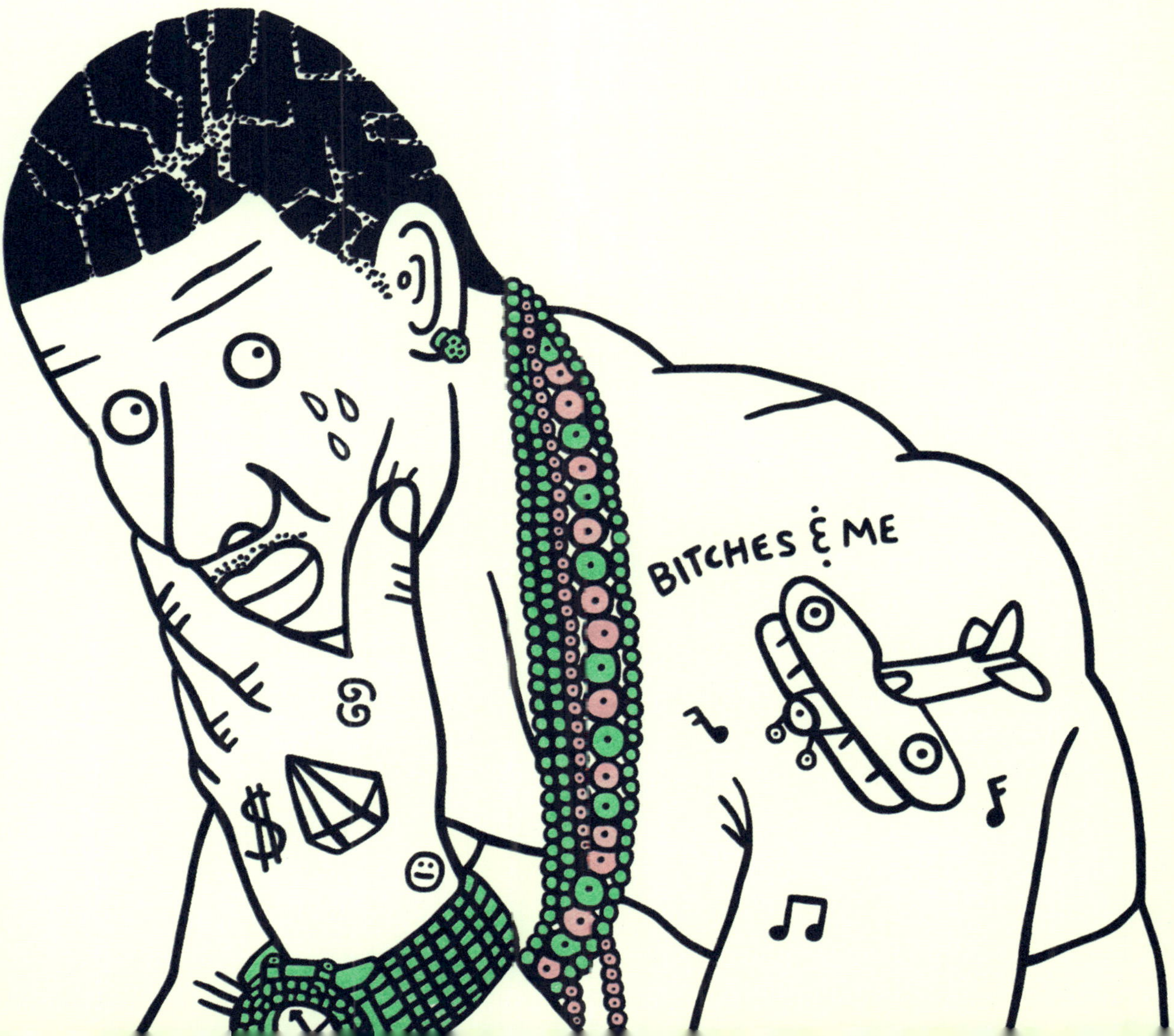
BITCHES & ME

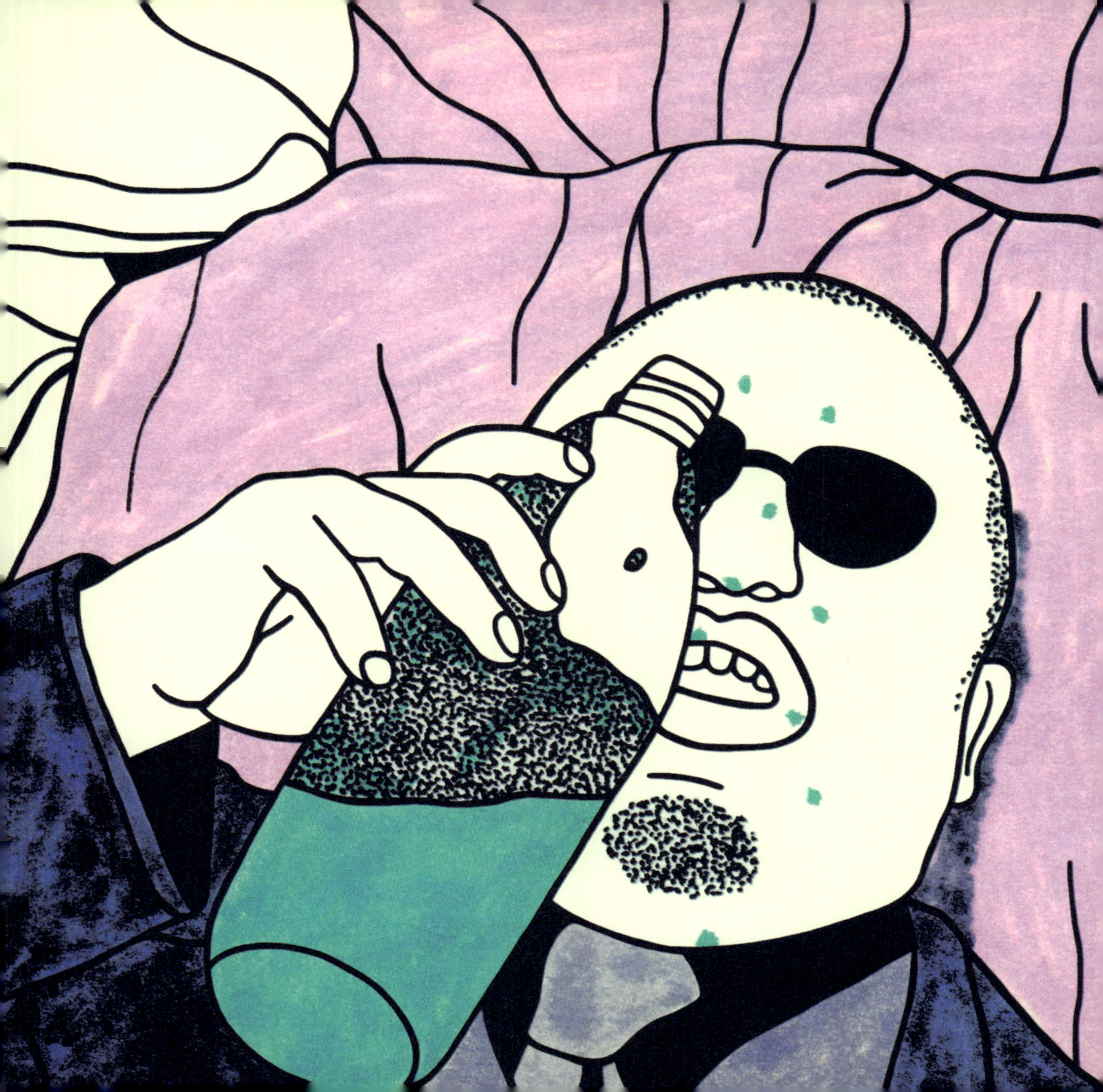

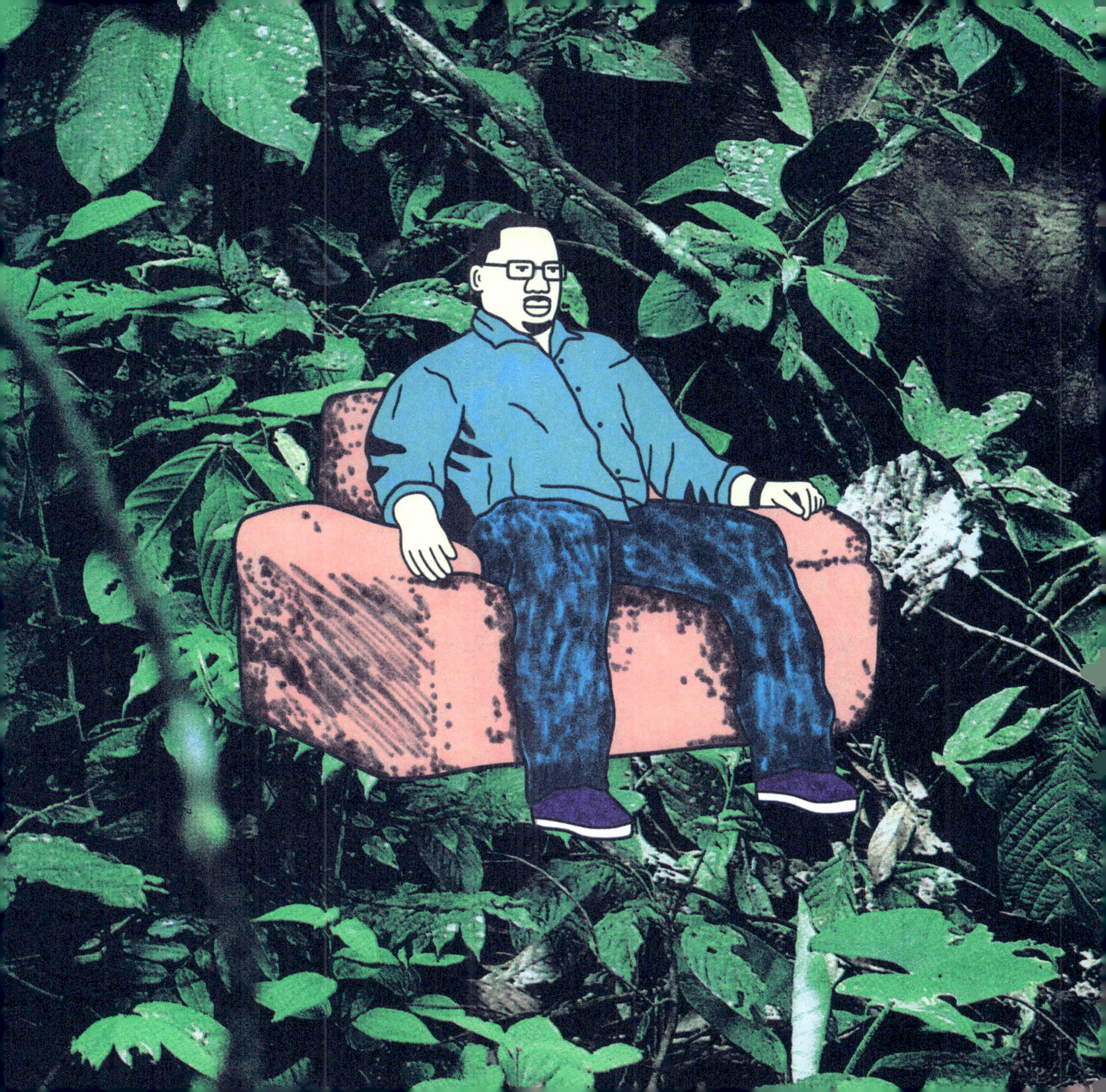

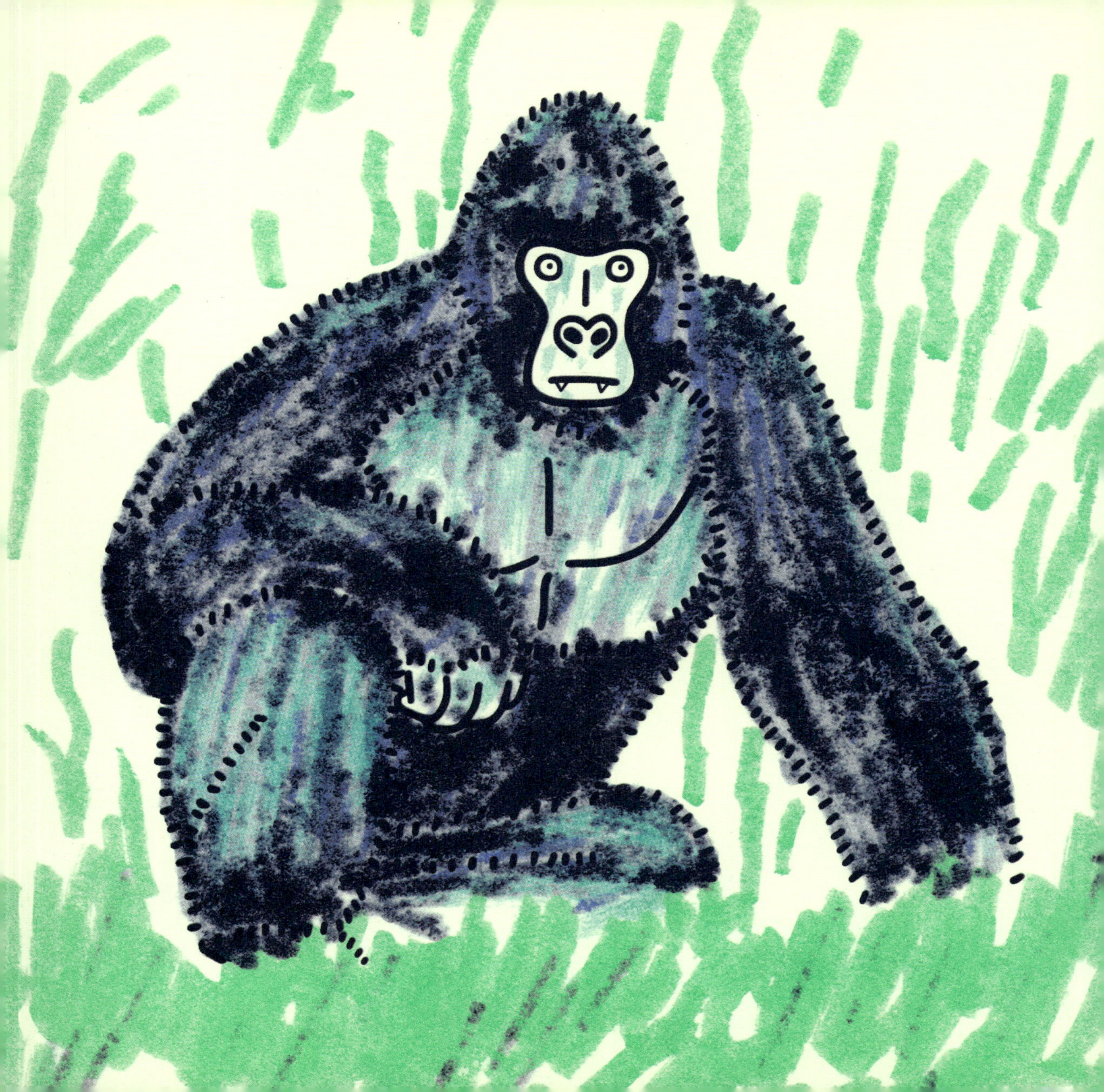

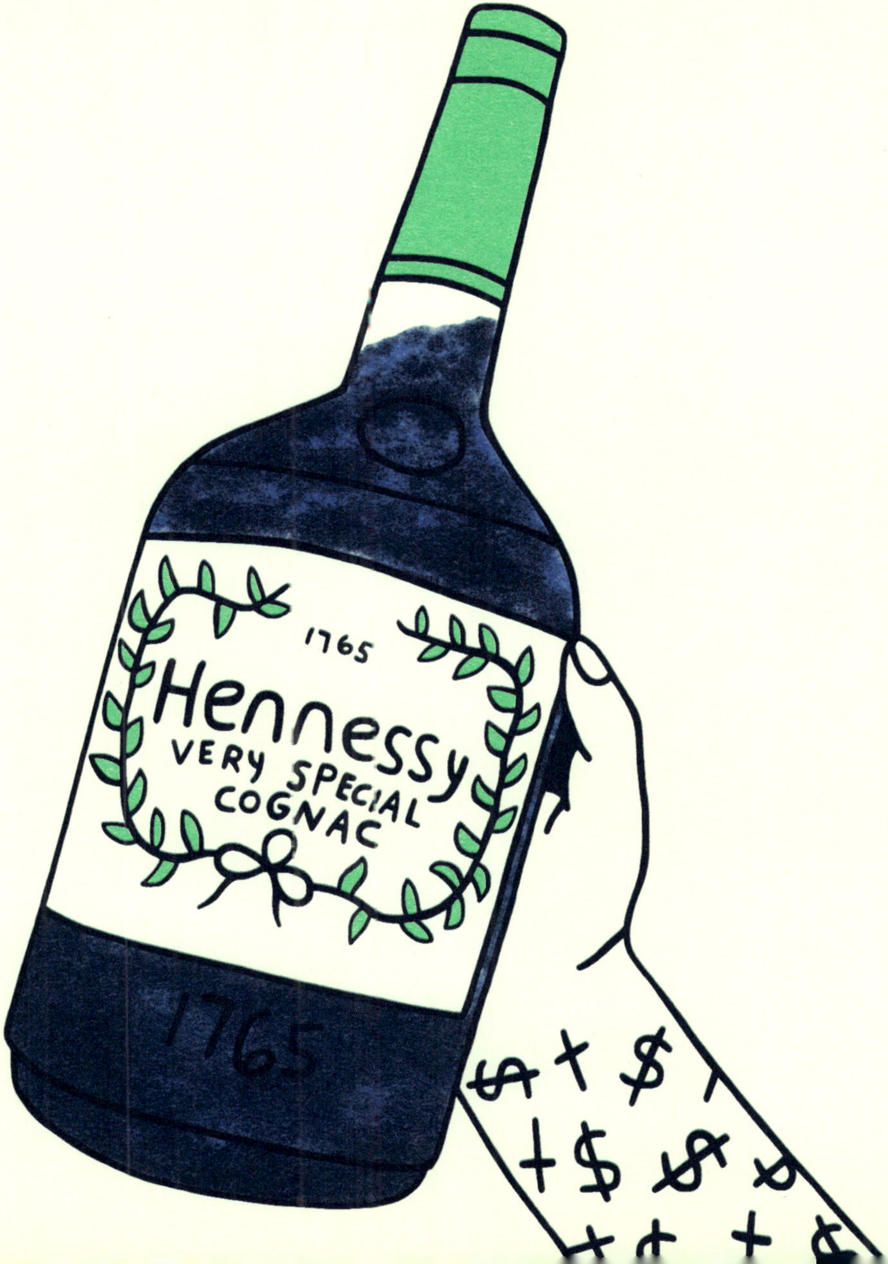
1765
Hennessy
VERY SPECIAL
COGNAC
1765

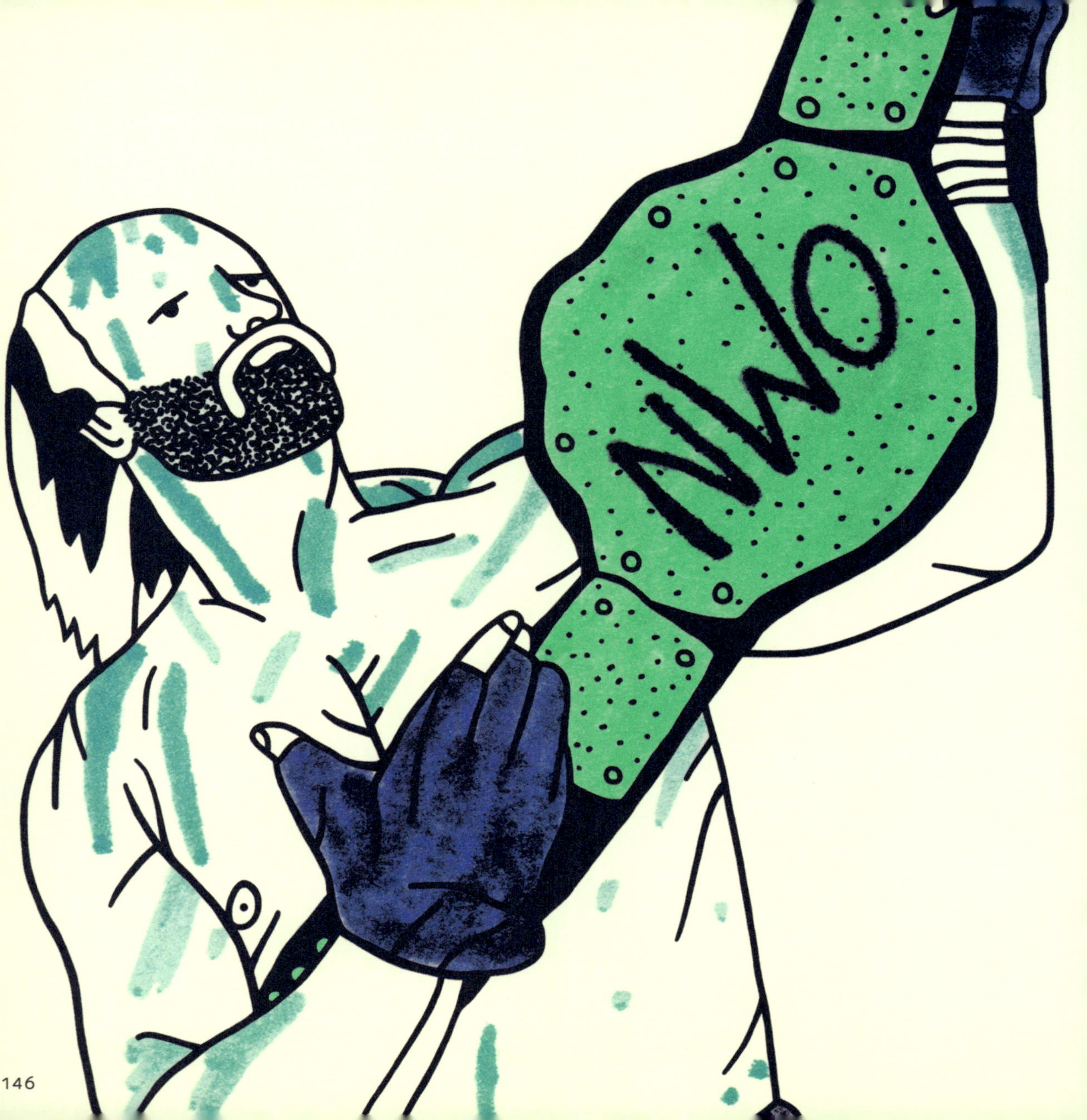
NWO

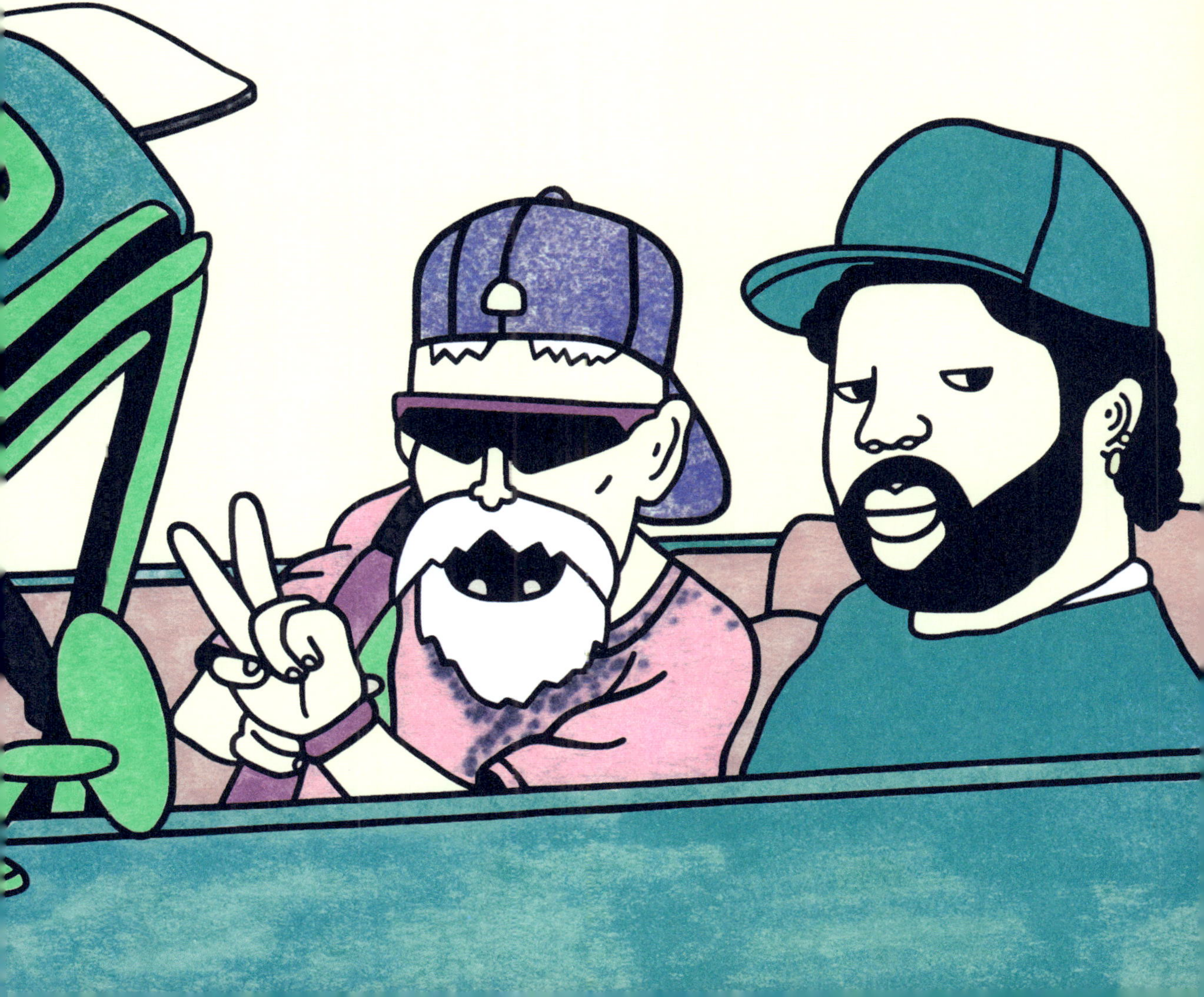

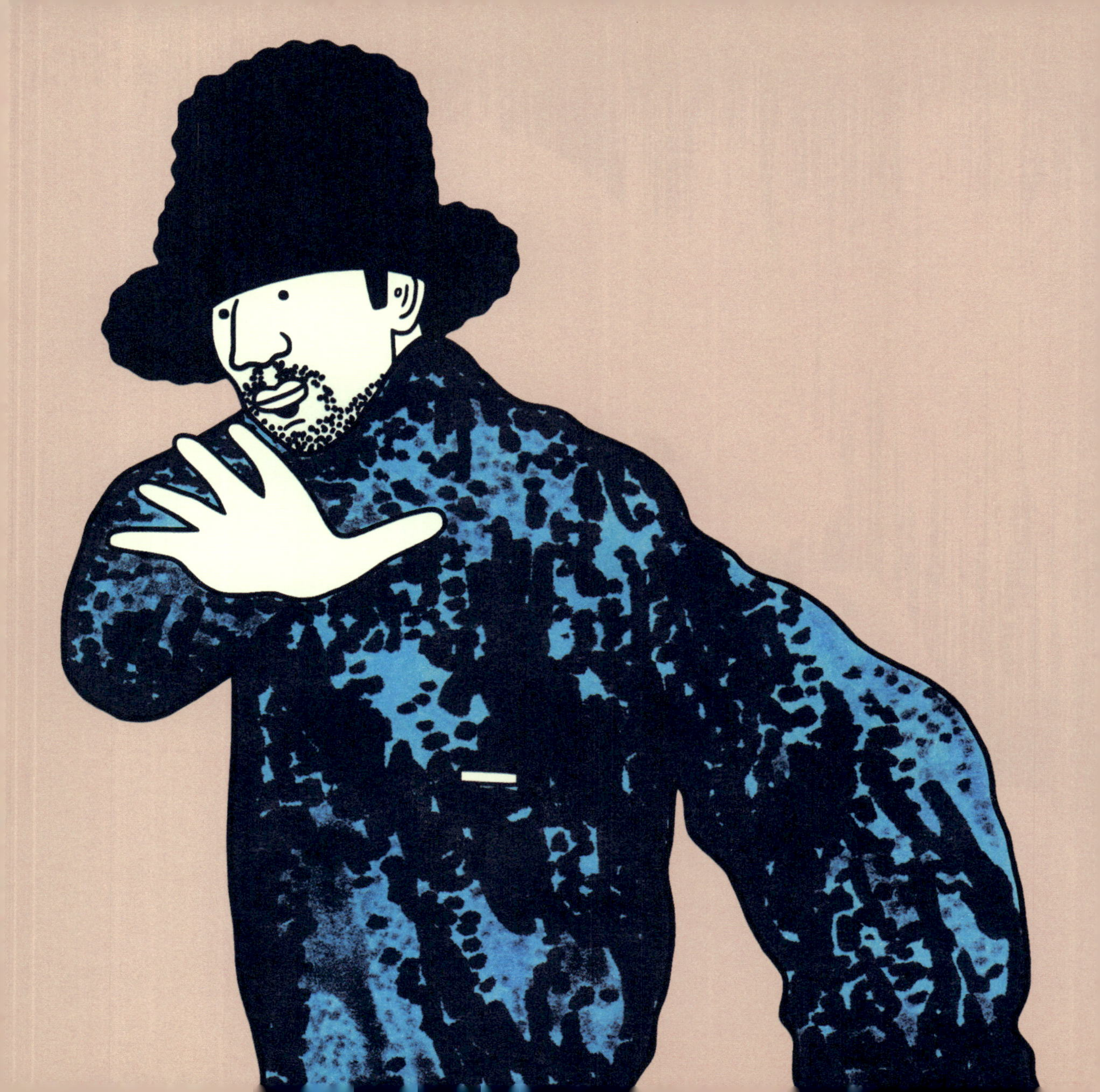

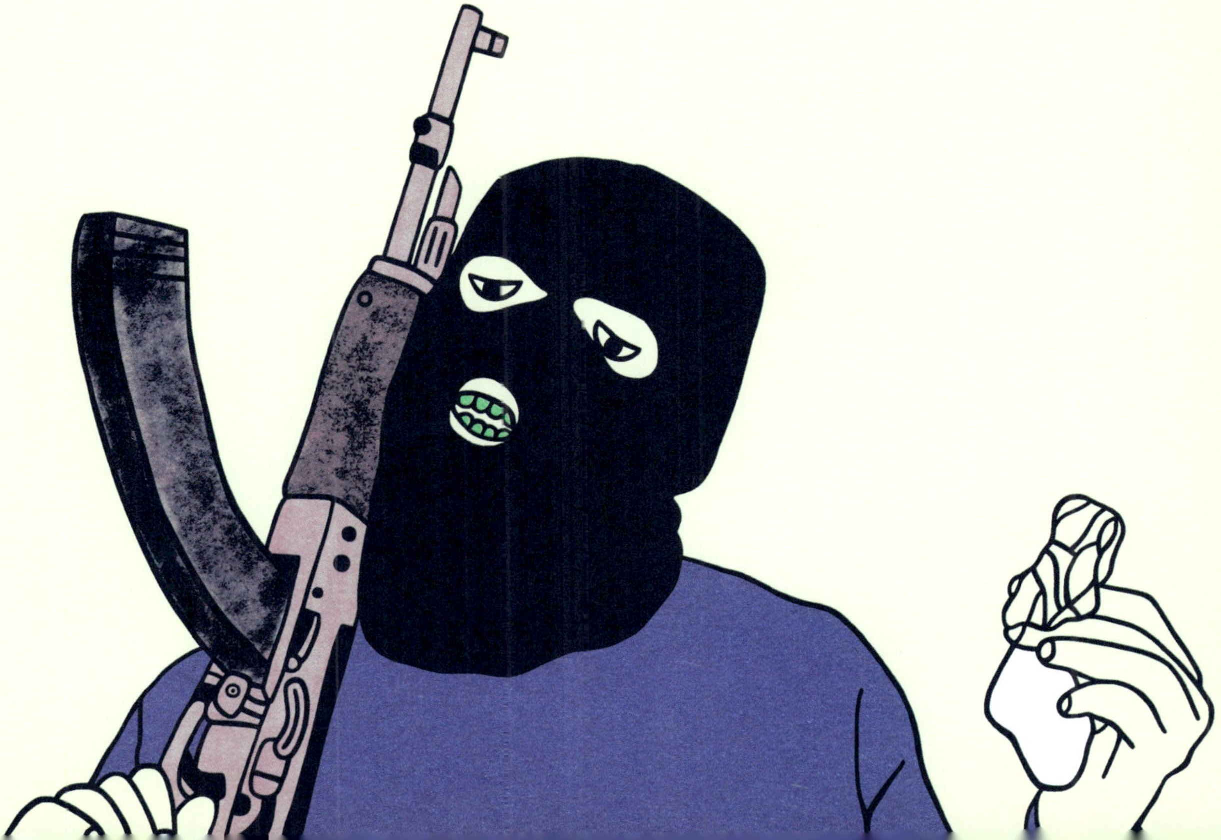

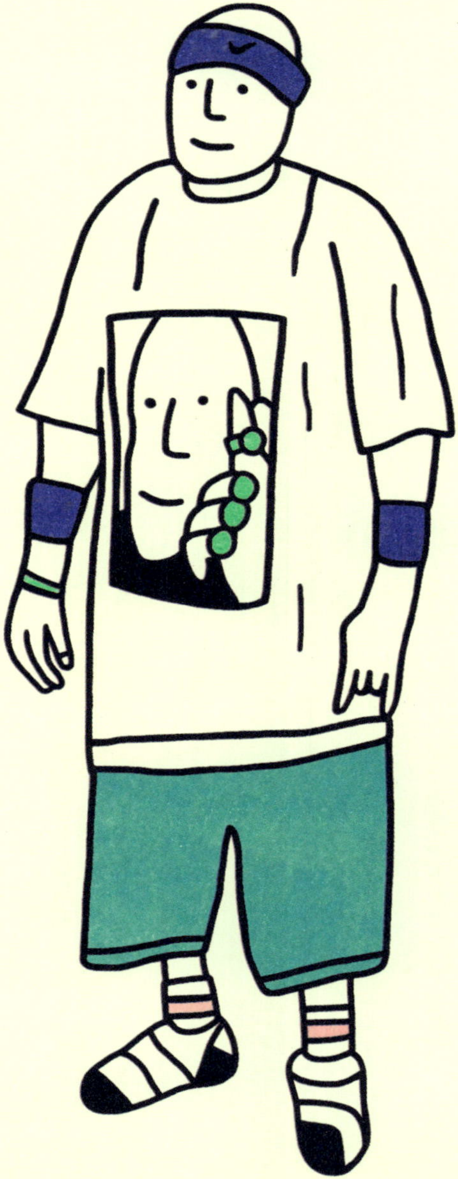

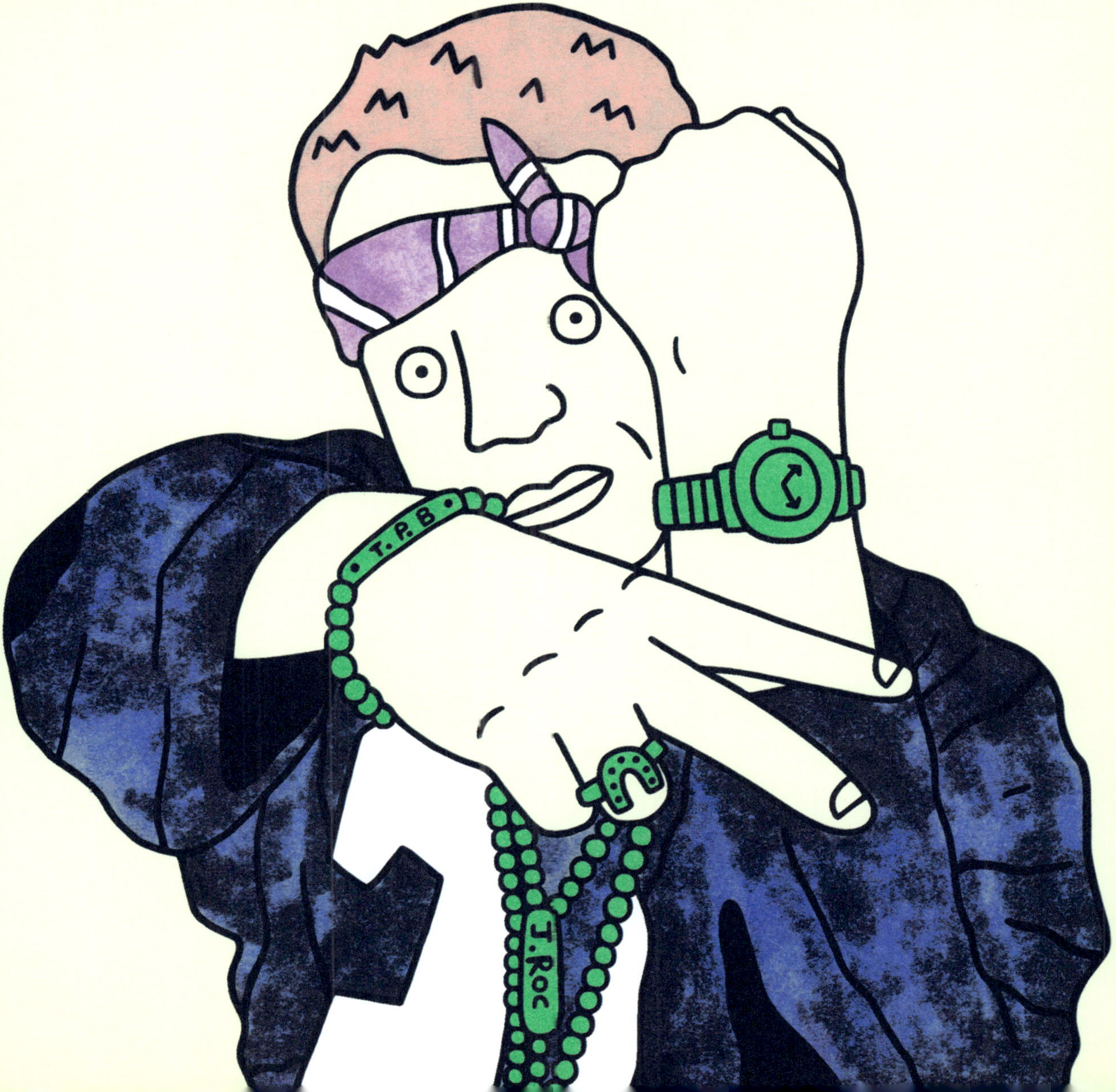
T.P.B
J.ROC

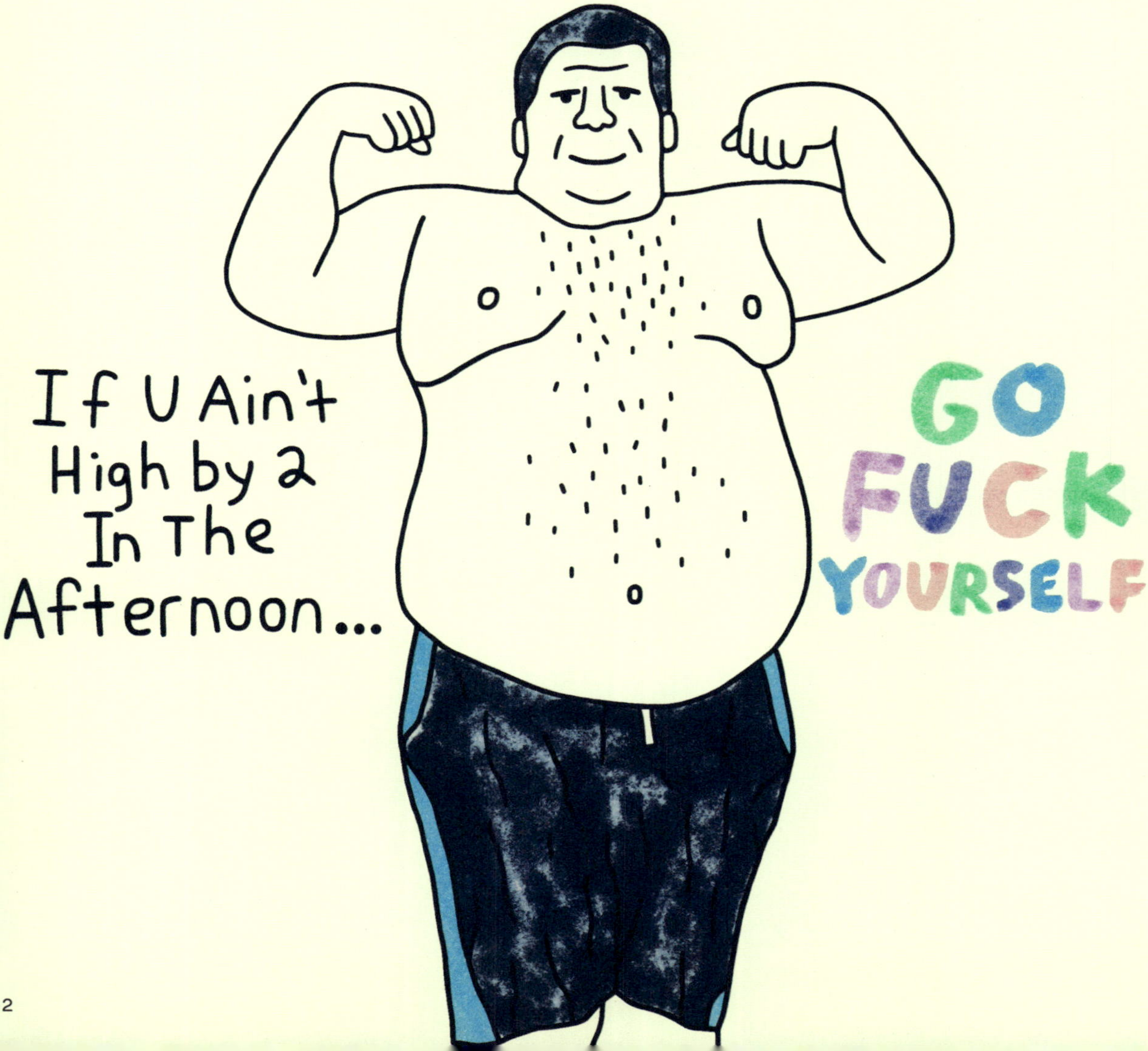
If U Ain't
High by 2
In The
Afternoon...
GO
FUCK
YOURSELF

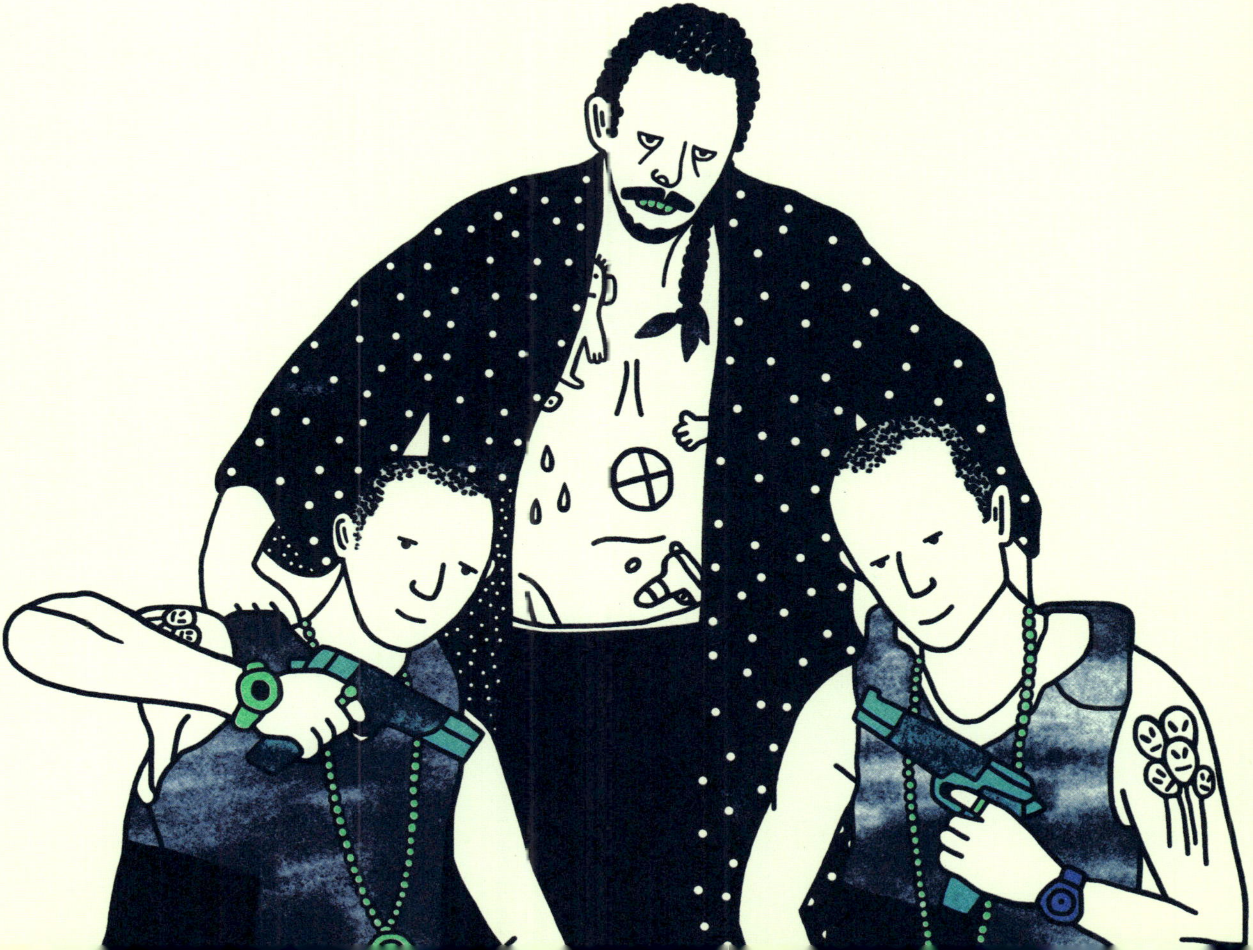

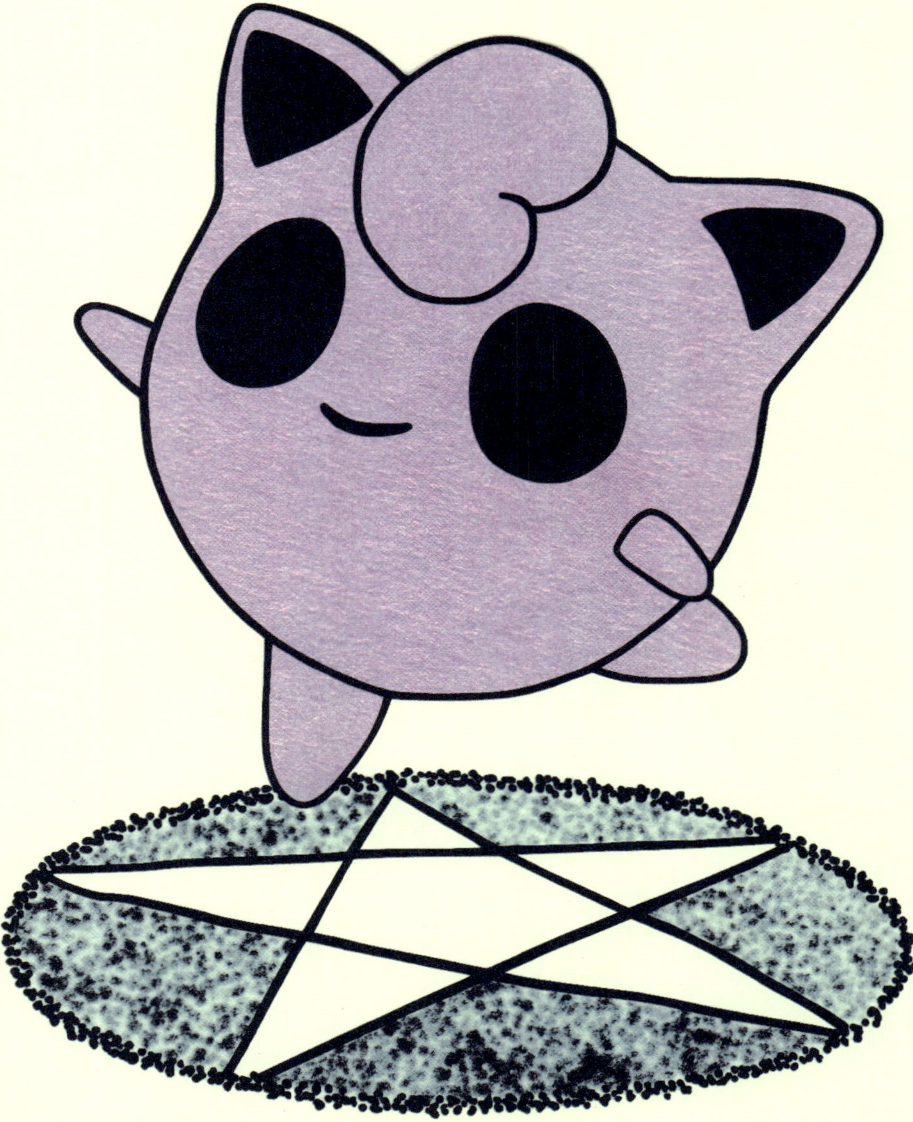

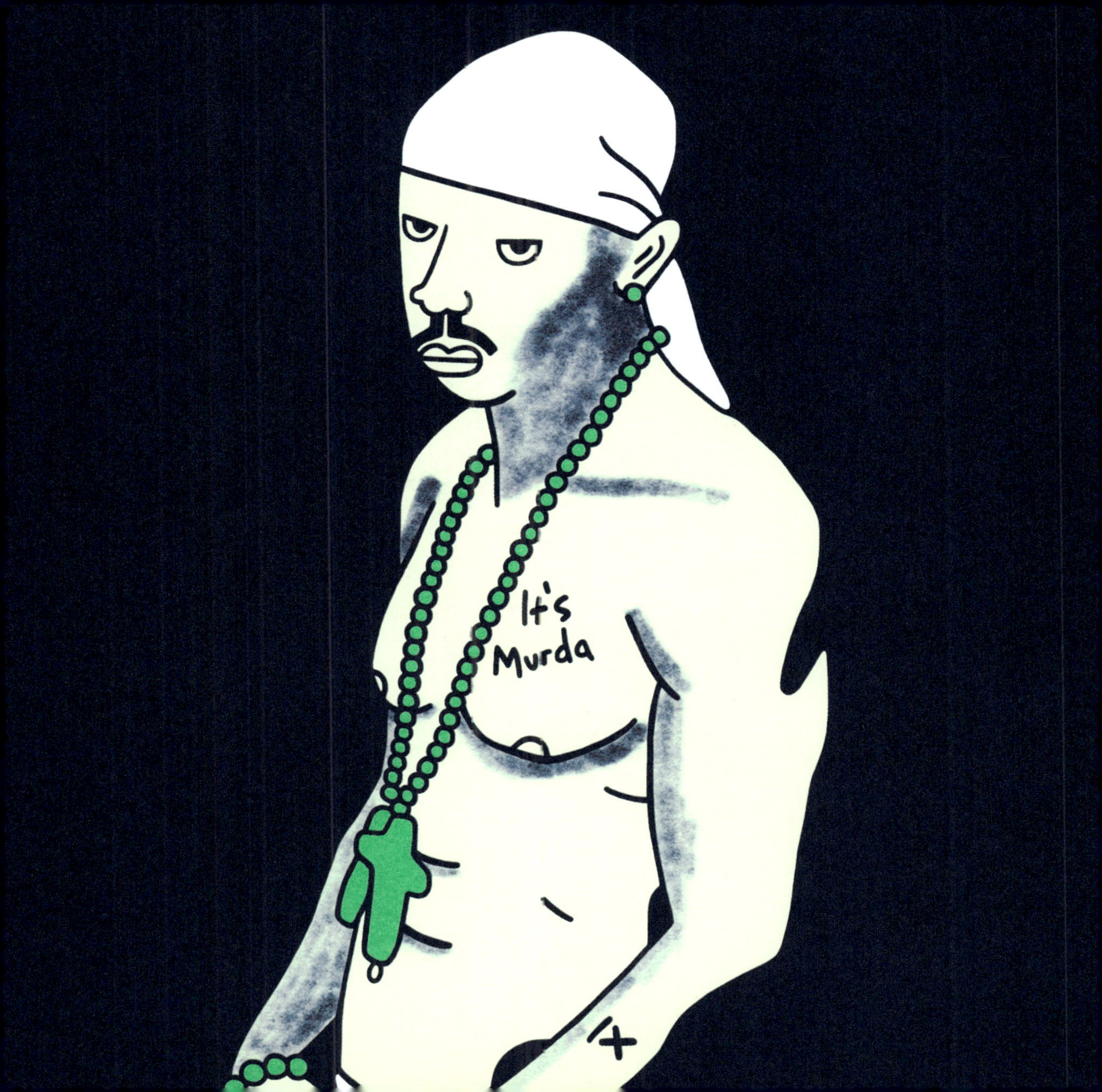
It's
Murda

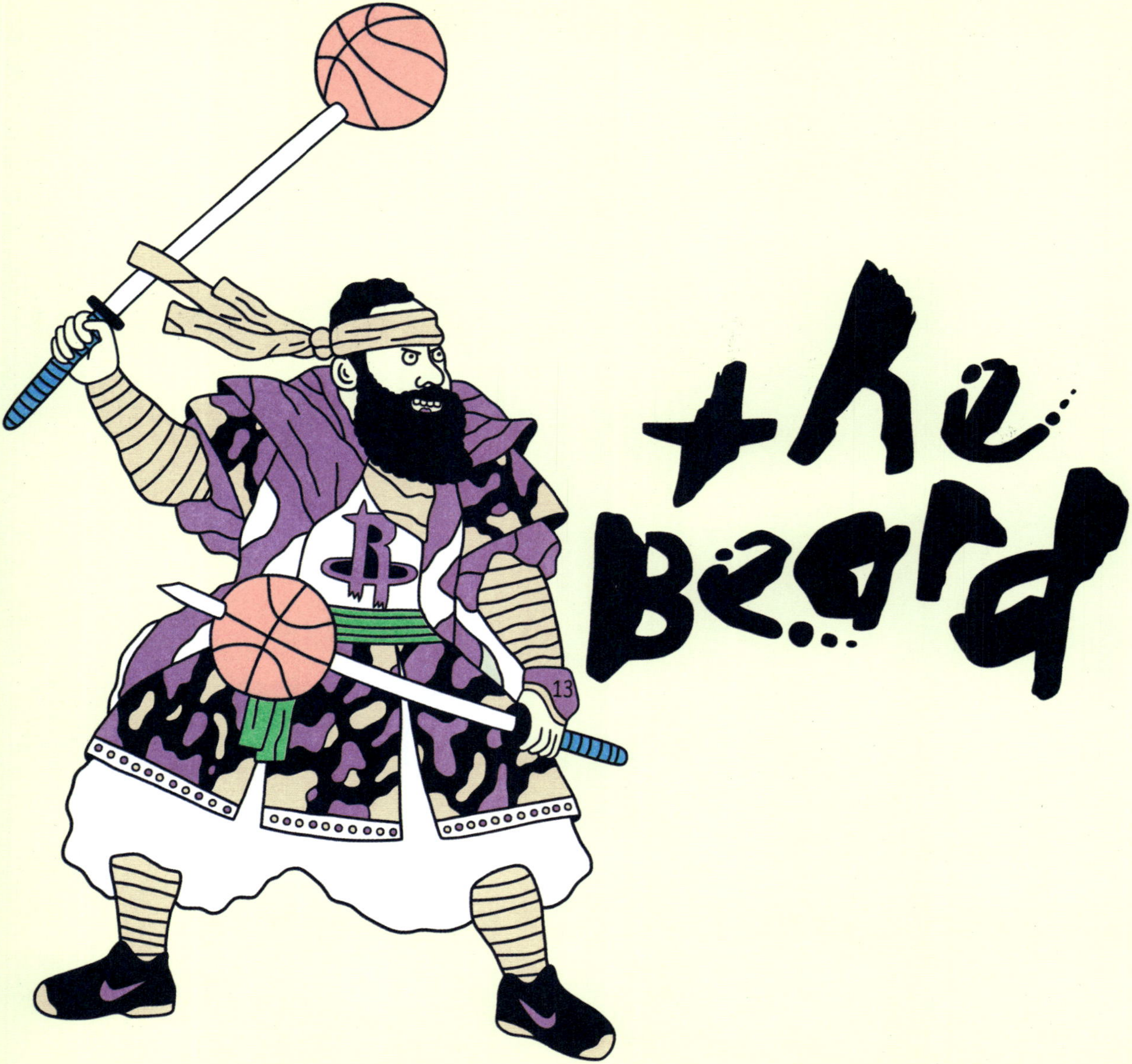
the Beard

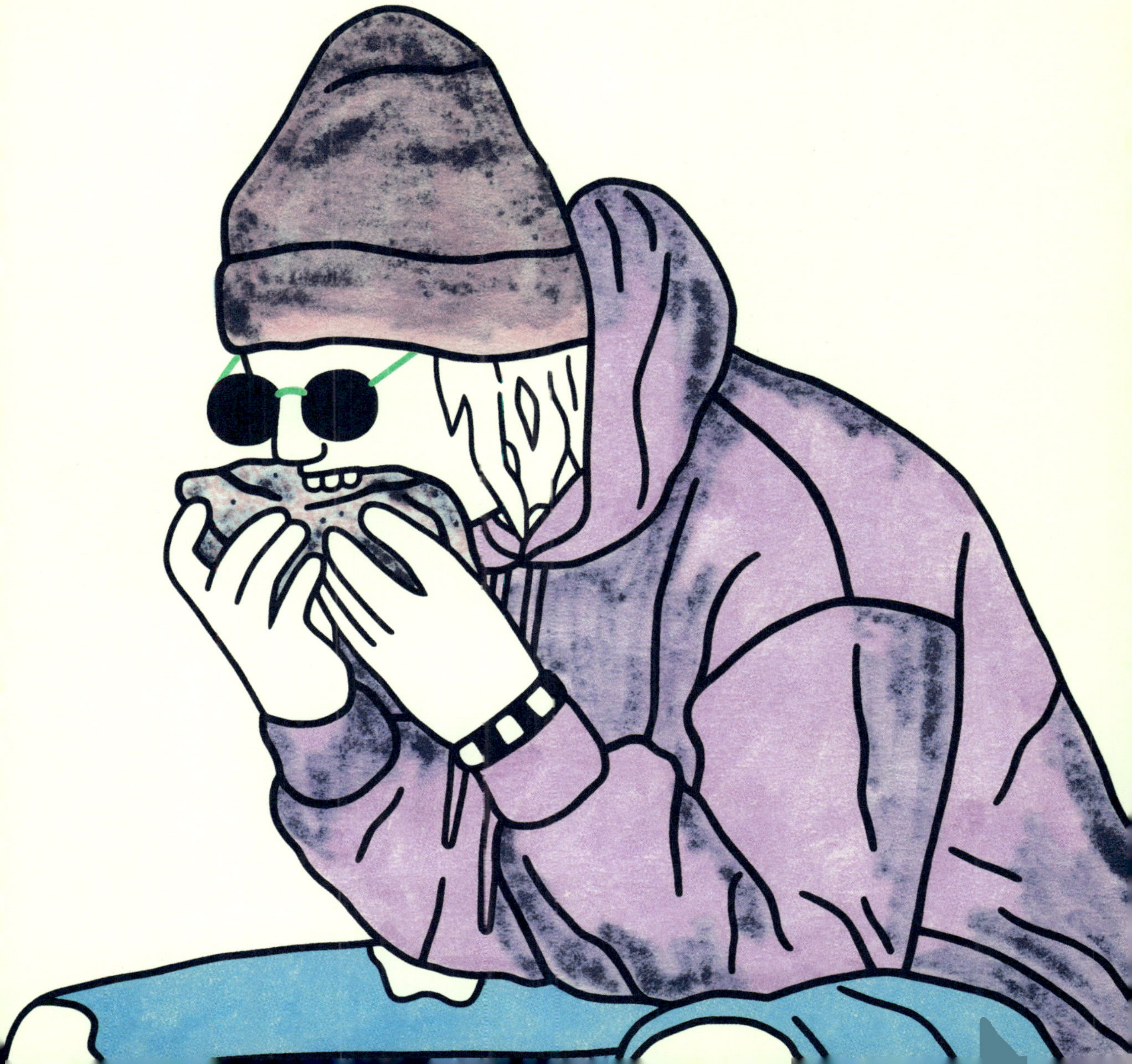

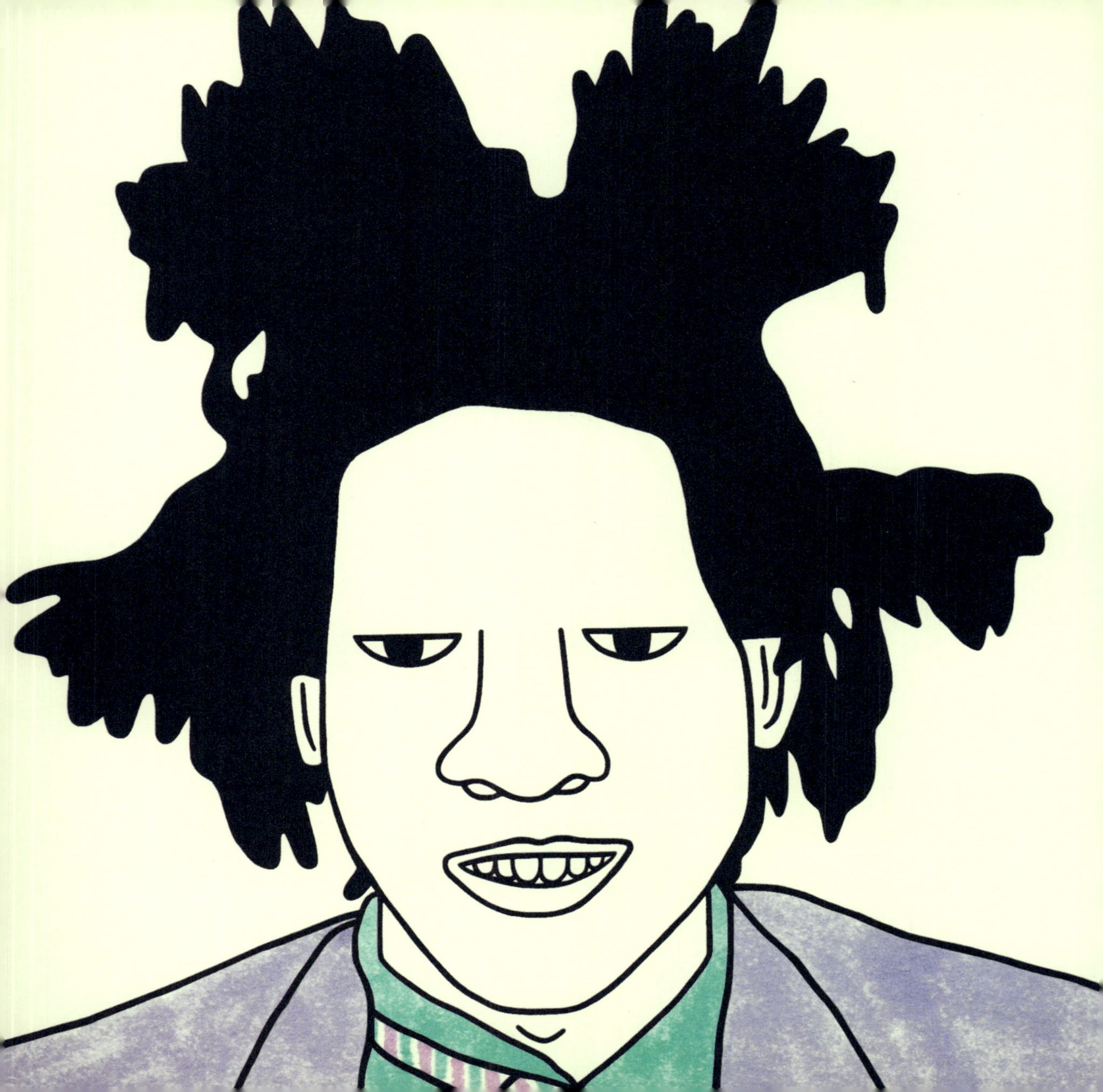

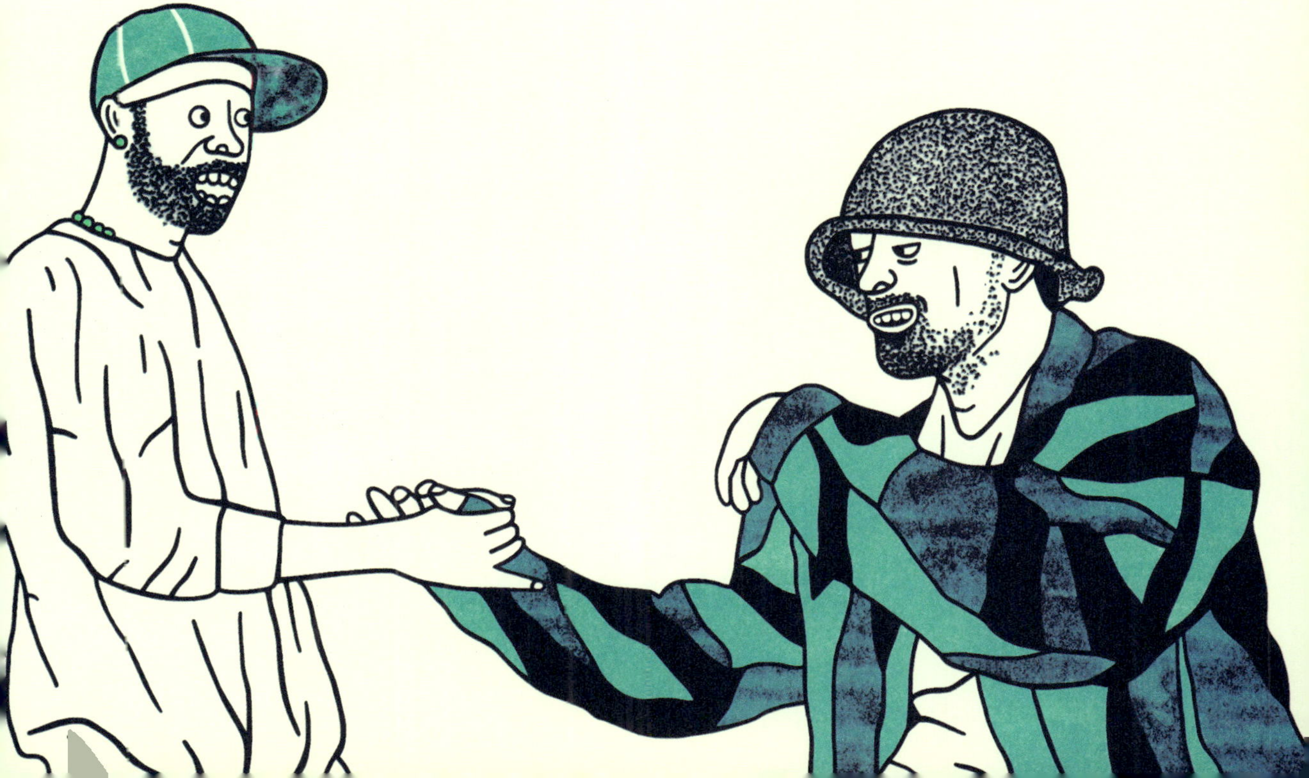

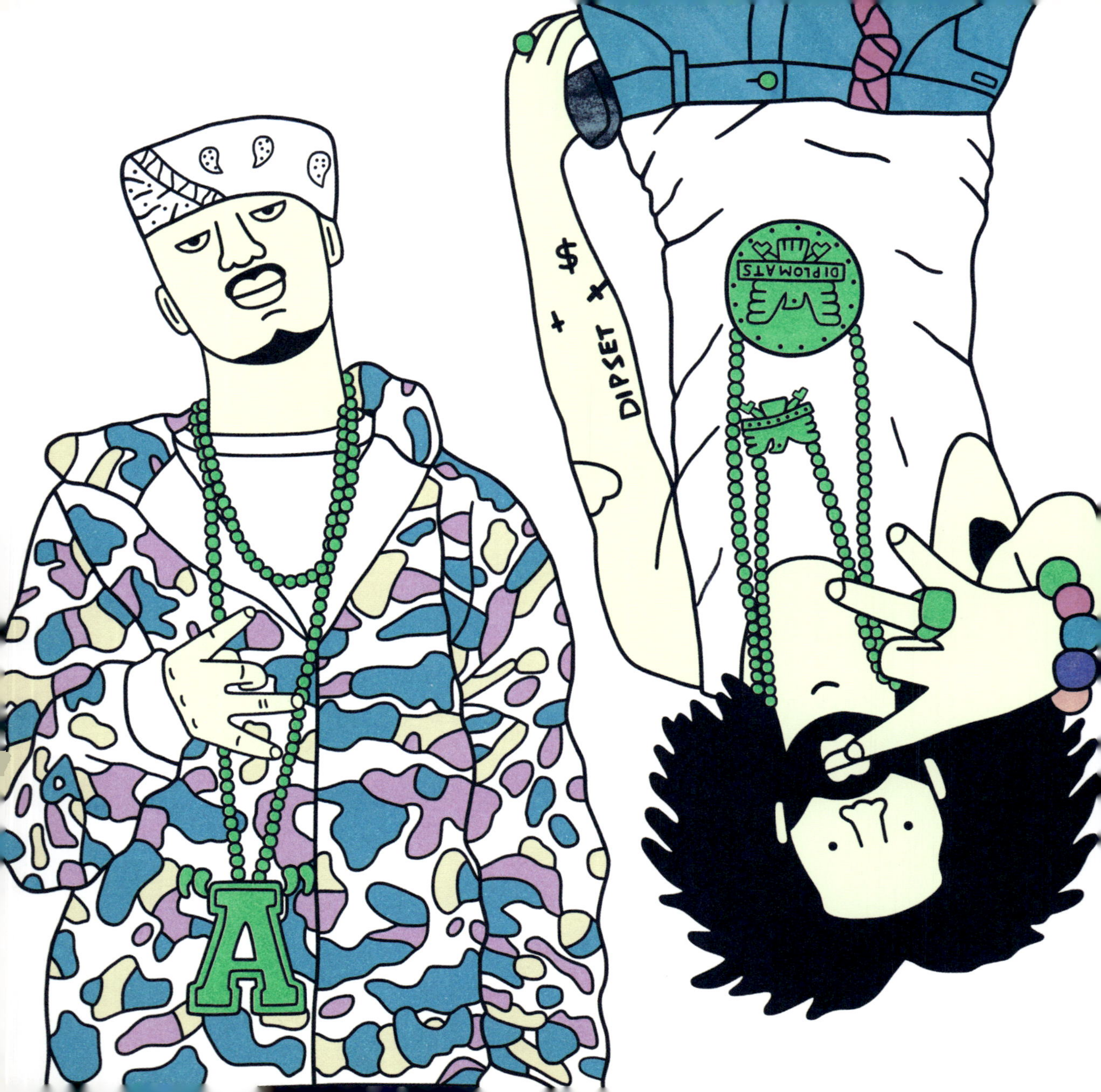
DIPSET
DIPLOMATS
A

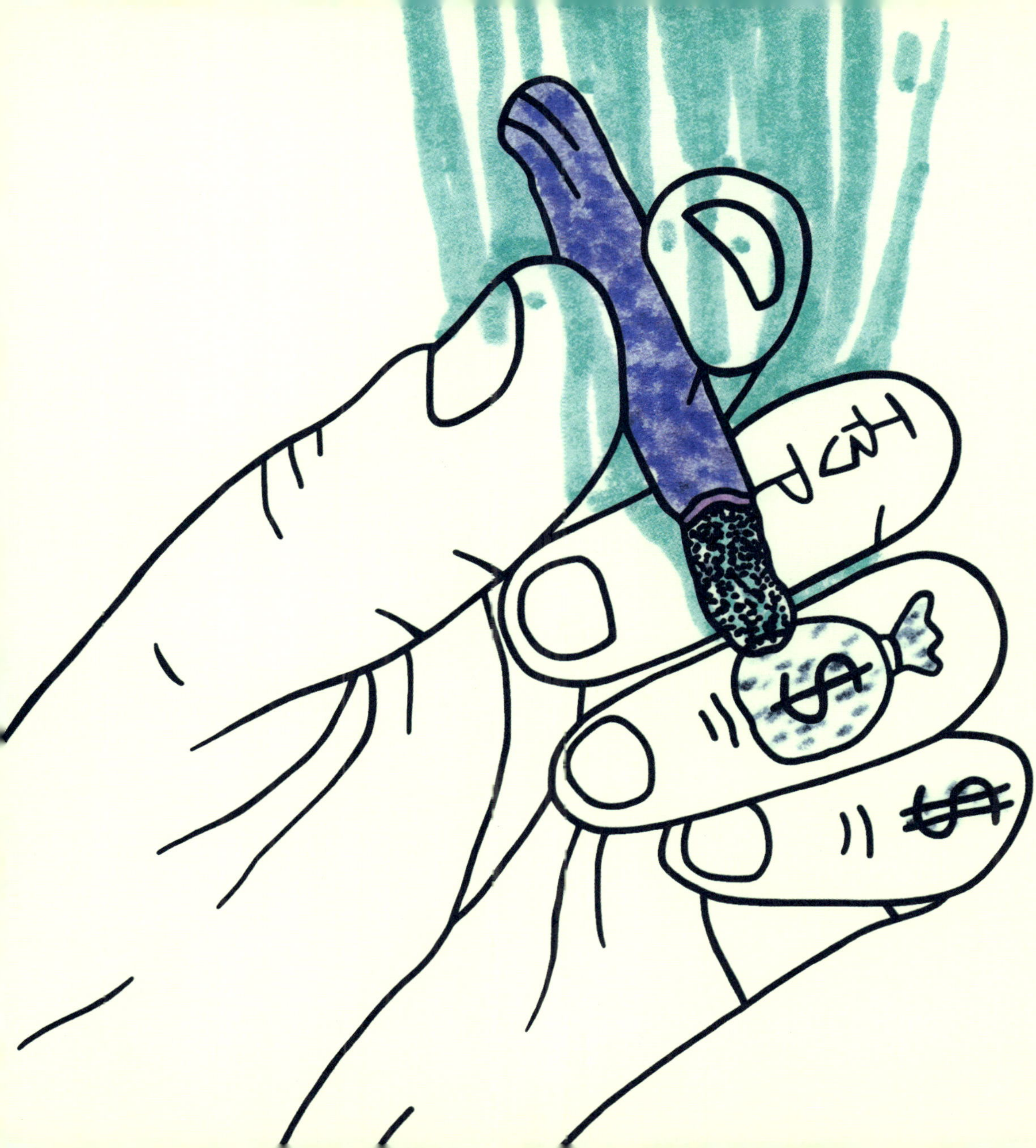

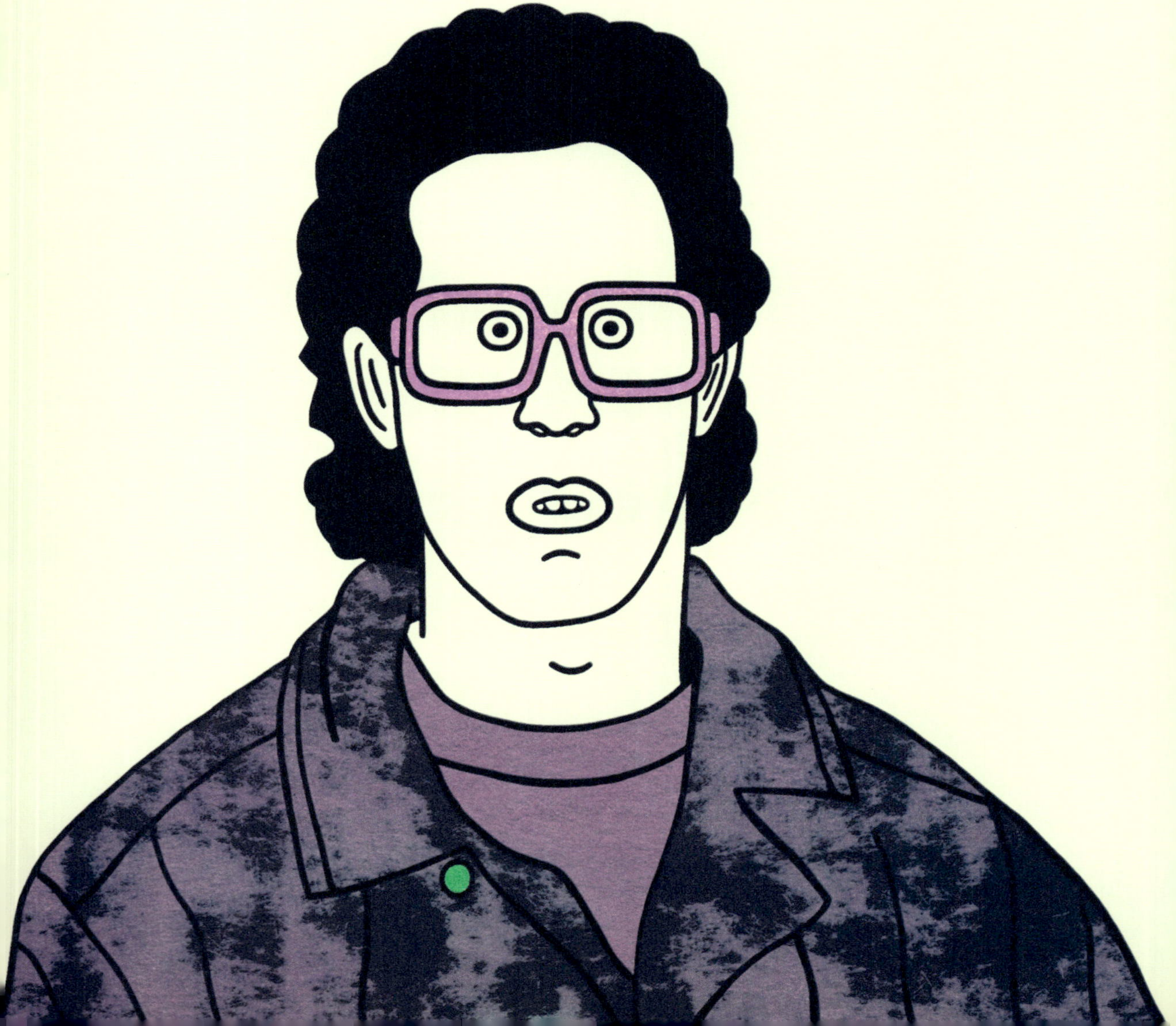

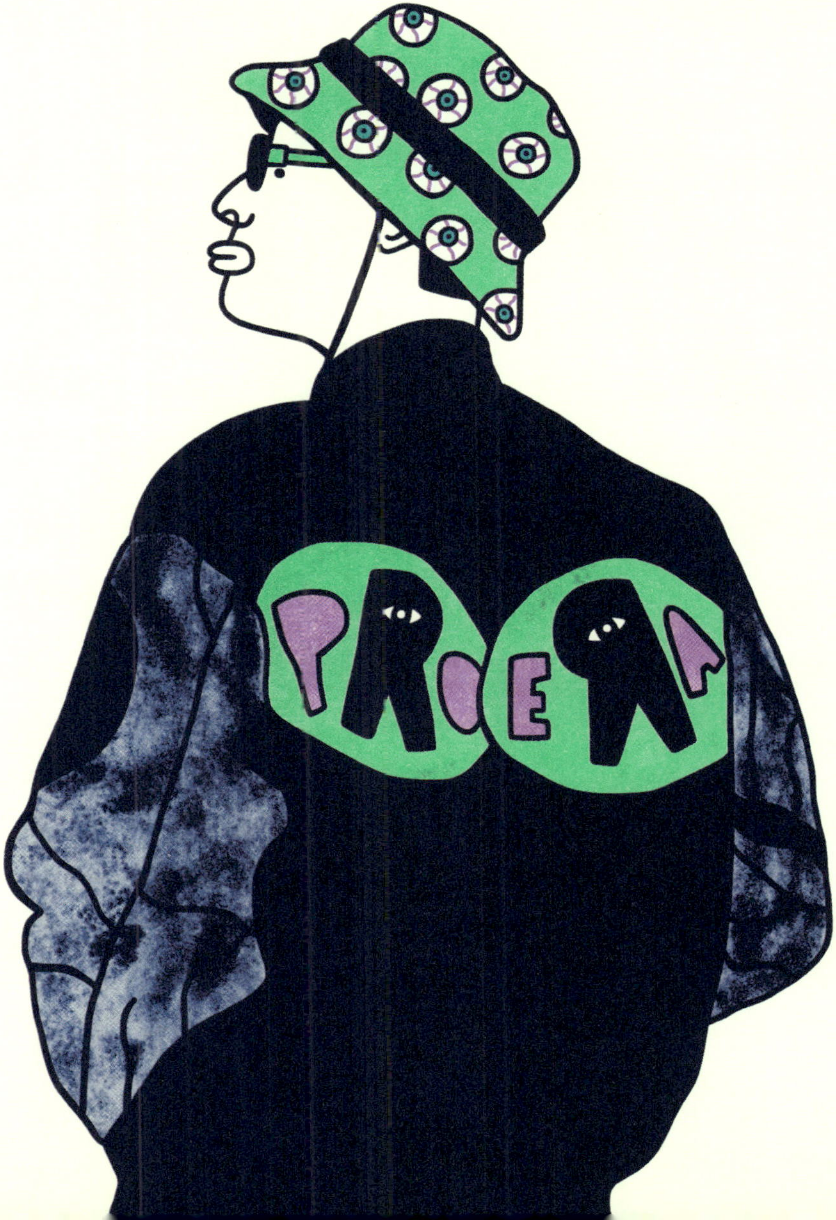

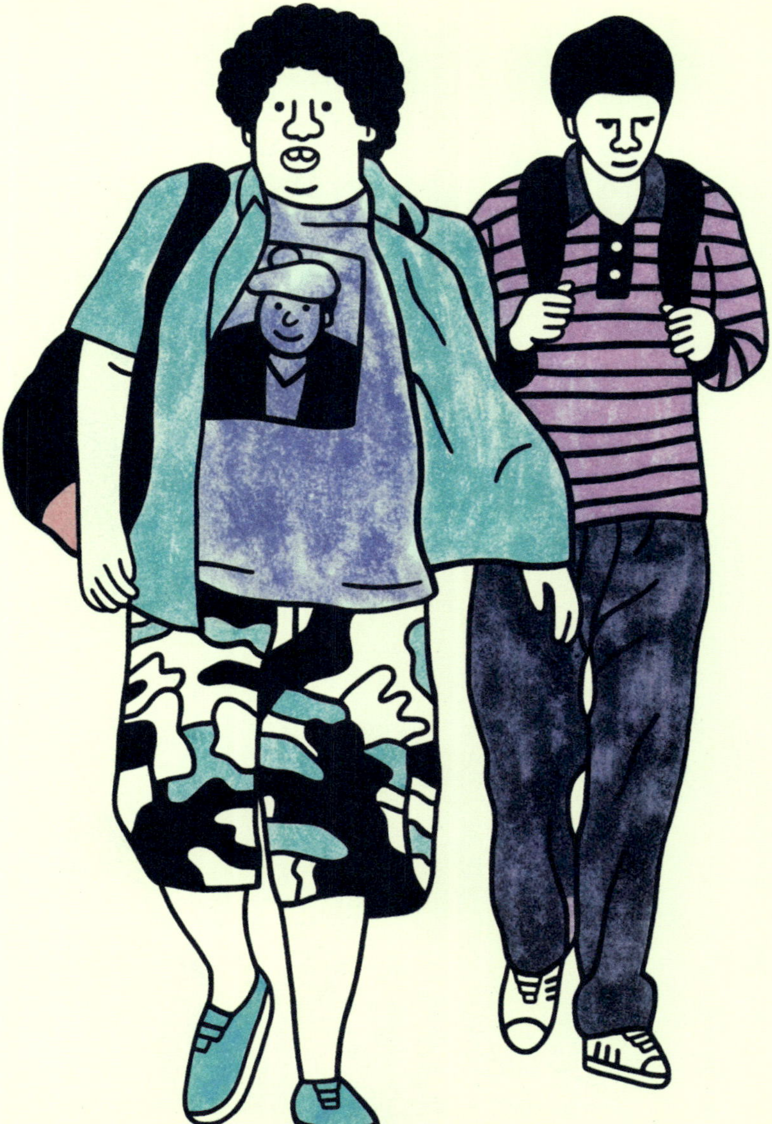

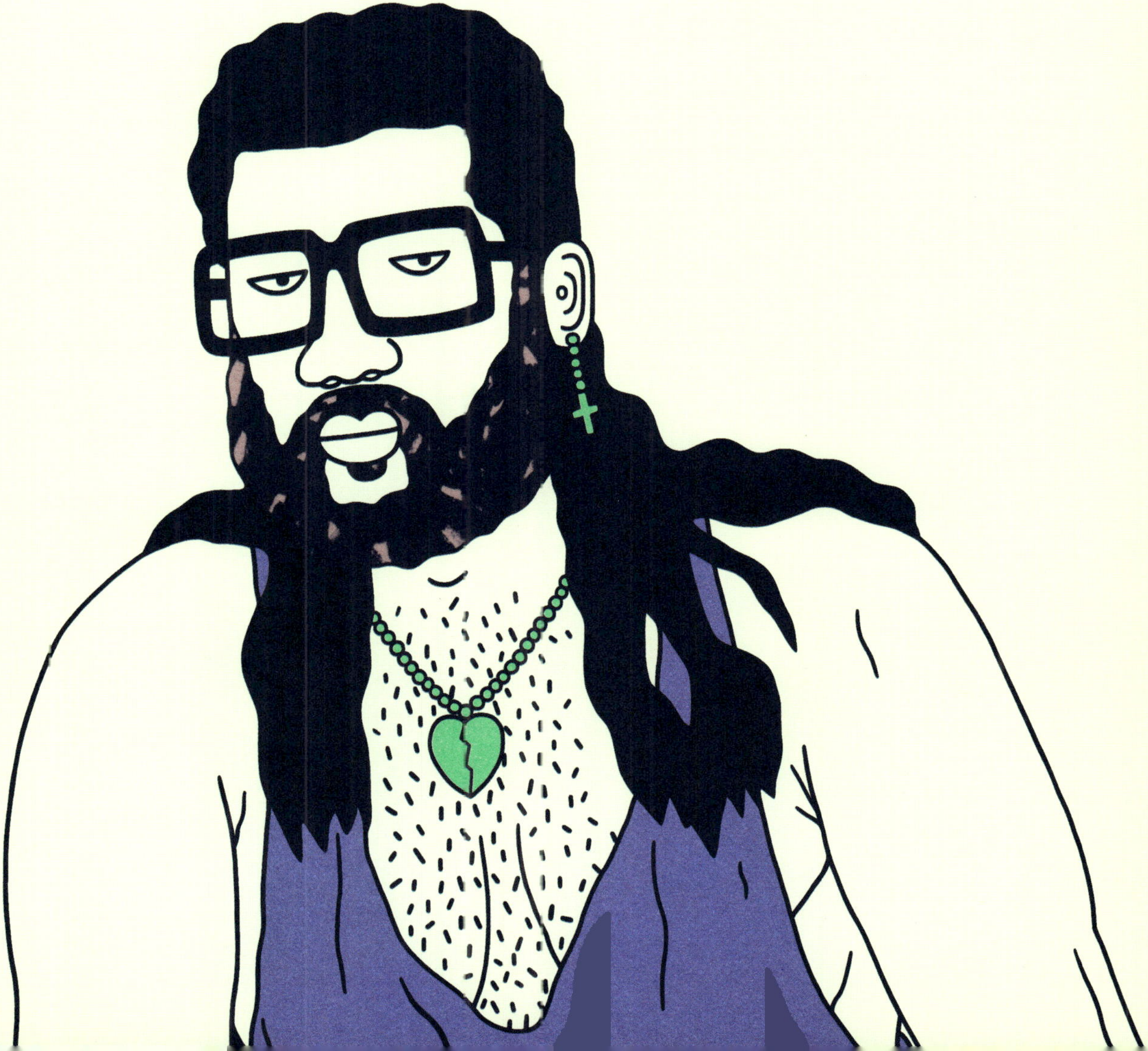

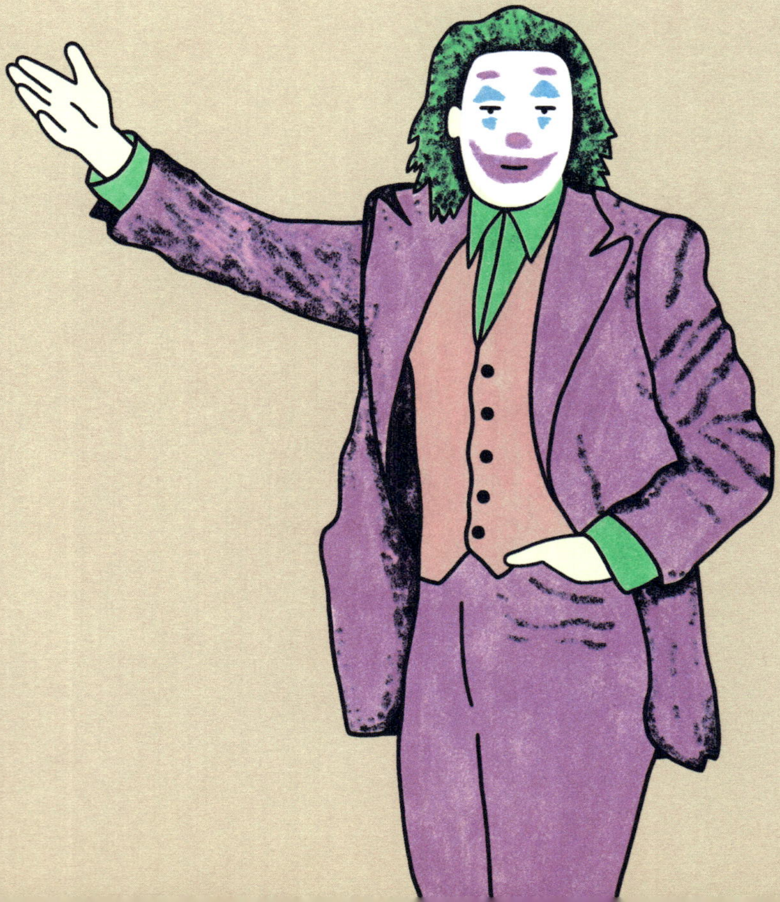

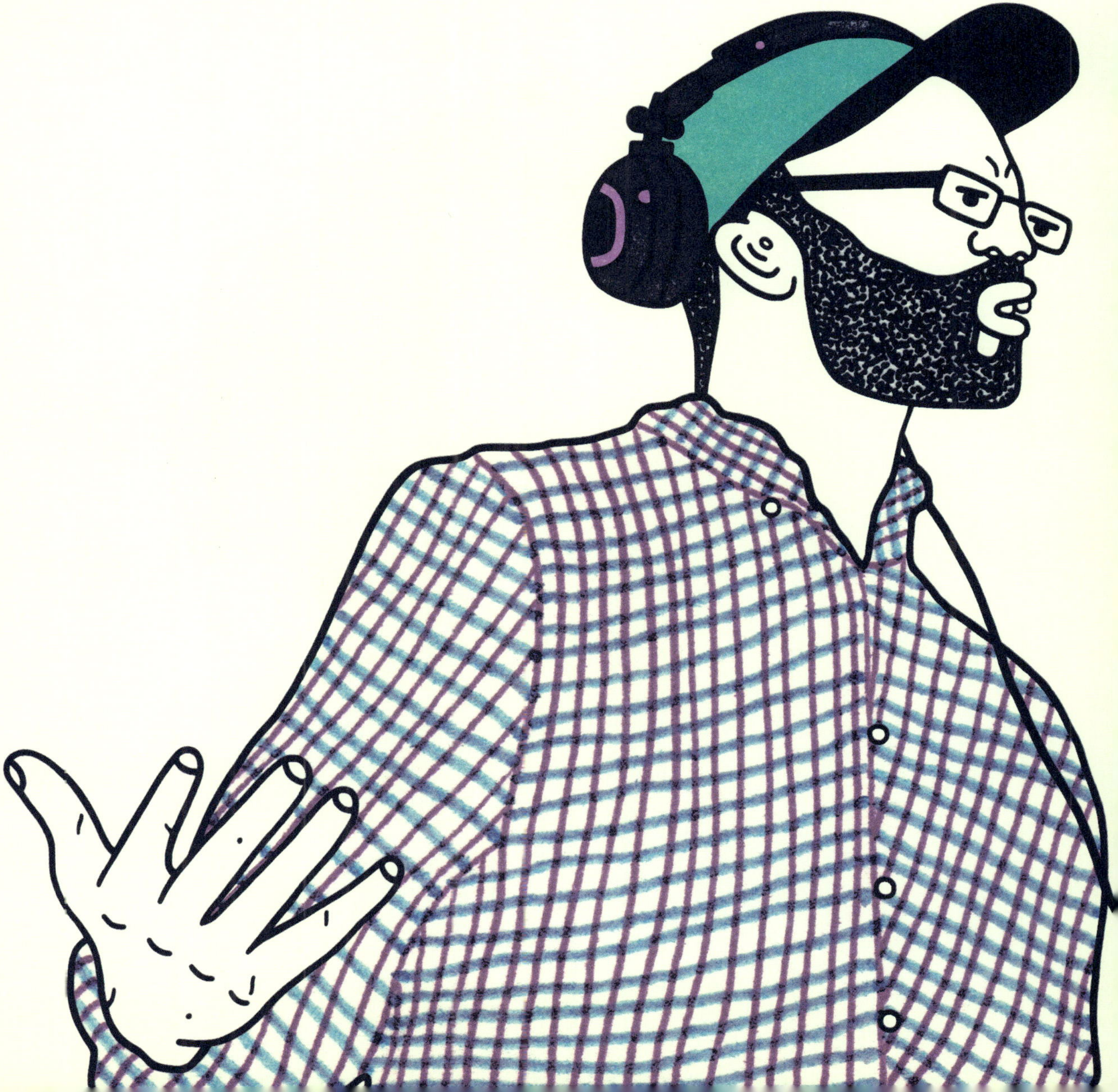

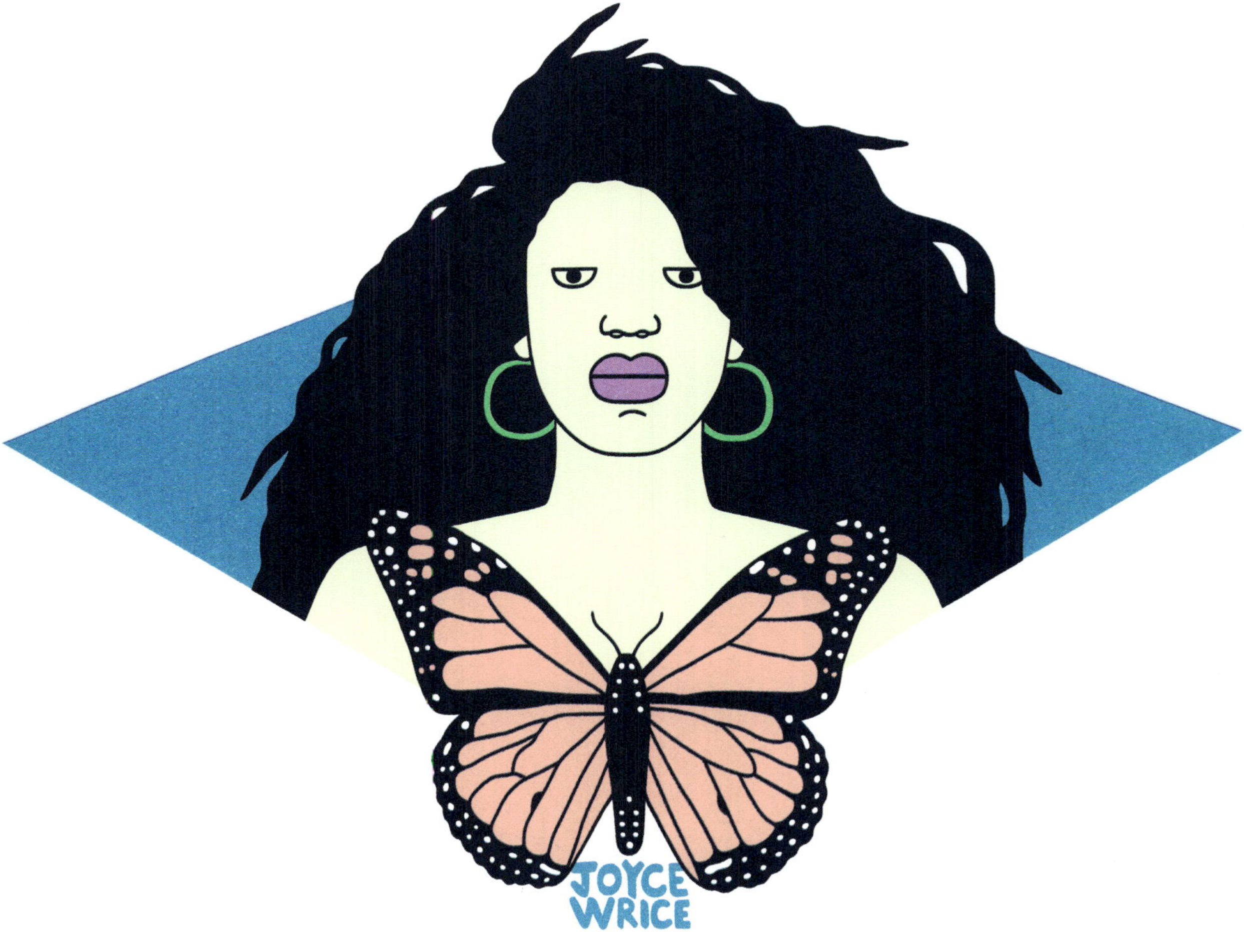
JOYCE
WRICE

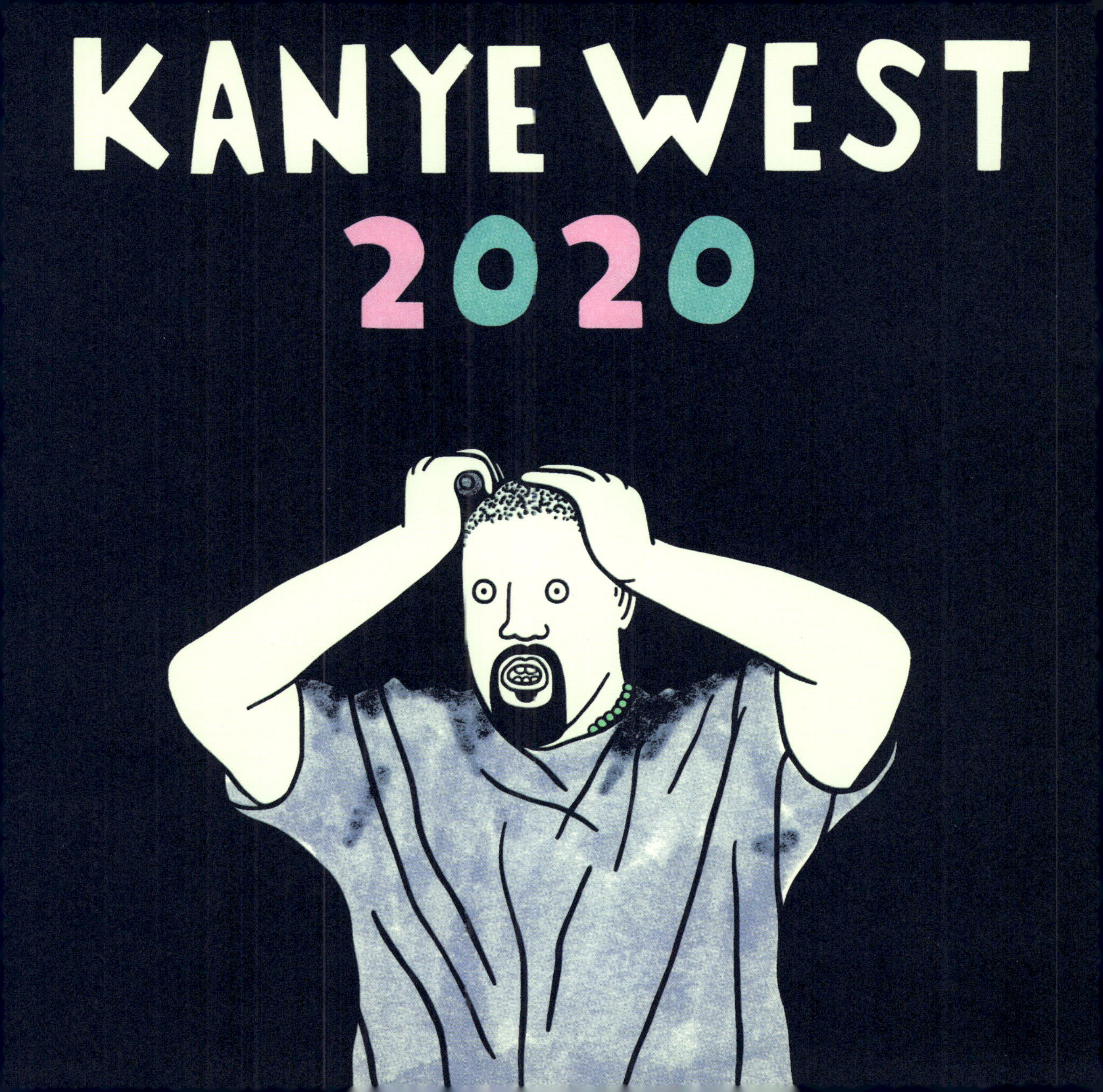
KANYE WEST
2020

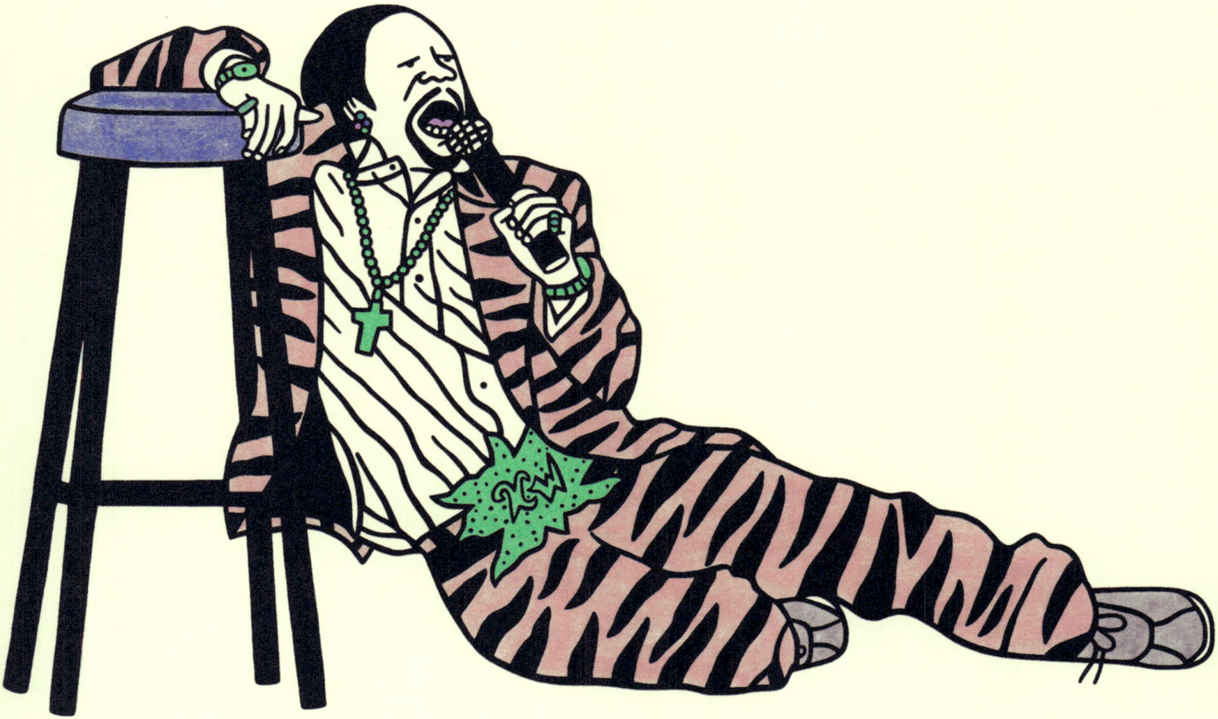

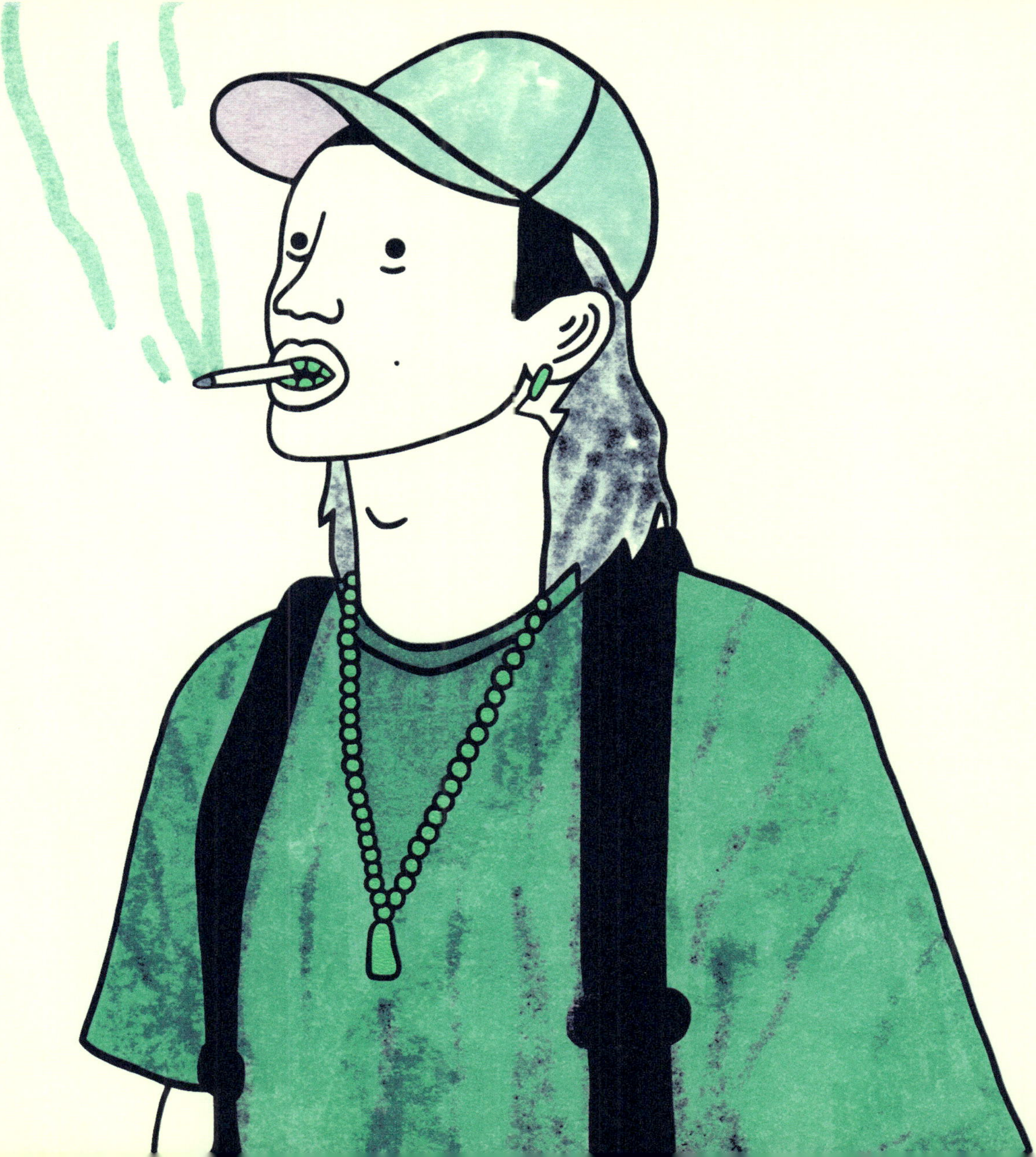

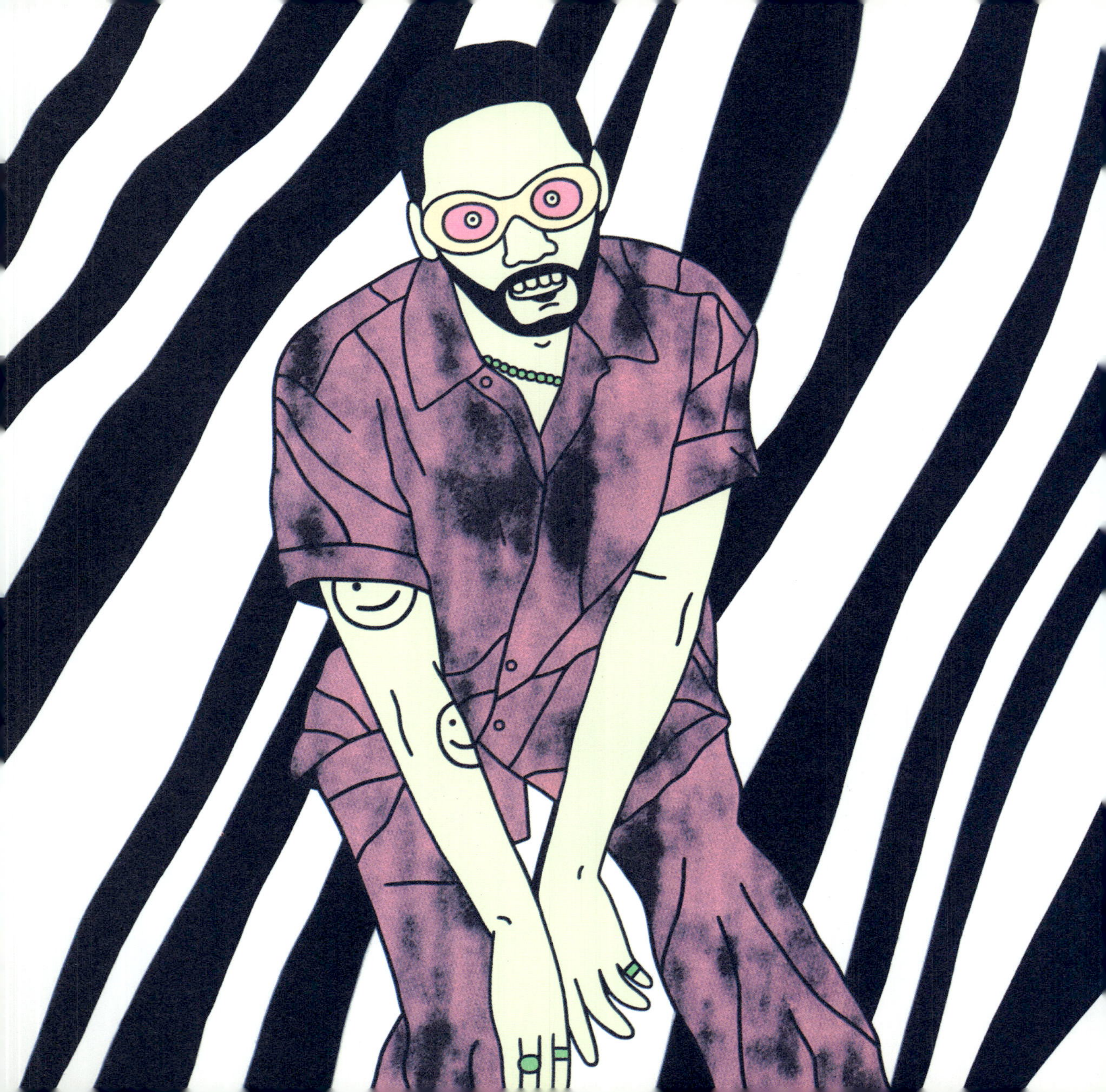

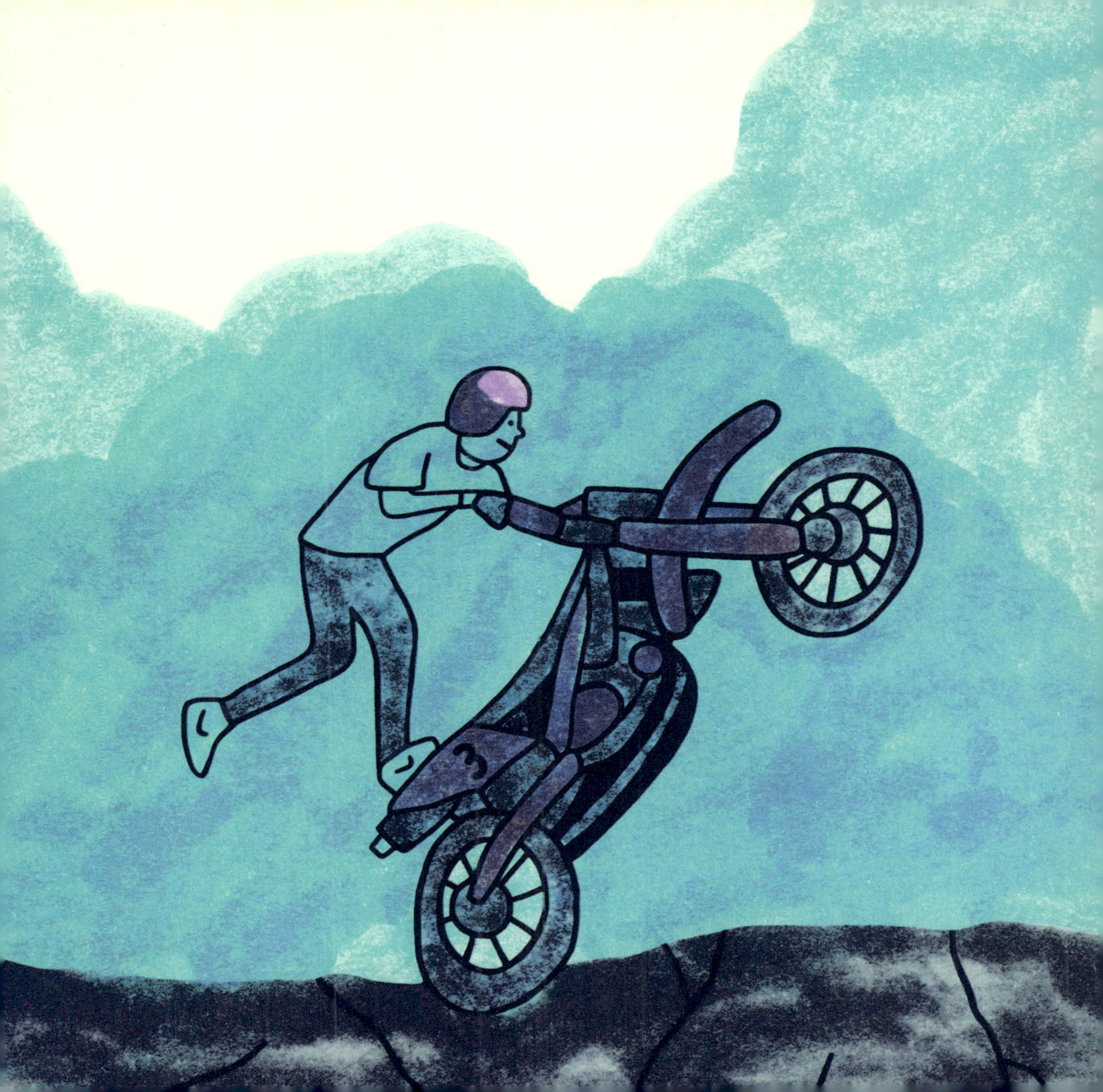

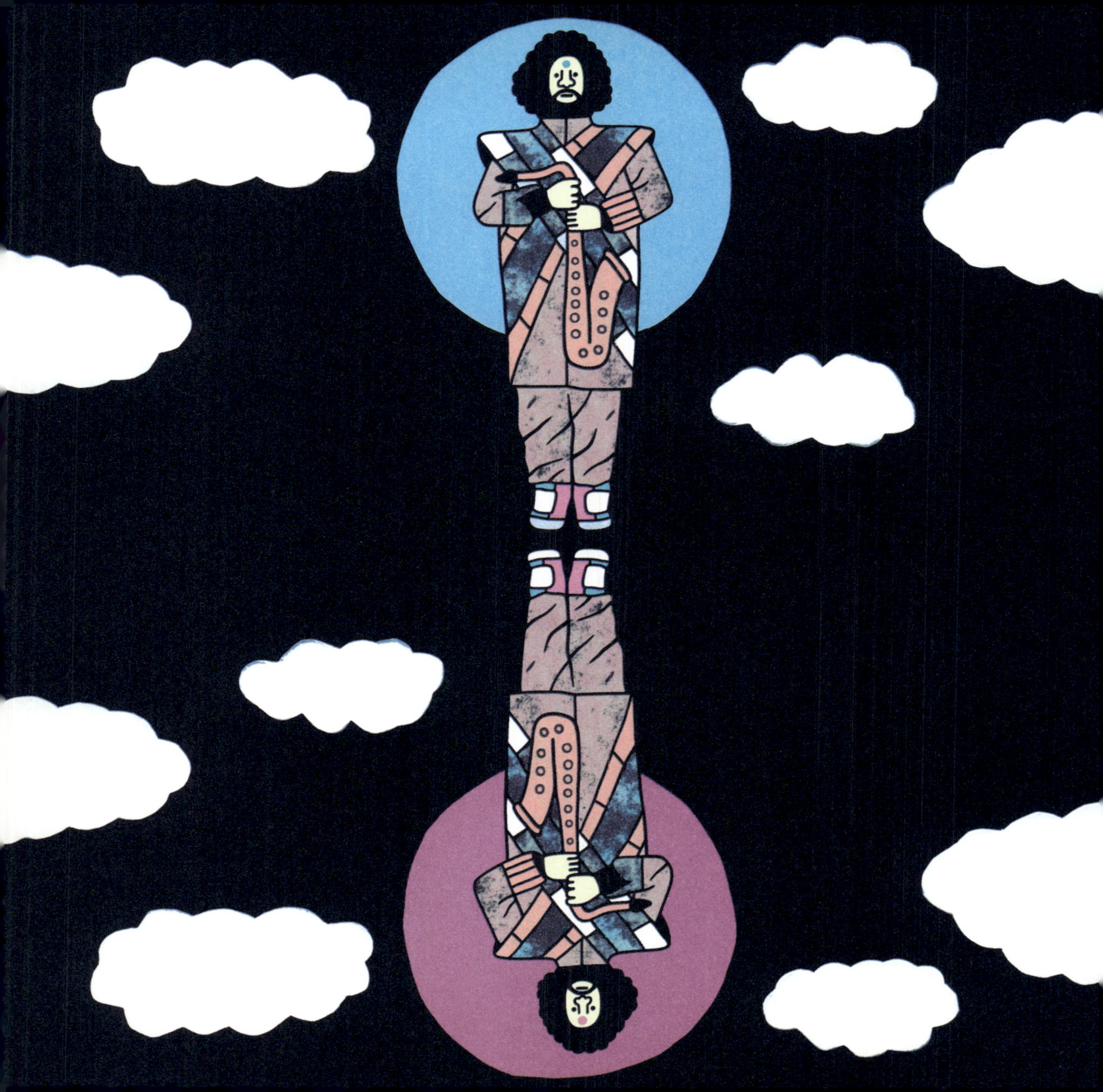

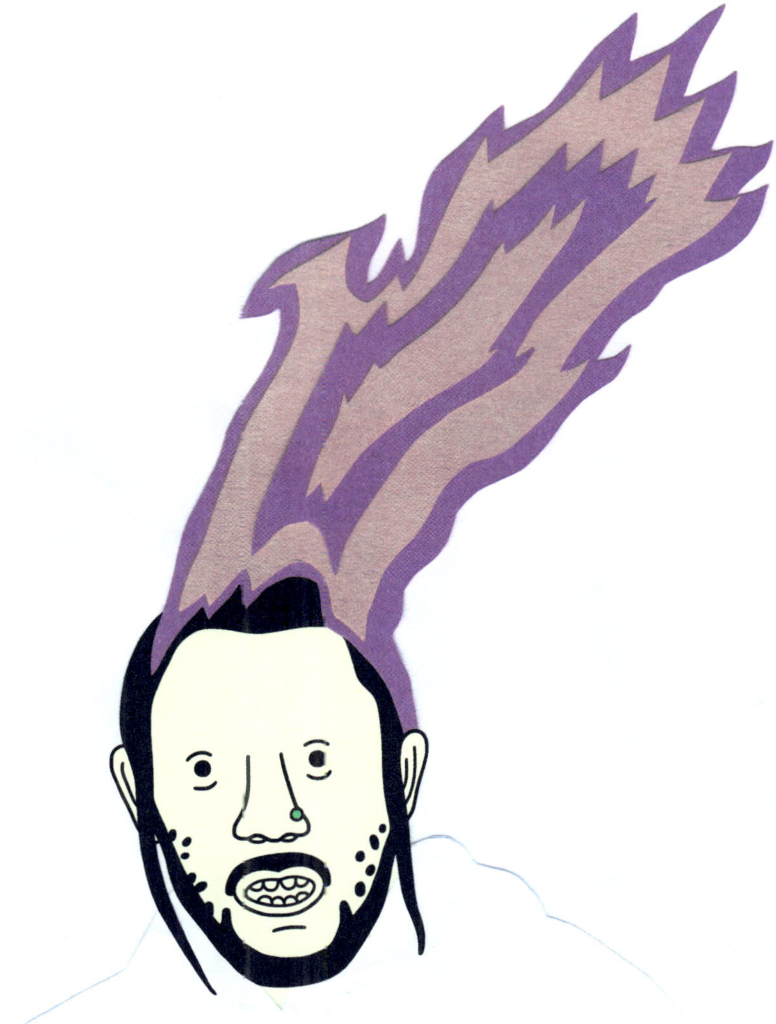

Dreamer

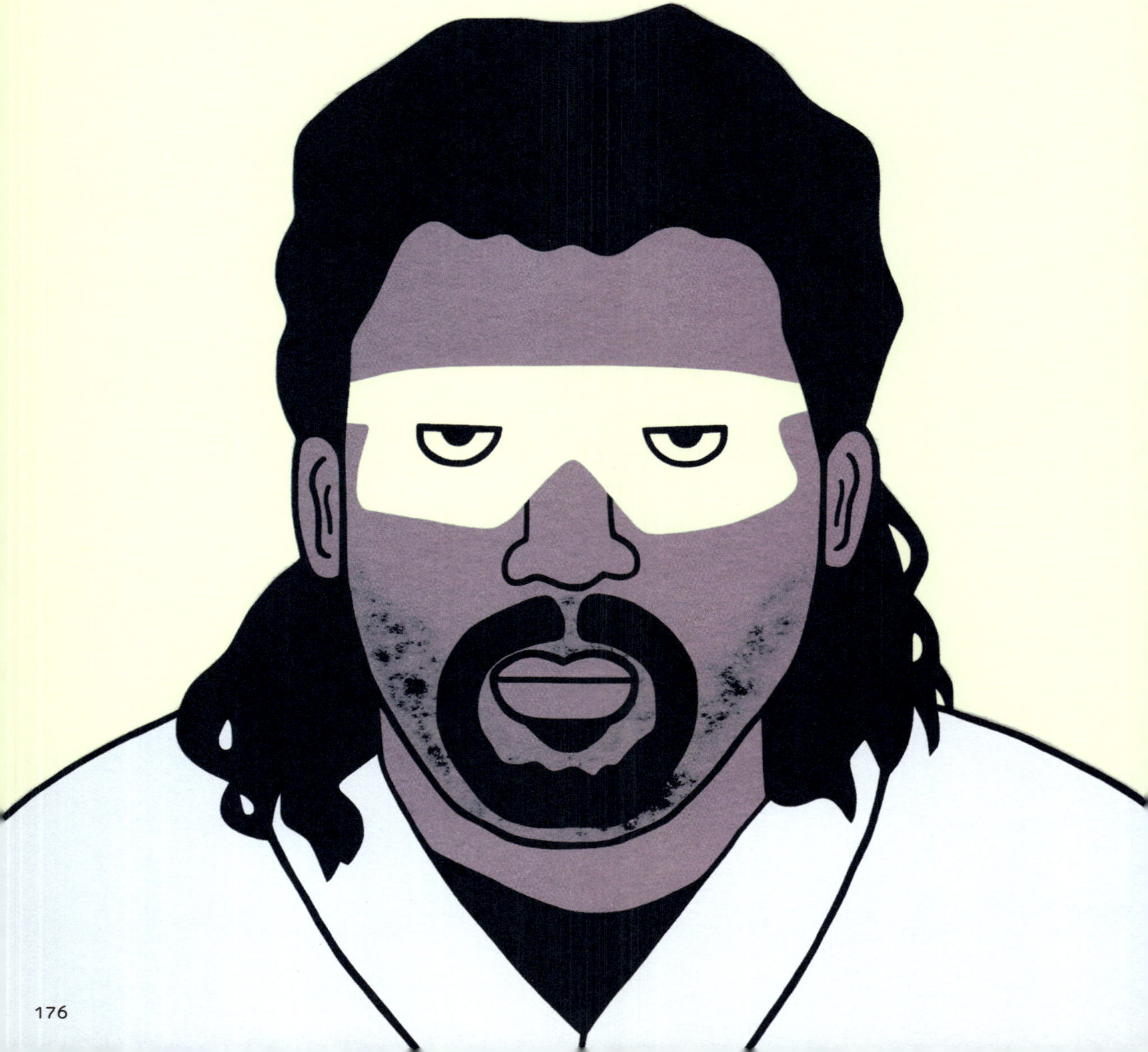

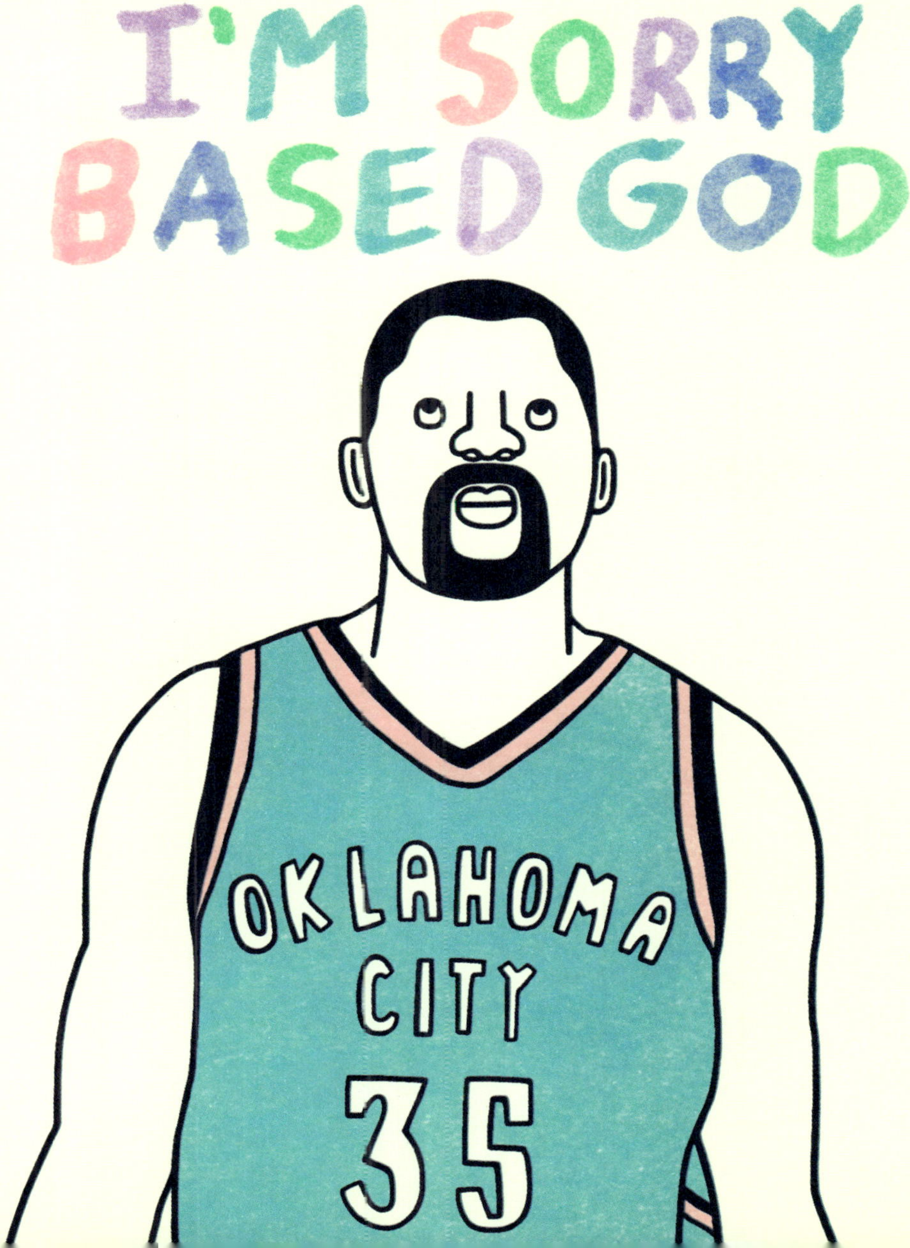
I'M SORRY BASED GOD
OKLAHOMA CITY
35

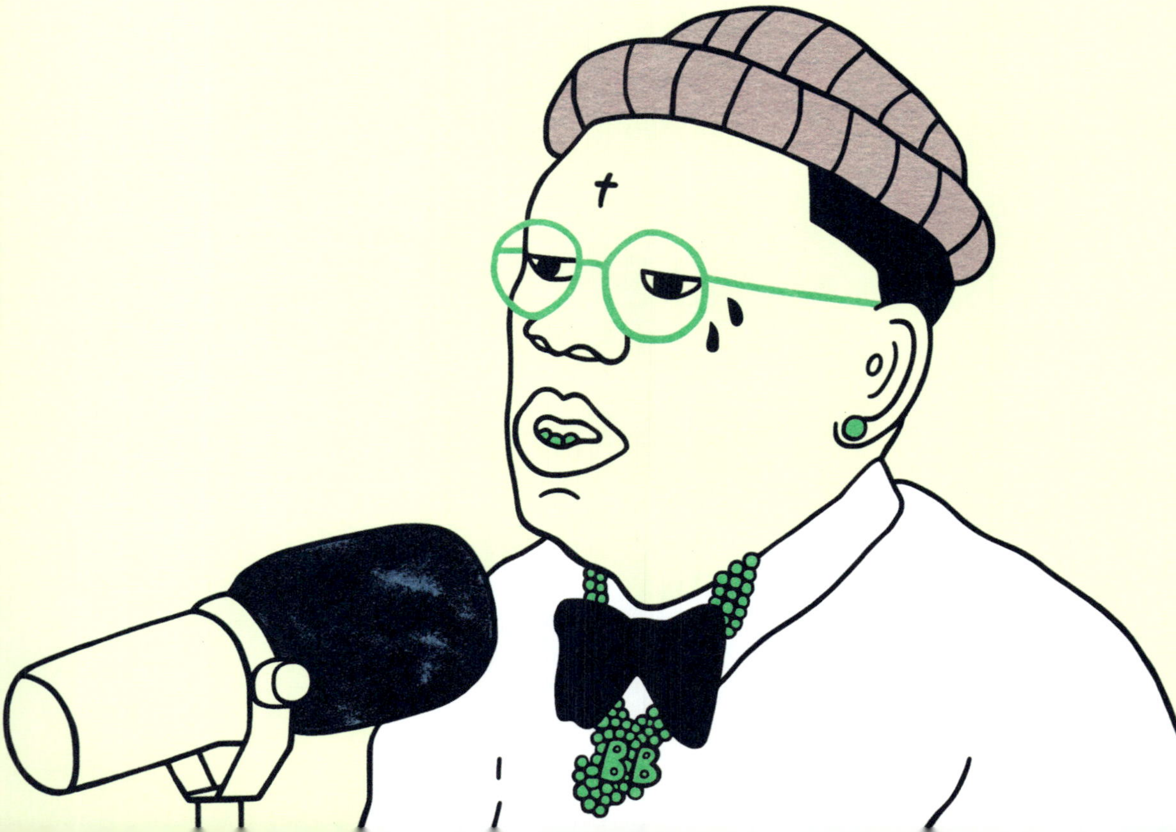
BB

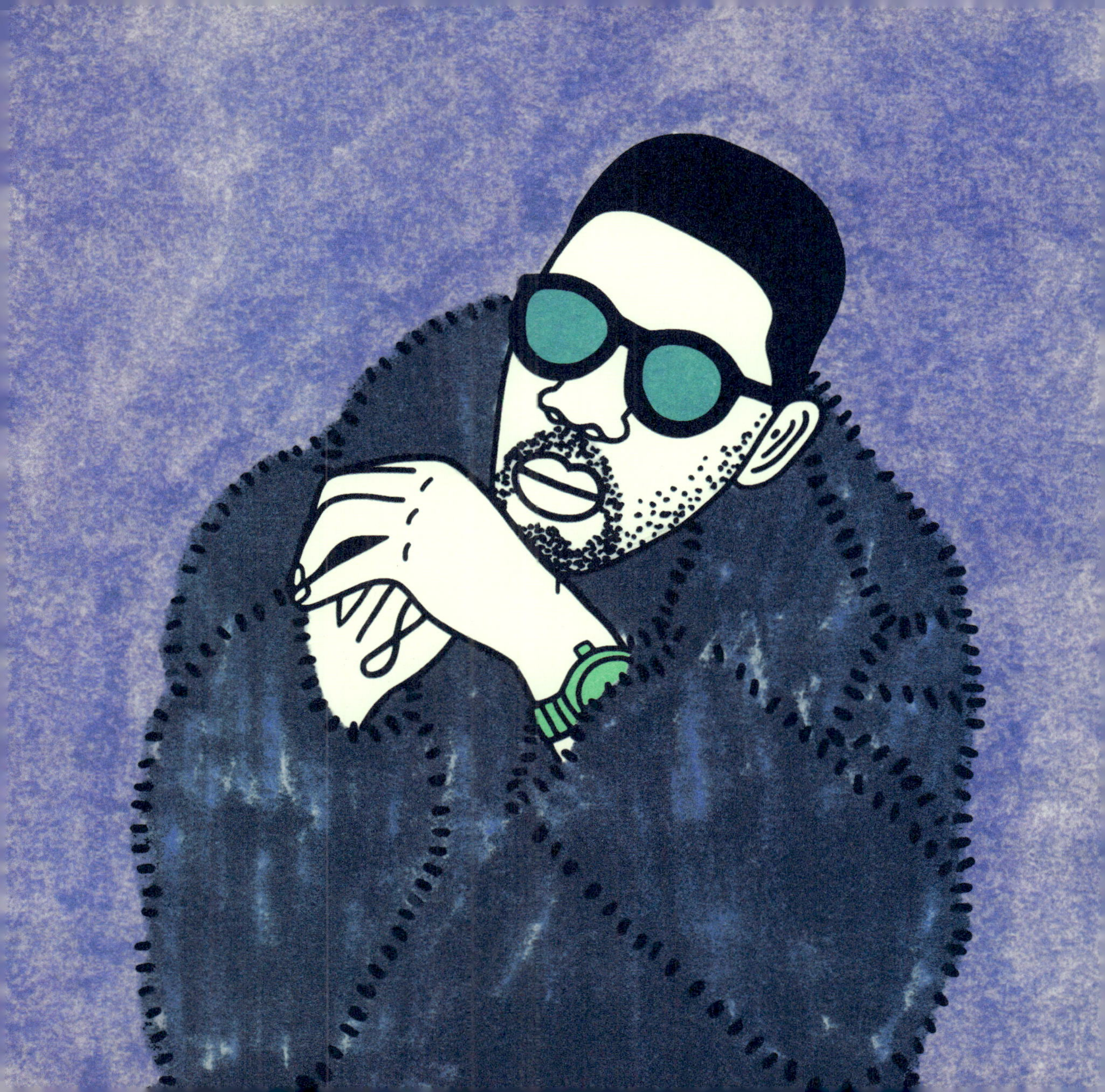

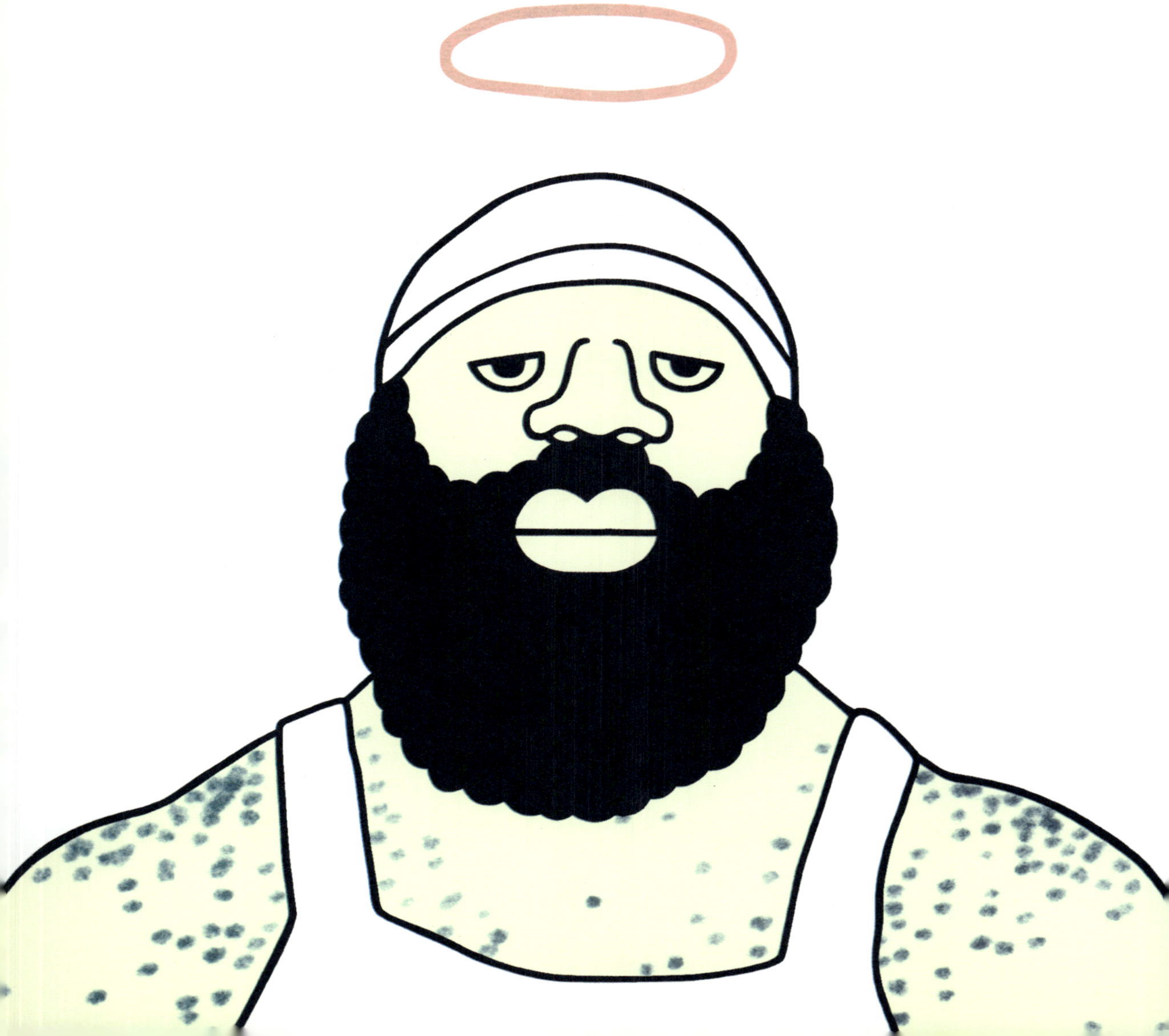

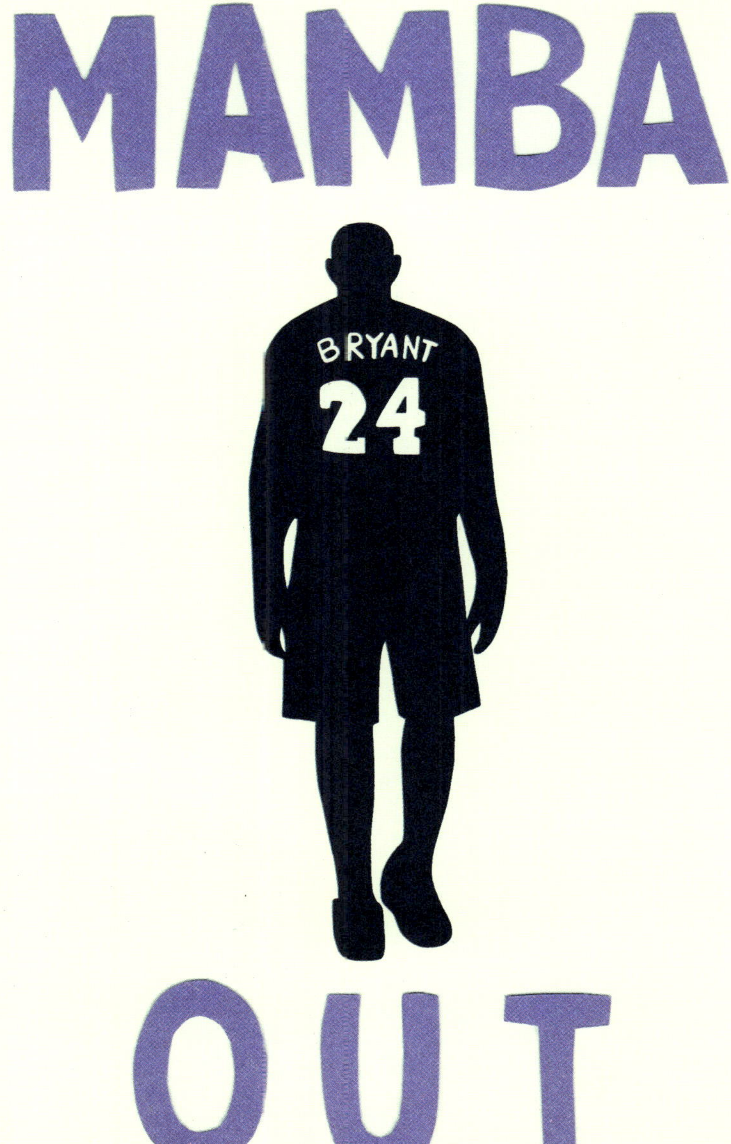
MAMBA
BRYANT
24
OUT

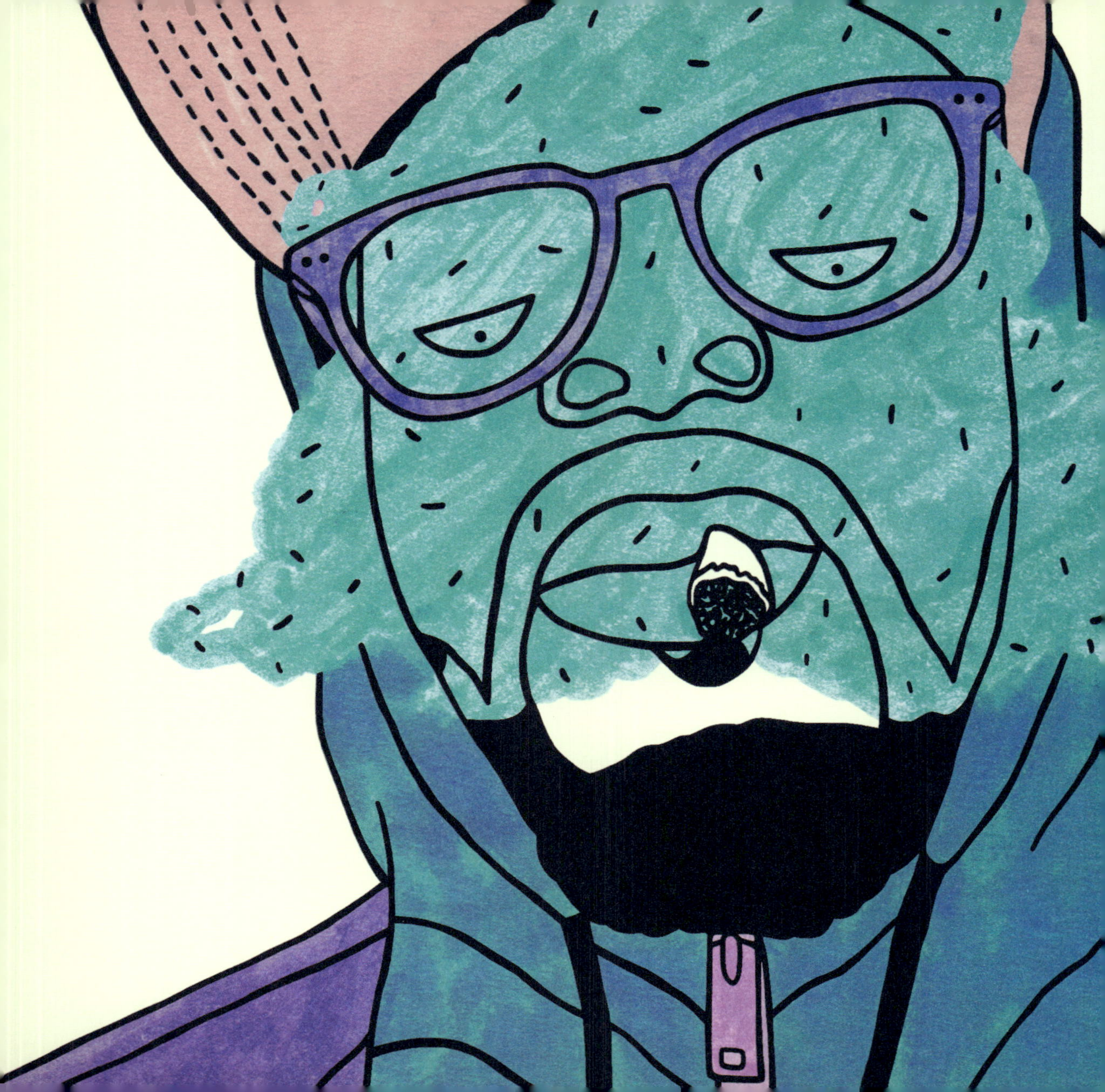

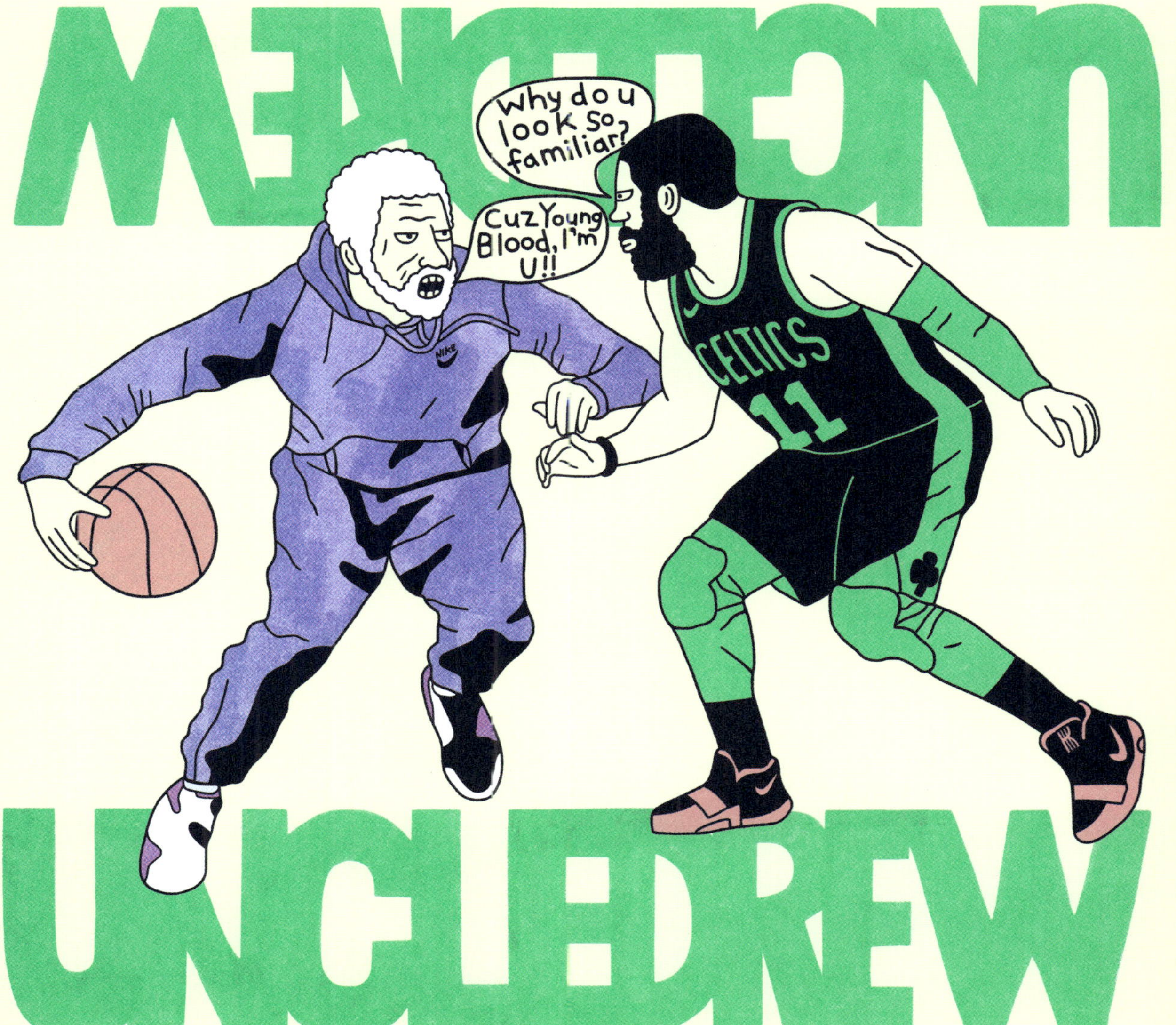
UNCLEDREW
Why do u look so familiar?
Cuz Young Blood, I'm U!!
NIKE
CELTICS
11
UNCLEDREW

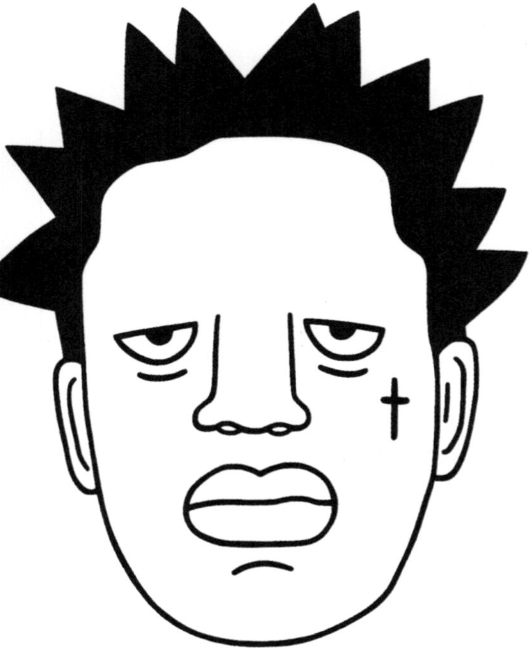

Kodak Black

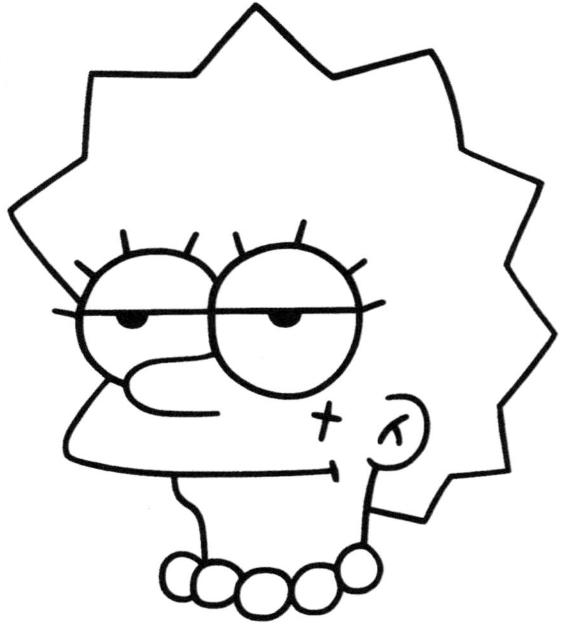

Lisa Simpson

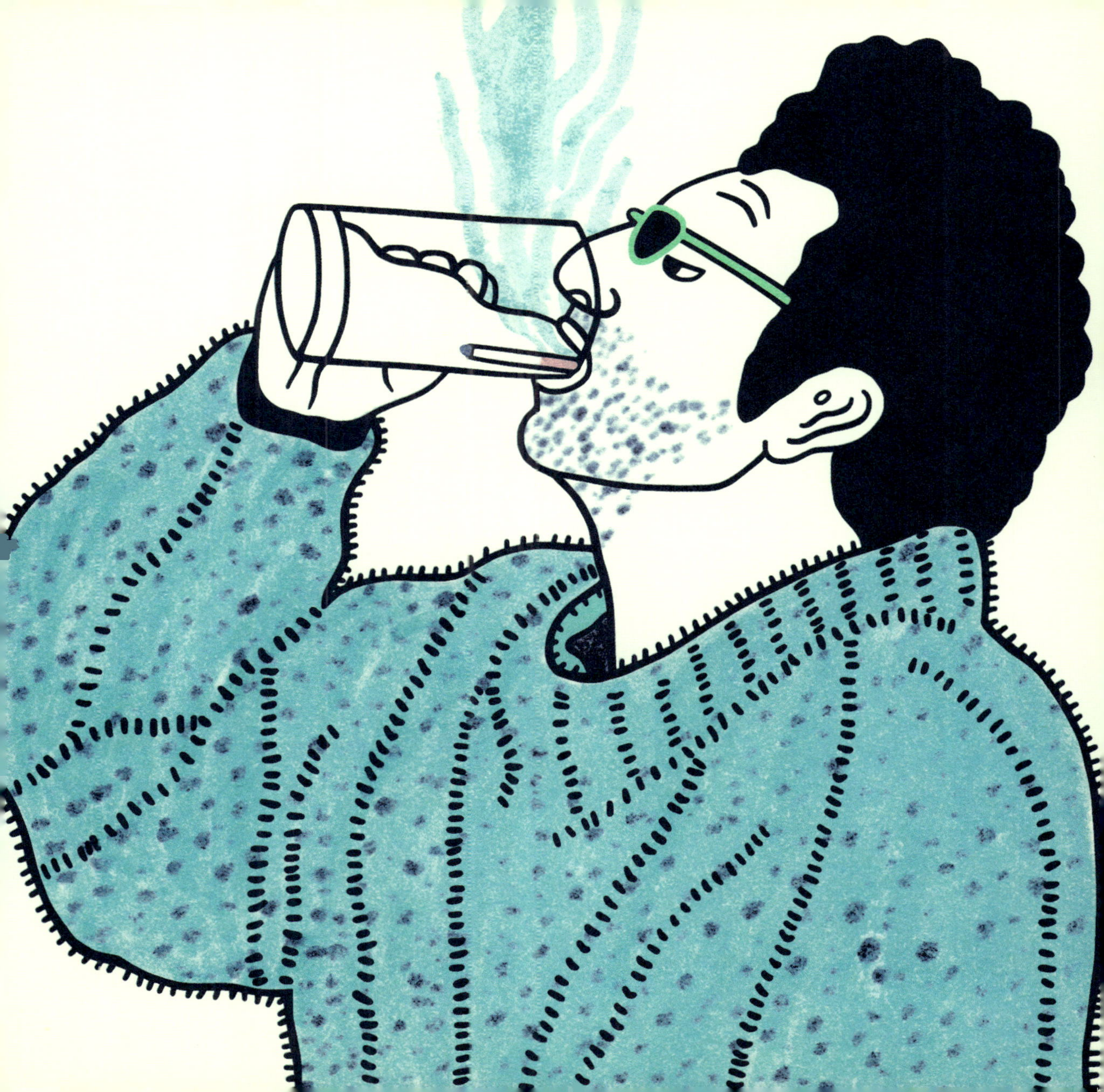

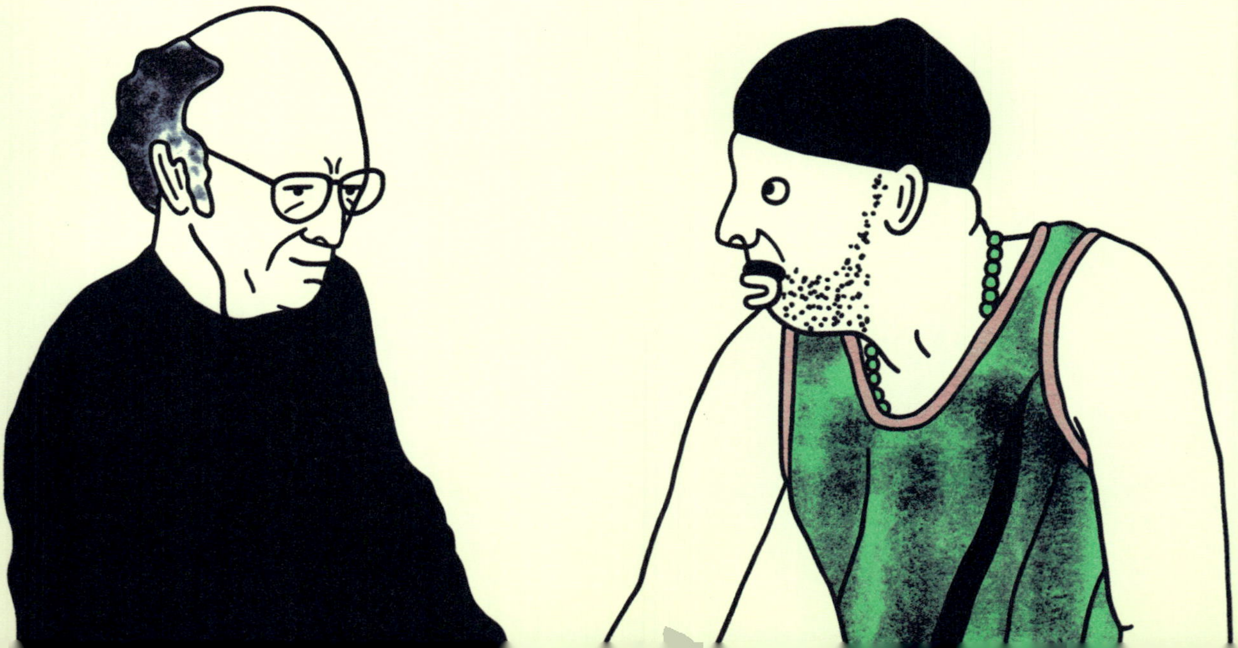

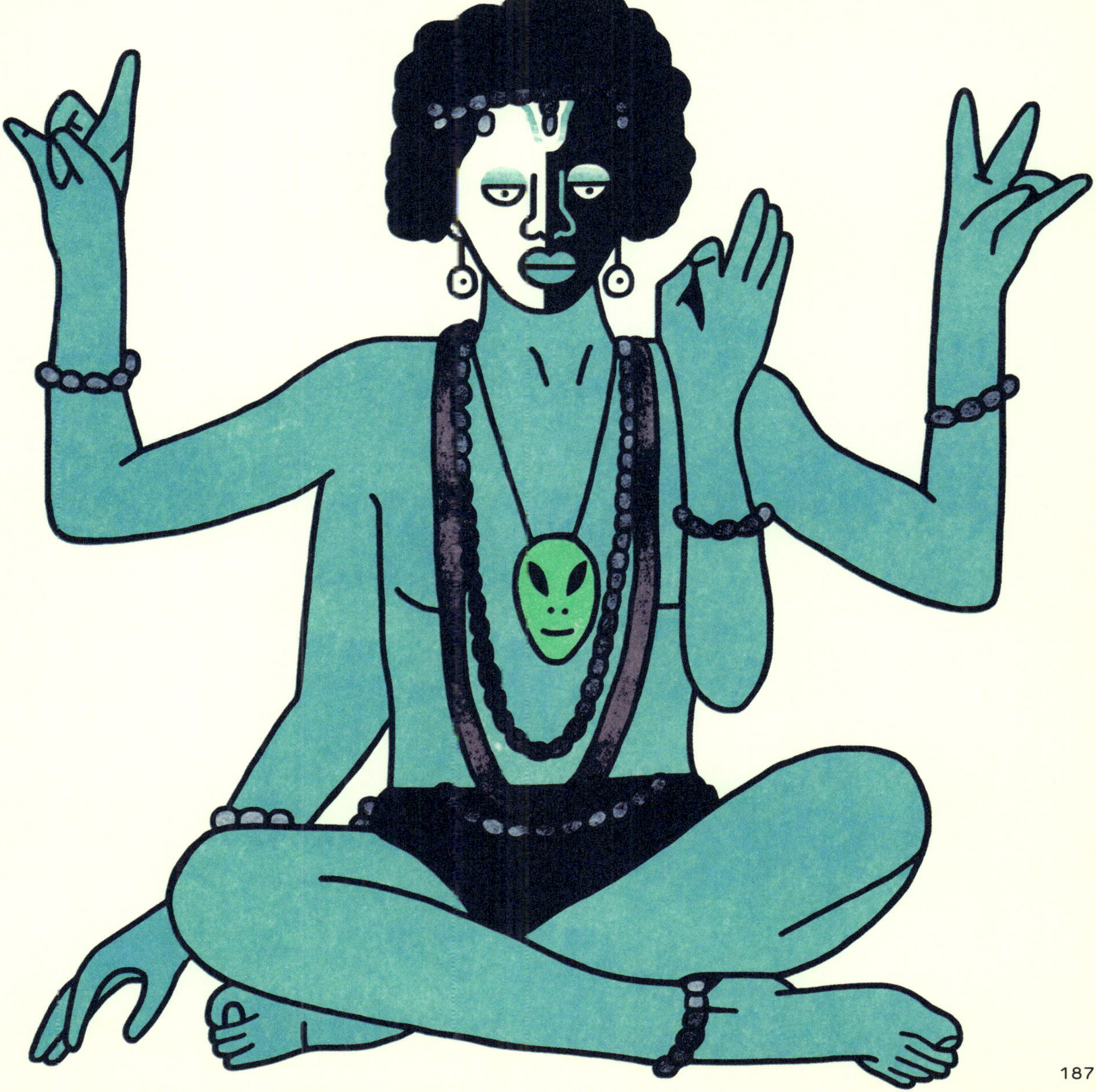

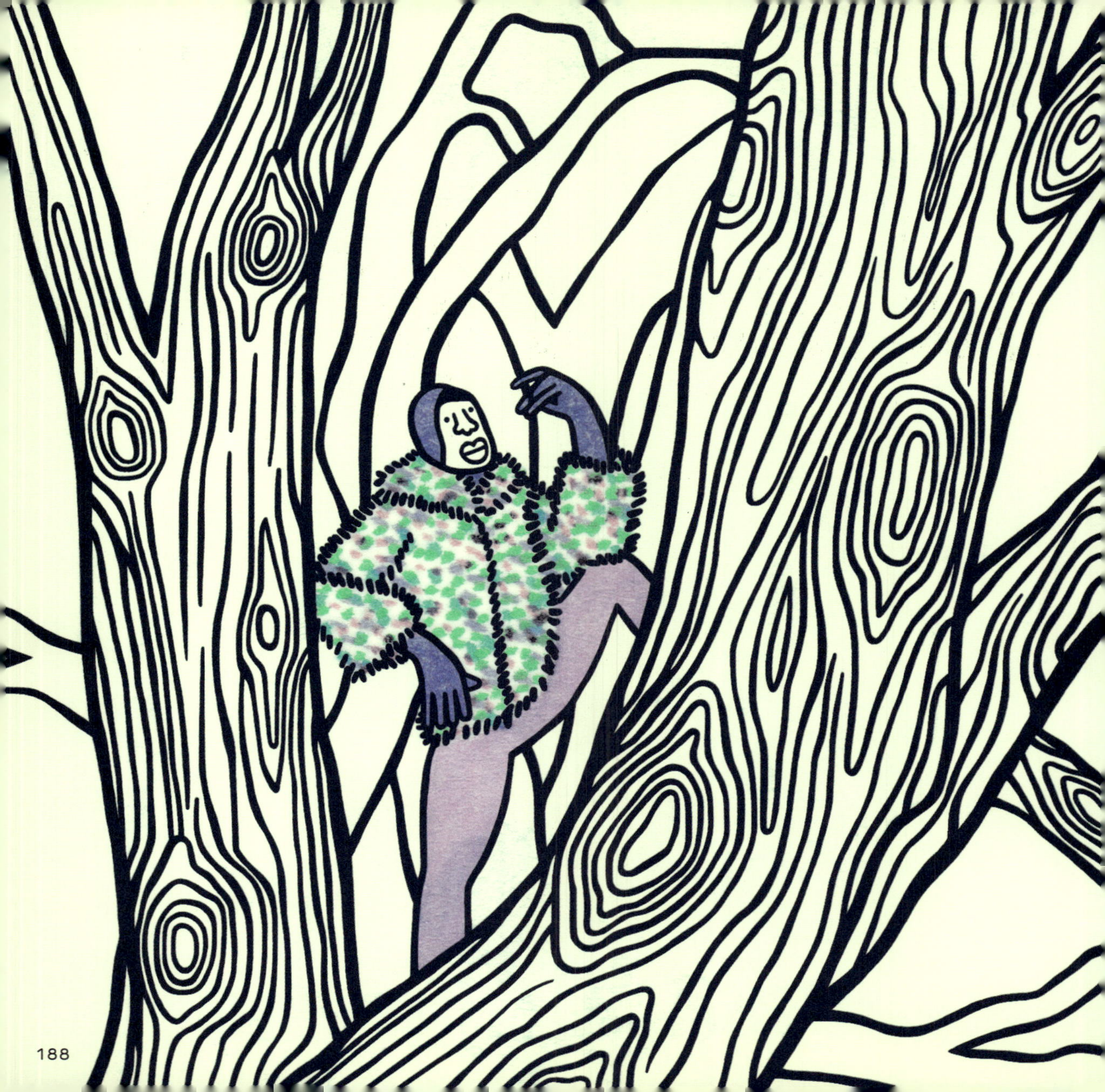

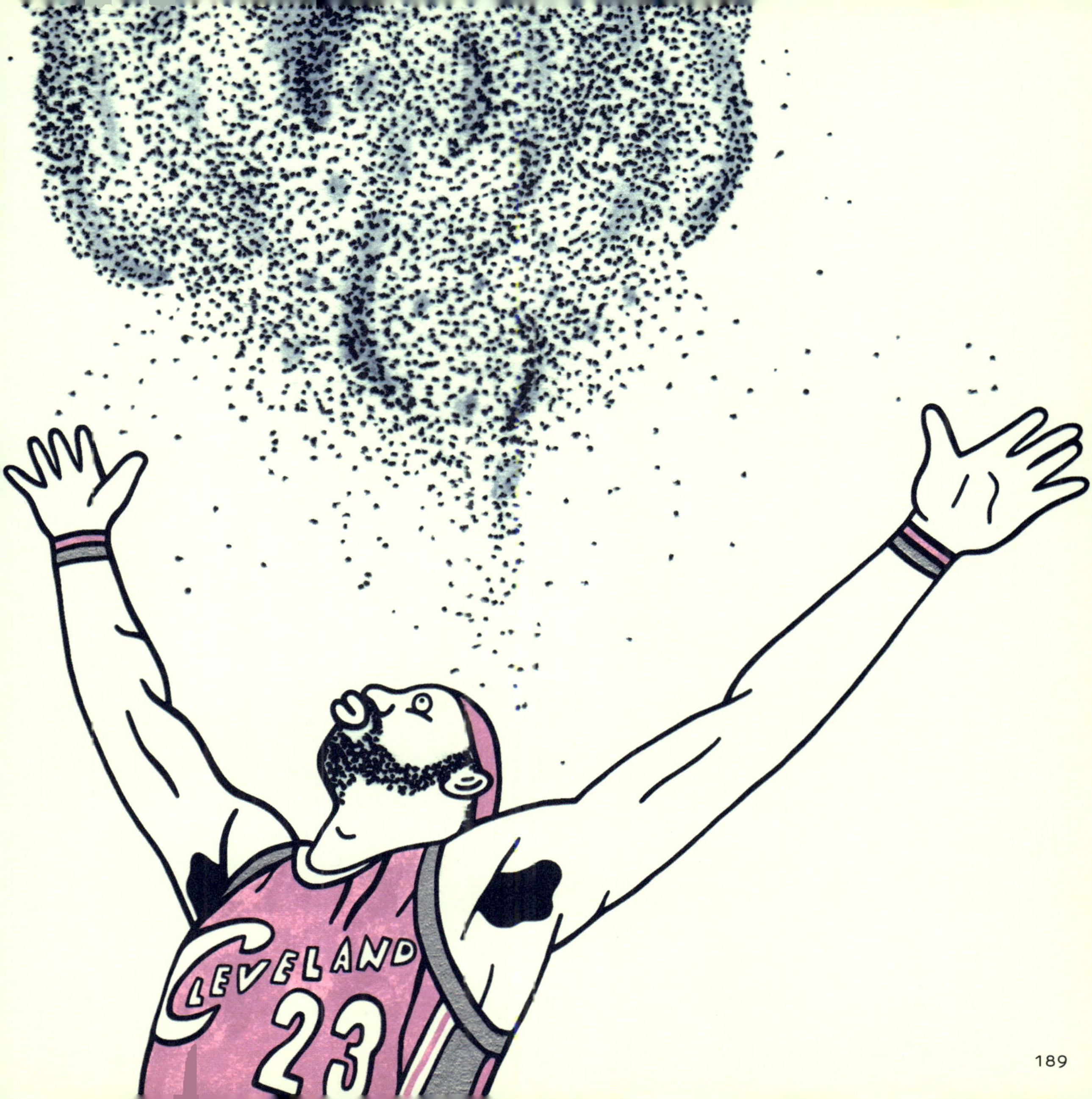
CLEVELAND
23

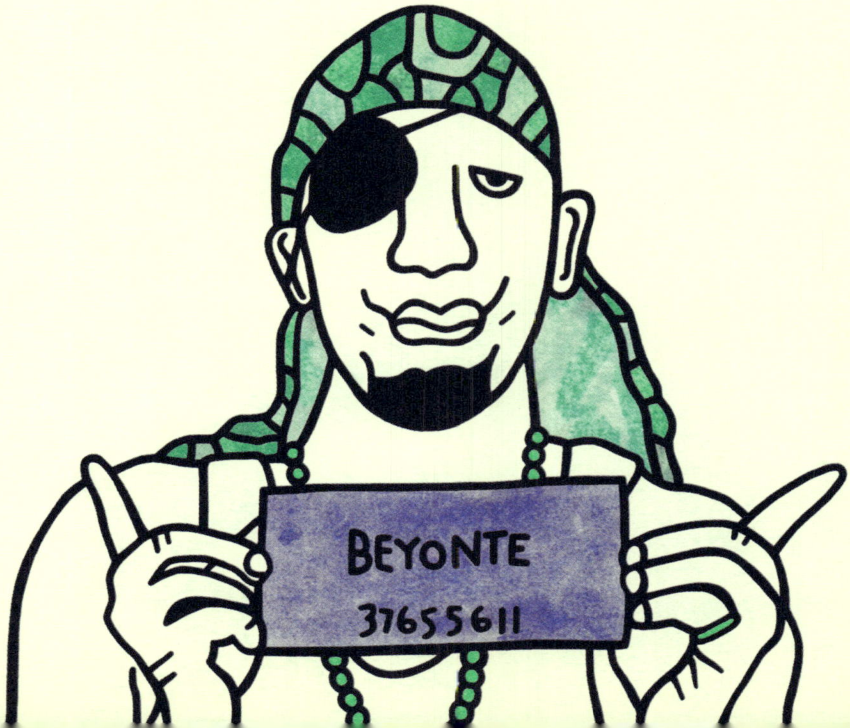
BEYONTE
37655611

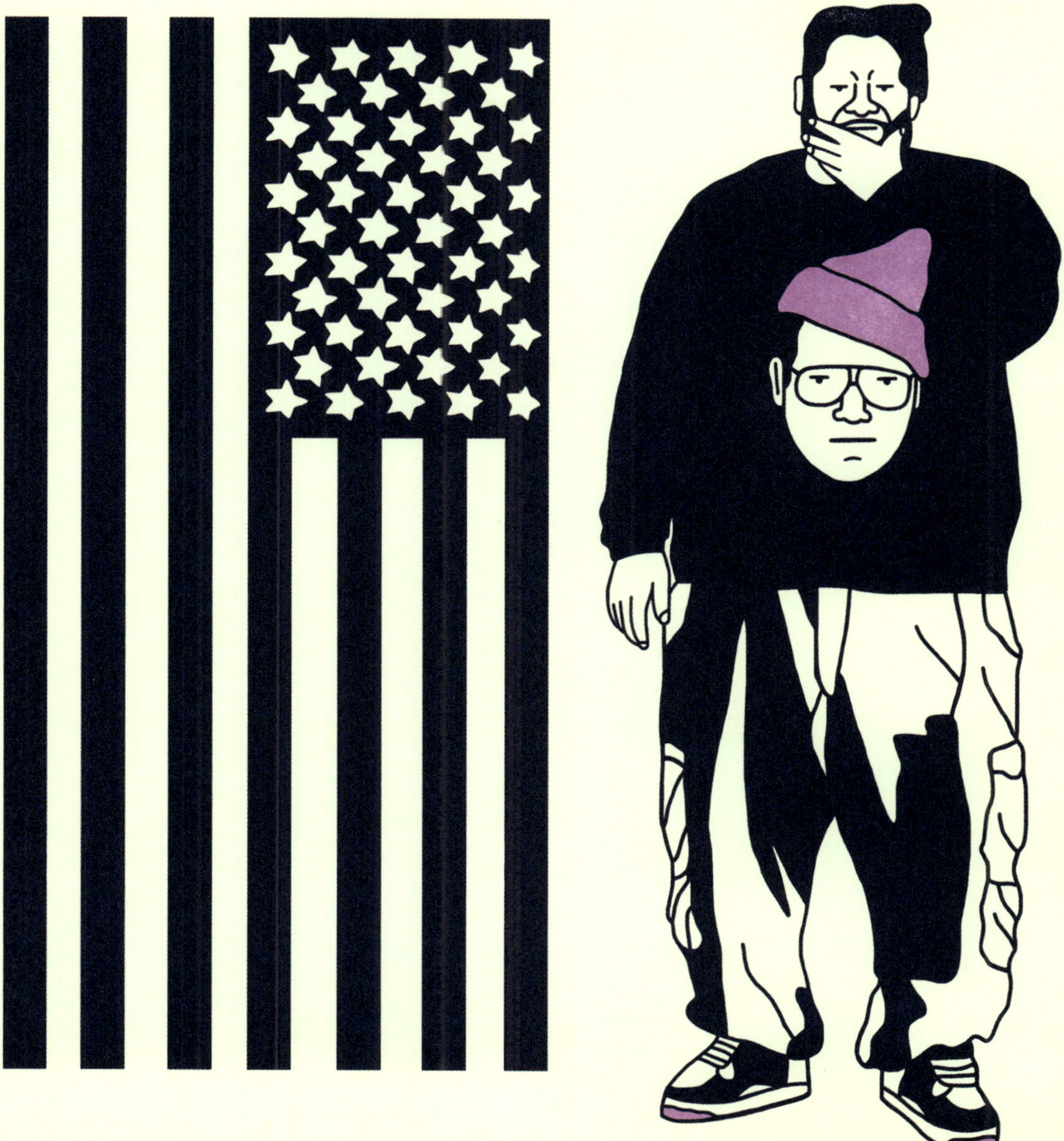

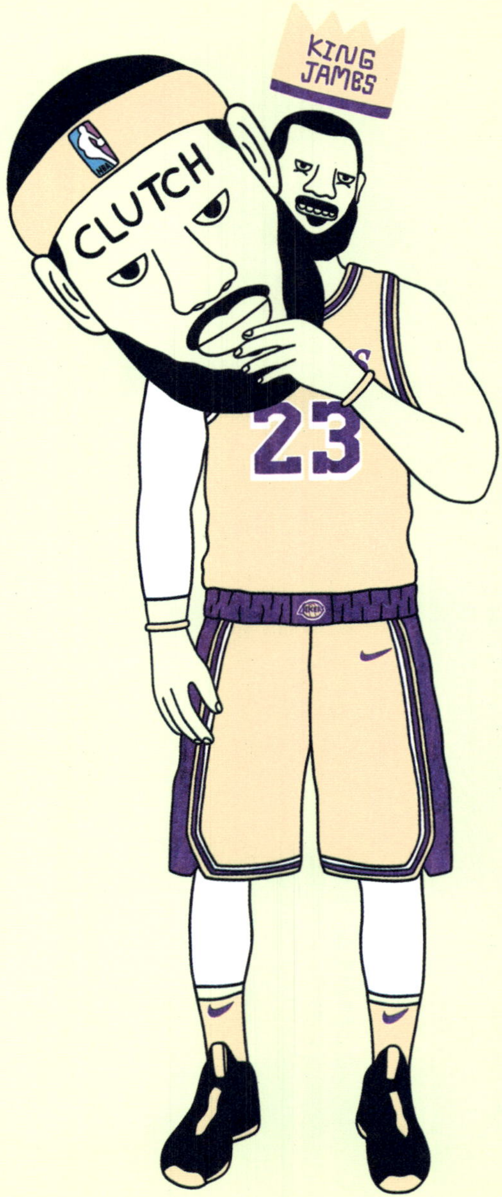
KING JAMES
CLUTCH
23

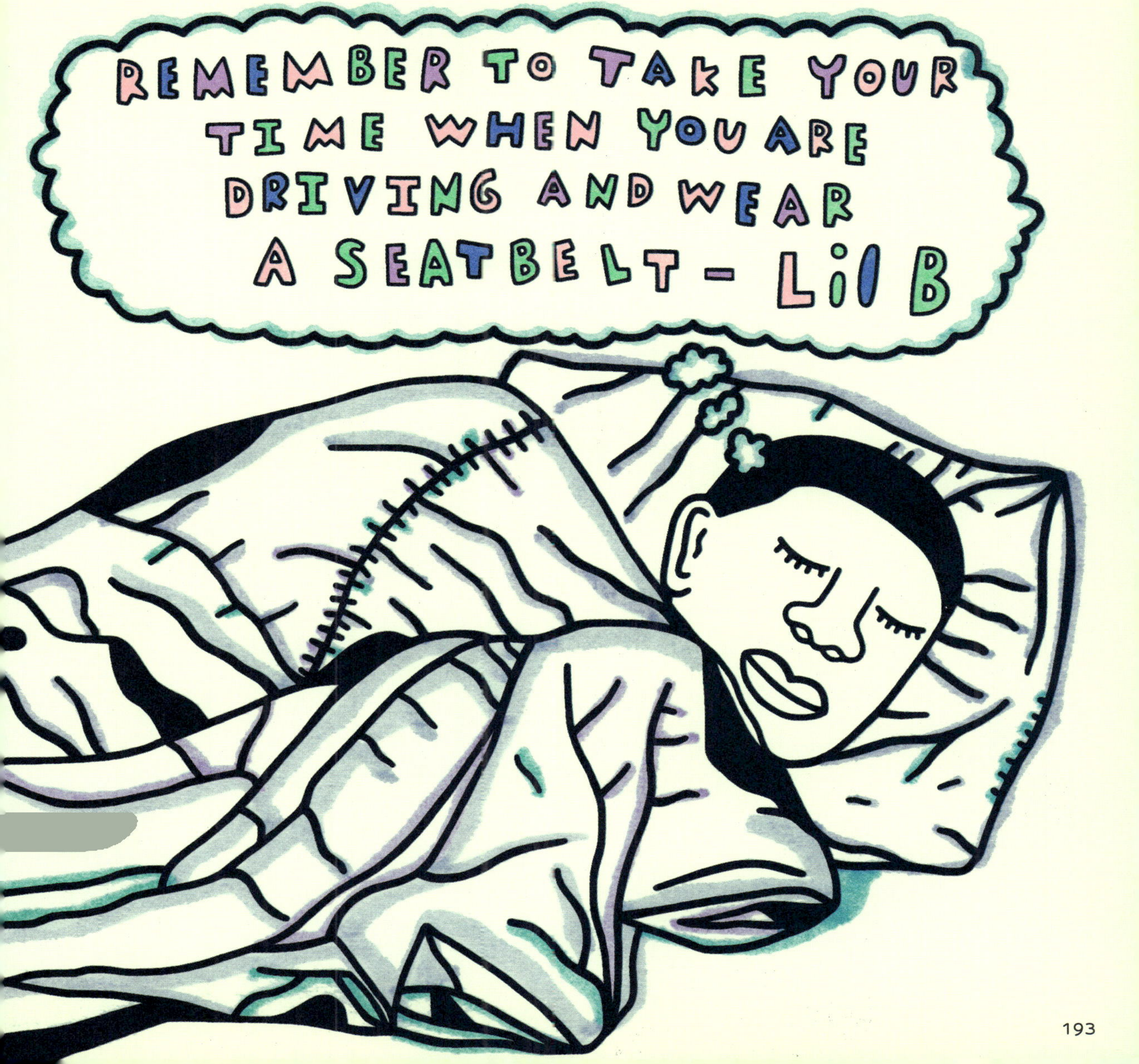
REMEMBER TO TAKE YOUR TIME WHEN YOU ARE DRIVING AND WEAR A SEATBELT - Lil B

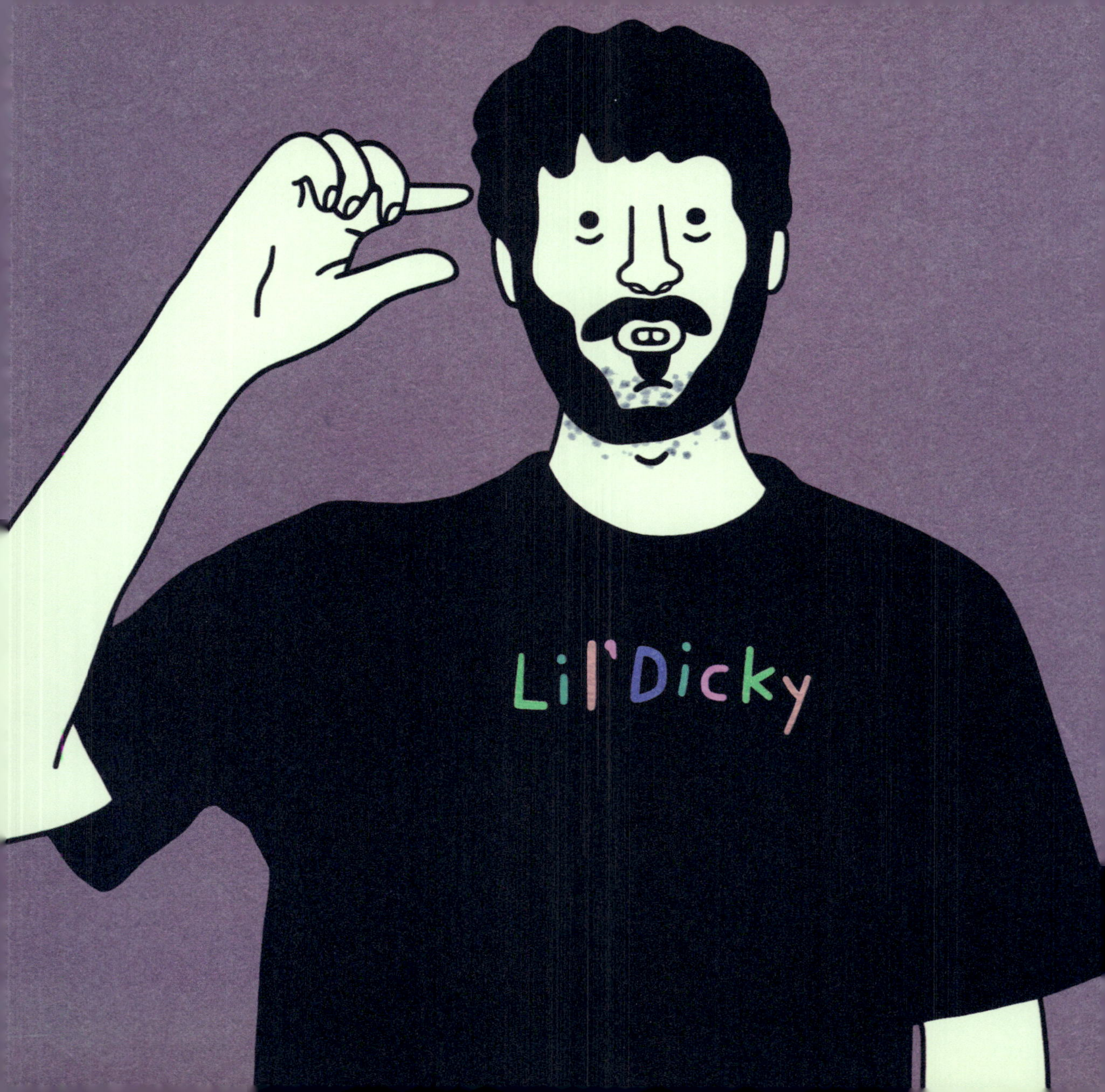
Lil'Dicky

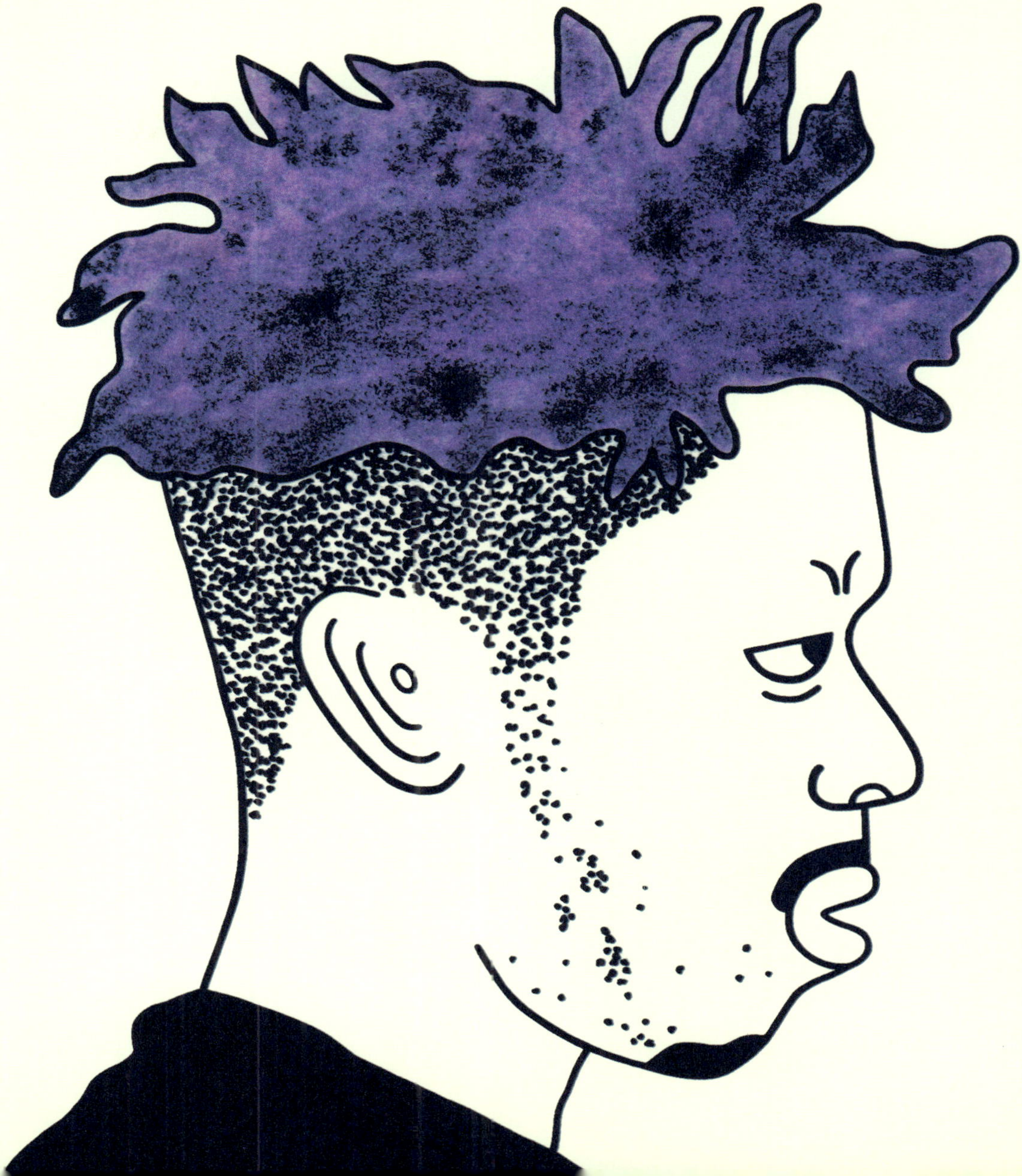

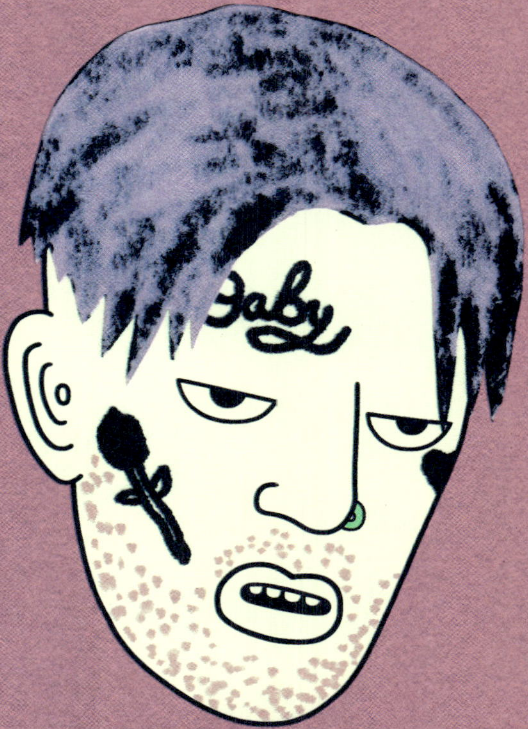
Baby

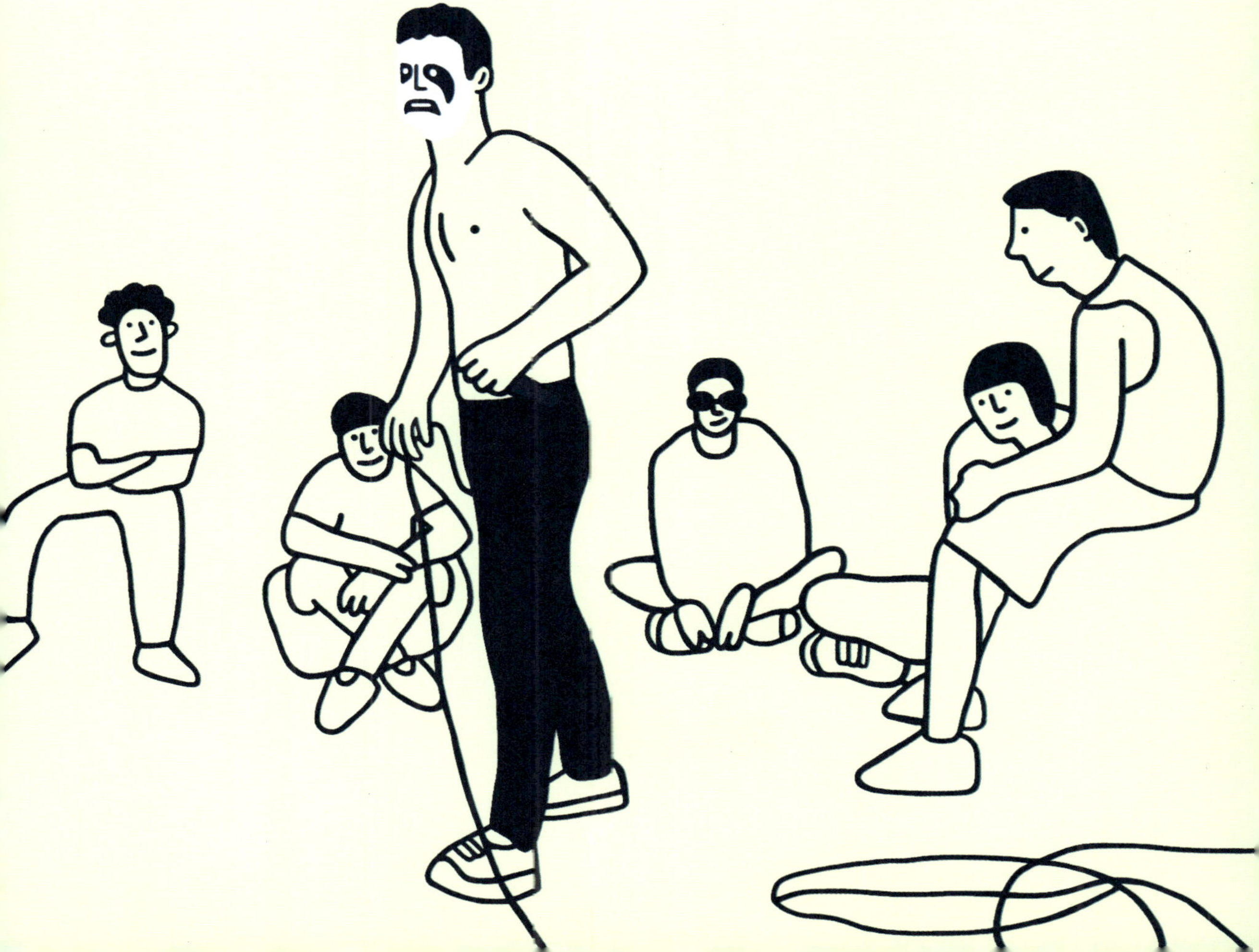

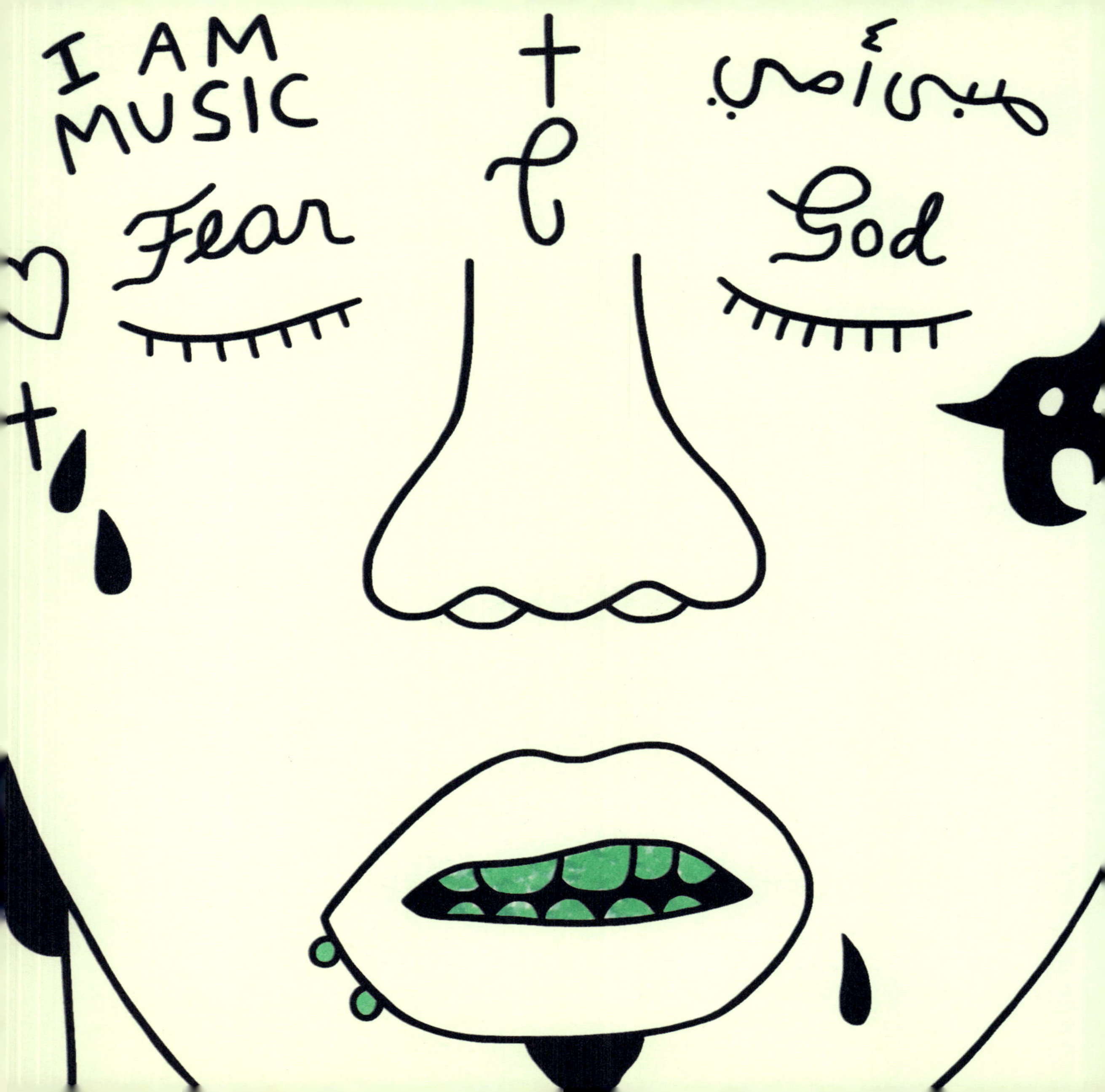
I AM
MUSIC
Fear
God

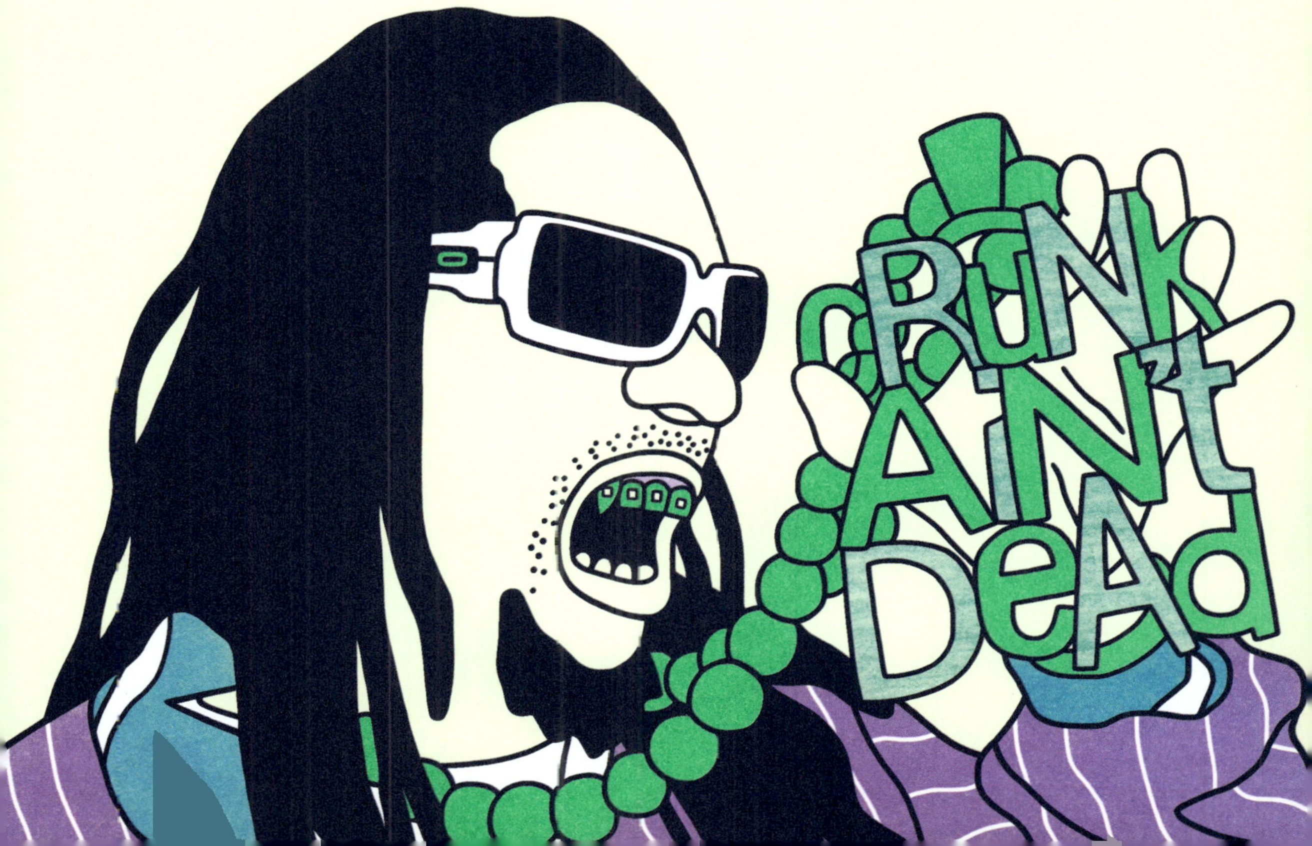
Crunk Ain't Dead

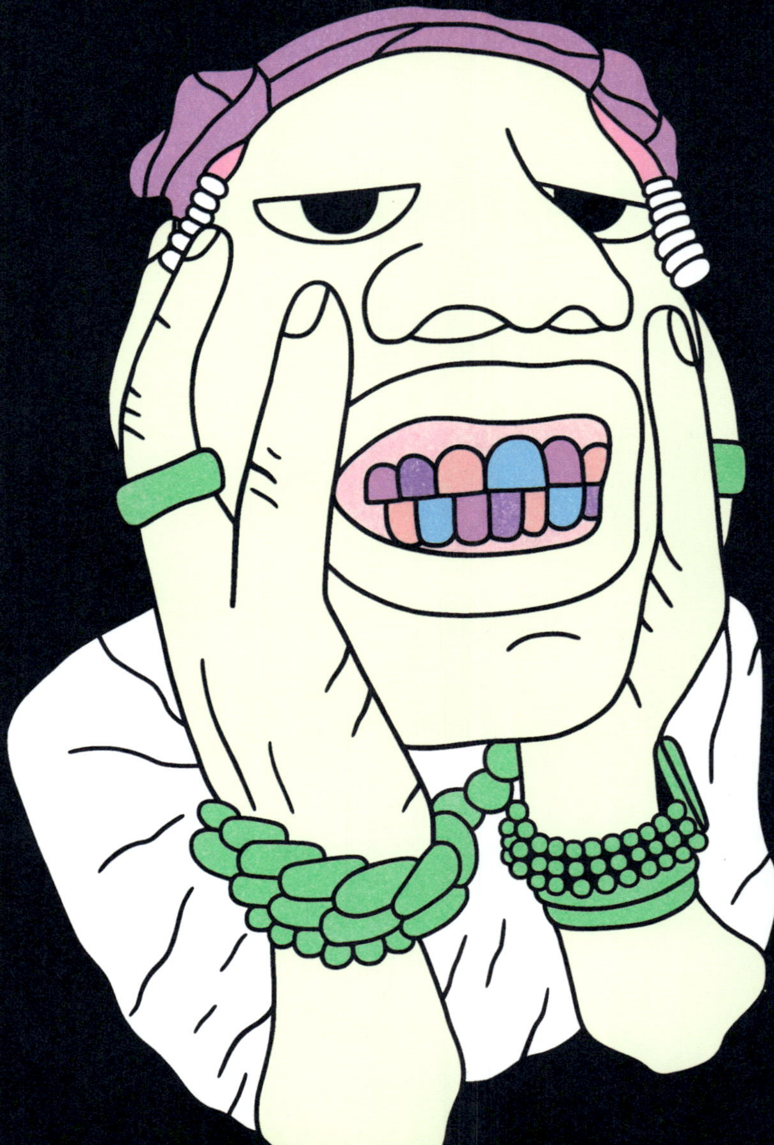

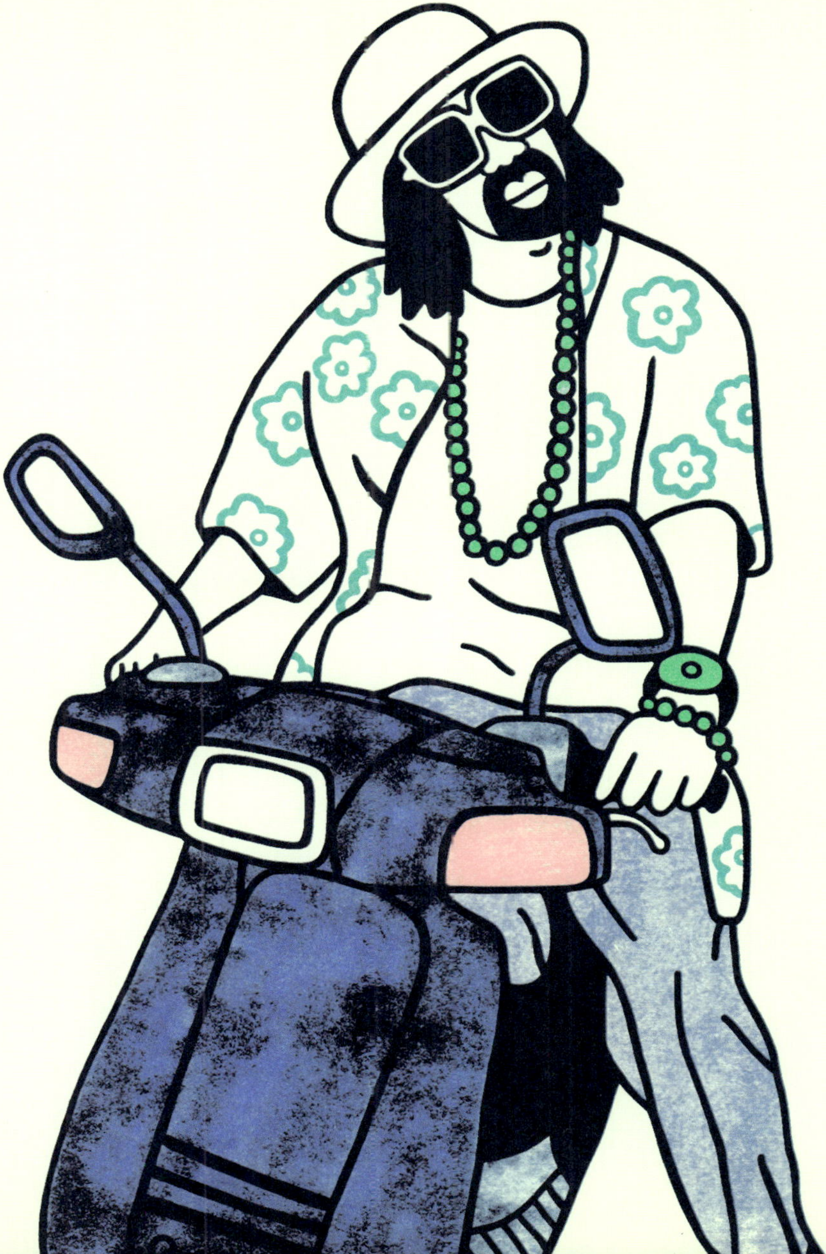

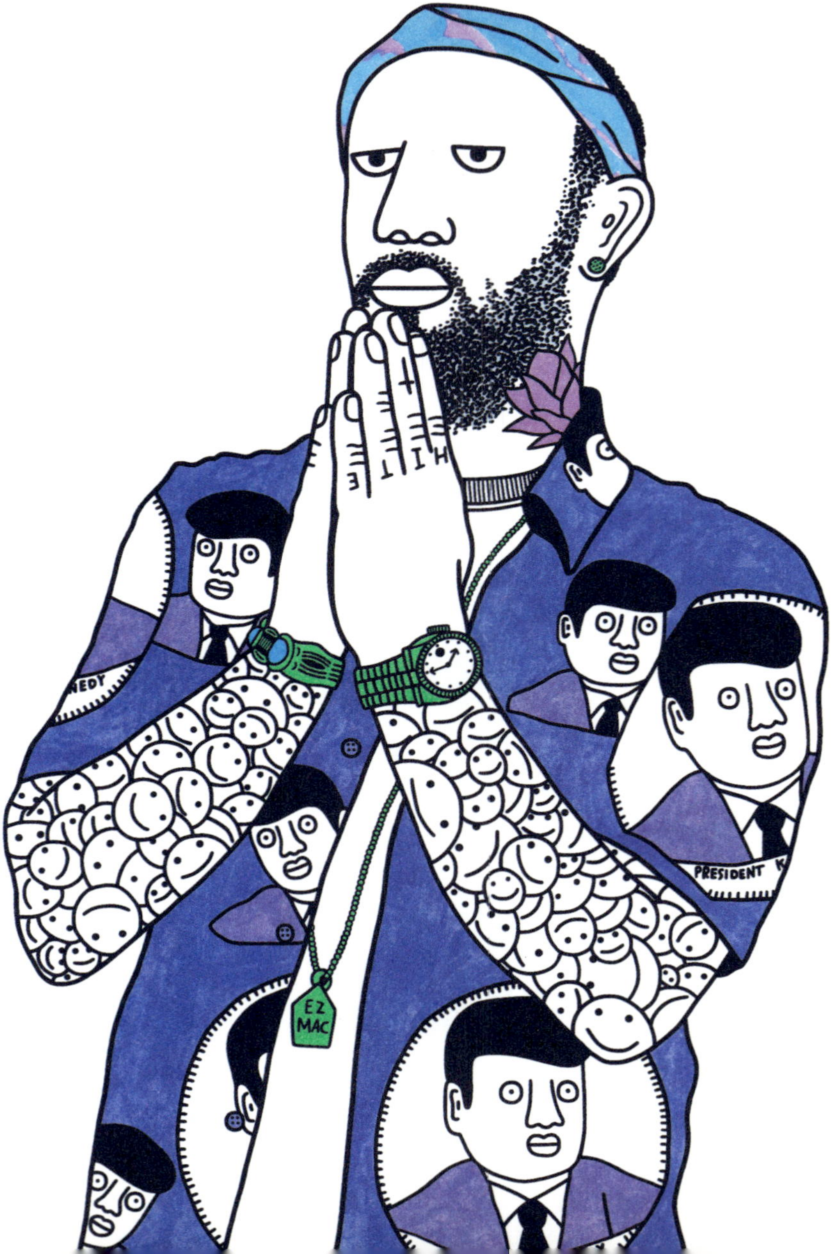
NEDY
PRESIDENT K
EZ MAC

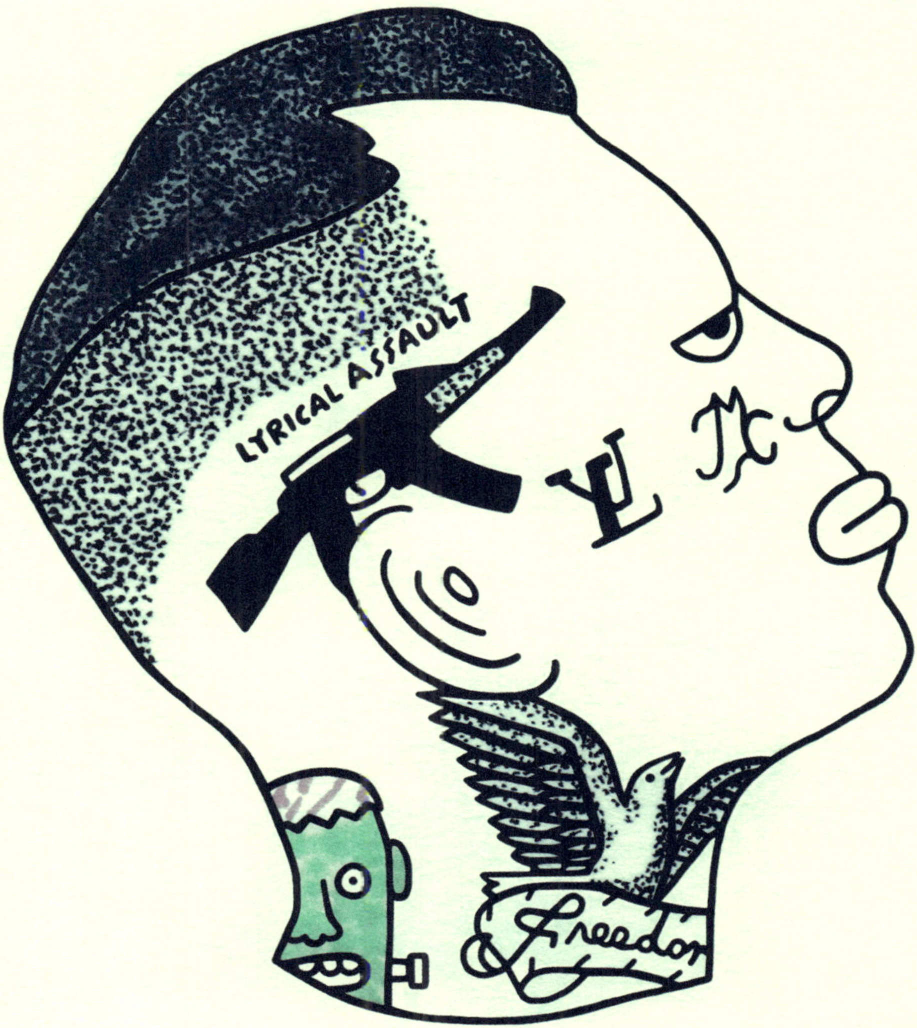
LYRICAL ASSAULT

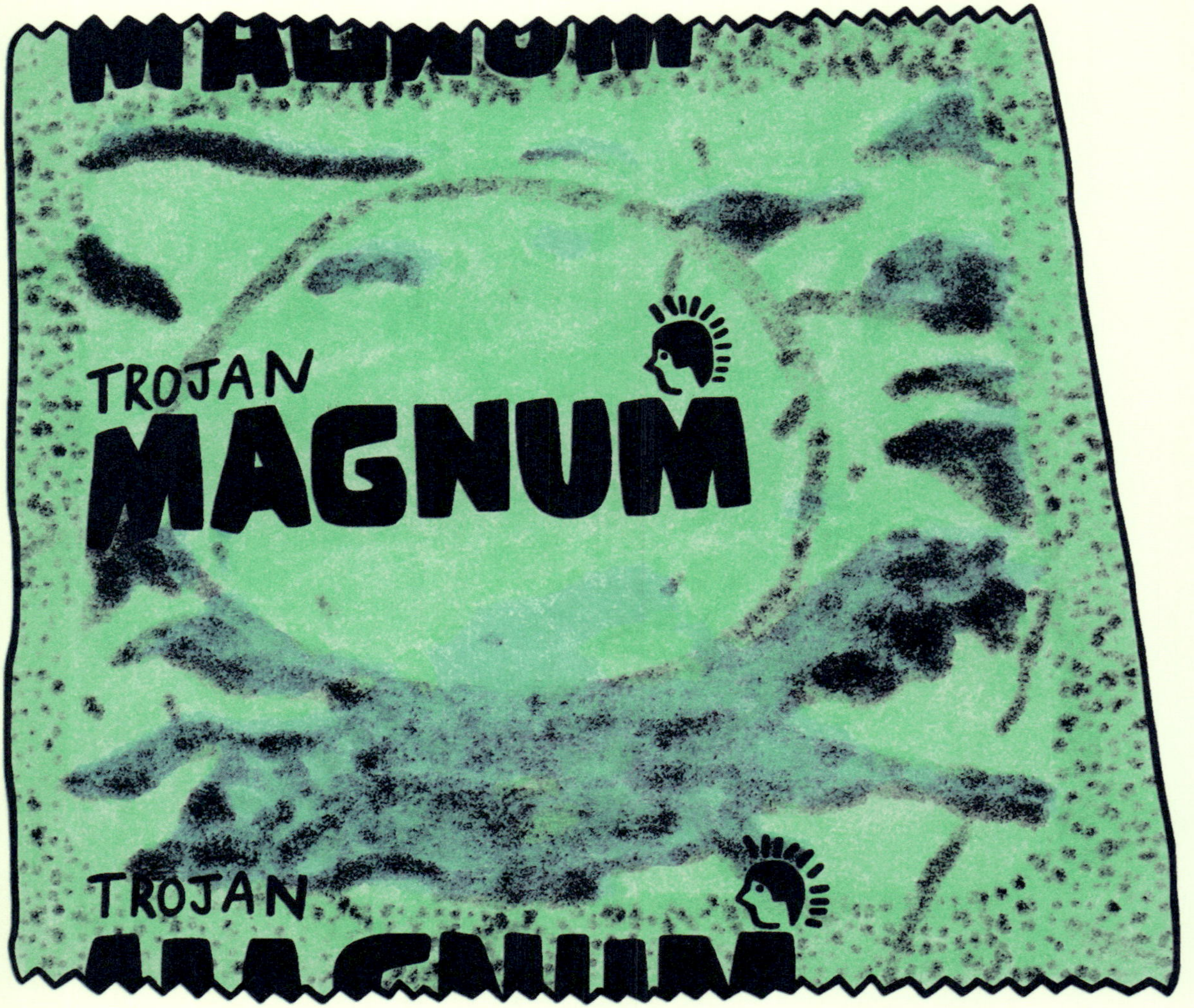
TROJAN
MAGNUM

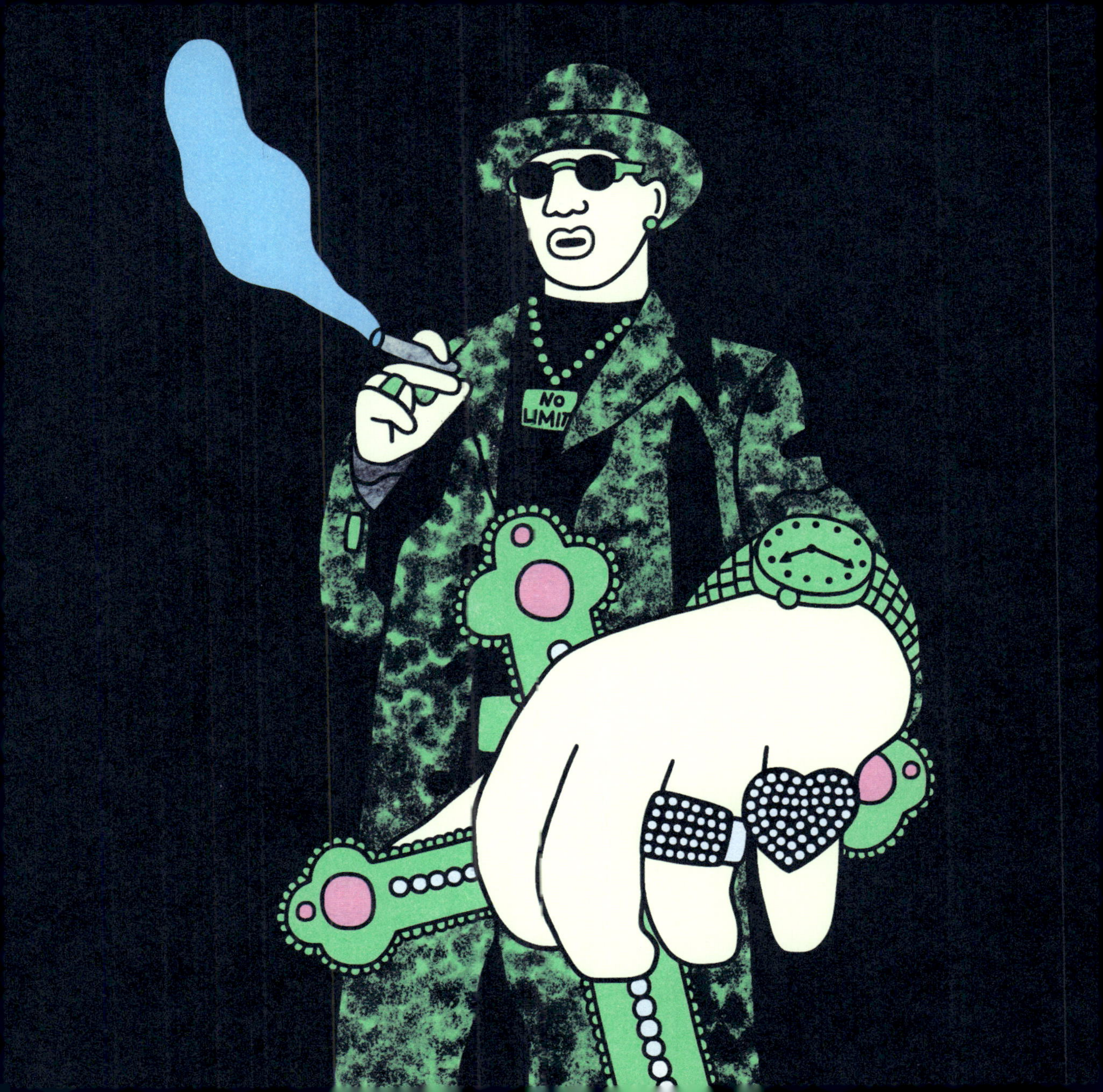
NO
LIMIT

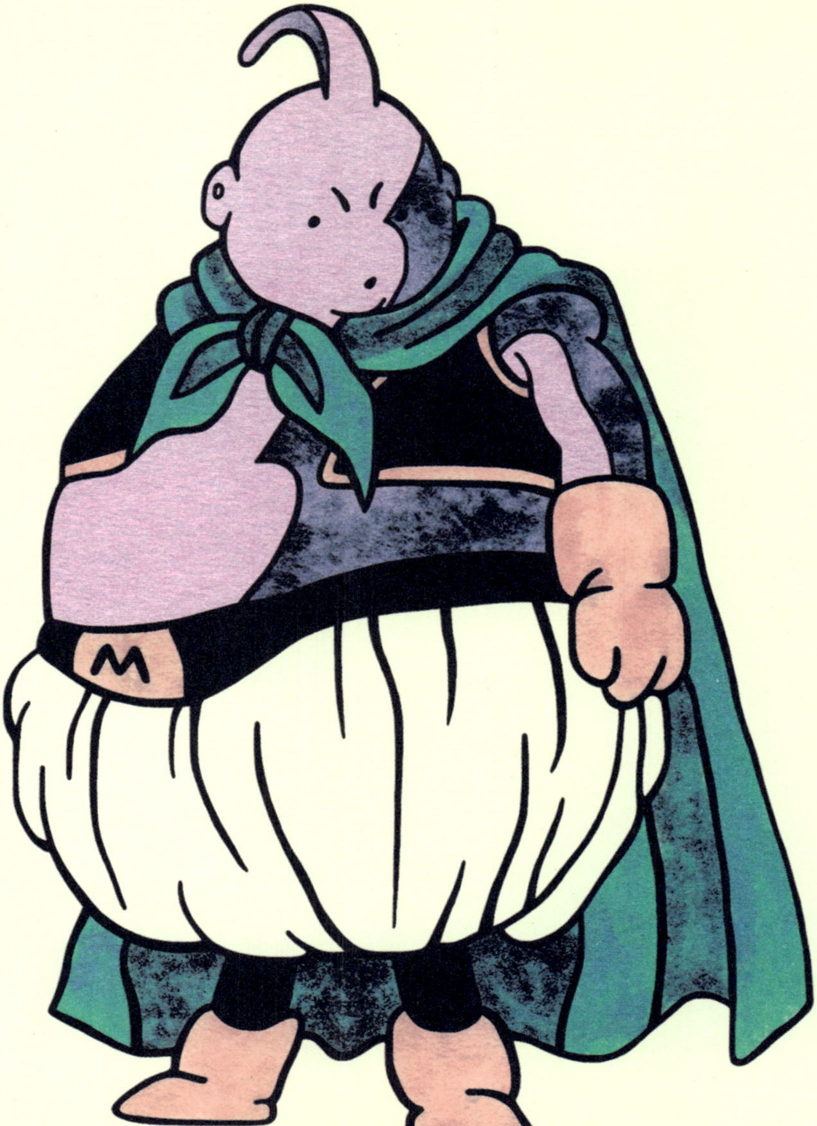
M

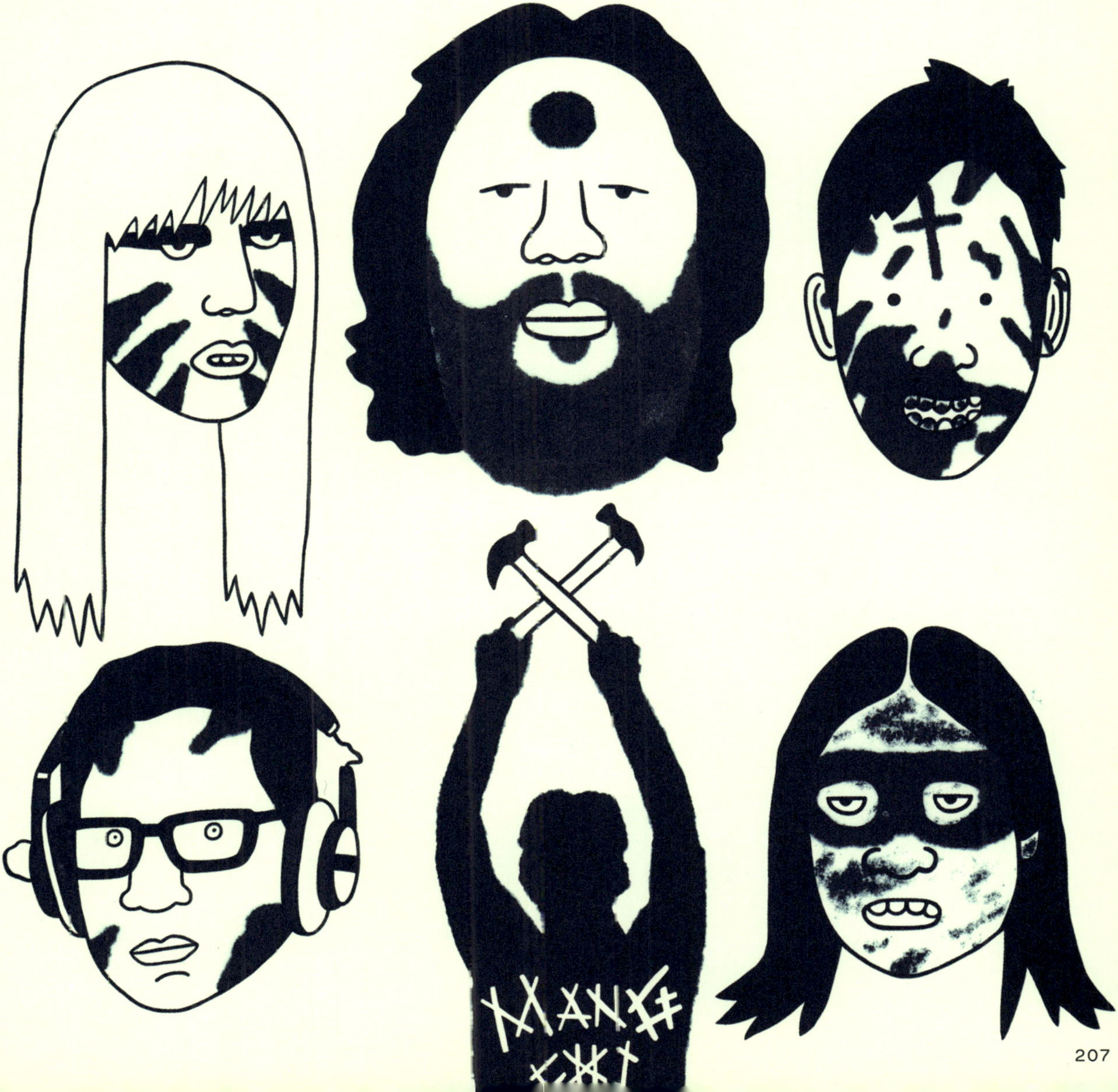

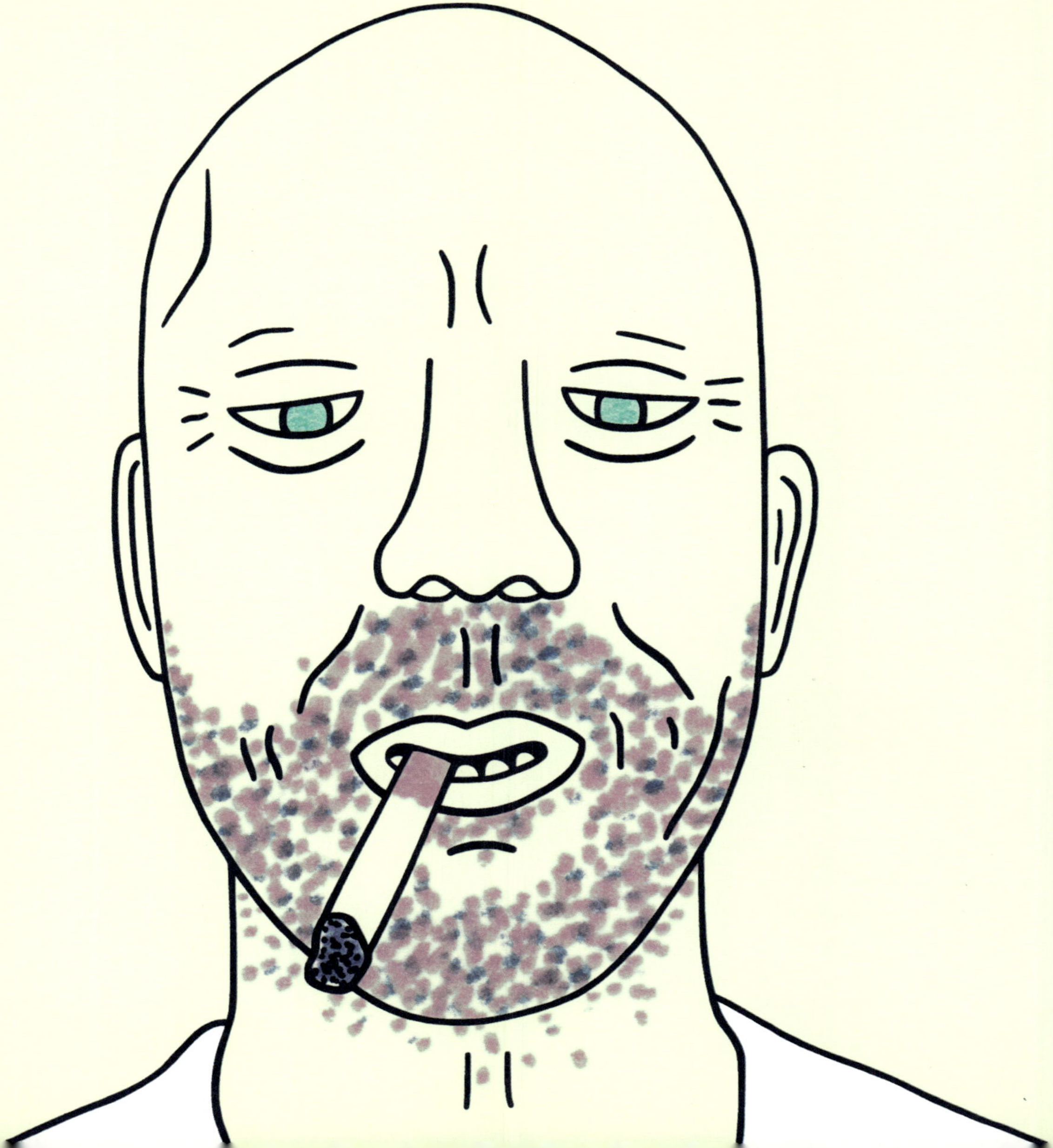

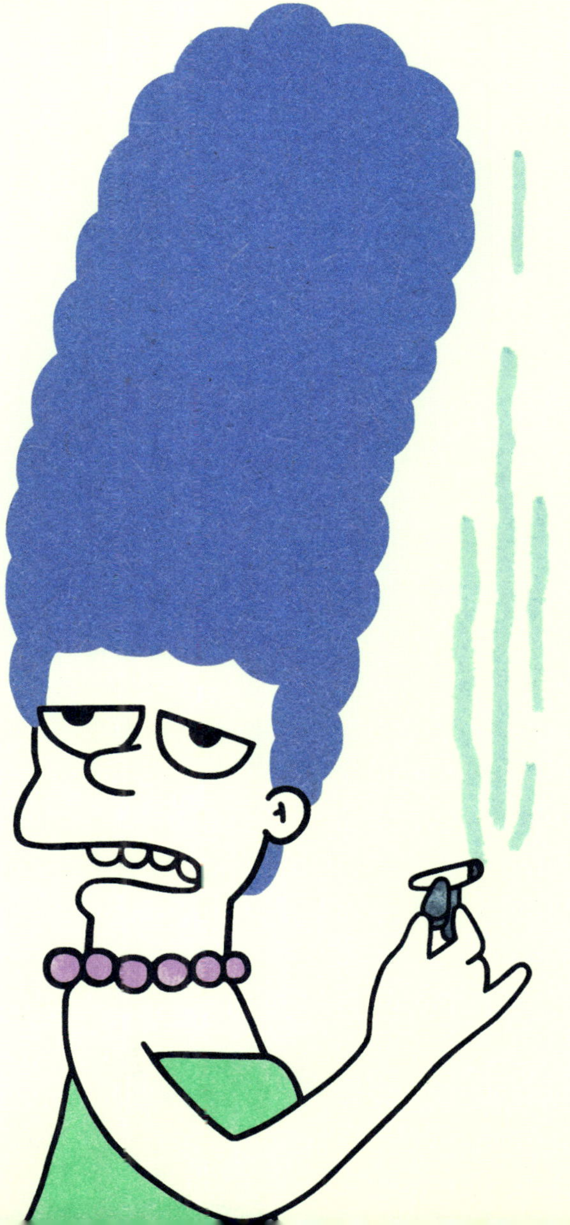

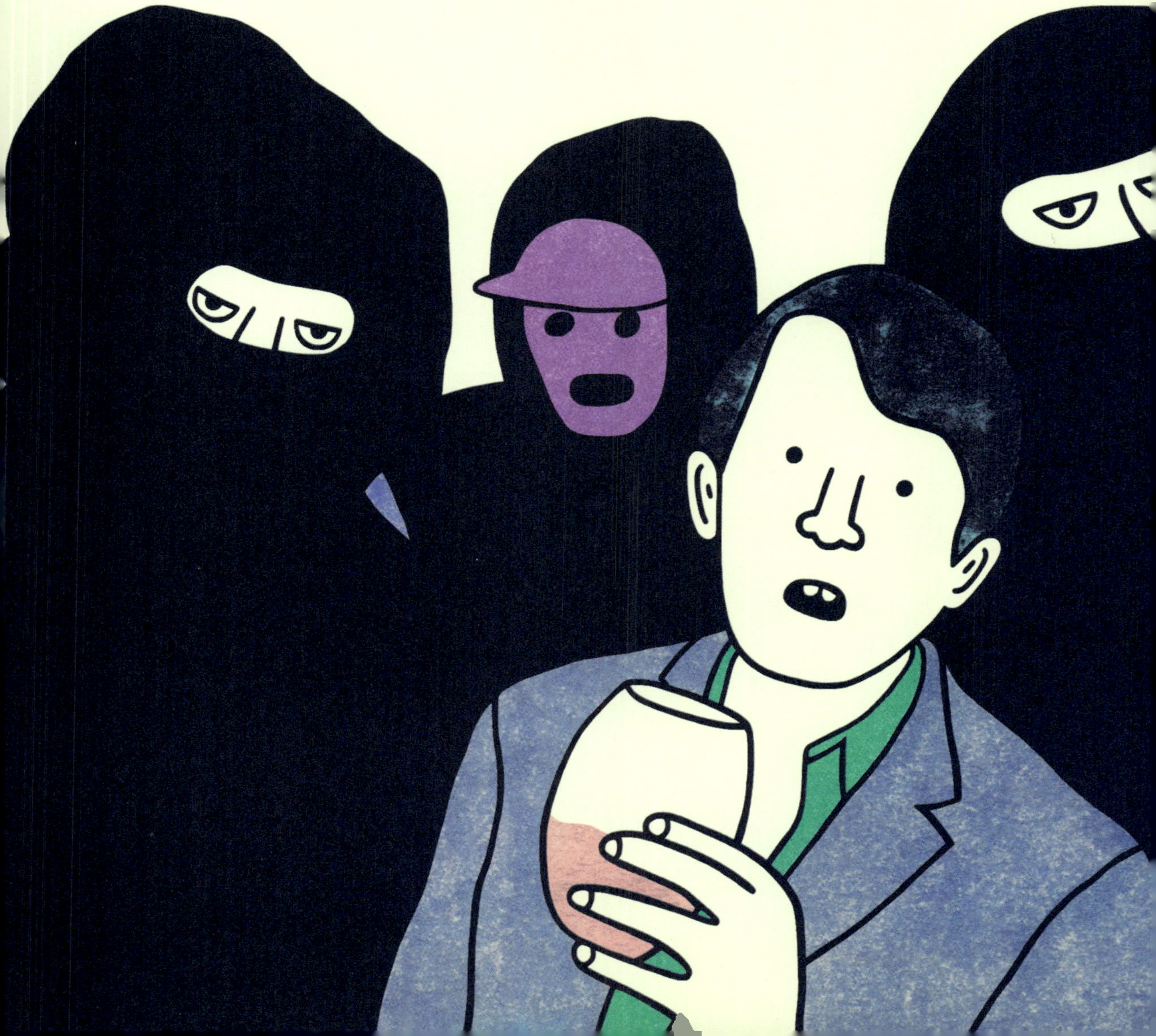

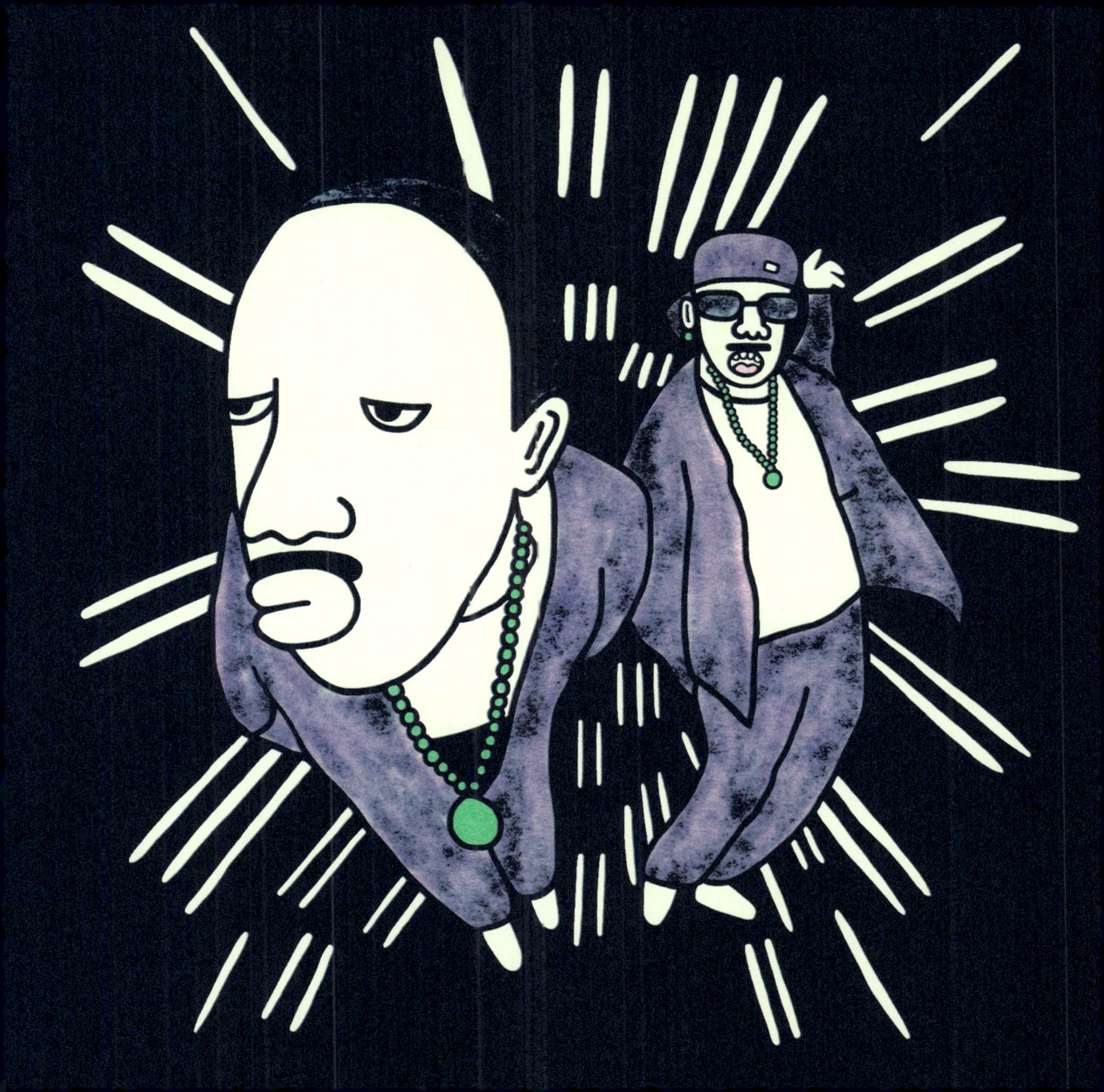

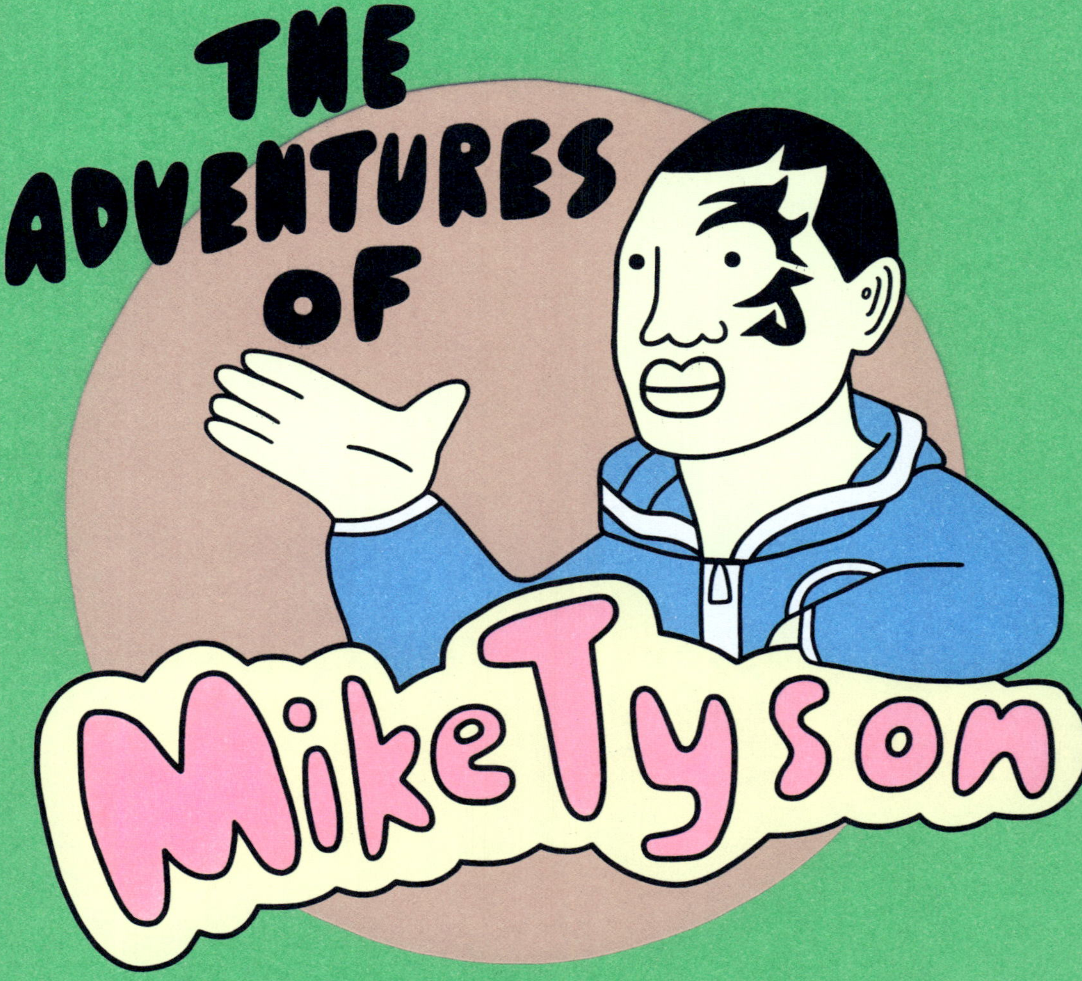
THE
ADVENTURES
OF
Mike Tyson

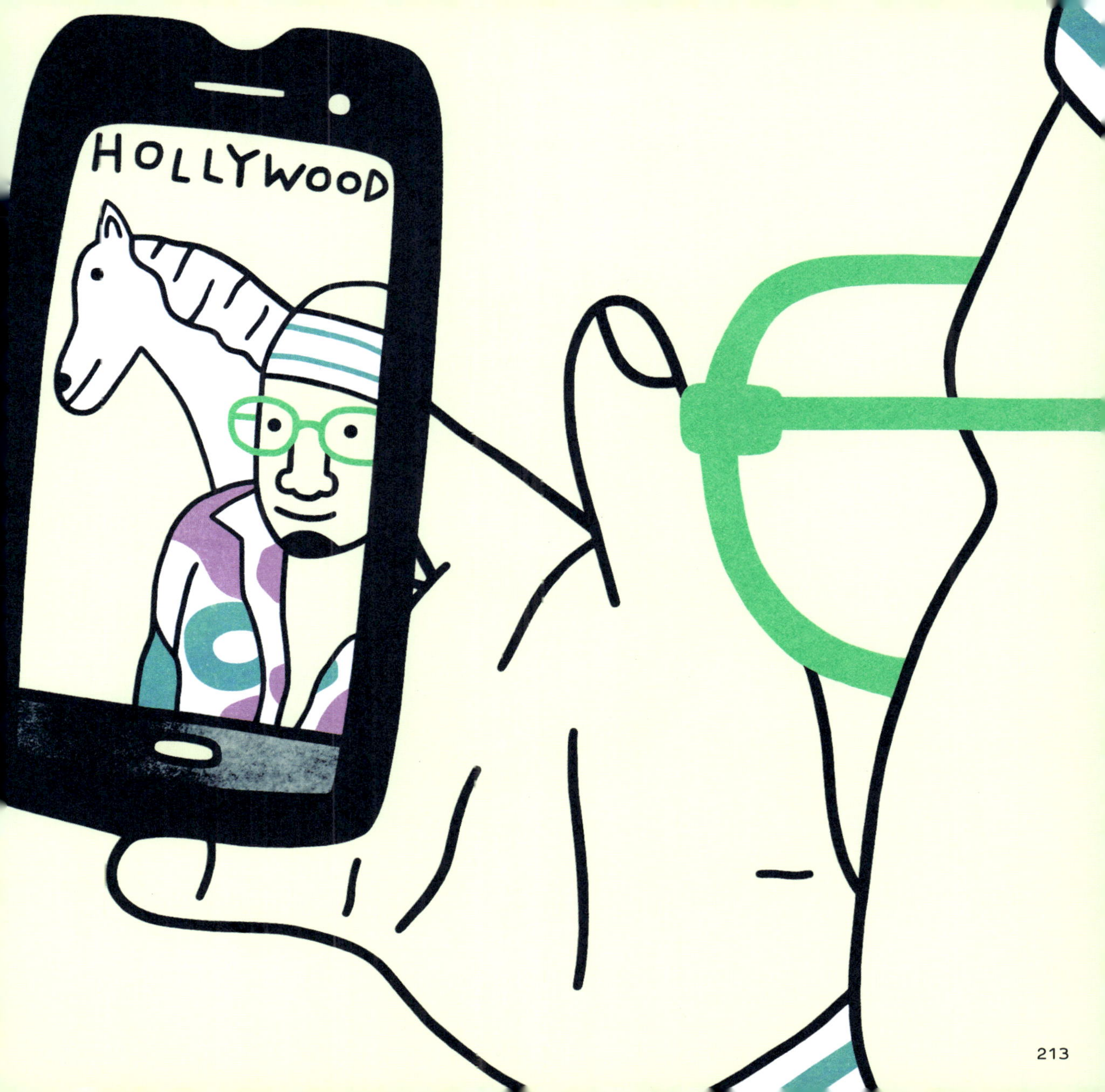
HOLLYWOOD

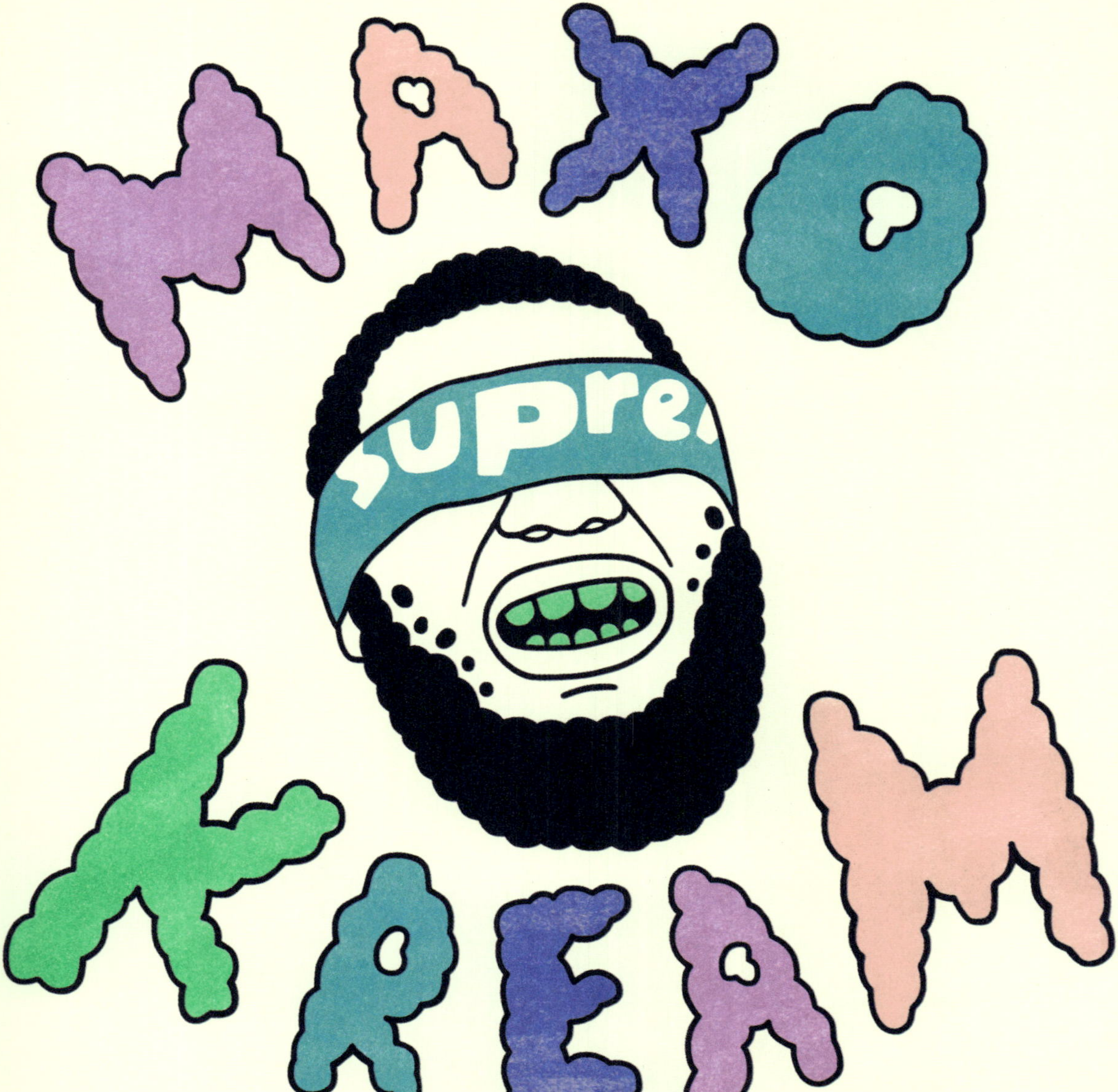
MAXO
supre
KREAM

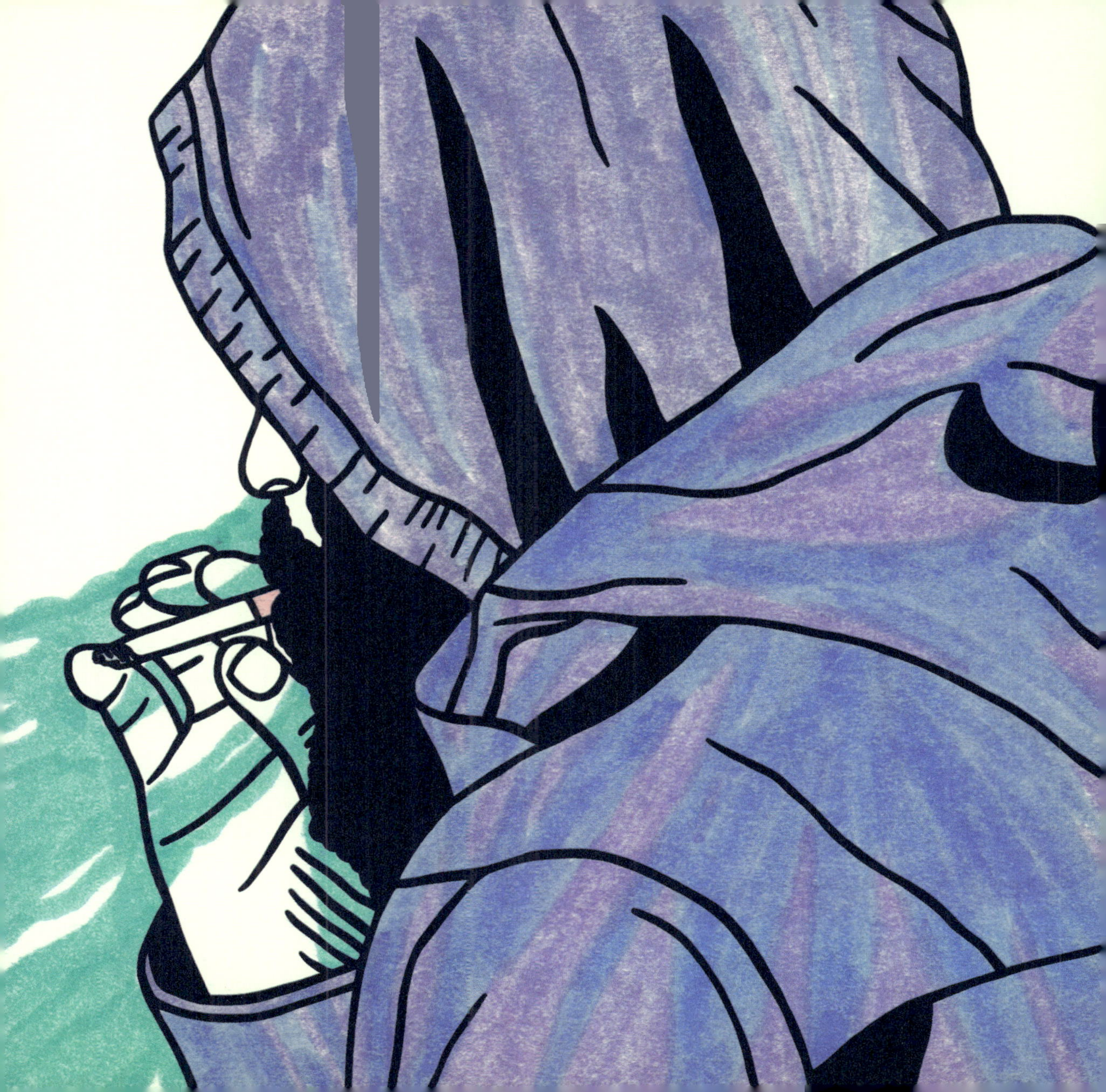

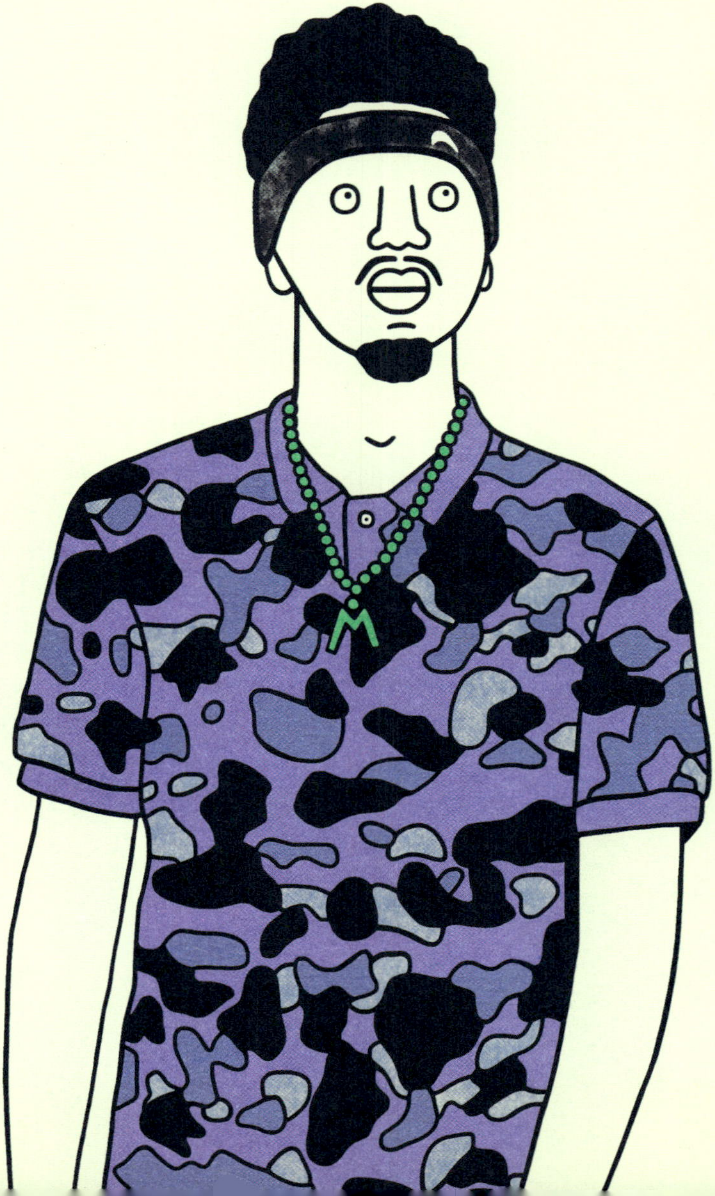
M

IF YOUNG METRO
DON'T TRUST U
I'M GON SHOOT

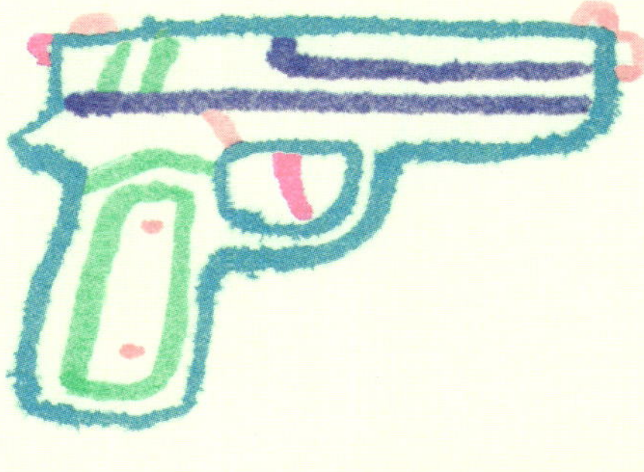

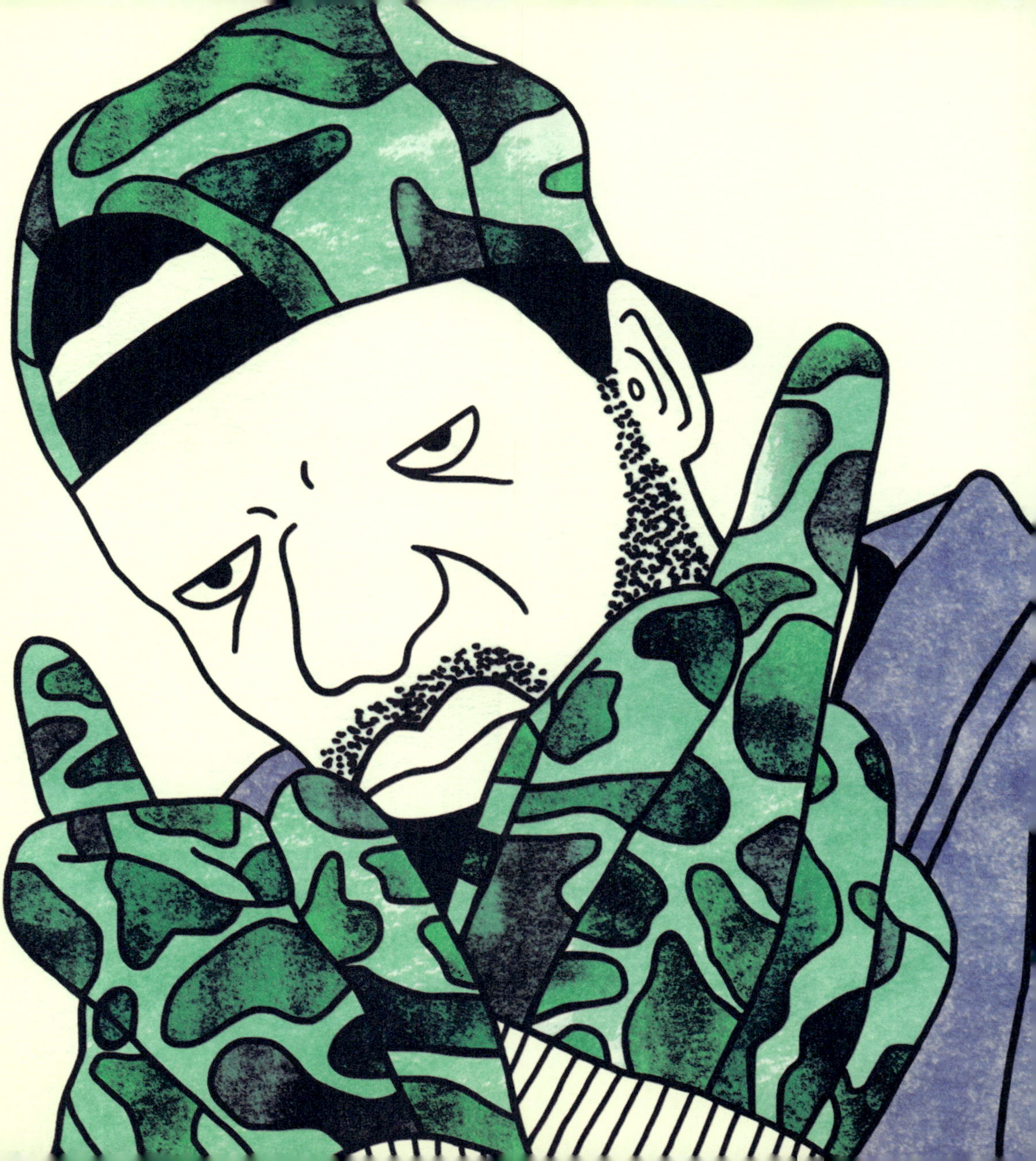

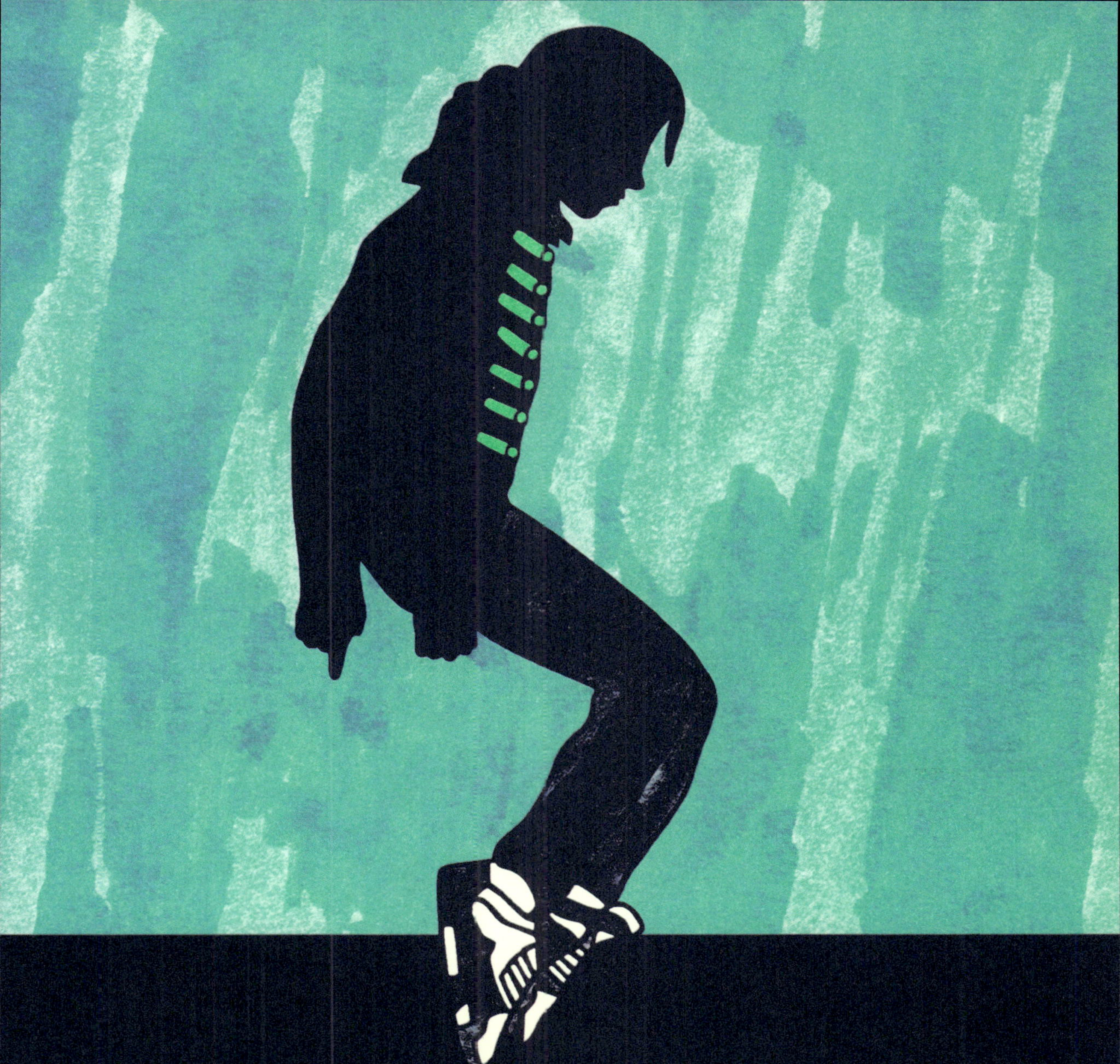

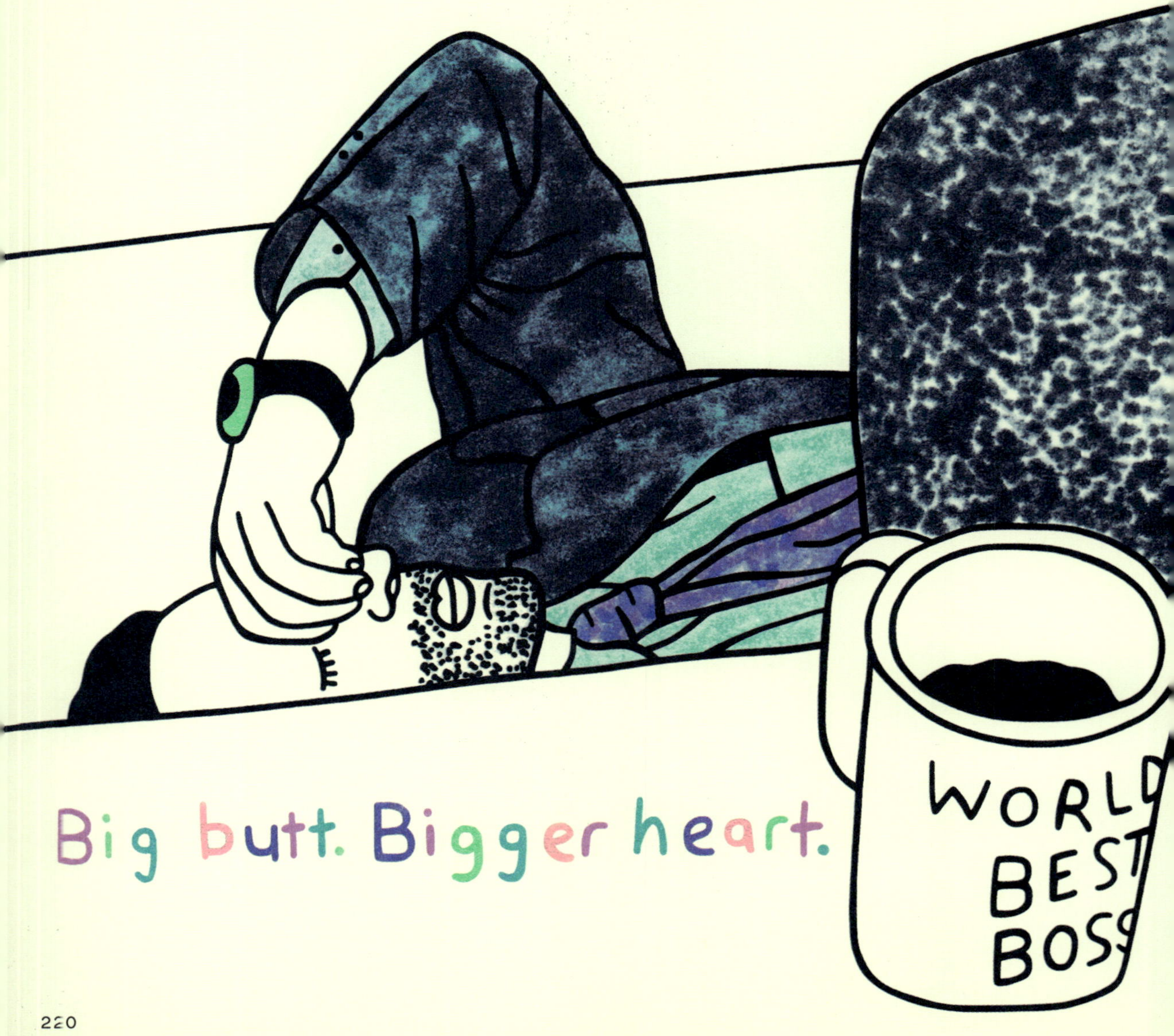

Big butt. Bigger heart.

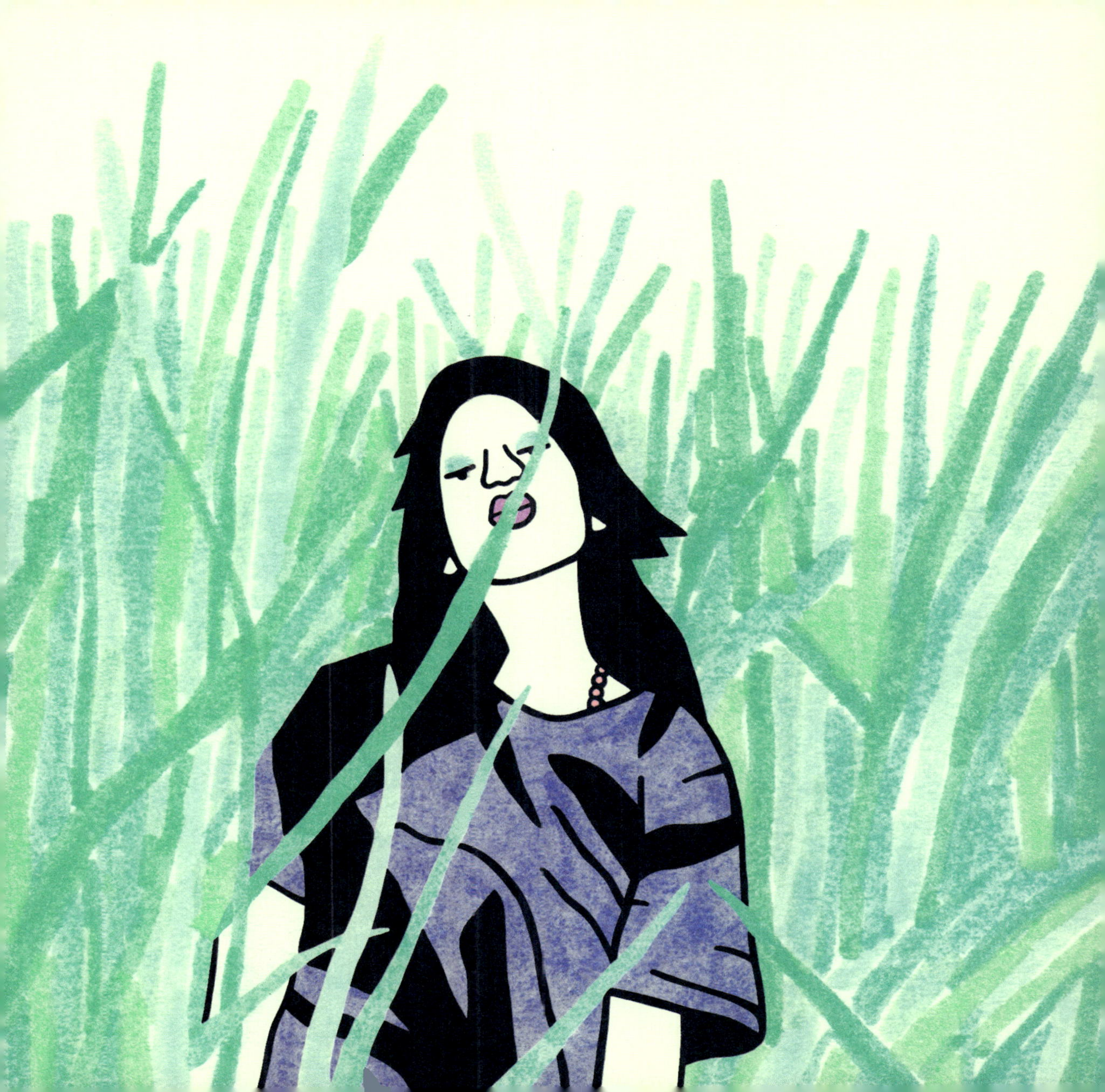

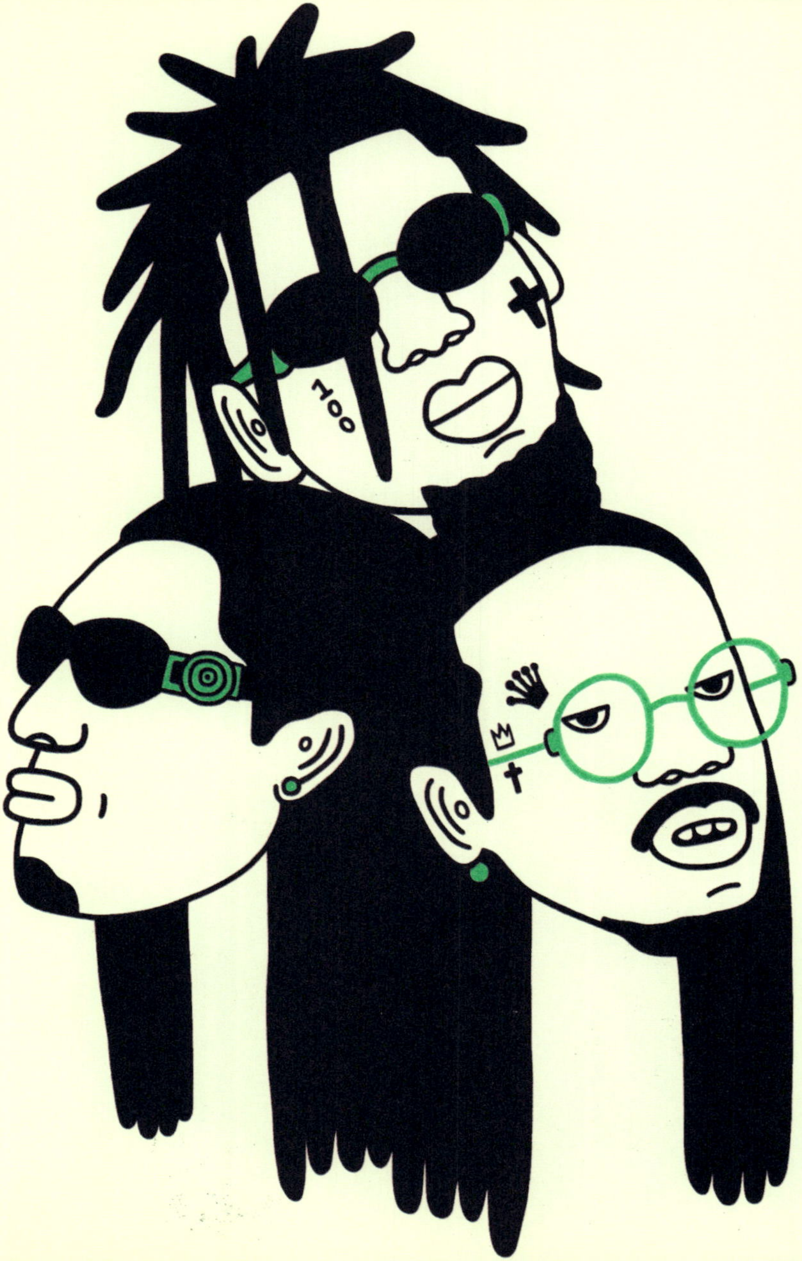

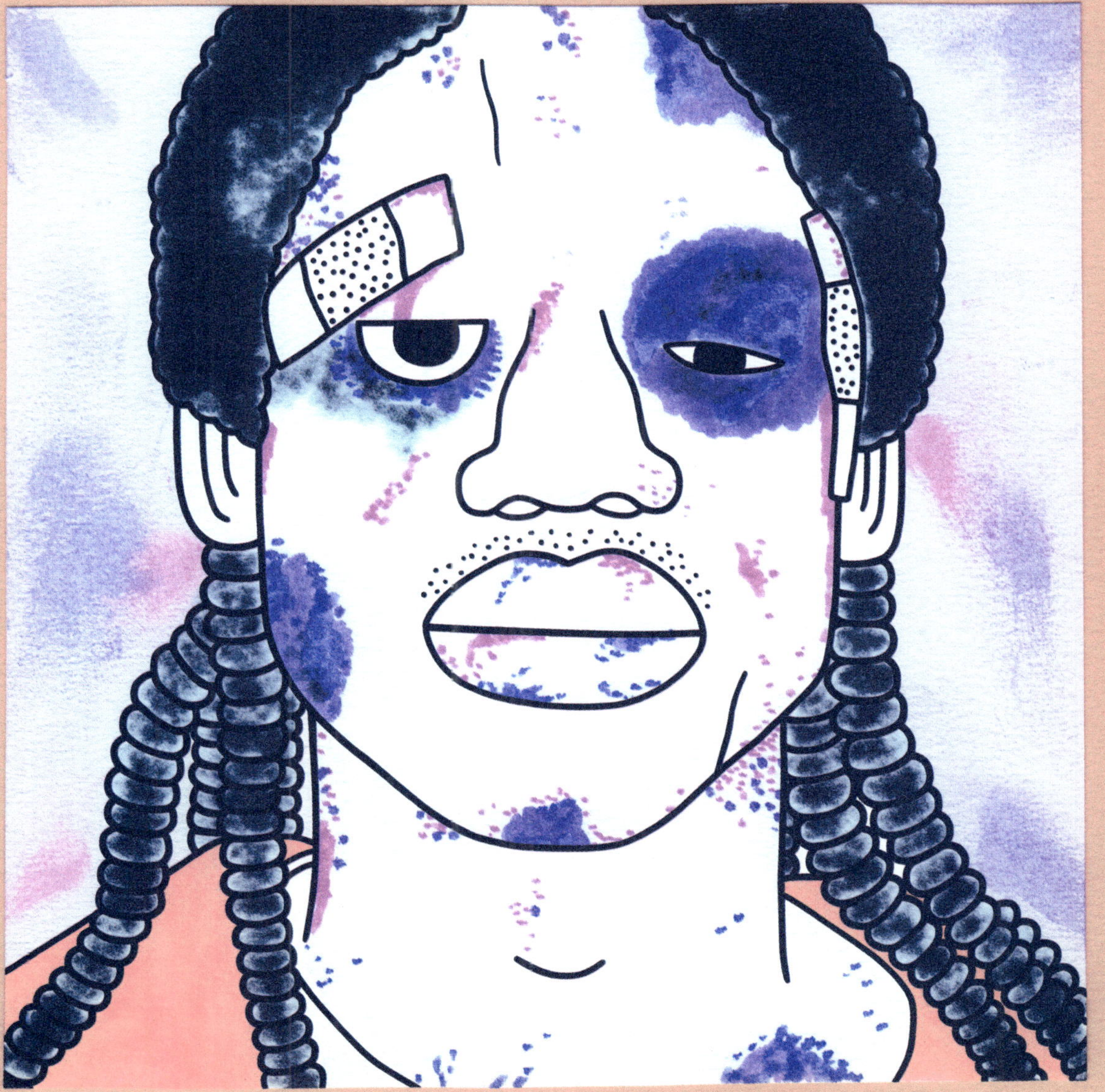

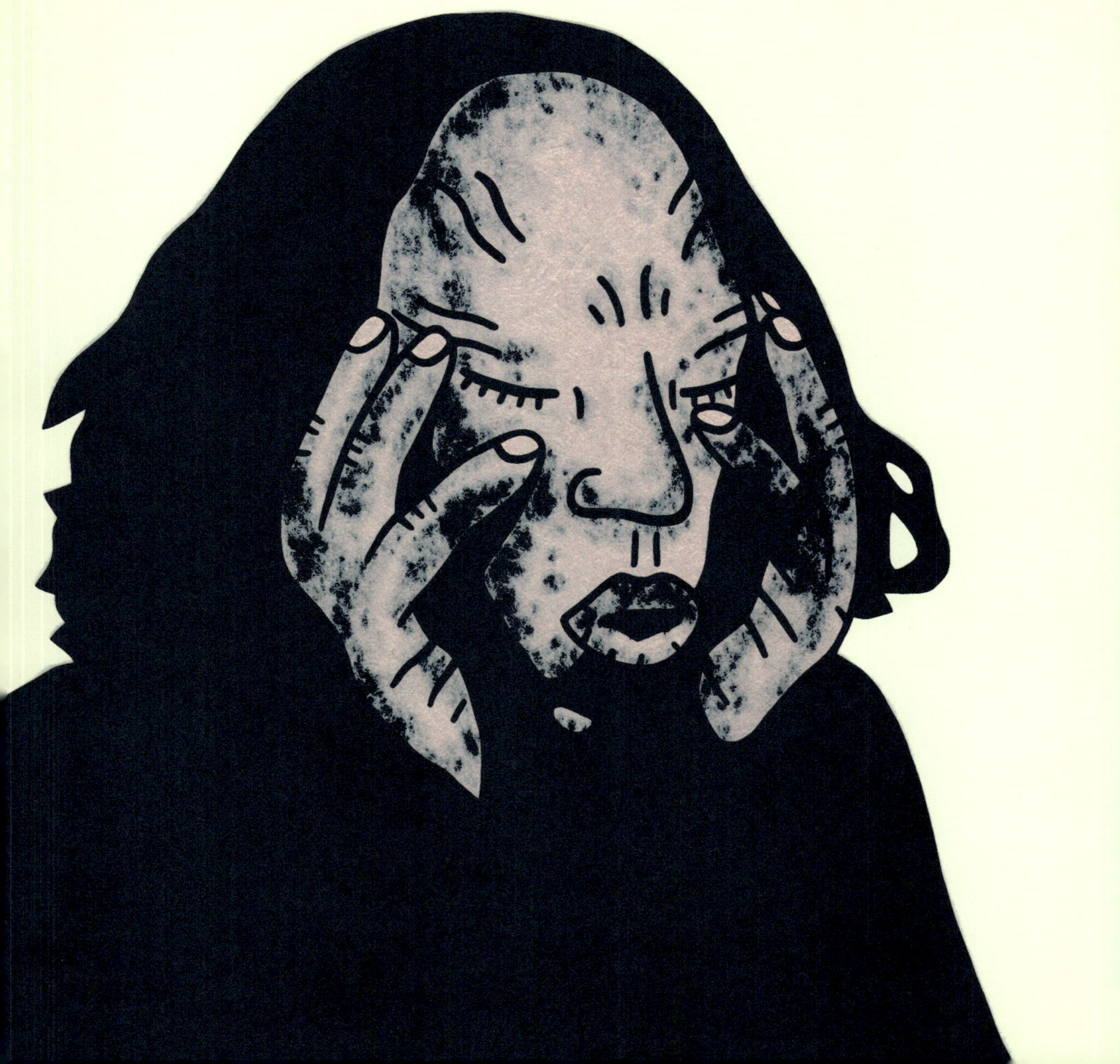

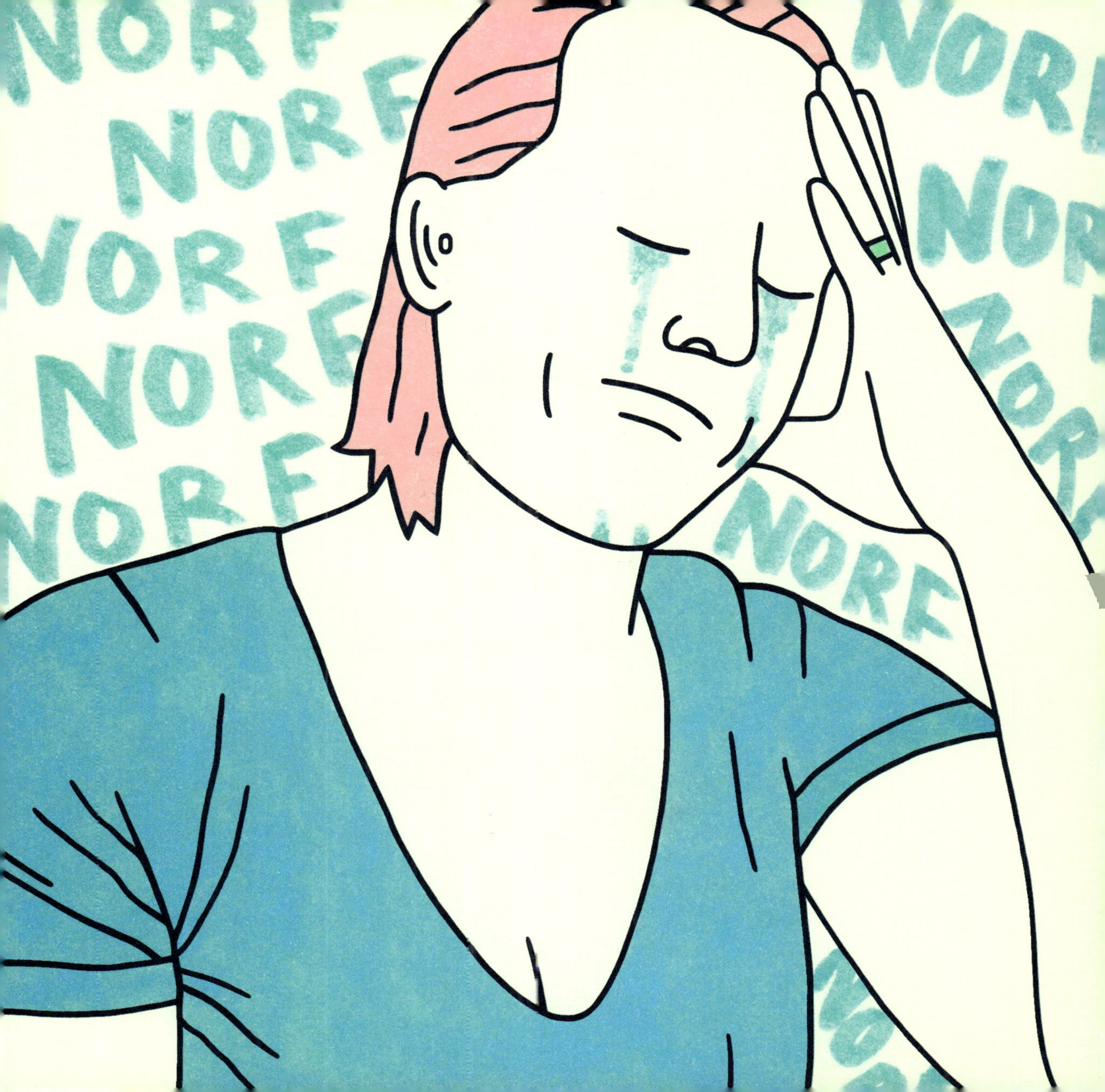
NORF
NORF
NORF
NORF
NORF
NORF

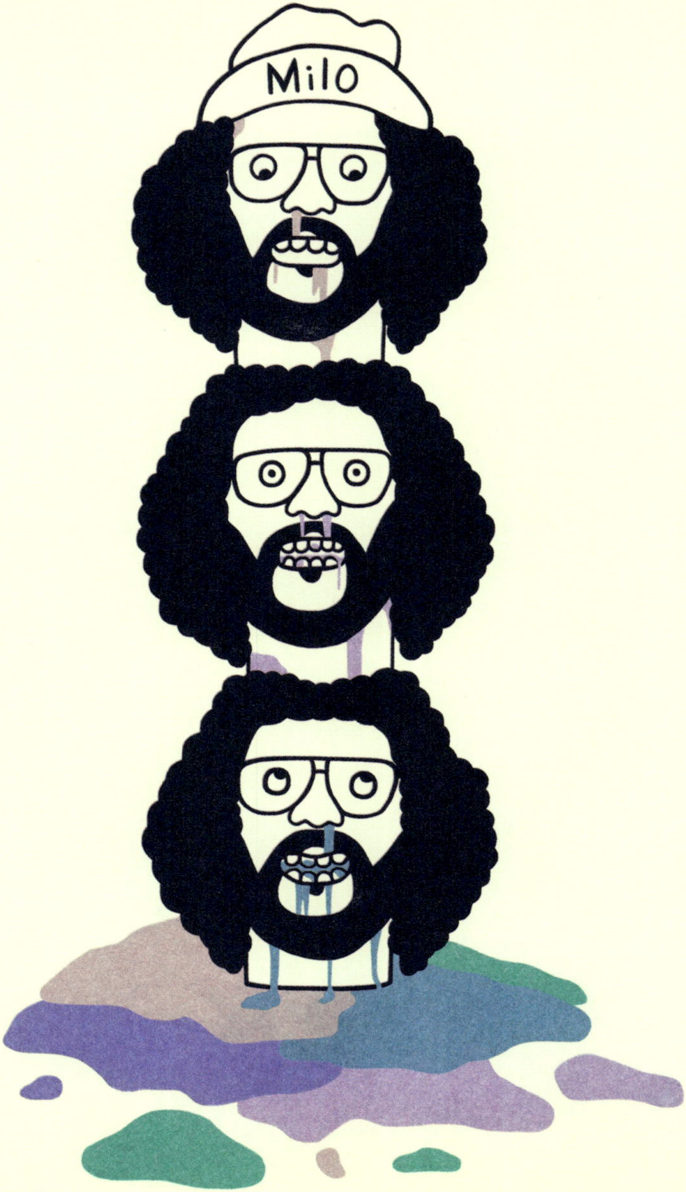
Milo

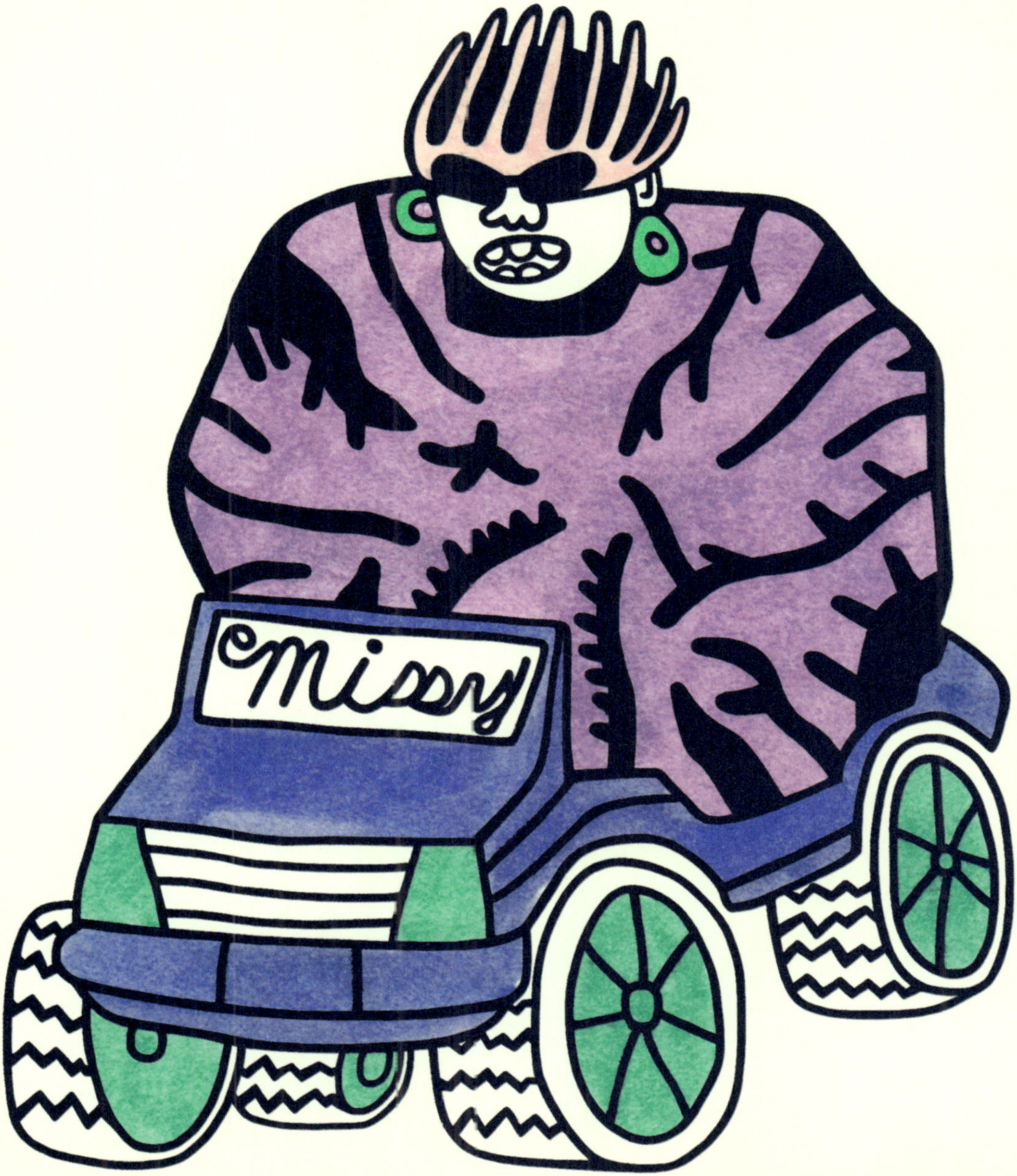
Missy

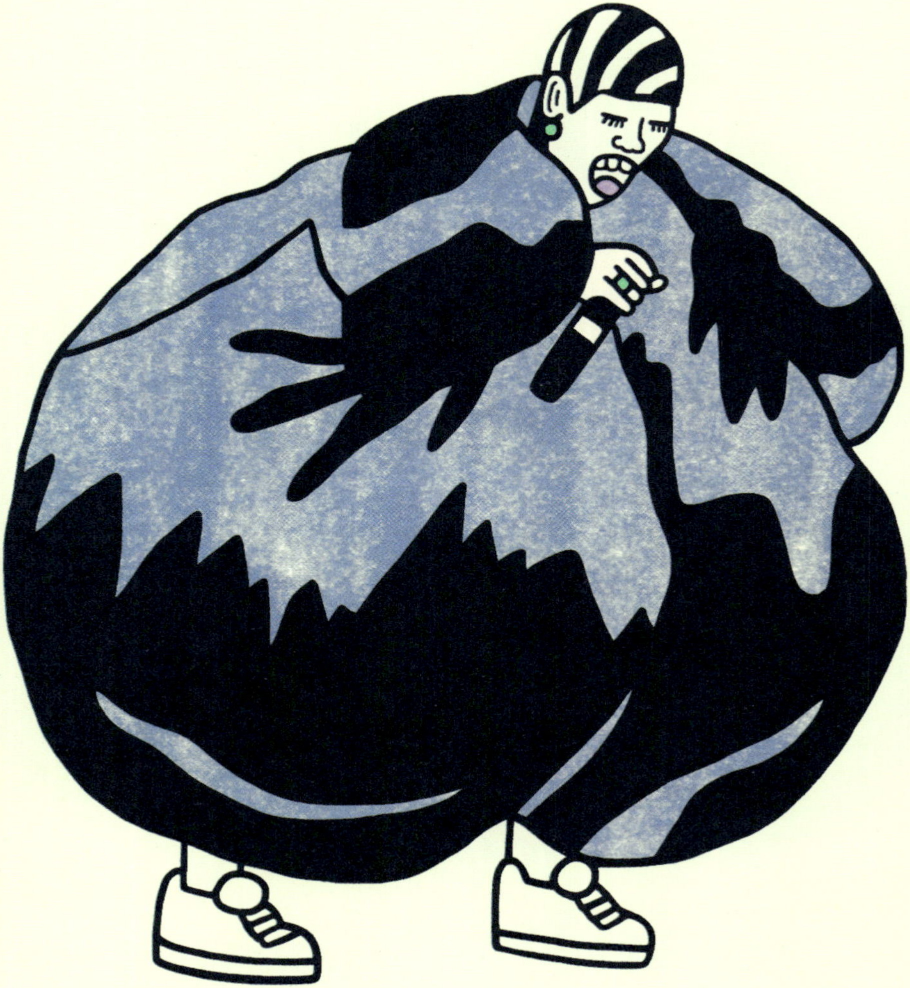

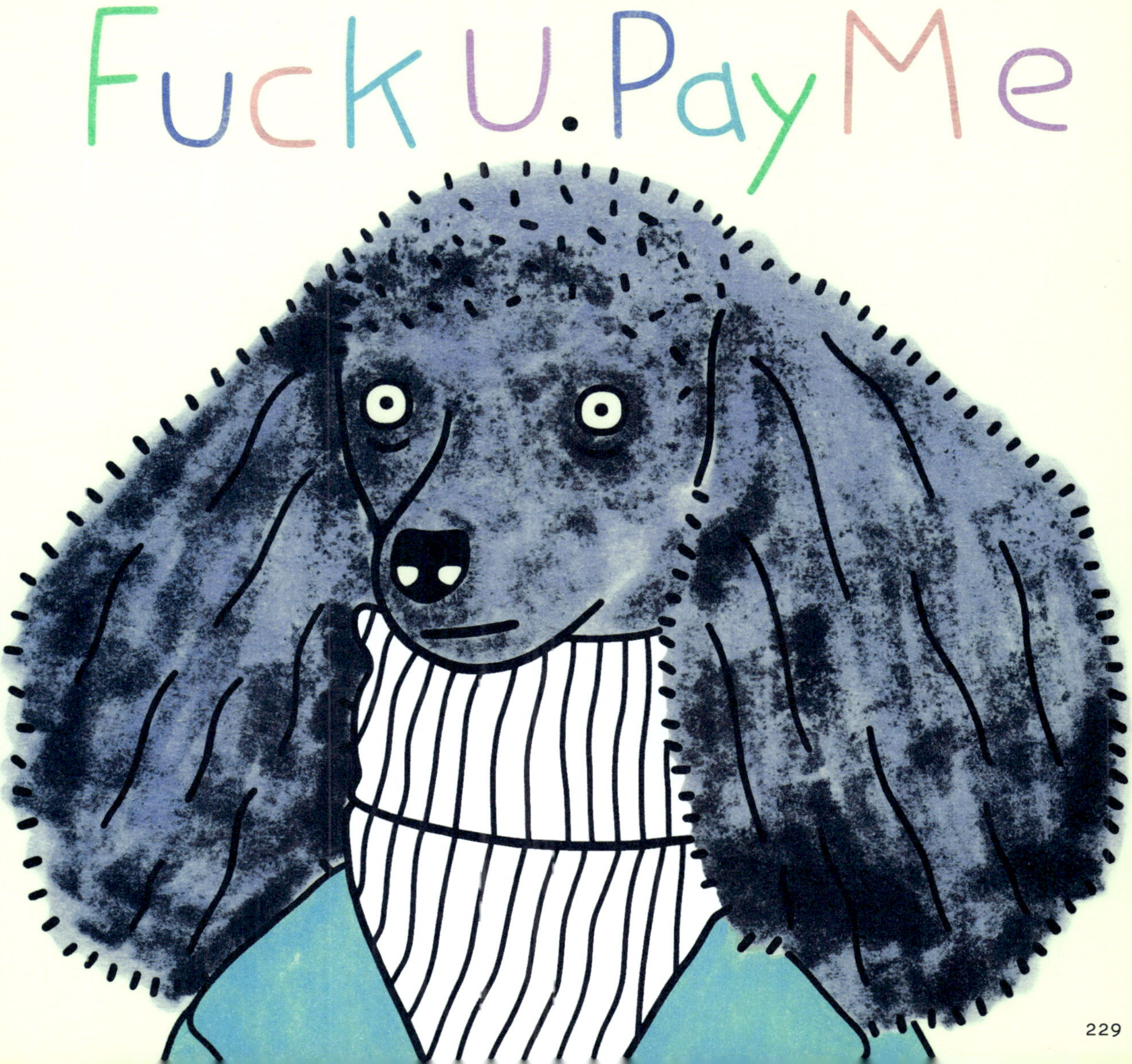
Fuck U. Pay Me

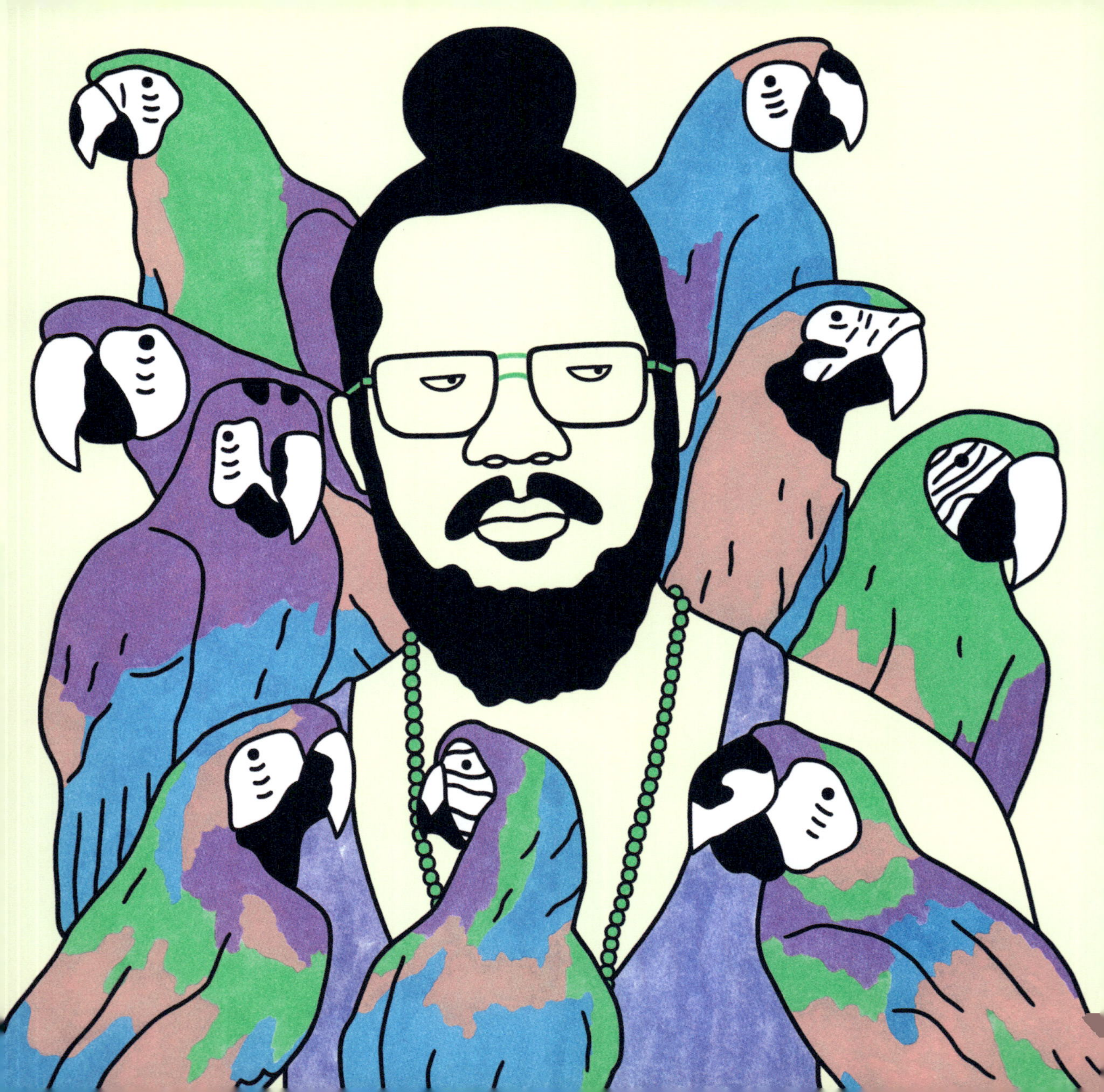

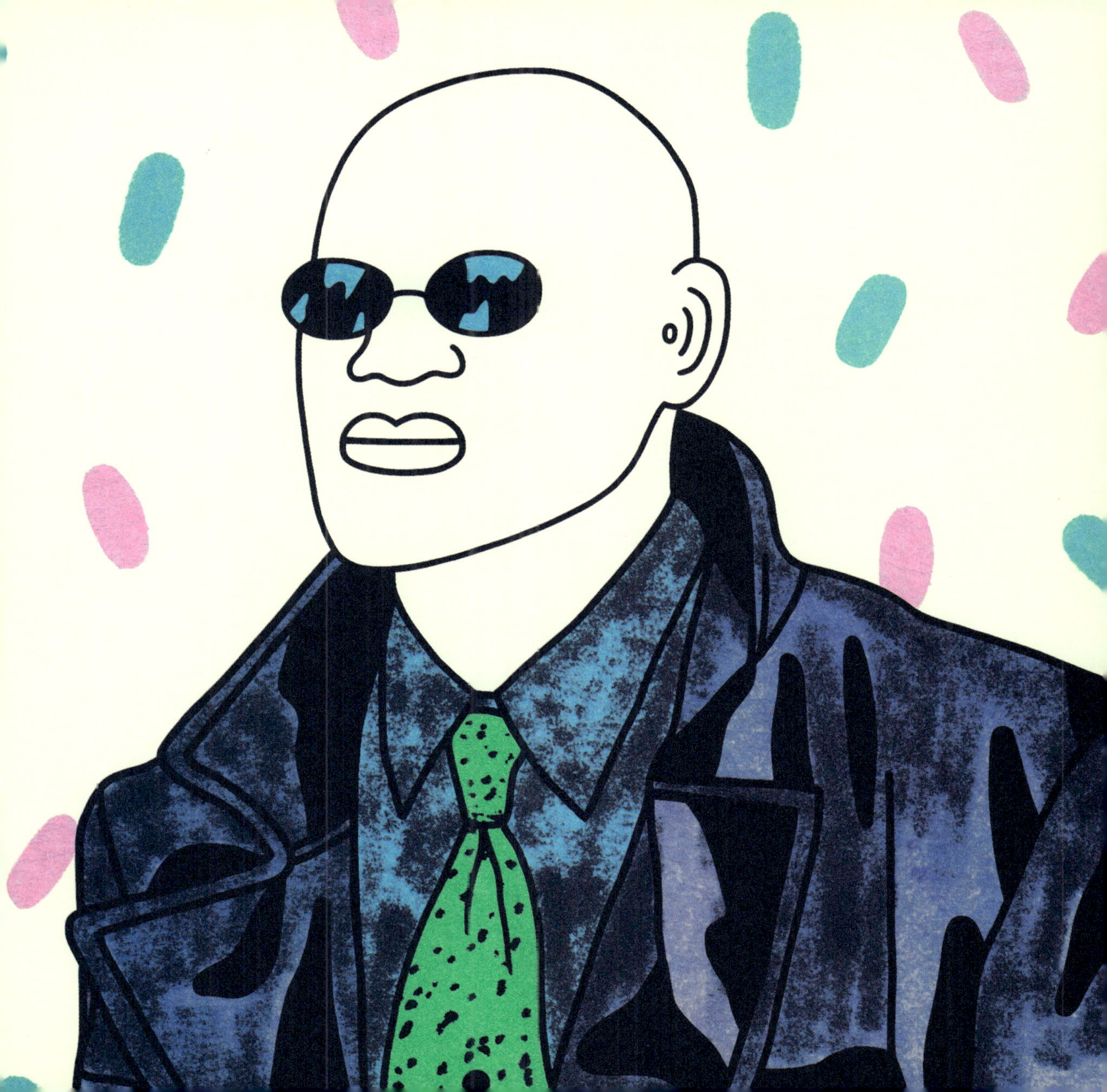

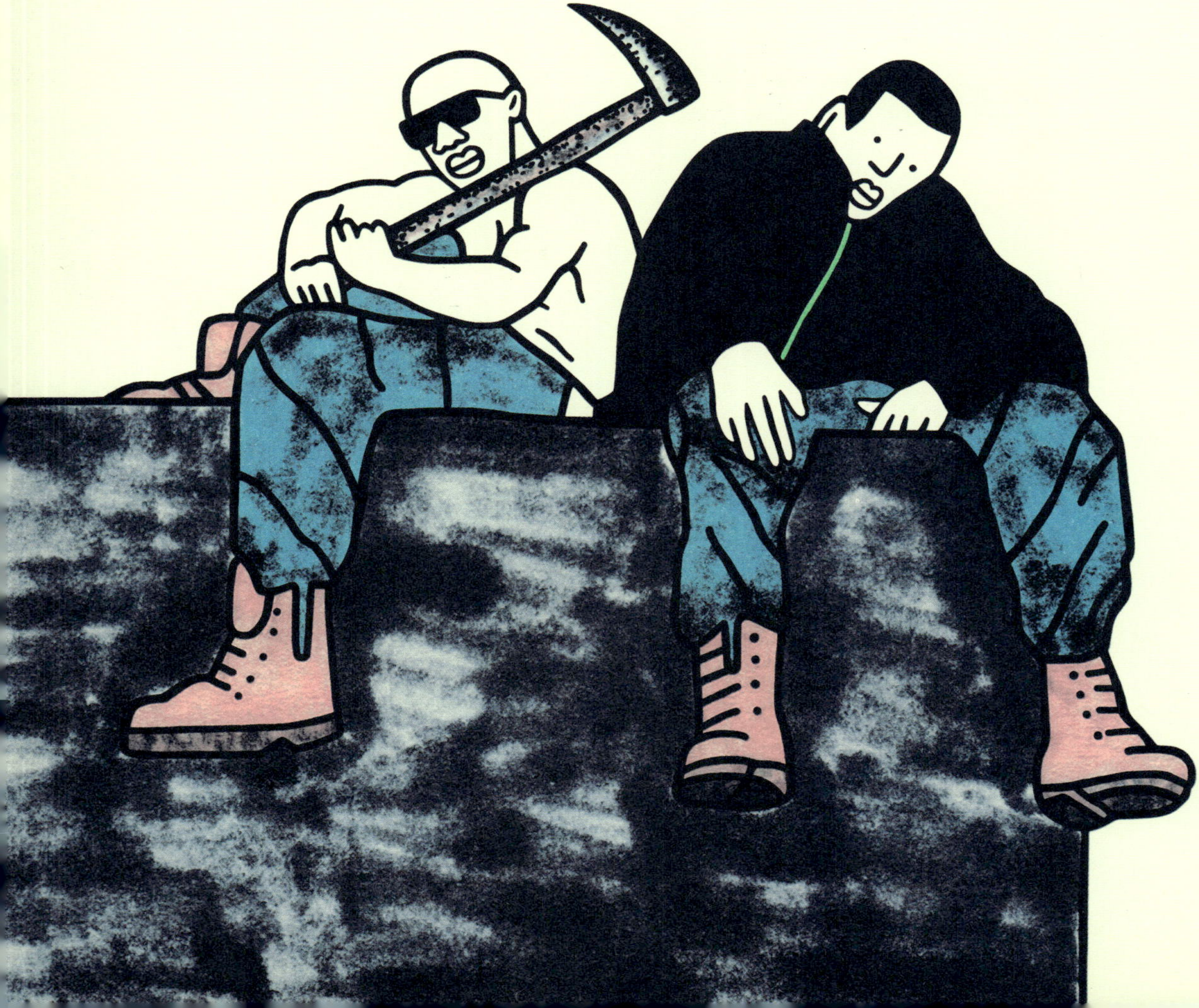

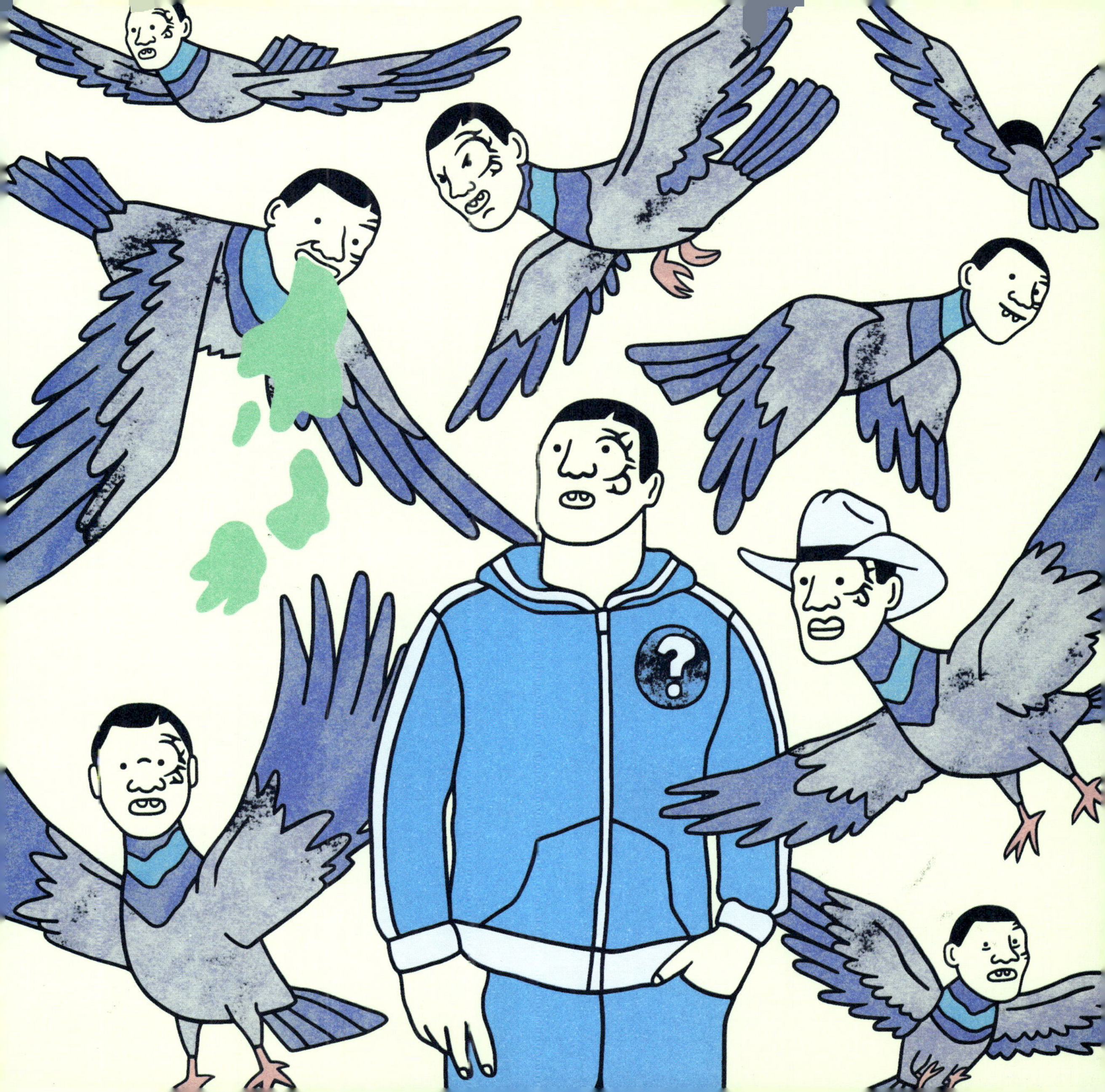

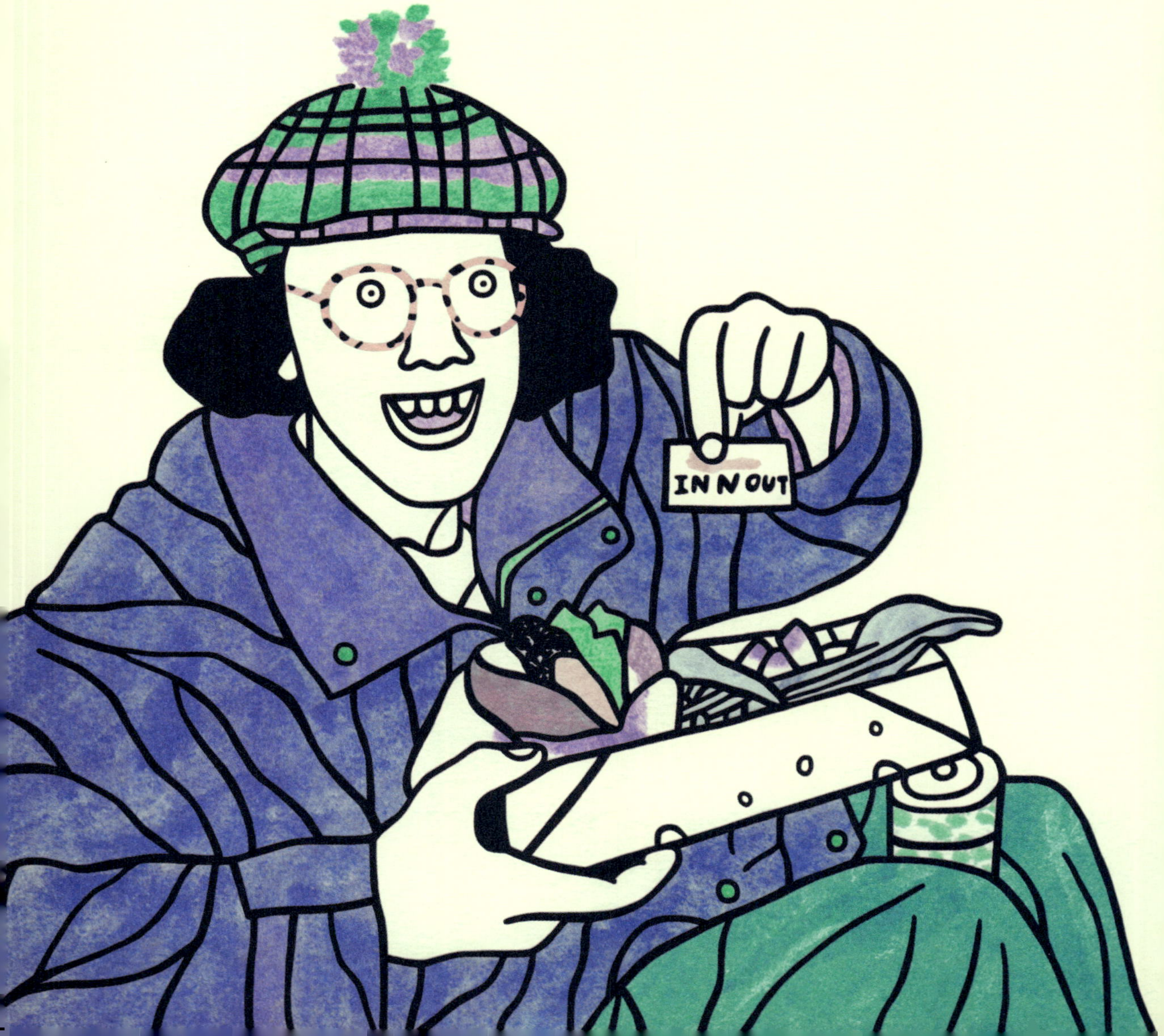
IN N OUT

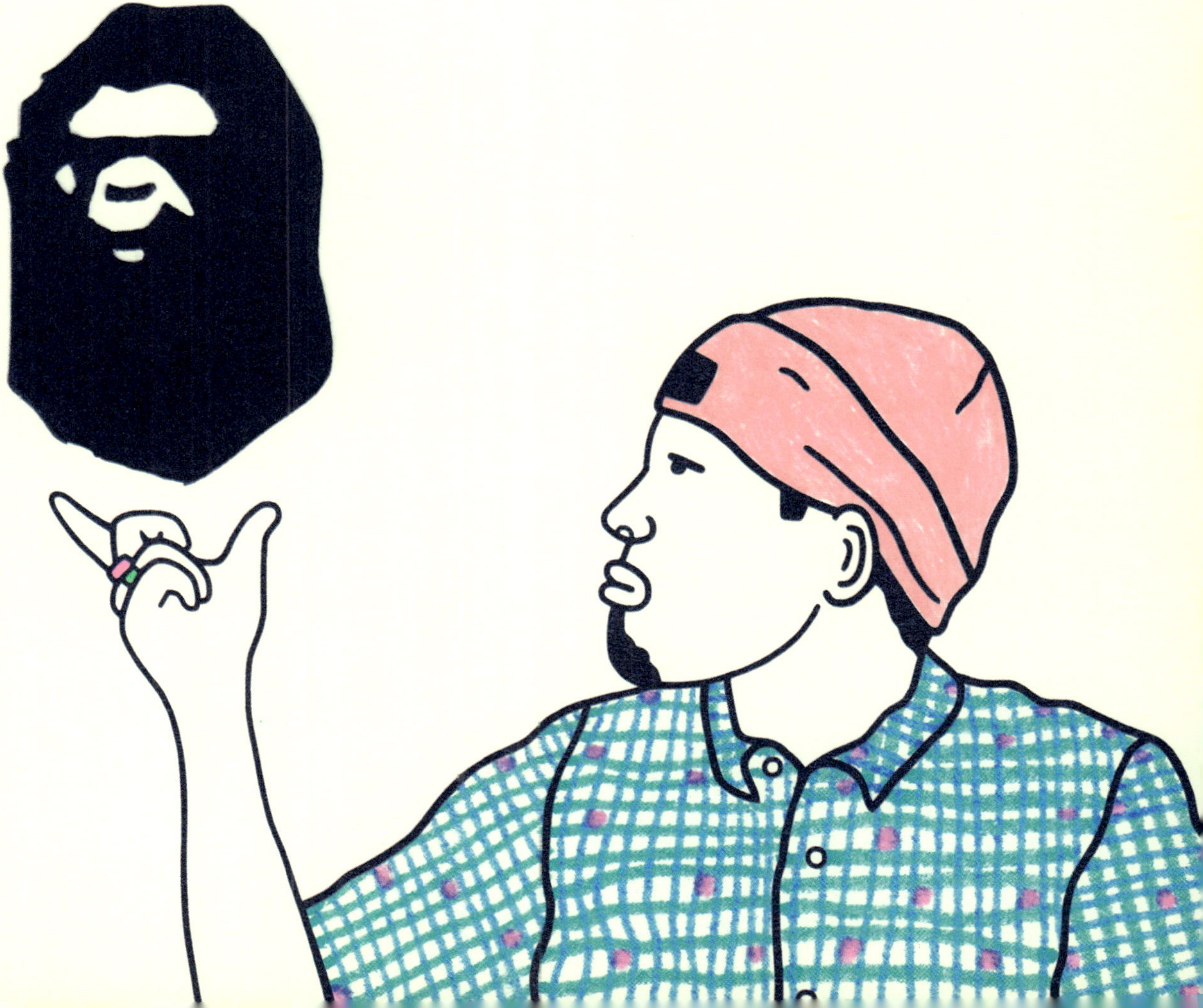

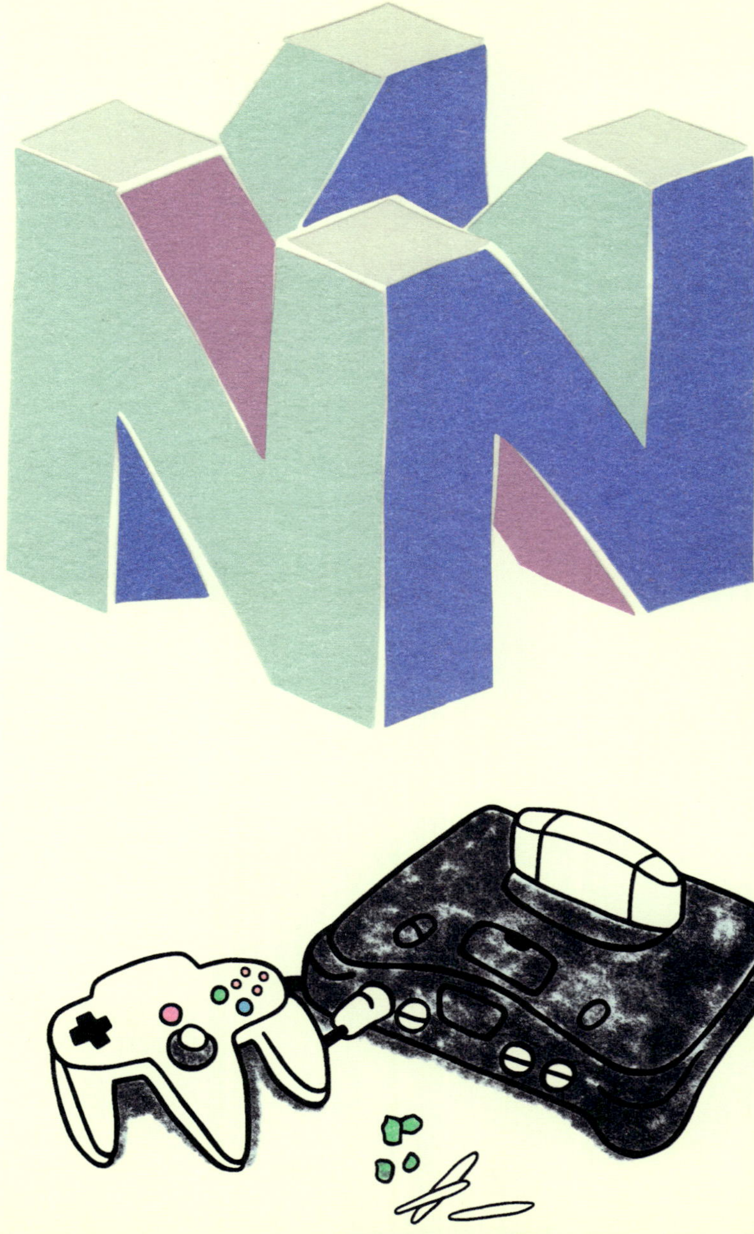

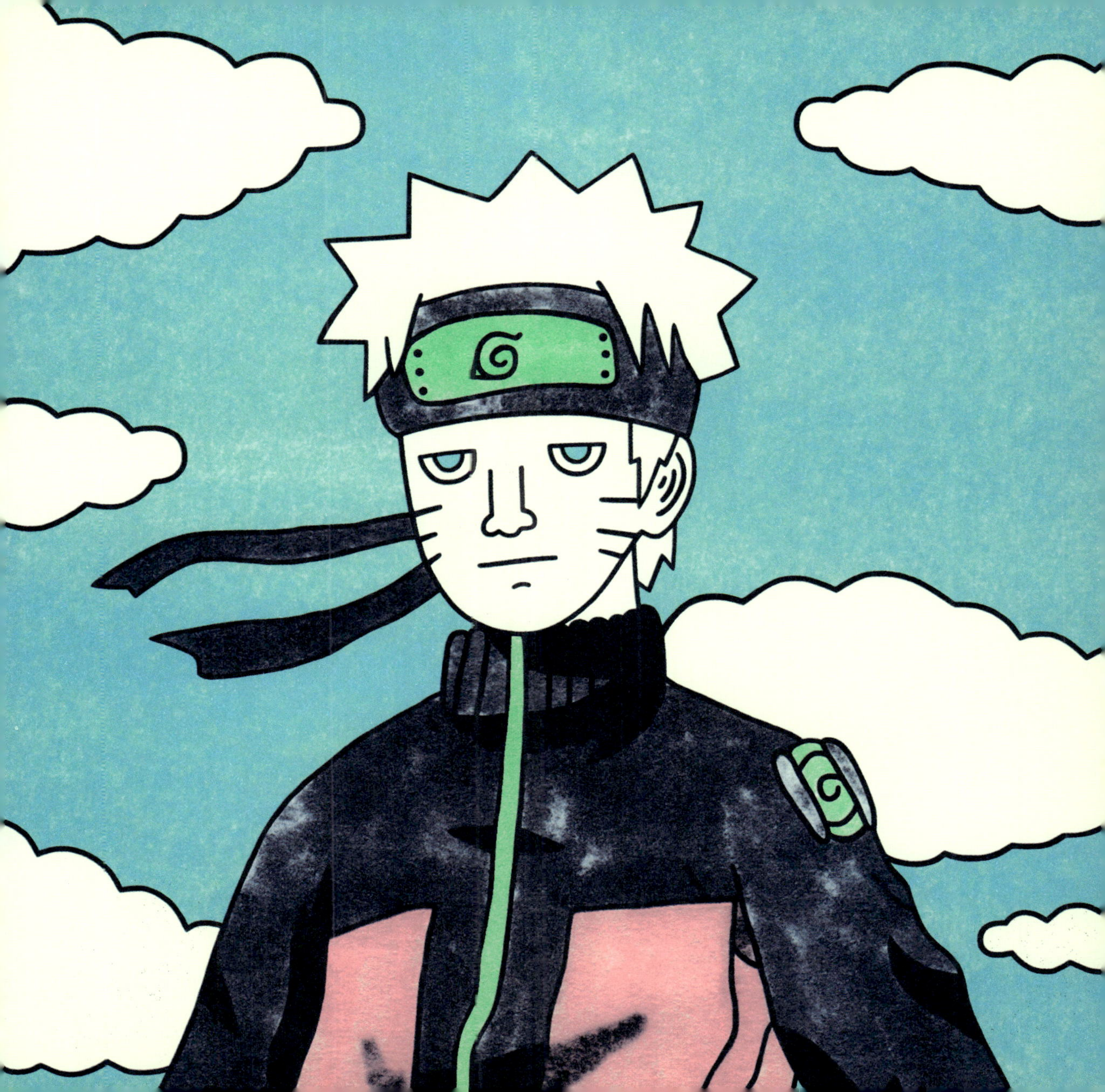

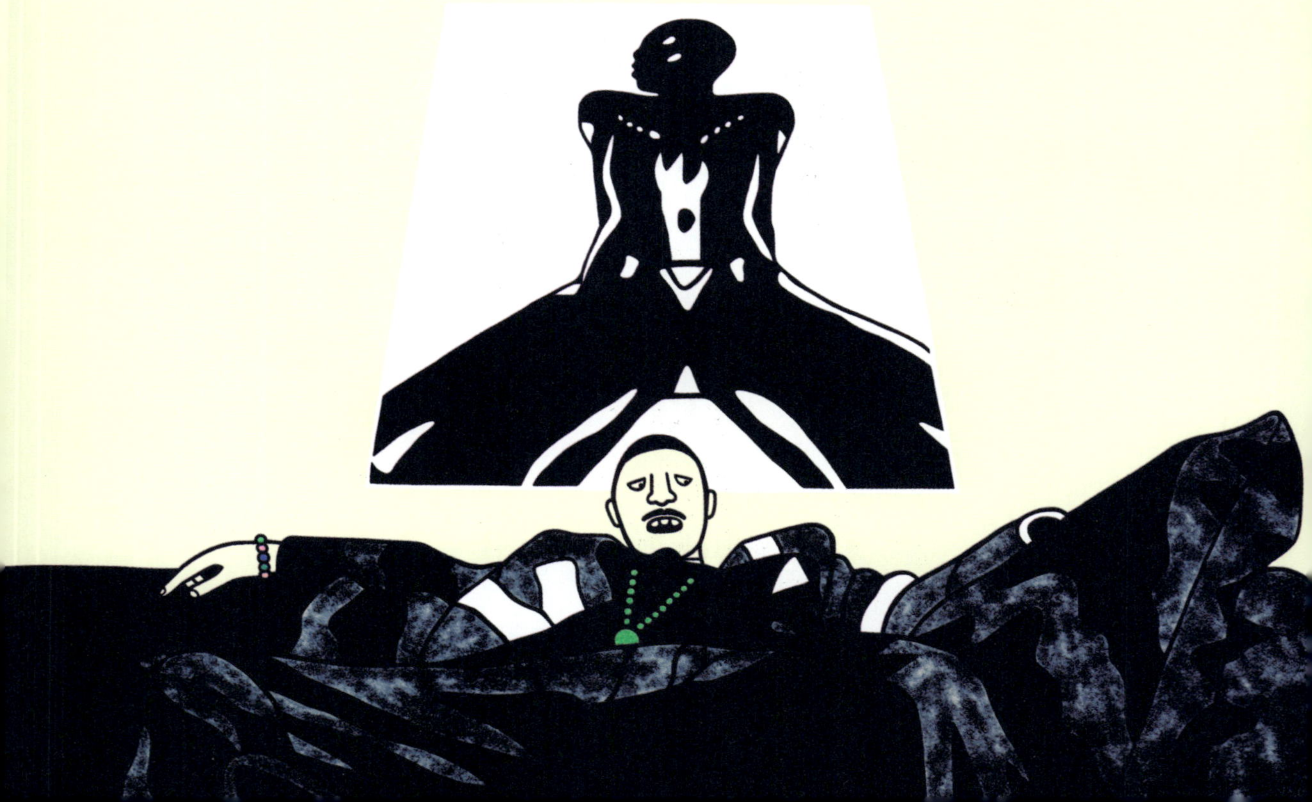

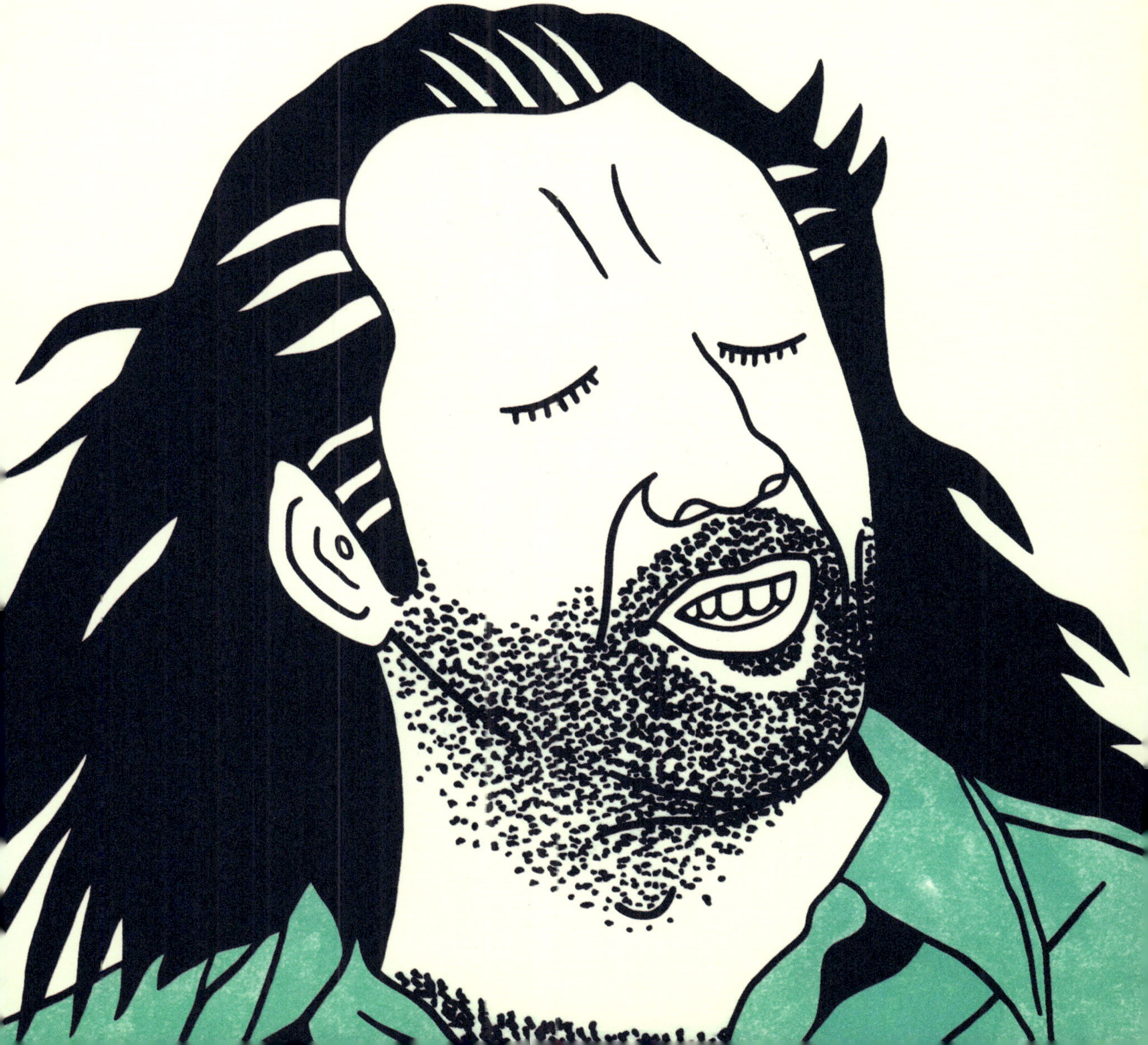

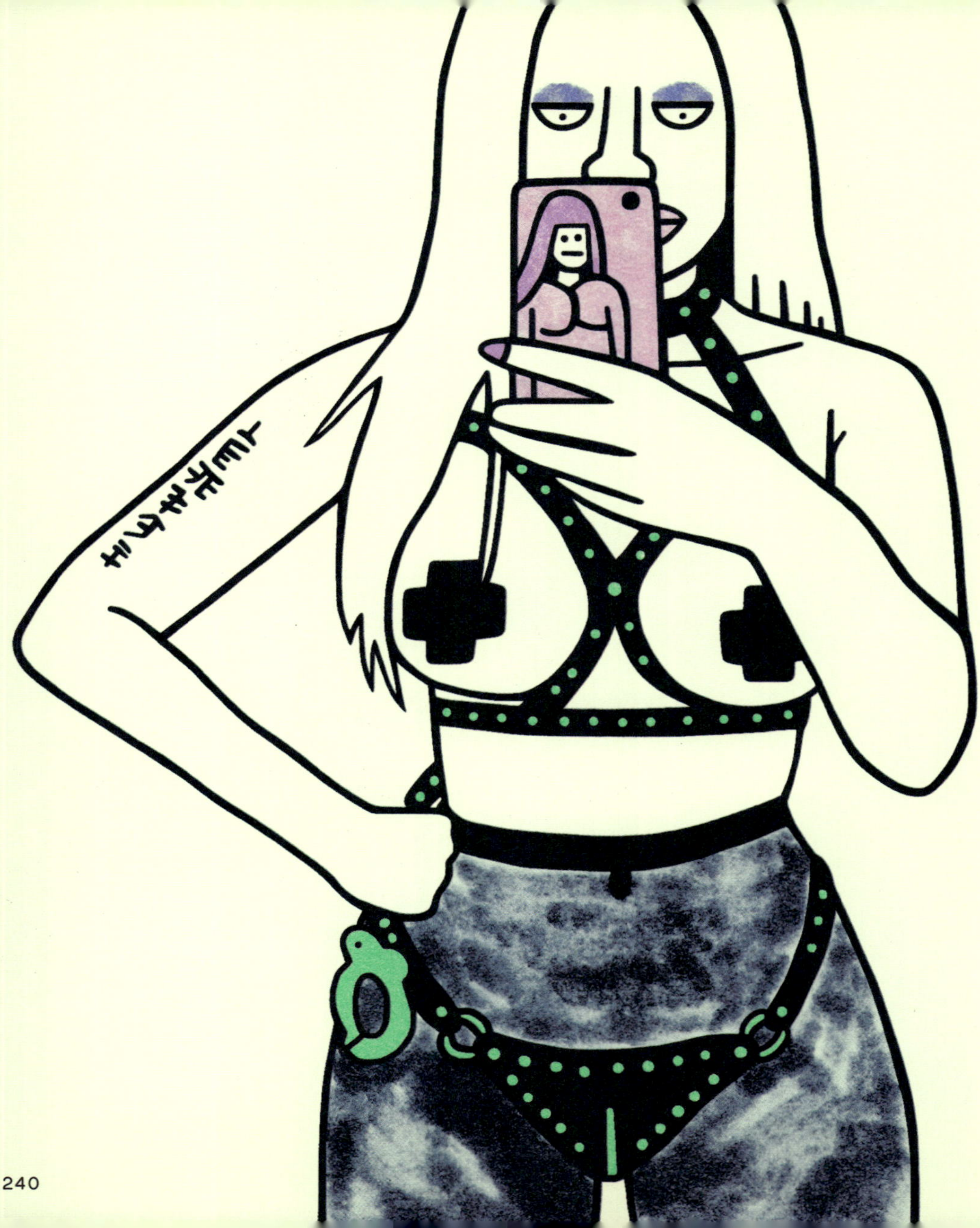

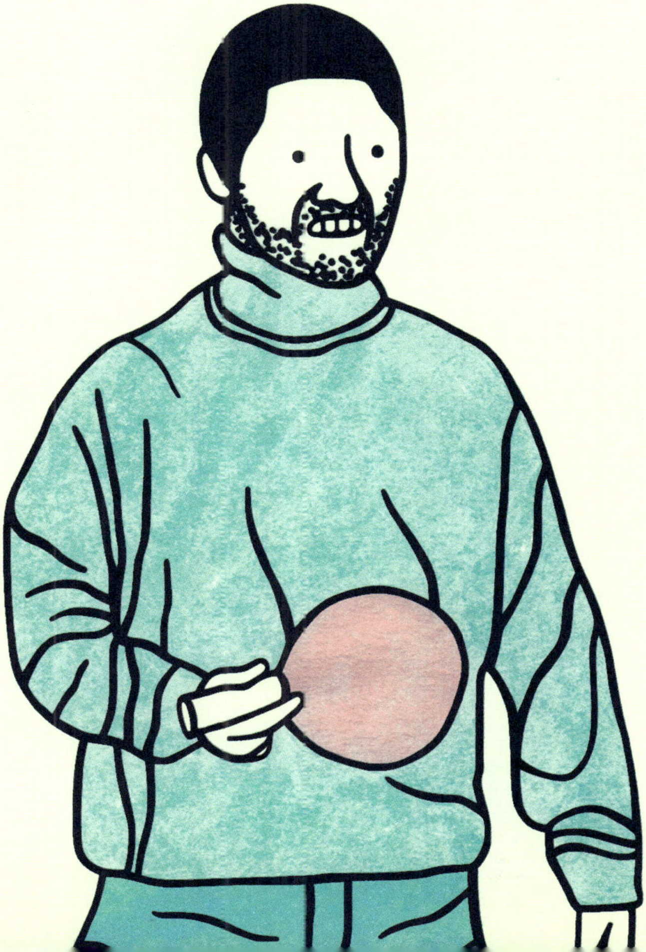

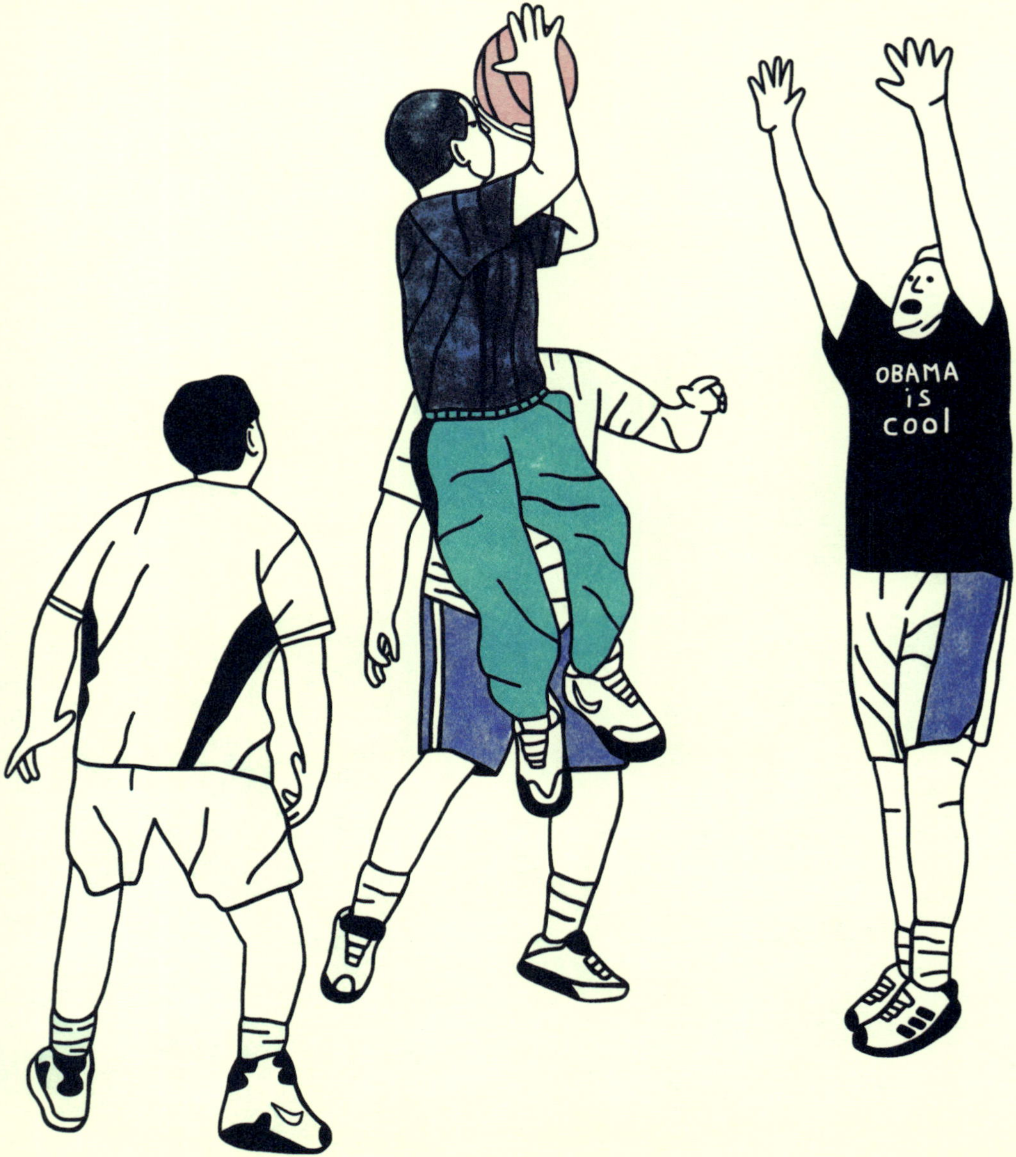
OBAMA
is
cool

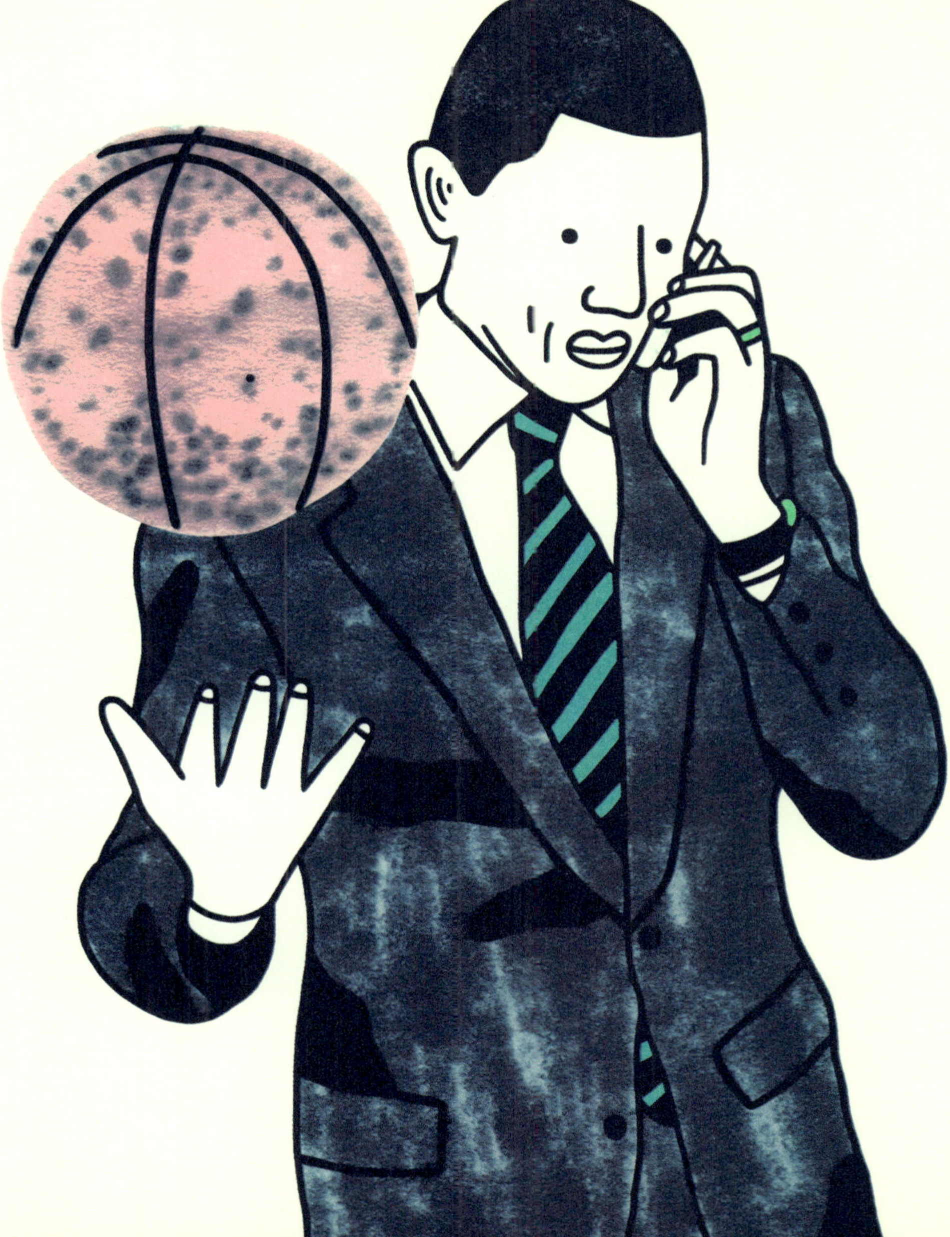

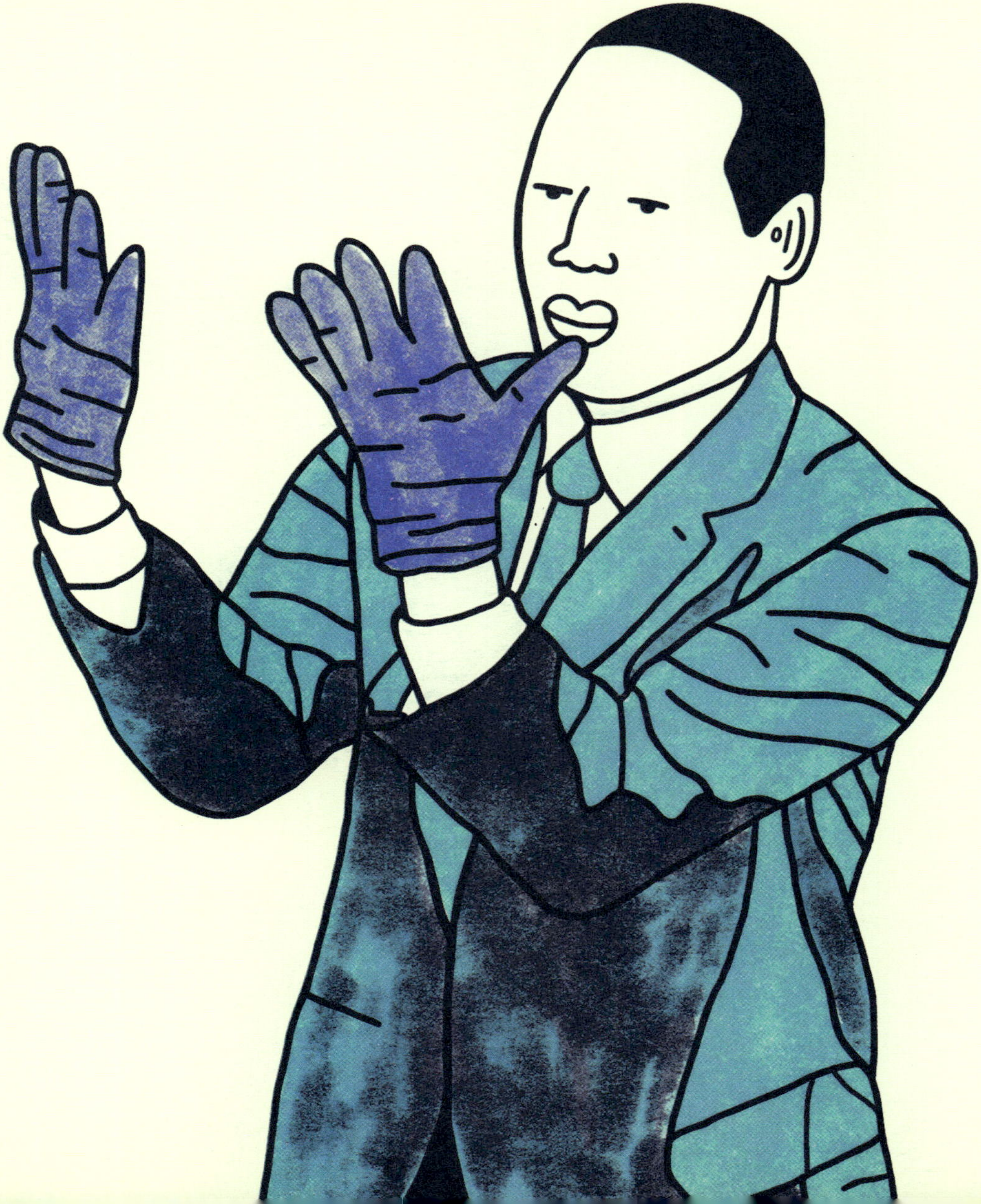

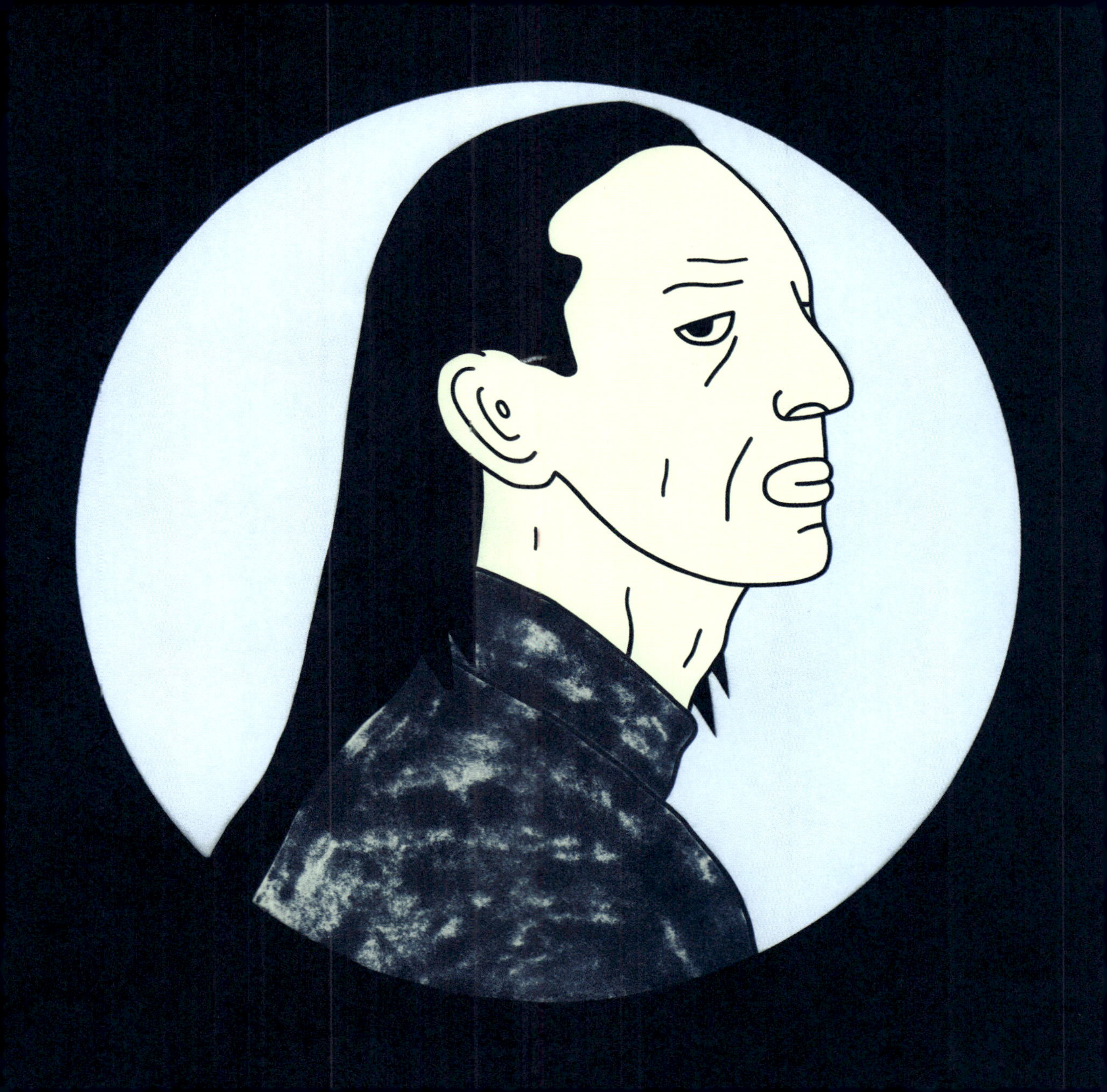

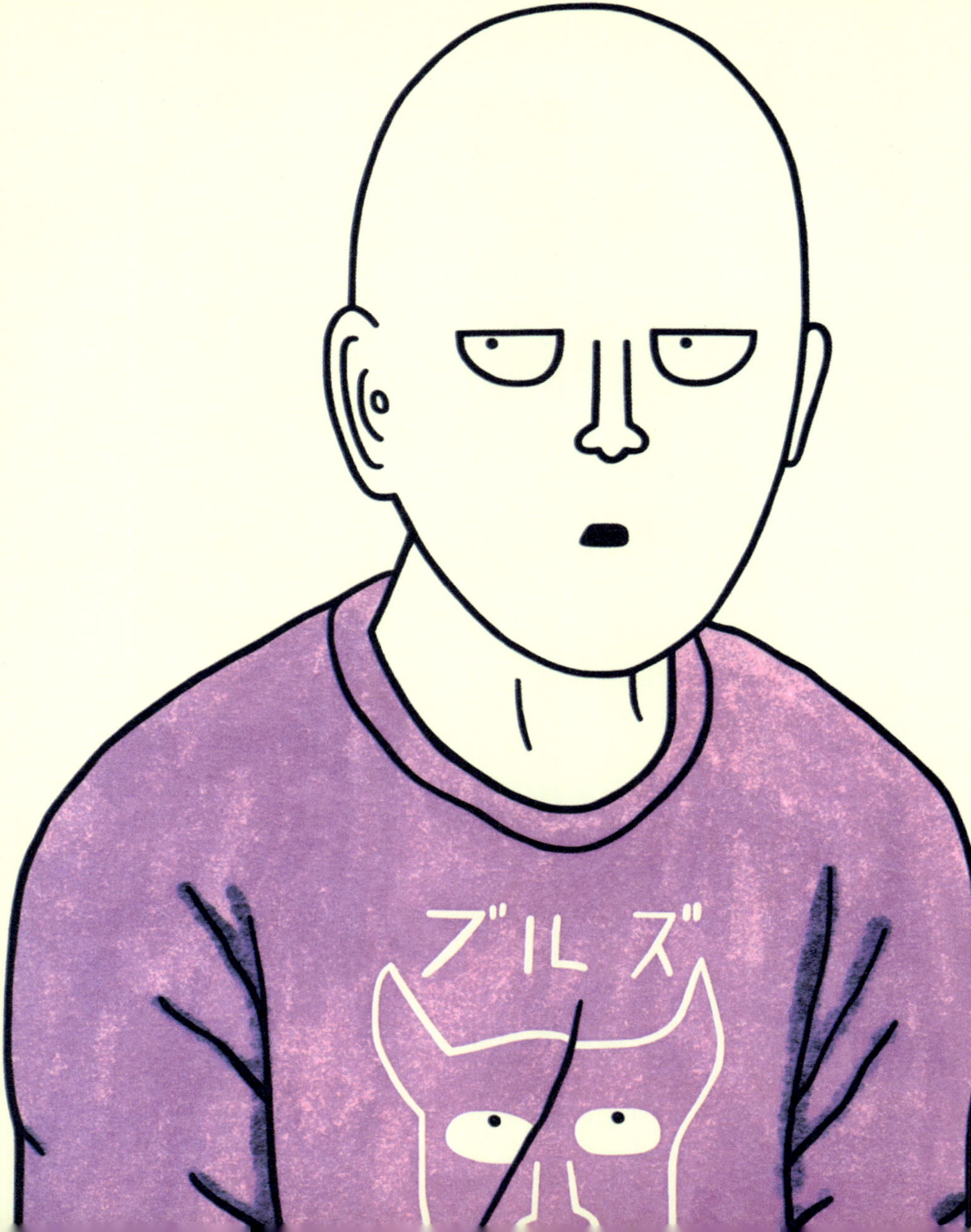
ブルズ

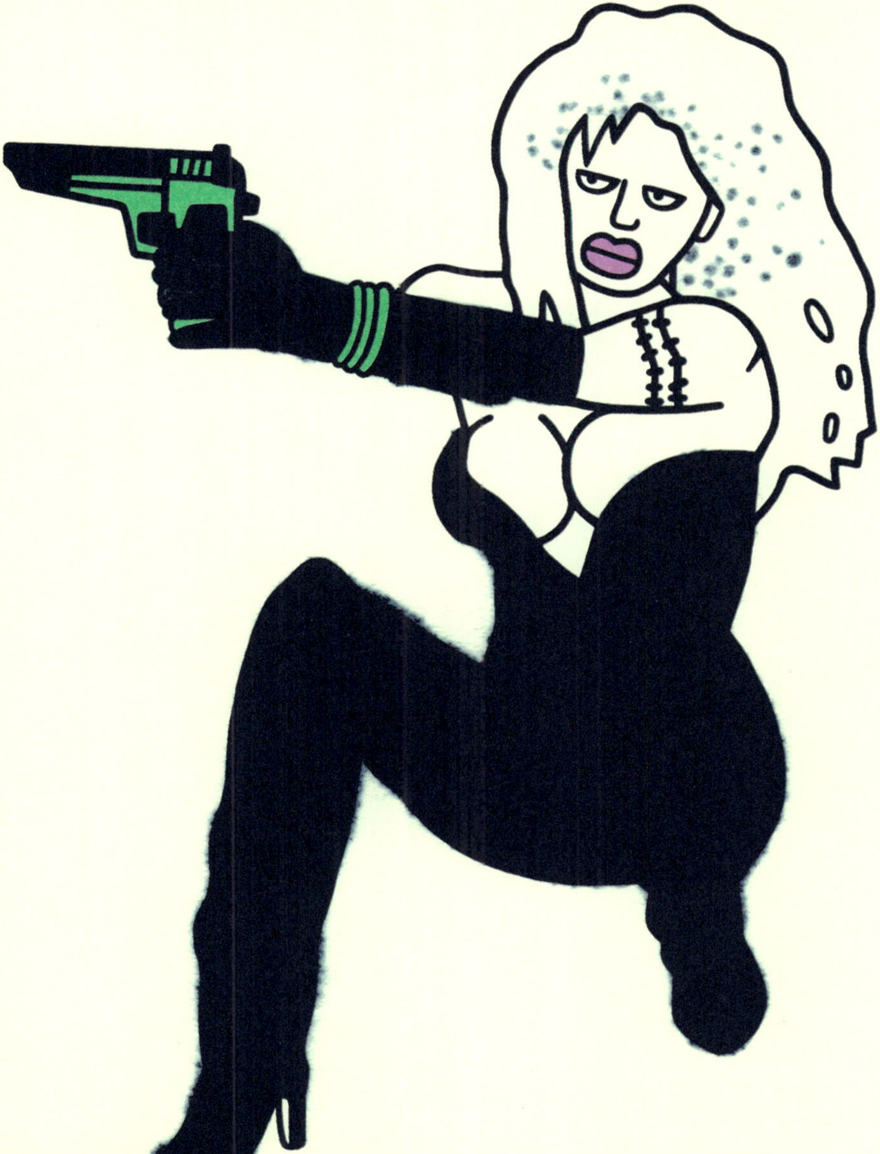

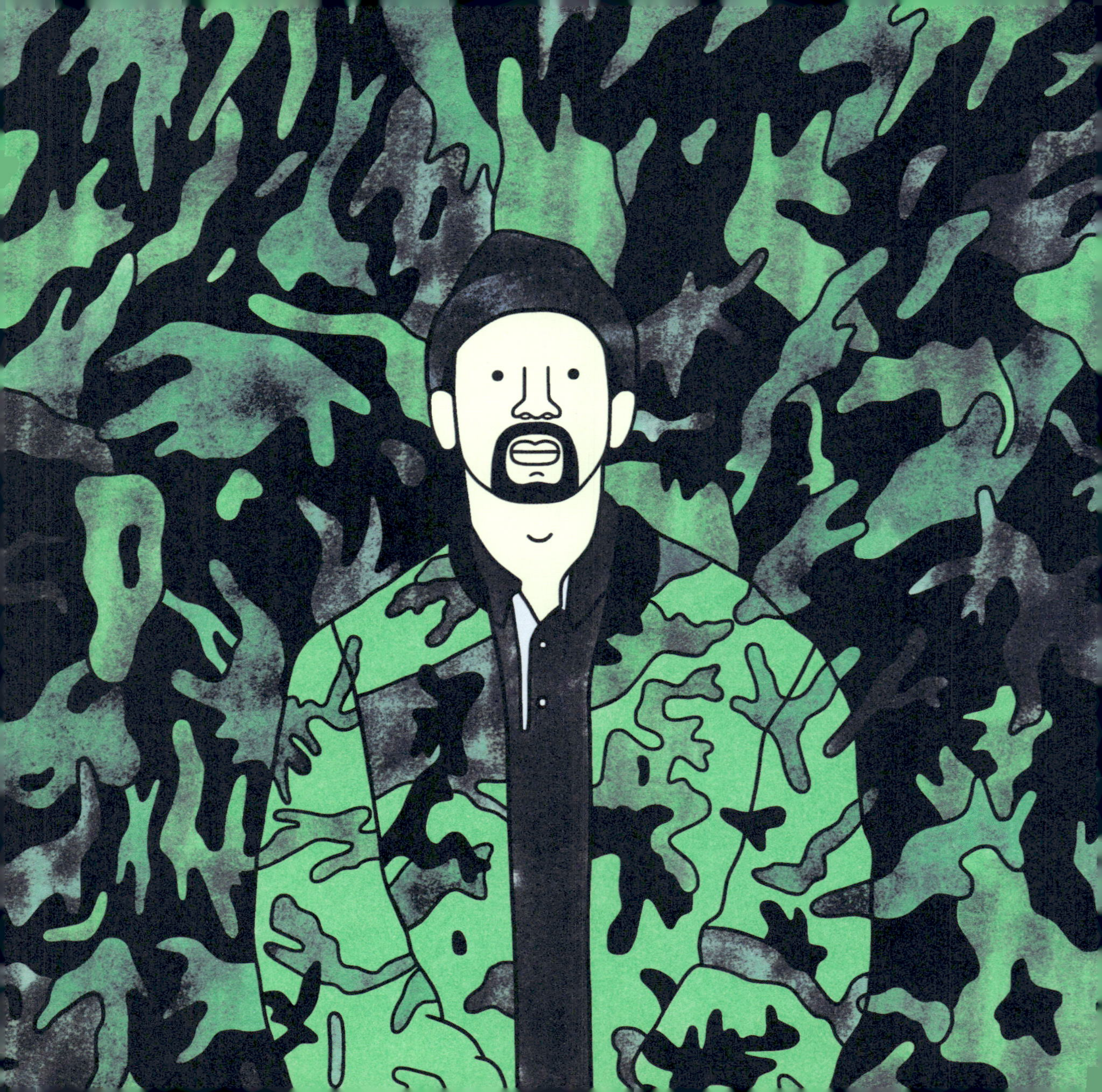

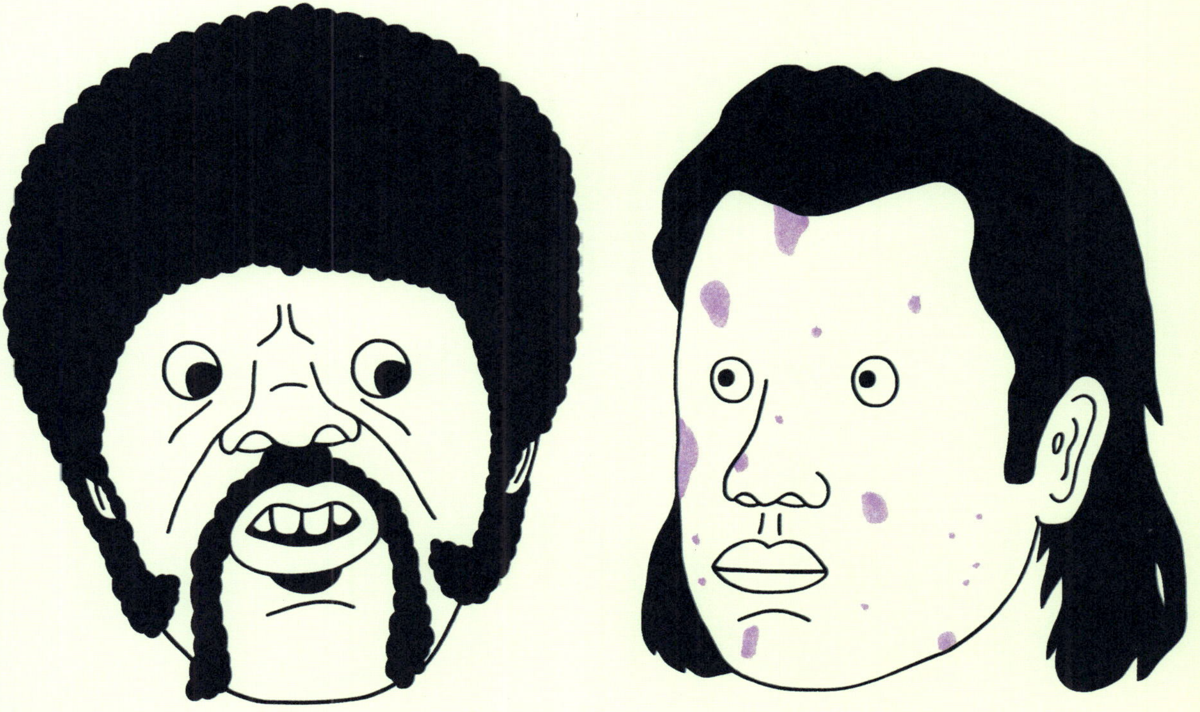

there's nothing worse than forcing yourself to give a fuck.

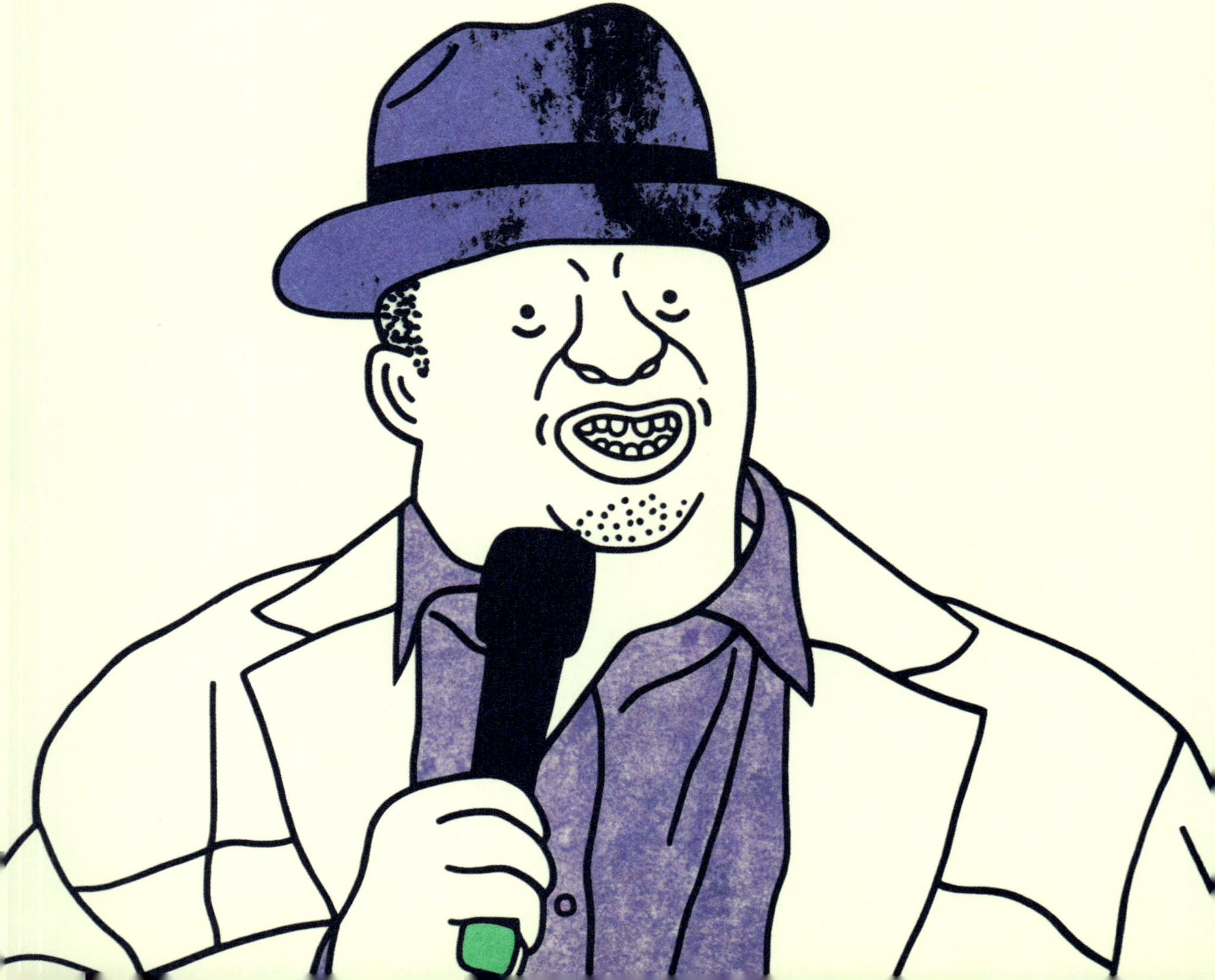

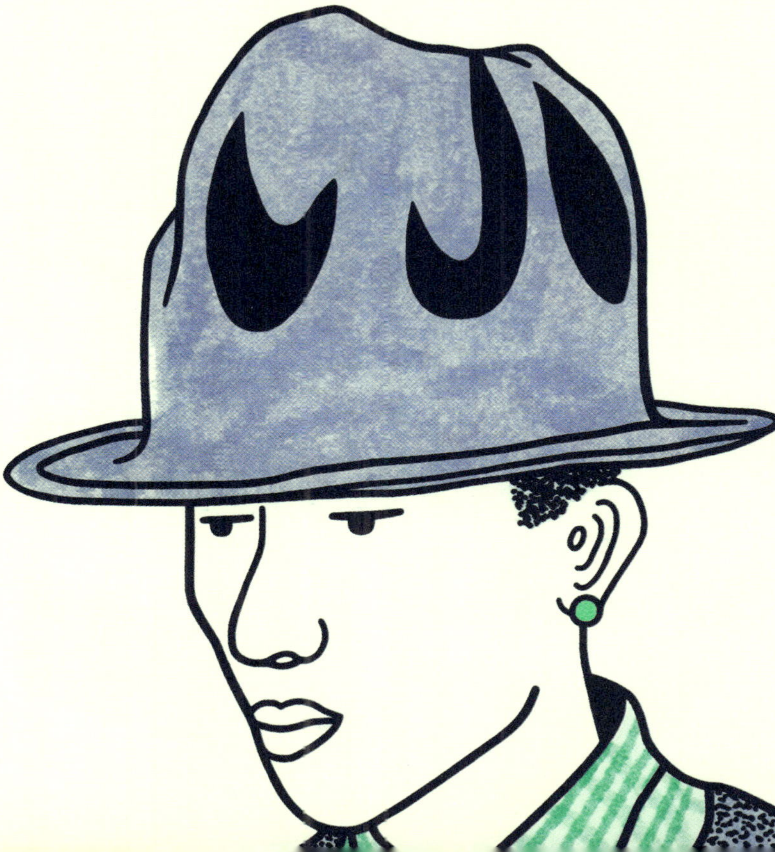

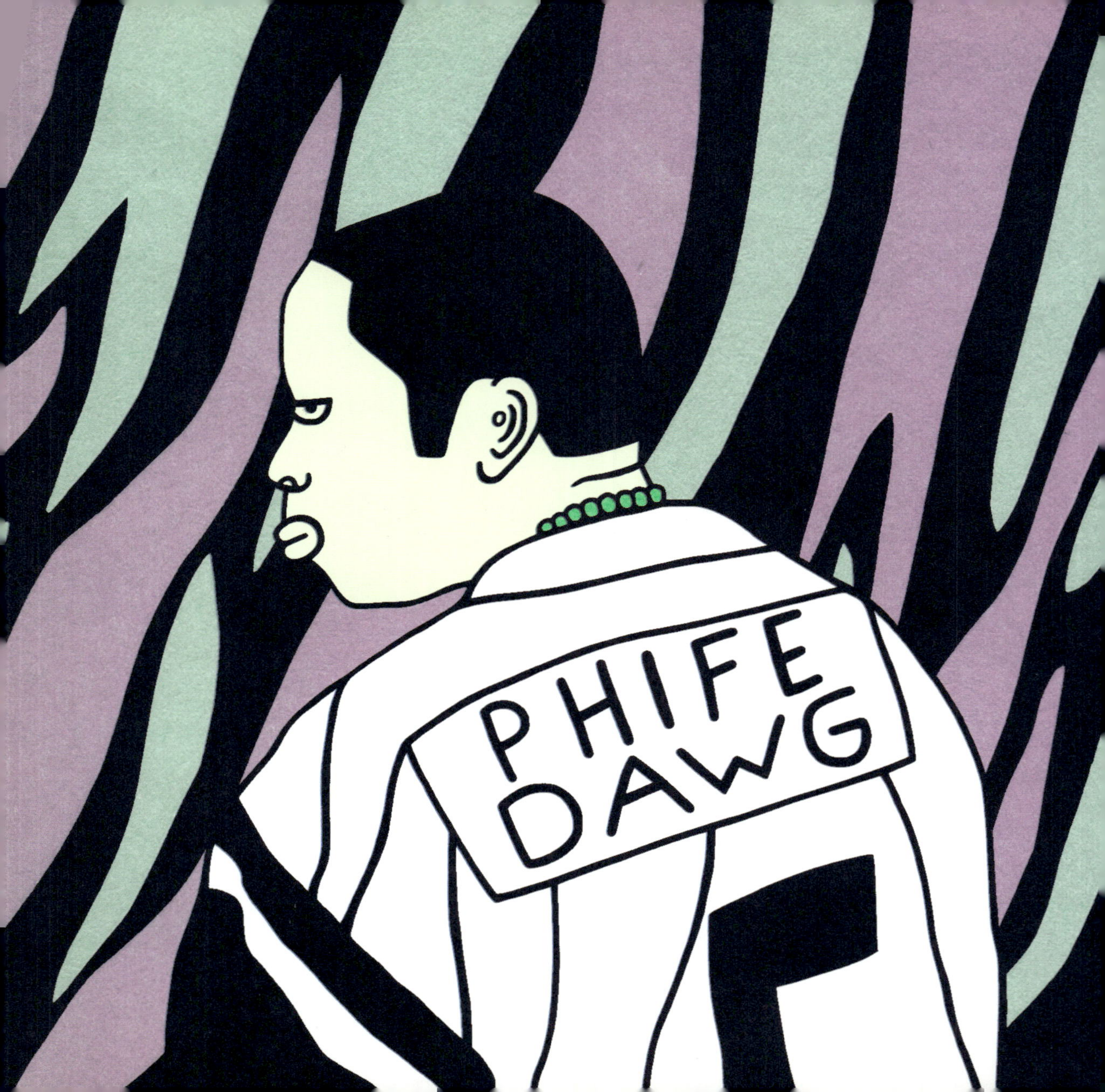
PHIFE
DAWG

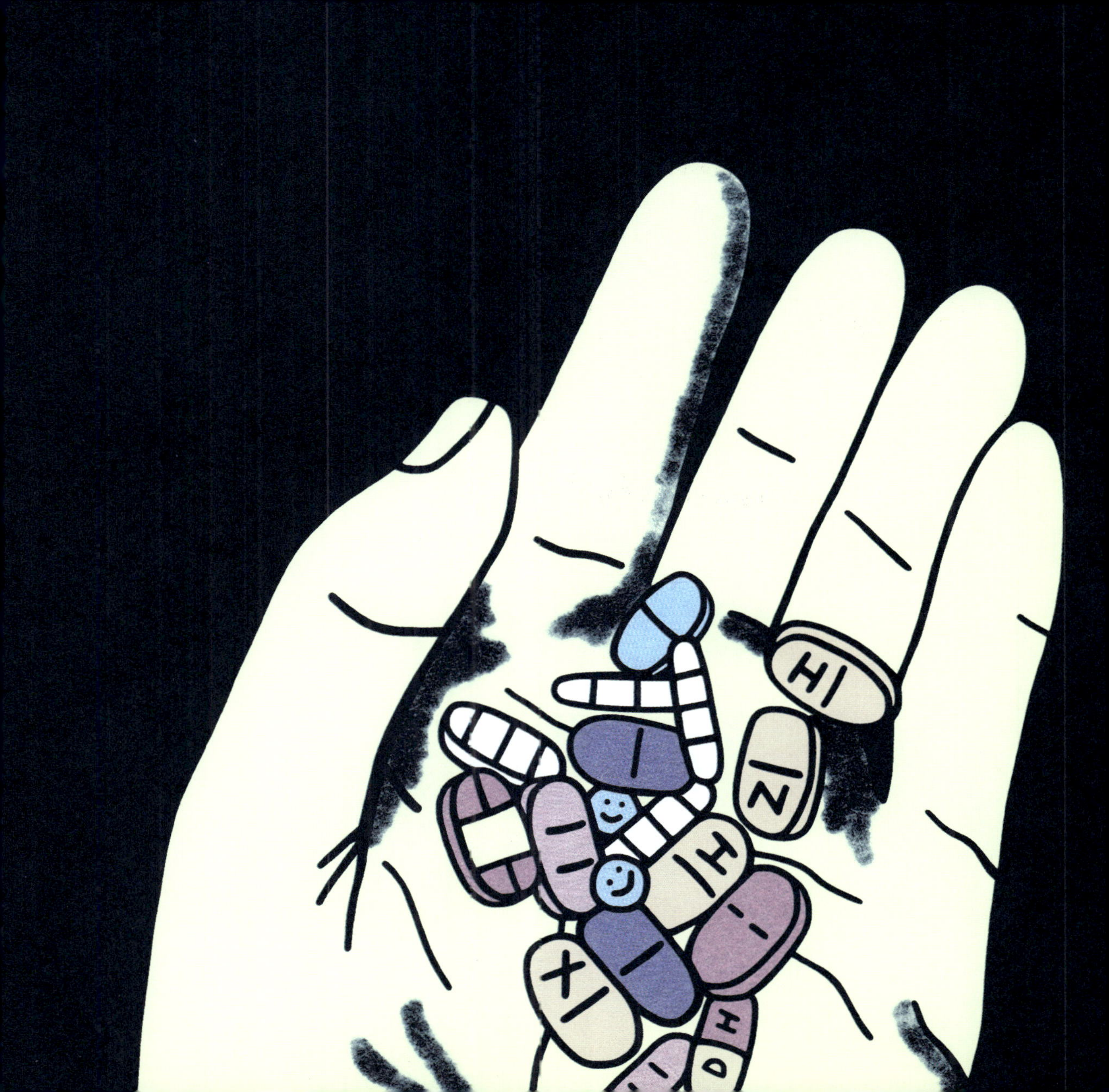

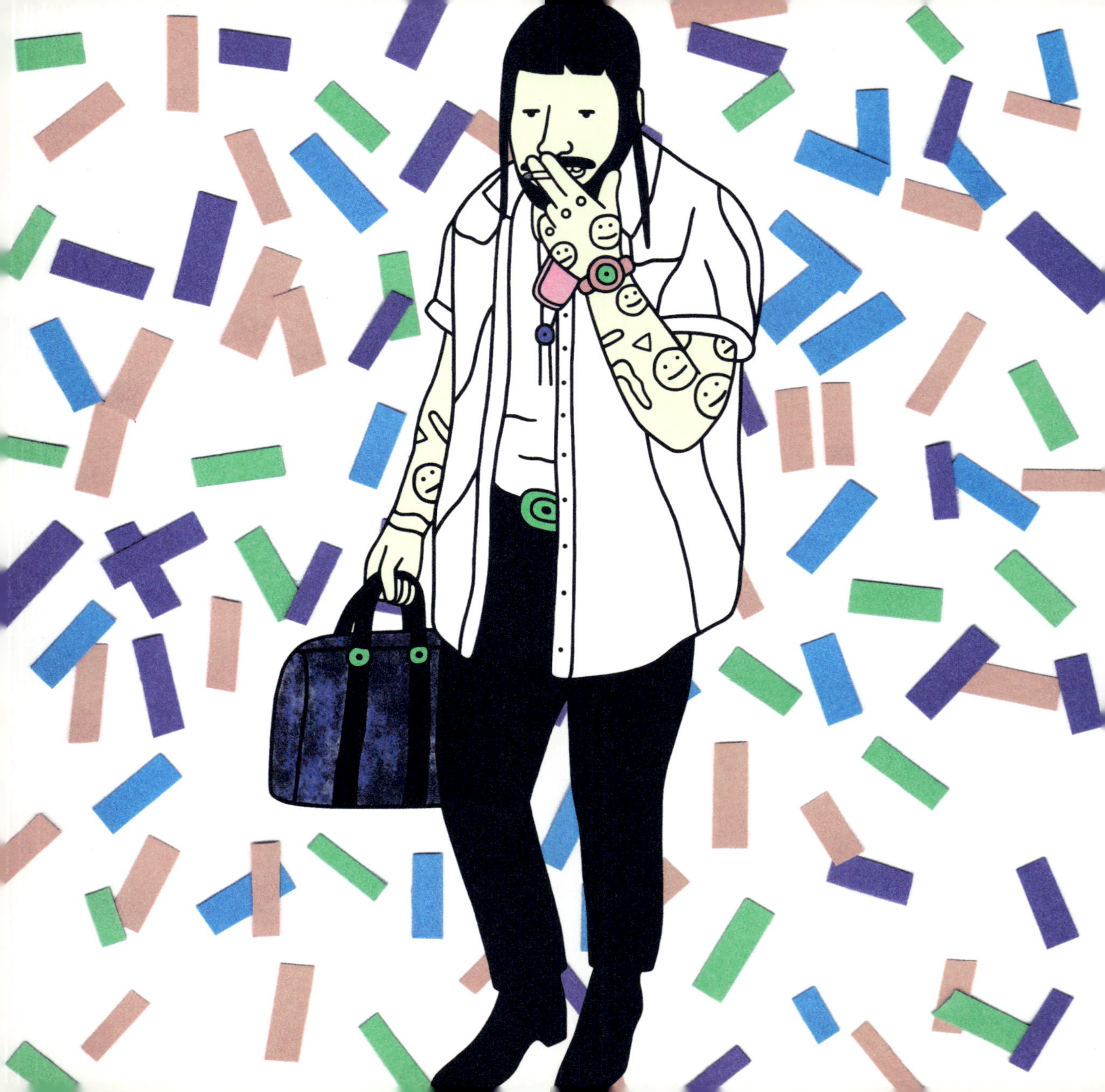

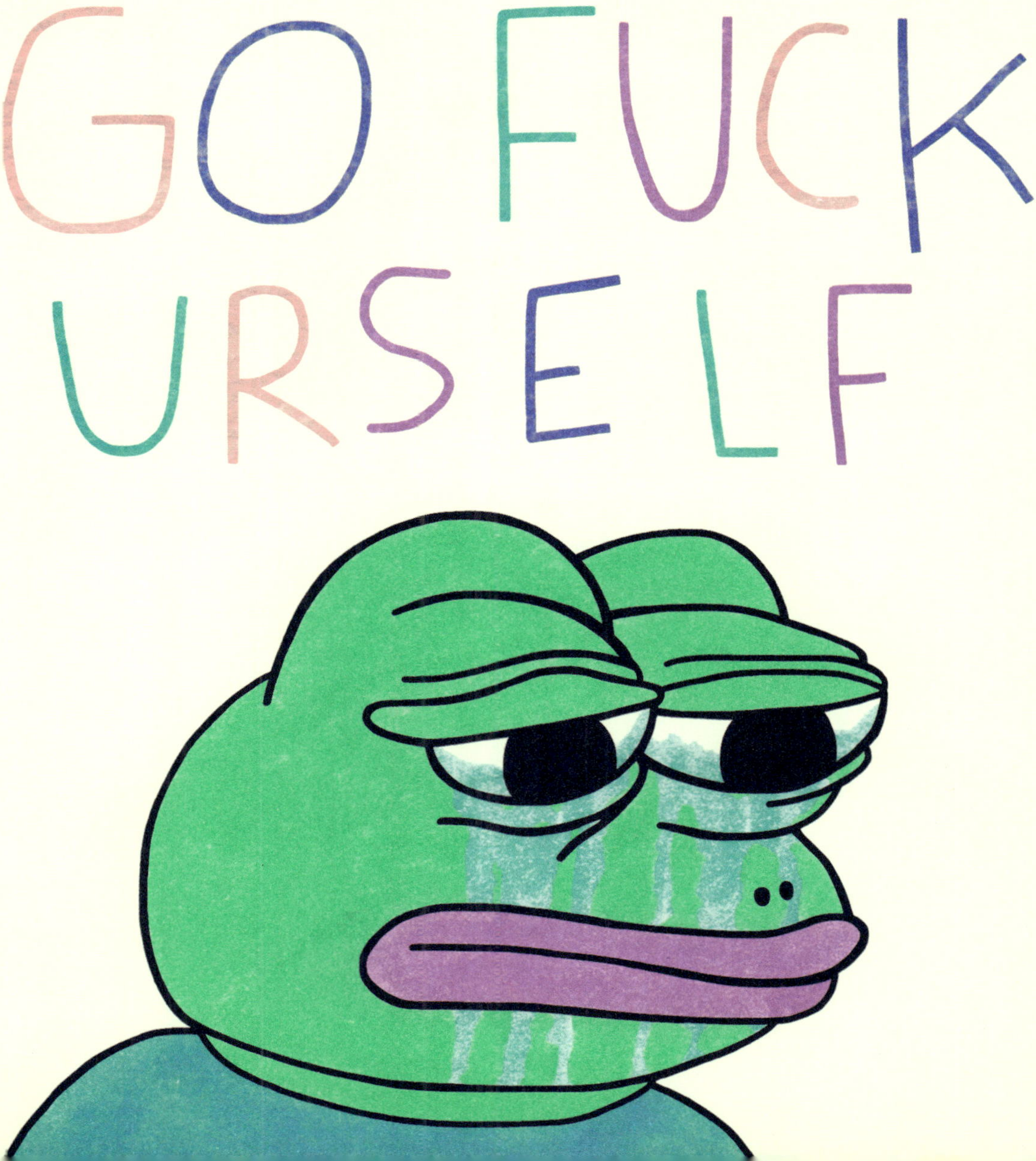
GO FUCK
URSELF

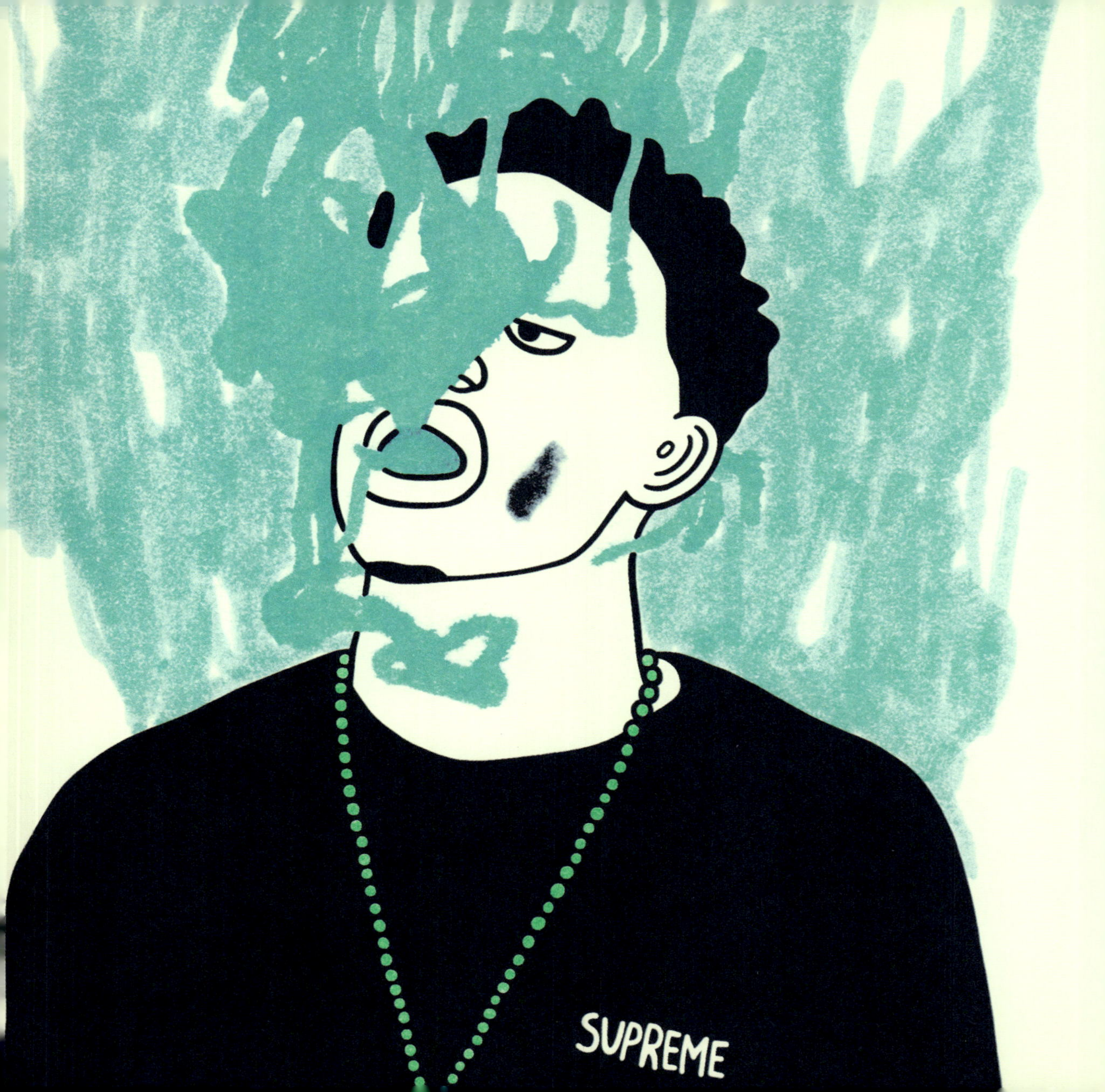
SUPREME

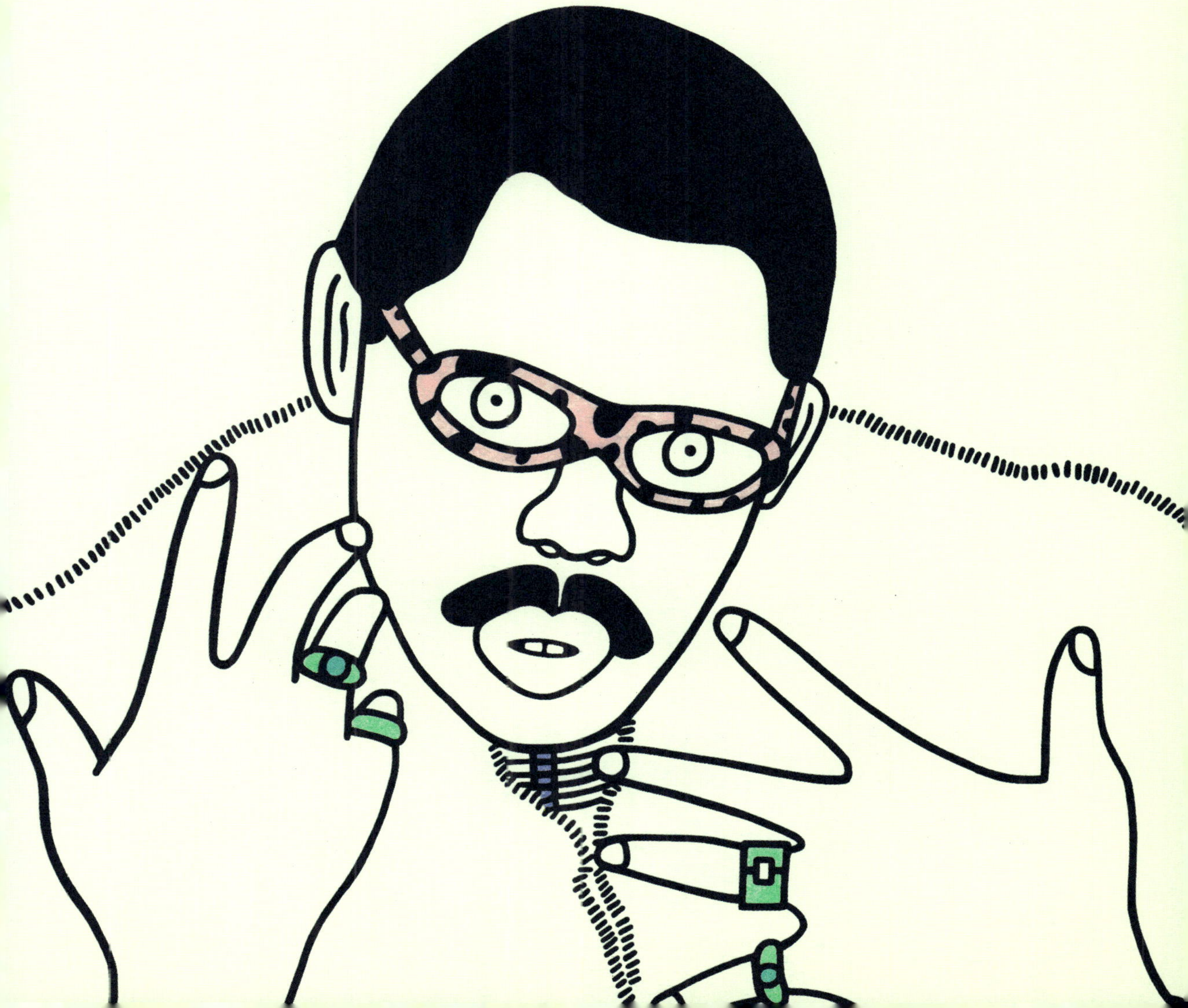

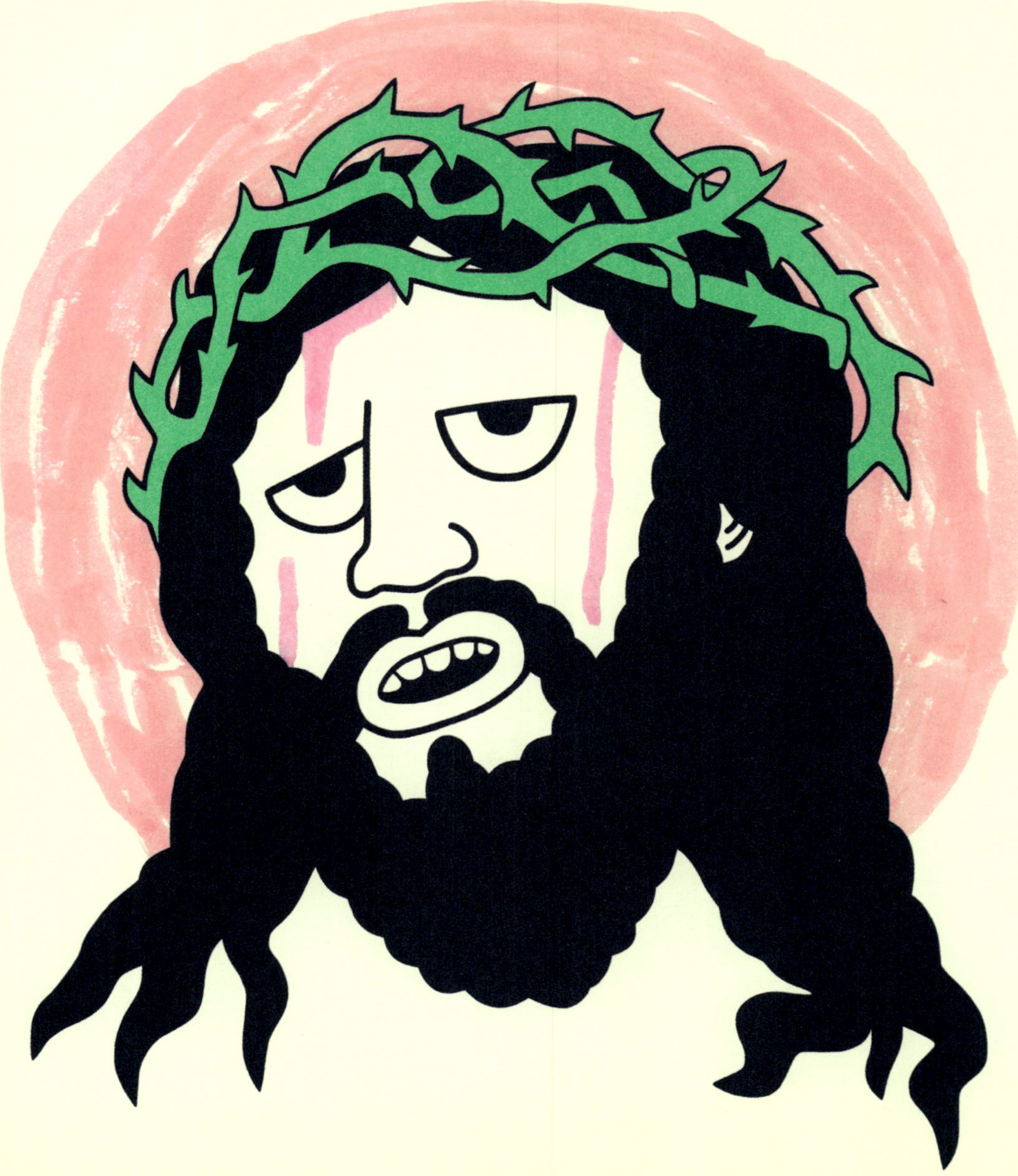

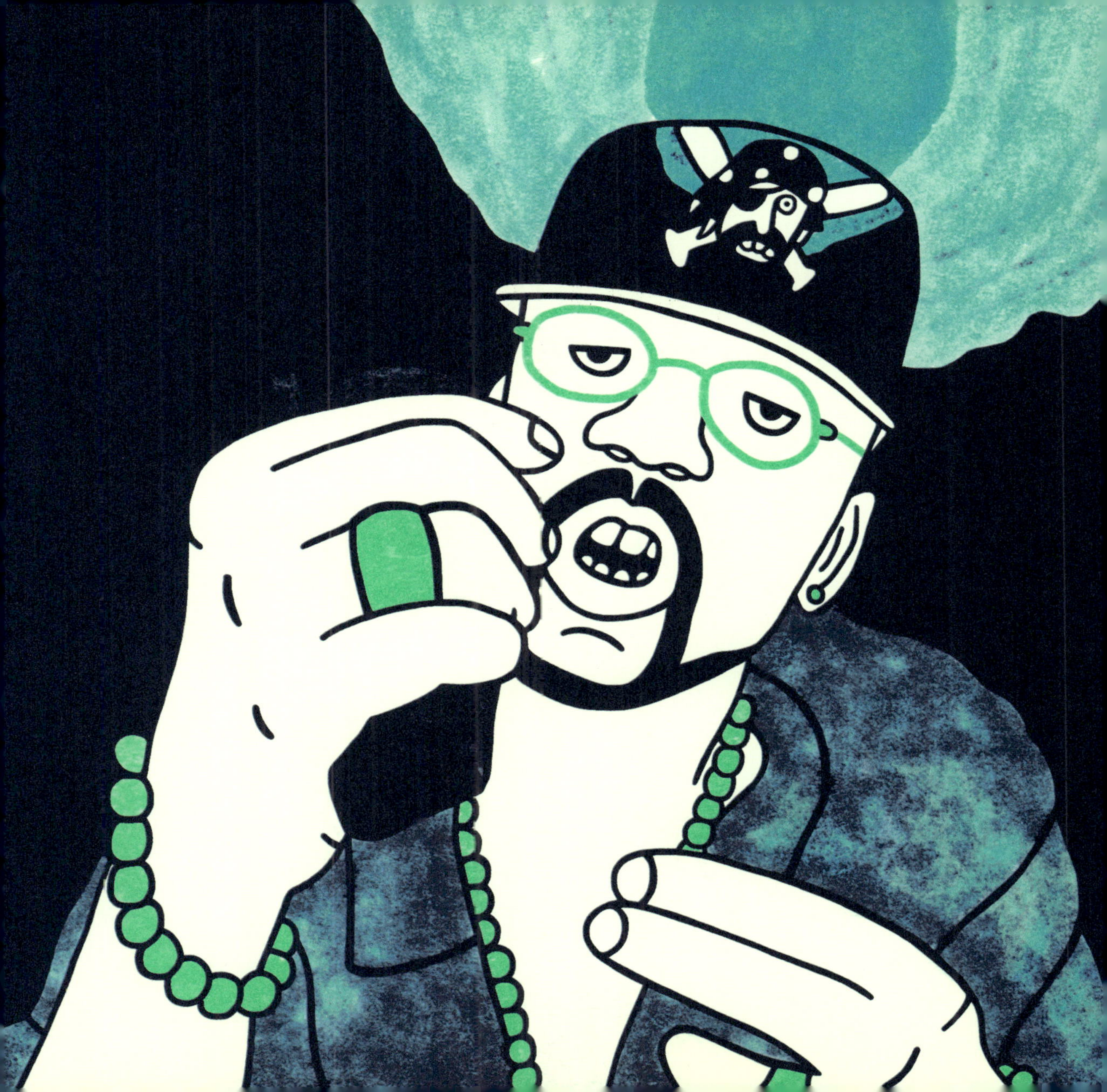

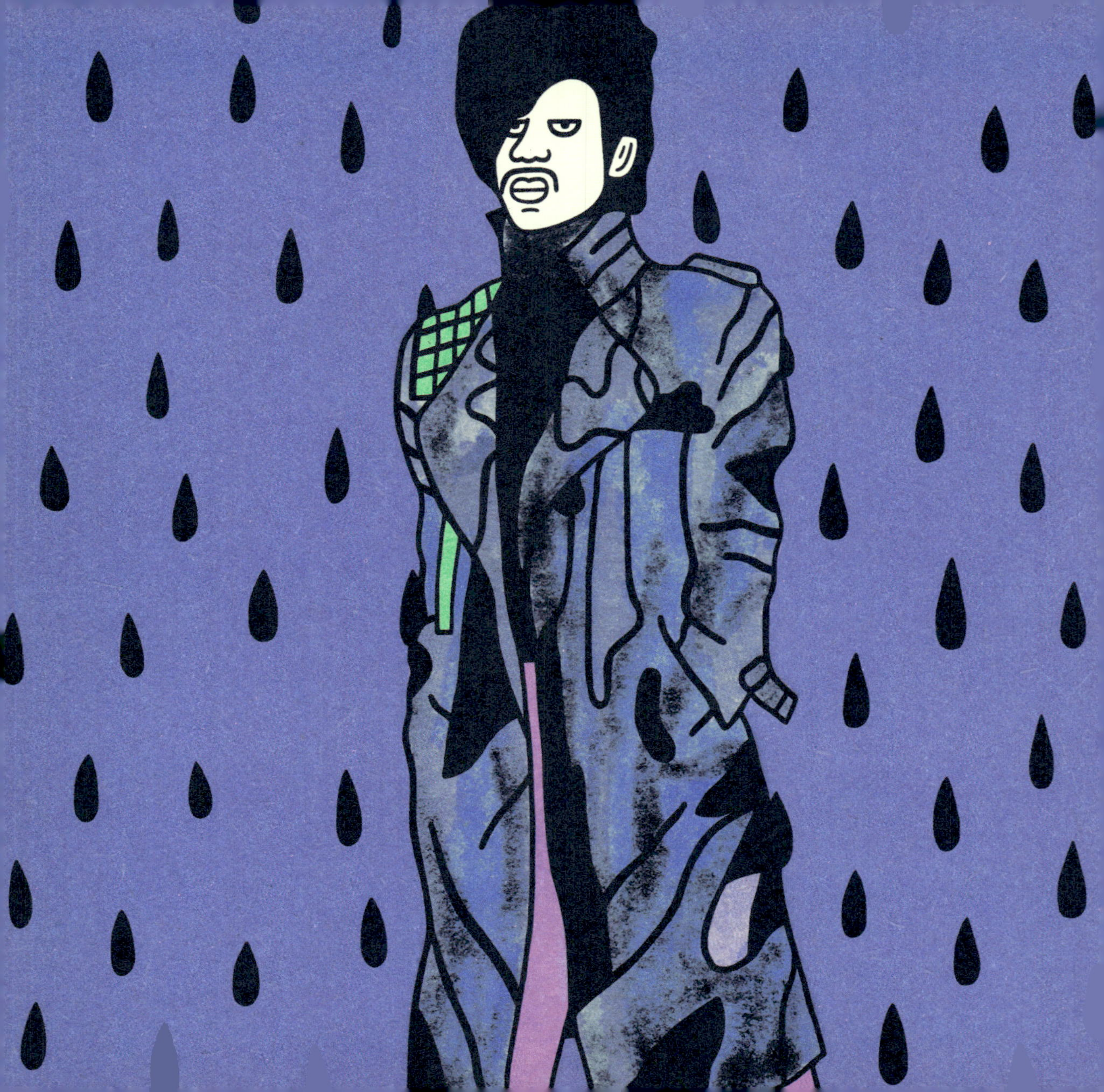

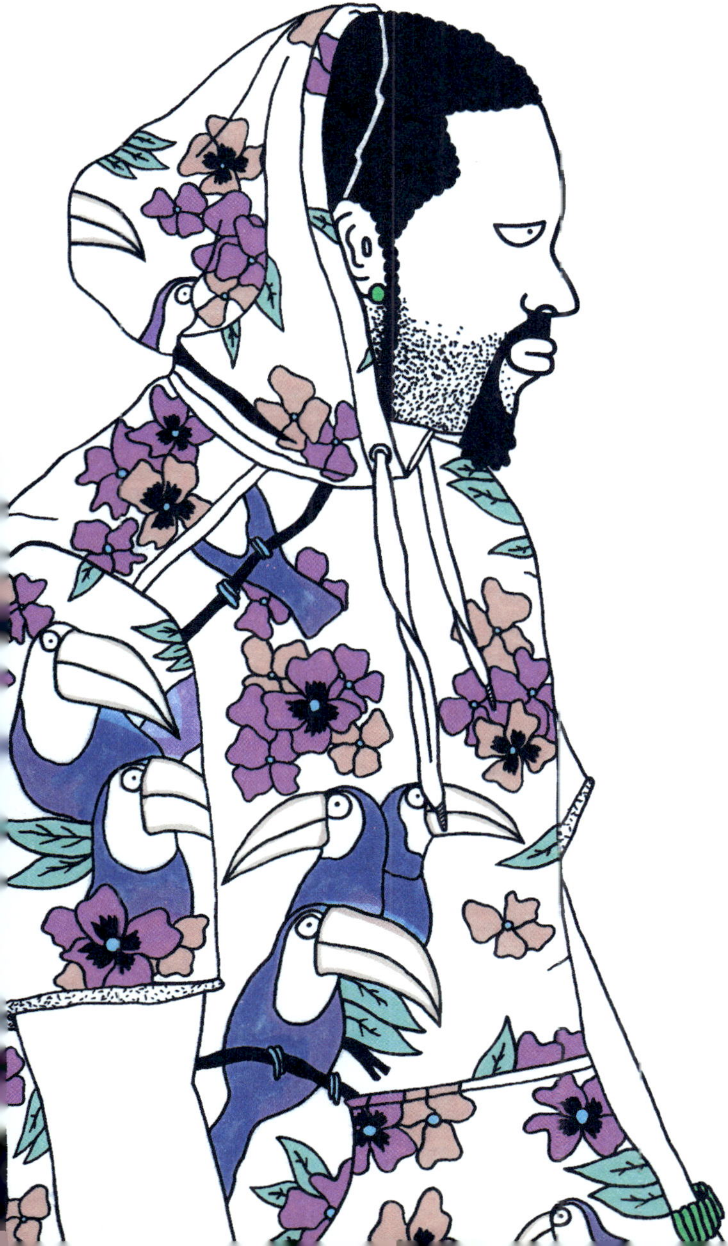

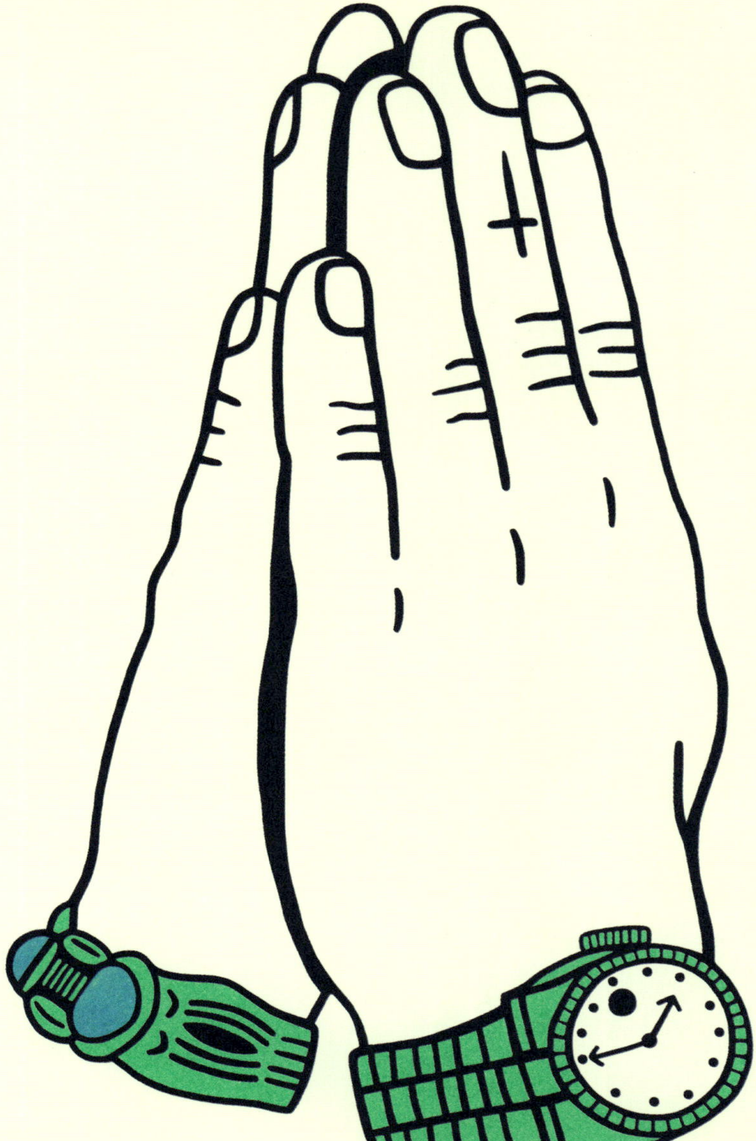

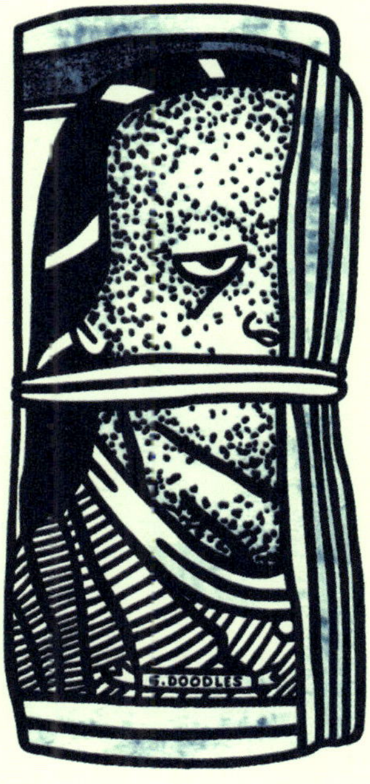
G. DOODLES

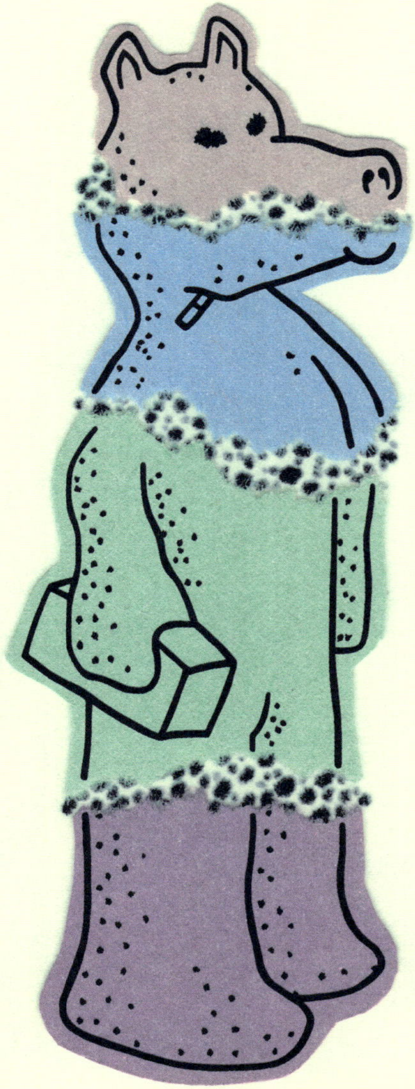

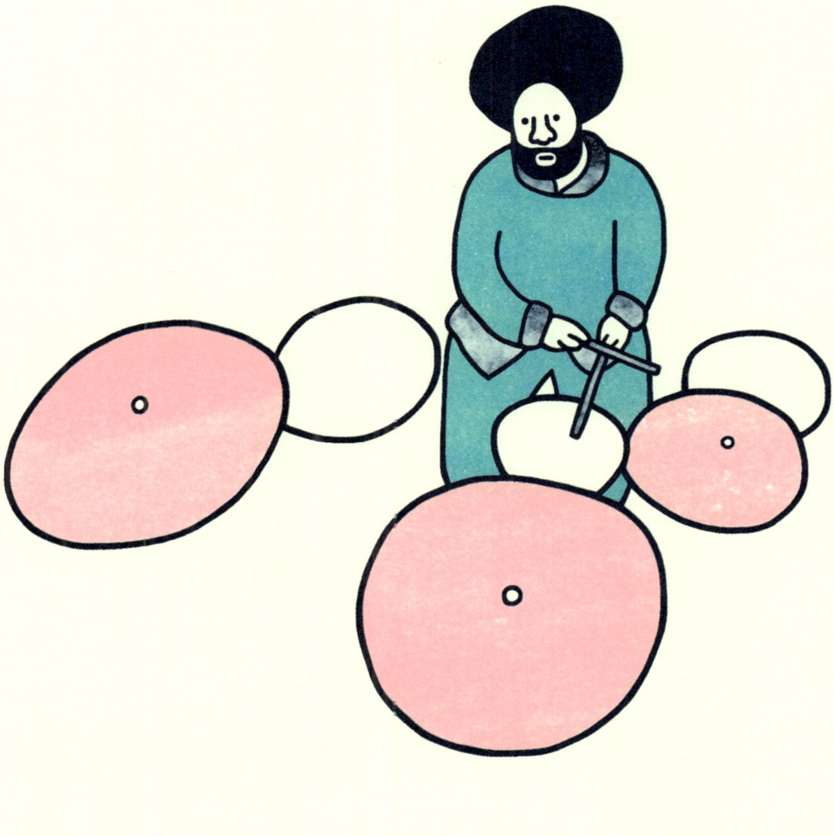

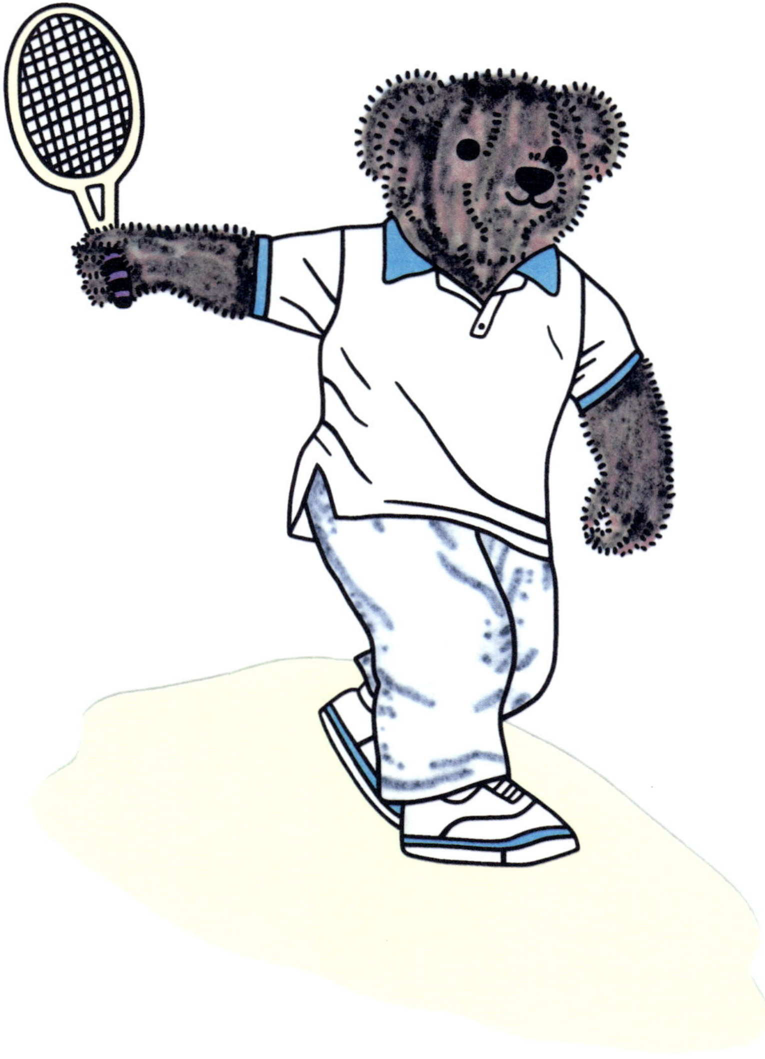

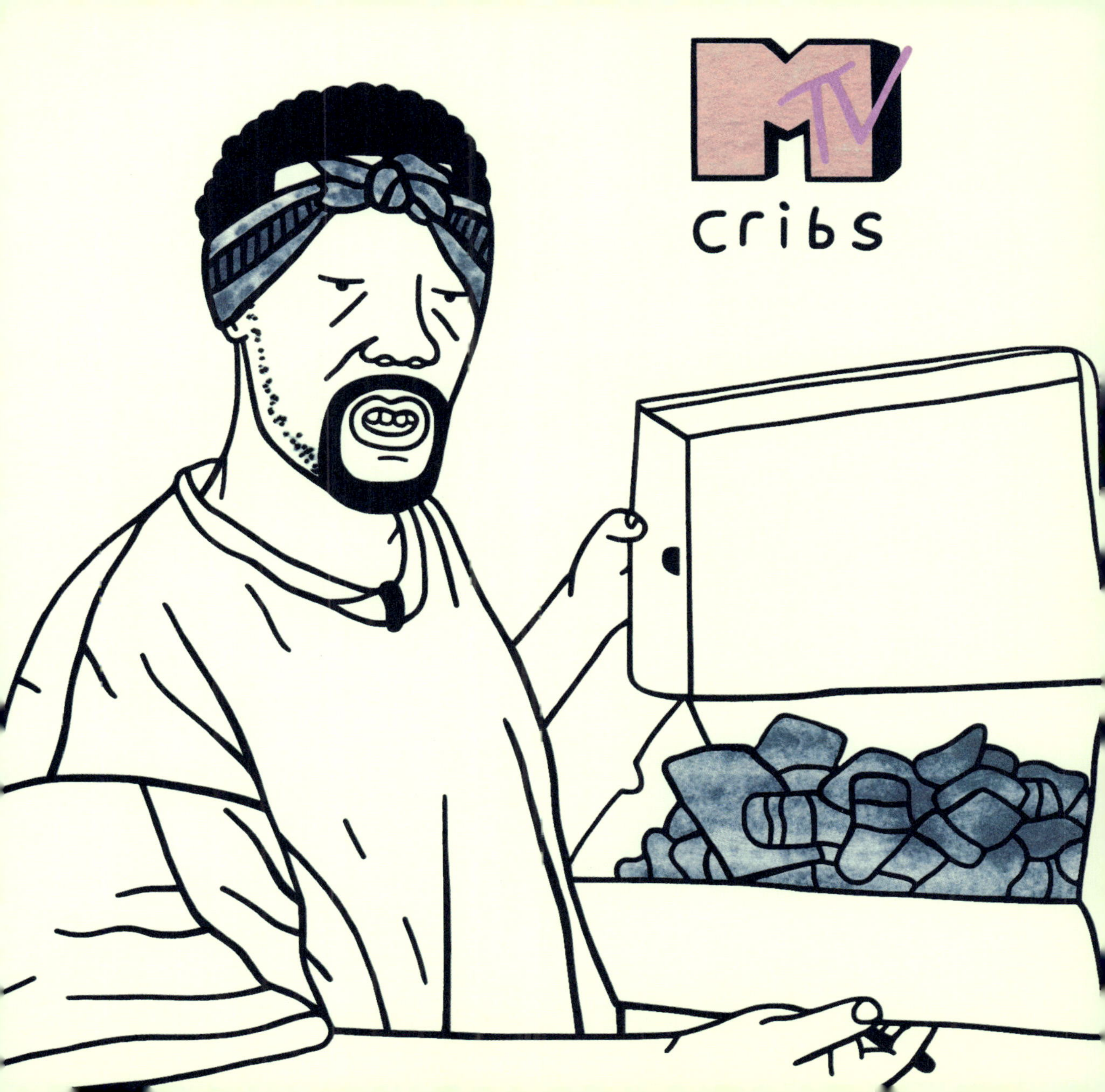
MTV
cribs

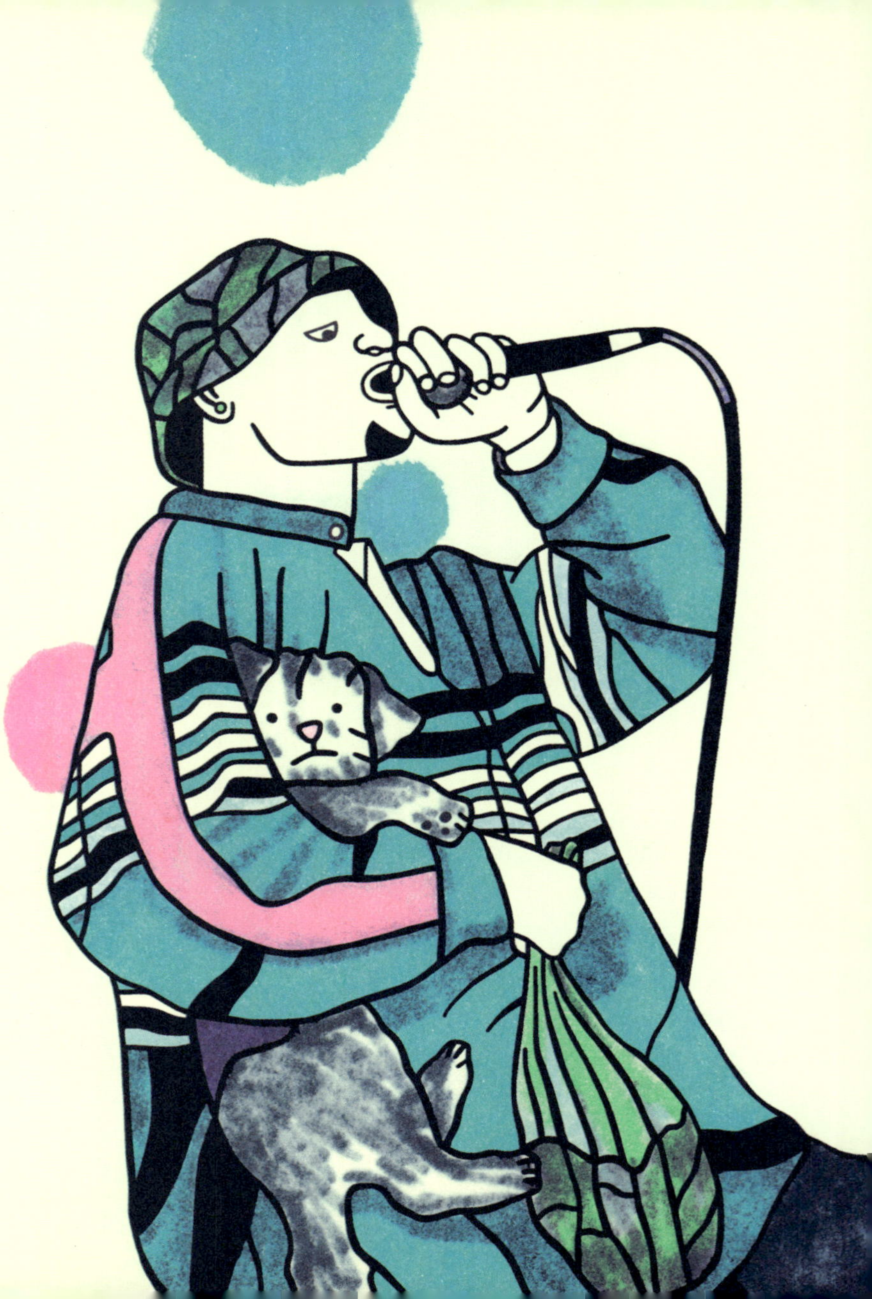

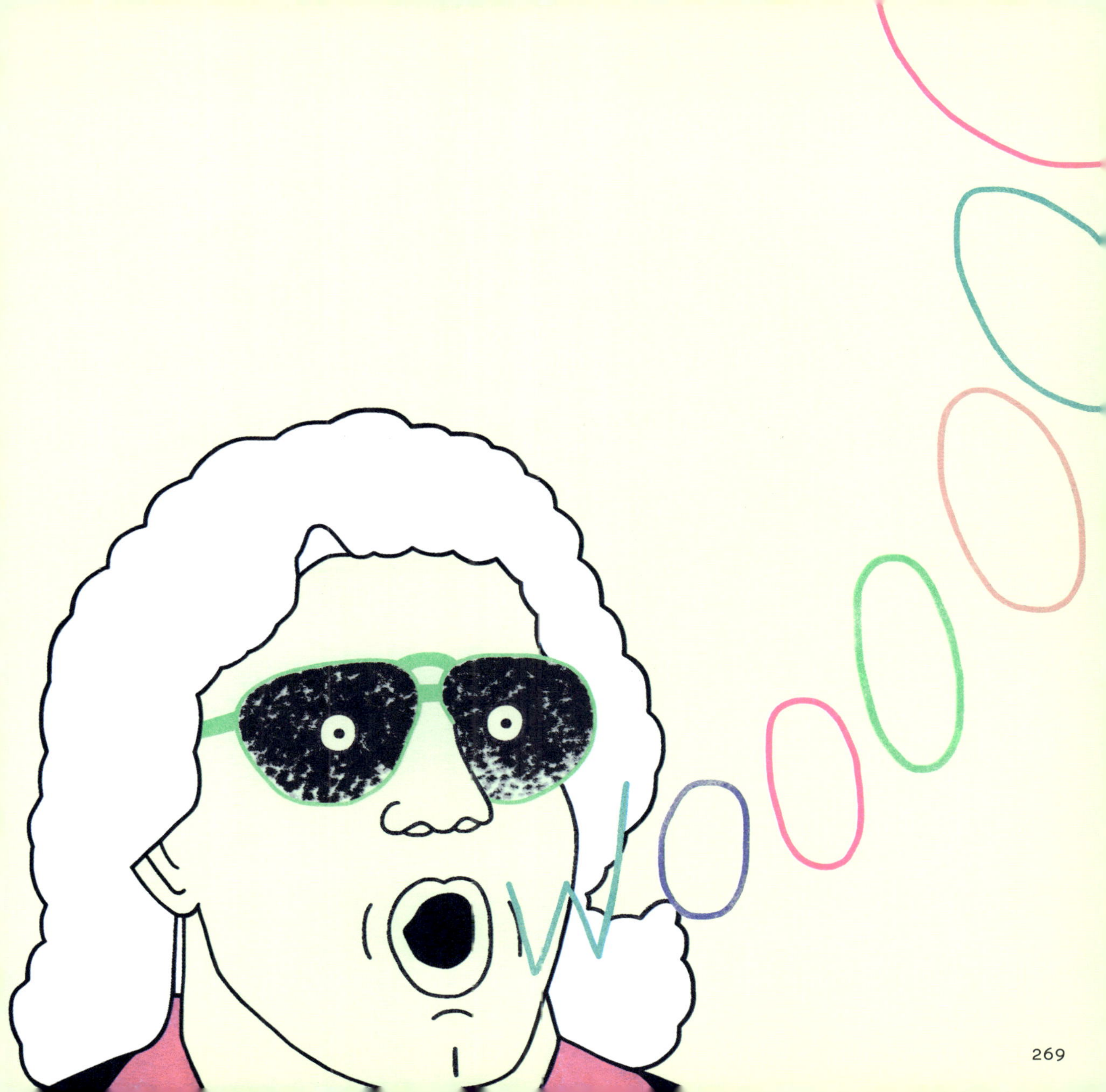
WOOOOOO

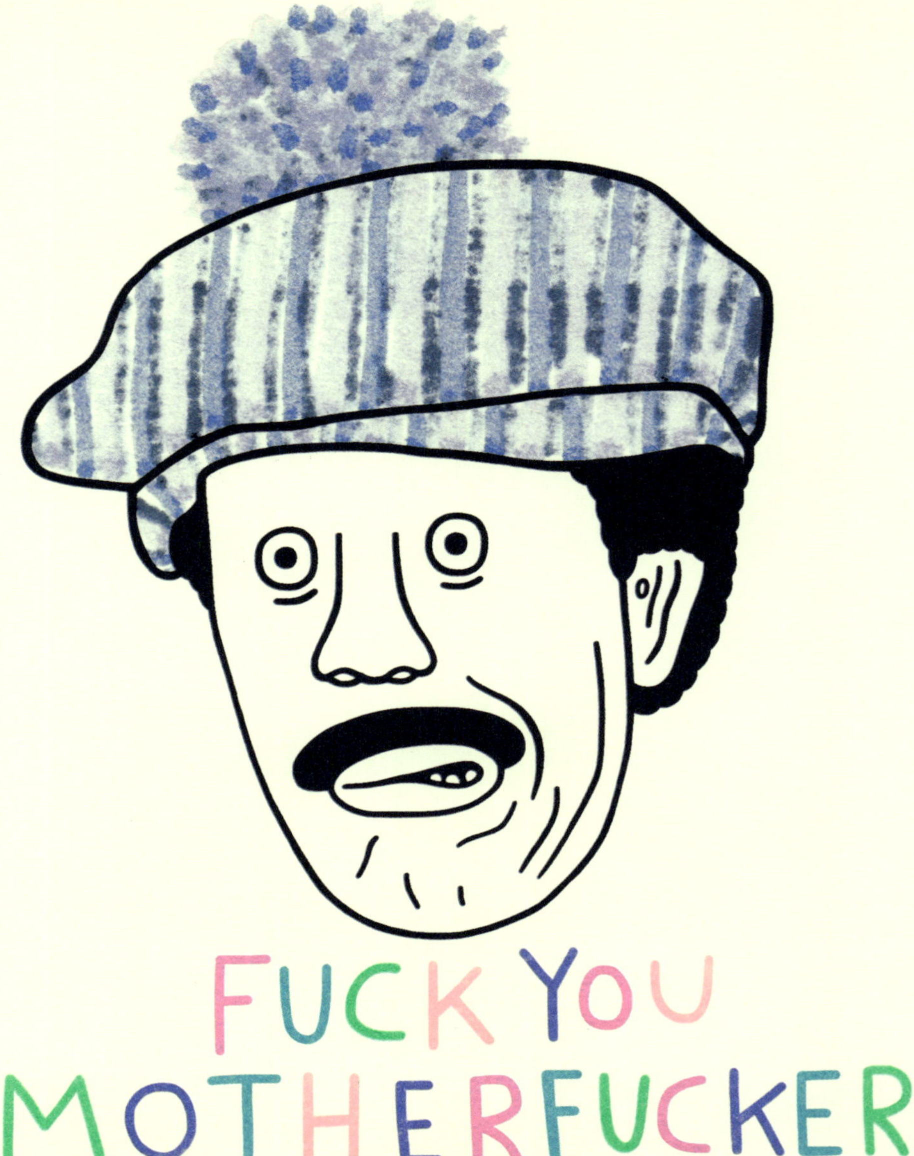
FUCK YOU
MOTHERFUCKER

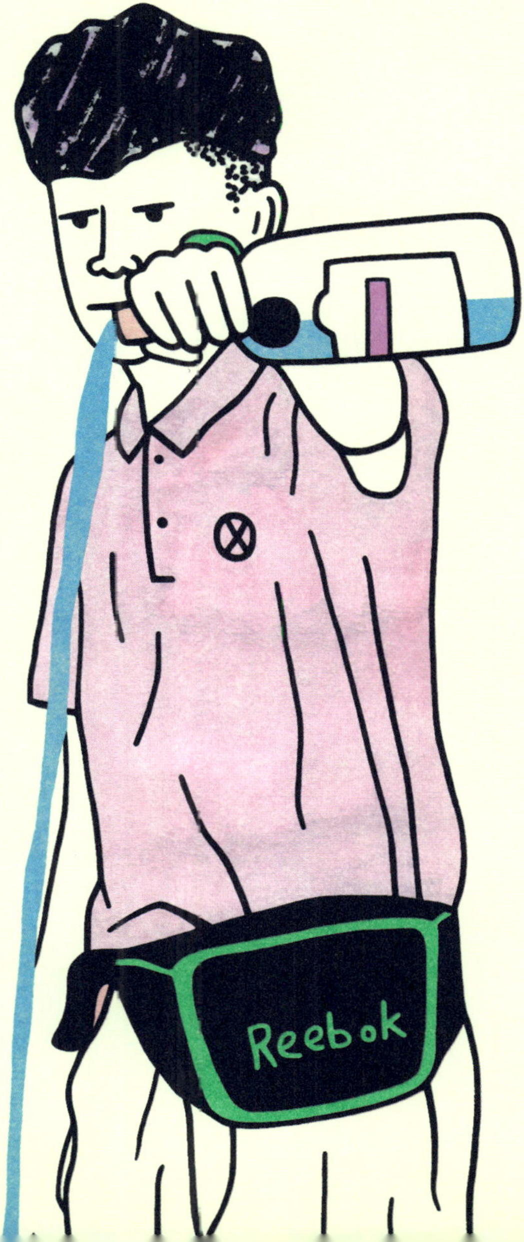
Reebok

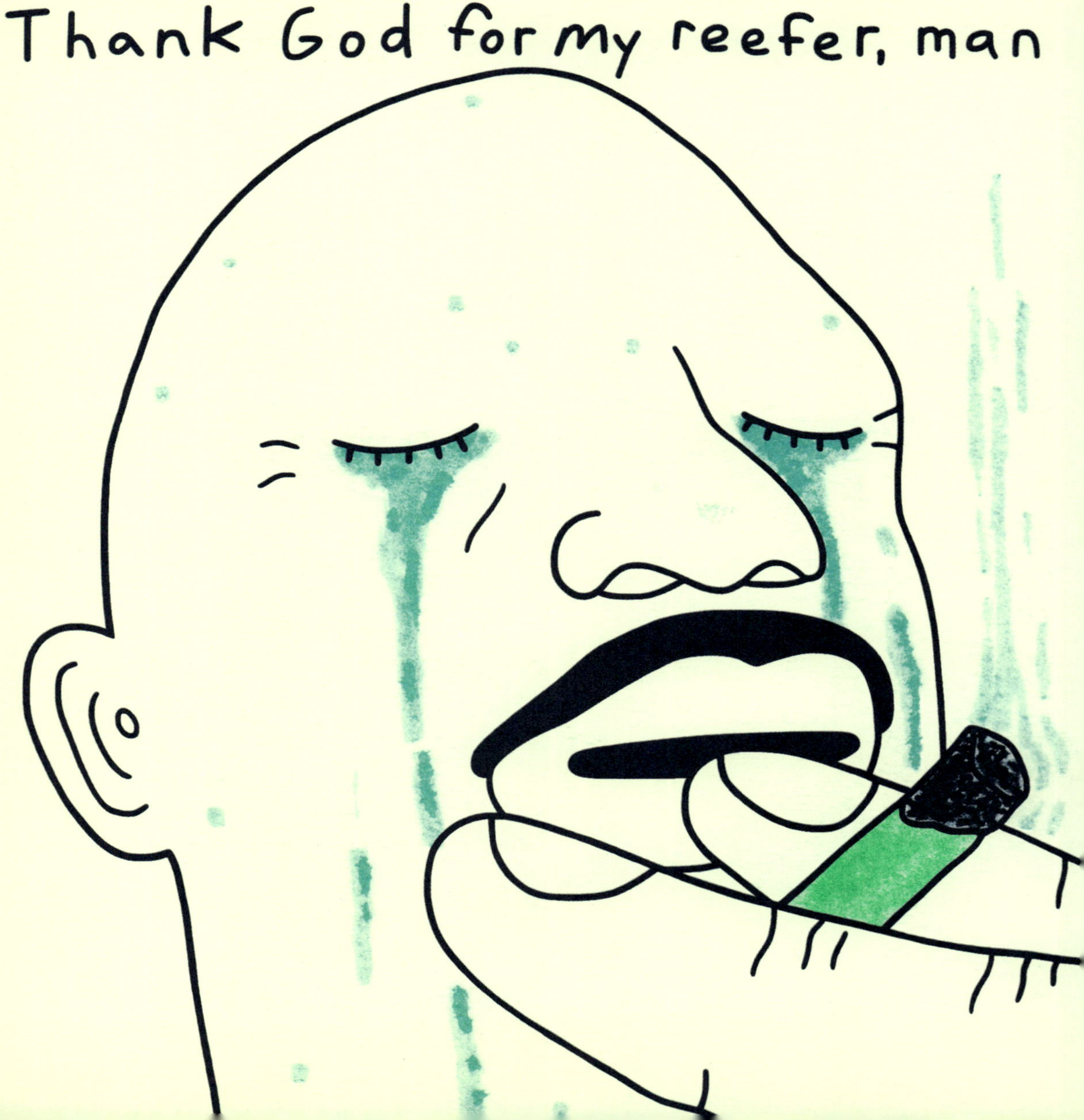
Thank God for my reefer, man

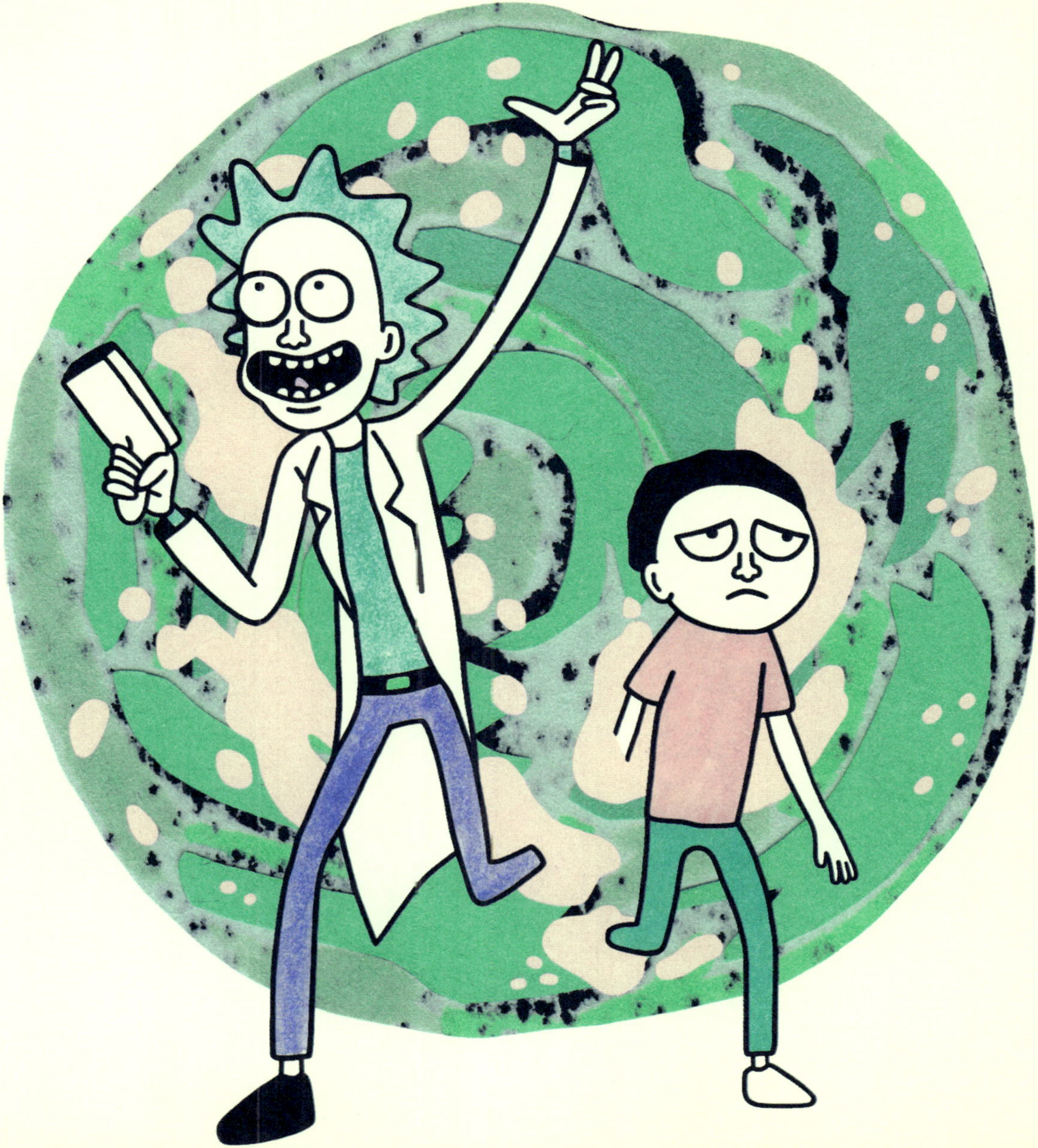

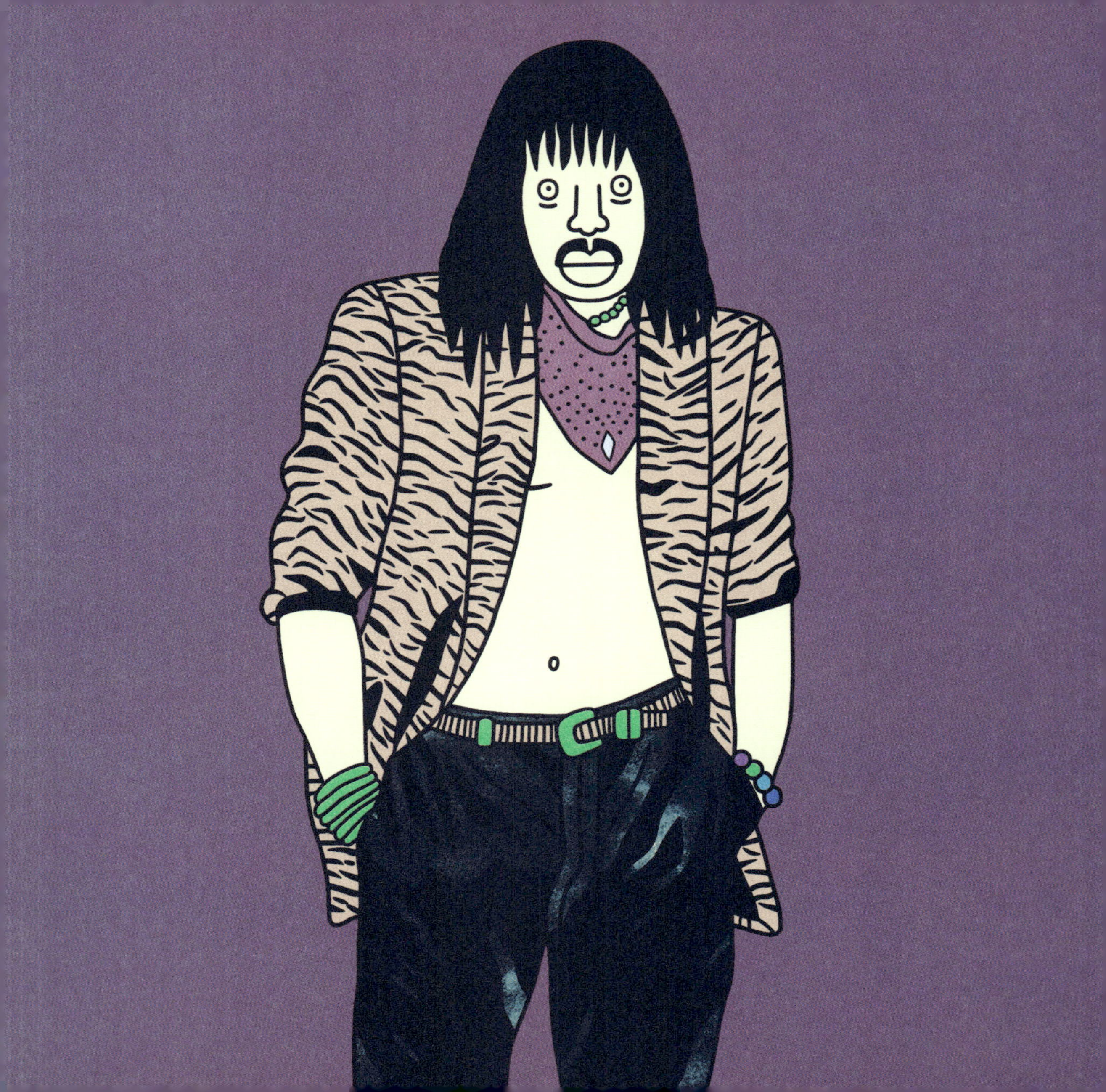

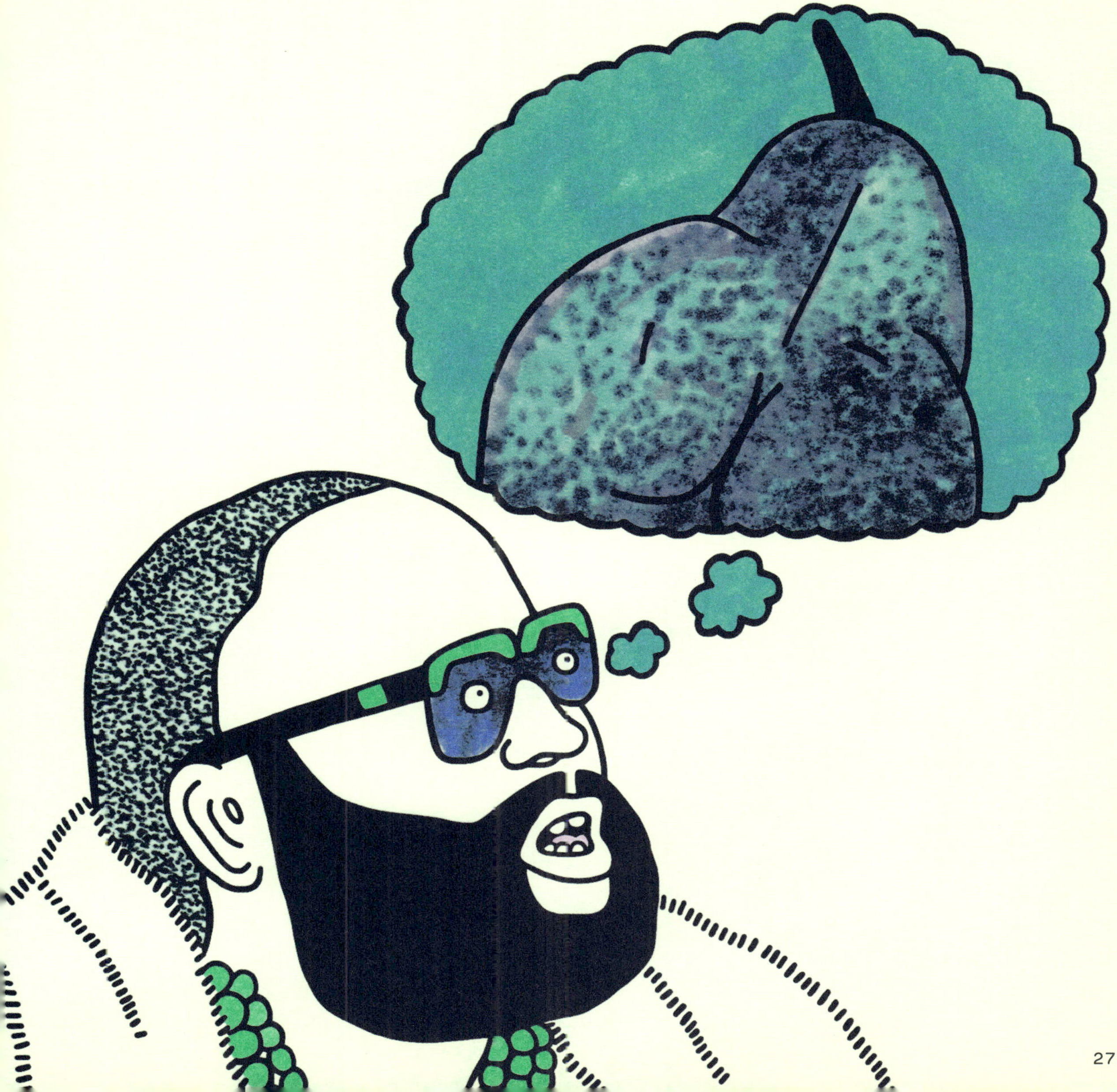

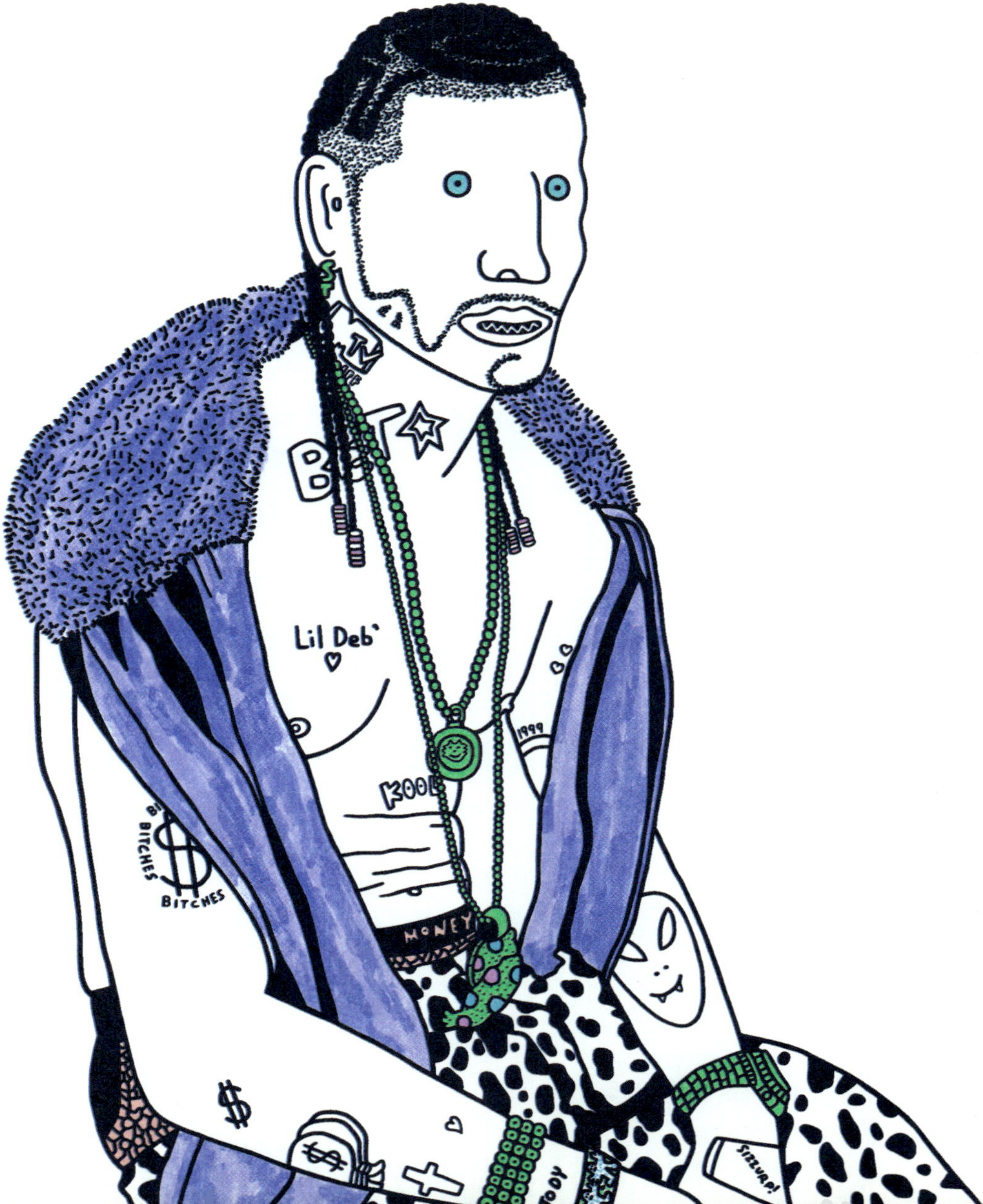
Lil Deb'
1999
KOOL
BITCHES
BITCHES
MONEY

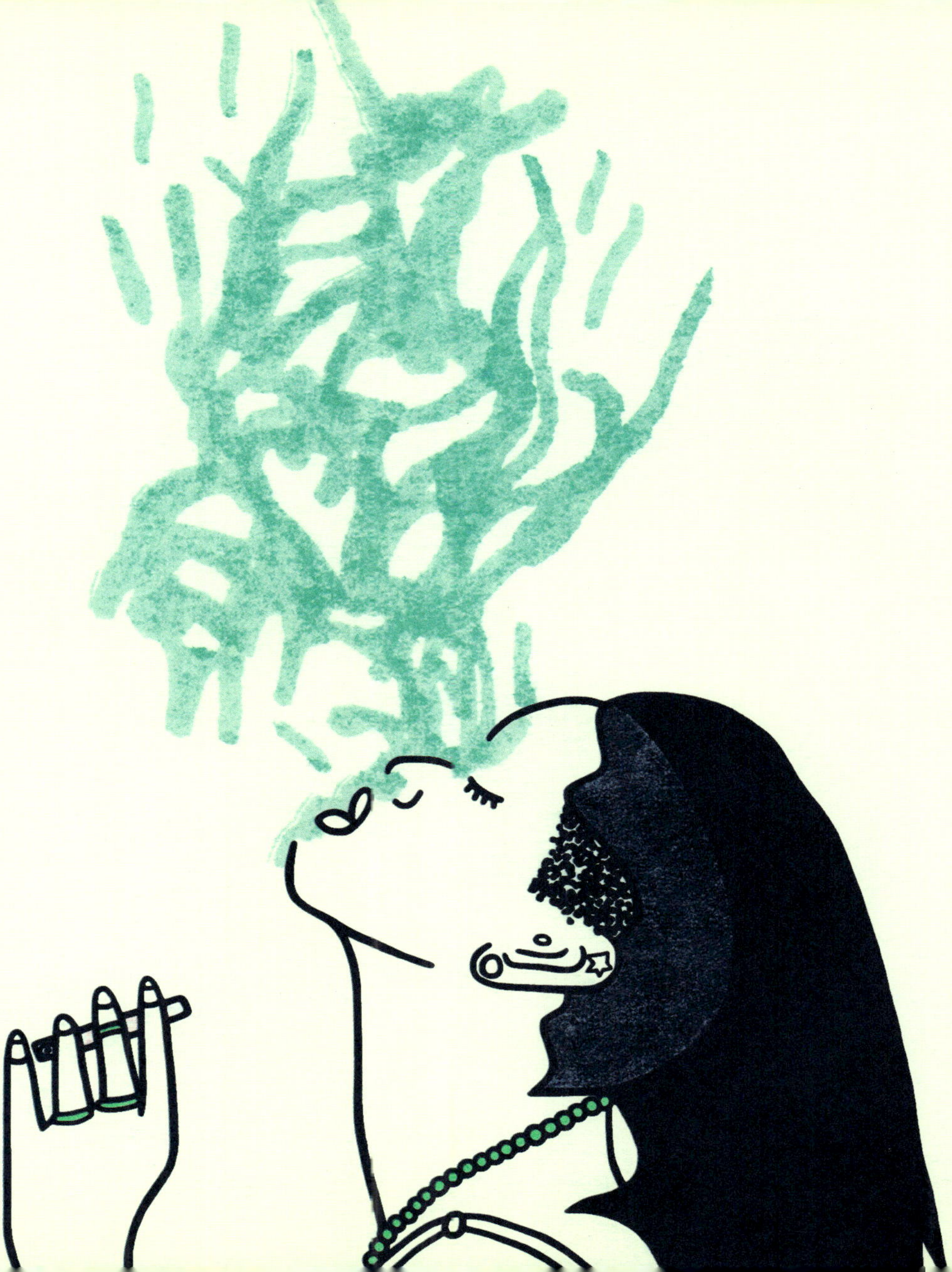

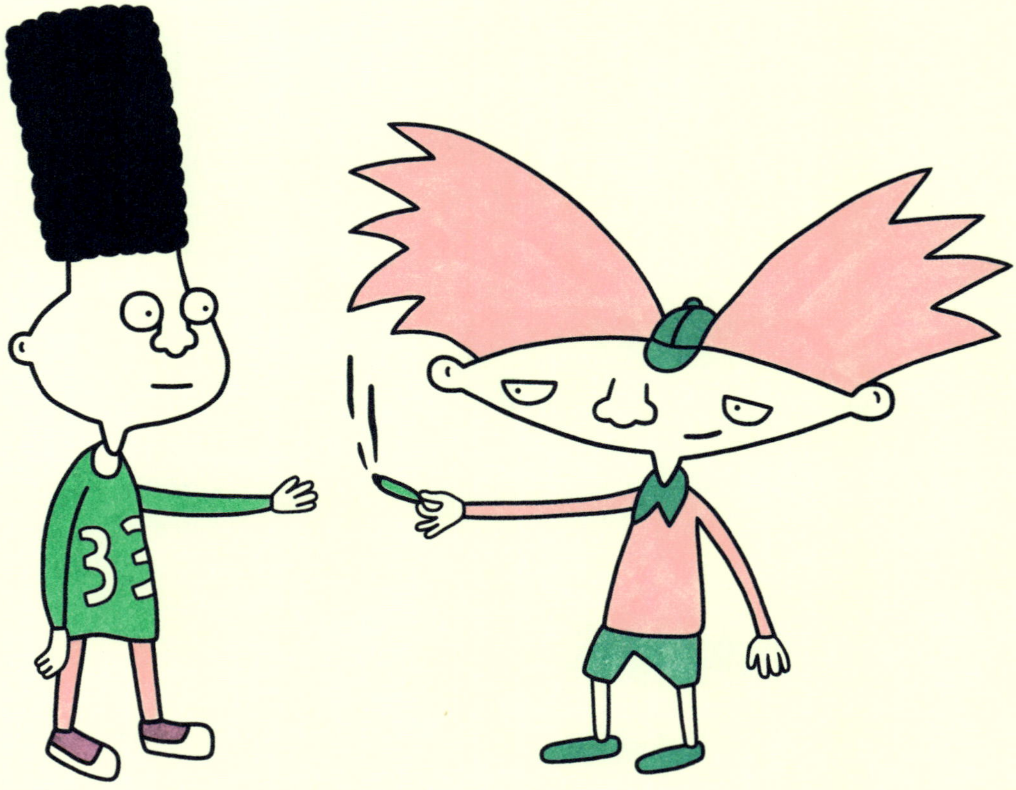

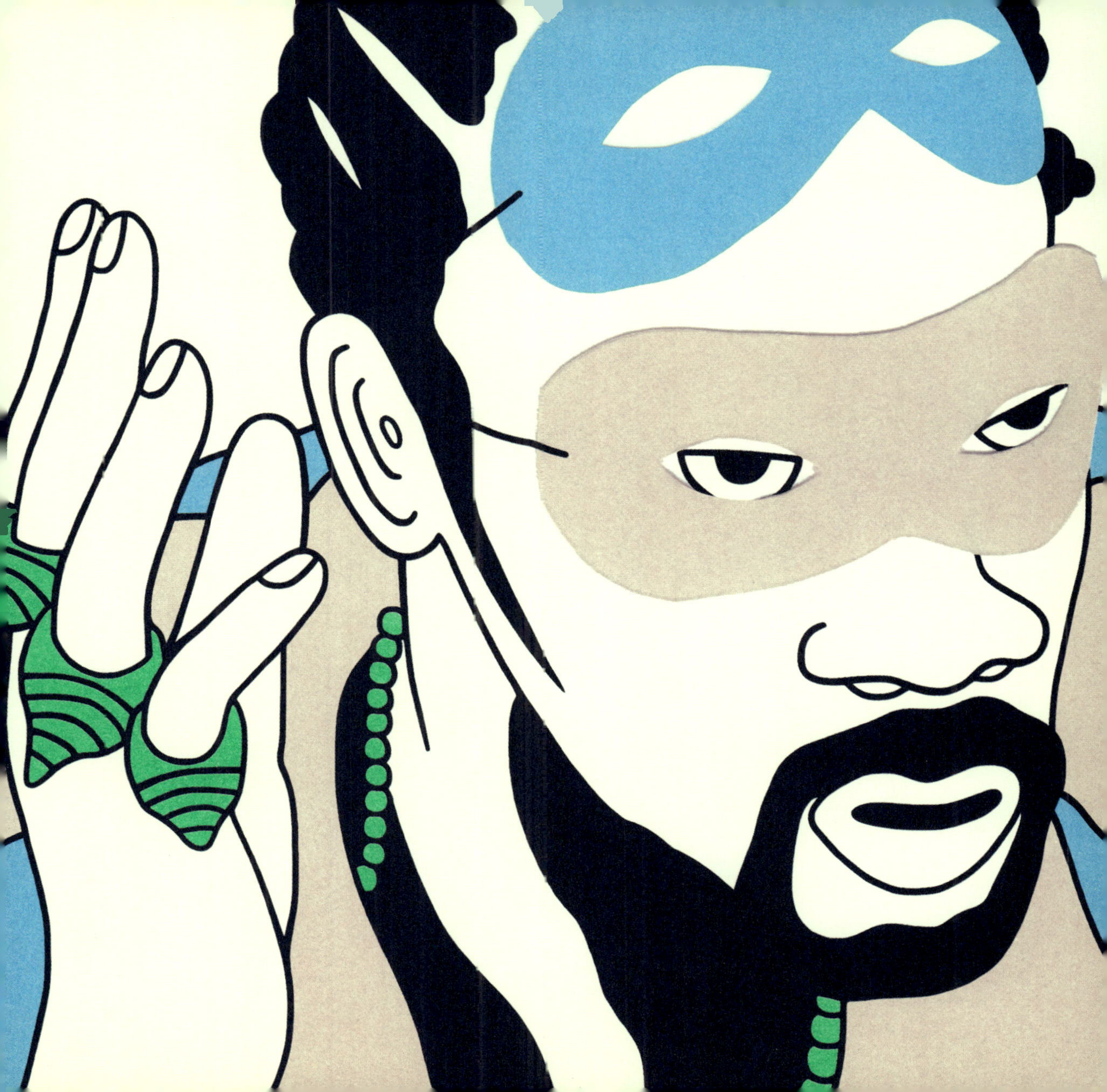

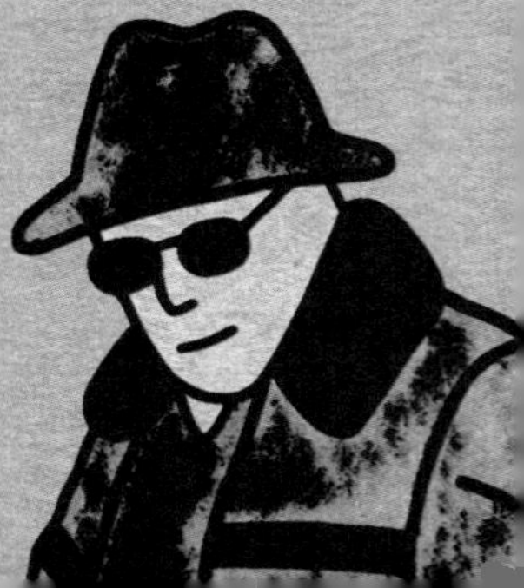

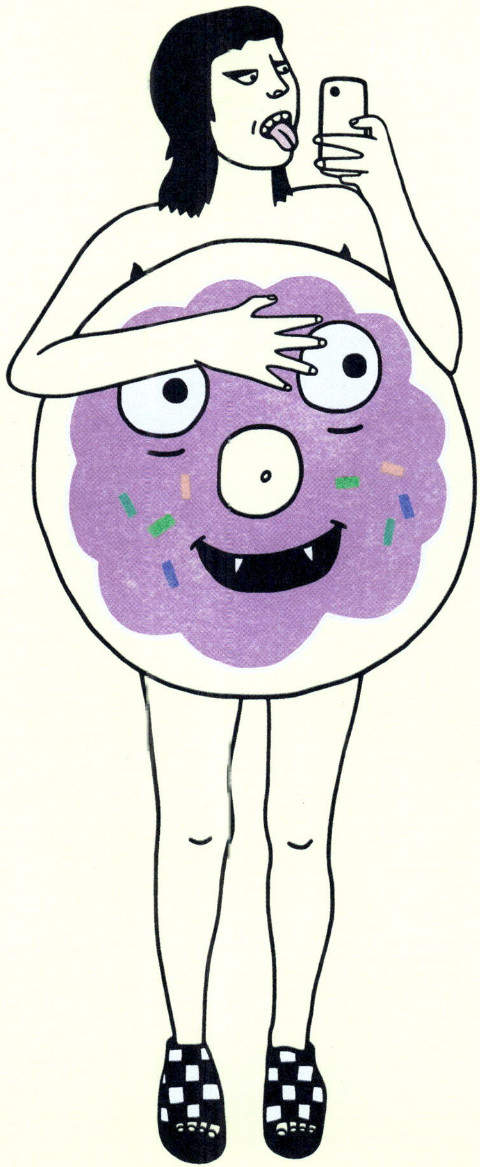

Shia Motivates

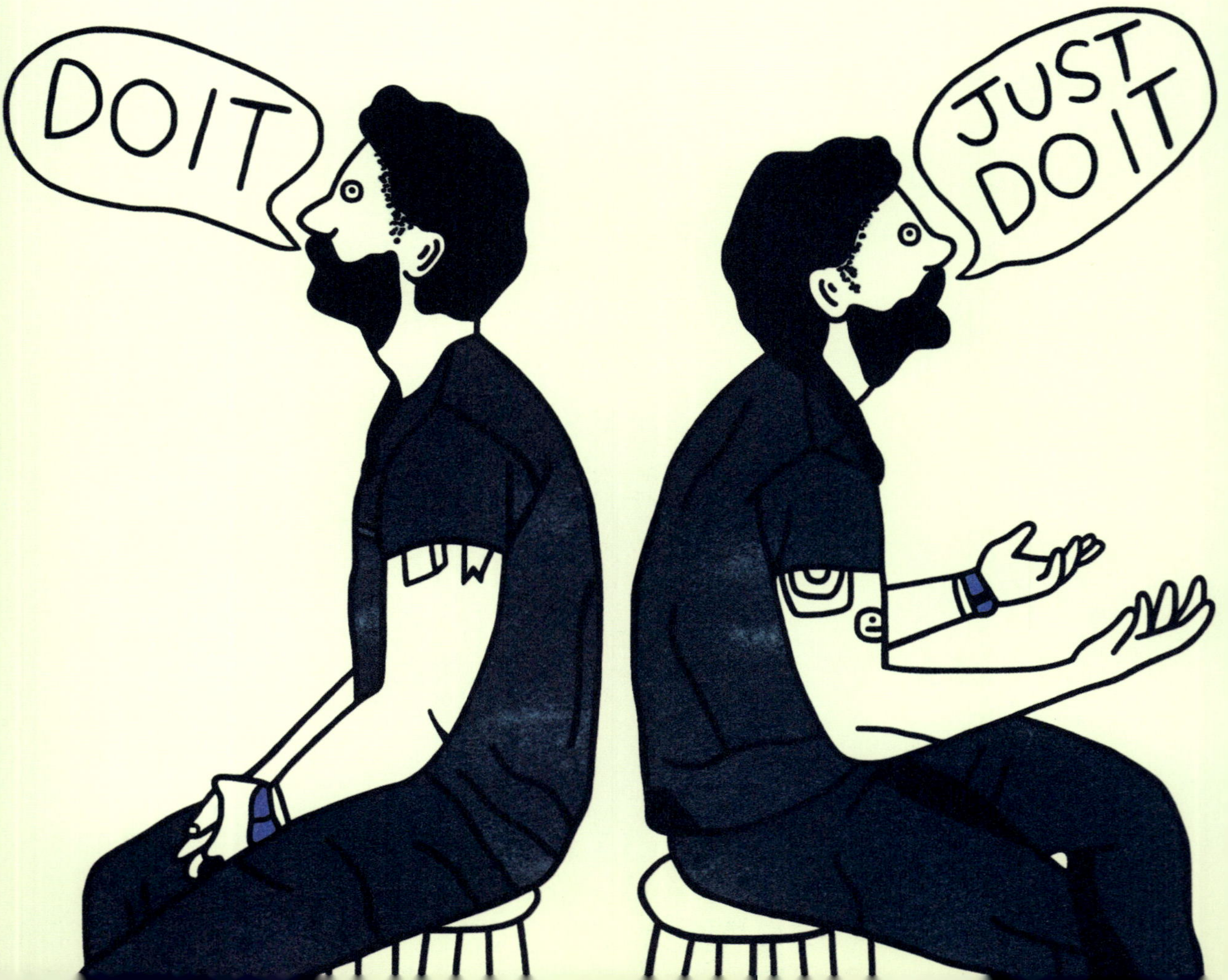

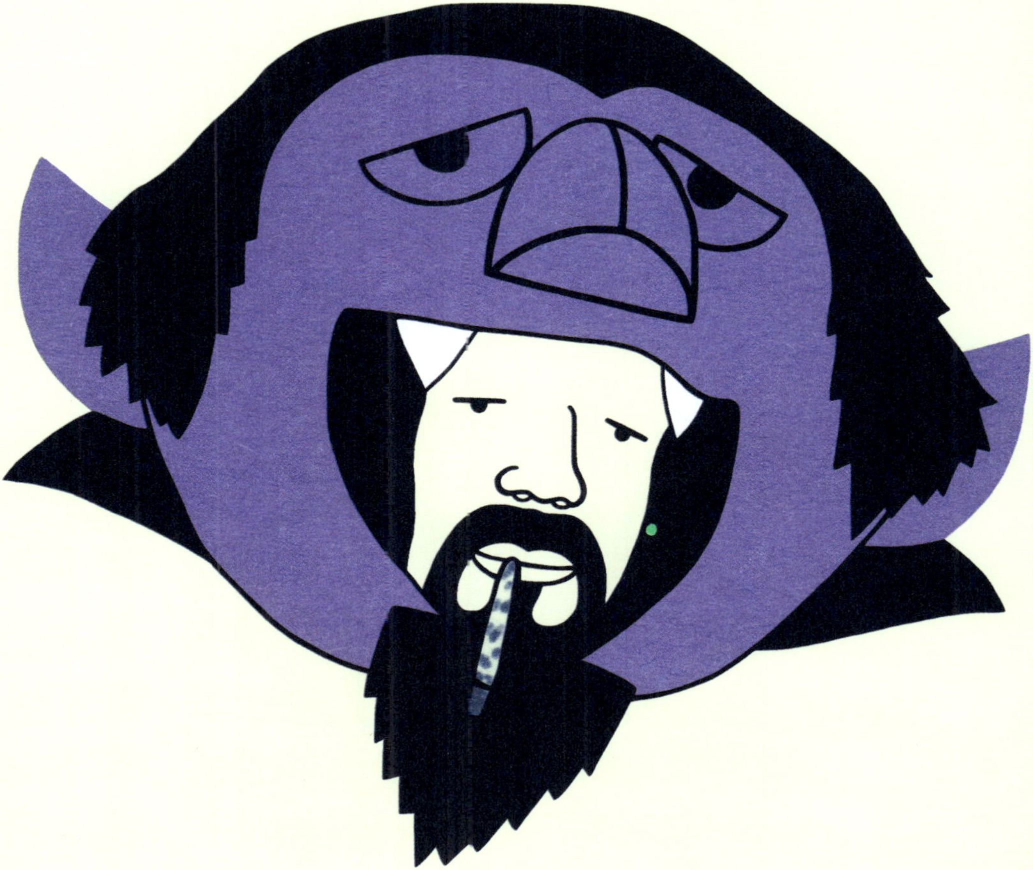

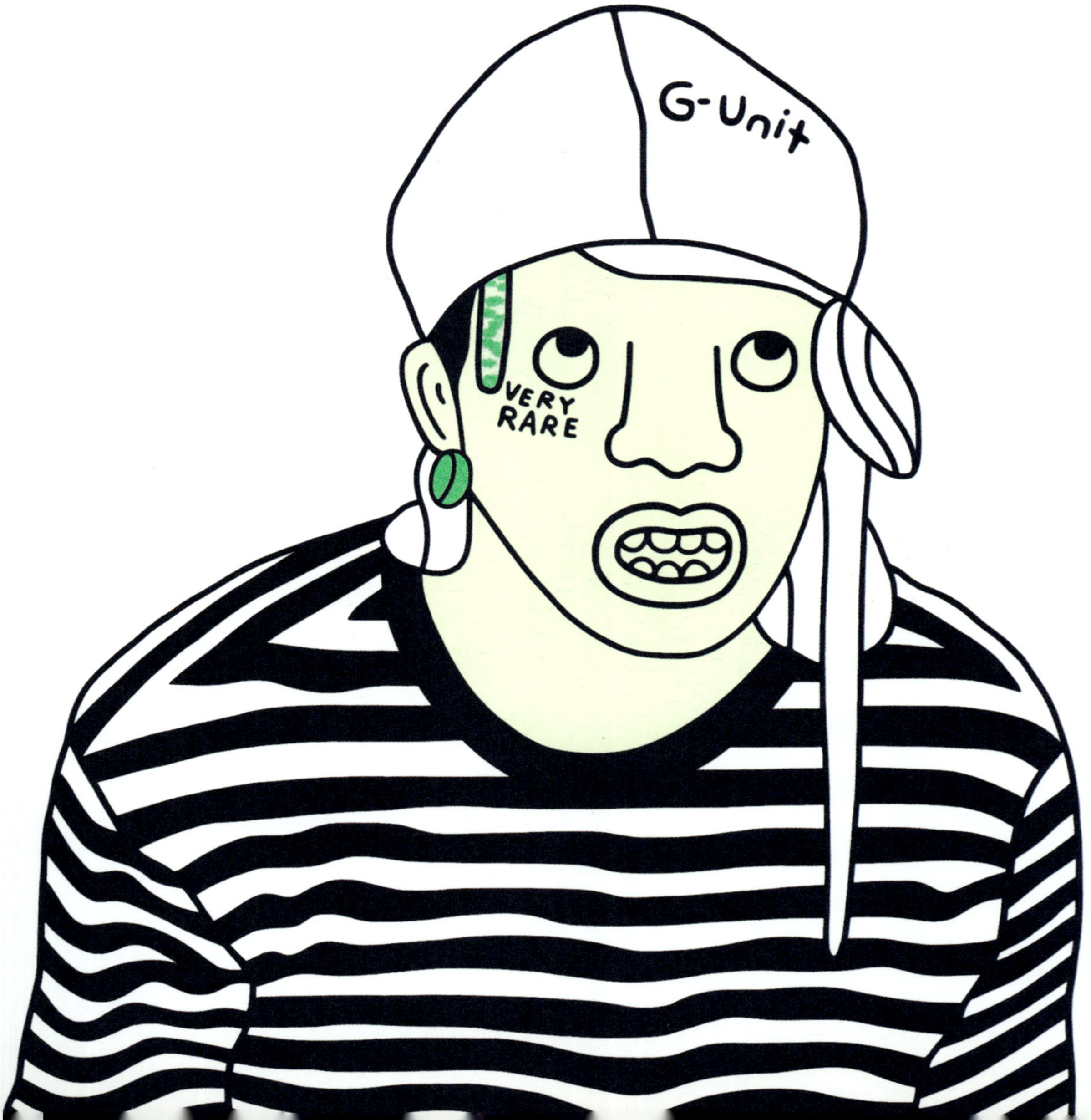
G-Unit
VERY
RARE

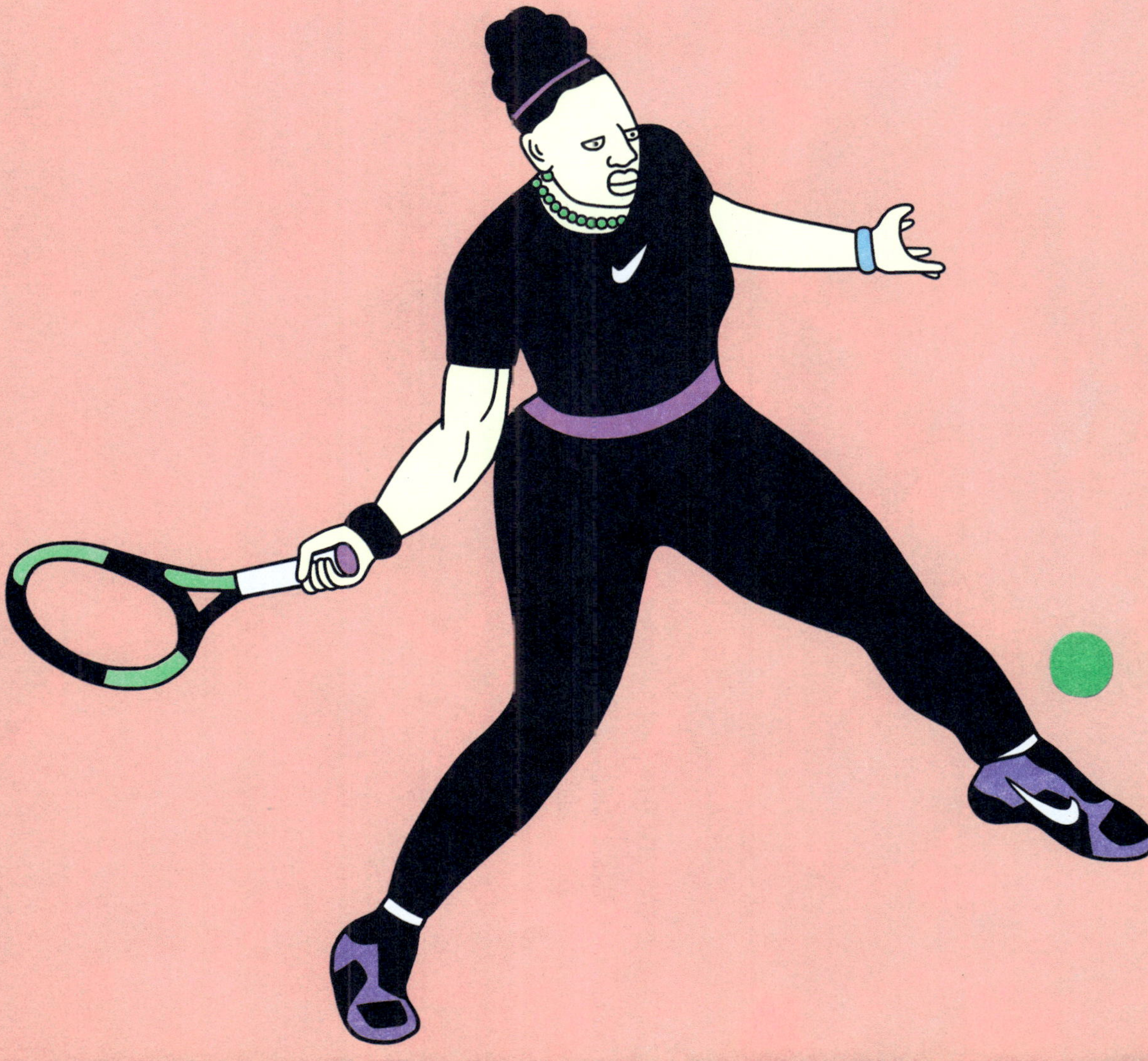

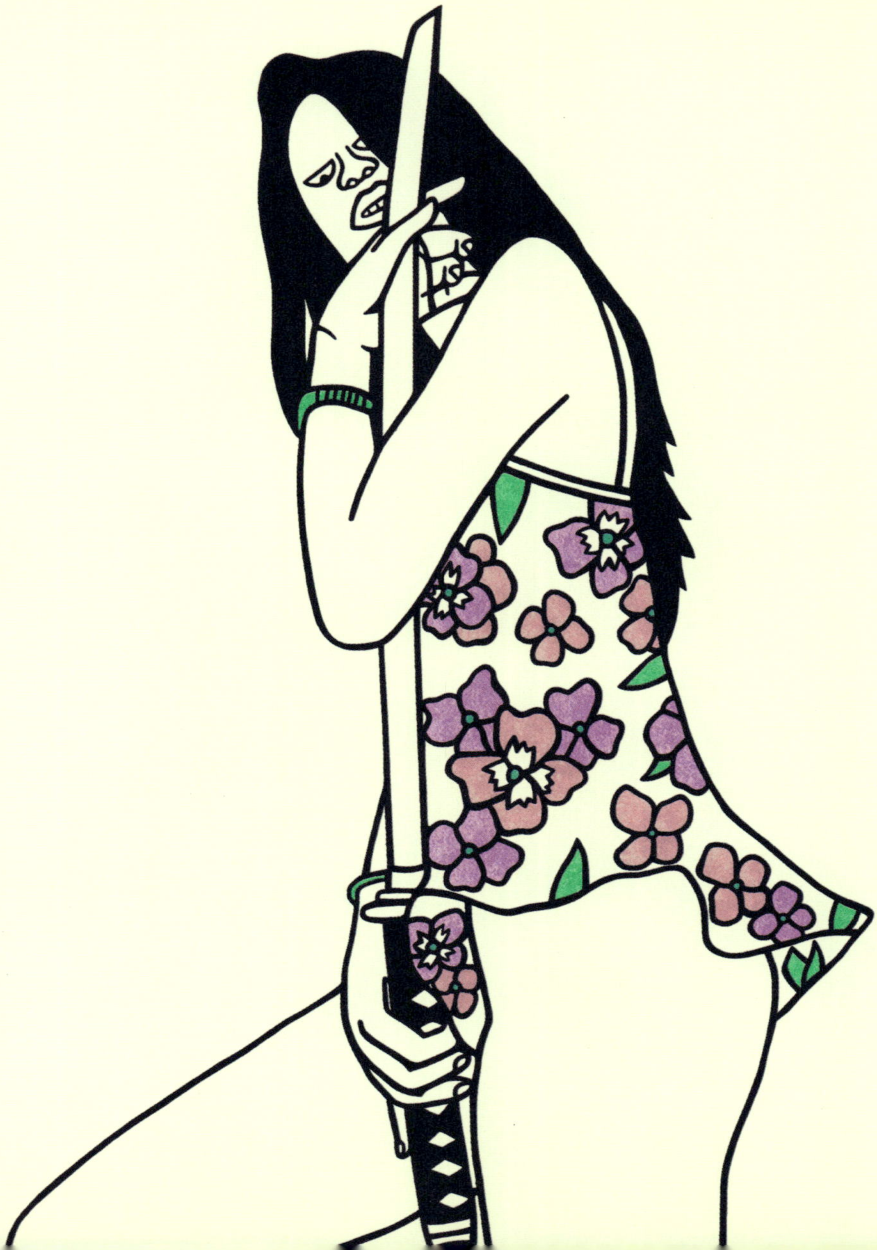

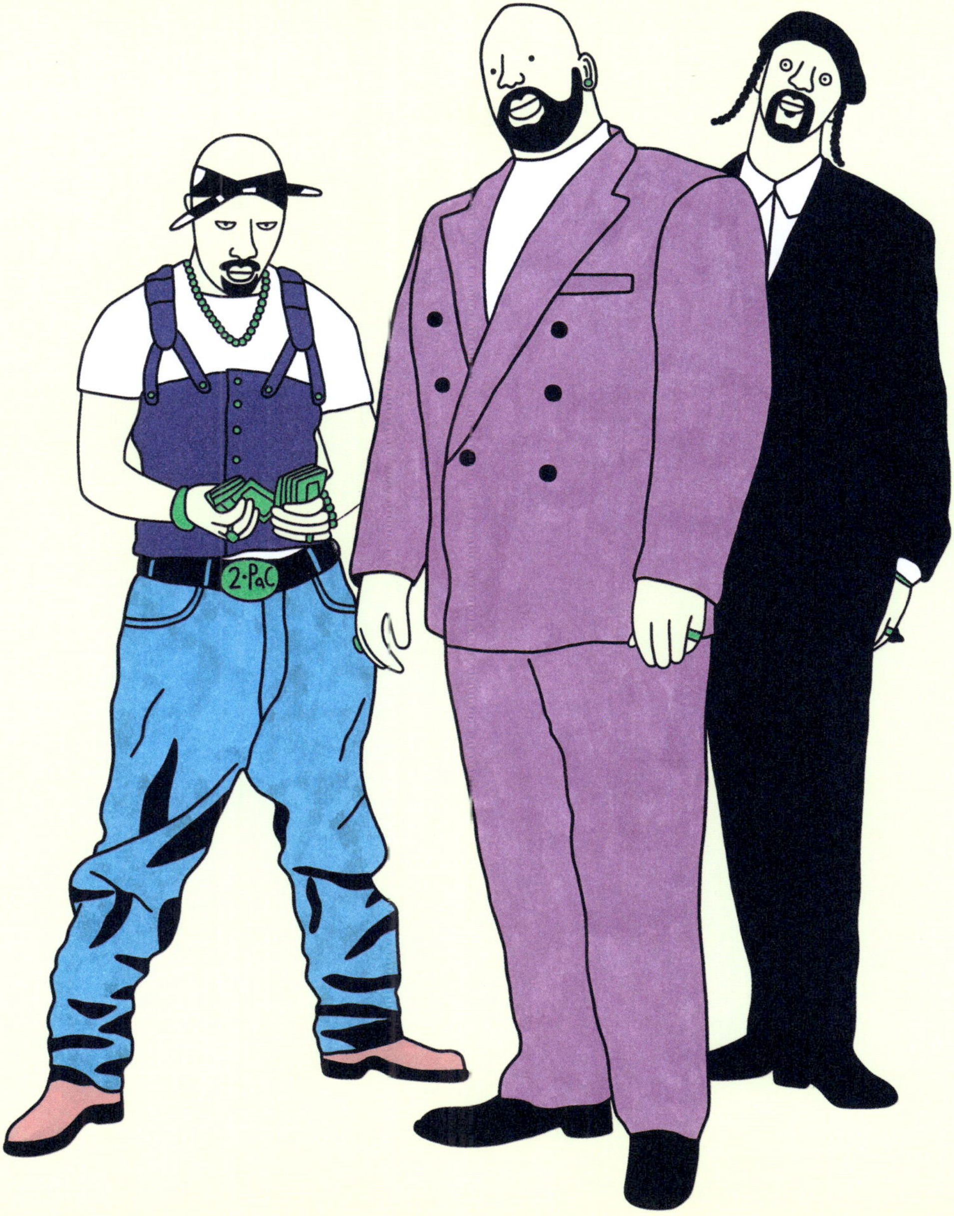
2·PaC

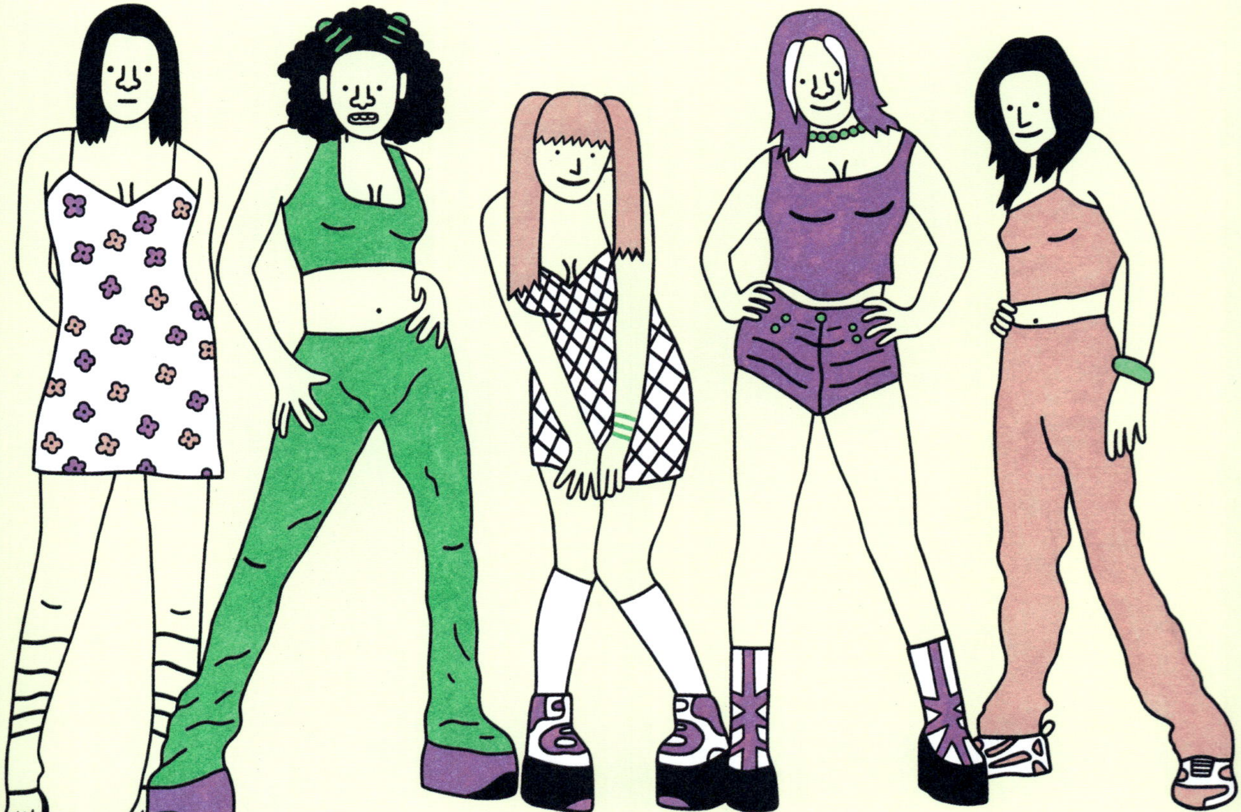

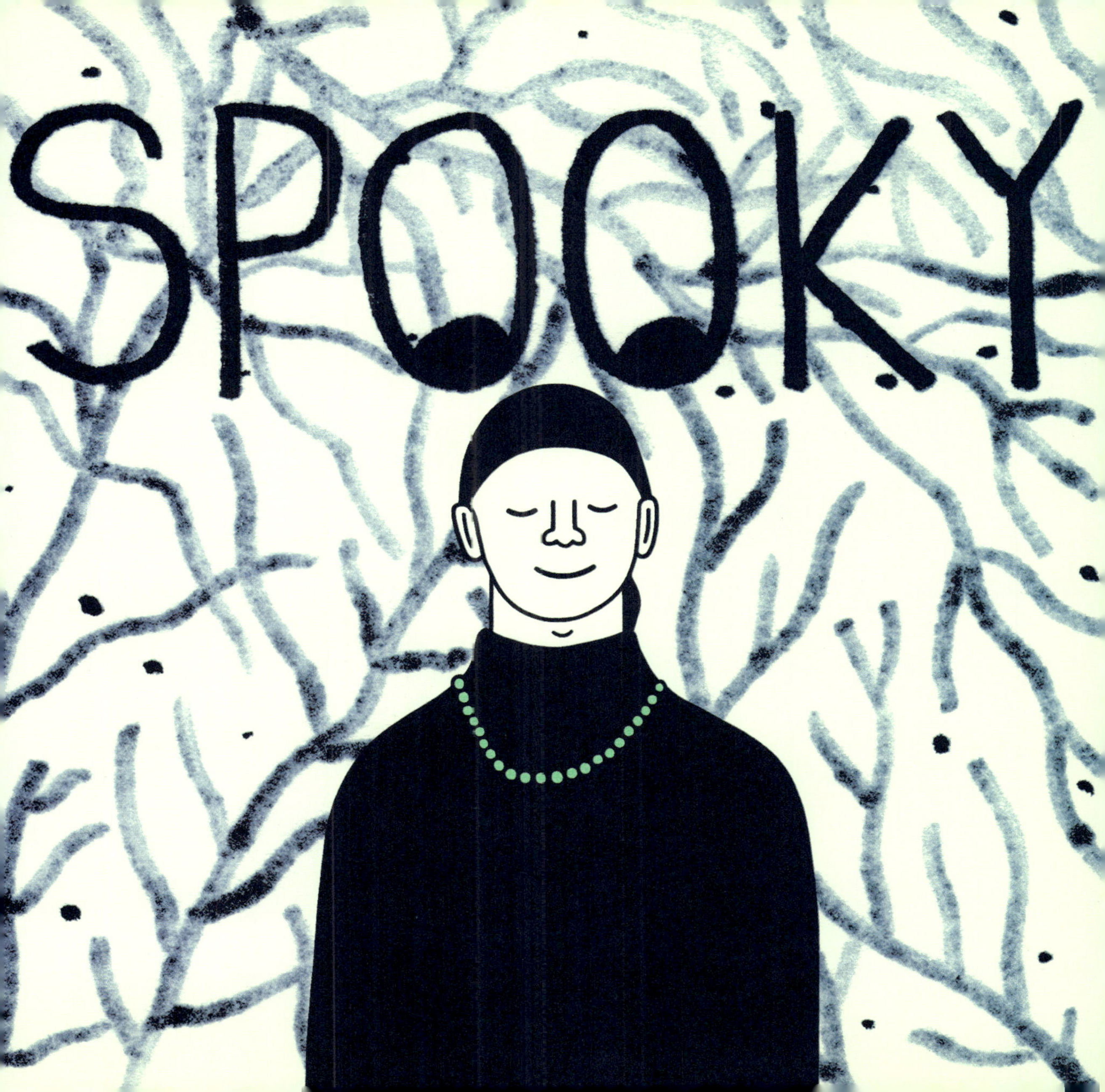
SPOOKY

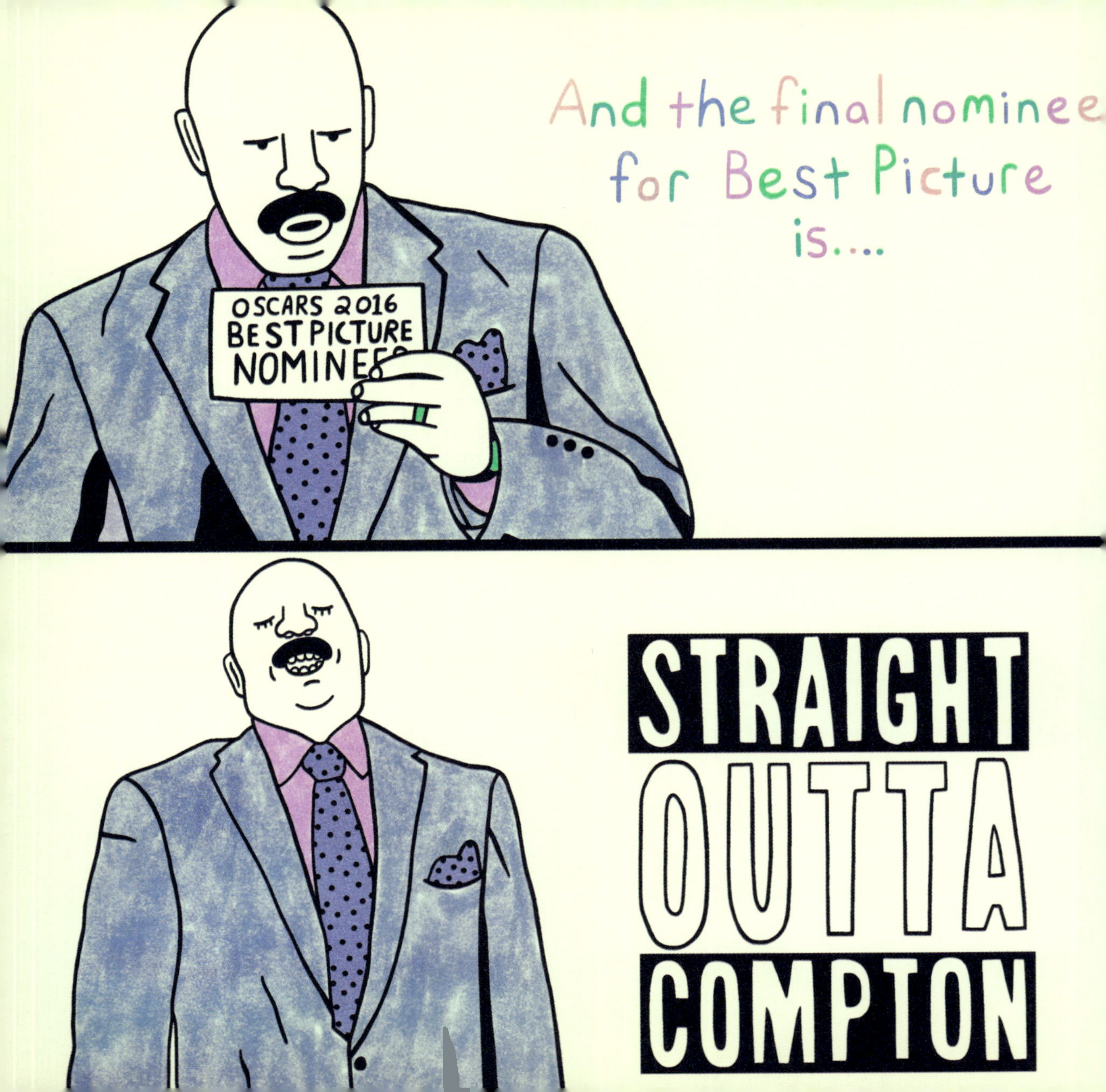
And the final nominee for Best Picture is....
OSCARS 2016 BEST PICTURE NOMINEES
STRAIGHT
OUTTA
COMPTON

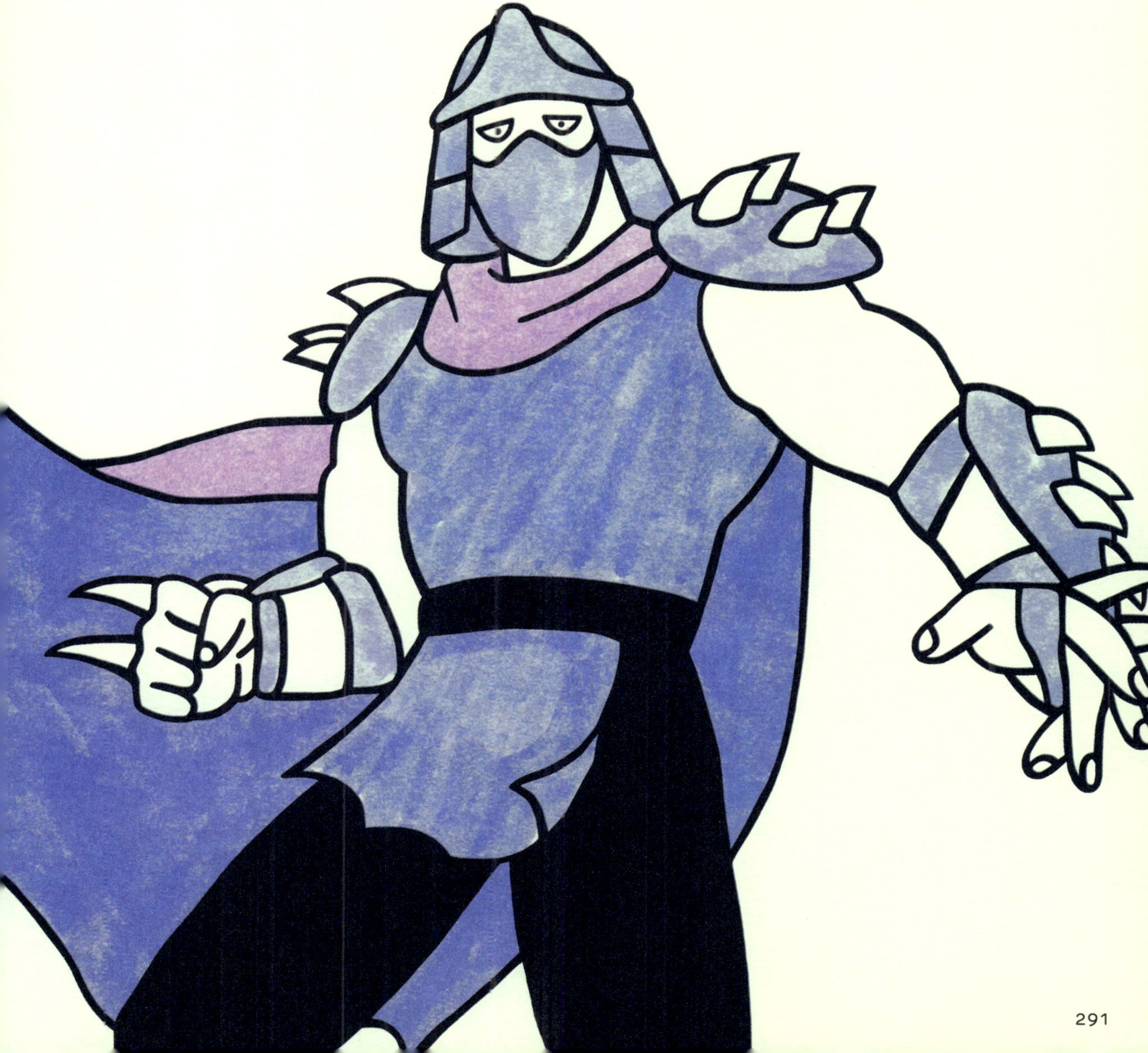

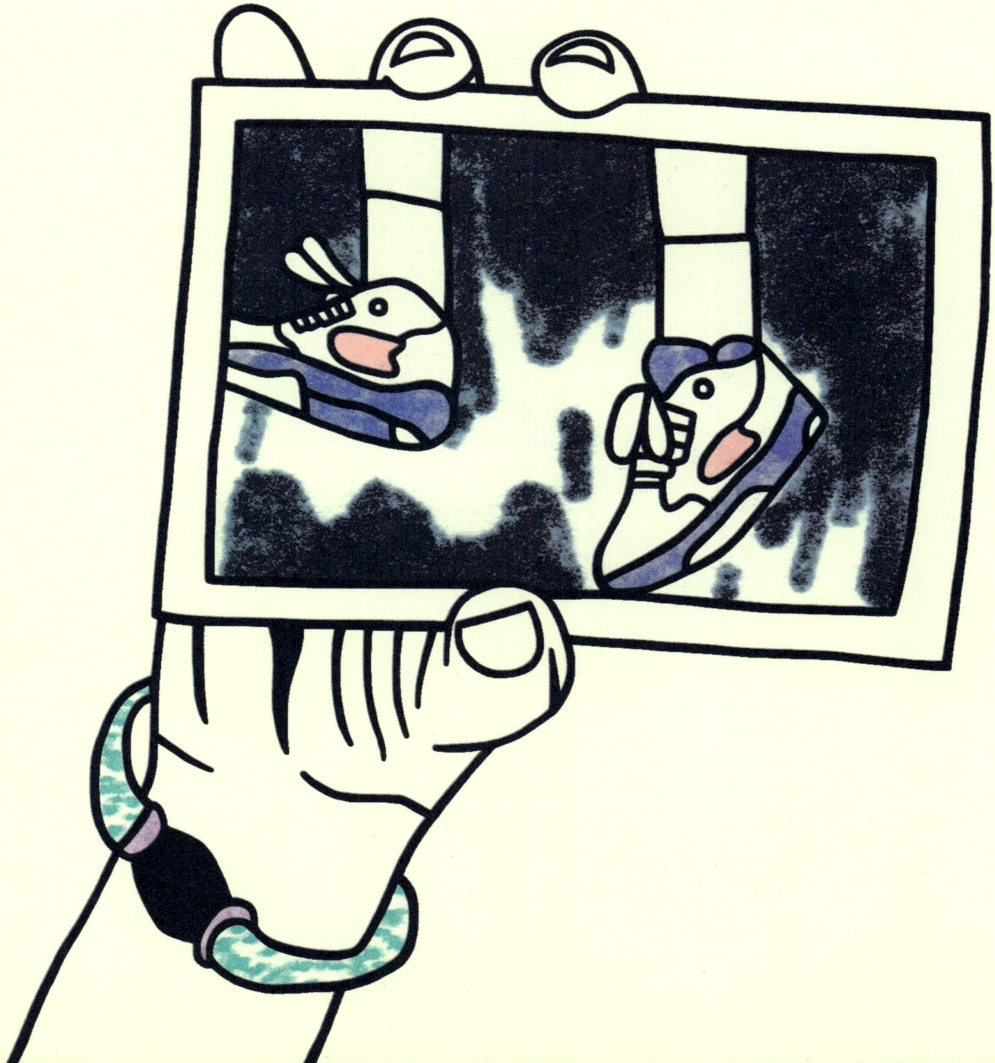

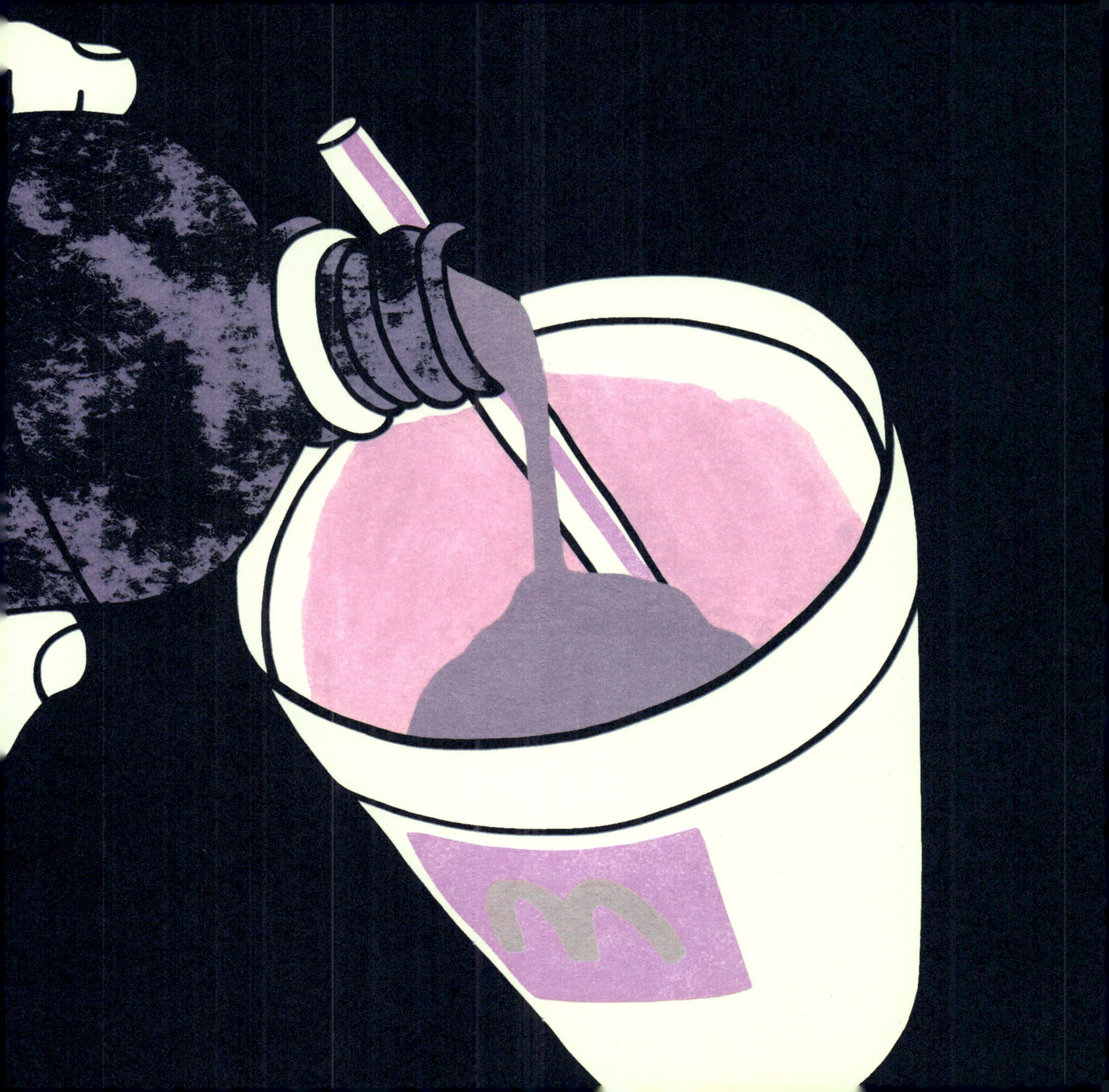

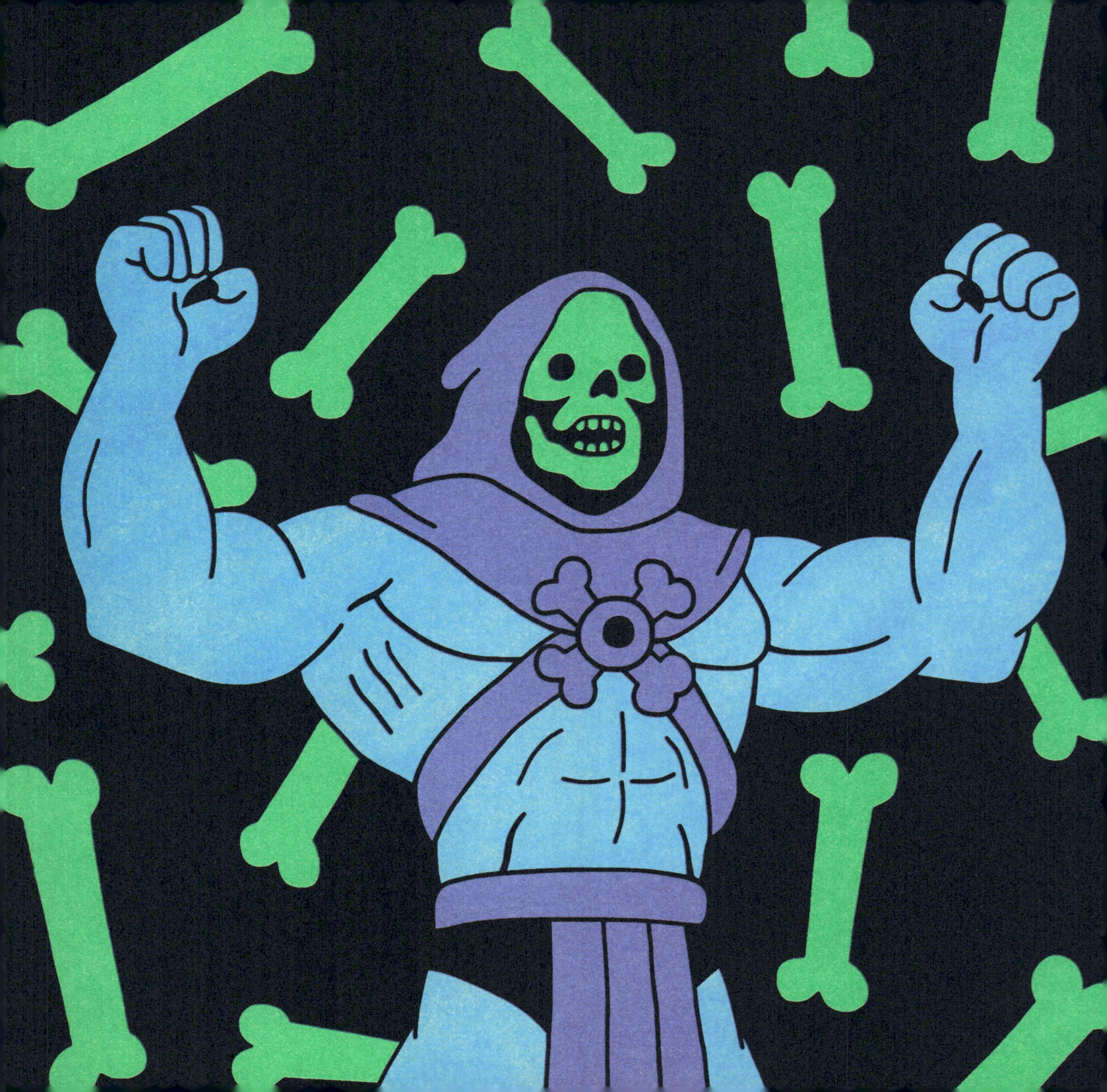

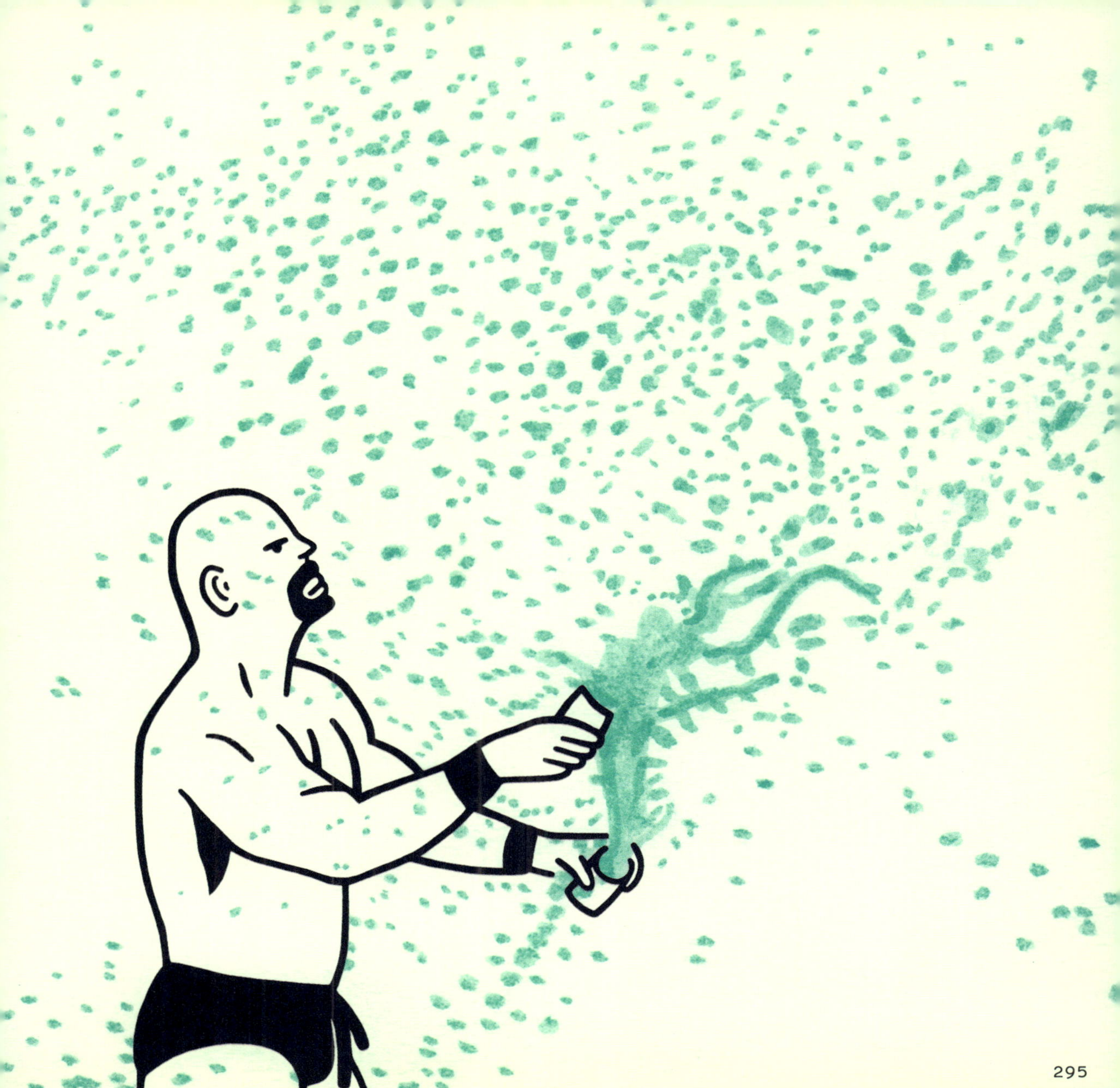

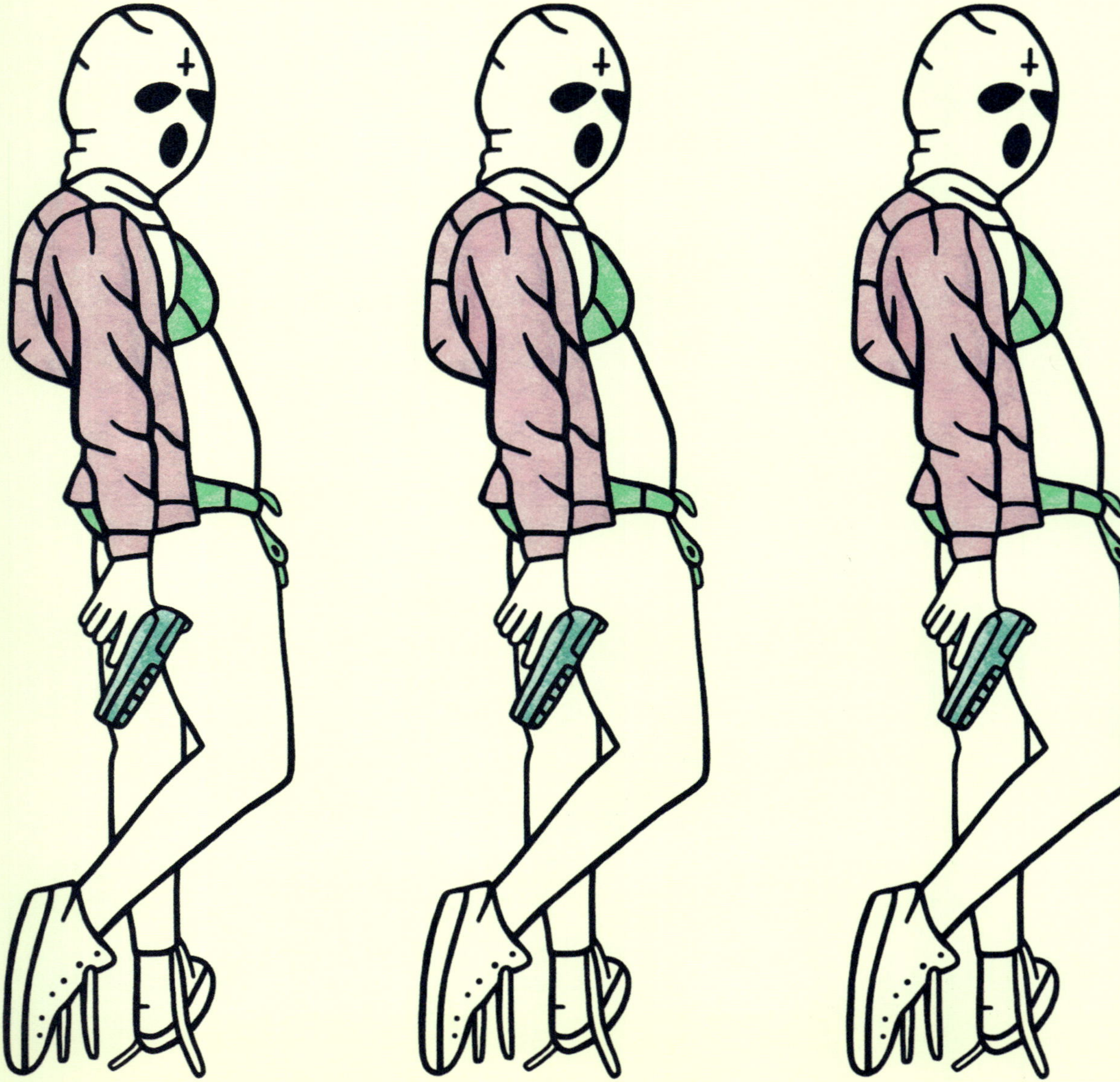

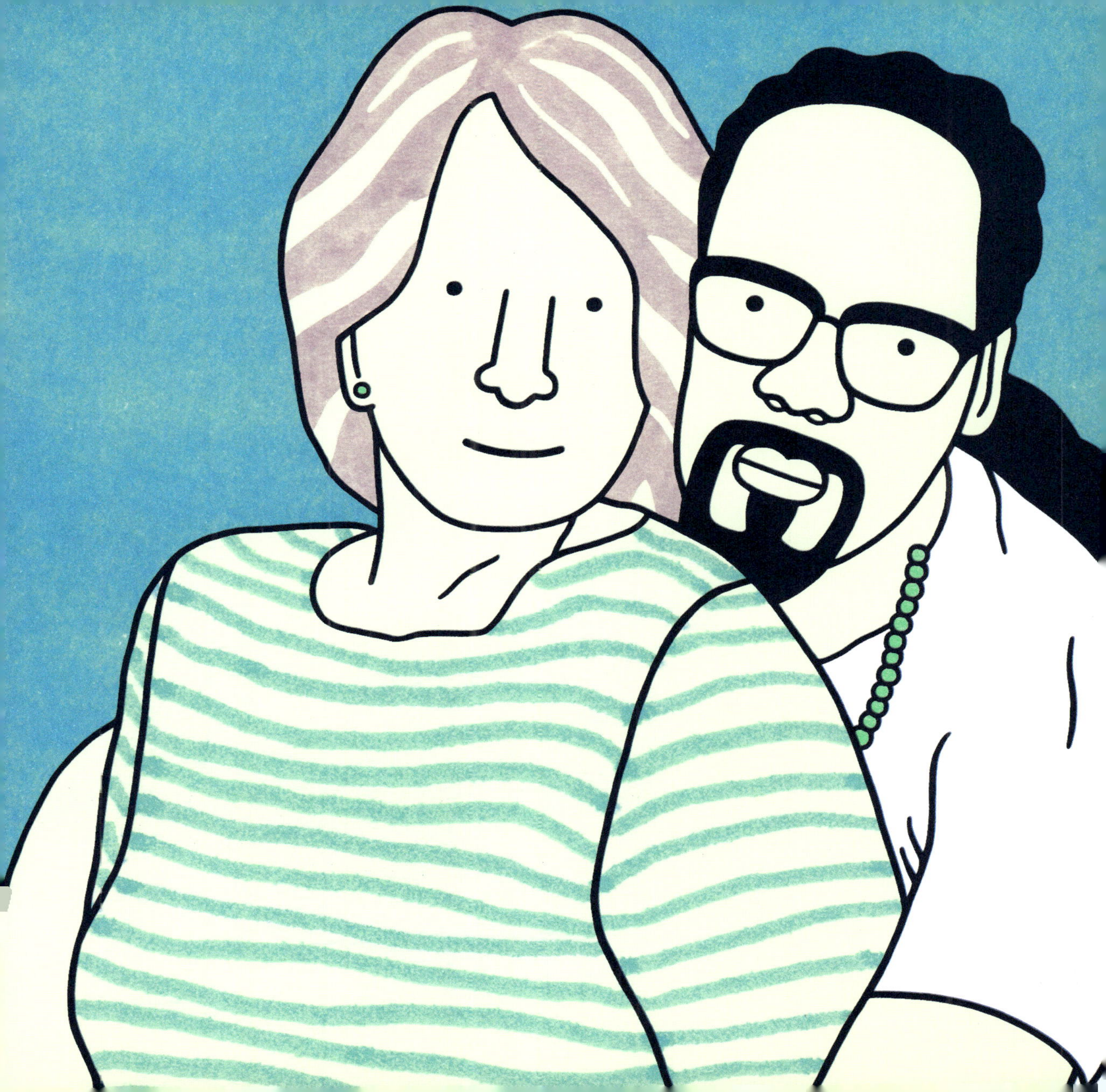

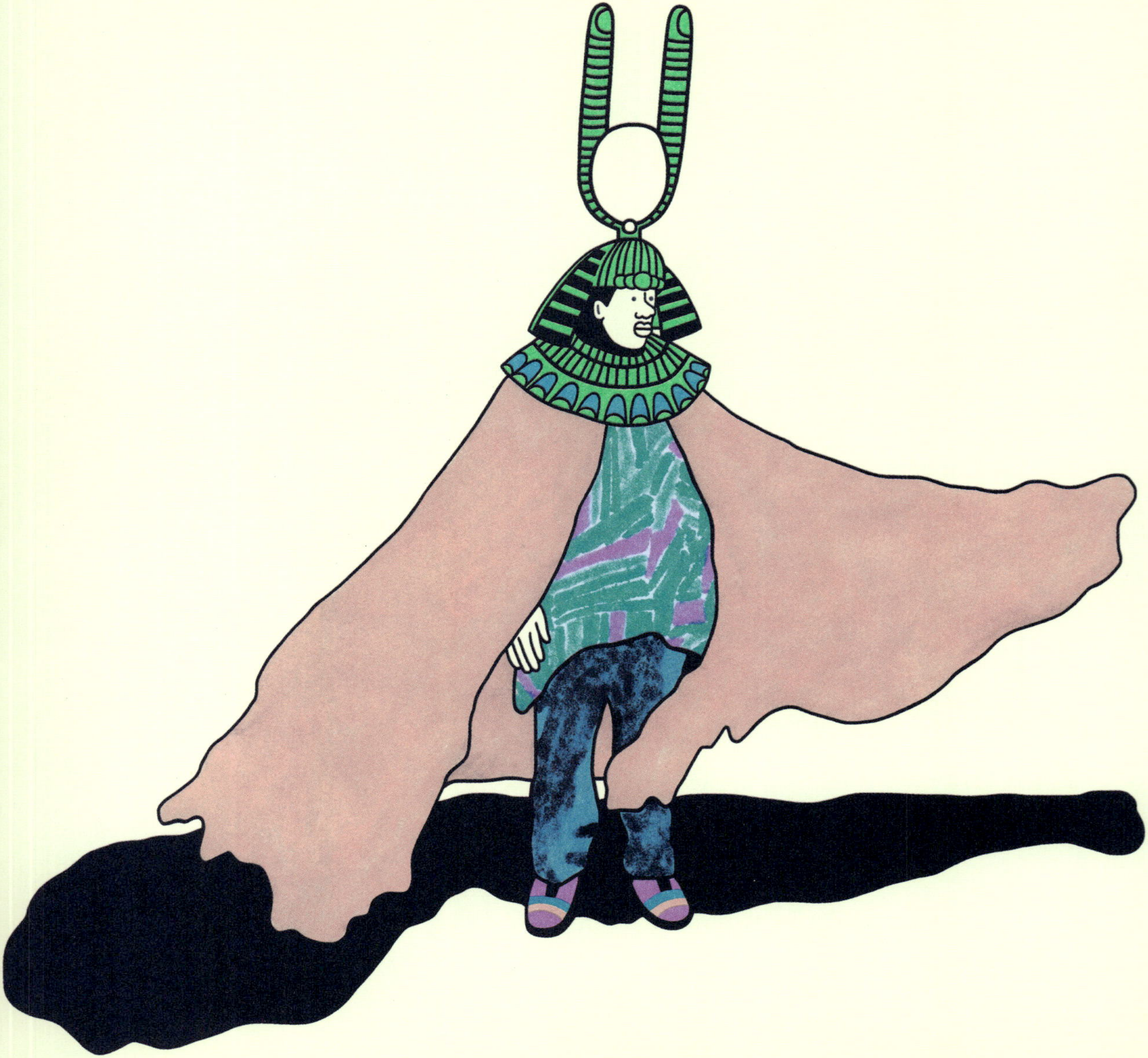

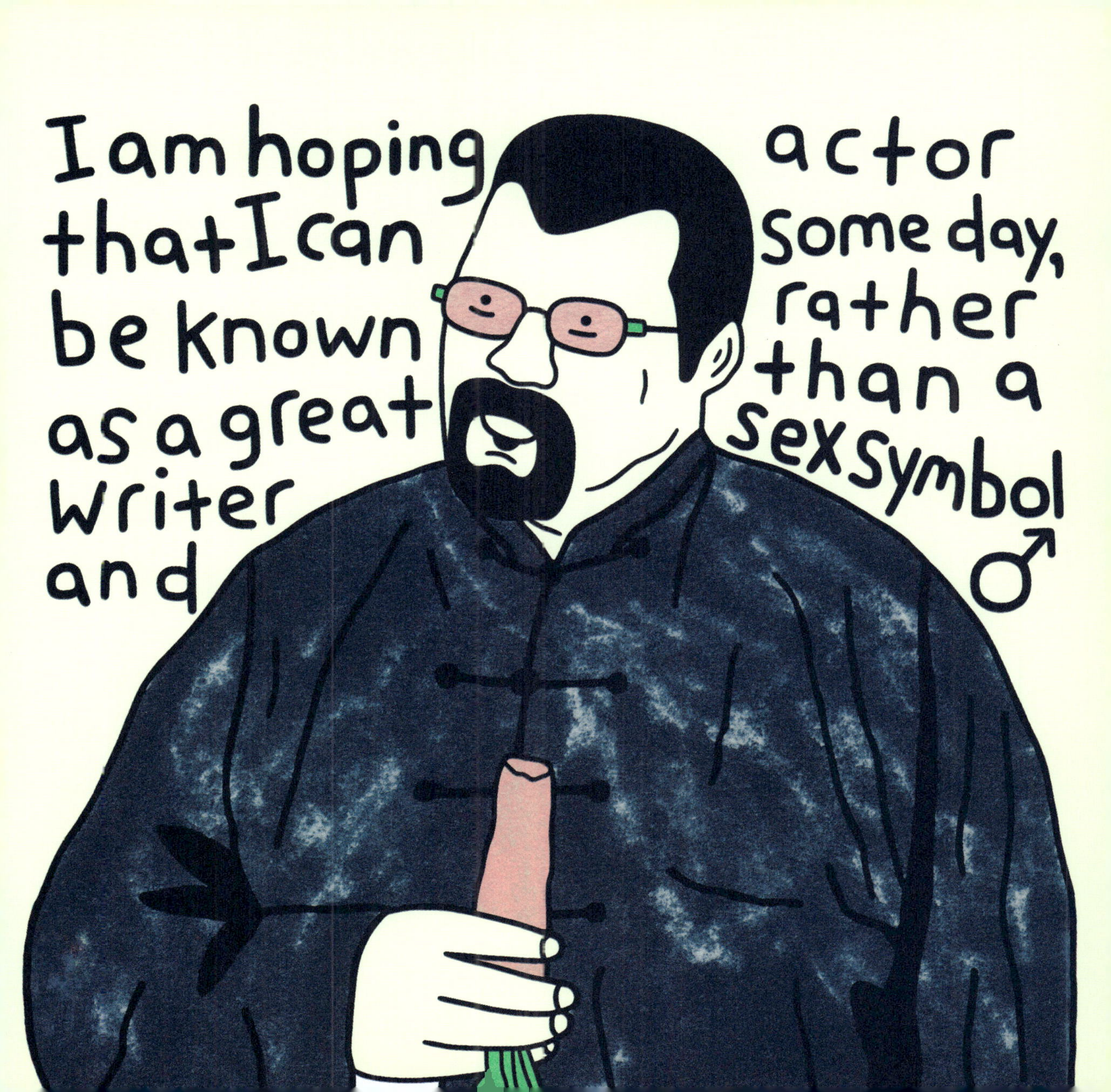
I am hoping that I can be known as a great writer and actor some day, rather than a sex symbol ♂

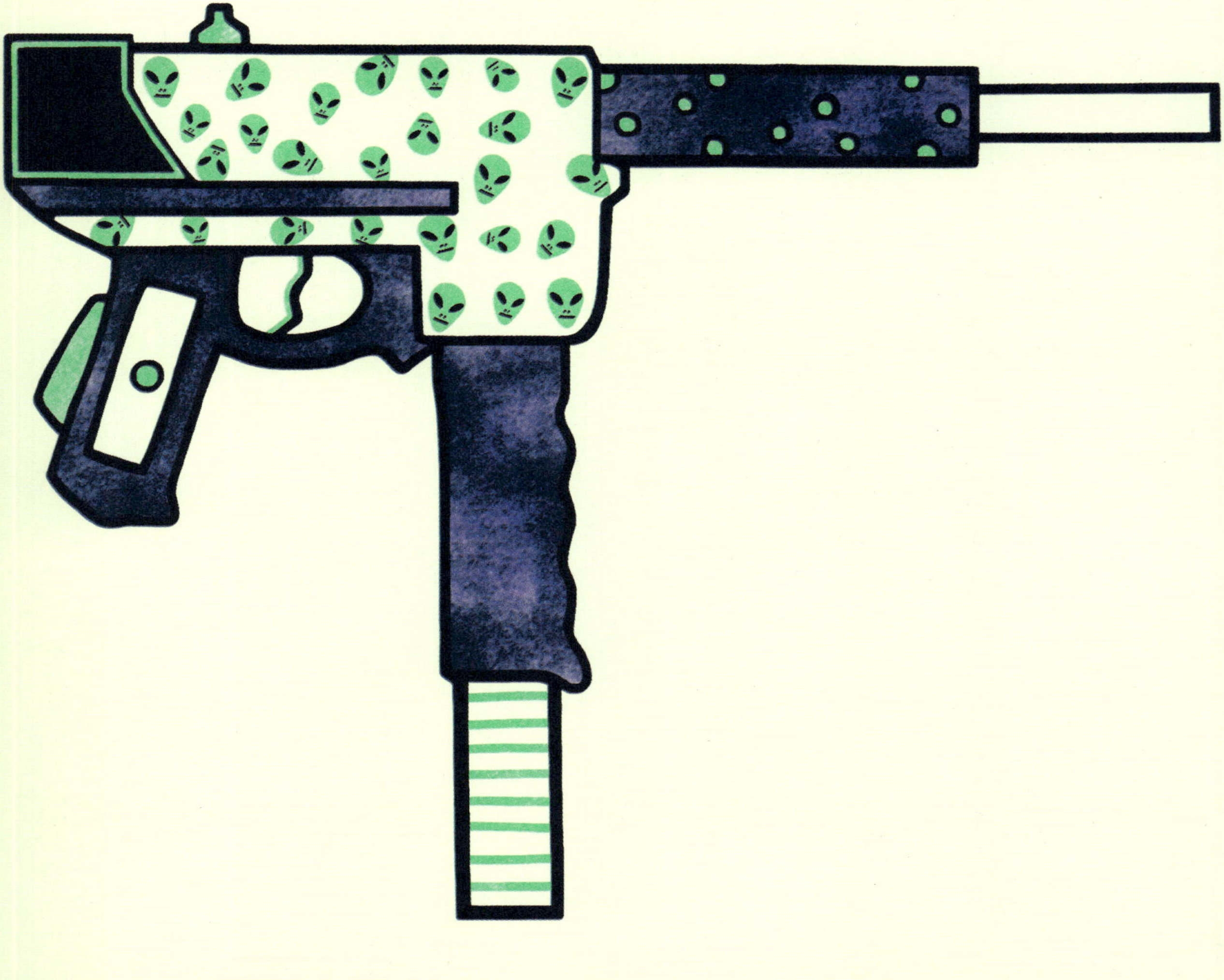

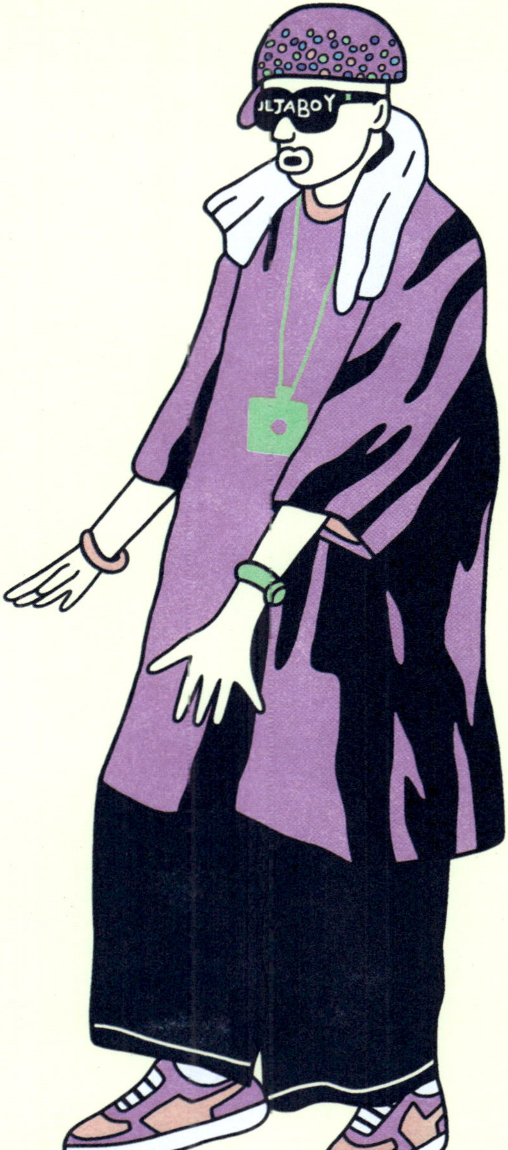

JIJABOY

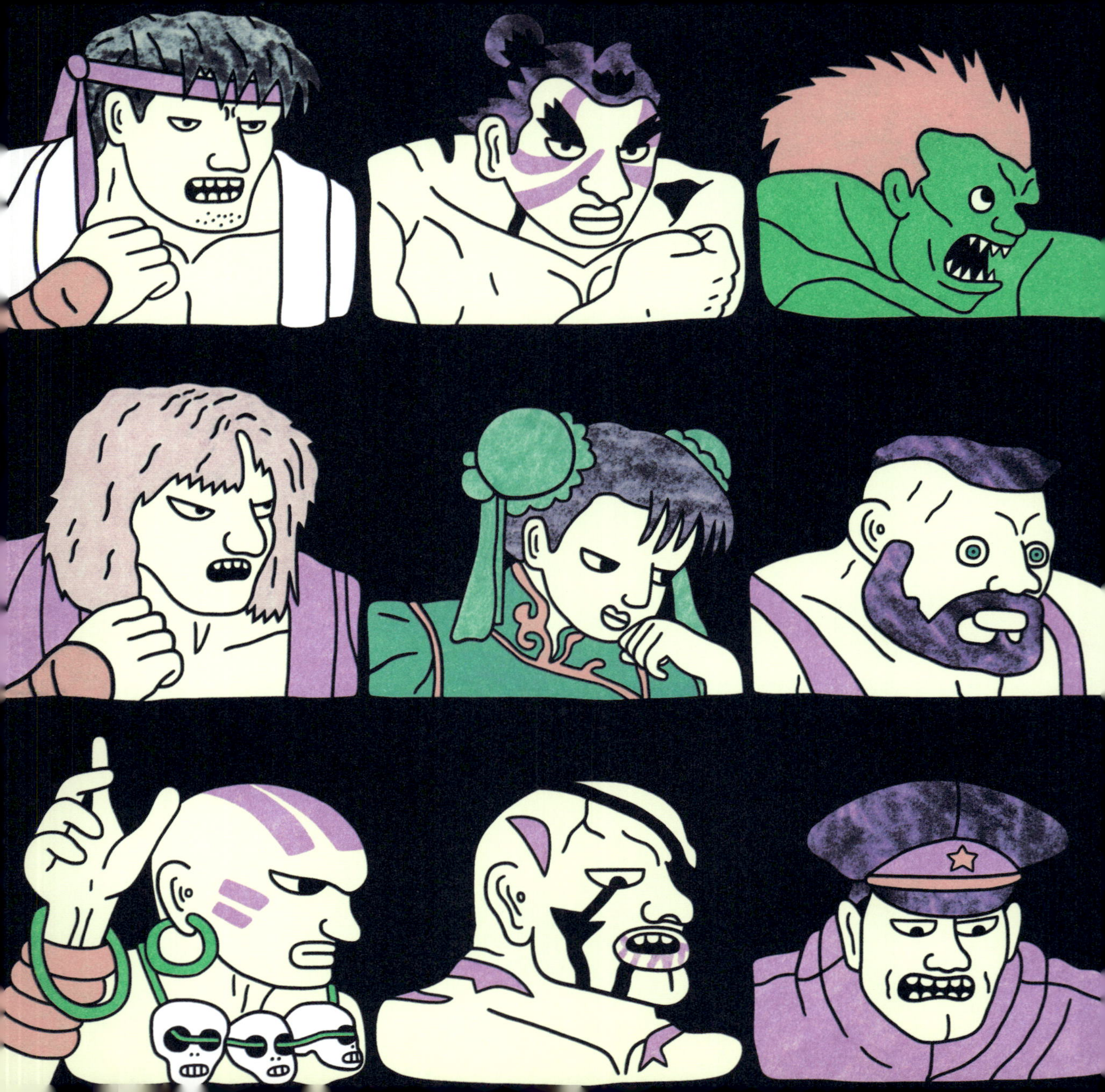

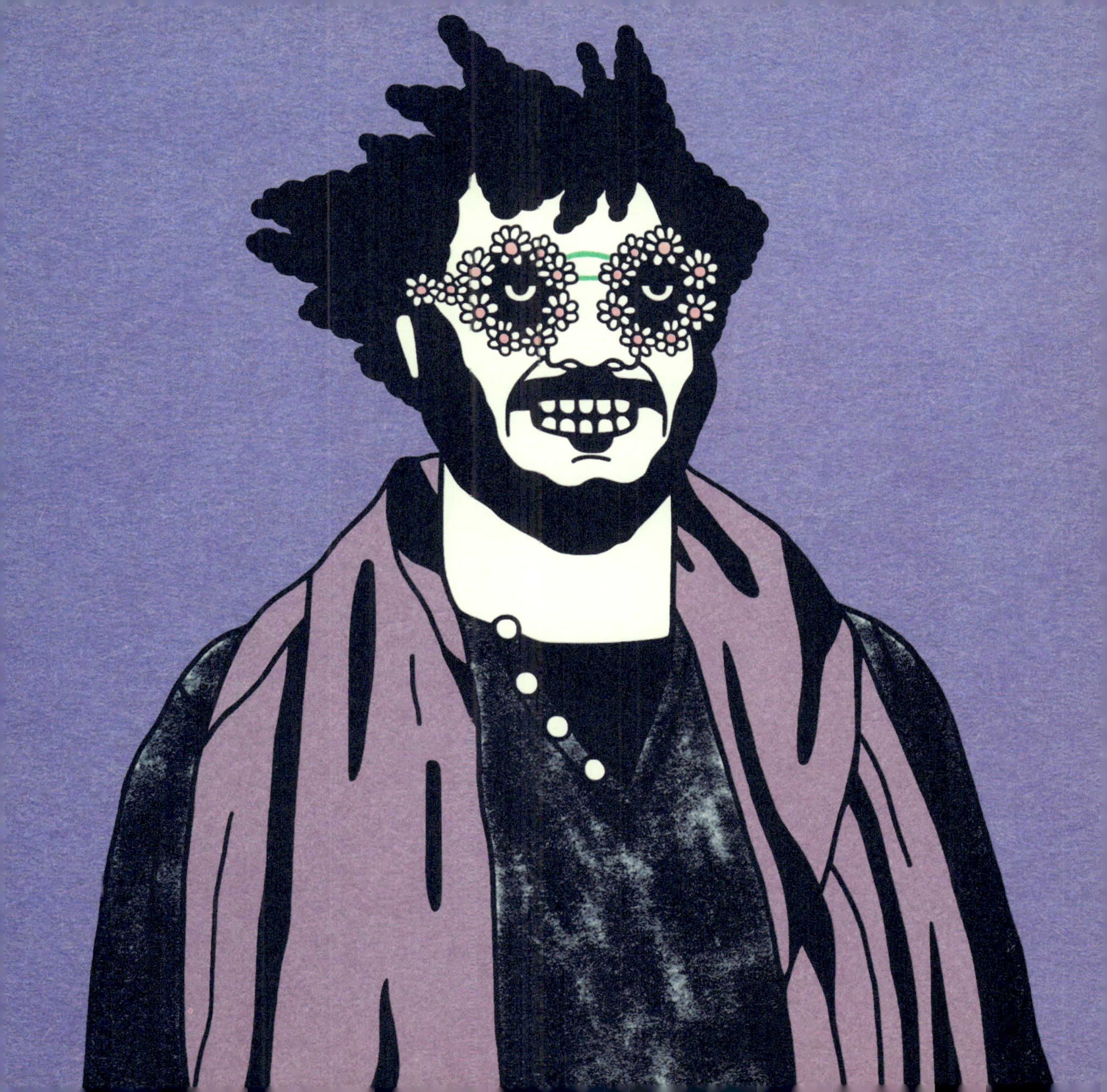

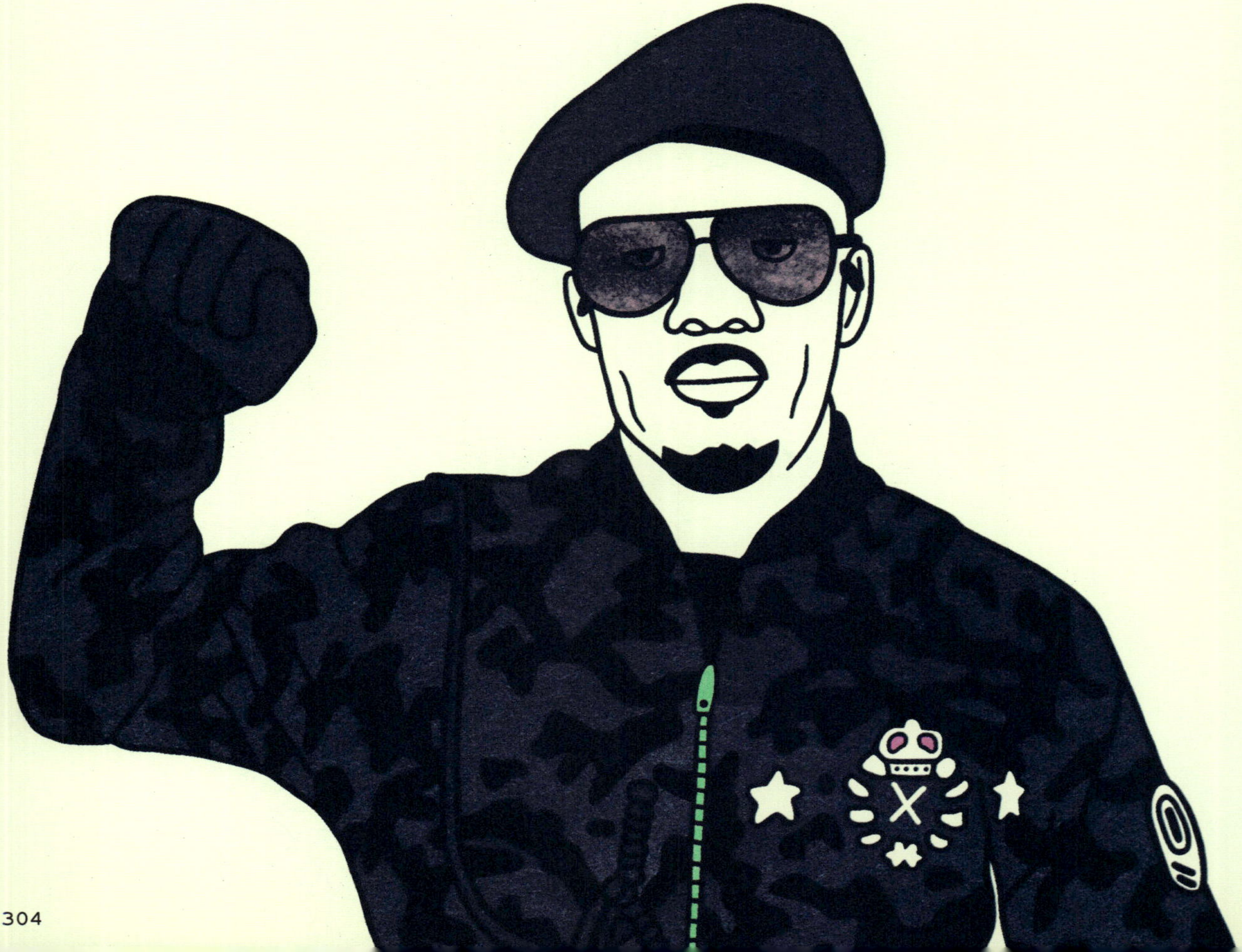

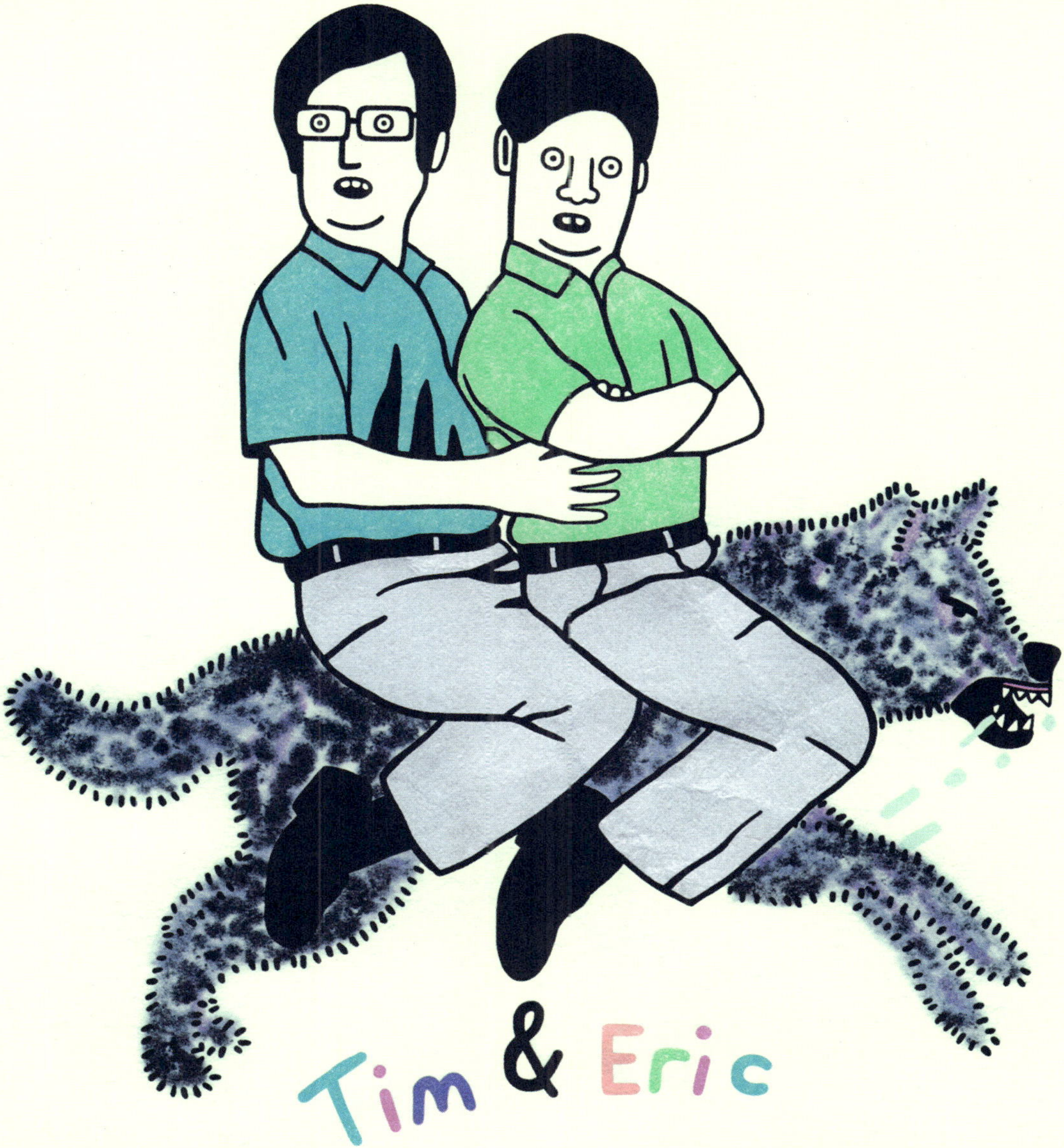
Tim & Eric

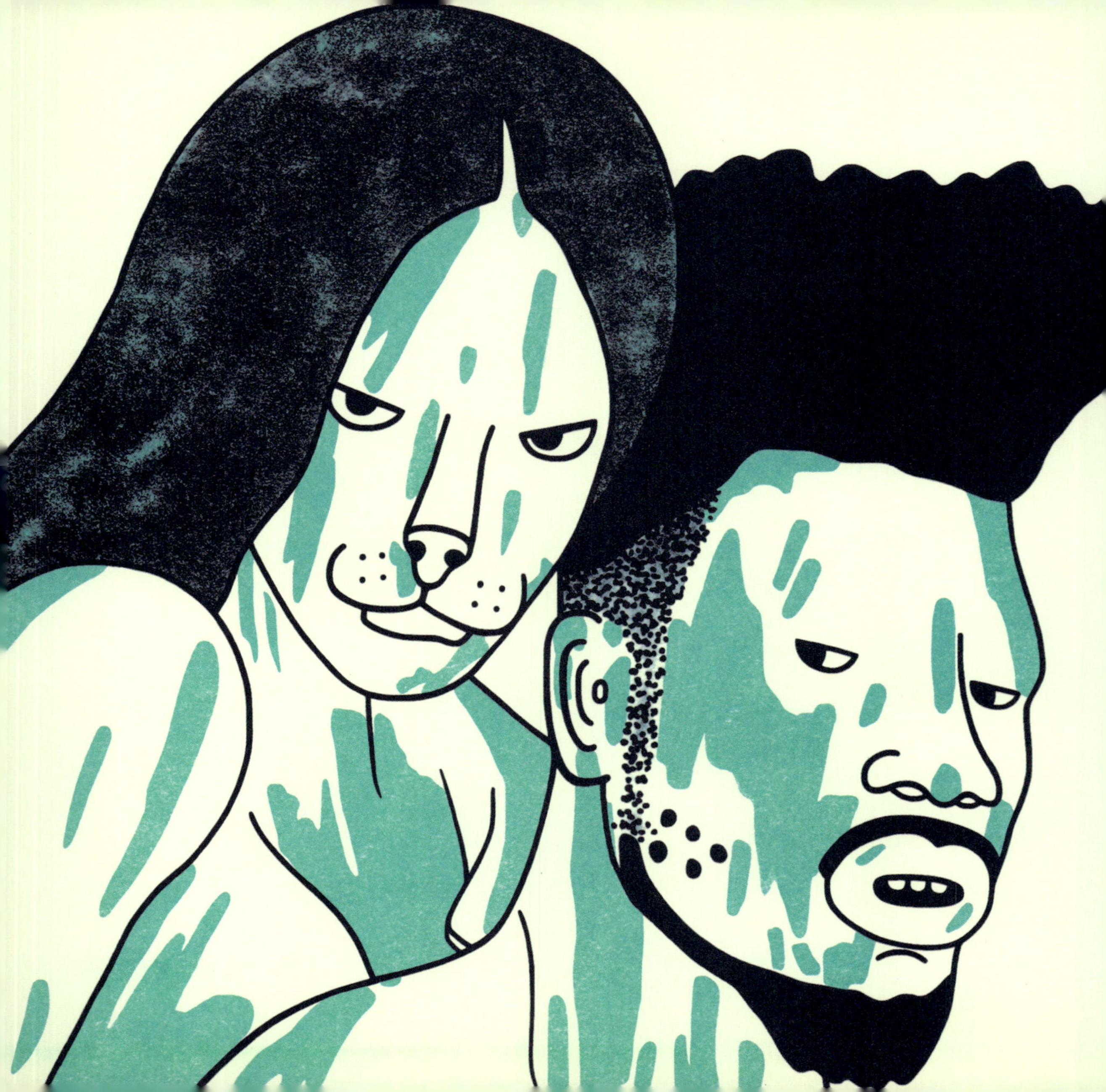

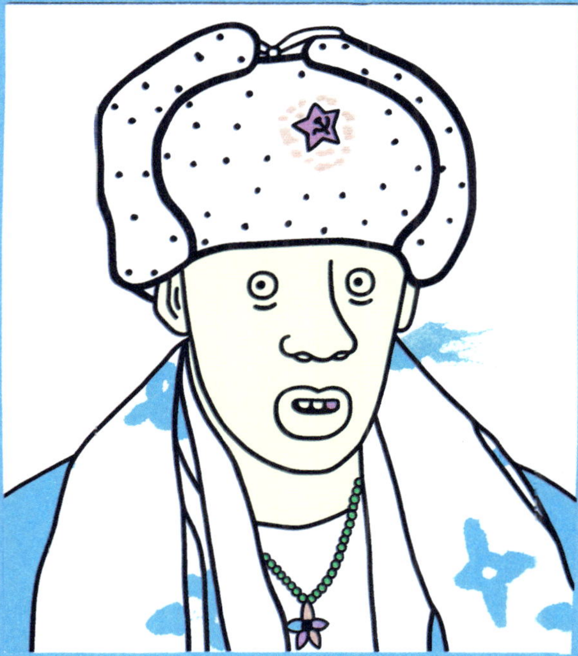
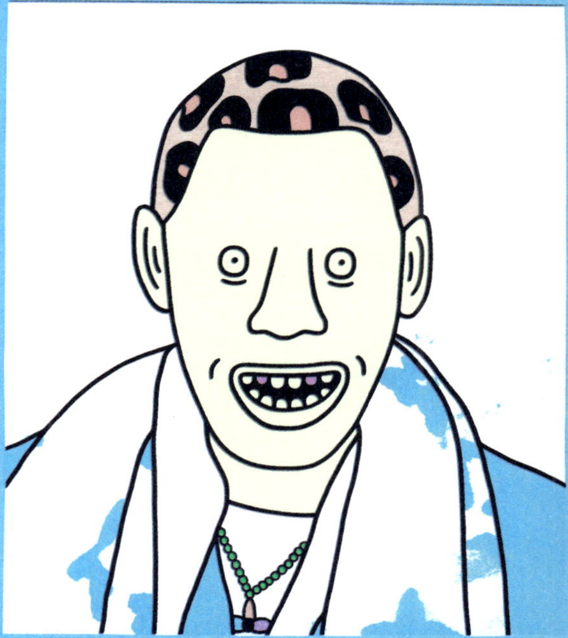

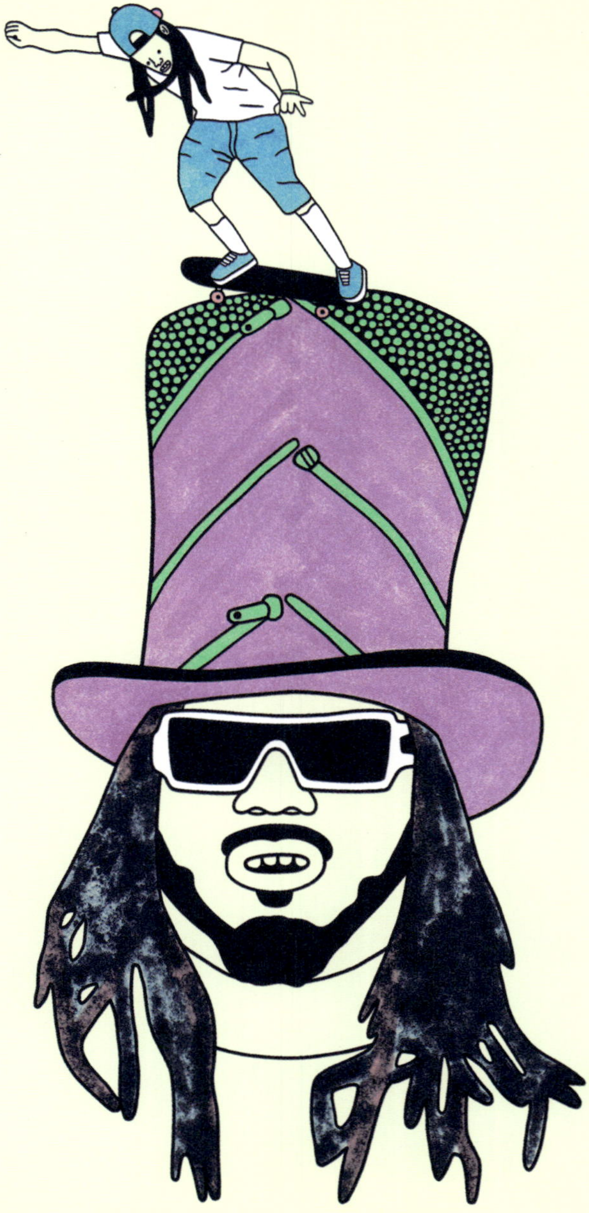

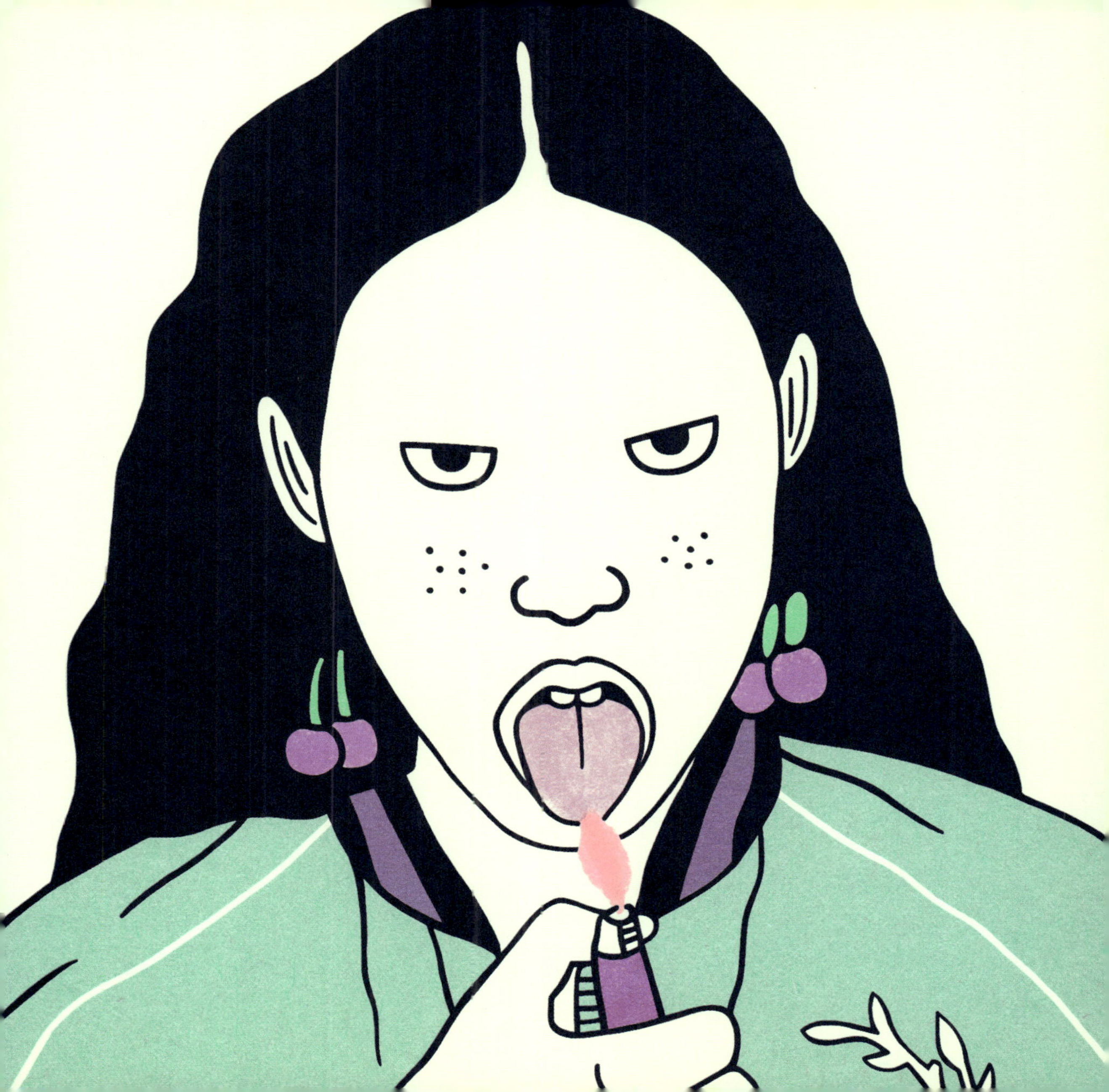

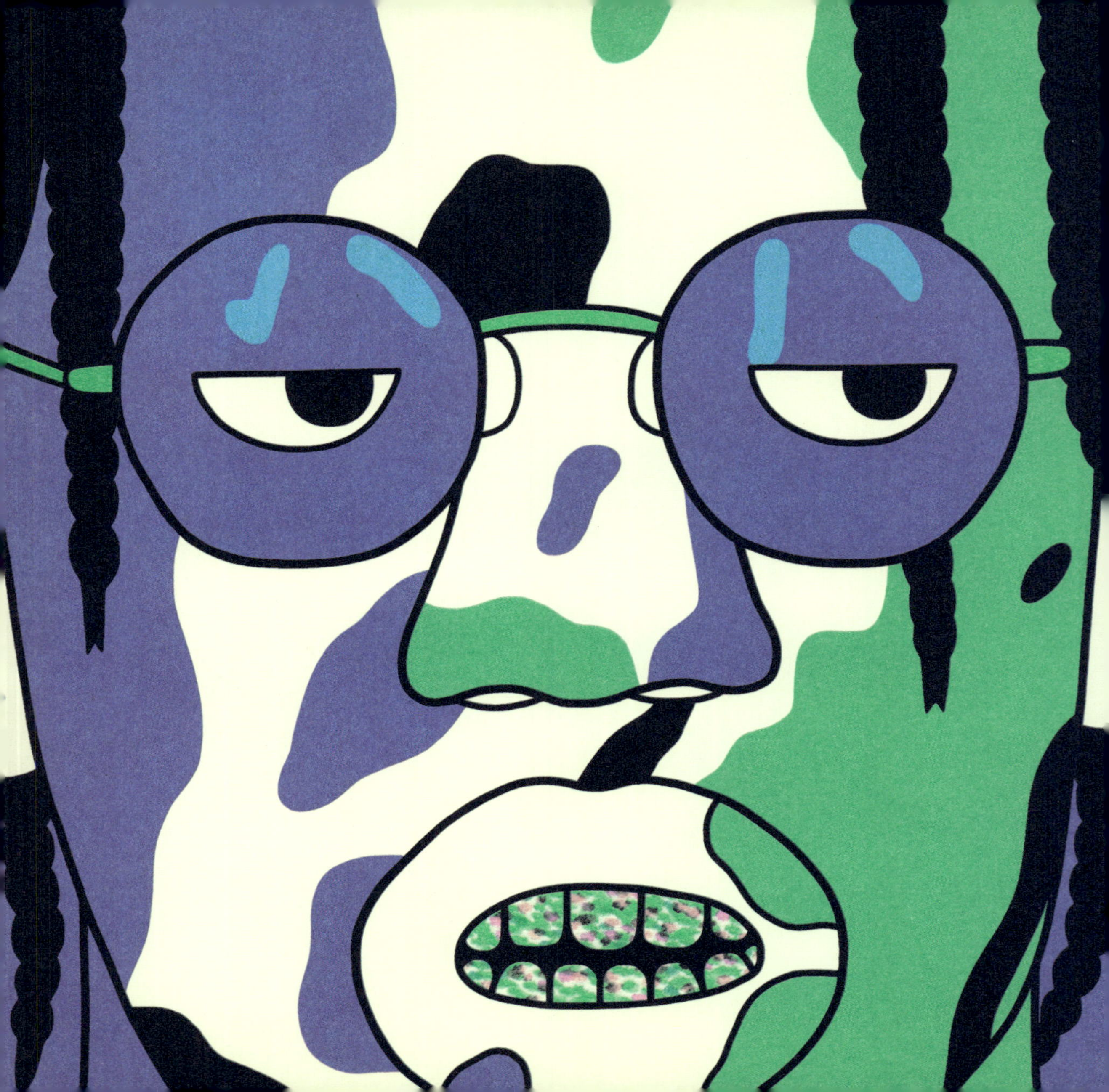

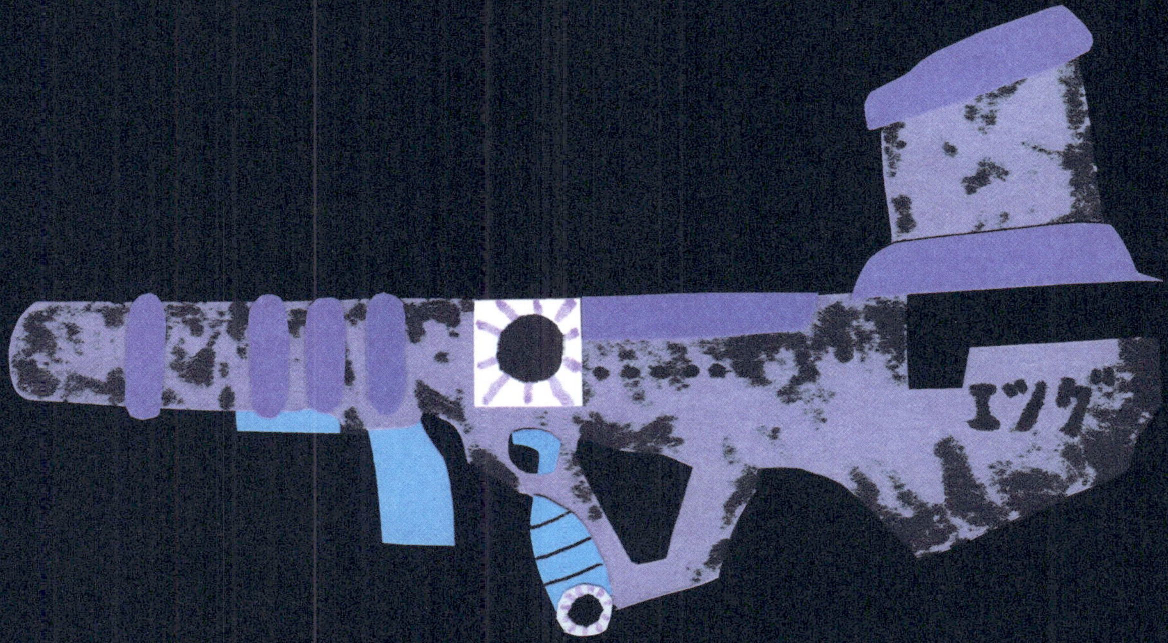
エッグ

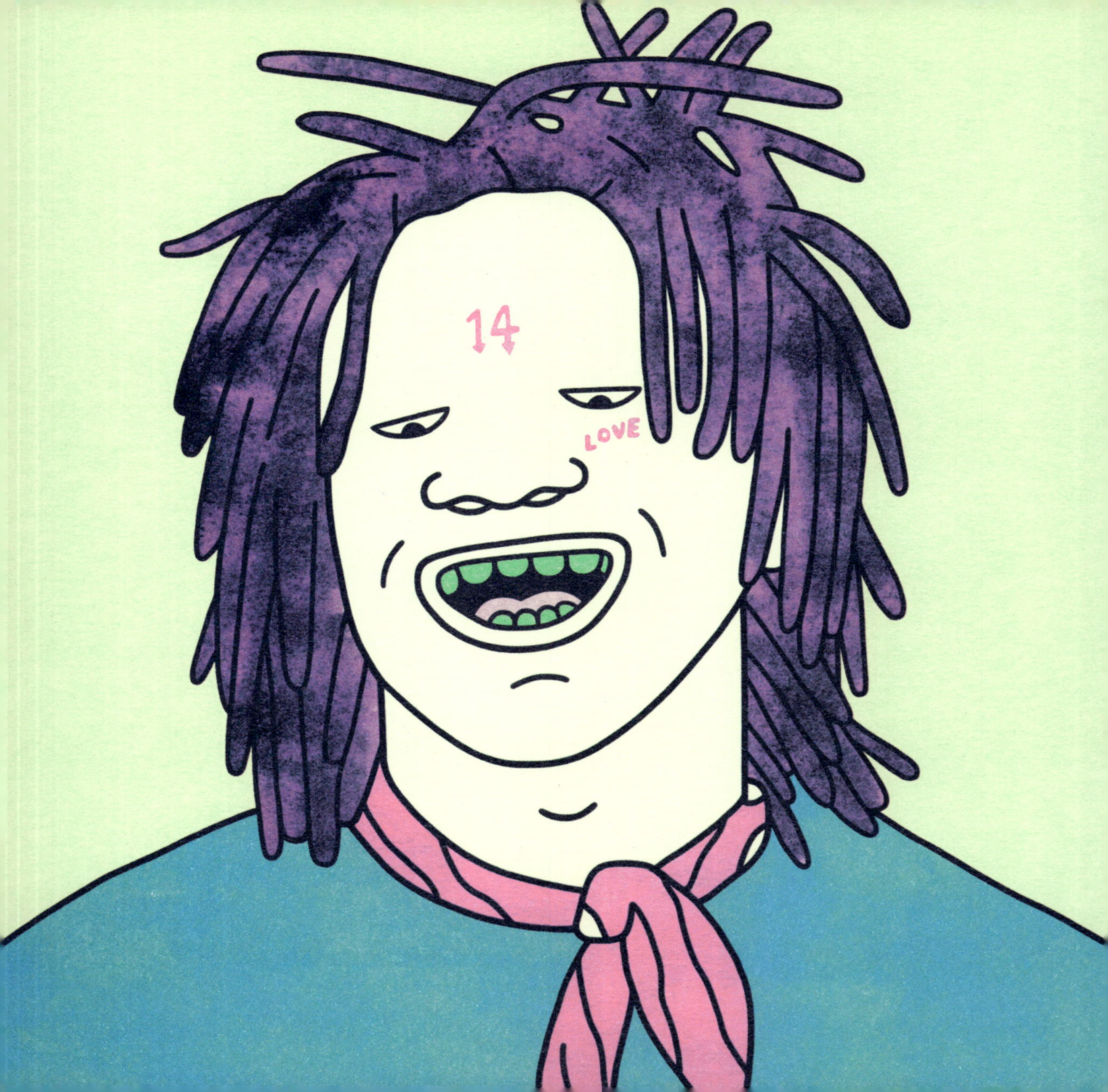
14
LOVE

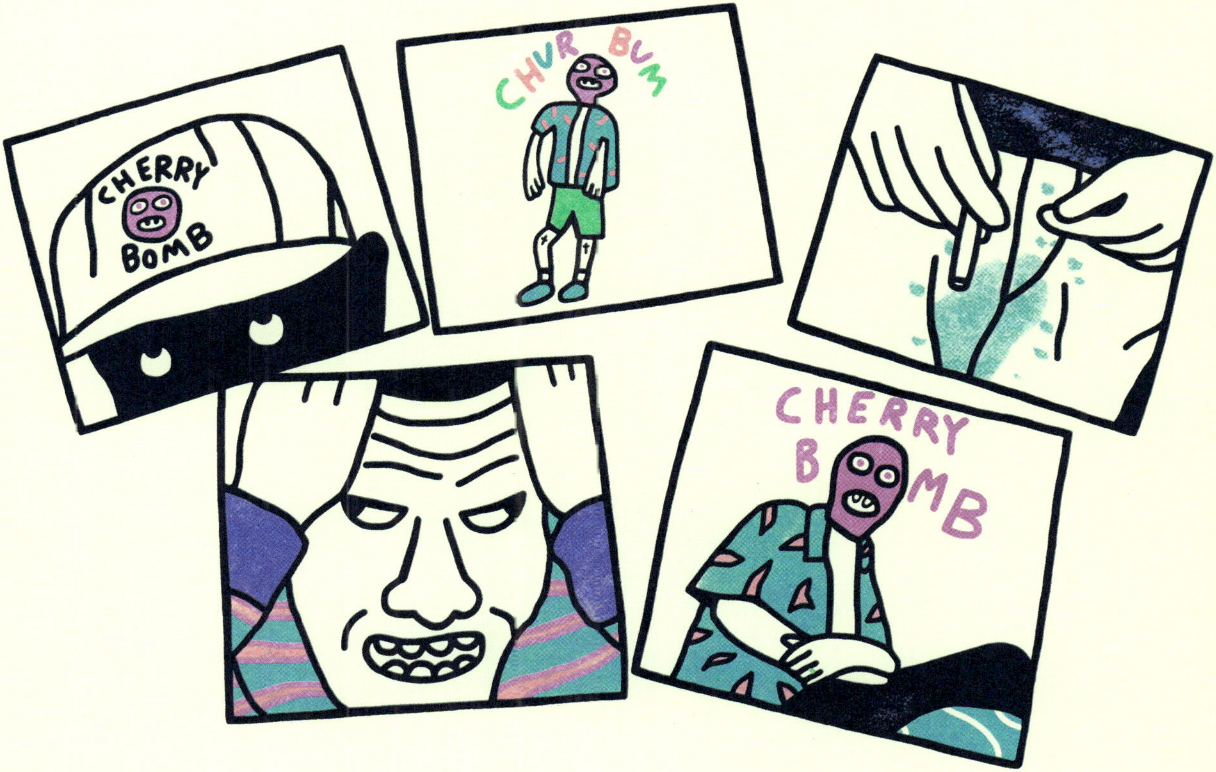
CHERRY BOMB
CHUR BUM
CHERRY BOMB

What more do you want from meeee?

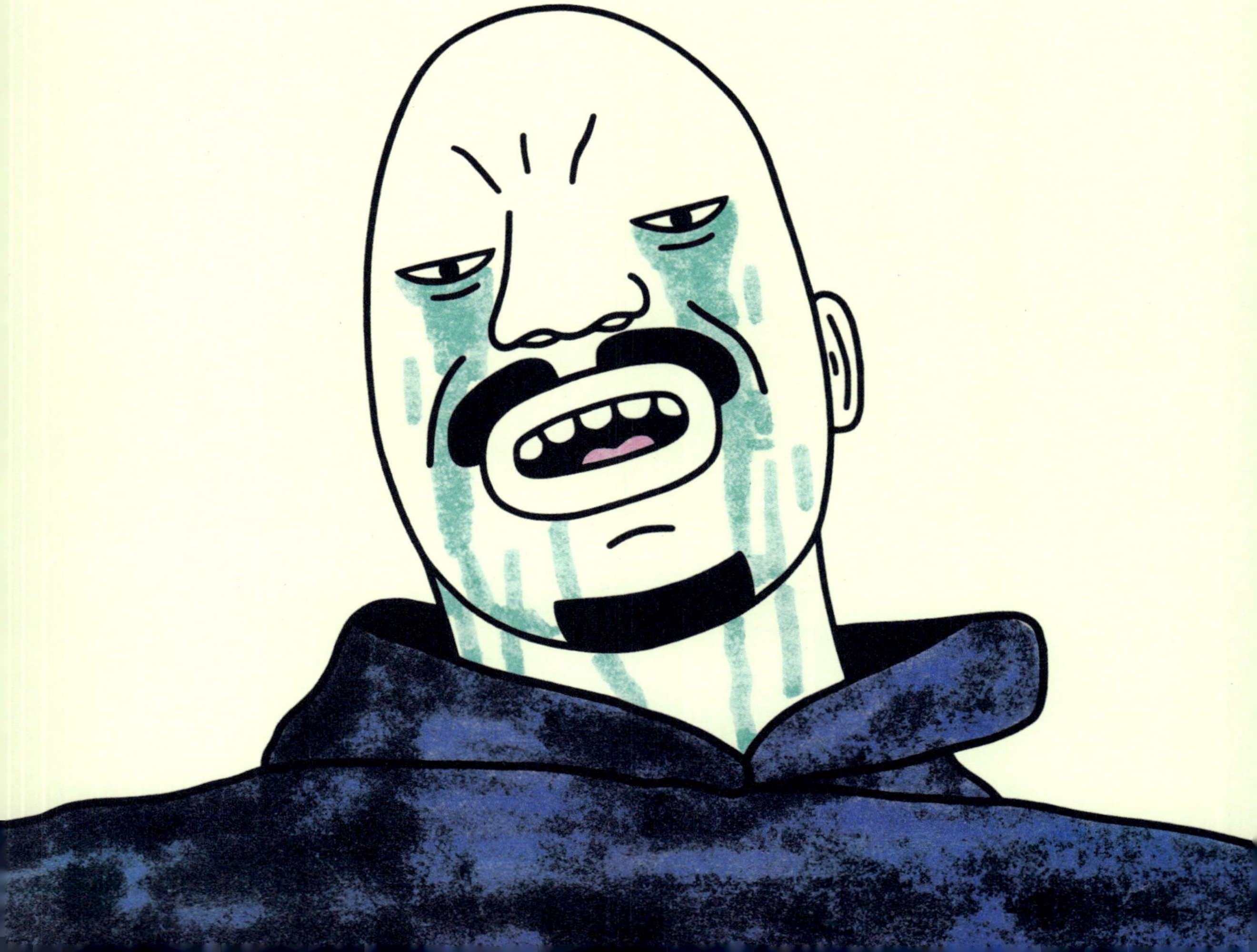

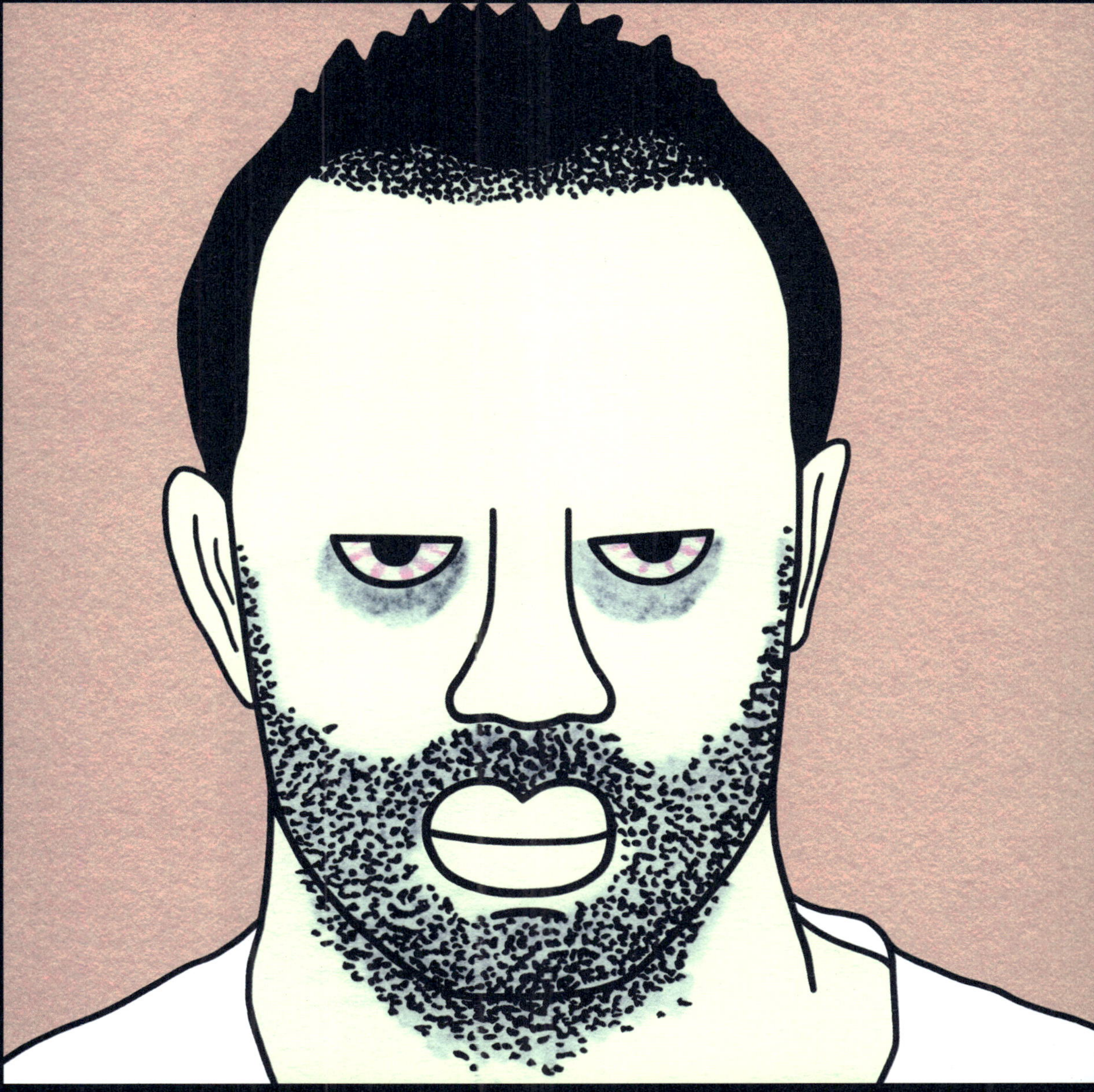

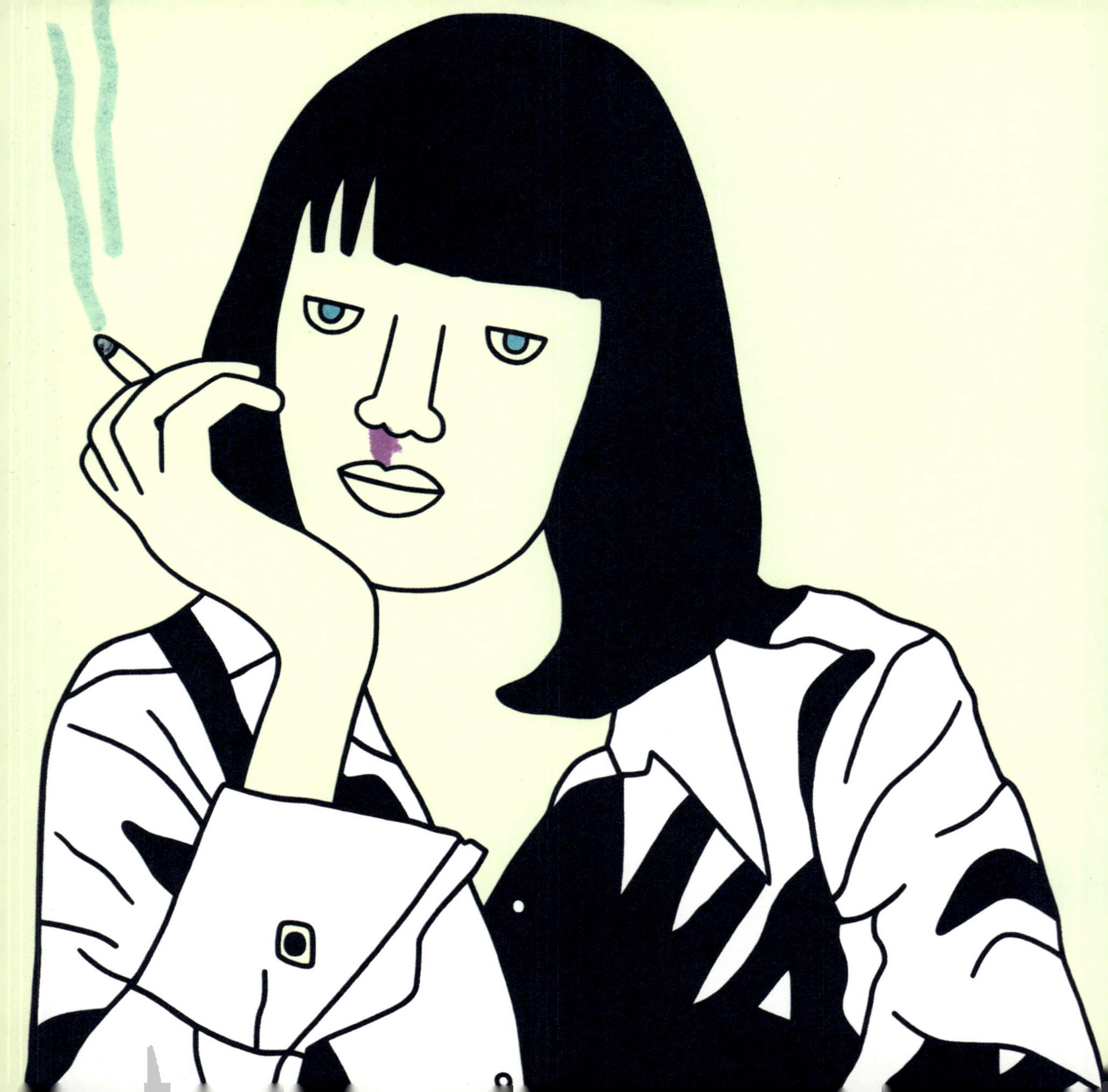

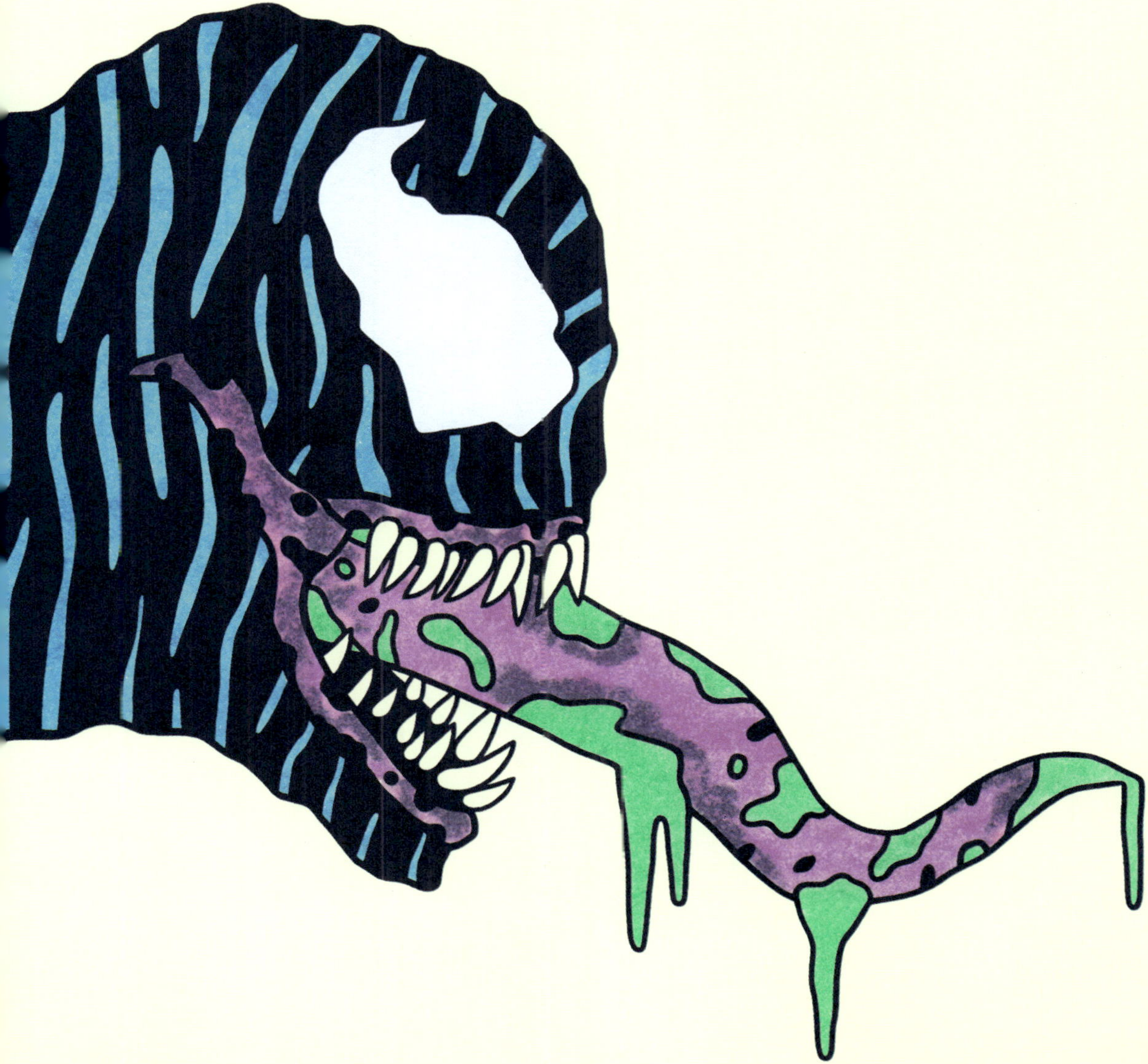

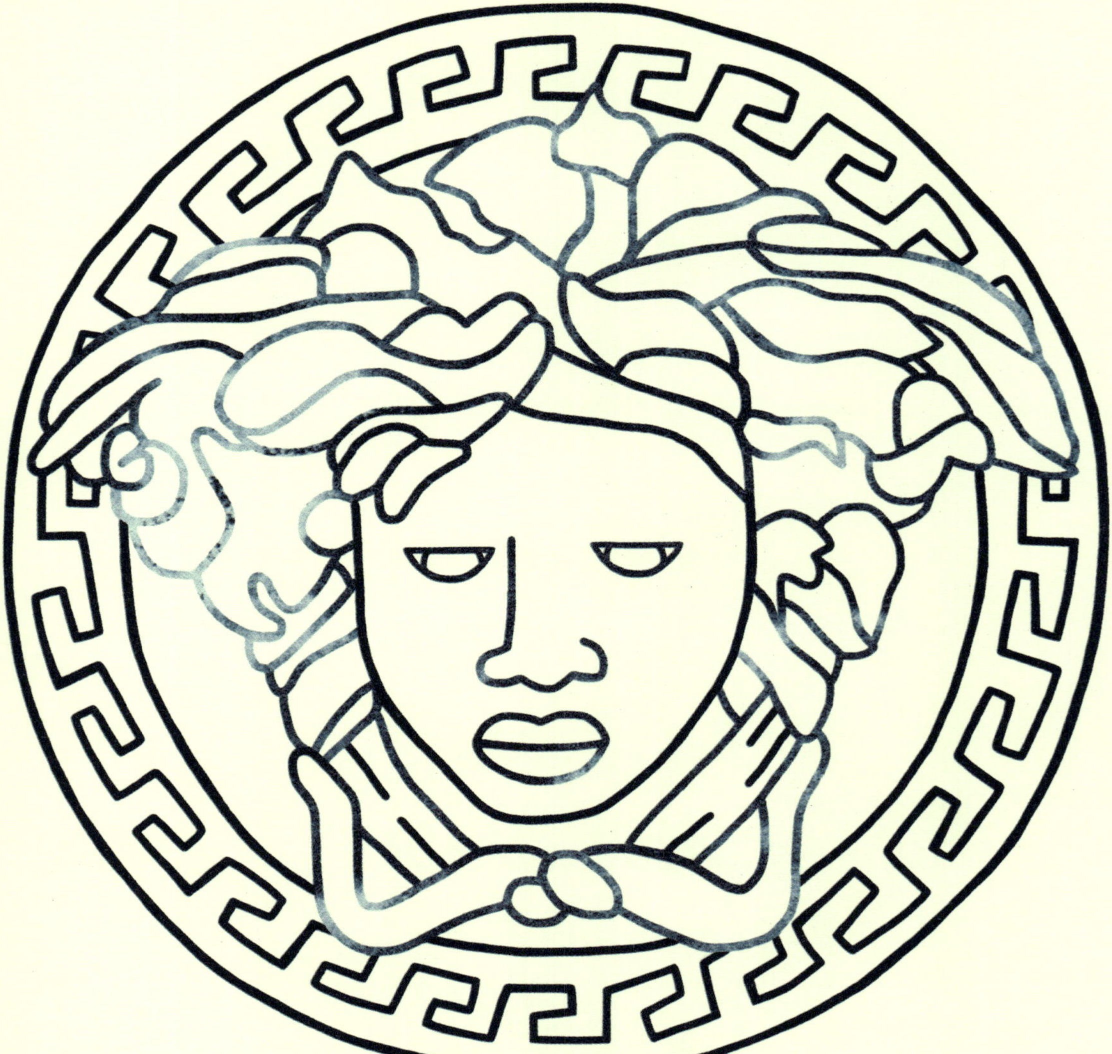

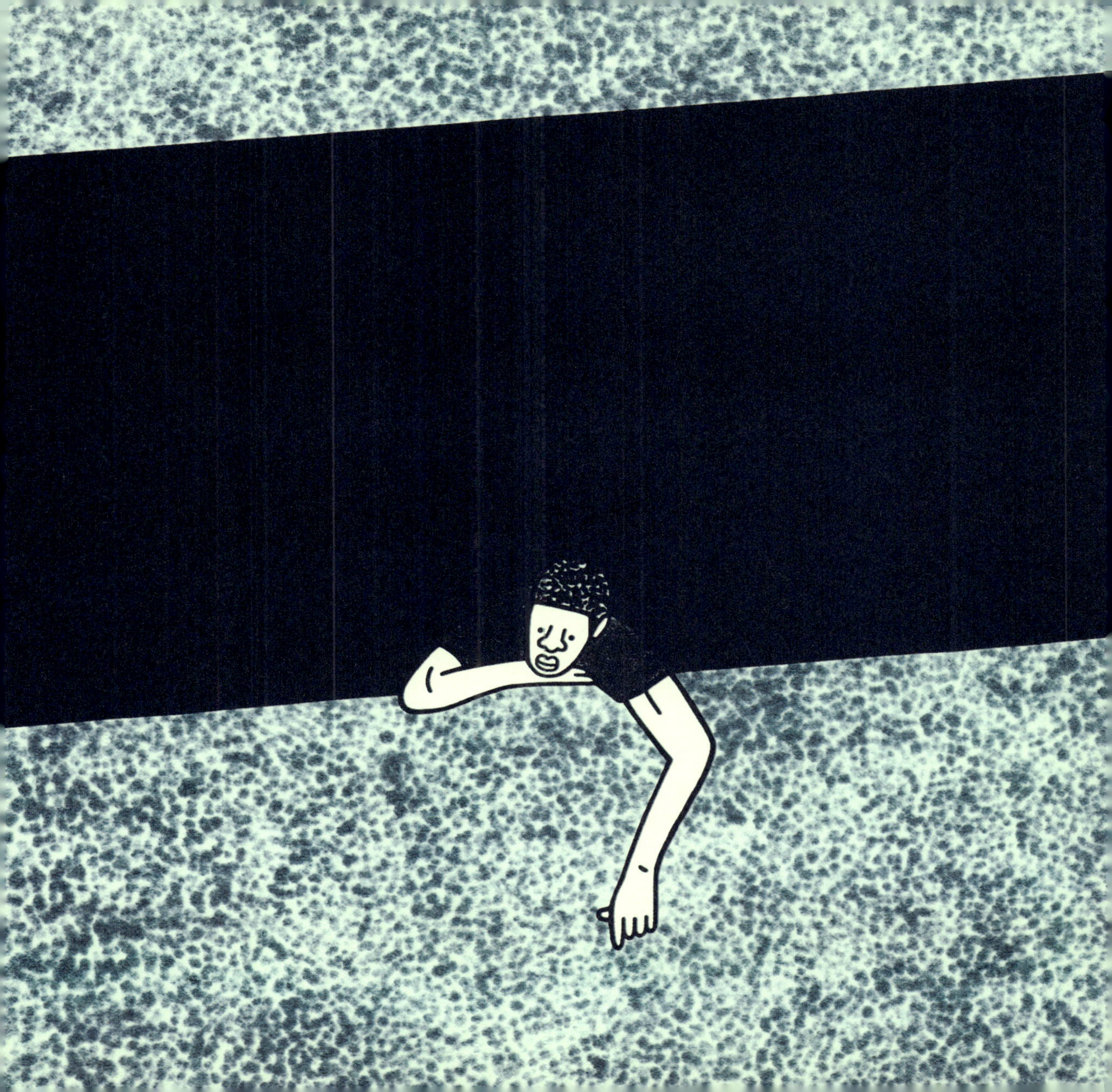

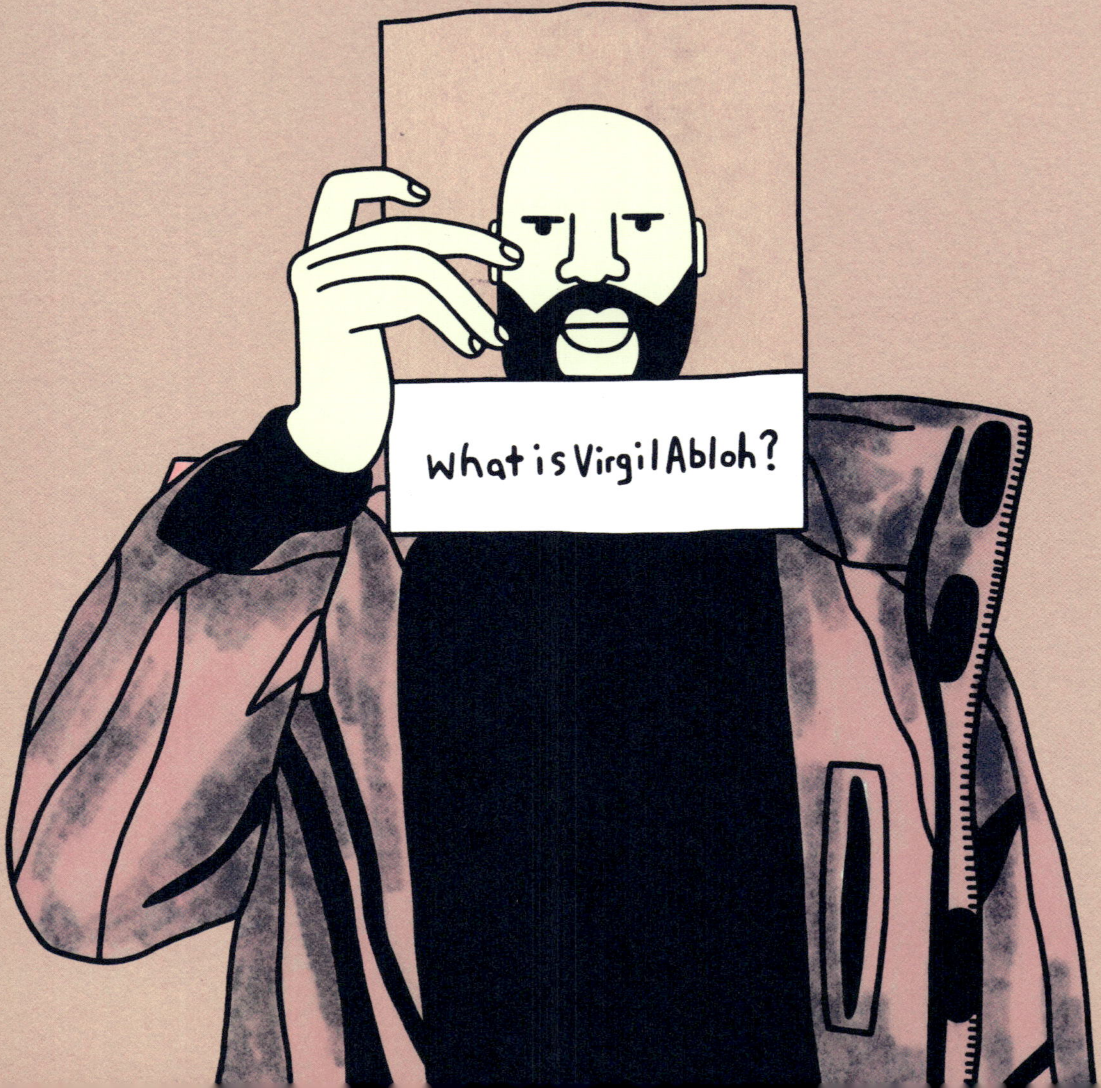
What is Virgil Abloh?

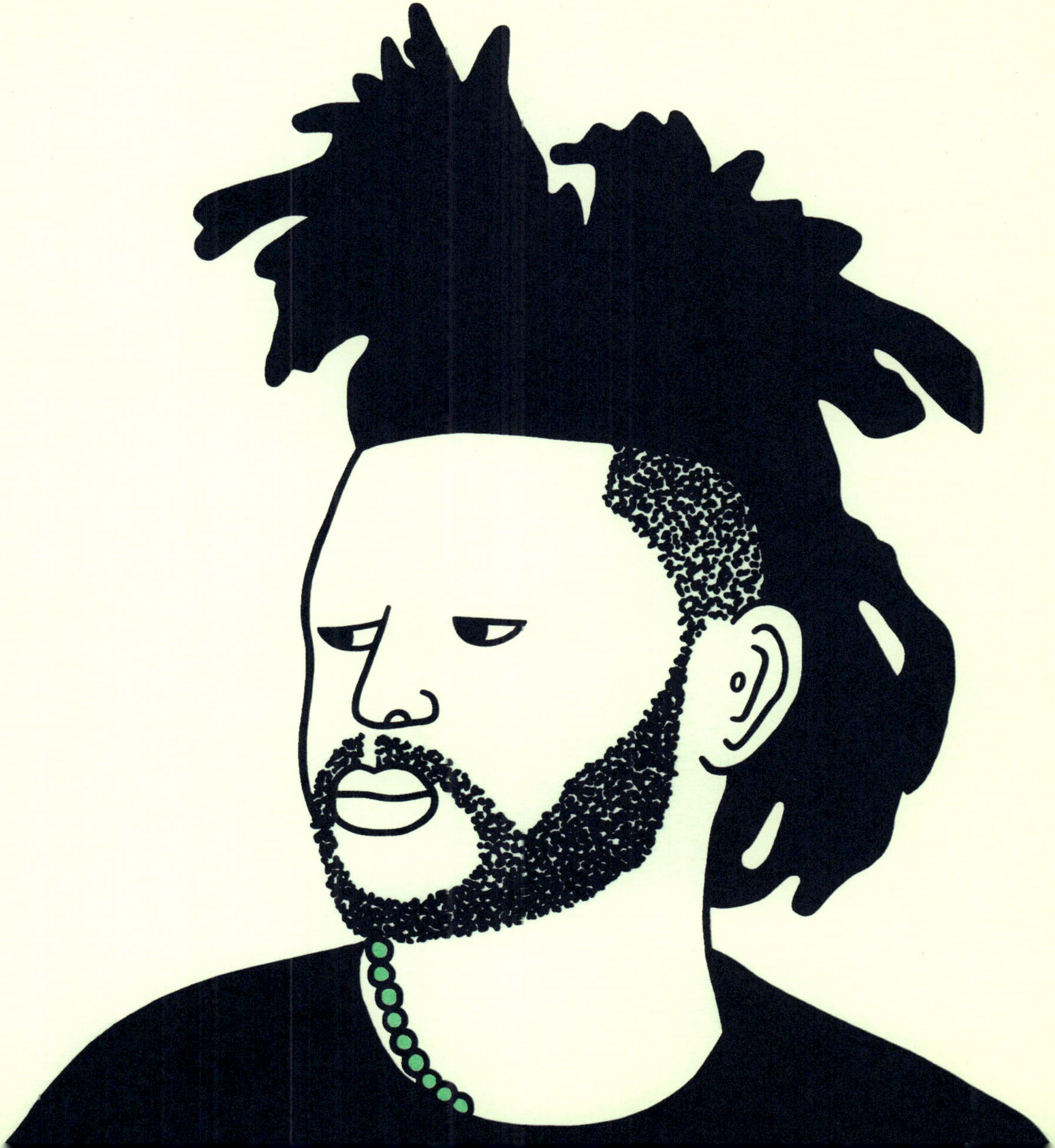

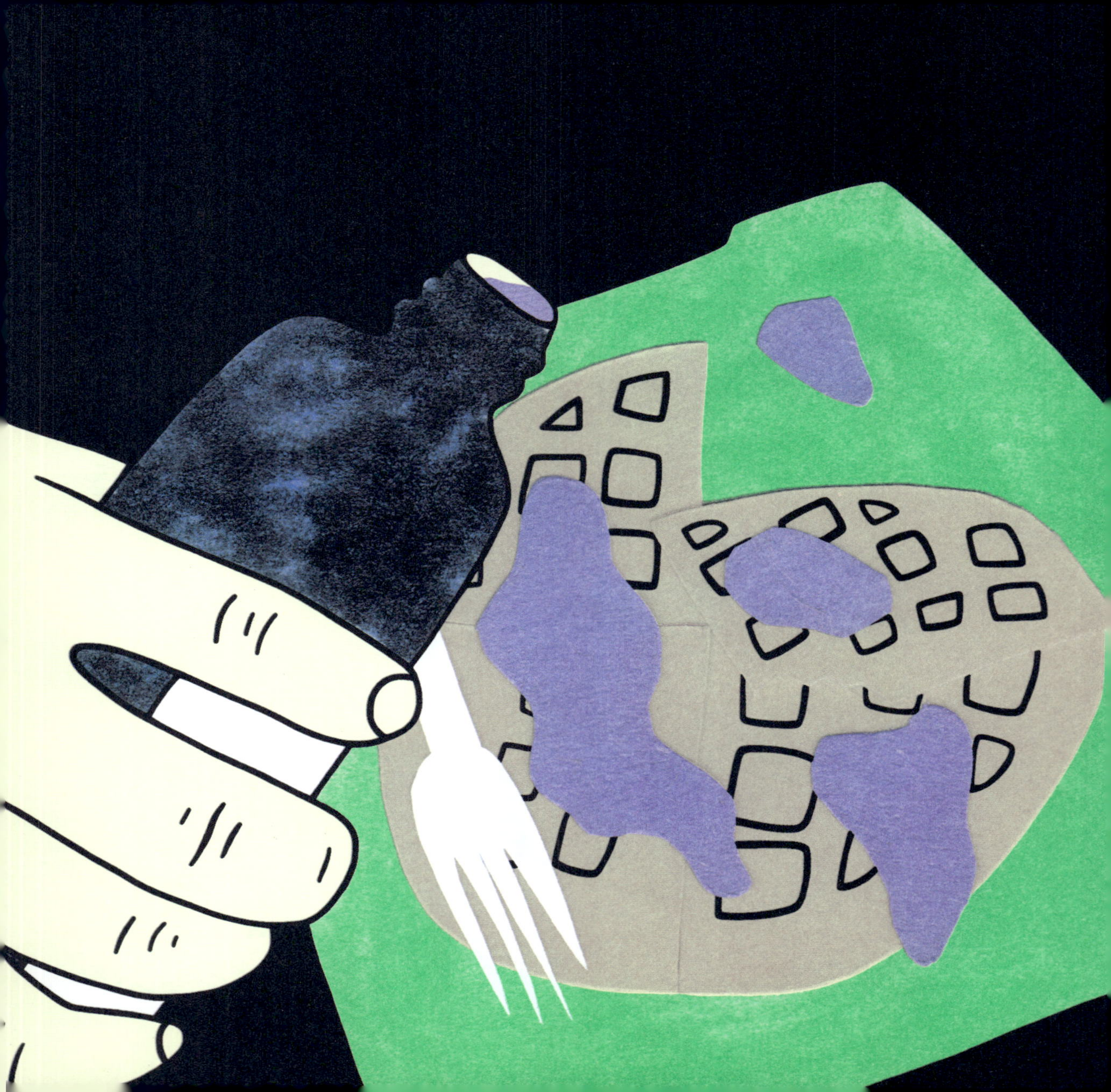

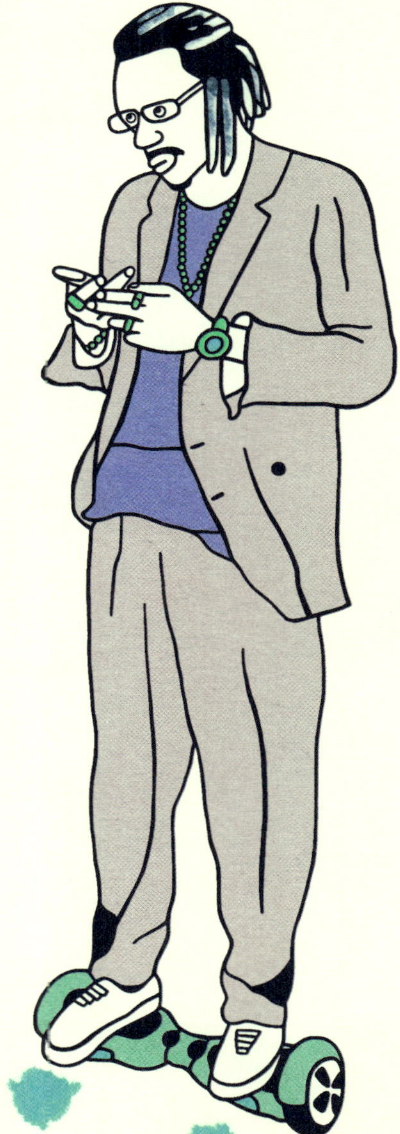

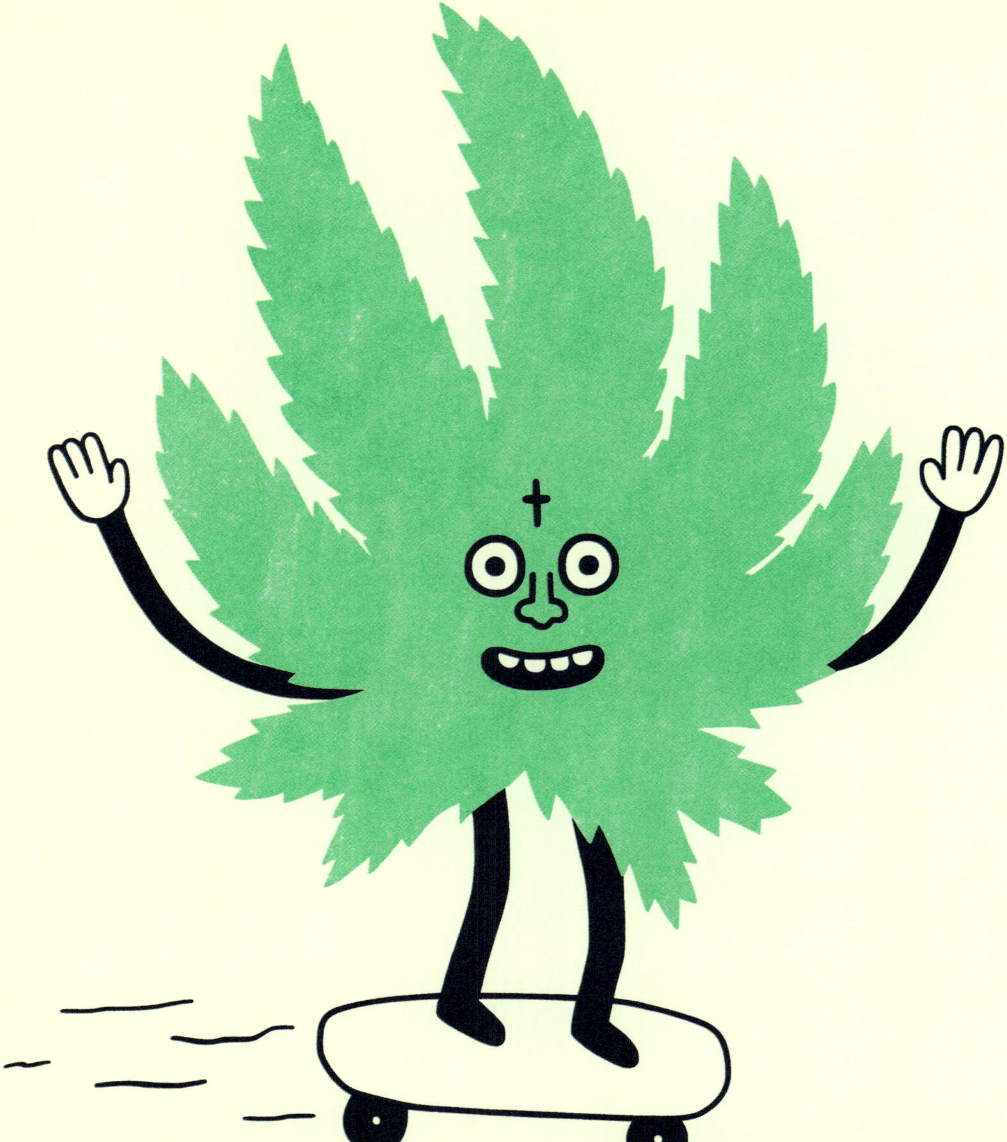

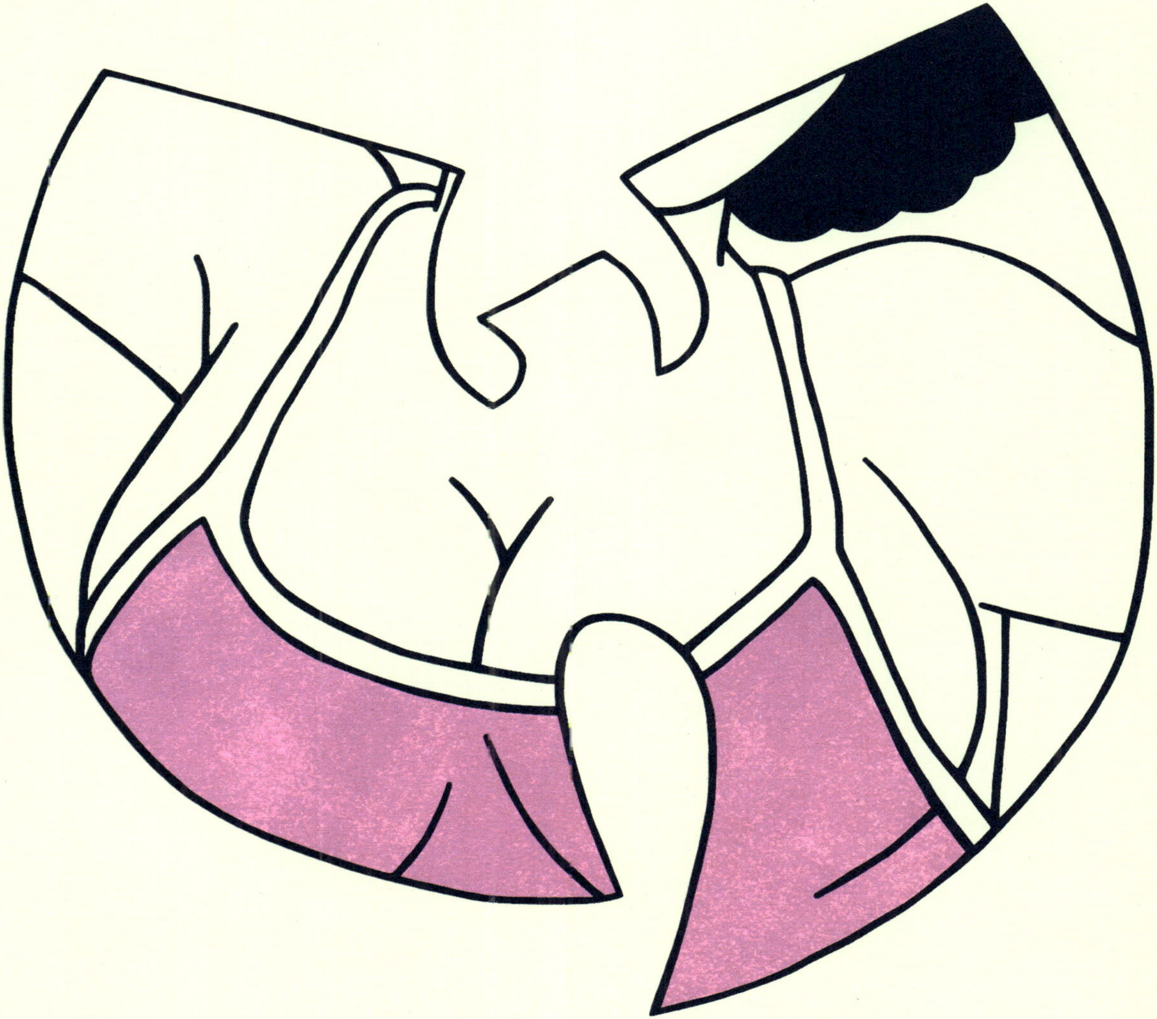

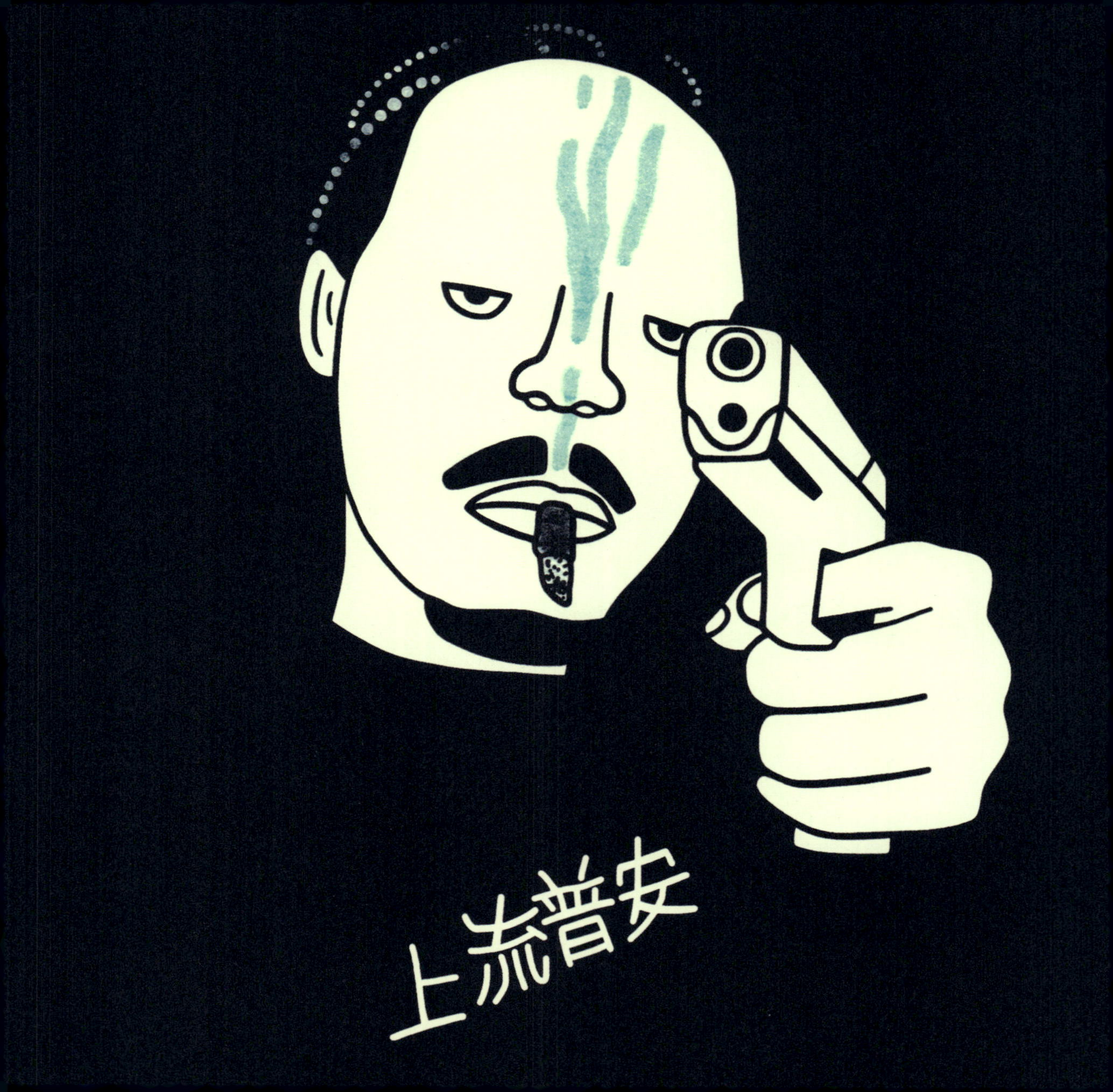
上流普安

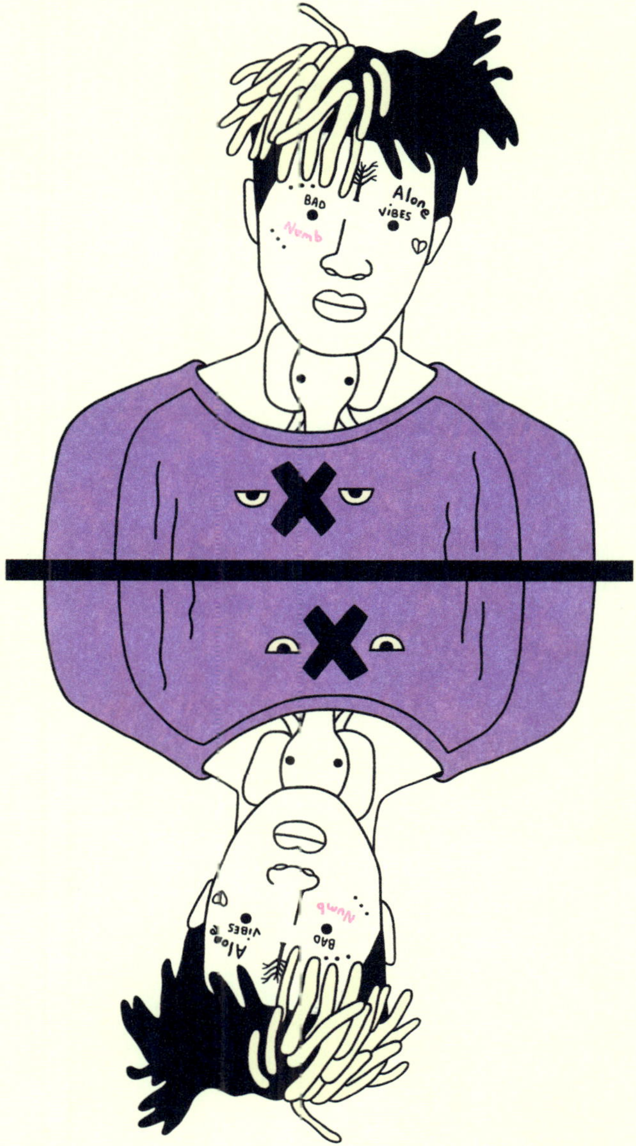
BAD
Alone
VIBES
Numb

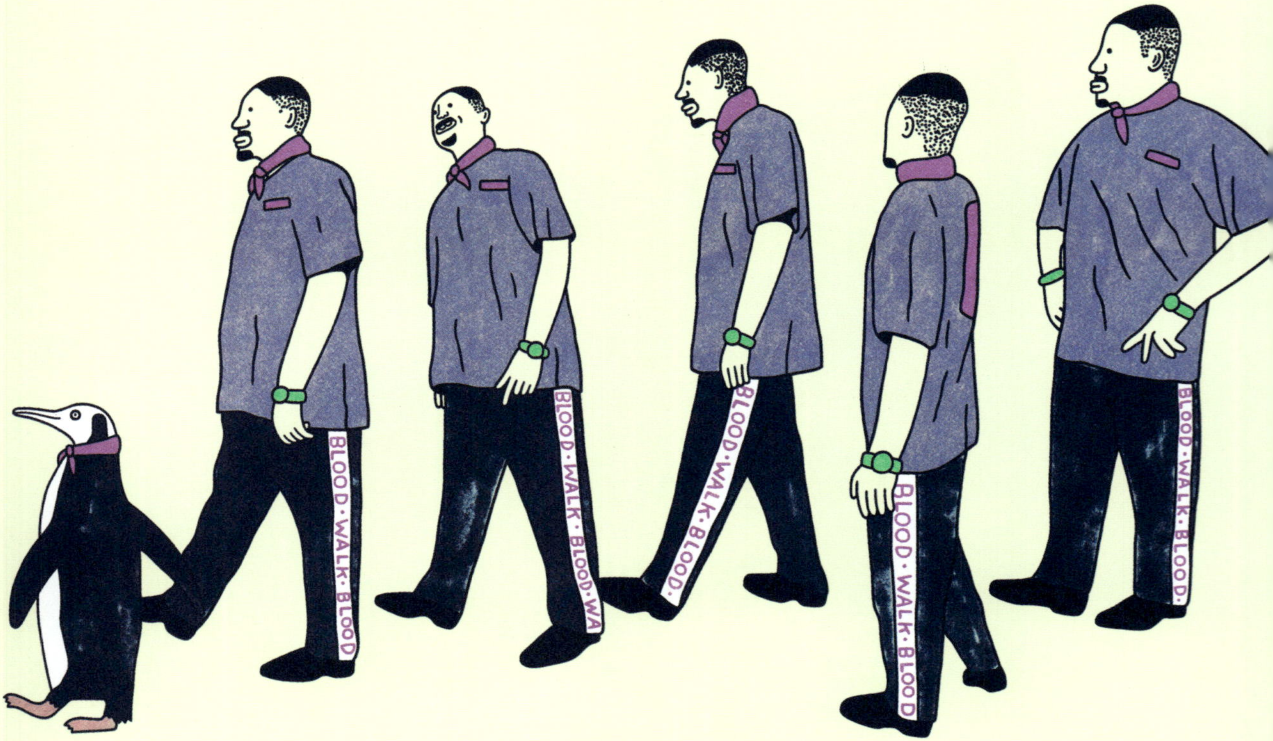
BLOOD·WALK·BLOOD
BLOOD·WALK·BLOOD·WA
BLOOD·WALK·BLOOD·
BLOOD·WALK·BLOOD
BLOOD·WALK·BLOOD·

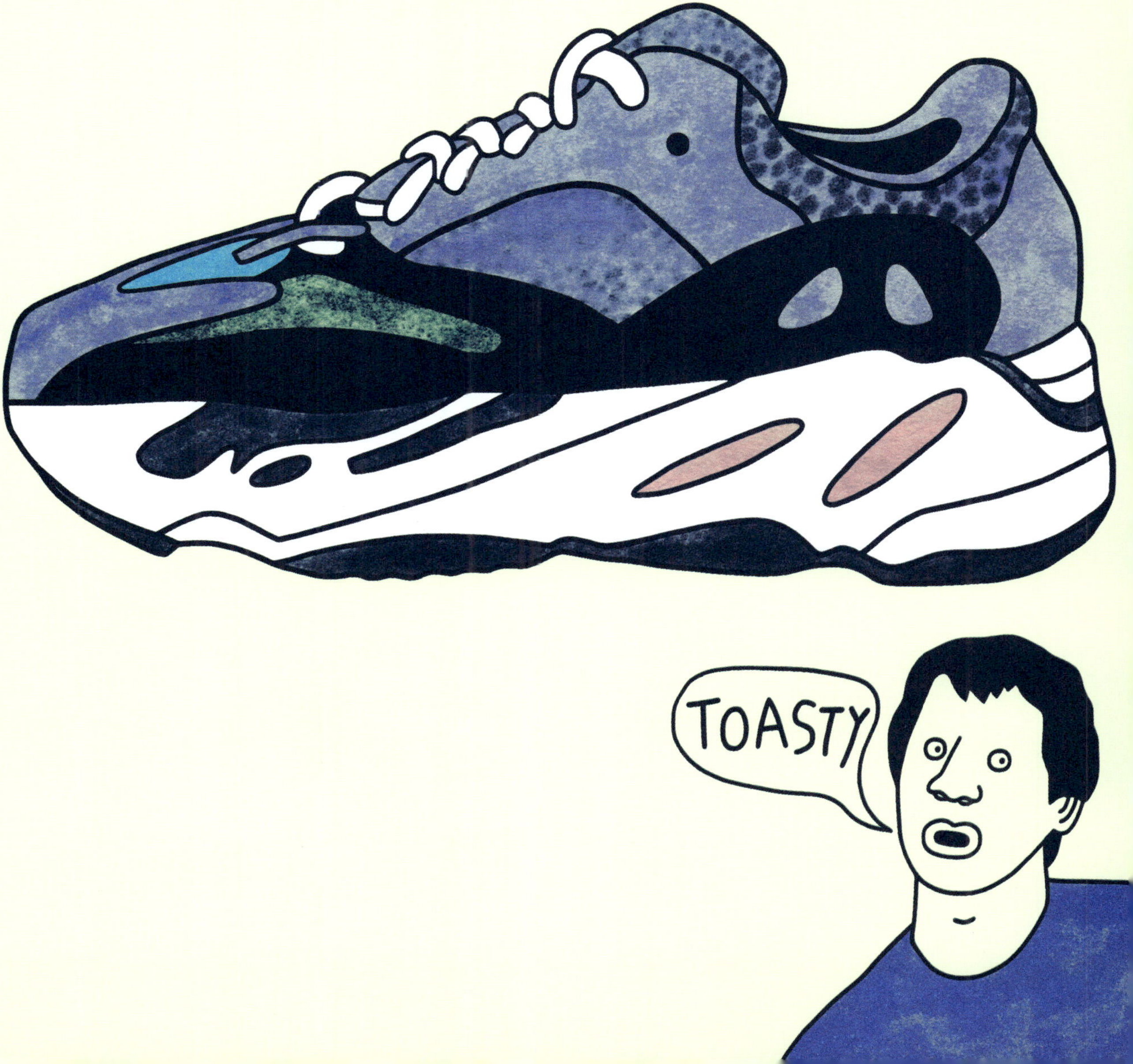
TOASTY

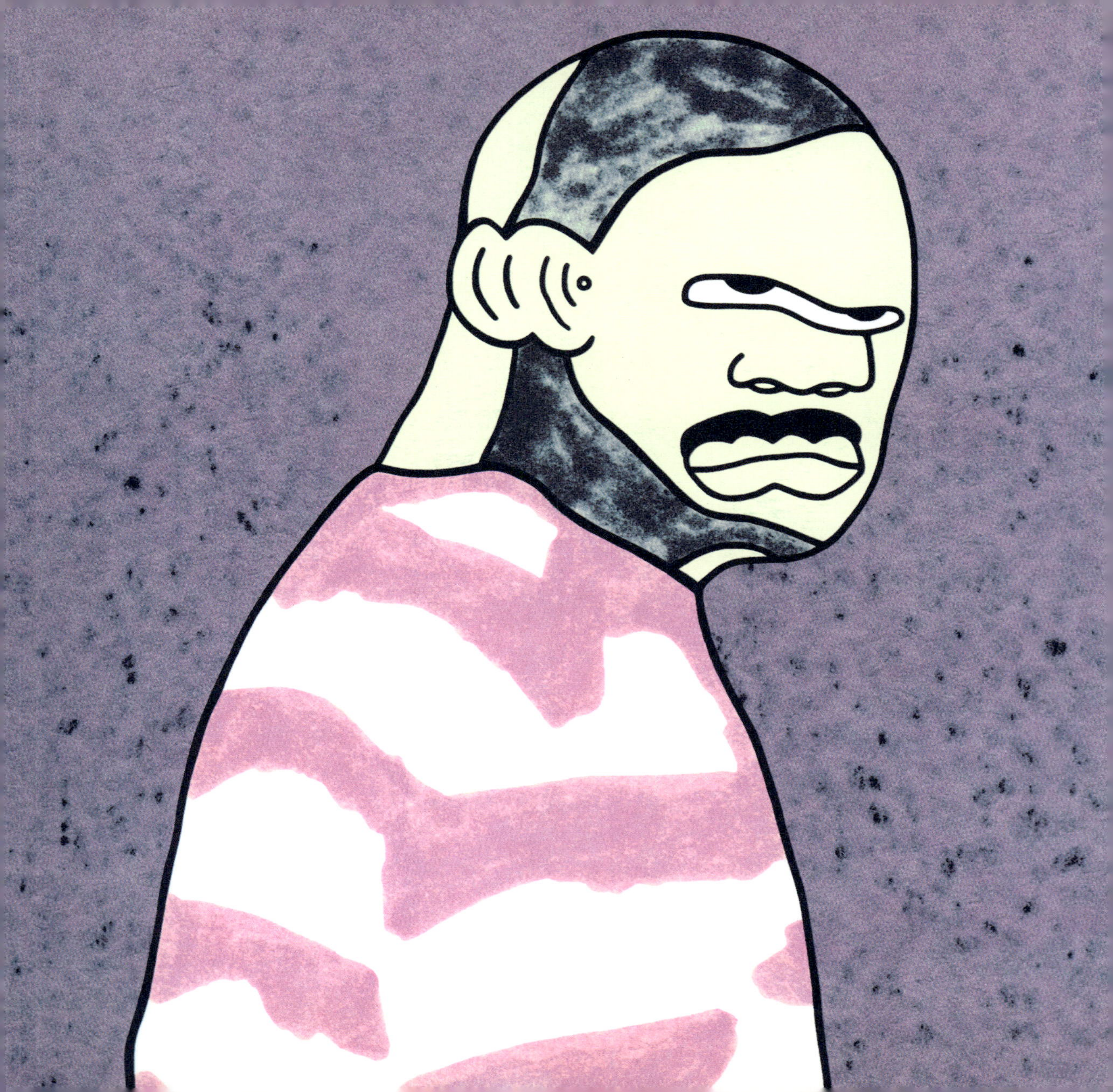

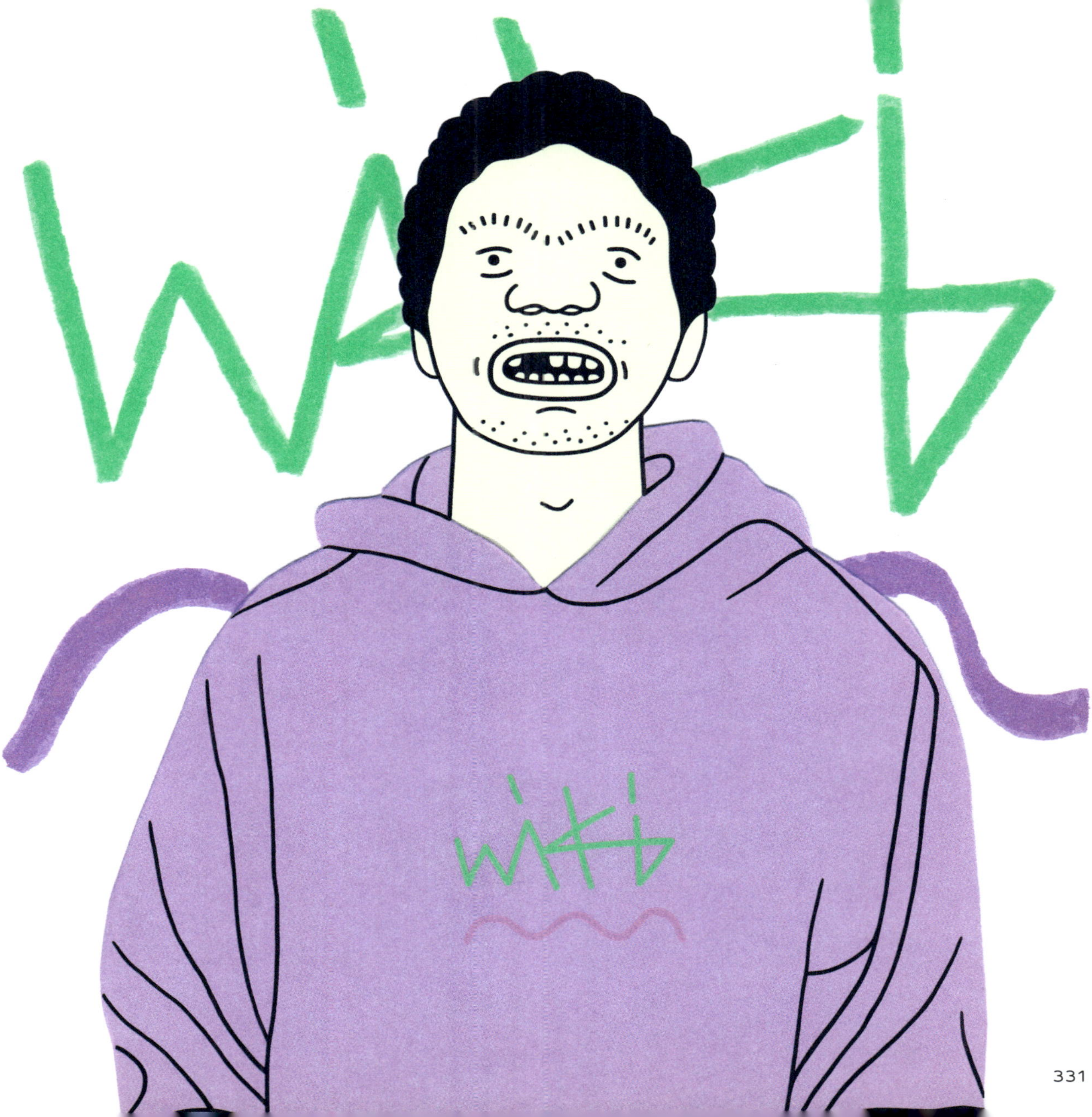

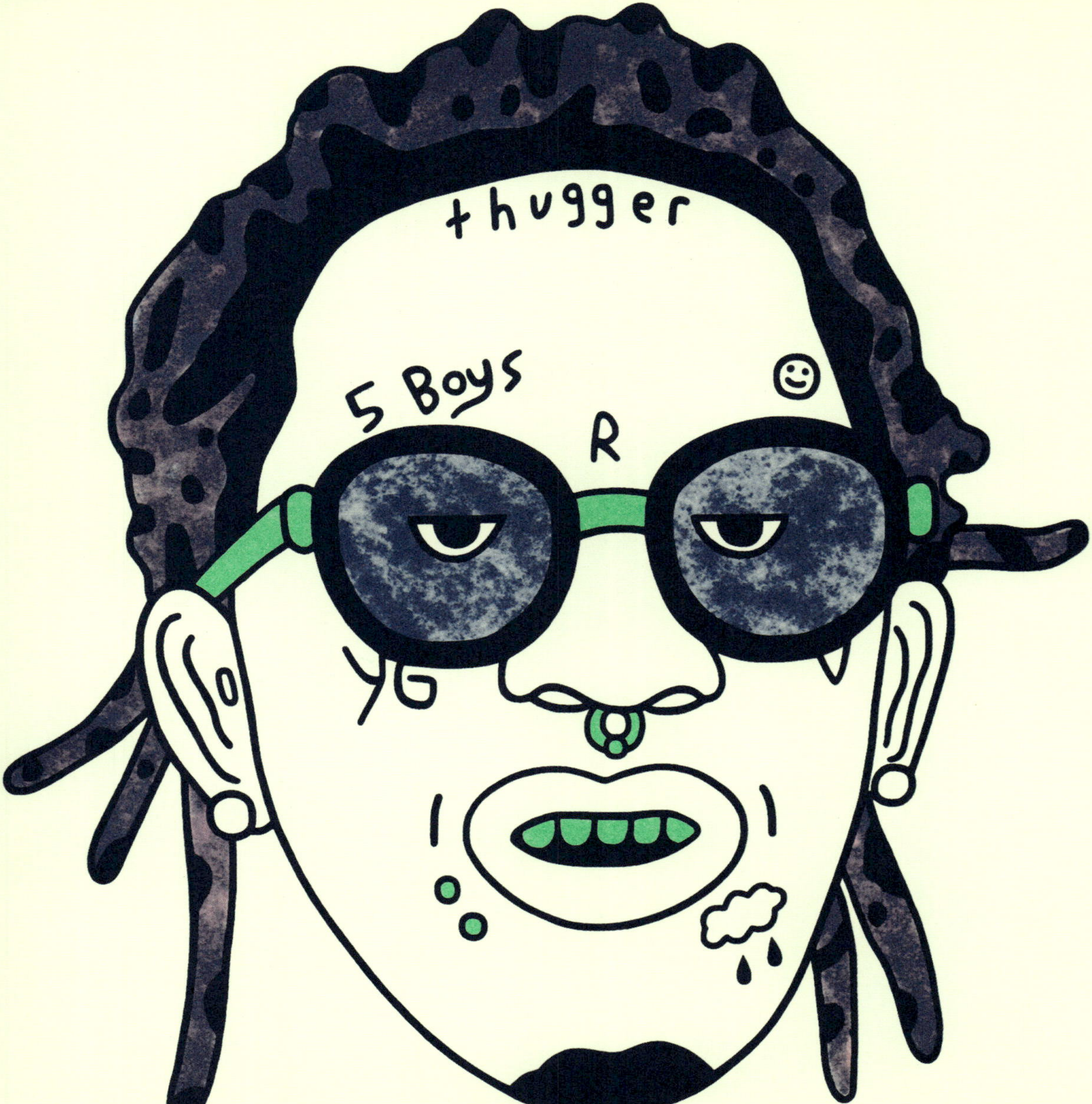
thugger
5 Boys
R
YG

Featured (in order of appearance)

Featured (in order of appearance)

Outro by Knxwledge

think about it. some humans out here hating themselves & hurting each other without even knowing or acknowledging each other for what we are (humans) like at the beginning there was a chance to choose or something. it's not easy for anyone, period.

we all have to work & self-medicate with something to keep us here.

all we kan do is our best.

learn before anything that one must love themselves before they kan love anything or anyone.

make your own way while you have the chance because we only get one.

depend on yourself because you kan do it.

thank your mother for allowing u to be here, brush your teeth every day, and you'll be aight.

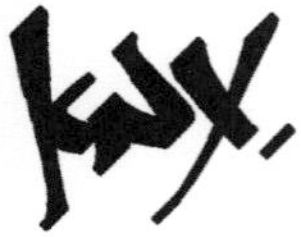